The Bartender's Companion ~ 5th Edition

The Original Guide to American Cocktails and Drinks

Robert Plotkin

BarMedia ~ 2004

OTHER BOOKS BY ROBERT PLOTKIN

- The Original Pocket Guide to American Cocktails and Drinks (2004)
- Drinks for All Ages: The Original Guide to
  Alcohol-Free Beverages and Drinks (2002)
- The Professional Bartender's Training Manual ~ 3rd Edition (2002)
- Caribe Rum: The Original Guide to Caribbean Rum and Drinks (2001)
- Successful Beverage Management: Proven Strategies for the
  On-Premise Operator (2000)
- ¡Toma! Margaritas! The Original Guide to Margaritas and Tequila (1999)
- Preventing Internal Theft: A Bar Owner's Guide ~ 2nd Edition (1998)
- Increasing Bar Sales: Creative Twists to Bigger Profits (1997)
- Reducing Bar Costs: A Survival Guide for the '90s (1993)
- 501 Questions Every Bartender Should Know How to Answer:
  A Unique Look at the Bar Business (1993)
- The Professional Guide to Bartending: The Encyclopedia of
  American Mixology (1991)
- The Intervention Handbook: The Legal Aspects of
  Serving Alcohol ~ 2nd Edition (1990)

Published by: **BarMedia**
P.O. Box 14486
Tucson, AZ 85732
520.747.8131
www.BarMedia.com

Copyright 2004 BarMedia
5th Edition

ISBN: 0-945562-30-6
Printed in China

M.S.
For Almost 40 years my friend and mentor.
R.P.

Contents

Glassware & Drink Preparation 303

An overview of selecting glassware when preparing cocktails and drinks, including sixty photos of creative glassware options. There are also explanations of the drink preparation instructions provided in each recipe.

Find a Drink ~ Special Index 307

An easy-to-use listing of every drink, listed both by main ingredient and drink type which references you back to the alphabetized recipes.

Responsible Service

The editors of this book advocate moderation in the consumption of alcohol. In addition, we strongly urge responsibility when serving alcohol. The information contained herein is intended to assist in the responsible service of alcohol with the understanding that certification from an alcohol-awareness program is beneficial for all servers of alcohol. Responsibility falls on each individual who serves alcohol. Whether at home or commercially, serve conscientiously and responsibly.

Furthermore, we would like to advance the following:

- A "strong drink" is not necessarily a "good drink." Increasing a drink's liquor portion increases both its alcoholic potency and cost. Over-portioning alcohol is an expensive and liability-laden practice.

- Not all drinks are created equally. For instance, a Martini served straight-up is more potent than one served on the rocks. Alcohol is soluble in water and will increase the rate at which ice melts. As a result, the melting ice will dilute the drink's alcohol, rendering it less potent.

- Similarly, a blended drink is less potent than one served on-the-rocks. Blending a drink with ice makes it more diluted. In most instances, the dominant ingredient in a blended drink is water (the ice).

- Neat drinks are prepared directly into the glass in which they are served. They are undiluted and high in alcohol concentration. Care should be taken with respect to their service.

- Shooters and layered cordials are conventionally consumed in one swallow, thereby dramatically increasing the rate the alcohol is absorbed into a person's bloodstream. Increased rate of consumption tends to accelerate intoxication.

- A "double" highball, containing 2 times the liquor of a standard highball and is more than twice as potent as two prepared regularly. A "double" will profoundly impact intoxication. Conversely, a "tall" highball, one prepared in a tall glass with significantly more mixer, is less potent than the same drink prepared in the regular manner.

Serve Responsibly
Drink Responsibly

Recipes

3D-ELIXIR
Rocks glass, ice
Build in glass
3/4 oz. Peppermint Schnapps
3/4 oz. Dark Crème de Cacao
3/4 oz. Triple Sec

24-KARAT NIGHTMARE
Presentation shot glass, chilled
Build in glass
1/2 fill Goldschläger
1/2 fill Rumple Minze Schnapps

38TH PARALLEL
Coffee mug, heated
Build in glass
3/4 oz. Chambord
1/2 oz. Baileys Irish Cream
1/2 oz. Dark Crème de Cacao
1/2 oz. Brandy
Near fill with hot coffee
Whipped cream garnish
Sprinkle nutmeg

.44 MAGNUM
Bucket glass, ice
Pour ingredients into iced mixing glass
1/2 oz. Light Rum
1/2 oz. Dark Rum
1/2 oz. Jamaican Rum
1/2 oz. Vodka
1/2 oz. Triple Sec
3/4 oz. pineapple juice
1 1/2 oz. sweet 'n' sour
Shake and strain
Fill with Seven-Up

'57 CHEVY
Bucket glass, ice
Pour ingredients into iced mixing glass
1/2 oz. Southern Comfort
1/2 oz. Disaronno Amaretto
1/2 oz. Vodka
1/2 oz. Light Rum
1/2 oz. Crème de Noyaux
1 1/2 oz. sweet 'n' sour
1 1/2 oz. pineapple juice
Shake and strain

'57 T-BIRD WITH ARIZONA PLATES
Bucket glass, ice
Build in glass
1/2 oz. Vodka
1/2 oz. Disaronno Amaretto
1/2 oz. Midori
1/2 oz. Peach Schnapps
1/2 oz. Triple Sec
1/2 oz. grenadine
1 oz. orange juice
1 oz. cranberry juice
Lemon wedge garnish

'57 T-BIRD WITH FLORIDA PLATES
Bucket glass, ice
Build in glass
1/2 oz. Vodka
1/2 oz. Disaronno Amaretto
1/2 oz. Grand Marnier
Fill with orange juice

'57 T-BIRD WITH HAWAIIAN PLATES
Bucket glass, ice
Build in glass
1/2 oz. Vodka
1/2 oz. Disaronno Amaretto
1/2 oz. Grand Marnier
Fill with pineapple juice

110 DEGREES IN THE SHADE
Beer glass, ice
Build in glass
1 1/4 oz. Jalapeño-infused Vodka
Fill with Modelo Especial Mexican Beer
Lime wedge and jalapeño slice garnish

1701 FOG
Cocktail glass, chilled
Pour ingredients into iced mixing glass
1 1/2 oz. Türi Vodka
3/4 oz. Chambord
1/2 oz. Rose's Lime Juice
1 oz. grapefruit juice
1 1/4 oz. sweet 'n' sour
Shake and strain
Orange and cherry garnish

GREY GOOSE® VODKA

Ultra-premium GREY GOOSE VODKA was released in 1997 and quickly began earning medals at competitions. Within months of its inception the vodka was ranked among the world's elite. In the United States, aficionados and enthusiasts made Grey Goose an immediate success and the brand has never looked back.

The vodka is made in the heart of Cognac. Grey Goose is distilled in small batches beginning in copper stills from a choice blend of grains. This pure grain vodka is produced with pristine, limestone-filtered water drawn from the famous Genté Springs. The spirit is then rigorously filtered and bottled at 80 proof.

A moment alone with Grey Goose Vodka will reveal why it has caught on big with consumers. The vodka has crystalline clarity and a supple, medium-weight body. The subtle, delicate bouquet is semisweet and inviting. Grey Goose enters the mouth without a trace of heat and features a grainy-sweet, thoroughly satisfying palate. The finish is crisp and eminently smooth.

Fans of Grey Goose Vodka will also want to check out their L'ORANGE, a vibrant, orange-infused vodka, LA VANILLE, a voluptuous spirit with an alluring, vanilla-laced bouquet and palate and the altogether refreshing, lemon-infused LE CITRON. Each of these versions of Grey Goose are worthy of the name and are ideally suited for use in scores of contemporary cocktails.

ABBEY ROAD
Coffee mug, heated
Build in glass
3/4 oz. Chambord
1/2 oz. Disaronno Amaretto
1/2 oz. Kahlúa
Near fill with hot coffee
Whipped cream garnish
Dust powdered cocoa

ABERDEEN ANGUS
Coffee mug, heated
Build in glass
1 1/2 oz. Scotch Whisky
3/4 oz. Drambuie
1 tbsp. honey
1/2 oz. fresh lemon juice
Fill with hot water
Lemon wedge garnish

ABO-TRON
Cocktail glass, chilled
Pour ingredients into iced mixing glass
1 oz. Absolut Citron Vodka
2 oz. RémyRed Red Berry Infusion
Stir and strain
Lemon twist garnish

ABSOLUTELY GRAND
Cocktail glass, chilled
Pour ingredients into iced mixing glass
1 1/2 oz. Absolut Vodka
3/4 oz. Grand Marnier
1/2 oz. fresh lime juice
Stir and strain

ABSOLUT MANDARINADE
Bucket glass, ice
Build in glass
1 1/2 oz. Absolut Mandarin Vodka
1/2 oz. Chambord
Fill with lemonade
Lemon slice garnish

ABSOLUT TROUBLE
Cocktail glass, chilled
Pour ingredients into iced mixing glass
1 1/2 oz. Absolut Citron Vodka
1 oz. Grand Marnier
1/2 oz. grenadine
1 oz. orange juice
Shake and strain

ACAPULCO
House specialty glass, ice
Pour ingredients into iced mixing glass
1 oz. Silver Tequila
1 oz. Light Rum
1 oz. grapefruit juice
3 oz. pineapple juice
Shake and strain
Pineapple wedge and cherry garnish

ACAPULCO BREEZE
House specialty glass, ice
Pour ingredients into iced mixing glass
1 1/2 oz. Corazón Silver Tequila
1/2 oz. Midori
2 oz. sweet 'n' sour
3 oz. cranberry juice
Shake and strain
Lemon wedge garnish

ACAPULCO GOLD
Highball glass, ice
Build in glass
3/4 oz. Gold Rum
3/4 oz. Peach Schnapps
Fill with orange juice

ACAPULCO SUNBURN
Bucket glass, ice
Build in glass
1 3/4 oz. Don Eduardo Añejo Tequila
1/2 oz. Agavero Liqueur
1/4 oz. fresh lime juice
1 oz. pineapple juice
1/2 fill cranberry juice
1/2 fill lemonade
Lemon wedge garnish

A CELLO MIA
Tea cup or coffee mug, heated
Build in glass
2 oz. Limoncello Liqueur
3/4 oz. Cointreau
Fill with hot herbal tea
Lemon wedge garnish

ACHING BACH
Presentation shot glass, chilled
Build in glass
1/3 fill Brandy
1/3 fill Kahlúa
1/3 fill Tequila

ADAM'S APPLE
Cocktail glass, chilled
Pour ingredients into iced mixing glass
1 1/2 oz. Sauza Gold Tequila
1/2 oz. DeKuyper Pucker Sour Apple
1 oz. sweet 'n' sour
1 oz. orange juice
Shake and strain
Green apple wedge garnish

A DAY AT THE BEACH
House specialty glass, ice
Pour ingredients into iced mixing glass
1 oz. Light Rum
1 oz. Malibu Caribbean Rum
1/2 oz. Disaronno Amaretto
1/2 oz. grenadine
4 oz. orange juice
Shake and strain
Pineapple wedge and orange slice garnish

ADIOS MOTHER
House specialty glass, ice
Pour ingredients into iced mixing glass
3/4 oz. Danzka Vodka
3/4 oz. Danzka Grapefruit Vodka
3/4 oz. DeKuyper Island Blue Pucker
3/4 oz. Blue Curaçao
2 oz. sweet 'n' sour
2 oz. orange juice
Shake and strain
Fill with Seven-Up

ADONIS
Cocktail glass, chilled
Pour ingredients into iced mixing glass
1/2 oz. Sweet Vermouth
1 1/2 oz. Dry Sherry
2 dashes orange bitters
Stir and strain
Orange twist garnish

AFTERBURNER
Presentation shot glass, chilled
Build in glass
3/4 oz. Kahlúa
3/4 oz. Jägermeister
1/2 oz. 151° Rum

AFTER EIGHT
Presentation shot glass, chilled
Layer ingredients
1/3 fill Kahlúa
1/3 fill Green Crème de Menthe
1/3 fill half & half cream

AFTER FIVE
Presentation shot glass, chilled
Layer ingredients
1/3 fill Kahlúa
1/3 fill Peppermint Schnapps
1/3 fill Baileys Irish Cream

AFTER HOURS COCKTAIL
Cocktail glass, chilled
Pour ingredients into iced mixing glass
1 1/2 oz. Plymouth Gin
1/2 oz. Cointreau
1/2 oz. fresh lime juice
1/2 oz. orange juice
Stir and strain
Orange twist garnish

COINTREAU® LIQUEUR

COINTREAU is recognized around the world as one of the timeless classic liqueurs. It was created in 1849 by Frenchman Edouard Cointreau in Angers in the Loire Valley. The recipe for Cointreau has since remained a secret and been passed down from generation to generation. Today only five members of the immediate family know the recipe.

Cointreau is crafted from a complex blend of sweet orange peels from Spain, France and Brazil, and bitter, unripe orange peels from South America. A portion of the peels are dried in the sun prior to distillation, the rest are distilled fresh. The peels are macerated in alcohol, and when the infusions have reached their peak flavor, they are double-distilled in copper alembic stills. The distillery has nineteen stills, each designed specifically to produce this incomparable liqueur.

Cointreau must be tasted neat to be fully appreciated. It is perfectly clear with a satiny textured, medium-weight body. The liqueur is impressively aromatic with a highly focused bouquet of freshly cut oranges. It glides over the palate with a tingling wash of sweet orange flavor. The citrus experience continues long into the lingering finish.

Cointreau is particularly versatile in drink making. It has a starring role in an impressively long list of cocktails, both classic and contemporary.

AFTER TAN (1)
House specialty glass, chilled
Pour ingredients into blender
3/4 oz. Cruzan Coconut Rum
3/4 oz. Cruzan Orange Rum
1/2 oz. Dark Crème de Cacao
2 scoops vanilla ice cream
Blend ingredients (with ice optional)
Whipped cream garnish
Drizzle 1/2 oz. Disaronno Amaretto

AFTER TAN (2)
House specialty glass, chilled
Pour ingredients into blender
1/2 oz. Malibu Caribbean Rum
1/2 oz. White Crème de Cacao
2 scoops vanilla ice cream
Blend ingredients (with ice optional)
Whipped cream garnish
Drizzle 1/2 oz. Disaronno Amaretto

AGGRAVATION
Rocks glass, ice
Build in glass
1 1/2 oz. Scotch Whisky
3/4 oz. Kahlúa
3/4 oz. half & half cream

ALABAMA SLAMMER (1)
Presentation shot glass, chilled
Layer ingredients
1/3 fill Southern Comfort
1/3 fill Sloe Gin
1/3 fill orange juice

ALABAMA SLAMMER (2)
Rocks glass, ice
Build in glass
1 oz. Disaronno Amaretto
1 oz. Southern Comfort
1/2 oz. Rose's Lime Juice
1/2 oz. grenadine

ALABAMA SLAMMER (3)
Bucket glass, ice
Pour ingredients into iced mixing glass
1 1/2 oz. Vodka
1/2 oz. Southern Comfort
1/2 oz. RémyRed Red Berry Infusion
1 1/2 oz. sweet 'n' sour
1 1/2 oz. orange juice
Shake and strain

ALABAMA SLAMMER (4)
Bucket glass, ice
Build in glass
1 oz. Southern Comfort
3/4 oz. Disaronno Amaretto
1/2 oz. Sloe Gin
Fill with orange juice

ALABAMA SLAMMER (5)
Rocks glass, chilled
Pour ingredients into iced mixing glass
1/2 oz. Southern Comfort
1/2 oz. Disaronno Amaretto
1/2 oz. Sloe Gin
1/4 oz. orange juice
1/4 oz. sweet 'n' sour
1/4 oz. Seven-Up
Shake and strain

ALASKA
Cocktail glass, chilled
Pour ingredients into iced mixing glass
1 1/2 oz. Gin
1/2 oz. Yellow Chartreuse
1/2 oz. Dry Sherry
Stir and strain
Lemon twist garnish

ALEXANDER THE GREAT
Cocktail glass, chilled
Pour ingredients into iced mixing glass
1 oz. Metaxa 5 Star Brandy
1/2 oz. Dark Crème de Cacao
1 1/2 oz. half & half cream
Shake and strain
Sprinkle nutmeg

ALICE IN WONDERLAND
aka **A.M.F., Dallas Alice**
Rocks glass, chilled
Pour ingredients into iced mixing glass
3/4 oz. Tia Maria
3/4 oz. Grand Marnier Centenaire
3/4 oz. El Tesoro Añejo Tequila
Stir and strain

ALIEN SECRETION
Bucket glass, ice
Build in glass
1 oz. Midori
1 oz. Malibu Caribbean Rum
Fill with pineapple juice

ALL AMERICAN WHISTLER
Bucket glass, ice
Build in glass
1 1/4 oz. Gin
Near fill with Squirt
Float 3/4 oz. Peach Schnapps
Lemon wedge garnish

ALL STAR CAST
Brandy snifter, ice
Build in glass
1 1/2 oz. Sauza Tres Generaciones
      Añejo Tequila
3/4 oz. Grand Marnier Centenaire
1/2 oz. Godiva Chocolate Liqueur

ALMOND JOY
Rocks glass, ice
Build in glass
1 1/2 oz. Disaronno Amaretto
3/4 oz. Dark Crème de Cacao
3/4 oz. half & half cream

ALPINE GLOW
House specialty glass, ice
Pour ingredients into iced mixing glass
1 1/2 oz. Gold Rum
1 1/2 oz. Brandy
1/2 oz. Orange Liqueur
1/2 oz. grenadine
2 oz. sweet 'n' sour
Shake and strain
Float 3/4 oz. Dark Rum
Lemon twist garnish

AMANGANI INDIAN PAINTBRUSH
House specialty glass, chilled
Pour ingredients into blender
2 oz. Light Rum
6 strawberries
1 oz. orange juice
2 oz. pineapple juice
Blend with ice
Strawberry garnish

AMARETTO CRUISE
House specialty glass, chilled
Pour ingredients into blender
1 1/4 oz. Bacardi Gold Rum
1 oz. Disaronno Amaretto
3/4 oz. Mount Gay Eclipse Rum
1/2 oz. DeKuyper Peachtree Schnapps
1 oz. sweet 'n' sour
1 oz. half & half cream
2 oz. orange juice
2 oz. cranberry juice
Blend with ice

AMBER CLOUD
Brandy snifter, heated
Build in glass
1 1/2 oz. VS Cognac
1/2 oz. Galliano Liqueur

AMBROSIA (1)
Champagne glass, chilled
Build in glass
1/2 fill apricot puree
1/2 fill Champagne

SAUZA® TRES GENERACIONES® AÑEJO TEQUILA

Tequila hasn't always been popular in the United States. Until the late '70s it was thought of as a minor spirit, considered only good for shots and Margaritas. Then came a new breed of tequilas that began to change consumers' perceptions of it as a premium spirit. One of the most enduring of these tequilas is SAUZA TRES GENERACIONES AÑEJO.

This super-premium añejo is a 100% agave tequila double-distilled in copper alembic stills. It is aged for a minimum of 3 years in 180-liter, white oak barrels. The craftsmanship necessary to make this tequila alone places it with an elite few.

For all of its accolades, Sauza Tres Generaciones Añejo is an understated tequila. Its easy-to-enjoy character is accessible to nearly any palate. The tequila has the pale golden color of white wine and a seamlessly smooth texture. Its alluring, floral bouquet has notes of earthy agave, caramel and spice. Tres Generaciones fills the mouth slowly but surely, delivering a palate amply endowed with the flavors of citrus, pepper and toasted oak. The tequila finishes warm and satisfying.

Tres Generaciones Añejo is a sought after brand, one favored by aficionados and novices alike. It should come as no surprise that the añejo is at its finest when served neat and savored slowly.

AMBROSIA (2)
Champagne glass, chilled
Pour ingredients into iced mixing glass
1 1/4 oz. Laird's Applejack Brandy
1/2 oz. Cointreau
3/4 oz. sweet 'n' sour
Shake and strain
Fill with Champagne
Orange twist garnish

AMBUSH
Coffee mug, heated
Build in glass
1 oz. Irish Whiskey
1 oz. Disaronno Amaretto
Near fill with hot coffee
Whipped cream garnish

AMERICAN DREAM
Presentation shot glass, chilled
Build in glass
1/4 fill Kahlúa
1/4 fill Disaronno Amaretto
1/4 fill Godiva Chocolate Liqueur
1/4 fill Frangelico

AMERICAN GRAFFITI
Bucket glass, ice
Pour ingredients into iced mixing glass
1 1/4 oz. Light Rum
3/4 oz. Rum
1/2 oz. Sloe Gin
1/2 oz. Southern Comfort
1/4 oz. Rose's Lime Juice
1 1/2 oz. pineapple juice
1 1/2 oz. sweet 'n' sour
Shake and strain
Orange slice and cherry garnish

AMERICANO
Rocks glass, ice
Build in glass
1 oz. Campari Aperitivo
1 oz. Sweet Vermouth
Lemon twist garnish

AMERICANO HIGHBALL
Highball glass, ice
Build in glass
3/4 oz. Campari Aperitivo
3/4 oz. Sweet Vermouth
Fill with club soda
Lemon twist garnish

A.M.F.
aka **Alice in Wonderland, Dallas Alice**
Brandy snifter (ice optional)
Build in glass
3/4 oz. Tia Maria
3/4 oz. Grand Marnier
3/4 oz. Jose Cuervo Especial Tequila

ANCIENT MARINER (1)
Brandy snifter, ice
Build in glass
1 1/4 oz. Bacardi 8 Reserva Rum
1 oz. Grand Marnier Centenaire

ANCIENT MARINER (2)
Brandy snifter, ice
Build in glass
1 1/4 oz. Pyrat Cask 23 Rum
1 oz. Grand Marnier Centenaire

ANDALUSIA
Brandy snifter, heated
Build in glass
1 1/2 oz. Bacardi 8 Reserva Rum
1/2 oz. VS Cognac
1/2 oz. Dry Sherry
1-2 dashes Angostura Bitters
Lemon twist garnish

ANDES SUMMIT
House specialty glass, chilled
Pour ingredients into blender
1 1/2 oz. Peppermint Schnapps
1 1/2 oz. Godiva Chocolate Liqueur
3 oz. milk
2 scoops vanilla ice cream
Blend ingredients (with ice optional)
Shaved chocolate garnish

AÑEJO SUNRISE
Bucket glass, ice
Build in glass
1 1/4 oz. Añejo Tequila
Near fill with orange juice
Float 1/4 oz. grenadine
Orange slice and cherry garnish

ANGEL KISS
Rocks glass, ice
Build in glass
1 oz. Türi Vodka
1 oz. Frangelico
Lime wedge garnish

ANGEL'S KISS
aka **Angel's Tip**
Cordial or sherry glass, chilled
Layer ingredients
3/4 fill Dark Crème de Cacao
1/4 fill half & half cream

APPENDECTOMY
Cocktail glass, chilled
Pour ingredients into iced mixing glass
1 oz. Gin
1/2 oz. Grand Marnier
1 1/2 oz. sweet 'n' sour
Shake and strain

APPENDICITIS
aka **White Lady**
Cocktail glass, chilled
Pour ingredients into iced mixing glass
1 oz. Gin
1/2 oz. Triple Sec
1 1/2 oz. sweet 'n' sour
Shake and strain

APPETIZER
Cocktail glass, chilled
Pour ingredients into iced mixing glass
3/4 oz. Gin
3/4 oz. Dubonnet Rouge
2-3 dashes Angostura Bitters
1 1/2 oz. orange juice
Shake and strain

APPLE A GO-GOGH
Cocktail glass, chilled
Rim glass with sugar
Pour ingredients into iced mixing glass
1 1/2 oz. Van Gogh Wild Appel Vodka
1/2 oz. Kahlúa
1/4 oz. DeKuyper Buttershots Schnapps
Shake and strain
Apple wedge garnish

APPLE BRANDY COOLER
House specialty glass, ice
Pour ingredients into iced mixing glass
1 oz. Light Rum
1 oz. Brandy
4 oz. apple juice
Shake and strain
Float 3/4 oz. Dark Rum
Lime wedge garnish

APPLE CART
Cocktail glass, chilled
Pour ingredients into iced mixing glass
1 oz. Laird's 12 Year Apple Brandy
1/2 oz. Cointreau
1 1/2 oz. sweet 'n' sour
Shake and strain

APPLE COOLER
Bucket glass, ice
Build in glass
1 1/4 oz. DeKuyper Pucker Sour Apple
3/4 oz. Citadelle Apple Vodka
2 oz. cranberry juice
Fill with club soda

BOMBAY® ORIGINAL DRY GIN

While gin best typifies chic and sophistication, it was BOMBAY ORIGINAL DRY GIN that taught all the other performers how to act. It is one of the world's most venerable brands of London Gin, one that can be found on back bars across the globe. Now in its third century, Bombay Original is considered a "must have" in any gin enthusiast's repertoire.

The brand originated in 1761 and to this day is still made using the same distilling techniques and according to the same closely guarded recipe of botanicals. The gin is produced using a series of Carter Head alembic stills, which are specifically designed for making gin.

The process begins with producing pure, neutral grain spirits. It is then redistilled with eight botanicals and aromatics using a unique method called vapor infusion. The 86 proof result is a magnificently dry and flavorful spirit.

Tasting Bombay Original for the first time is like awakening taste buds that long ago went dormant. The gin has a lightweight body, satin-like texture and a compact, yet eminently pleasing herbal bouquet. It washes over the palate with hardly a trace of heat and slowly subsides into a flavor-enriched finale.

The singular character of Bombay Original is ideally enjoyed chilled, or better yet with a splash of crisp tonic water.

APPLE GRAND MARNIER
Cappuccino cup, heated
Build in glass
3/4 oz. Grand Marnier
3/4 oz. Calvados Apple Brandy
3/4 oz. VS Cognac
Near fill with hot espresso coffee
Top with frothed milk
Dust powdered cocoa

APPLEJACK CREAM
Cocktail glass, chilled
Pour ingredients into iced mixing glass
1 1/2 oz. Laird's Applejack Brandy
1 oz. apple cider
1 tsp. sugar
2 oz. half & half cream
Shake and strain
Sprinkle cinnamon

APPLE SPICE
Bucket glass, ice
Build in glass
1 1/4 oz. Jim Beam White Label Bourbon
1/2 oz. DeKuyper Pucker Sour Apple
1/4 oz. Cinnamon Schnapps
Fill with apple cider
Apple wedge garnish

APPLE STING
Brandy snifter (ice optional)
Build in glass
1 1/2 oz. Laird's Applejack Brandy
1/2 oz. Peppermint Schnapps

APPLE TINKER
Cocktail glass, chilled
Pour ingredients into iced mixing glass
1 3/4 oz. Tanqueray Nº Ten Gin
1/2 oz. DeKuyper Pucker Sour Apple
1/2 oz. Rose's Lime Juice
1 1/2 oz. sweet 'n' sour
Shake and strain
Lemon twist garnish

APPLE TODDY
Coffee mug, heated
Build in glass
1 oz. Laird's Applejack Brandy
1/2 oz. simple syrup
Fill with frothed milk
Sprinkle nutmeg

APPLETON BLAST
House specialty glass, ice
Build in glass
1 1/2 oz. Appleton Estate V/X Jamaica Rum
1/2 oz. Disaronno Amaretto
1/2 oz. DeKuyper Peachtree Schnapps
Fill with cranberry juice
Orange slice garnish

APPLETON BREEZE
House specialty glass, ice
Build in glass
1 1/2 oz. Appleton Estate V/X Jamaica Rum
1/2 oz. Rose's Lime Juice
3 oz. cranberry juice
3 oz. grapefruit juice
Lime wedge garnish

APPLETON PLANTER'S PUNCH
House specialty glass, chilled
Pour ingredients into blender
1 1/2 oz. Appleton Estate V/X Jamaica Rum
1 oz. simple syrup
2 oz. fresh lime juice
2 oz. pineapple juice
3 large, peeled and cored pineapple slices
Blend with ice
Float 3/4 oz. Appleton Estate
    V/X Jamaica Rum
Pineapple wedge and cherry garnish

APPLE WORKS
Coffee mug, heated
Build in glass
1 1/4 oz. Bacardi Light Rum
3/4 oz. Mount Gay Extra Old Rum
1/2 oz. Laird's 12 Year Apple Brandy
1/2 fill warm cranberry juice
1/2 fill warm apple cider
Cinnamon stick garnish

APRÉS SKI
Coffee mug, heated
Build in glass
1 oz. Laird's Applejack Brandy
3/4 oz. Laird's 12 Year Apple Brandy
Fill with hot apple cider
Cinnamon stick garnish

APRIL IN PARIS
Champagne glass, chilled
Build in glass
1 oz. Grand Marnier Centenaire
Swirl and coat inside of glass
Fill with Champagne
Orange twist garnish

AQUA ZEST
Bucket glass, ice
Build in glass
1 1/4 oz. Jose Cuervo Clásico Tequila
3/4 oz. Blue Curaçao
1/2 oz. Rose's Lime Juice
1/2 fill orange juice
1/2 fill lemonade

ARCTIC MINT
House specialty glass, chilled
Rim glass with powdered cocoa (optional)
Pour ingredients into blender
1 oz. Peppermint Schnapps
3/4 oz. chocolate syrup
3 oz. milk
2 scoops chocolate mint ice cream
Blend ingredients (with ice optional)
Chocolate covered pretzel garnish

AREA 151
Rocks glass, ice
Build in glass
3/4 oz. Añejo Tequila
3/4 oz. 151° Rum
1/2 oz. Kahlúa
1/2 oz. Peppermint Schnapps

ARIANA'S DREAM
House specialty glass, chilled
Pour ingredients into blender
1 oz. RedRum
1 oz. VooDoo Spiced Rum
1 oz. White Crème de Cacao
3 oz. orange juice
Blend with ice
Orange slice and strawberry garnish

ARTIFICIAL INTELLIGENCE
House specialty glass, ice
Pour ingredients into iced mixing glass
3/4 oz. Mount Gay Eclipse Rum
3/4 oz. Bacardi Select Rum
3/4 oz. Appleton Estate V/X Jamaica Rum
3/4 oz. Malibu Caribbean Rum
1 oz. fresh lime juice
3 oz. pineapple juice
Shake and strain
Float 3/4 oz. Midori
Lime, lemon and orange wedge garnish

A.S. MACPHERSON
House specialty glass, ice
Pour ingredients into iced mixing glass
3 oz. orange juice
2 oz. apple cider
1 1/2 oz. sweet 'n' sour
3 dashes Angostura Bitters
Shake and strain
Fill with club soda
Orange slice and cherry garnish

COURVOISIER® INITIALE EXTRA® COGNAC

Located in the heart of Jarnac, France, the House of Courvoisier creates its cognacs from the finest brandies distilled in the premiere *crus*, or growing regions. The brandies are then cellared in handmade Limousin and Tronçais oak barrels. Since aging is so crucial to achieving excellence, the experts at Courvoisier hand select which trees are to be used for the casks, seasoning the staves in the open air for 3 years before they are assembled into finished barrels.

Few cognacs better illustrate the Chateau's artistry and centuries old expertise than COURVOISIER INITIALE EXTRA. It is a blend of rare, exceptionally old cognacs from the Grande Champagne and Borderies districts. The youngest brandy in the blend is over 50 years old, with some that have been aged for over a century.

The Initiale Extra is an unqualified masterpiece. The brandy has a voluminous bouquet redolent with the savory aromas of vanilla, citrus, cocoa and cinnamon. The palate is full of nuances and fills the mouth with the sumptuous flavors of almonds, fruit and baking spices. The finish is long, relaxed and exquisitely flavorful.

Whether in a snifter at a quiet moment or in the middle of a crowded dance floor, it is next to impossible to do anything but thoroughly savor Courvoisier Initiale Extra.

ASPEN COFFEE
Coffee mug, heated
Build in glass
3/4 oz. Kahlúa
3/4 oz. Baileys Irish Cream
3/4 oz. Frangelico
Near fill with hot coffee
Whipped cream garnish
Sprinkle shaved chocolate

AUGUST MOON
Presentation shot glass, chilled
Build in glass
1/3 fill Triple Sec
1/3 fill Disaronno Amaretto
Near fill with orange juice
Whipped cream garnish

AUNT BEA'S CURE-ALL HOT MILK PUNCH
Coffee mug, heated
Build in glass
1 oz. Brandy
1 oz. Spiced Rum
1/2 oz. Vanilla Rum
Fill with hot milk
Sprinkle nutmeg

AVIATION COCKTAIL
Cocktail glass, chilled
Pour ingredients into iced mixing glass
2 oz. Miller's London Dry Gin
1/2 oz. Chambord
1 3/4 oz. sweet 'n' sour
Shake and strain
Lemon twist garnish

B-52
Presentation shot glass, chilled
Layer ingredients
1/3 fill Kahlúa
1/3 fill Baileys Irish Cream
1/3 fill Grand Marnier

B & B
Sherry glass or brandy snifter, heated
Build in glass
1/2 fill Brandy
1/2 fill Benedictine

BABY GRAND COCKTAIL
Brandy snifter, heated
Build in glass
3/4 oz. B & B Liqueur
1/2 oz. Baileys Irish Cream

BACARDI COCKTAIL
Cocktail glass, chilled
Pour ingredients into iced mixing glass
1 1/2 oz. Bacardi Light Rum
3/4 oz. grenadine
2 oz. sweet 'n' sour
Shake and strain

BACARDI TROPICAL DREAM
House specialty glass, chilled
Pour ingredients into blender
1 3/4 oz. Bacardi Gold Rum
1 1/4 oz. Orange Rum
3/4 oz. Disaronno Amaretto
1/2 oz. Rose's Lime Juice
1 1/2 oz. sweet 'n' sour
2 oz. orange juice
Blend with ice
Lime, lemon and orange wedge garnish

BADDA-BING
House specialty glass, ice
Pour ingredients into iced mixing glass
3/4 oz. Absolut Vodka
3/4 oz. Bacardi Gold Rum
3/4 oz. Vox Raspberry Vodka
1/2 oz. Gran Gala Orange Liqueur
1/2 oz. sweet 'n' sour
1 oz. orange juice
1 oz. cranberry juice
1 oz. pineapple juice
Shake and strain
Float 1/2 oz. Razzmatazz Raspberry Liqueur
Pineapple wedge garnish

BAHAMA MAMA (1)
House specialty glass, ice
Pour ingredients into iced mixing glass
1 1/2 oz. Light Rum
5 oz. pineapple juice
Shake and strain
Float 1/2 oz. Appleton Estate
   V/X Jamaica Rum
Float 1/2 oz. Gosling's Black Seal Rum

BAHAMA MAMA (2)
House specialty glass, ice
Pour ingredients into iced mixing glass
1 1/4 oz. Light Rum
1/2 oz. 151° Rum
1/2 oz. Coconut Rum
1/2 oz. Kahlúa
1/2 oz. Rose's Lime Juice
1 1/2 oz. sweet 'n' sour
3 oz. pineapple juice
Shake and strain
Lime, lemon and orange wedge garnish

BAILEYS BUTTERBALL
Presentation shot glass, chilled
Build in glass
3/4 oz. Baileys Irish Cream
3/4 oz. DeKuyper Buttershots Schnapps
3/4 oz. Kahlúa Especial

BAILEYS COMET
Rocks glass, ice
Build in glass
1 1/2 oz. Vox Raspberry Vodka
3/4 oz. Baileys Irish Cream

BAILEYS EXPRESS
Coffee mug, heated
Build in glass
1 1/4 oz. Baileys Irish Cream
Near fill with hot espresso coffee
Whipped cream garnish
Dust powdered cocoa

BAILEYS FIZZ
Highball glass, ice
Build in glass
1 1/4 oz. Baileys Irish Cream
Fill with club soda

BAILEYS MALIBU RUM YUM
Rocks glass, chilled
Pour ingredients into iced mixing glass
1 oz. Baileys Irish Cream
1 oz. Malibu Caribbean Rum
1 oz. half & half cream
Shake and strain

BAILEYS MINT KISS
Coffee mug, heated
Build in glass
3/4 oz. Baileys Irish Cream
3/4 oz. Kahlúa
3/4 oz. Rumple Minze Schnapps
Near fill with hot coffee
Whipped cream garnish
Dust powdered cocoa

BALALAIKA
Cocktail glass, chilled
Pour ingredients into iced mixing glass
1 1/2 oz. Stolichnaya Razberi Vodka
1/2 oz. Triple Sec
1 1/2 oz. sweet 'n' sour
Shake and strain
Lime wedge garnish

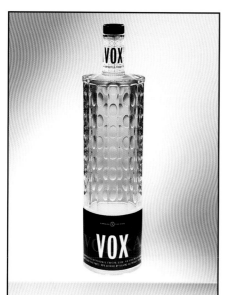

VOX® VODKA

If you're in the market for a sophisticated vodka to call your own, look no further. VOX VODKA from the Netherlands is a pristine, ultra-premium spirit bred for a chilled cocktail glass and the unhurried time to enjoy it. The vodka is meticulously produced from 100% wheat selected for its mild taste. It is distilled five times, then repeatedly filtered through screens made of inert material to achieve its essential purity. The demineralized water used to dilute the vodka to proof is filtered to remove all traces of color, taste and odor.

Ultra-premium Vox Vodka has single-handedly turned neutral into something beautiful. It possesses brilliant clarity, a nearly weightless body, an impeccably clean palate and a cool, crisp finish. The 80 proof vodka is appropriately packaged in a striking, sculpted bottle made of Austrian glass.

In 2003, Jim Beam debuted VOX RASPBERRY. This all-world vodka has a sultry body, a generous, true-to-fruit bouquet, and a full, rounded palate that fills the mouth with the flavor of sun-drenched raspberries. The vodka tapers off without burn or unwanted heat, leaving behind the lingering flavor of fresh picked raspberries.

Both Vox Vodkas exist in a universe of unlimited creative possibilities. While perhaps best served in a cocktail, they are also primed and ready for any vodka-related assignment.

BALASHI BREEZE
House specialty glass, chilled
Pour ingredients into blender
1 1/2 oz. Midori
1/2 oz. Blue Curaçao
1/2 oz. Light Rum
1 oz. cranberry juice
2 1/2 oz. coconut cream syrup
4 oz. pineapple juice
Blend with ice

BALL BEARING
Presentation shot glass, chilled
Build in glass
1/2 fill Cherry Marnier
1/2 fill Champagne

BALL JOINT
House specialty glass, chilled
Pour ingredients into iced mixing glass
1 oz. Ketel One Vodka
3/4 oz. Grand Marnier
3 oz. orange juice
Shake and strain

BALTIMORE ZOO
House specialty glass, ice
Pour ingredients into iced mixing glass
1 oz. Vodka
1/2 oz. Rum
3/4 oz. Triple Sec
1/2 oz. Sloe Gin
1/2 oz. Rose's Lime Juice
2 oz. orange juice
Shake and strain
Fill with Guinness Stout

BAM BE
Presentation shot glass, chilled
Layer ingredients
1/3 fill Tia Maria
1/3 fill Baileys Irish Cream
1/3 fill B & B Liqueur

BANALINI
Champagne glass, chilled
Build in glass
3/4 oz. Peach Schnapps
3/4 oz. Cruzan Banana Rum
Fill with Champagne
Banana slice garnish

BANANA BAY
Bucket glass, ice
Build in glass
1 1/2 oz. Cruzan Banana Rum
Fill with cola

BANANA COW

House specialty glass, chilled
Pour ingredients into blender
1 1/2 oz. Cruzan Estate Diamond Rum
1 oz. Cruzan Banana Rum
1 oz. Cruzan Orange Rum
1/2 oz. grenadine syrup
3/4 oz. half & half cream
2 scoops vanilla ice cream
Blend ingredients (with ice optional)
Banana slice garnish

BANANA FROST

House specialty glass, chilled
Pour ingredients into blender
1 oz. Disaronno Amaretto
1 oz. Vanilla Rum
1 ripe banana
1 oz. half & half cream
2 scoops vanilla ice cream
Blend ingredients (with ice optional)
Banana slice garnish

BANANA FRUIT PUNCH

(makes two servings)
2 house specialty glasses, chilled
Pour ingredients into blender
2 1/2 oz. Bacardi Gold Rum
1 3/4 oz. Mount Gay Eclipse Rum
4-5 slices cored, peeled pineapple
3 ripe bananas
5 oz. orange juice
4 oz. sweet 'n' sour
2 oz. fresh lime juice
1/2 tsp. nutmeg
Blend with ice
Float into each 3/4 oz. Dark Rum

BANANA MILKSHAKE

House specialty glass, chilled
Pour ingredients into blender
1 1/2 oz. Gold Rum
3/4 oz. Dark Rum
2 ripe bananas
1 oz. honey
1 cup milk
2 scoops vanilla ice cream
Blend ingredients (with ice optional)
Whipped cream garnish
Drizzle chocolate syrup

BANANA MONKEY

House specialty glass, chilled
Pour ingredients into iced mixing glass
2 oz. Mount Gay Extra Old Rum
1 oz. Mount Gay Eclipse Rum
1 oz. Crème de Banana
1 oz. fresh lime juice
3/4 oz. grenadine
Shake and strain
Lime wedge garnish

BANANA NUTS

Cocktail glass, chilled
Rim glass with sugar (optional)
Pour ingredients into iced mixing glass
1 1/4 oz. Cruzan Banana Rum
3/4 oz. Crème de Banana
1/2 oz. Frangelico
1/2 oz. orange juice
1/2 oz. grapefruit juice
Shake and strain
Orange slice garnish

BANANA POPSICLE

House specialty glass, chilled
Pour ingredients into blender
1 oz. Crème de Banana
3/4 oz. Cruzan Banana Rum
1 1/2 oz. orange juice
1 ripe banana
1 oz. half & half cream
Blend with ice

BANANA SANDWICH

aka **Monkey's Lunch**
Presentation shot glass, chilled
Layer ingredients
1/3 fill Kahlúa
1/3 fill Crème de Banana
1/3 fill Baileys Irish Cream

BANANAS BARBADOS

House specialty glass, chilled
Pour ingredients into blender
1 oz. Mount Gay Eclipse Rum
1/2 oz. Crème de Banana
2 oz. sweet 'n' sour
1 dash vanilla extract
1 ripe banana
Blend with ice
Float 1 oz. Mount Gay Extra Old Rum

BANANAS OVER YOU

House specialty glass, chilled
Pour ingredients into blender
1 oz. Frangelico
1 oz. Crème de Banana
1/2 oz. White Crème de Cacao
1 ripe banana
2 oz. half & half cream
2 scoops vanilla ice cream
Blend ingredients (with ice optional)
Strawberry garnish

GRAND MARNIER® LIQUEUR

GRAND MARNIER ranks among the finest liqueurs on the planet. People speak of it with justifiable reverence. Grand Marnier is the creation of the Lapostolle family, who in 1827, founded a distillery to produce liqueurs in the chateau country of France. By 1870, the firm was experimenting with different blends of cognac-based liqueurs at their distillery in Cognac. Family member Louis-Alexandre Marnier hit on the notion of combining the peels of bitter Haitian oranges with Fine Champagne cognac. After a decade in development, Grand Marnier was introduced to the world in 1880.

The liqueur is made in Neauphle-le-Château and crafted exactly as it was 120 years ago. The orange peels are first slowly macerated in cognac. The infused-spirit is redistilled, blended with the finest cognacs from each of the growing regions, and sweetened with sugar syrup. The liqueur is then barrel-aged at the Marnier-Lapostolle cognac cellars at Château de Bourg.

To describe Grand Marnier as exquisite may be underselling it a bit. The liqueur has the captivating color of cognac with radiant yellow and gold highlights. Its lightweight body has the texture of satin and the generous citrus bouquet is laced with the aroma of brandy. The palate is an elegant array of sweet and sour orange flavors followed closely by a lingering cognac finish.

BANANA SPLIT
House specialty glass, chilled
Pour ingredients into blender
3/4 oz. White Crème de Menthe
3/4 oz. White Crème de Cacao
3/4 oz. Crème de Banana
2 scoops strawberry ice cream
Blend ingredients (with ice optional)
Whipped cream garnish

BANANA STIGMA
Cocktail glass, chilled
Pour ingredients into iced mixing glass
2 oz. Spudka Vodka
3/4 oz. Whaler's Banana Rum
3/4 oz. Whaler's Vanille Cream
3/4 oz. half & half cream
Shake and strain
Lime wedge garnish

BANDERA
Presentation shot glasses (3), chilled
Build in glasses
First glass - fresh lime juice
Second glass - Añejo Tequila
Third glass - Bloody Mary Mix

BANILLA BOAT
House specialty glass, chilled
Pour ingredients into blender
1 oz. B & B Liqueur
3/4 oz. Crème de Banana
2 scoops vanilla ice cream
Blend ingredients (with ice optional)
Float 3/4 oz. Chambord
Banana slice garnish

BANK SHOT
Rocks glass, chilled
Pour ingredients into iced mixing glass
1 1/4 oz. Absolut Kurant Vodka
1/2 oz. Chambord
1 1/2 oz. orange juice
Shake and strain

BANSHEE
aka **White Monkey**
Cocktail glass, chilled
Pour ingredients into iced mixing glass
1/2 oz. Crème de Banana
1/2 oz. White Crème de Cacao
2 oz. half & half cream
Shake and strain
Banana slice garnish (optional)

BARBARY COAST
Cocktail glass, chilled
Pour ingredients into iced mixing glass
3/4 oz. Scotch Whisky
3/4 oz. Gin
3/4 oz. White Crème de Cacao
3/4 oz. half & half cream
Shake and strain

BARCELONA COFFEE
Coffee mug, heated
Build in glass
1 3/4 oz. Licor 43 (Cuarenta y Tres)
1 oz. Brandy
Near fill with hot coffee
Top with frothed milk
Dust powdered cocoa

BARN RAISER
House specialty glass, ice
Build in glass
1 oz. Vodka
1 oz. Light Rum
1/2 oz. grenadine
2 oz. orange juice
2 oz. pineapple juice
Float 3/4 oz. Dark Rum

BASIN STREET BALM
Cocktail glass, chilled
Pour ingredients into iced mixing glass
1 oz. Brandy
3/4 oz. Peach Schnapps
1 1/2 oz. sweet 'n' sour
Shake and strain
Orange slice and cherry garnish

BAT BITE
Highball glass, ice
Build in glass
1 1/4 oz. Dark Rum
Fill with cranberry juice

BATIDA
Bucket glass, ice
Build in glass
1 1/2 oz. Ypioca Cachaça
1/2 fill orange juice
1/2 fill pineapple juice

BAY AREA GARTER
Coffee mug, heated
Build in glass
3/4 oz. Kahlúa Especial
1/2 oz. Frangelico
1/2 oz. Godiva Chocolate Liqueur
1/2 oz. chocolate syrup
Near fill with hot coffee
Whipped cream garnish
Dust powder cocoa

BAYBREEZE
aka **Downeaster**
Highball glass, ice
Build in glass
1 1/4 oz. Vodka
1/2 fill cranberry juice
1/2 fill pineapple juice

BAY BRIDGE COMMUTER (1)
Bucket glass, ice
Pour ingredients into iced mixing glass
1 3/4 oz. Absolut Peppar Vodka
1/2 tsp. horseradish
3-4 dashes Tabasco Sauce
4 oz. gazpacho
Shake and strain
Lime wedge and prawn garnish

BAY BRIDGE COMMUTER (2)
Bucket glass, ice
Pour ingredients into iced mixing glass
1 1/2 oz. Aquavit
1/2 tsp. horseradish
3-4 dashes Tabasco Sauce
4 oz. gazpacho
Shake and strain
Lime wedge and prawn garnish

BAY BRIDGE
COMMUTER SHOOTER
Rocks glass, chilled
Build in glass
1 1/2 oz. Aquavit
1/2 tsp. horseradish
2 dashes Tabasco Sauce
2 oz. gazpacho
Lime wedge and prawn garnish

BBC
Presentation shot glass, chilled
Build in glass
1/3 fill Baileys Irish Cream
1/3 fill B & B Liqueur
1/3 fill Cointreau

BEACH BLONDE
House specialty glass, ice
Pour ingredients into iced mixing glass
1 1/2 oz. Light Rum
1 oz. Disaronno Amaretto
3/4 oz. grenadine
3/4 oz. Rose's Lime Juice
2 1/2 oz. orange juice
Shake and strain
Near fill with Seven-Up
Float 3/4 oz. Dark Rum

JOSE CUERVO®
RESERVA DE LA FAMILIA®

Clear some space on the top-shelf for ultra-premium JOSE CUERVO RESERVA DE LA FAMILIA TEQUILA, or better yet, build another shelf. First introduced in 1995 to celebrate the distillery's 200th anniversary, this magnificent, vintage dated tequila is museum quality and will likely redefine your concept of luxury living.

As the name would imply, this highly sought-after tequila was once the private domain of the descendants of Jose Maria Guadalupe Cuervo. Reserva De La Familia is a mature, well-rested 100% agave tequila, crafted from the finest stocks of añejos in the Jose Cuervo cellars. The blend is comprised of tequilas that were aged in both new charred French and American oak barrels. The limited edition spirit is hand-bottled, labeled, numbered and sealed in wax.

You can tell you're in for a special treat from the moment the tequila hits your glass. The 2003 vintage has a deep, lustrous, amber color and a supple, medium-weight body. Minutes after it is poured the tequila releases its full bouquet, one laced with the aromas of flora, ripe fruit and oaky vanilla. As it rolls over the palate the tequila fills the mouth with a savory array of flavors, and then gradually subsides into a cognac-like finish.

Reserva De La Familia is a highly prized tequila, one that could only have been created by Jose Cuervo.

BEACH BUM BLUE
House specialty glass, ice
Rim glass with sugar (optional)
Pour ingredients into iced mixing glass
1 1/4 oz. Espolon Reposado Tequila
1 oz. Blue Curaçao
1/2 oz. DeKuyper Peach Pucker
1 1/2 oz. sweet 'n' sour
Shake and strain
Lime wedge garnish

BEACHCOMBER (1)
House specialty glass, ice
Pour ingredients into iced mixing glass
1 1/2 oz. Light Rum
1/2 oz. Triple Sec
1/2 oz. Chambord
1/2 oz. Rose's Lime Juice
1 1/2 oz. sweet 'n' sour
Shake and strain

BEACHCOMBER (2)
Cocktail glass, chilled
Pour ingredients into iced mixing glass
1 1/4 oz. Light Rum
3/4 oz. Mount Gay Eclipse Rum
1/2 oz. Triple Sec
1/2 oz. grenadine
1 oz. sweet 'n' sour
Shake and strain
Lime wedge garnish

BEAM ME UP, SCOTTIE
Presentation shot glass, chilled
Layer ingredients
1/3 fill Kahlúa
1/3 fill Crème de Banana
1/3 fill Baileys Irish Cream

BEARING STRAIT
Cocktail glass, chilled
Pour ingredients into iced mixing glass
1 1/2 oz. Original Cristall Vodka
1/2 oz. Grand Marnier
1/2 oz. Rose's Lime Juice
Stir and strain
Lime wedge garnish

BEAURITA
Presentation shot glass, chilled
Rim glass with salt (optional)
Build in glass
2 dashes Tabasco Sauce
1/4 oz. fresh lime juice
2 oz. Tequila

BEAUTIFUL IN BLUE
Champagne glass, chilled
Build in glass
2 oz. Hpnotiq Liqueur
Fill with champagne
Lemon twist garnish

BEAUTIFUL THING
Rocks glass, ice
Build in glass
1 oz. Baileys Irish Cream
1 oz. Rumple Minze Schnapps

BEAUTY AND THE BEAST
Brandy snifter, heated
Build in glass
3/4 oz. B & B Liqueur
3/4 oz. Black Sambuca

BEER BUSTER
Beer glass or mug, chilled
Build in glass
1 oz. Vodka
3 dashes Tabasco Sauce
Fill with Draft Beer

BEE'S KNEES
Cocktail glass, chilled
Pour ingredients into iced mixing glass
1 oz. Gin
1/2 oz. honey
1 1/2 oz. sweet 'n' sour
Shake and strain

BELGIAN WAFFLE
Tankard or pilsner glass, chilled
Build in glass
1/2 fill Tommyknocker Maple Nut Ale
1/2 fill Pete's Strawberry Blonde Ale

BELLINI
Champagne glass, chilled
Build in glass
1/2 fill peach puree
1/2 fill Champagne

BELLINISIMO
Champagne glass, chilled
Build in glass
1 oz. Chambord
1 oz. pear puree
Fill with Champagne
Lemon twist garnish

BELLISIMO
House specialty glass, ice
Pour ingredients into iced mixing glass
1 1/4 oz. Bacardi Limón Rum
3/4 oz. RémyRed Red Berry Infusion
2 dashes orange bitters
1 1/2 oz. sweet 'n' sour
3 oz. orange juice
Shake and strain
Orange slice garnish

BENSON BOMBER
Bucket glass, ice
Build in glass
1/2 oz. Dark Crème de Cacao
1/2 oz. Brandy
1/2 oz. Kahlúa
1/2 oz. Disaronno Amaretto
1/2 fill cola
1/2 fill half & half cream

BERLIN WALL
Rocks glass, ice
Build in glass
1 1/2 oz. Rumple Minze Schnapps
1/2 oz. Baileys Irish Cream

BERMUDA TRIANGLE (1)
Bucket glass, ice
Build in glass
1 1/2 oz. Gosling's Black Seal Rum
1 oz. DeKuyper Peachtree Schnapps
3/4 oz. VooDoo Spiced Rum
Fill with orange juice
Orange slice garnish

BERMUDA TRIANGLE (2)
Bucket glass, ice
Build in glass
1 1/2 oz. Gosling's Black Seal Rum
2 oz. cranberry juice
2 oz. orange juice
Orange slice garnish

BERMUDA TRIANGLE (3)
Cocktail glass, chilled
Pour ingredients into iced mixing glass
1 1/2 oz. Mount Gay Eclipse Rum
3/4 oz. Cointreau
1/2 oz. Rose's Lime Juice
1/2 oz. cranberry juice
Stir and strain
Lime wedge garnish

BERRIES JUBILEE
House specialty glass, chilled
Pour ingredients into blender
1 3/4 oz. Chambord
1/2 oz. coconut cream syrup
1 oz. half & half cream
2 1/2 oz. pineapple juice
Blend with ice
Whipped cream garnish (optional)

BERRY COOLER
House specialty glass, ice
Build in glass
3/4 oz. DeKuyper Raspberry Pucker
1/4 oz. Disaronno Amaretto
Fill with Seven-Up

GLENMORANGIE® SINGLE HIGHLAND MALT SCOTCH

Located in the northern Highlands, Glenmorangie was established in 1843 at the site of a former brewery. Today, the distillery only produces single malts and the anchor of their portfolio is the revered GLENMORANGIE 10 YEAR OLD SINGLE HIGHLAND MALT SCOTCH.

Perennially ranked as Scotland's best-selling single malt, Glenmorangie's 10 year old whisky is a magnificent dram, one that typifies why single malts are all the rage. It may well be one of the most accessible whiskies ever made, with a broad bouquet and a delicious palate graced with toasty and fruity flavors. It lingers like a pleasant dream.

Glenmorangie's latest handcrafted release is named ELEGANCE, a luxurious, 21 year old single malt. The full-bodied whisky is robust, aromatic and smoky with a long, spicy finish.

Glenmorangie has over the past several years released a glorious array of intriguing, 12 year old single malts finished for up to 2 years in a second, different wood. These distinctive whiskies include PORT WOOD FINISH (port pipes), MADEIRA WOOD FINISH (Malmsey Madeira drums) and SHERRY WOOD FINISH (Oloroso sherry casks).

The distillery has also released several limited bottlings, including a FIRST GROWTH CLARET WOOD FINISH, CÔTE DE NUITS WOOD FINISH and FINO SHERRY WOOD FINISH.

BETELGEUSE
Champagne glass, chilled
Pour ingredients into iced mixing glass
1 oz. Stolichnaya Vanil Vodka
1 oz. Whaler's Original Vanille Rum
1/2 oz. Rose's Lime Juice
1 oz. White Zinfandel
Shake and strain
Fill with Champagne
Orange slice garnish

BETSY ROSS
Cocktail glass, chilled
Pour ingredients into iced mixing glass
1 oz. Brandy
1 oz. Tawny Port
1/2 oz. Cointreau
2 dashes Angostura Bitters
Stir and strain

BETTER THAN N.E.1
Bucket glass, ice
Build in glass
1 1/4 oz. Bourbon
1/2 oz. Saké
1/2 fill lemonade
1/2 fill cranberry juice
Lemon wedge garnish

BETTOR'S DREAM
Cocktail glass, chilled
Pour ingredients into iced mixing glass
1 1/2 oz. Canadian Whisky
1/2 oz. Grand Marnier
2 oz. sweet 'n' sour
Shake and strain
Orange slice and cherry garnish

BETTY GRABLE
Coffee mug, heated
Build in glass
1 1/4 oz. Dark Rum
1/2 oz. Disaronno Amaretto
1/2 oz. Chambord
Near fill with hot apple cider
Whipped cream and cinnamon
   stick garnish
Sprinkle nutmeg

BETWEEN THE SHEETS
Bucket glass, ice
Pour ingredients into iced mixing glass
1 oz. Brandy
3/4 oz. Light Rum
1/2 oz. Triple Sec
2 oz. sweet 'n' sour
Shake and strain

BEVERLY HILLBILLY
Presentation shot glass, chilled
Layer ingredients
1/2 fill Goldschläger
1/2 fill Jägermeister

BEVERLY HILLS COOLER
Champagne glass, chilled
Pour ingredients into iced mixing glass
1 oz. VSOP Cognac
1/2 oz. B & B Liqueur
3 oz. orange juice
Shake and strain
Fill with Champagne
Orange twist garnish

BIBLE BELT (1)
Cocktail glass, chilled
Pour ingredients into iced mixing glass
1 oz. Southern Comfort
1/2 oz. Triple Sec
1 1/2 oz. sweet 'n' sour
Shake and strain
Lime wedge garnish

BIBLE BELT (2)
Cocktail glass, chilled
Rim glass with sugar (optional)
Pour ingredients into iced mixing glass
1 1/4 oz. Jack Daniel's Tennessee Whiskey
3/4 oz. Grand Marnier
1/2 oz. Rose's Lime Juice
1 1/4 oz. sweet 'n' sour
Shake and strain

BIG BAMBOO (1)
House specialty glass, ice
Pour ingredients into iced mixing glass
1 oz. Gold Rum
1 oz. 151° Rum
3/4 oz. Chambord
1 oz. pineapple juice
1 oz. orange juice
1 oz. fresh lime juice
Shake and strain
Float 3/4 oz. Grand Marnier
Orange slice garnish

BIG BAMBOO (2)
House specialty glass, ice
Pour ingredients into iced mixing glass
1 1/4 oz. KéKé Beach Cream Liqueur
3/4 oz. Dark Rum
3/4 oz. Banana Rum
1 1/2 oz. sweet 'n' sour
1 1/2 oz. pineapple juice
Shake and strain

BIG BLUE SHOOTER
Rocks glass, chilled
Pour ingredients into iced mixing glass
1 1/4 oz. Pyrat XO Reserve Rum
1 oz. Malibu Caribbean Rum
3/4 oz. Captain Morgan Spiced Rum
3/4 oz. Blue Curaçao
3 oz. pineapple juice
Shake and strain
Lime wedge garnish

BIG CHILL
House specialty glass, chilled
Pour ingredients into blender
1 1/2 oz. Dark Rum
1 oz. Coconut Rum
3/4 oz. Rose's Lime Juice
1 oz. pineapple juice
1 1/2 oz. cranberry juice
1 1/2 oz. orange juice
Blend with ice
Float 3/4 oz. Jamaican Rum
Pineapple wedge and cherry garnish

BIG FAT MONKEY KISS
Presentation shot glass, chilled
Build in glass
1/2 oz. Disaronno Amaretto
1/2 oz. Peach Schnapps
1/2 oz. Crème de Banana
1/2 oz. cranberry juice

BIKINI LINE
Presentation shot glass, chilled
Build in glass
1/3 fill Tia Maria
1/3 fill Chambord
1/3 fill Vox Raspberry Vodka

BISMARK
Tankard or pilsner glass, chilled
Build in glass
1/2 fill Beck's Dark Lager
1/2 fill Champagne

BITCHES FROM HELL
Presentation shot glass, chilled
Build in glass
1/3 fill Jägermeister
1/3 fill Crème de Banana
1/3 fill half & half cream

BIT-O-HONEY
Presentation shot glass, chilled
Layer ingredients
1/2 fill Butterscotch Schnapps
1/2 fill Baileys Irish Cream

SEA WYNDE®
POT STILL RUM

If you're in the market for a rare and remarkable rum, the likes of which hasn't been seen in more than three decades, then look no further than ultra-premium SEA WYNDE POT STILL RUM, a rum crafted in a traditional style made famous by the British Royal Navy.

Most rums are produced in column stills, which is an economical method of producing large quantities of light-bodied spirits. The rums used to create Sea Wynde are distilled in pot stills, a significantly more laborious and expensive process.

The ultra-premium Sea Wynde blend is comprised of five magnificent, yet distinctively different pure pot still rums. They are distilled in Jamaica and Guyana and aged in oak barrels for 5 to 11 years. The rum is bottled at 92 proof.

There may not be a more coveted, eminently satisfying rum on the planet than Sea Wynde. It is in all respects near perfection. Sea Wynde has a marvelous, full body, a generous bouquet and a palate bursting at the seams with the flavors of vanilla, honey, fruit and roasted coffee. Its long, warm and sultry finish is reminiscent of an aged malt whisky.

While this robust and highly aromatic rum is ideally served neat or straight-up, it is also substantial enough to feature in cocktails.

BLACK & BLUE BAYOU
Bucket glass, ice
Build in glass
1 1/2 oz. RémyRed Grape Berry Infusion
3/4 oz. Blue Curaçao
1/2 fill pineapple juice
1/2 fill grapefruit juice

BLACK AND BROWN
Tankard or pilsner glass, chilled
Build in glass
1/2 fill Guinness Stout
1/2 fill Newcastle Brown Ale

BLACK AND TAN
Beer or ale glass, chilled
Build in glass
1/2 fill Bass Ale
1/2 fill Guinness Stout

BLACK AND WHITE
Presentation shot glass, chilled
Layer ingredients
1/2 fill Kahlúa
1/2 fill Chambord

BLACK APE
Tankard or pilsner glass, chilled
Build in glass
1/2 fill Guinness Stout
1/2 fill Pyramid Apricot Ale

BLACKBEARD'S TREASURE
House specialty glass, chilled
Pour ingredients into blender
1 1/2 oz. Spiced Rum
1 oz. Mount Gay Eclipse Rum
1 oz. Chambord
2 oz. raspberry puree
2 oz. sweet 'n' sour
Blend with ice
Pineapple wedge and cherry garnish

BLACK BEAUTY (1)
Rocks glass, ice
Build in glass
3/4 oz. Van Gogh Vodka
1/2 oz. Van Gogh Chocolate Vodka
1/2 oz. Frangelico
1/2 oz. Kahlúa Especial
3/4 oz. half & half cream

BLACK BEAUTY (2)
Cocktail glass, chilled
Rim glass with sugar (optional)
Pour ingredients into iced mixing glass
1 1/2 oz. Jim Beam Black Label Bourbon
1 oz. DeKuyper Peachtree Schnapps
1/2 oz. cranberry juice
Stir and strain

BLACK CAT
Bucket glass, ice
Build in glass
1 1/2 oz. DeKuyper Cherry Pucker
1/2 oz. RémyRed Grape Berry Infusion
1/2 fill cranberry juice
1/2 fill cherry soda

BLACK CHERRY SONIC
Highball glass, ice
Build in glass
1 1/4 oz. Ultimat Black Cherry Vodka
1/2 fill club soda
1/2 fill tonic water
Orange wedge garnish

BLACK CITRUS SIN
Rocks glass, ice
Pour ingredients into iced mixing glass
1 oz. Jim Beam Black Label Bourbon
1/2 oz. Poire (Pear) William Eau-de-Vie
3/4 oz. simple syrup
3/4 oz. orange juice
3/4 oz. cranberry juice
3/4 oz. lemon juice
Shake and strain
Pear slice garnish

BLACK DEATH
Pilsner glass, chilled
Build in glass
1/2 fill Guinness Stout
1/2 fill Woodchuck Cider

BLACK DIAMOND
Cocktail glass, chilled
Pour ingredients into iced mixing glass
1 3/4 oz. Irish Whiskey
1/2 oz. RémyRed Red Berry Infusion
1/2 oz. Dry Vermouth
Stir and strain
Lemon twist garnish

BLACK-EYED SUSAN
aka **Kentucky Screwdriver**
Highball glass, ice
Build in glass
1 1/4 oz. Bourbon
Fill with orange juice

BLACK HAWAIIAN
Rocks glass, ice
Pour ingredients into iced mixing glass
Build in glass
2 oz. Pearl Lo Coco Vodka
1 oz. Kahlúa

BLACK HOOTER
Rocks glass, chilled
Pour ingredients into iced mixing glass
1 oz. Blackberry Brandy
1 oz. Chambord
Shake and strain
Splash Seven-Up

BLACK JACK
Coffee mug, heated
Build in glass
1 oz. Jack Daniel's Tennessee Whiskey
1 oz. Rumple Minze Schnapps
Fill with hot coffee

BLACK JAMAICAN
Rocks glass, ice
Build in glass
1 1/2 oz. Appleton Estate V/X Jamaica Rum
1/2 oz. Tia Maria

BLACK JEWELED RUSSIAN
Rocks glass, ice
Build in glass
1 1/2 oz. Stolichnaya Vodka
1/2 oz. Drambuie
1/2 oz. Kahlúa Especial
1/2 oz. Sylk Cream Liqueur

BLACK KNIGHT
Coffee mug, preheated
Build in glass
1 1/4 oz. Jim Beam Black Label Bourbon
1/2 oz. Cinnamon Schnapps
1/4 tsp. honey
Fill with hot apple cider
Garnish with cinnamon stick and
    apple wedge

BLACK MARIA
Coffee mug, heated
Build in glass
1 1/2 oz. Kuya Fusion Rum
1 1/2 oz. Tia Maria
3/4 oz. Dark Crème de Cacao
Near fill with hot coffee
Whipped cream garnish

BLACK MASS
Presentation shot glass, chilled
Layer ingredients
1/3 fill Kahlúa
1/3 fill Sambuca
1/3 fill Dark Rum

ABSOLUT® VODKA

Lars Olsen Smith was a giant in the Swedish vodka industry, who by the 1870s controlled the majority of the country's spirits production. Armed with a state of the art facility equipped with a revolutionary new column still, Smith began bottling a vodka of unprecedented purity in 1879. Appropriately labeled *Absolut Renat Brannvin* (absolutely pure vodka), it is this spirit that inspired the creation of ABSOLUT VODKA.

The world-renowned brand is distilled in Ahus, a picturesque town on the southern coast of Sweden, by the state-consortium V. & S. Vin and Spirits Company. Absolut Vodka is made entirely from a mash of locally grown wheat and purified well water. It is quadruple-distilled in a six-column, continuous still and emerges at extremely high proof. The vodka is not subjected to filtration before being reduced with water to 80 proof.

Introduced in the United States in 1979, Absolut is now the best-selling imported vodka in this country. It has pristine clarity and a lightweight body with the lush texture of velvet. The vodka has a subtle bouquet of citrus, pine and clover, and a clean, marvelously neutral palate. The finish is crisp and refreshing.

The famed Absolut line of vodkas also includes VANILIA (vanilla), CITRON (citrus), PEPPAR (pepper), KURANT (currant) and MANDARIN (mandarin orange).

BLACK 'N' BLUE
Cocktail glass, chilled
Pour ingredients into iced mixing glass
1 1/2 oz. Polar Ice Vodka
3/4 oz. Blue Curaçao
3/4 oz. white cranberry juice
1/2 oz. fresh lime juice
Stir and strain
Lime wedge garnish

BLACK ORCHID
Bucket glass, ice
Pour ingredients into iced mixing glass
1 oz. Dark Rum
1 oz. Blue Curaçao
1 1/2 oz. grenadine
1 1/2 oz. cranberry juice
Shake and strain
Float 3/4 oz. Jamaican Rum
Orange slice garnish

BLACK RUBY
Coffee mug, heated
Build in glass
1 oz. Opal Nera Black Sambuca
3/4 oz. Tuaca
1 pinch each, sugar and cinnamon
Add lemon and orange zest
Fill with hot coffee

BLACK RUSSIAN
Rocks glass, ice
Build in glass
1 1/2 oz. Vodka
3/4 oz. Kahlúa

BLACK SMOOTH & SOUR
Bucket glass, cracked ice
Pour ingredients into iced mixing glass
2 oz. Jim Beam White Label Bourbon
1 oz. Disaronno Amaretto
1 oz. Triple Sec
2 oz. sweet 'n' sour
2 oz. lemon-lime soda
Shake and strain
Lemon wedge garnish

BLACK STOCKINGS
Cocktail glass, chilled
Pour ingredients into iced mixing glass
2 oz. Vox Raspberry Vodka
3/4 oz. Chambord
3/4 oz. Godiva Chocolate Liqueur
Stir and strain
Lemon twist garnish

BLACK SUN
Bucket glass, ice
Build in glass
1 1/2 oz. Mount Gay Eclipse Rum
3/4 oz. Cointreau
3/4 oz. sweet 'n' sour
Fill with cola
Lime wheel garnish

BLACK TEQUILA ROSE
Brandy snifter
Layer in bottom of glass
1 oz. Razzmatazz Raspberry Liqueur
Add ice
Pour into center of glass
1 1/4 oz. Tequila Rose Cream Liqueur

BLACK VELVET
Tankard or pilsner glass, chilled
Build in glass
1/2 fill Guinness Stout
1/2 fill Champagne

BLACK VELVETEEN
Tankard or pilsner glass, chilled
Build in glass
1/2 fill Guinness Stout
1/2 fill hard apple cider

BLACK WATCH
Rocks glass, ice
Build in glass
1 1/2 oz. Scotch Whisky
1/2 oz. Kahlúa
Lemon twist garnish

BLACK WIDOW
Bucket glass, ice
Build in glass
1 oz. Grey Goose Vodka
1 oz. Disaronno Amaretto
Near fill with orange juice
Splash club soda
Orange slice garnish

BLAST FROM THE PAST
Cappuccino cup, heated
Build in glass
1/2 oz. Tia Maria
1/2 oz. Grand Marnier
1/2 oz. Chambord
Near fill with hot espresso coffee
Top with frothed milk
Sprinkle shaved chocolate

BLAST-OFF PUNCH
House specialty glass, ice
Pour ingredients into iced mixing glass
3/4 oz. Light Rum
3/4 oz. Gold Rum
3/4 oz. Blue Curaçao
1/2 oz. Orange Rum
1 1/2 oz. sweet 'n' sour
1 1/2 oz. orange juice
Shake and strain
Float 3/4 oz. Dark Rum
Lime, lemon and orange wedge garnish

BLEACHER'S TWIST
Presentation shot glass, chilled
Layer ingredients
1/3 fill Kahlúa Especial
1/3 fill Chambord
1/3 fill Baileys Irish Cream

BLENDED FROG
House specialty glass, chilled
Pour ingredients into blender
1 oz. DeKuyper Peachtree Schnapps
1 oz. DeKuyper Raspberry Pucker
3 oz. cranberry juice
2 scoops vanilla ice cream
Blend ingredients (with ice optional)

BLING BLING
Rocks glass, chilled
Pour ingredients into iced mixing glass
1 oz. RedRum
1 oz. Hpnotiq Liqueur
2 oz. pineapple juice
Shake and strain
Splash lemon-lime soda

BLITZ KNIGHT
Cocktail glass, chilled
Pour ingredients into iced mixing glass
2 1/2 oz. Wet by Beefeater
1/8 oz. fresh lime juice
Stir and strain
Lemon twist garnish

BLIZZARD (1)
House specialty glass, chilled
Pour ingredients into blender
2 oz. Bourbon
1/2 oz. Rose's Lime Juice
1/2 oz. grenadine
1 1/2 oz. cranberry juice
2 oz. sweet 'n' sour
Blend with ice
Orange slice and cherry garnish

DISARONNO® ORIGINALE

Legend has it that DISARONNO ORIGINALE was created in Saronno, Italy in 1525. The recipe for the original amaretto was passed through the creator's family for generations until it was acquired in 1817 by Carlo Dominico Reina, who began selling the liqueur in his apothecary. After World War I one of Reina's descendents began to market the liqueur outside of Saronno.

In 1939, the century-old firm of Illva Saronno began producing the famous liqueur under the name Amaretto di Saronno. Its proprietary recipe is still made with a base of premium Italian grape spirits, which is patiently steeped with 17 herbs and fruits, including apricot kernel oil. Once fully infused with flavor, the liqueur is sweetened with caramelized sugar and bottled at 56 proof.

Disaronno Originale is a *grand dame* of liqueurs; one often imitated, yet never equaled. It has a burnished, copper hue and medium-weight, satiny smooth body. The generous bouquet is laced with the aromas of marzipan and citrus zest. Its palate rapidly fills the mouth with the marvelous, semisweet flavors of almonds, oranges and vanilla. The finish is long and eminently flavorful.

Disaronno Originale is altogether indispensable behind the bar, as evidenced by the exceptionally large numbers of drinks in which it is featured. Accept no substitute.

BLIZZARD (2)
House specialty glass, chilled
Pour ingredients into blender
1 1/4 oz. Dark Rum
3/4 oz. Brandy
3/4 oz. Cruzan Rum Cream
3/4 oz. half & half cream
2 scoops chocolate ice cream
Blend ingredients (with ice optional)
Whipped cream garnish
Drizzle 3/4 oz. Kahlúa
Sprinkle nutmeg

BLONDE TEASER (1)
Bucket glass, ice
Build in glass
3/4 oz. Ketel One Vodka
3/4 oz. DeKuyper Buttershots Schnapps
Fill with cola

BLONDE TEASER (2)
Bucket glass, ice
Build in glass
3/4 oz. Vanilla Rum
3/4 oz. DeKuyper Buttershots Schnapps
Fill with cola

BLOOD AND SAND (1)
Highball glass, ice
Build in glass
3/4 oz. Scotch Whisky
3/4 oz. Cherry Brandy
Fill with orange juice

BLOOD AND SAND (2)
Cocktail glass, chilled
Pour ingredients into iced mixing glass
1 1/4 oz. Scotch Whisky
1/2 oz. Sweet Vermouth
1/2 oz. Cherry Brandy
1 oz. orange juice
Shake and strain
Orange twist garnish

BLOOD AND SAND (3)
Cocktail glass, chilled
Pour ingredients into iced mixing glass
3/4 oz. Scotch Whisky
3/4 oz. Cherry Heering
3/4 oz. Sweet Vermouth
3/4 oz. orange juice
Stir and strain
Orange slice and cherry garnish

BLOOD ORANGE CHAMPAGNE COCKTAIL
Champagne glass, chilled
Build in glass
1/2 fill blood orange juice
1/2 fill Champagne
Lemon twist garnish

BLOODY BRAIN
Presentation shot glass, chilled
Build in glass
1 oz. Baileys Irish Cream
1 oz. Peach Schnapps
3 drops grenadine

BLOODY MARIA
Bucket glass, ice
Rim glass with salt (optional)
Build in glass
1 1/4 oz. Tequila
Fill with Bloody Mary mix
Lime wedge and celery garnish

BLOODY MARY
Bucket glass, ice
Rim glass with salt (optional)
Build in glass
1 1/4 oz. Vodka
Fill with Bloody Mary mix
Lime wedge and celery garnish

BLOODY MARY, BLOODHOUND
Bucket glass, ice
Rim glass with salt (optional)
Build in glass
1 oz. Vodka
1 oz. Dry Sack Sherry
Fill with Bloody Mary mix
Lime wedge and celery garnish

BLOODY MARY,
BLOODY BASTARD
Bucket glass, ice
Rim glass with salt (optional)
Build in glass
1/2 fill Bass Ale
1/2 fill Bloody Mary mix
1/2 tbsp. horseradish
Lime wedge and shrimp garnish

BLOODY MARY, BLOODY BISON
Bucket glass, ice
Rim glass with salt (optional)
Build in glass
1 1/4 oz. Zubrówka Bison Brand Vodka
Fill with Bull Shot
Lime wedge and celery garnish
Note: "Bull Shot" is 1/2 Bloody Mary mix
and 1/2 beef broth

BLOODY MARY, BLOODY BULL
Bucket glass, ice
Rim glass with salt (optional)
Build in glass
1 1/4 oz. Vodka
Fill with Bull Shot
Lime wedge and celery garnish
Note: "Bull Shot" is 1/2 Bloody Mary mix
and 1/2 beef broth

BLOODY MARY,
BLOODY CAESAR
House specialty glass, ice
Rim glass with salt (optional)
Build in glass
1 1/4 oz. Vodka
Fill with Clamato juice
Lime wedge and celery garnish
Note: "Bloody Clam" may be substituted for
    Clamato juice (a mix of 1 1/2 oz. clam
    juice per serving of Bloody Mary mix)

BLOODY MARY, BLOODY CAJUN
Bucket glass, ice
Rim glass with salt (optional)
Build in glass
1 1/2 oz. Vodka
1/2 tsp. onion powder
1/4 tsp. crushed thyme leaves
1 pinch red pepper
2 pinches paprika
Fill with Bloody Mary mix
Lime wedge and celery garnish

BLOODY MARY,
BLOODY FRENCH GOOSE
Bucket glass, ice
Rim glass with salt (optional)
Build in glass
1 1/2 oz. Grey Goose Vodka
1/4 tsp. Italian seasoning
2 pinches each, garlic powder and paprika
1/2 oz. fresh lime juice
Fill with Bloody Mary mix
Roasted garlic and celery garnish

BLOODY MARY,
BLOODY ITALIAN
Bucket glass, ice
Rim glass with salt (optional)
Build in glass
1 1/2 oz. Vodka
1/4 tsp. Italian seasoning
2 pinches each, garlic powder and paprika
Fill with Bloody Mary mix
Lime wedge and celery garnish

BLOODY MARY, BLOODY MOOSE
Bucket or house specialty glass, ice
Rim glass with salt (optional)
Build in glass
1 1/2 oz. Zubrówka Bison Brand Vodka
Fill with Bloody Mary mix
Lime wedge and beef jerky garnish

EL TESORO® PLATINUM
100% AGAVE TEQUILA

Renowned El Tesoro de Don Felipe 100% Agave Tequilas are handmade at a small distillery located high in the Los Altos Mountains named La Alteña. There, the Camarena family makes tequila the same way they have for over 50 years, using methods long since abandoned by other distillers as too expensive.

The range of artisan tequilas is anchored by the altogether remarkable EL TESORO PLATINUM. It is aromatic, peppery and loaded with the robust character and clean, crisp flavor of blue agave. The tequila is bottled within 24 hours of distillation—unfiltered and unaltered, exactly as it came out of the still. The distillery also makes EL TESORO REPOSADO, which is barrel-aged between 6 and 9 months, and EL TESORO AÑEJO, which is matured for 2 to 3 years in small, oak bourbon barrels. It has a deep, satisfying bouquet, an exceptionally rich, well-rounded flavor and a long, lingering finish.

EL TESORO PARADISO is an innovative style of tequila. It is a 5 year old añejo, hand-crafted from a blend of El Tesoro tequilas that are further aged in French oak barrels previously used to age A. de Fussigny Cognac. Paradiso strikes a sublime balance between the elegance of cognac and the sultry character of tequila, both of which are deeply imbued in its bouquet, body, flavor and finish.

BLOODY MARY, BLOODY NOSE (1)
Bucket or house specialty glass, ice
Rim glass with salt (optional)
Build in glass
1 1/2 oz. Vodka
Near fill with Bloody Mary mix
Float raw oyster
Lime wedge and celery garnish

BLOODY MARY, BLOODY NOSE (2)
Bucket or house specialty glass, ice
Rim glass with salt (optional)
Build in glass
1 1/2 oz. Absolut Peppar Vodka
1/2 tbsp. horseradish
Near fill with Bloody Mary mix
Float raw oyster
Lime wedge and celery garnish

BLOODY MARY, BLOODY RUSSIAN BASTARD
Bucket or house specialty glass, ice
Rim glass with salt (optional)
Build in glass
1 1/4 oz. Stolichnaya Citros Vodka
2 oz. Bass Ale
1/2 tbsp. horseradish
Fill with Bloody Mary mix
Lime wedge and shrimp garnish

BLOODY MARY, BLOODY TEX-MEX
Bucket or house specialty glass, ice
Rim glass with salt (optional)
Build in glass
1 1/2 oz. Vodka
1/2 oz. chili powder
2 pinches each, ground cumin and paprika
Fill with Bloody Mary mix
Lime wedge and celery garnish

BLOODY MARY, BLOODY WRIGHT
Bucket glass, ice
Rim glass with salt (optional)
Build in glass
1 1/2 oz. Cruzan Estate Light Rum
Fill with Bloody Mary mix
Lime wedge and celery garnish

BLOODY MARY, DANISH (1)
Bucket glass, ice
Rim glass with salt (optional)
Build in glass
1 1/2 oz. Aquavit
1/2 tsp. horseradish
2 oz. Clamato juice
Fill with Bloody Mary mix
Lime wedge and celery garnish

BLOODY MARY, DANISH (2)
Bucket glass, ice
Rim glass with salt (optional)
Build in glass
1 1/4 oz. Aquavit
Fill with Bloody Mary mix
Lime wedge and celery garnish

BLOODY MARY, DIRTY
Bucket glass, ice
Rim glass with salt (optional)
Build in glass
1 1/2 oz. Vodka
1/4 oz. olive juice (brine)
Fill with Bloody Mary mix
Olive and celery garnish

BLOODY MARY, DIRTY BLOODY CAJUN
Bucket glass, ice
Rim glass with salt (optional)
Build in glass
1 1/2 oz. Vodka
1/2 tsp. onion powder
1/4 tsp. crushed thyme leaves
1 pinch red pepper
2 pinches paprika
1/4 oz. olive juice (brine)
Fill with Bloody Mary mix
Lime wedge, olive and celery

BLOODY MARY, GIN
aka **Gin Mary**, **Red Snapper**
Bucket glass, ice
Rim glass with salt (optional)
Build in glass
1 1/4 oz. Gin
Fill with Bloody Mary mix
Lime wedge and celery garnish

BLOODY MARY, JÄGER SALSA
House specialty glass, ice
Rim glass with salt (optional)
Build in glass
1 1/4 oz. Jägermeister
2 tsp. salsa, medium-hot
Fill with Bloody Mary mix
Lime wedge and celery garnish

BLOODY MARY, MANGO
Bucket glass, ice
Rim glass with salt (optional)
Build in glass
1 1/4 oz. Mango-infused Vodka
Fill with Mango Bloody Mary mix
Lime wedge, celery and mango slice garnish
Note: See Mars Mango Infusion and Mango Bloody Mary Mix

BLOODY MARY, MICHILATA
Pint glass, ice
Rim glass with salt (optional)
Pour ingredients into iced mixing glass
1 1/2 oz. Reposado Tequila
3/4 oz. fresh lime juice
1/2 oz. fresh lemon juice
4 dashes Tabasco Sauce
1/4 oz. white wine vinegar
2 pinches each, salt, black pepper and seasoned salt
3 oz. tomato juice
Shake and strain
Fill with Tecate Mexican Beer
Lime wedge garnish

BLOODY MARY MIX
Large covered jar
Mix per instructions
46 oz. tomato juice
2 oz. Worcestershire sauce
6 dashes Tabasco Sauce
2 tbsp. celery salt
1 tbsp. black pepper
1/2 tbsp. salt
2 dashes Angostura Bitters
Thoroughly mix ingredients and taste-test over ice. Keep refrigerated.
Optional ingredients: prepared horseradish; V-8; clamato juice; clam juice; pureed Mexican salsa; Mexican hot sauce; fresh lemon juice; fresh lime juice; beef bouillon; seasoned salt; cayenne pepper; onion powder; garlic salt/powder; diced or pureed jalapeño pepper; cilantro; A-1 sauce; chili powder; Italian seasonings; paprika; red pepper; crushed thyme leaves; ground cumin.

BLOODY MARY MIX, MANGO
Large covered jar
Pour ingredients into blender
2 cups mango cubes
1 tsp. chili powder
1 tsp. ginger powder
1 tbsp. black pepper, cracked
1 dash Tabasco Sauce
1/2 tsp. horseradish
4 cups V-8 juice
Thoroughly blend ingredients
Taste test, serve over ice
Note: See Mango Bloody Mary

BLOODY MARY, VIRGIN
aka **Bloody Shame**
Bucket or house specialty glass, ice
Rim glass with salt (optional)
Build in glass
Fill with Bloody Mary mix
Lime wedge and celery garnish

KAHLÚA® ESPECIAL LIQUEUR

In 2002, Kahlúa introduced a new version of their liqueur into the American market called KAHLÚA ESPECIAL. Once available only in duty-free stores, the super-premium liqueur is made entirely from high-grade, Arabica coffee beans from South America. The beans are cultivated under shady, high altitude conditions, which allow them to ripen slowly. They are handpicked and carefully roasted in small batches. For coffee aficionados, Kahlúa Especial is the real deal.

This exquisite liqueur has a silky smooth, richly textured body and a captivating aroma of roasted coffee, vanilla and milk chocolate. The lightweight liqueur immediately fills the mouth with an array of luxurious flavors, a lavish affair of freshly brewed espresso, dark chocolate and mocha. Perhaps best of all, the delectable flavors persist well into the relaxed finish. The overall effect is without equal.

In a country that finds tremendous joy in coffee, Kahlúa Especial is a 70 proof phenomenon waiting to happen. There simply is no other liqueur that comes as close to capturing the robust, mouth-watering essence of espresso.

Kahlúa Especial is bound to cause a stir in the mixology community. Its elevated proof, lighter body and exuberant character make it a prime candidate for inclusion in a broad range of creative Martinis and contemporary cocktails.

BLOODY MARY, WHARF POPPER
Bucket glass, ice
Build in glass
1 1/2 oz. Aquavit
1/2 oz. fresh lemon juice
2 pinches basil
Fill with Bloody Mary mix
Lime wedge and scallion garnish

BLOODY MARY, WHAT? ME WORRY
House specialty glass, ice
Rim glass with salt (optional)
Build in glass
4 oz. Alcohol-free Beer
Fill with Bloody Mary mix
Lime wedge and shrimp garnish

BLOW JOB (1)
Presentation shot glass, chilled
Build in glass
1/3 fill Grand Marnier
1/3 fill Crème de Banana
Near fill with Tia Maria
Whipped cream garnish

BLOW JOB (2)
Presentation shot glass, chilled
Build in glass
1/2 fill Grand Marnier
Near fill with Baileys Irish Cream
Whipped cream garnish

BLUE BAYOU (1)
Bucket glass, ice
Build in glass
1 1/2 oz. Vodka
1 oz. Midori
1/2 fill grapefruit juice
1/2 fill pineapple juice
Float 1 oz. DeKuyper Island Blue Pucker
Lime wedge garnish

BLUE BAYOU (2)
House specialty glass, chilled
Pour ingredients into blender
1 1/2 oz. Light Rum
1 oz. Blue Curaçao
3/4 oz. half & half cream
2 scoops French vanilla ice cream
Blend ingredients (with ice optional)
Orange slice and cherry garnish

BLUEBERRY LEMON FIZZ
House specialty glass, chilled
Pour ingredients into blender
6 oz. blueberry yogurt
1/2 oz. grenadine
2 oz. lemon-lime soda
2 scoops lemon sherbet
Blend ingredients (with ice optional)
Pineapple wedge garnish

BLUEBERRY TEA
Tea cup or coffee mug, heated
Build in glass
3/4 oz. Grand Marnier
3/4 oz. Disaronno Amaretto
Fill with hot tea
Lemon wedge garnish

BLUE BLAZER
Mug or tankard
Build in glass
2 oz. Scotch Whisky
3/4 oz. honey
1/4 oz. fresh lemon juice
3 oz. hot water
Combine ingredients and bring slowly
    to a boil allowing honey to dissolve
    before serving.
Note: Traditionally prepared aflame, this
    is an extremely dangerous and highly
    discouraged practice.

BLUE DEVIL
aka **Blue Moon**
Cocktail glass, chilled
Pour ingredients into iced mixing glass
2 oz. Magellan Gin
1/2 oz. Blue Curaçao
1 3/4 oz. sweet 'n' sour
Shake and strain

BLUE DUCK
Bucket glass, ice
Build in glass
1 1/2 oz. Vodka
3/4 oz. Gin
3/4 oz. Peach Schnapps
1/4 oz. Blue Curaçao
1/4 oz. fresh lemon juice
Fill with tonic water
Lime wheel garnish

BLUE FLUTE
Champagne glass, chilled
Build in glass
1 1/4 oz. Disaronno Amaretto
3/4 oz. Blue Curaçao
Fill with Champagne
Orange twist garnish

BLUE HAWAII
House specialty glass, chilled
Pour ingredients into blender
1 1/2 oz. Cruzan Estate Light Rum
1 oz. Blue Curaçao
3/4 oz. White Crème de Cacao
3/4 oz. half & half cream
2 scoops vanilla ice cream
Blend ingredients (with ice optional)
Orange slice and cherry garnish

BLUE HAWAIIAN
Collins or bucket glass, ice
Pour ingredients into iced mixing glass
1 1/2 oz. Light Rum
1 oz. Mount Gay Eclipse Rum
1 oz. Blue Curaçao
1 1/2 oz. sweet 'n' sour
1 1/2 oz. pineapple juice
1 1/2 oz. coconut cream syrup
Shake and strain
Pineapple wedge and orange slice garnish

BLUE LADY
Cocktail glass, chilled
Pour ingredients into iced mixing glass
2 oz. Hpnotiq Liqueur
1/2 oz. Gin
1 1/2 oz. sweet 'n' sour
Shake and strain

BLUE LAGOON (1)
Bucket glass, ice
Build in glass
1 1/2 oz. Cruzan Coconut Rum
3/4 oz. Cruzan Pineapple Rum
Near fill with pineapple juice
Float 3/4 oz. Blue Curaçao

BLUE LAGOON (2)
Bucket glass, ice
Build in glass
1 oz. Malibu Caribbean Rum
Near fill with pineapple juice
Float 3/4 oz. Blue Curaçao

BLUE LEMONADE
Bucket glass, ice
Build in glass
1 1/2 oz. Citrus Vodka
3/4 oz. Blue Curaçao
Fill with lemonade

BLUE MARLIN
Cocktail glass, chilled
Pour ingredients into iced mixing glass
1 1/2 oz. Appleton Estate V/X Jamaica Rum
1 1/4 oz. Mount Gay Eclipse Rum
3/4 oz. Blue Curaçao
1/2 oz. Citrónge Orange Liqueur
1 oz. fresh lime juice
Shake and strain
Lime wedge garnish

BLUE MIMOSA
Champagne glass, chilled
Build in glass
3/4 oz. VSOP Cognac
2 oz. Hpnotiq Liqueur
1/2 fill orange juice
1/2 fill Champagne
Orange slice garnish

KNAPPOGUE CASTLE® IRISH SINGLE MALT WHISKEY

Irish whiskies continue to flourish in the United States and the 1993 vintage of KNAPPOGUE CASTLE IRISH SINGLE MALT WHISKEY has fanned the flames. The whiskey is about the most luxurious malt whiskey to ever grace a glass.

Knappogue Castle Single Malt is triple-distilled in small batches at the famed Bushmill Distillery in the heart of County Antrim. The malt whiskies selected for this prestigious bottling are aged in oak bourbon barrels until it is determined they have reached their fullest potential.

The '93 vintage of the Knappogue (pronounced nah-POG) Castle is an extraordinary single malt whiskey, one worthy of the many accolades it has received. Unlike many Scotch malts, Knappogue Castle is not dominated by a smoky, peaty character. It is light and eminently drinkable. It has an alluring bouquet with fresh notes of grain and herbs. On the palate, the silky textured whiskey is ideally balanced with the delightfully sweet flavor of malt, spice and caramel. The finish is long and relaxed with a slightly sweet flavor.

Knappogue Castle is a delectable top-shelf performer. It is an affordable, highly versatile whiskey, one equally at home served neat in a snifter as it is mixed in a cocktail. The 1994 vintage promises to be as good if not better.

BLUE MOON CAFÉ
Sherry glass, chilled
Build in glass
1/3 fill Blue Curaçao
1/3 fill orange juice
1/3 fill Champagne

BLUE TAIL FLY
Cocktail glass, chilled
Pour ingredients into iced mixing glass
1/2 oz. White Crème de Cacao
1/2 oz. Blue Curaçao
2 oz. half & half cream
Shake and strain

BLUE TRAIN SPECIAL
Champagne glass, chilled
Pour ingredients into iced mixing glass
1 oz. Brandy
1 oz. pineapple juice
Shake and strain
Fill with Champagne
Lemon twist garnish

BLUE WAVE (1)
Bucket glass, ice
Build in glass
1 1/2 oz. Tarantula Azul
3/4 oz. Blue Curaçao
Fill with lemonade
Orange slice and cherry garnish

BLUE WAVE (2)
Tall house specialty glass, ice
Pour ingredients into iced mixing glass
2 oz. Hpnotiq Liqueur
2 oz. White Wine
3/4 oz. Blue Curaçao
1 oz. orange juice
1 oz. white cranberry juice
1 1/2 oz. sweet 'n' sour
Shake and strain
Orange slice and apple wedge garnish

BLUE WHALE
Bucket glass, ice
Build in glass
1 1/2 oz. Peach Schnapps
3/4 oz. Blue Curaçao
Fill with Seven-Up

BLUSHING ANGEL
Champagne glass, chilled
Pour ingredients into iced mixing glass
1 1/2 oz. Dubonnet Rouge
2 1/2 oz. cranberry juice
Shake and strain
Fill with Champagne
Lemon twist garnish

BLUSHING BERRY COOLER

House specialty glass, chilled
Pour ingredients into blender
1 1/2 oz. Kahlúa
4 oz. strawberry puree or 1/2 cup frozen
   strawberries
2 1/2 oz. milk
2 oz. plain lowfat yogurt
2 oz. orange juice concentrate, frozen
Blend with ice

BOBBY BURNS

Cocktail glass, chilled
Pour ingredients into iced mixing glass
1 1/2 oz. Scotch Whisky
1/2 oz. Sweet Vermouth
1/2 oz. Drambuie
Stir and strain

BOBSLEDDER'S BANSHEE

House specialty glass, chilled
Pour ingredients into blender
1 oz. Peppermint Schnapps
1 oz. Baileys Irish Cream
3/4 oz. half & half cream
2 chocolate chip cookies
2 scoops vanilla ice cream
Blend ingredients (with ice optional)
Chocolate chip cookie garnish

BOCCI BALL

Highball glass, ice
Build in glass
1 1/4 oz. Disaronno Amaretto
Near fill with orange juice
Splash club soda

BOCCI SHOOTER

Presentation shot glass, chilled
Build in glass
1/2 fill Disaronno Amaretto
Near fill with orange juice
Splash club soda

BODY WARMER

Tea cup or coffee mug, heated
Build in glass
1 1/4 oz. Grand Marnier
1/2 oz. simple syrup (optional)
Fill with hot tea

BOG FOG

Highball glass, ice
Build in glass
1 1/4 oz. Light Rum
1/2 fill cranberry juice
1/2 fill orange juice

BOGS & BUBBLES

Champagne glass, chilled
Build in glass
1/2 fill cranberry juice
1/2 fill Champagne

BOILERMAKER

Shot glass and beer mug
Build in shot glass
1 1/2 oz. Whiskey
Build in mug
Fill with Draft Beer

BOINA ROJA

House specialty glass, ice
Pour ingredients into iced mixing glass
1 1/2 oz. Light Rum
3/4 oz. Gold Rum
1/2 oz. grenadine
1 oz. fresh lime juice
1 1/2 oz. sweet 'n' sour
Shake and strain
Mint sprig and cherry garnish

BOMB

House specialty glass, ice
Pour ingredients into iced mixing glass
1 oz. Dewar's White Label Scotch Whisky
1 oz. Jim Beam Black Label Bourbon
1/2 oz. Spiced Rum
1 1/2 oz. orange juice
1 1/2 oz. pineapple juice
Shake and strain
Float 3/4 oz. Raspberry Liqueur

BOMBAY GRAND

Cocktail glass, chilled
Pour ingredients into iced mixing glass
1 oz. Bombay Gin
1/2 oz. Grand Marnier
1 1/2 oz. sweet 'n' sour
Shake and strain
Orange twist garnish

BOMBAY SPIDER

Bucket glass, ice
Build in glass
1 1/4 oz. Bombay Sapphire London Dry Gin
3 dashes Angostura Bitters
Fill with ginger ale

BOMB POP

Bucket glass, ice
Build in glass
1 oz. Vodka
1 oz. Midori
1 oz. DeKuyper Watermelon Pucker
3/4 oz. sweet 'n' sour
Fill with Seven-Up

VAN GOGH®
WILD APPEL VODKA

Ultra-premium Van Gogh Flavored Vodkas are crafted at the Dirkzwager Distillery in Schiedam, Holland. None better typify their top-shelf status than VAN GOGH WILD APPEL VODKA.

Distilled in extremely small batches from a proprietary blend of premium grains and purified water, the Wild Appel Vodka is an amazingly delicious spirit infused with organic, tree-ripened apples. The first of its type, it must be tasted to be fully appreciated.

VAN GOGH CITROEN VODKA has a light, appealing bouquet and a vibrant palate of freshly cut citrus. Made from Spanish Valencia oranges and Mediterranean blood oranges, VAN GOGH ORANJE VODKA is imbued with a floral bouquet and sensational orange taste. The famed line also includes VAN GOGH MELON, VANILLA, RASPBERRY and PINEAPPLE VODKAS.

If you're into chocolate, be prepared to be wowed by VAN GOGH DUTCH CHOCOLATE VODKA. True to its name, the vodka has the prominent smell and taste of Dutch chocolate. Even though it is jammed with chocolate flavor, the spirit is perfectly balanced.

The Van Gogh family of flavored vodkas are indispensable behind the bar. With a simple flick of the wrist, you can add a delightful splash of robust flavor to any cocktail without adding the slightest trace of sweetness.

BONAPARTE
Brandy snifter, heated
Build in glass
1 3/4 oz. Courvoisier VSOP Cognac
3/4 oz. Grand Marnier Centenaire

BORINQUEN
House specialty glass, chilled
Pour ingredients into blender
1 1/2 oz. Cruzan Estate Diamond Rum
1 oz. Rhum Barbancourt 8-Star
3/4 oz. Rose's Lime Juice
2 oz. orange juice
2 oz. passion fruit syrup
2 oz. fresh lime juice
Blend with ice
Float 3/4 oz. Matusalem Gran Reserva Rum
Pineapple wedge and cherry garnish

BOSOM CARESSER
Cocktail glass, chilled
Pour ingredients into iced mixing glass
1 1/2 oz. Brandy
1/2 oz. Triple Sec
3 dashes grenadine
1 egg yolk (optional)
Shake and strain

BOSSA NOVA
House specialty glass, ice
Pour ingredients into iced mixing glass
2 oz. Bacardi Limón Rum
1 1/2 oz. fresh lime juice
2 oz. sweet 'n' sour
2 oz. passion fruit juice
Shake and strain
Float 1 oz. Dark Rum
Lime wedge and orange slice garnish

BOTTOM BOUNCER
Presentation shot glass, chilled
Build in glass
1 oz. Baileys Irish Cream
1 oz. DeKuyper Buttershots Schnapps

BOURBON BALL
Cocktail glass, chilled
Pour ingredients into iced mixing glass
1 oz. Woodford Reserve Bourbon
1 oz. Dark Crème de Cacao
1 oz. Tuaca
Stir and strain
Strawberry Garnish

BRAHMA BULL
Rocks glass, ice
Build in glass
1 1/2 oz. Jose Cuervo Especial Tequila
3/4 oz. Tia Maria

BRAIN SHOOTER
Cordial or sherry glass, chilled
Build in glass
3/4 oz. Baileys Irish Cream
1/2 oz. Peppermint Schnapps
3 drops grenadine in center

BRAINSTORM COCKTAIL
Cocktail glass, chilled
Pour ingredients into iced mixing glass
1 1/2 oz. Irish (or Rye) Whiskey
1/2 oz. B & B Liqueur
1/2 oz. Dry Vermouth
Stir and strain
Orange twist garnish

BRANDY ALEXANDER
Cocktail glass, chilled
Pour ingredients into iced mixing glass
3/4 oz. Brandy
3/4 oz. Dark Crème de Cacao
1 1/2 oz. half & half cream
Shake and strain
Sprinkle nutmeg

BRANDY EGG NOG (1)
House specialty glass, ice
Pour ingredients into iced mixing glass
1 1/2 oz. Brandy
1 tsp. sugar
1 egg (optional)
3 dashes vanilla extract
4 oz. half & half cream
Shake and strain
Sprinkle nutmeg

BRANDY EGG NOG (2)
Coffee mug, heated
Build in glass
3/4 oz. Brandy
3/4 oz. Dark Crème de Cacao
Fill with hot milk
Sprinkle nutmeg

BRANDY GUMP
Cocktail glass, chilled
Pour ingredients into iced mixing glass
1 oz. Brandy
1/2 oz. grenadine
1 1/2 oz. sweet 'n' sour
Shake and strain

BRASS MONKEY
Cocktail glass, chilled
Pour ingredients into iced mixing glass
1 1/2 oz. Sea Wynde Pot Still Rum
1 1/2 oz. Grey Goose Vodka
3/4 oz. orange juice
Shake and strain

BRAVE AGAVE
Rocks glass, ice
Build in glass
1 1/2 oz. Añejo Tequila
3/4 oz. Agavero Liqueur

BRAVE BULL
Rocks glass, ice
Build in glass
1 1/2 oz. Tequila
3/4 oz. Kahlúa

BRAWNY BROTH
Coffee mug, heated
Build in glass
1 1/4 oz. Vodka
Fill with hot beef bouillon
1 dash lemon pepper
Lemon wedge garnish

BRAZIL
Cocktail glass, chilled
Pour ingredients into iced mixing glass
1 oz. Dry Vermouth
1 oz. Dry Sherry
1/4 oz. Pernod
2-3 dashes Angostura Bitters
Stir and strain
Lemon twist garnish

BROOKLYN
Cocktail glass, chilled
Pour ingredients into iced mixing glass
1/2 oz. Dry Vermouth
1 1/2 oz. Bourbon
1 dash Amer Picon or Angostura Bitters
Stir and strain

BROWN COW
Rocks glass, ice
Build in glass
1 1/2 oz. Bourbon
3/4 oz. Hershey's chocolate syrup
3/4 oz. half & half cream

BROWN COW MILKSHAKE
House specialty glass, chilled
Pour ingredients into blender
2 oz. Bourbon
1 1/2 oz. Hershey's chocolate syrup
1 oz. half & half cream
2 scoops vanilla ice cream
Blend ingredients (with ice optional)
Whipped cream garnish
Sprinkle shaved chocolate

BROWN DERBY
House specialty glass, ice
Build in glass
1 1/2 oz. Raspberry Vodka
3 oz. Dr. Pepper
Fill with Guinness Stout

PLYMOUTH® GIN

If you are looking for a gin that is fundamentally different from all the others, then open up a bottle of PLYMOUTH GIN. This marvelously delicious spirit could well be called the gin that launched a thousand ships. The landmark brand has a long, storied history with the British Royal Navy, in fact it is distilled within walking distance of the naval base at Plymouth.

Plymouth Gin continues to be made where it originated over 200 years ago, at England's oldest, continuously operating distillery—the historic Coates & Co. Black Friars Distillery. Distilled in a large copper alembic still, this distinguished gin is exceedingly dry and highly aromatic.

Venerable Plymouth Gin has an expansive, citrus and juniper bouquet and a seamlessly smooth body. It immediately fills the mouth with the exuberant flavors of juniper, coriander, orange and lemon. The 82.4 proof gin finishes long, dry and brimming with flavor. It's little wonder why the BBC consistently names Plymouth as England's finest gin.

It should be noted that in 1896 the first published recipe for the Martini called for the use of Plymouth Gin and remains an ideal brand to choose when creating a signature Martini. Its bold, assertive character is perfectly suited for any type of gin-based assignment.

Come see why Plymouth Gin is still the daily issue to officers in the British Royal Navy.

BROWN SQUIRREL
Cocktail glass, chilled
Pour ingredients into iced mixing glass
1/2 oz. Disaronno Amaretto
1/2 oz. Dark Crème de Cacao
2 oz. half & half cream
Shake and strain

BROWN VELVET
Tankard or pilsner glass, chilled
Build in glass
2 oz. Tawny Port
Fill with Anchor Steam Beer

BRUT 'N' BOGS
Champagne glass, chilled
Build in glass
1 oz. Chambord
1/2 fill cranberry juice
1/2 fill Champagne

B-STING
Cocktail glass, chilled
Pour ingredients into iced mixing glass
1 1/2 oz. B & B Liqueur
1/2 oz. Peppermint Schnapps
Stir and strain

BUBBLE GUM
Rocks glass, chilled
Pour ingredients into iced mixing glass
1/2 oz. Southern Comfort
1/2 oz. Disaronno Amaretto
1/2 oz. Crème de Banana
1/2 oz. milk
2 dashes grenadine
Shake and strain

BUBBLE ZAZA
Champagne glass, chilled
Pour ingredients into iced mixing glass
1 1/4 oz. Vox Raspberry Vodka
3/4 oz. DeKuyper Island Blue Pucker
3/4 oz. orange juice
Shake and strain
Fill with Champagne
Lemon twist garnish

BUCK
Highball glass, ice
Build in glass
1 1/4 oz. requested liquor
Fill with ginger ale
Lemon wedge garnish

BUCKHEAD ROOT BEER
Highball glass, ice
Build in glass
1 1/4 oz. Jägermeister
Fill with club soda
Lime wedge garnish

BUCKING BRONCO
Rocks glass, chilled
Pour ingredients into iced mixing glass
3/4 oz. Jägermeister
3/4 oz. Myers's Jamaican Rum
3/4 oz. Orange Rum
3/4 oz. pineapple juice
Shake and strain
Lime wedge garnish

BUDDHA SHOOTER
Presentation shot glass, chilled
Build in glass
1 oz. Saké
1 oz. Añejo Tequila

BUFFALO SWEAT
Presentation shot glass, chilled
Build in glass
1 3/4 oz. Bourbon
3 dashes Tabasco Sauce

BUKHARA COFFEE
House specialty glass, chilled
Pour ingredients into blender
1 1/4 oz. Stolichnaya Vanil Vodka
3/4 oz. Baileys Irish Cream
1/2 oz. White Crème de Cacao
2 oz. coffee
2 scoops vanilla ice cream
Blend ingredients (with ice optional)
Whipped cream garnish
Sprinkle shaved chocolate

BULL AND BEAR
Cocktail glass, chilled
Pour ingredients into iced mixing glass
1 1/2 oz. Bourbon
3/4 oz. Grand Marnier
1/4 oz. Crème de Cassis
1/2 oz. Rose's Lime Juice
Stir and strain
Orange slice and cherry garnish

BULLFIGHTER
Presentation shot glass, chilled
Layer ingredients
1/2 fill Patrón XO Café Coffee Liqueur
1/2 fill Patrón Silver Tequila

BULLFROG (1)
Highball glass, ice
Build in glass
1 1/4 oz. Vodka
Fill with lemonade
Lemon twist garnish

BULLFROG (2)
Bucket glass, ice
Build in glass
1 1/2 oz. Southern Comfort
3/4 oz. Midori
2 1/2 oz. sweet 'n' sour
Fill with Seven-Up

BUMBLE BEE
Pilsner glass, chilled
Build in glass
1/2 fill with Honey Lager
1/2 fill with Guinness Stout

BURGUNDY BISHOP
Bucket glass, ice
Pour ingredients into iced mixing glass
1 1/2 oz. Light Rum
2 oz. sweet 'n' sour
3 oz. Dry Red Wine
Shake and strain
Lime, lemon and orange wedge garnish

BURGUNDY COCKTAIL
Wine glass, chilled
Pour ingredients into iced mixing glass
3 oz. Dry Red Wine
3/4 oz. VS Cognac
1/2 oz. Chambord
Stir and strain
Lemon twist garnish

BURNT SIENNA
House specialty glass, ice
Pour ingredients into iced mixing glass
3/4 oz. Bourbon
3/4 oz. Yukon Jack Liqueur
3/4 oz. Midori
1/4 oz. Chambord
1 oz. orange juice
1 oz. cranberry juice
2 oz. sweet 'n' sour
Shake and strain
Lime wedge garnish

BUSH TICKLER
House specialty glass, chilled
Pour ingredients into blender
1 1/2 oz. Dark Rum
1 oz. Amber Rum
3/4 oz. Dark Crème de Cacao
3/4 oz. half & half cream
2 oz. coconut cream syrup
3 oz. pineapple juice
Blend with ice
Float 3/4 oz. Kahlúa
Pineapple wedge and cherry garnish

BAILEYS® ORIGINAL IRISH CREAM LIQUEUR

The makers of BAILEYS ORIGINAL IRISH CREAM LIQUEUR are justifiably proud of being the world's first cream liqueur. Now often imitated, the brand became an international sensation upon its 1979 introduction and is now the best-selling liqueur in the world.

Created by R. & A. Bailey Company of Dublin, Ireland, the liqueur is made from a base of dairy cream not more than 2 hours old. The cream is infused with aged, triple-distilled Irish whiskey and natural vanilla and chocolate flavorings. The liqueur is homogenized to ensure that the flavors fully amalgamate, then pasteurized and bottled at 34 proof.

Baileys Irish Cream is an elegant taste sensation that well deserves its international preeminence. The liqueur has a beige hue and a luscious, medium-weight body. The bouquet is decidedly creamy with engaging aromas of whiskey and chocolate. It spreads a wealth of flavors over the palate, alternating notes of vanilla, chocolate and whiskey. The dairy-wrapped flavors persist long into the luxurious finish.

Baileys Irish Cream is absolutely marvelous served chilled, straight-up, or over ice. To overlook its versatility behind the bar would be to deny it of its pub heritage. Baileys is a liqueur with unlimited creative uses, as evidenced by the long list of cocktails in which it is featured.

BUSHWACKER
House specialty glass, chilled
Pour ingredients into blender
1 1/4 oz. Light Rum
1 oz. Dark Rum
3/4 oz. half & half cream
2 1/2 oz. coconut cream syrup
Blend with ice
Float 3/4 oz. Kahlúa
Pineapple wedge and cherry garnish

BUSTED RUBBER
Presentation shot glass, chilled
Layer ingredients
1/3 fill DeKuyper Raspberry Pucker
1/3 fill Baileys Irish Cream
1/3 fill Grand Marnier

BUTTERFINGER
Presentation shot glass, chilled
Layer ingredients
1/3 fill Godiva Chocolate Liqueur
1/3 fill DeKuyper Buttershots Schnapps
1/3 fill Baileys Irish Cream

BUTTERSCOTCH HOP
House specialty glass, chilled
Pour ingredients into blender
3/4 oz. DeKuyper Buttershots Schnapps
3/4 oz. Kahlúa Especial
3/4 oz. Whaler's Original Vanille Rum
2 scoops vanilla ice cream
Blend ingredients (with ice optional)

BUTTERSCOTCH SLIDE
House specialty glass, chilled
Pour ingredients into blender
3/4 oz. Baileys Irish Cream
3/4 oz. Kahlúa
3/4 oz. DeKuyper Buttershots Schnapps
2 oz. milk
Blend with ice

BUZZ BOMB
Champagne glass, chilled
Pour ingredients into iced mixing glass
1/2 oz. VS Cognac
1/2 oz. B & B Liqueur
1/2 oz. Cointreau
1/2 oz. sweet 'n' sour
Shake and strain
Fill with Champagne
Lemon wheel garnish

BYRRH COCKTAIL
Cocktail glass, chilled
Pour ingredients into iced mixing glass
1 oz. Byrrh
1 oz. Gin
1/2 oz. Dry Vermouth (optional)
Stir and strain
Lemon twist garnish

CABIN FEVER CURE
Coffee mug, heated
Build in glass
3/4 oz. VooDoo Spiced Rum
1/2 oz. Dark Crème de Cacao
1/2 oz. Rumple Minze Schnapps
Near fill with hot chocolate
Whipped cream garnish
Sprinkle shaved chocolate

CACTUS JUICE
Bucket glass, ice
Build in glass
1 1/4 oz. El Tesoro Platinum Tequila
3/4 oz. Agavero Liqueur
Fill with lemonade
Lemon wedge garnish

CACTUS MOON
Bucket glass, ice
Build in glass
1 1/2 oz. Original Cristall Lemon Vodka
1/2 oz. Grand Marnier
1/2 oz. Limoncello Liqueur
Fill with lemonade
Lemon wedge garnish

CAFÉ A LA CABANA
Coffee mug, heated
Build in glass
3/4 oz. Pyrat XO Reserve Rum
3/4 oz. Licor 43 (Cuarenta y Tres)
1/2 oz. Godiva Chocolate Liqueur
Near fill with hot coffee
Whipped cream garnish

CAFÉ AMORE
Coffee mug, heated
Build in glass
1/2 oz. Godiva Chocolate Liqueur
1/2 oz. Disaronno Amaretto
1/2 oz. Tia Maria
1/2 oz. VS Cognac
Near fill with hot coffee
Whipped cream garnish

CAFÉ BRÛLOT
2 Demitasse cups, heated
Heat in a shallow bowl
1 oz. Laird's 12 Year Apple Brandy
1 oz. Cointreau
Lemon and orange horse's neck
   (a continuous peel)
1 cinnamon stick
4 cloves
Ignite mixture
Ladle flaming liquid over orange peel
1 1/2 cups hot coffee
Slowly pour hot coffee into bowl
   to extinguish flame
Pour into demitasse cups

CAFÉ CHARLES
2 Irish coffee glasses, heated
Build in one glass
3/4 oz. Metaxa 5 Star Brandy
3/4 oz. Galliano Liqueur
3/4 oz. Patrón XO Café Coffee Liqueur
Ignite and split flaming mixture
   between glasses
Near fill each glass with hot coffee
   to extinguish flames
Whipped cream garnish
Sprinkle shaved chocolate

CAFÉ CHOCOLATE (1)
Coffee mug, heated
Build in glass
3/4 oz. Kahlúa Especial
3/4 oz. Baileys Irish Cream
1/2 oz. Dark Crème de Cacao
1/2 oz. Grand Marnier
1 oz. chocolate syrup
Near fill with hot coffee
Whipped cream garnish
Sprinkle shaved chocolate

CAFÉ CHOCOLATE (2)
Coffee mug, heated
Build in glass
3/4 oz. Orange Liqueur
3/4 oz. Kahlúa
3/4 oz. Baileys Irish Cream
1/2 oz. Dark Crème de Cacao
1 oz. Hershey's chocolate syrup
Near fill with hot coffee
Whipped cream garnish
Sprinkle shaved chocolate

CAFÉ CONTENTÉ
Coffee mug, heated
Build in glass
3/4 oz. Dark Rum
3/4 oz. Kahlúa
3/4 oz. Chambord
Fill with hot coffee
Whipped cream garnish

CAFÉ CORRECTO
Coffee mug, heated
Build in glass
1 oz. Brandy
Near fill with hot espresso coffee
Whipped cream garnish
Dust powdered cocoa

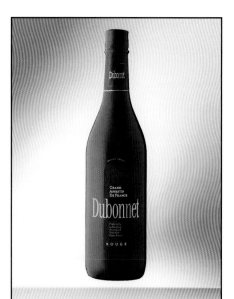

DUBONNET® ROUGE

Dubonnet is the best-selling aperitif in America. Best described as a sweetened and fortified wine, its original calling was as an aperitif wine, one typically consumed before dinner to awaken and stimulate the appetite. While still popular as an aperitif, the brand has also become an ingredient in many contemporary cocktails.

Considered the *grand dame* of aperitifs, Dubonnet was created by Frenchman Joseph Dubonnet in 1846 as a restorative elixir for the French Foreign Legion on their missions to Africa and Asia. The brand's two versions are still made according to the same secret recipes.

Light and refreshing, DUBONNET ROUGE is produced on a base of premium red wine that is infused with a proprietary blend of herbs, spices, peels and quinine. The wine is fortified with grape spirits to an elevated strength of 19% alcohol by volume. The famed aperitif is characteristically aromatic with a delicate body and a palate of tangy fruit. The finish is long and vaguely effervescent.

DUBONNET BLONDE is crafted on a base of white wine, fortified with grape spirits and infused with botanicals. It is drier than its red wine counterpart.

While both versions are a genuine pleasure to sip neat or over ice, they are enormously delicious when featured in signature cocktails.

CAFÉ DIABLO
Coffee mug, heated
Build in glass
3/4 oz. VS Cognac
3/4 oz. Grand Marnier
3/4 oz. Sambuca
1/2 oz. simple syrup
Fill with hot coffee
Sprinkle grated orange rind, cloves, cinnamon and allspice
Orange twist garnish

CAFÉ DUBLIN
Coffee mug, heated
Build in glass
1 oz. Irish Whiskey
1 oz. Irish Mist
1/2 oz. Kahlúa
Near fill with hot coffee
Top with frothed milk
Dust powdered cocoa

CAFÉ FOSTER
Coffee mug, heated
Build in glass
1 1/2 oz. Rhum Barbancourt 5-Star
3/4 oz. Godiva Chocolate Liqueur
3/4 oz. Crème de Banana
Near fill with hot coffee
Whipped cream garnish
Drizzle chocolate syrup

CAFÉ FRAMBOISE
Cocktail glass, chilled
Pour ingredients into iced mixing glass
1 3/4 oz. Citadelle Raspberry Vodka
3/4 oz. Kahlúa
1/2 oz. cold espresso coffee
3/4 oz. half & half cream
Shake and strain

CAFÉ GATES
Presentation shot glass, chilled
Build in glass
1/3 fill Grand Marnier
1/3 fill Tia Maria
1/3 fill Dark Crème de Cacao

CAFÉ KINGSTON
Coffee mug, heated
Build in glass
1/2 oz. Appleton Estate V/X Jamaica Rum
1/2 oz. Cruzan Rum Cream
1/2 oz. Tia Maria
1/2 oz. Hershey's chocolate syrup
Near fill with hot coffee
Whipped cream garnish
Sprinkle shaved chocolate

CAFÉ REGGAE
Coffee mug, heated
Build in glass
3/4 oz. Kuya Fusion Rum
1/2 oz. Dark Crème de Cacao
Near fill with hot coffee
Whipped cream garnish
Drizzle 3/4 oz. Tia Maria

CAFÉ ROYALE
Coffee mug, heated
Build in glass
1/2 oz. simple syrup (optional)
1 oz. VS Cognac
Fill with hot coffee
Note: May be requested made with Brandy

CAFÉ ST. ARMANDS
Coffee mug, heated
Build in glass
1 oz. Dark Crème de Cacao
1/2 oz. Licor 43 (Cuarenta y Tres)
Near fill with hot coffee
Whipped cream garnish

CAIPIRINHA (1)
Rocks or old fashion glass
Build in glass
4 large lime wedges
3/4 oz. simple syrup
Muddle contents
2 1/2 oz. Ypioca Cachaça
Add cracked ice

CAIPIRINHA (2)
Rocks or old fashion glass
Build in glass
4 large lime wedges
3/4 oz. simple syrup
Muddle contents
1 1/2 oz. Licor 43 (Cuarenta y Tres)
1 1/2 oz. Light Rum
Add cracked ice

CAIPIRISSMA
Rocks or old fashion glass
Build in glass
4 large lime wedges
3/4 oz. simple syrup
Muddle contents
2 1/2 oz. Light Rum
Add crushed ice
Lime wedge garnish

CAIPIROSHKA
Rocks or old fashion glass
Build in glass
4 large lime wedges
3/4 oz. simple syrup
Muddle contents
2 1/2 oz. Vodka
Add cracked ice

CAJUN MIMOSA
Champagne glass, chilled
Build in glass
1/2 fill Champagne
1/4 oz. jalapeño pepper juice
Fill with orange juice
Orange slice and pepper garnish

CALIFORNIA LEMONADE
Bucket glass, ice
Pour ingredients into iced mixing glass
1 1/2 oz. Seagram's 7 Whisky
1/2 oz. Rose's Lime Juice
1/2 oz. grenadine
1 1/2 oz. sweet 'n' sour
Shake and strain
Fill with club soda
Orange slice and cherry garnish

CALIFORNIAN
Highball glass, ice
Build in glass
1 1/4 oz. Chambord
1/2 fill orange juice
Near fill with sweet 'n' sour
Splash Seven-Up

CALIFORNIA ROOT BEER
Highball glass, ice
Build in glass
3/4 oz. Kahlúa
3/4 oz. Galliano Liqueur
Fill with club soda

CALIFORNIA SCREW
aka **California Split**, **Desert Screw**
Highball glass, ice
Build in glass
1 1/4 oz. Vodka
1/2 fill orange juice
1/2 fill grapefruit juice

CALYPSO COFFEE
aka **Spanish Coffee**
Coffee mug, heated
Build in glass
1 oz. Light Rum
1 oz. Tia Maria
Near fill with hot coffee
Whipped cream garnish
Sprinkle shaved chocolate

MAKER'S MARK®
BOURBON WHISKY

As the country's first small batch whiskey, MAKER'S MARK is generally credited with bourbon's phenomenal resurgence. The distinctive, red wax-dipped bottle has secured its place on top-shelves across the country and is one of the most recognizable whiskeys in the world.

Maker's Mark is crafted at the Star Hill Distillery in Loretto, Kentucky, which is among the smallest distilleries in the state and on the registry of National Historic Landmarks. The brand is one of only a few bourbons to include wheat instead of rye in its mash bill, which also includes corn, barley malt and a sour mash component. The whiskey is made with a yeast strain that is purported to be the oldest in Kentucky. For all intents and purposes, the hugely successful brand is a handmade product.

Maker's Mark Bourbon, 90 proof, has a soft, supple body and a captivating bouquet of honey, vanilla, spices and fruit. The color is rich with the red hue of aged wood. The palate is loaded with the flavors of caramel, butter and notes of toasty oak. The whiskey has a relaxed and slightly smoky finish.

Here's a world-class whiskey that doesn't cost a week's paycheck. While its captivating array of flavors and aromas come alive with a splash of spring water, Maker's Mark is unsurpassed in a Manhattan or specialty cocktail.

CALYPSO HIGHWAY
House specialty glass, ice
Pour ingredients into iced mixing glass
1 oz. Dark Rum
1 oz. Banana Rum
3/4 oz. Blue Curaçao
2 dashes vanilla extract
1 oz. coconut cream syrup
2 oz. pineapple juice
2 oz. orange juice
Shake and strain
Float 3/4 oz. 151° Rum
Pineapple wedge and cherry garnish

CAMPARI & SODA
Highball glass, ice
Build in glass
1 1/4 oz. Campari Aperitivo
Fill with club soda
Lemon twist garnish

CANADIAN
aka **Canada**
Cocktail glass, chilled
Pour ingredients into iced mixing glass
1 1/2 oz. Canadian Whisky
1/2 oz. Triple Sec
2 dashes Angostura Bitters
1/2 oz. simple syrup
1 oz. sweet 'n' sour
Shake and strain

CANADIAN BLISS
Rocks glass, ice
Build in glass
2 oz. Canadian Whisky
3/4 oz. Limoncello Liqueur
Lemon twist garnish

CANADIAN FOOT WARMER
Coffee mug, heated
Build in glass
1 1/4 oz. Canadian Whisky
3/4 oz. Cinnamon Schnapps
1/2 oz. Kahlúa
Near fill with hot chocolate
Whipped cream garnish
Dust powdered cocoa

CANADIAN STONE FENCE
House specialty glass, ice
Pour ingredients into iced mixing glass
1 1/2 oz. Canadian Whisky
1/2 oz. Triple Sec
1/2 oz. sugar syrup
2 oz. apple cider
Shake and strain

CANADIAN TART
Rocks glass, ice
Build in glass
2 oz. Canadian Whisky
3/4 oz. RémyRed Red Berry Infusion
Cherry garnish

C. & C.
Brandy snifter, heated
Build in glass
1 1/2 oz. VS Cognac
1/2 oz. Green Chartreuse

CANDY APPLE
Bucket glass, ice
Build in glass
1 3/4 oz. Cruzan Vanilla Rum
3/4 oz. DeKuyper Pucker Sour Apple
Near fill with club soda
Float 1/2 oz. grenadine

CANNONBALL
Bucket glass, ice
Build in glass
2 oz. Pusser's British Navy Rum
1/2 oz. Rose's Lime Juice
1 oz. cranberry juice
1 oz. pineapple juice
1 oz. orange juice
Lime wedge garnish

CANYON QUAKE (1)
House specialty glass, chilled
Pour ingredients into blender
3/4 oz. Baileys Irish Cream
3/4 oz. Brandy
3/4 oz. Kahlúa
2 oz. half & half cream
Blend with ice

CANYON QUAKE (2)
Rocks glass, chilled
Pour ingredients into iced mixing glass
1 oz. Disaronno Amaretto
3/4 oz. Baileys Irish Cream
3/4 oz. Brandy
3/4 oz. half & half cream
Shake and strain

CANYON SLIDER
Presentation shot glass, chilled
Layer ingredients
1/2 fill Peppermint Schnapps
1/2 fill Bourbon

CAPE CODDER
aka **Cape Cod**
Highball glass, ice
Build in glass
1 1/4 oz. Vodka
Fill with cranberry juice

CAPERS COCKTAIL
House specialty glass, ice
Rim glass with salt (optional)
Build in glass
1 oz. Citadelle Apple Vodka
3/4 oz. Limoncello Liqueur
Fill with lemonade
Lemon wheel garnish

CAPO DI SOPRANOS
Coffee mug or glass, heated
Build in glass
1 oz. Limoncello Liqueur
3/4 oz. Baileys Irish Cream
1/2 oz. Sambuca
Fill with hot coffee
Whipped cream garnish
Drizzle 1/2 oz. Kahlúa

CAPPA 21
Cappuccino cup, heated
Build in glass
1 1/2 oz. Dark Rum
1/2 oz. Tia Maria
1/2 oz. Brandy
Square of Ghirardelli chocolate
Near fill with hot espresso coffee
Top with frothed milk
Sprinkle shaved chocolate

CAPPO DE TUTTI CAPPI
Cappuccino cup, heated
Build in glass
1/2 oz. Tia Maria
1/2 oz. Brandy
1/2 oz. Dark Rum
1 piece Ghirardelli chocolate
Near fill with hot espresso coffee
Top with frothed milk
Sprinkle shaved chocolate

CAPTAIN'S COFFEE (1)
Coffee mug, heated
Build in glass
1 1/2 oz. Pusser's British Navy Rum
1 oz. Patrón XO Café Coffee Liqueur
Near fill with hot coffee
Whipped cream garnish (optional)
Drizzle 1/2 oz. Patrón XO Café
    Coffee Liqueur

CAPTAIN'S COFFEE (2)
Coffee mug, heated
Build in glass
1 oz. Captain Morgan Spiced Rum
1 oz. Kahlúa
2 dashes Angostura Bitters
Near fill with hot coffee
Whipped cream garnish
Sprinkle nutmeg

KETEL ONE® VODKA

Phenomenally popular KETEL ONE VODKA can trace its origins to 1691, when the Nolet family built a distillery in Schiedam, Holland. For ten generations, the Nolet family has been distilling the finest handmade spirits using the techniques and recipes perfected by Joannes Nolet and his successors.

Ketel One Vodka is triple-distilled in small batches entirely from wheat using the alembic copper pot still method. The final distillation occurs in a centuries old, alembic copper pot still, referred to as "Ketel #1." The Ketel One name is derived from the original "Distiller Ketel #1." After distillation, the vodka is rested in tile-lined tanks.

Ketel One is a handcrafted vodka. It has pristine clarity and a round, flawlessly textured body. The vodka's subtle yet pleasing bouquet is laced with citrus and toasted cereal aromas. The pleasures continue as the vodka fills the mouth with layers of sweet and spicy flavors. The finish is elegant and long lasting.

The famed distillery also makes citrus-infused KETEL ONE CITROEN VODKA. It has a pale yellow hue and a wafting bouquet of fresh limes and lemons. The zesty palate is endowed with a refreshing, bona fide citrus flavor that persists well into the extended finish.

The exemplary Ketel One sisters are sophisticated vodkas that know no creative limitations.

CAPTAIN'S COOLER
Bucket glass, ice
Pour ingredients into iced mixing glass
1 1/4 oz. Captain Morgan Spiced Rum
1 oz. Triple Sec
1/2 oz. Rose's Lime Juice
1/2 oz. cranberry juice
1 oz. orange juice
Shake and strain
Fill with Seven-Up

CAR BOMB
Shot glass and tankard glass, chilled
Build in shot glass
1 1/2 oz. Baileys Irish Cream
Build in tankard glass
3/4 fill Guinness Stout
Drop shot glass of Baileys into Guinness

CARAMEL APPLE
Presentation shot glass, chilled
Pour ingredients into iced mixing glass
1 1/2 oz. DeKuyper Pucker Sour Apple
3/4 DeKuyper Buttershots Schnapps
Stir and strain

CARDINAL PUNCH
Bucket glass, ice
Pour ingredients into iced mixing glass
3 oz. cranberry juice
1 1/2 oz. orange juice
1 oz. sweet 'n' sour
Shake and strain
Fill with ginger ale

CARDINALI
Bucket glass, ice
Pour ingredients into iced mixing glass
3 oz. cranberry juice
2 oz. sweet 'n' sour
Shake and strain
Lime wheel garnish

CARIBBEAN BERRY
House specialty glass, chilled
Pour ingredients into blender
3/4 oz. Dark Rum
3/4 oz. Disaronno Amaretto
1/2 oz. Crème de Banana
1/2 cup strawberries
1 1/2 oz. sweet 'n' sour
Blend with ice
Float 3/4 oz. Jamaican Rum
Banana slice and strawberry garnish

CARIBBEAN CHAMPAGNE
Champagne glass, chilled
Build in glass
3/4 oz. Light Rum
3/4 oz. Crème de Banana
Fill with Champagne
Banana slice and cherry garnish

CARIBBEAN CONTESSA
Champagne glass, chilled
Pour ingredients into iced mixing glass
1/2 oz. Light Rum
1/2 oz. Grand Marnier
1/2 oz. cranberry juice
1/2 oz. orange juice
Shake and strain
Fill with Champagne
Lemon twist garnish

CARIBBEAN CRUISE (1)
House specialty glass, chilled
Pour ingredients into blender
1 oz. Appleton Estate V/X Jamaica Rum
1 oz. Mount Gay Eclipse Rum
3/4 oz. Dark Rum
3/4 oz. half & half cream
2 oz. coconut cream syrup
3 oz. pineapple juice
Blend with ice
Float 3/4 oz. Patrón XO Café Coffee Liqueur
Pineapple wedge and cherry garnish

CARIBBEAN CRUISE (2)
House specialty glass, ice
Pour ingredients into iced mixing glass
1 1/2 oz. Dark Rum
3/4 oz. Orange Liqueur
1 1/2 oz. sweet 'n' sour
1 1/2 oz. orange juice
Shake and strain
Float 3/4 oz. Jamaican Rum
Orange slice garnish

CARIBBEAN CRUISE (3)
Cocktail glass, chilled
Pour ingredients into iced mixing glass
1 1/2 oz. Light Rum
3/4 oz. Orange Liqueur
1/2 oz. fresh lime juice
2 oz. sweet 'n' sour
Shake and strain
Orange twist garnish

CARIBBEAN DREAM (1)
Coffee mug, heated
Build in glass
1 oz. Mount Gay Eclipse Rum
1/2 oz. Myers's Jamaican Rum
1/2 oz. Crème de Banana
1/2 oz. White Crème de Cacao
Near fill with hot coffee
Whipped cream garnish

CARIBBEAN DREAM (2)
House specialty glass, chilled
Pour ingredients into blender
1 oz. Bacardi Light Rum
3/4 oz. Disaronno Amaretto
3/4 oz. White Crème de Cacao
1/2 oz. fresh lime juice
3 oz. pineapple juice
Blend with ice
Float 3/4 oz. Rhum Barbancourt 5-Star
Pineapple wedge and cherry garnish

CARIBBEAN GRIDLOCK
House specialty glass, chilled
Pour ingredients into blender
3/4 oz. Appleton Estate V/X Jamaica Rum
3/4 oz. Bacardi Light Rum
3/4 oz. Mount Gay Eclipse Rum
3/4 oz. Rose's Lime Juice
2 oz. sweet 'n' sour
2 oz. orange juice
Blend with ice
Float 3/4 oz. Gosling's Black Seal Rum
Lime, lemon and orange wedge garnish

CARIBBEAN ROMANCE
House specialty glass, ice
Pour ingredients into iced mixing glass
1 1/2 oz. Light Rum
1 oz. Disaronno Amaretto
1 1/2 oz. orange juice
1 1/2 oz. pineapple juice
1/2 oz. grenadine
Shake and strain
Float 3/4 oz. Mount Gay Extra Old Rum
Lime, lemon and orange wedge garnish

CARIBBEAN SOUR
Cocktail glass, chilled
Pour ingredients into iced mixing glass
1 1/2 oz. Kuya Fusion Rum
3/4 oz. Banana Rum
3/4 oz. Chambord
1/2 oz. grenadine
2 oz. sweet 'n' sour
Shake and strain
Orange slice garnish

CARIBBEAN SUNSET
Presentation shot glass, chilled
Build in glass
1/3 fill Kahlúa
1/3 fill Chambord
1/3 fill Tia Maria

HPNOTIQ® LIQUEUR

HPNOTIQ (pronounced "hypnotic") is a classy, irresistible liqueur from France. It's guaranteed that you've never tasted anything like Hpnotiq before, simply because there is nothing else like it. The aquamarine hued gem is made from an ultra-premium blend of triple-distilled vodka, aged cognac and a proprietary mix of natural tropical fruit juices. Try as you might you won't be able to detect their individual identities.

Calling Hpnotiq a liqueur is almost a misnomer. While as versatile as a liqueur, the product is more like a skillfully crafted cocktail in a cork-finished bottle. The cognac used in its production is a blend of brandies from the Petite Champagne, Fins Bois and Borderies regions.

The moment Hpnotiq hits the glass you know you're in for a singular treat. The liqueur has an alluring turquoise blue color and a light, spirit-like body. Its prominent bouquet is laced with the aromas of ripe fruit and citrus. The mouth-filling palate is tart and loaded with nuance, an intriguing mix with a taste reminiscent of grapefruit, mandarin and a hint of brandy on the finish.

Hpnotiq is a bona fide pleasure to work with behind the bar. It was obviously created for a cocktail glass and is outstanding served chilled straight-up, or on the rocks.

CARIBE SUNSET
Presentation shot glass
Build in glass
1/4 fill Chambord
1/4 fill Dark Crème de Cacao
1/4 fill Tia Maria
1/4 fill hot coffee

CARIBE SURFSIDER
House specialty glass, chilled
Pour ingredients into blender
3/4 oz. Light Rum
3/4 oz. Dark Rum
1/2 oz. Crème de Banana
1/2 oz. Blackberry Brandy
3/4 oz. grenadine
3/4 oz. fresh lime juice
1/2 cup strawberries
2 oz. sweet 'n' sour
Blend with ice
Pineapple wedge and strawberry garnish

CARTE BLANCHE
Coffee mug, heated
Build in glass
1/2 oz. Christian Brothers Brandy
1/2 oz. White Crème de Menthe
1/2 oz. Godiva Chocolate Liqueur
Near fill with hot chocolate
Whipped cream garnish
Drizzle 1/2 oz. Green Crème de Menthe

CARTEL BUSTER
Presentation shot glass, chilled
Layer ingredients
1/3 fill Tia Maria
1/3 fill Grand Marnier
1/3 fill Jose Cuervo Especial Tequila

CARTEL SHOOTER
Presentation shot glass, chilled
Build in glass
1/2 oz. Chambord
1/2 oz. Orange Vodka
1/2 oz. grapefruit juice
1/2 oz. lemonade

CARTLAND CURE
House specialty glass, chilled
Pour ingredients into blender
3 oz. milk
1 egg (optional)
1 ripe banana
2 tbsp. yogurt, plain
1 tbsp. powdered cocoa
1 tsp. honey
1 tsp. wheat germ
Blend with ice

CASTLE COFFEE
Coffee mug, heated
Build in glass
1 oz. Knappogue Castle Irish Whiskey
1 oz. Celtic Crossing Irish Liqueur
1/2 oz. Grand Marnier
Near fill with hot coffee
Whipped cream garnish
Drizzle 1/2 oz. Kahlúa Especial

CASTLE IN THE CLOUDS
Cocktail glass, chilled
Pour ingredients into iced mixing glass
2 oz. Knappogue Castle Irish Whiskey
1/2 oz. Dubonnet Rouge
1/2 oz. Limoncello Liqueur
Stir and strain
Lemon twist garnish

CATHERINE WAS GREAT
House specialty glass, chilled
Pour ingredients into blender
1 3/4 oz. Vodka
1/2 oz. Disaronno Amaretto
1/2 oz. Bacardi Limón Rum
2 oz. orange juice
2 oz. sweet 'n' sour
Blend with ice
Orange slice garnish

CAYMAN COCKTAIL
Cocktail glass, chilled
Pour ingredients into iced mixing glass
1 1/2 oz. Vodka
1 1/2 oz. Peach Schnapps
1/2 oz. orange juice
1/2 oz. pineapple juice
1/2 oz. grenadine
Shake and strain
Splash Seven-Up
Orange slice garnish

C.C. RIDER
Presentation shot glass, chilled
Build in glass
1/2 fill Chambord
1/2 fill Champagne

CELESTE'S COCKTAIL
House specialty glass, ice
Pour ingredients into iced mixing glass
1 oz. Canadian Whisky
1 oz. Cinnamon Schnapps
1/2 oz. RémyRed Red Berry Infusion
1/2 oz. orange juice
1 1/2 oz. Hawaiian Punch
Shake and strain

CELESTIAL FIZZ
Champagne glass, chilled
Pour ingredients into iced mixing glass
1 oz. VS Cognac
3/4 oz. Grand Marnier
1 oz. sweet 'n' sour
1 1/2 oz. cranberry juice
Shake and strain
Fill with Champagne
Orange slice garnish

CELLO AMORE
Cocktail glass, chilled
Rim glass with powdered cocoa
Pour ingredients into iced mixing glass
1 3/4 oz. Limoncello Liqueur
1 oz. Disaronno Amaretto
1 oz. Kahlúa
Shake and strain

CELLO BLANCO
Cocktail glass, chilled
Pour ingredients into iced mixing glass
1 3/4 oz. Limoncello Liqueur
3/4 oz. White Crème de Cacao
3/4 oz. Southern Comfort
Stir and strain
Lemon wheel garnish

CELLO FELLOW
Bucket glass, ice
Build in glass
1 3/4 oz. Limoncello Liqueur
1 oz. Vodka
3/4 oz. Disaronno Amaretto
Fill with orange juice
Orange slice garnish

CELTIC KISS
Rocks glass, ice
Build in glass
1 1/2 oz. Celtic Crossing Irish Liqueur
3/4 oz. Baileys Irish Cream

CEMENT MIXER
Presentation shot glass, chilled
Build in glass
1 oz. Baileys Irish Cream
1 oz. Citrus Vodka
Swirl in mouth before swallowing

CENSORED ON THE BEACH
Highball glass, ice
Build in glass
1 oz. Peach Schnapps
1 oz. Vodka
1/2 fill cranberry juice
1/2 fill orange juice

JÄGERMEISTER® LIQUEUR

The mere mention of JÄGERMEISTER LIQUEUR is enough to raise a knowing smile to the face of any seasoned imbiber. The popular, "must have" elixir has become a classic rite of passage and can be found behind nearly every bar on the planet.

The Mast family founded the Mast-Jägermeister Company in 1878 in Wolfenbüttel, Germany. Jägermeister in German means "master of the hunt." The herbal liqueur was first bottled and widely marketed in 1935.

Renowned Jägermeister is comprised of a sophisticated blend of 56 roots, herbs and spices from around the world, including gentian roots, valerian, poppy seeds, ginseng and chamomile blossoms. The various botanicals are individually macerated in neutral spirits for up to 6 weeks. They are then filtered and matured in charred oak barrels for a minimum of one year prior to blending. The liqueur is bottled at 70 proof.

Jägermeister is a singular sensation not to be missed. It has a reddish brown hue and a wafting bouquet loaded with spice and peppery aromas. The liqueur immediately fills the mouth with a montage of flavors ranging from bittersweet to spicy hot. The finish is long and spectacular.

Jägermeister is at its best served chilled and enjoyed as an ice cold shot. It is also the featured performer in scores of contemporary cocktails.

CESAR RITZ
Champagne glass, chilled
Pour ingredients into iced mixing glass
1/2 oz. Armagnac
1/2 oz. Peach Schnapps
1/4 oz. grenadine
1 tbsp. vanilla ice cream
Shake and strain
Fill with Champagne
Lemon twist garnish

CHAMBORD DREAM
Cocktail glass, chilled
Pour ingredients into iced mixing glass
1/2 oz. Chambord
1/2 oz. Dark Crème de Cacao
2 oz. half & half cream
Shake and strain

CHAMBORD REPOSE
Coffee mug, heated
Build in glass
3/4 oz. Chambord
1/2 oz. Dark Crème de Cacao
1/2 oz. Tia Maria
Near fill with hot coffee
Top with frothed milk
Sprinkle shaved chocolate

CHAMPAGNE COCKTAIL
Champagne glass, chilled
Build in glass
Sugar cube soaked w/Angostura Bitters
Fill with Champagne
Lemon twist garnish

CHAMPAGNE CORNUCOPIA
House specialty glass, chilled
Pour ingredients into blender
1 oz. Vodka
3/4 oz. Peach Schnapps
1 1/2 oz. cranberry juice
2 scoops orange sorbet
Blend ingredients (with ice optional)
Fill with Champagne
Orange slice and cherry garnish

CHAMPAGNE FRAMBOISE
Champagne glass, chilled
Build in glass
Near fill with Champagne
Float 3/4 oz. Chambord
Lemon twist garnish

CHAMPAGNE IMPERIAL
Champagne glass, chilled
Build in glass
Sugar cube soaked w/Angostura Bitters
1/2 oz. Courvoisier VSOP Cognac
1/2 oz. Grand Marnier Centenaire
Fill with Champagne
Lemon twist garnish

CHAMPAGNE JUBILEE
Champagne glass, chilled
Build in glass
1 1/2 oz. Disaronno Amaretto
2 oz. cranberry juice
Fill with Champagne
Orange twist garnish

CHAMPAGNE MARSEILLE
Champagne glass, chilled
Pour ingredients into iced mixing glass
3/4 oz. Grand Marnier
3/4 oz. Disaronno Amaretto
1/2 oz. Vodka
1 1/2 oz. orange juice
Shake and strain
Fill with Champagne

CHAMPAGNE NORMANDE
Champagne glass, chilled
Build in glass
1 oz. Calvados Apple Brandy
1/2 oz. simple syrup
2 dashes Angostura Bitters
Fill with Champagne
Orange twist garnish

CHAMPS ELYSEES COCKTAIL (1)
Cocktail glass, chilled
Pour ingredients into iced mixing glass
1 oz. Brandy
1/2 oz. B & B Liqueur
2 dashes Angostura Bitters
1 1/2 oz. sweet 'n' sour
Shake and strain

CHAMPS ELYSEES COCKTAIL (2)
Champagne glass, chilled
Pour ingredients into iced mixing glass
1 oz. VSOP Cognac
1 oz. B & B Liqueur
2 dashes Angostura Bitters
1 1/2 oz. sweet 'n' sour
Shake and strain
Fill with Champagne

CHARISMA COCKTAIL
Cocktail glass, chilled
Pour ingredients into iced mixing glass
1 1/2 oz. Van Gogh Chocolate Vodka
3/4 oz. Grey Goose La Vanille Vodka
3/4 oz. Kahlúa Especial
1/2 oz. Rumple Minze Schnapps
Shake and strain

CHEAP SHADES
House specialty glass, chilled
Pour ingredients into blender
1 oz. Midori
1 oz. Peach Schnapps
1 oz. sweet 'n' sour
2 oz. orange juice
2 oz. pineapple juice
Blend with ice
Fill with Seven-Up

CHEAP SUNGLASSES
Bucket glass, ice
Build in glass
1 1/4 oz. Vodka
1/2 fill cranberry juice
1/2 fill Seven-Up

CHEESY CHEERLEADER
House specialty glass, ice
Pour ingredients into iced mixing glass
1 1/2 oz. KéKé Beach Cream Liqueur
3/4 oz. Citrus Rum
3/4 oz. Limoncello Liqueur
1 1/2 oz. pink lemonade
1 1/2 oz. pineapple juice
Shake and strain

CHEF DIETER'S
APPLE PIE COCKTAIL
Coffee mug, heated
Build in glass
1 oz. Laird's Applejack Brandy
1 oz. Bärenjäger Honey Liqueur
1/4 tsp. mulling spices
4 oz. hot apple cider
Cinnamon stick garnish

CHERRILLO
Presentation shot glass, chilled
Build in glass
1 oz. Limoncello Liqueur
1 oz. Chambord
1 oz. Baileys Irish Cream
Speared cherry garnish

CHERRY AMORE
Champagne glass, chilled
Pour ingredients into iced mixing glass
1 1/4 oz. Brandy
1/2 oz. maraschino cherry juice
2 oz. sweet 'n' sour
Shake and strain
Fill with Champagne

CHERRY BEAN
Presentation shot glass, chilled
Layer ingredients
1/2 fill Anisette
1/2 fill Cherry Brandy

PATRÓN® 100% AGAVE AÑEJO TEQUILA

The famed artisan tequilas of Patrón are skillfully distilled and blended in the high altitudes of the mountains surrounding Jalisco. These 100% agave tequilas have remained preeminent since they were introduced in America in the mid-1980s, due largely to the enormous following of the brand's flagship, PATRÓN AÑEJO.

The entire range of Patrón tequilas is made relying on time-proven techniques. The mature agaves are baked, crushed and slowly fermented. They are then double-distilled in copper pot stills, balanced to 80 proof and repeatedly filtered for purity. Aging takes place in small, 180-liter American oak barrels.

Patrón Añejo is an incomparable masterpiece with a luxurious, satiny smooth gold body. The tequila is generously aromatic with light fruity notes. Its palate is a rich complex of caramel, citrus and spice. The finish is long and semisweet.

PATRÓN SILVER is a rare and exuberant gem, loaded with the fresh aromas of lemon and white pepper. The supple body delivers on the promise of buttery sweet and peppery flavors. It is a supremely elegant blanco tequila.

The latest addition to the family is PATRÓN REPOSADO. It is aged a minimum of 6 months, during which it picks up a trace of golden color and a splash of toasted oak flavor. The tequila is mellow and inviting with a relaxed finish.

CHERRY BLOSSOM
Cocktail glass, chilled
Pour ingredients into iced mixing glass
1 1/2 oz. Cherry Brandy
1 oz. Brandy
3/4 oz. sweet 'n' sour
1 dash Triple Sec
1 dash grenadine
Shake and strain
Cherry garnish

CHERRY BOMB
Presentation shot glass, chilled
Layer ingredients
1/4 fill Kahlúa
1/4 fill Crème de Banana
1/4 fill Baileys Irish Cream
1/4 fill DeKuyper Cherry Pucker

CHICAGO
Champagne glass, chilled
Rim glass with salt (optional)
Pour ingredients into iced mixing glass
1 oz. Brandy
1/2 oz. Triple Sec
2 dashes Angostura Bitters
Stir and strain
Fill with Champagne
Lemon twist garnish

CHICAGO TIMES
Coffee mug, heated
Build in glass
1/2 oz. Disaronno Amaretto
1/2 oz. Tuaca
1/2 oz. Baileys Irish Cream
1/2 fill hot coffee
Near fill with hot chocolate
Whipped cream garnish
Drizzle 1/2 oz. Frangelico
Dust powdered cocoa

CHI-CHI
House specialty glass, chilled
Pour ingredients into blender
1 oz. Vodka
2 oz. coconut cream syrup
3 oz. pineapple juice
3/4 oz. half & half cream (optional)
Blend with ice
Pineapple wedge and cherry garnish

CHIHUAHUA
Bucket glass, ice
Rim glass with salt (optional)
Build in glass
1 1/4 oz. Tequila
Fill with grapefruit juice

CHILLER
Highball glass, ice
Build in glass
1 1/4 oz. requested liquor/liqueur
Fill with ginger ale

CHILL-OUT CAFÉ
Coffee mug or glass, ice
Build in glass
1/2 oz. Kahlúa
1/2 oz. Disaronno Amaretto
1/2 oz. Dark Crème de Cacao
Fill with iced coffee
Mint sprig garnish

CHIMAYO COCKTAIL
House specialty glass, ice
Pour ingredients into iced mixing glass
1 oz. Añejo Tequila
1/2 oz. Crème de Cassis
1/2 oz. fresh lime juice
3 oz. unfiltered apple cider
Shake and strain

CHIP SHOT
Presentation shot glass
Layer ingredients
1/3 fill Kahlúa
1/3 fill Disaronno Amaretto
1/3 fill hot coffee

CHIQUITA PUNCH
House specialty glass, chilled
Pour ingredients into blender
1 oz. Crème de Banana
1/2 oz. Kahlúa
1/2 oz. Dark Crème de Cacao
3/4 oz. grenadine
1 1/2 oz. half & half cream
1 1/2 oz. orange juice
Blend with ice
Banana slice garnish

CHOCOLATE ALMOND KISS
House specialty glass, chilled
Pour ingredients into blender
1 oz. Frangelico
1/2 oz. Dark Crème de Cacao
1/2 oz. Vodka
2 scoops vanilla ice cream
Blend ingredients (with ice optional)
Sprinkle shaved chocolate

CHOCOLATE BANANA (1)
House specialty glass, chilled
Pour ingredients into blender
1 1/4 oz. Crème de Banana
1 oz. chocolate syrup
1 ripe banana
2 scoops vanilla ice cream
Blend ingredients (with ice optional)
Whipped cream garnish
Sprinkle shaved chocolate

CHOCOLATE BANANA (2)
Presentation shot glass, chilled
Build in glass
1 oz. Cruzan Banana Rum
1 oz. Godiva Chocolate Liqueur
1/2 oz. half & half cream

CHOCOLATE COVERED BANANA (1)
House specialty glass, chilled
Pour ingredients into blender
1 1/2 oz. Appleton Estate V/X Jamaica Rum
1 1/2 oz. Godiva Chocolate Liqueur
2 ripe bananas
3/4 oz. half & half cream
2 scoops vanilla ice cream
Blend ingredients (with ice optional)
Whipped cream garnish
Drizzle 3/4 oz. Rhum Barbancourt 5-Star
Sprinkle shaved chocolate

CHOCOLATE COVERED BANANA (2)
House specialty glass, chilled
Pour ingredients into blender
1 3/4 oz. Baileys Irish Cream
1 oz. Banana Rum
1 oz. chocolate syrup
1 ripe banana
2 scoops banana ice cream
Blend ingredients (with ice optional)
Whipped cream garnish
Drizzle chocolate syrup
Banana slice garnish

CHOCOLATE CREAM SODA
Bucket glass, ice
Build in glass
1 1/2 oz. Godiva Chocolate Liqueur
2 oz. milk
Fill with club soda

CLASSIC® 12
BY CANADIAN CLUB®

For more than a century, Canadian Club has been the best-selling brand of Canadian whisky in the world. The release of the CLASSIC 12 by CANADIAN CLUB will go a long way to solidify the brand's preeminence.

Made by Hiram Walker at their distillery in Ontario, Classic 12 is a blend comprised of corn whisky and lesser proportions of rye, malted rye and malted barley whiskies. The constituent whiskies are blended together prior to aging, allowing them to become thoroughly integrated. The whisky is then aged for a minimum of 12 years in used bourbon barrels.

Canadian Club's Classic 12 has a brilliant amber hue, medium-weight body and a wafting bouquet loaded with the aromas of vanilla, fruit and citrus. It is imbued with the flavors of honey, toffee, cocoa and spice that persist long into the soft, lingering finish. This thoroughly engaging whisky is a bona fide treat for anyone with a taste for great spirits.

Perennial all-star CANADIAN CLUB is a 6 year old Canadian blended whisky. It has a dry, rounded body and a creamy, pronounced bouquet. The whisky lilts over the palate without a trace of bitterness, leaving behind the lip-smacking flavors of caramel, butter, orange zest and notes of cereal. The whisky finishes long and relaxed.

CHOCOLATE ICE CREAM FLOAT
House specialty glass, chilled
Pour ingredients into blender
1 3/4 oz. Jack Daniel's Tennessee Whiskey
2 oz. Hershey's chocolate syrup
2 scoops chocolate ice cream
Blend ingredients (with ice optional)
Pour into glass
Near fill with club soda
Float 1 scoop chocolate ice cream
Drizzle chocolate syrup
Graham cracker garnish

CHOCOLATE MILK COOLER
House specialty glass, chilled
Pour ingredients into blender
1 1/2 oz. Kahlúa Especial
1 1/4 oz. Christian Brothers Brandy
8 oz. chocolate milk
1 tsp. vanilla extract
Blend with ice
Whipped cream garnish
Sprinkle shaved chocolate

CHOCO LATÉ ORANGE
Brandy snifter, ice
Build in glass
1 oz. Van Gogh Vodka
1 oz. Van Gogh Oranje Vodka
1 oz. Godiva Chocolate Liqueur
1/2 oz. Grand Marnier
Orange twist garnish

CHOCOLATE SQUIRREL
Cocktail glass, chilled
Pour ingredients into iced mixing glass
3/4 oz. Disaronno Amaretto
3/4 oz. Frangelico
1/2 oz. Dark Crème de Cacao
1/2 oz. Brandy
1 1/2 oz. half & half cream
Shake and strain

CHOCOLATE WHITE RUSSIAN
Rocks glass, ice
Build in glass
1 1/2 oz. Van Gogh Chocolate Vodka
1 oz. Godiva Chocolate Liqueur
1 oz. milk

CIAO BELLO
Coffee mug or glass, heated
Build in glass
3/4 oz. Limoncello Liqueur
3/4 oz. Kahlúa
Near fill with hot coffee
Whipped cream garnish
Sprinkle shaved chocolate

CINDERELLA
House specialty glass, chilled
Pour ingredients into blender
1/2 oz. grenadine
1 1/2 oz. orange juice
1 1/2 oz. sweet 'n' sour
1 1/2 oz. pineapple juice
Blend with ice
Fill with club soda

CINNAMON SLING
Bucket glass, ice
Pour ingredients into iced mixing glass
1 oz. Gin
1 oz. Cinnamon Schnapps
2 1/2 oz. sweet 'n' sour
Shake and strain
Fill with club soda
Orange slice and cherry garnish

CINNFUL APPLE
Highball glass, ice
Build in glass
1 1/4 oz. Cinnamon Schnapps
Fill with apple cider

CIRCUS PEANUT
Presentation shot glass, chilled
Build in glass
1/3 fill Midori
1/3 fill Crème de Banana
1/3 fill half & half cream

CITROEN LEMON DROP
Cocktail glass, chilled
Rim glass with sugar
Pour ingredients into iced mixing glass
2 oz. Ketel One Citroen Vodka
1/2 tsp. sugar
1/2 oz. fresh lemon juice
Shake and strain
Sprinkle 1/2 tsp. sugar
Lemon wheel garnish

CITRON NEON
House specialty glass, chilled
Pour ingredients into blender
1 1/2 oz. Absolut Citron Vodka
1 oz. Midori
3/4 oz. DeKuyper Island Blue Pucker
1/2 oz. Rose's Lime Juice
2 oz. sweet 'n' sour
Blend with ice

CITRUS SAMURAI
Rocks glass, ice
Build in glass
1 1/2 oz. Citrus Vodka
1/2 oz. Triple Sec
1 oz. lemonade
Lemon wedge garnish

CITY TAVERN COOLER
Bucket glass, ice
Build in glass
1 1/2 oz. Dark Rum
1 oz. Bourbon
3/4 oz. Peach Schnapps
4 oz. apple cider
Apple wedge garnish

CLAM DIGGER
Bucket glass, ice
Rim glass with salt (optional)
Build in glass
1 1/2 oz. Gin
3 dashes red pepper sauce
Fill with clam juice

CLAM FOGGER
Highball glass, ice
Build in glass
1 1/4 oz. Vodka
1/3 fill cranberry juice
1/3 fill grapefruit juice
1/3 fill orange juice

CLASSIC VETTE
Cocktail glass, chilled
Rim glass with sugar (optional)
Pour ingredients into iced mixing glass
1 oz. Brandy
3/4 oz. Cointreau
1/2 oz. Limoncello Liqueur
2 oz. sweet 'n' sour
Shake and strain
Lemon twist garnish

CLEAR AND PRESENT DANGER
House specialty glass, ice
Pour ingredients into iced mixing glass
1 oz. Ketel One Citroen Vodka
3/4 oz. Midori
3/4 oz. DeKuyper Peachtree Schnapps
3/4 oz. grape juice
1 1/2 oz. cranberry juice
2 oz. orange juice
Shake and strain

CLOVER CLUB
Cocktail glass, chilled
Pour ingredients into iced mixing glass
1 1/2 oz. Gin
1/2 oz. grenadine
1 1/2 oz. sweet 'n' sour
1 egg white (optional)
Shake and strain

ORIGINAL CRISTALL® VODKA

The world-renowned Cristall Distillery in the heart of Moscow is at the center of the Russian vodka universe. For the better part of a century they have endeavored to craft increasingly finer, more delectable vodkas. The distillery's crowning achievement is acknowledged to be ORIGINAL CRISTALL VODKA.

This incomparable vodka is available in the United States, and we as a country are better for it. Its appealing character is the result of being triple-distilled from winter wheat and pristine glacier water. The vodka is filtered through quartz crystals and birch charcoal to ultimately achieve its impeccable quality and ultra-clean finish.

Original Cristall is an exceptional vodka with crystalline clarity and an enticing floral bouquet. Its full, supple body immediately warms the mouth and then slowly ebbs to a finish marked with notes of chocolate and vanilla. While often showcased in cocktails, Original Cristall is ideally served straight-up or over ice.

To add to their already long list of accomplishments, the distillery has created the super-premium ORIGINAL CRISTALL LEMON VODKA. Infused with natural lemon flavor, the silky smooth spirit has a delightful citrus personality. It makes a superb Martini or the base for a Cosmopolitan. Also available from Cristall is STARAYA MOSKVA, a sensationally smooth vodka with a moderate price tag.

CLUB MACANUDO
Cocktail glass, chilled
Pour ingredients into iced mixing glass
2 oz. Grey Goose Vodka
1/2 oz. VSOP Cognac
1/2 oz. Dubonnet Rouge
Shake and strain
Splash Champagne

CLUB SHERRY
Rocks glass, ice
Build in glass
1 1/2 oz. Canadian Club Whisky
3/4 oz. Sherry

C-NOTE A-FLOAT
Cocktail glass, chilled
Pour ingredients into iced mixing glass
1 1/2 oz. Irish Mist Irish Liqueur
1/2 oz. Godiva Chocolate Liqueur
1/2 oz. Green Crème de Menthe
1/2 oz. Kahlúa
Shake and strain

COCAINE SHOOTER (1)
Rocks glass, chilled
Pour ingredients into iced mixing glass
3/4 oz. Vodka
3/4 oz. Chambord
1/2 oz. Southern Comfort
3/4 oz. orange juice
3/4 oz. cranberry juice
Shake and strain

COCAINE SHOOTER (2)
Rocks glass, chilled
Pour ingredients into iced mixing glass
1 1/2 oz. Vodka
3/4 oz. Chambord
1/4 oz. sweet 'n' sour
1/4 oz. Seven-Up
Shake and strain

COCO LOCO
House specialty glass, chilled
Pour ingredients into blender
1 oz. Tequila
2 oz. coconut cream syrup
3 oz. pineapple juice
1/2 oz. Rose's Lime Juice
Blend with ice
Pineapple wedge and cherry garnish

COCOMACOQUE

House specialty glass, ice
Pour ingredients into iced mixing glass
1 1/2 oz. Gold Rum
1 1/2 oz. Red Wine
1 1/2 oz. sweet 'n' sour
1 1/2 oz. pineapple juice
1 1/2 oz. orange juice
Shake and strain
Float 3/4 oz. Dark Rum
Pineapple wedge and cherry garnish

COCO MOCHA

House specialty glass or
   large coffee mug, chilled
Pour ingredients into blender
3 oz. cold coffee
1/2 tsp. chocolate syrup
4 oz. coconut cream syrup
Blend with ice
Whipped cream garnish
Sprinkle nutmeg

COCOMOTION

House specialty glass, chilled
Pour ingredients into blender
1 1/2 oz. Mount Gay Eclipse Rum
1 oz. Bacardi Gold Rum
3/4 oz. Tia Maria
1 oz. fresh lime juice
2 oz. coconut cream syrup
3 oz. pineapple juice
Blend with ice
Float 3/4 oz. Appleton Estate
   V/X Jamaica Rum
Pineapple wedge and cherry garnish

COCONUT BREEZE

House specialty glass, ice
Pour ingredients into iced mixing glass
1 1/4 oz. Light Rum
1 oz. Coconut Rum
1/2 oz. simple syrup
1 oz. fresh lime juice
2 oz. mango juice
2 oz. pineapple juice
Shake and strain
Fill with Seven-Up
Lime wedge garnish

COCONUT COFFEE POT

Cocktail glass, chilled
Pour ingredients into iced mixing glass
1 3/4 oz. Pearl Lo Coco Vodka
1/2 oz. Malibu Caribbean Rum
1/2 oz. Tia Maria
Stir and strain

COCONUT CREAM PIE

Cocktail glass, chilled
Pour ingredients into iced mixing glass
1 oz. Vanilla Rum
1 oz. Malibu Caribbean Rum
1 1/2 oz. half & half cream
Shake and strain
Shredded coconut garnish

CODE RED

Champagne glass, chilled
Build in glass
2 1/2 oz. RémyRed Red Berry Infusion
Fill with Champagne
Orange twist garnish

COFFEE NUTCAKE

House specialty glass, chilled
Pour ingredients into blender
1 1/2 oz. Kahlúa Especial
3/4 oz. Frangelico
1/2 oz. Dark Crème de Cacao
2 dashes grenadine
2 scoops French vanilla ice cream
Blend ingredients (with ice optional)

COGNAC RITZ

Champagne glass, chilled
Pour ingredients into iced mixing glass
1 oz. Courvoisier VSOP Cognac
1 oz. orange juice
1 oz. sweet 'n' sour
Shake and strain
Fill with Champagne
Lemon twist garnish

COLD FUSION

House specialty glass, ice
Pour ingredients into iced mixing glass
3/4 oz. Vodka
3/4 oz. Midori
1/2 oz. Triple Sec
1/2 oz. Rose's Lime Juice
1/2 oz. fresh lemon juice
1 1/2 oz. sweet 'n' sour
Shake and strain
Lime wedge garnish

COLD GOLD

Highball glass, ice
Build in glass
3/4 oz. Cruzan Orange Rum
Near fill with orange juice
Float 3/4 oz. Blue Curaçao

GENTLEMAN JACK®
RARE TENNESSEE WHISKEY

GENTLEMAN JACK RARE TENNESSEE WHISKEY is the first new whiskey released by Jack Daniel's Distillery in almost 100 years. It is handcrafted from a recipe created by Jack Daniel himself at the turn of the century, and the result is an unqualified American masterpiece.

The exact mash bill used to make this superb whiskey is a closely guarded secret, however, it is no doubt still made with the same limestone water from the Cave Spring Hollow that helped make Jack Daniel's Tennessee Whiskey a worldwide brand.

The whiskey is aged in oak barrels for a minimum of 4 years and then mellowed twice through Tennessee sugar maple charcoal, once before being put in wood and once again after.

A whiskey this wonderful could only have been conceived by Jack Daniel himself. The bouquet is a complex affair with ribbons of honey, raisins, oak and a hint of smoke. The whiskey has a medium-weight body that slides effortlessly over the palate, leaving behind a marvelous array of sweet honey and maple flavors. The finish is warm, flavorful and lingering.

To best appreciate how rare Gentleman Jack really is, present it neat with some spring water on the side. But don't stop there, this whiskey is spry enough to be the featured attraction in numerous cocktails.

COLLINS
Collins or bucket glass, ice
Pour ingredients into iced mixing glass
1 1/4 oz. requested liquor/liqueur
2 oz. sweet 'n' sour
Shake and strain
Fill with club soda
Orange slice and cherry garnish

COLLINS, BEVERLY HILLS
Collins or bucket glass, ice
Pour ingredients into iced mixing glass
1 1/4 oz. Citadelle Gin
2 oz. sweet 'n' sour
Shake and strain
Fill with Perrier mineral water
Orange slice and cherry garnish

COLLINS, FIFI
Collins or bucket glass, ice
Pour ingredients into iced mixing glass
1 1/4 oz. VS Cognac
2 oz. sweet 'n' sour
Shake and strain
Fill with club soda
Orange slice and cherry garnish

COLLINS, JACK
aka **Apple Collins**
Collins or bucket glass, ice
Pour ingredients into iced mixing glass
1 1/4 oz. Laird's Applejack Brandy
2 oz. sweet 'n' sour
Shake and strain
Fill with club soda
Orange slice and cherry garnish

COLLINS, JAMIE
Collins or bucket glass, ice
Pour ingredients into iced mixing glass
1 1/4 oz. Bourbon
1/2 oz. Limoncello Liqueur
2 oz. sweet 'n' sour
Shake and strain
Fill with Squirt
Orange slice and cherry garnish

COLLINS, JEFF
Collins or bucket glass, ice
Pour ingredients into iced mixing glass
1 1/4 oz. Citrus Vodka
3/4 oz. cranberry juice
1 1/2 oz. sweet 'n' sour
Shake and strain
Fill with club soda
Lemon wedge garnish

COLLINS, JIM
Collins or bucket glass, ice
Pour ingredients into iced mixing glass
1 1/4 oz. Scotch Whisky
2 oz. sweet 'n' sour
Shake and strain
Fill with club soda
Orange slice and cherry garnish

COLLINS, JOE
aka **Mike Collins**
Collins or bucket glass, ice
Pour ingredients into iced mixing glass
1 1/4 oz. Irish Whiskey
2 oz. sweet 'n' sour
Shake and strain
Fill with club soda
Orange slice and cherry garnish

COLLINS, JOHN
aka **Colonel Collins**
Collins or bucket glass, ice
Pour ingredients into iced mixing glass
1 1/4 oz. Bourbon
2 oz. sweet 'n' sour
Shake and strain
Fill with club soda
Orange slice and cherry garnish

COLLINS, PEDRO
Collins or bucket glass, ice
Pour ingredients into iced mixing glass
1 1/4 oz. Light Rum
2 oz. sweet 'n' sour
Shake and strain
Fill with club soda
Orange slice and cherry garnish

COLLINS, PIERRE
Collins or bucket glass, ice
Pour ingredients into iced mixing glass
1 1/4 oz. VS Cognac
2 oz. sweet 'n' sour
Shake and strain
Fill with club soda
Orange slice and cherry garnish

COLLINS, RED TURKEY
Collins or bucket glass, ice
Pour ingredients into iced mixing glass
1 1/4 oz. Wild Turkey Bourbon
1/2 oz. RémyRed Red Berry Infusion
2 oz. sweet 'n' sour
Shake and strain
Fill with club soda
Orange slice and cherry garnish

COLLINS, RODEO DRIVE
House specialty glass, ice
Build in glass
2 oz. Damrak Amsterdam Gin
3/4 oz. Cointreau
Fill with Perrier mineral water
Float 3/4 oz. Oro di Mazzetti
    Grappa Liqueur
Orange slice and lemon garnish

COLLINS, TOM
aka **Gin Fizz**
Collins or bucket glass, ice
Pour ingredients into iced mixing glass
1 1/4 oz. Gin
2 oz. sweet 'n' sour
Shake and strain
Fill with club soda
Orange slice and cherry garnish

COLLINS, VODKA
Collins or bucket glass, ice
Pour ingredients into iced mixing glass
1 1/4 oz. Vodka
2 oz. sweet 'n' sour
Shake and strain
Fill with club soda
Orange slice and cherry garnish

COLOMBIAN NECKTIE
Rocks glass, chilled
Build in glass
3/4 oz. Rumple Minze Schnapps
3/4 oz. 151° Rum
2-3 dashes Tabasco Sauce
1/2 oz. Cinnamon Schnapps

COLORADO AVALANCHE
Coffee mug, heated
Build in glass
1/2 oz. Kahlúa
1/2 oz. Dark Crème de Cacao
1/2 oz. Chambord
Near fill with hot Nestle's Alpine
    White Cocoa
Whipped cream garnish
Dust powdered cocoa

COLORADO BULLDOG
Bucket glass, ice
Build in glass
1 1/2 oz. Vodka
3/4 oz. Kahlúa
1/2 fill cola
1/2 fill half & half cream

COLORADO RIVER COOLER
Brandy snifter, ice
Build in glass
4 oz. White Zinfandel Wine
1 oz. Midori
Fill with club soda

MIDORI® MELON LIQUEUR

MIDORI MELON LIQUEUR burst into the limelight in the early 1980s and the brand can now be found on nearly every back bar in the world. In fact, its popularity continues to grow as steadily increasing numbers of contemporary drinks incorporate it into their recipes.

Midori is produced in Japan from a base of neutral spirits and proprietary flavors, the most readily identifiable of which is honeydew melon. Its lustrous, emerald green color is absolutely intriguing, which has certainly played a role in the liqueur's meteoric success.

Midori has medium-weight body and a lively bouquet with the aromas of melon, banana and strawberry. Its slightly sweet palate immediately fills the mouth with the fresh fruit flavors of honeydew, cantaloupe and bananas. The liqueur has excellent persistence of flavor.

It's difficult to imagine operating a bar without Midori. Like most great supporting actors, it receives little fanfare, but among professionals, it ranks on the short list of "must have" back bar entries. Without it, a large segment of popular mixology drops off-line.

In a world of substitutes and knock-offs, it's interesting to note that no brand has even made an attempt to go head-to-head with Midori. Some things just can't be duplicated.

COME-ON-I-WANNA-LEI-YA
House specialty glass, chilled
Pour ingredients into blender
1 1/4 oz. Cruzan Vanilla Rum
3/4 oz. Cruzan Coconut Rum
3/4 oz. Cruzan Orange Rum
2 scoops vanilla ice cream
Blend ingredients (with ice optional)
Whipped cream garnish
Drizzle 1/2 oz. Disaronno Amaretto

COMFORT KIT
Bucket glass, ice
Build in glass
1 oz. Sauza Hornitos Tequila
Near fill with orange juice
Float 3/4 oz. Southern Comfort

COMFORTABLE CRUSH
Bucket glass, ice
Build in glass
3/4 oz. Chambord
3/4 oz. Southern Comfort
1/2 oz. Peach Schnapps
Fill with lemonade
Lemon wedge garnish

COMFORTABLE SCREW
aka **Southern Screw**
Highball glass, ice
Build in glass
1 1/4 oz. Southern Comfort
Fill with orange juice

COMMODORE
Cocktail glass, chilled
Pour ingredients into iced mixing glass
1 1/2 oz. Gold Rum
2 dashes grenadine
1 egg white (optional)
1/2 oz. simple syrup
1 1/2 oz. sweet 'n' sour
Shake and strain

CONCORDE
Champagne glass, chilled
Build in glass
1 1/2 oz. Stolichnaya Citros Vodka
Near fill with Champagne
Float 3/4 oz. Grand Marnier

COOKIE MINT ROOKIE
House specialty glass, ice
Pour ingredients into blender
1 oz. Kahlúa
3/4 oz. Baileys Irish Cream
3/4 oz. Brandy
3/4 oz. White Crème de Menthe
2 oz. cold espresso coffee
2 scoops vanilla ice cream
1 oz. Hershey's chocolate syrup
Blend ingredients
Chocolate chips garnish

COOKIES 'N' CREAM
House specialty glass, chilled
Pour ingredients into blender
1 oz. Dark Crème de Cacao
1 oz. half & half cream
2-3 Oreo cookies
2 scoops vanilla ice cream
Blend ingredients (with ice optional)

COOL CAPTAIN
Presentation shot glass, chilled
Build in glass
1 oz. Captain Morgan Spiced Rum
3/4 oz. Peppermint Schnapps
1/4 oz. grenadine

COOL CARLOS
House specialty glass, ice
Pour ingredients into iced mixing glass
1 1/2 oz. Dark Rum
1 oz. Orange Curaçao
1 1/2 oz. sweet 'n' sour
2 oz. cranberry juice
2 oz. pineapple juice
Shake and strain
Float 3/4 oz. Jamaican Rum
Pineapple wedge and orange slice garnish

COOL MINT LISTERINE
Presentation shot glass, chilled
Build in glass
1/3 fill Vodka
1/3 fill Peppermint Schnapps
1/3 fill Blue Curaçao

CORAZÓN DE LEÓN
Cocktail glass, chilled
Rim glass with salt (optional)
Pour ingredients into iced mixing glass
1 1/2 oz. Corazón Reposado Tequila
1/2 oz. Cointreau
1/2 oz. Grand Marnier
1/2 oz. fresh lime juice
1/2 oz. orange juice
1 1/2 oz. sweet 'n' sour
Shake and strain
Lime wheel garnish

CORK STREET COFFEE (1)
Coffee mug, heated
Build in glass
1 1/2 oz. Gold Rum
1/2 oz. Cruzan Rum Cream
1/2 oz. Frangelico
Near fill with hot coffee
Whipped cream garnish
Drizzle chocolate syrup

CORK STREET COFFEE (2)
Coffee mug, heated
Build in glass
3/4 oz. Baileys Irish Cream
3/4 oz. Frangelico
1/2 oz. Gold Rum
Near fill with hot coffee
Whipped cream garnish
Dust powdered cocoa

CORONATION
Wine goblet (ice optional)
Build in glass
1 oz. Dry Vermouth
1 1/2 oz. Dry Sherry
1 dash Maraschino Liqueur
2 dashes Angostura Bitters
5 oz. White Wine
Fill with club soda

CORPSE REVIVER (1)
Cocktail glass, chilled
Pour ingredients into iced mixing glass
3/4 oz. Calvados Apple Brandy
3/4 oz. VS Cognac
1/2 oz. Sweet Vermouth
Stir and strain
Lemon twist garnish

CORPSE REVIVER (2)
Cocktail glass, chilled
Pour ingredients into iced mixing glass
1 oz. Fernet Branca
1 oz. Brandy
1 oz. White Crème de Cacao
Stir and strain

COSMOPOLITAN
Cocktail glass, chilled
Pour ingredients into iced mixing glass
1 1/2 oz. Absolut Citron Vodka
1/2 oz. Cointreau
1/2 oz. Rose's Lime Juice
1/2 oz. cranberry juice
Stir and strain
Orange twist garnish

TEQUILA CORAZÓN® DE AGAVE BLANCO

While there is something supremely sublime about sipping a well aged tequila, it is not the end all. Most spirit aficionados eventually gravitate to drinking the blanco tequilas because of their pure and unadulterated character. They are unaffected by the aging process and therefore illustrate exactly how the tequilas taste directly from the still. TEQUILA CORAZÓN DE AGAVE BLANCO is an excellent example.

The entire Tequila Corazón range is distilled in the highlands of Arandas. These handcrafted, 100% agave tequilas are produced on the sprawling Destiladora San Nicholas Estate using traditional, century-old methods abandoned by most as cost prohibitive.

The 80 proof tequilas are made from mature, estate grown agaves. After harvesting, the agaves are baked in stone ovens, slowly fermented and distilled in the estate's copper pot stills. The result is highly sophisticated spirits worthy of *grand cru* status.

Tequila Corazón Blanco is drawn directly from the still and rested for 24 hours before being bottled. The tequila has a fresh, exuberant personality that can only be found in an unaged spirit. It has a lightweight, supple body and a wafting floral bouquet. The palate fills the mouth with long lasting spicy, peppery flavors. The overall effect is delectable and thoroughly satisfying.

COSMOPOLITAN, CARIBBEAN COSMO
Cocktail glass, chilled
Pour ingredients into iced mixing glass
1 1/2 oz. Cruzan Orange Rum
1 1/2 oz. Cruzan Light Rum
1/2 oz. fresh lime juice
3/4 oz. cranberry juice
Stir and strain
Lime wedge garnish

COSMOPOLITAN, CELLO
Cocktail glass, chilled
Pour ingredients into iced mixing glass
1 1/2 oz. Limoncello Liqueur
1/2 oz. Cointreau
1/2 oz. Rose's Lime Juice
1/2 oz. cranberry juice
Stir and strain
Lime wedge garnish

COSMOPOLITAN, CHI CHI
Cocktail glass, chilled
Pour ingredients into iced mixing glass
1 1/2 oz. Pineapple Rum
3/4 oz. Coconut Rum
1/2 oz. Orange Liqueur
1/2 oz. cranberry juice
3/4 oz. sweet 'n' sour
Stir and strain
Frozen cranberry garnish

COSMOPOLITAN, COMFORT
Cocktail glass, chilled
Pour ingredients into iced mixing glass
1 oz. Southern Comfort
1/2 oz. Cointreau
1/2 oz. fresh lime juice
2 oz. cranberry juice
Stir and strain
Lime wedge garnish

COSMOPOLITAN, COSMORITA
Cocktail glass, chilled
Pour ingredients into iced mixing glass
1 1/2 oz. Sauza Tres Generaciones
  Plata Tequila
3/4 oz. Agavero Liqueur
1/2 oz. Rose's Lime Juice
1/2 oz. cranberry juice
Stir and strain
Lime wedge garnish

COSMOPOLITAN, DISARONNO
Cocktail glass, chilled
Pour ingredients into iced mixing glass
1 oz. Disaronno Amaretto
1 oz. Bacardi Limón Rum
1/2 oz. cranberry juice
Stir and strain
Lime wedge garnish

COSMOPOLITAN, DUBONNET
Cocktail glass, chilled
Pour ingredients into iced mixing glass
1 1/4 oz. Citrus Vodka
3/4 oz. Dubonnet Rouge
1/2 oz. Cointreau
1/2 oz. Rose's Lime Juice
1/2 oz. cranberry juice
1/4 oz. fresh lime juice
Stir and strain
Lime wheel garnish

COSMOPOLITAN, EURO
Cocktail glass, chilled
Pour ingredients into iced mixing glass
2 oz. Citadelle Raspberry Vodka
3/4 oz. Chambord
1/2 oz. Cointreau
1/2 oz. fresh lime juice
1 oz. white cranberry juice
Stir and strain
Lemon wheel garnish

COSMOPOLITAN, HPNOTIQ
Cocktail glass, chilled
Pour ingredients into iced mixing glass
1 1/2 oz. Citrus Vodka
1 oz. Hpnotiq Liqueur
1/2 oz. fresh lime juice
1 oz. white cranberry juice
Stir and strain
Lime wedge garnish

COSMOPOLITAN, LEMON TWISTED
Cocktail glass, chilled
Pour ingredients into iced mixing glass
2 oz. Van Gogh Citron Vodka
1 oz. Van Gogh Wild Appel Vodka
3/4 oz. Van Gogh Oranje Vodka
1/2 oz. fresh lime juice
3/4 oz. cranberry juice
Shake and strain
Lemon twist garnish

COSMOPOLITAN, LIMÓN
Cocktail glass, chilled
Pour ingredients into iced mixing glass
1 1/2 oz. Bacardi Limón Rum
1/2 oz. Cointreau
1/2 oz. Rose's Lime Juice
1/2 oz. cranberry juice
Stir and strain
Orange twist garnish

COSMOPOLITAN, LONDON
Cocktail glass, chilled
Pour ingredients into iced mixing glass
1 3/4 oz. Beefeater London Dry Gin
1/2 oz. Cointreau
1/2 oz. Rose's Lime Juice
1/2 oz. white cranberry juice
Stir and strain
Orange twist garnish

COSMOPOLITAN, MARGARITA COSMO
Cocktail glass, chilled
Rim glass with salt (optional)
Pour ingredients into iced mixing glass
2 oz. Sauza Tres Generaciones Plata Tequila
3/4 oz. Grand Marnier
1/2 oz. Rose's Lime Juice
3/4 oz. cranberry juice
Stir and strain
Lime wedge garnish

COSMOPOLITAN, MELON
Cocktail glass, chilled
Pour ingredients into iced mixing glass
1 1/2 oz. Vodka
1 oz. Midori
1/2 oz. Cointreau
1/2 oz. Rose's Lime Juice
1/2 oz. cranberry juice
Stir and strain
Lime wedge garnish

COSMOPOLITAN, MEXICALI
Cocktail glass, chilled
Pour ingredients into iced mixing glass
1 1/2 oz. Patrón Añejo Tequila
3/4 oz. Cointreau
1/2 oz. Rose's Lime Juice
1/2 oz. cranberry juice
Stir and strain
Lime wedge garnish

COSMOPOLITAN, MIDNIGHT BLUE
Cocktail glass, chilled
Pour ingredients into iced mixing glass
1 3/4 oz. Citrus Vodka
1 oz. Hpnotiq Liqueur
1/2 oz. Blue Curaçao
1/2 oz. Rose's Lime Juice
1 oz. white cranberry juice
Stir and strain
Lime wedge garnish

ABERLOUR® A'BUNADH SINGLE SPEYSIDE MALT

Aberlour is one of the most esteemed whisky distilleries in Scotland, if not the world. It is located in the heart of the Highlands, an easy walk from the river Spey, ensconced among towering trees and a gurgling natural spring. Master distiller Douglas Cruickshank leads a small group of craftsmen and together they create a range of single malt Scotches ranging from the Aberlour 12 year old Single Speyside Malt to the highly sought after 30 year old Stillman's Dram.

Once only sold in duty-free shops around the world, ABERLOUR A'BUNADH SINGLE SPEYSIDE MALT is certainly one of the most extraordinary malts sold in a bottle. It is a robust, unadulterated whisky. The whisky is left in a pristine state—unfiltered, undiluted and bottled at cask strength; our tasting sample was 119.2 proof.

For whisky aficionados, Aberlour a'bunadh is a mother lode, definitely in the "too good to share" category. It has an expansive nose and a full, creamy palate that features the malty, smoky flavors of sherry, chocolate and fruit. This magnificent whisky has one of the truly memorable finishes.

Aberlour a'bunadh was bred to be savored after dinner and should be served neat, or with a splash of spring water to be fully appreciated.

COSMOPOLITAN, ORCHARD PEACH
Cocktail glass, chilled
Pour ingredients into iced mixing glass
2 oz. Grey Goose L'Orange Vodka
3/4 oz. DeKuyper Peachtree Schnapps
1/2 oz. Rose's Lime Juice
1 oz. white cranberry juice
Stir and strain
Peach slice garnish

COSMOPOLITAN, PURPLE (1)
Cocktail glass, chilled
Pour ingredients into iced mixing glass
1 1/2 oz. RémyRed Grape Berry Infusion
1/2 oz. Blue Curaçao
1/2 oz. cranberry juice
1/2 oz. fresh lime juice
Stir and strain
Lime wedge garnish

COSMOPOLITAN, PURPLE (2)
Cocktail glass, chilled
Pour ingredients into iced mixing glass
1 1/2 oz. Citrus Vodka
3/4 oz. Blue Curaçao
1/2 oz. Chambord
1/2 oz. Rose's Lime Juice
1/2 oz. cranberry juice
Stir and strain
Lime wheel garnish

COSMOPOLITAN, RASPBERRY (1)
Cocktail glass, chilled
Pour ingredients into iced mixing glass
2 oz. Vodka
3/4 oz. Chambord
3/4 oz. Cointreau
1/2 oz. fresh lime juice
Stir and strain
Lemon wheel garnish

COSMOPOLITAN, RASPBERRY (2)
Cocktail glass, chilled
Pour ingredients into iced mixing glass
1 1/2 oz. Vox Raspberry Vodka
3/4 oz. Cointreau
1/2 oz. fresh lime juice
1 oz. cranberry juice
Stir and strain
Lime wedge garnish

COSMOPOLITAN, RED LIGHT
Cocktail glass, chilled
Pour ingredients into iced mixing glass
1 oz. Dubonnet Rouge
1 1/2 oz. Absolut Citron Vodka
1/4 oz. fresh lemon juice
1 oz. cranberry juice
Stir and strain
Lime wheel garnish

COSMOPOLITAN, SONORAN
Cocktail glass, chilled
Pour ingredients into iced mixing glass
1 1/2 oz. Jose Cuervo Tradicional Tequila
3/4 oz. Grand Marnier
1/2 oz. Cointreau
1/2 oz. Rose's Lime Juice
1/2 oz. cranberry juice
Stir and strain
Lime wheel garnish

COSMOPOLITAN, SUMMER DAZE
Cocktail glass, chilled
Pour ingredients into iced mixing glass
3/4 oz. Citrus Vodka
3/4 oz. Raspberry Vodka
1/2 oz. Cointreau
1/2 oz. Rose's Lime Juice
1 oz. sweet 'n' sour
1 oz. cranberry juice
Stir and strain
Lime wedge garnish

COSMOPOLITAN, TRES COSMO
Cocktail glass, chilled
Pour ingredients into iced mixing glass
1 1/2 oz. Sauza Tres Generaciones
    Añejo Tequila
1 oz. Cointreau
1 oz. fresh lime juice
1 oz. cranberry juice
Shake and strain
Lime twist garnish

COSMOPOLITAN, WHITE
Cocktail glass, chilled
Pour ingredients into iced mixing glass
1 1/2 oz. Absolut Citron Vodka
3/4 oz. Cointreau Liqueur
1/2 oz. Rose's Lime Juice
3/4 oz. white grape juice
Stir and strain
Lime wheel garnish

COVE COOLER
Bucket glass, ice
Build in glass
1 1/4 oz. Pusser's British Navy Rum
1 1/2 oz. sweet 'n' sour
Near fill with pineapple juice
Splash club soda
Orange slice garnish

COWBOY KILLER
House specialty glass, ice
Pour ingredients into iced mixing glass
1/2 oz. Disaronno Amaretto
1/2 oz. DeKuyper Cherry Pucker
1/2 oz. Southern Comfort
1/2 oz. grenadine
1 oz. sweet 'n' sour
2 oz. orange juice
Shake and strain
Orange slice and cherry garnish

CRABAPPLE
Bucket glass, ice
Build in glass
1 1/2 oz. DeKuyper Pucker Sour Apple
3/4 oz. Vodka
Near fill with Squirt
Float 1/2 oz. grenadine

CRAB HOUSE SHOOTER
Rocks glass, chilled
Pour ingredients into iced mixing glass
1/2 oz. Disaronno Amaretto
1/2 oz. Southern Comfort
1/2 oz. Chambord
1/4 oz. sweet 'n' sour
1/4 oz. Rose's Lime Juice
1/4 oz. pineapple juice
1/4 oz. cranberry juice
1/4 oz. orange juice
Shake and strain

CRANBERRY SQUEEZE
Bucket glass, ice
Build in glass
1 1/4 oz. Stolichnaya Cranberi Vodka
3/4 oz. Chambord
Fill with lemonade
Lemon wedge garnish

CREAM OF GIN
Cocktail glass, chilled
Pour ingredients into iced mixing glass
3/4 oz. London Dry Gin
1/2 oz. White Crème de Menthe
1/2 oz. White Crème de Cacao
2 oz. half & half cream
Shake and strain

APPLETON ESTATE® V/X JAMAICA RUM

The surging popularity of rum in this country is due to a large degree to the uncompromised rums of Appleton Estate. Produced continuously since 1749, it is now the most highly sought after rum from Jamaica. One sip of APPLETON ESTATE V/X JAMAICA RUM and you'll learn why their reputation for greatness is well deserved.

Every step of production takes place on the Appleton Estate in St. Elizabeth Parish. The estate mills its own sugar cane and distills both light-bodied, continuous-distilled spirits and fuller, more complex pot-distilled rums. These rums are skillfully blended together and then aged in charred, American oak barrels.

Appleton Estate V/X Jamaica Rum is a spirit masterpiece. The rums used to make up its blend have an average age of 5 to 10 years. After blending, the rum is rested in huge oak vats to allow the constituent elements to become fully integrated. It is bottled at 80 proof.

The V/X on the labels stands for "very exceptional," which is definitely an understatement. The rum has a deep golden-amber color and a generous bouquet of oranges and molasses. The rum's medium body fills the mouth with the semisweet flavors of caramel, vanilla and spice. Possibly its best feature is the creamy, long lasting and flavor enriched finish.

CREAMSICLE (1)
Cocktail glass, chilled
Pour ingredients into iced mixing glass
3/4 oz. Crème de Banana
3/4 oz. Triple Sec
1 oz. orange juice
1 oz. half & half cream
Shake and strain

CREAMSICLE (2)
House specialty glass, chilled
Pour ingredients into blender
1 1/4 oz. Disaronno Amaretto
3/4 oz. Gran Gala Orange Liqueur
2 oz. orange juice
1 scoop each, vanilla ice cream and
    orange sorbet
Blend ingredients (with ice optional)
Whipped cream garnish

CREAMY BULL
Cocktail glass, chilled
Pour ingredients into iced mixing glass
3/4 oz. Tequila
3/4 oz. Kahlúa
2 oz. half & half cream
Shake and strain

CREAMY DREAMY ISOTOPE
Bucket glass, ice
Pour ingredients into iced mixing glass
3/4 oz. Orange Rum
3/4 oz. B & B Liqueur
3/4 oz. Galliano Liqueur
3/4 oz. Brandy
1 oz. orange juice
1 oz. half & half cream
Shake and strain

CREOLE
Rocks glass, ice
Pour ingredients into iced mixing glass
1 1/2 oz. Light Rum
2 dashes Tabasco Sauce
1 tsp. fresh lemon juice
1 1/2 oz. beef bouillon
Salt and pepper to taste
Shake and strain
Lemon wedge garnish

CRIMSON ROSE
House specialty glass, chilled
Pour ingredients into blender
1 1/4 oz. Tequila Rose Cream Liqueur
2 oz. Triple Sec
3 oz. frozen strawberries
Blend with ice
Strawberry garnish

CRUZAN RUM PUNCH
House specialty glass, ice
Pour ingredients into iced mixing glass
1/2 oz. Cruzan Coconut Rum
1/2 oz. Cruzan Orange Rum
1/2 oz. Cruzan Banana Rum
1/2 oz. Cruzan Pineapple Rum
1/2 oz. Cruzan Citrus Rum
1/2 oz. Cruzan Mango Rum
3/4 oz. grenadine
2 oz. orange juice
2 oz. pineapple juice
Shake and strain
Orange, papaya and cherry garnish

CRYPTO NUGGET
Rocks glass, chilled
Pour ingredients into iced mixing glass
3/4 oz. DeKuyper Pucker Sour Apple
3/4 oz. DeKuyper Island Blue Pucker
3/4 oz. Absolut Mandarin Vodka
1/4 oz. fresh lime juice
1 1/4 oz. sweet 'n' sour
Shake and strain

CUBA LIBRE
Highball glass, ice
Build in glass
1 1/4 oz. Light Rum
Fill with cola
Lime wedge garnish

CUBAN COCKTAIL
Cocktail glass, chilled
Pour ingredients into iced mixing glass
2 oz. Matusalem Light Dry Rum
2 oz. sweetened lime juice
Shake and strain
Lime wedge garnish

CUBAN PEACH
Cocktail glass, chilled
Pour ingredients into iced mixing glass
1 1/2 oz. Matusalem Light Dry Rum
1 oz. DeKuyper Peachtree Schnapps
1/2 oz. Rose's Lime Juice
1 dash simple syrup
Shake and strain
Mint sprig garnish

CUBAN SPECIAL
Cocktail glass, chilled
Pour ingredients into iced mixing glass
1 1/2 oz. Matusalem Light Dry Rum
1/2 oz. Triple Sec
1/2 oz. fresh lime juice
3/4 oz. pineapple juice
Shake and strain
Lime wedge garnish

CUERVO NATION COCKTAIL
Bucket glass, ice
Build in glass
1 1/2 oz. Jose Cuervo Especial Tequila
1 1/2 oz. pineapple juice
1 1/2 oz. orange juice
Float 3/4 oz. Blue Curaçao
Orange wedge garnish

CULTURE SHOCK
House specialty glass, chilled
Pour ingredients into blender
1/2 oz. Cruzan Coconut Rum
1/2 oz. Cruzan Banana Rum
1/2 oz. Cruzan Estate Diamond Rum
1/2 oz. RémyRed Red Berry Infusion
1 1/2 oz. orange juice
1 1/2 oz. pineapple juice
Blend with ice
Float 3/4 oz. Cruzan Estate Diamond Rum
Orange slice and cherry garnish

CURAÇAO COOLER
House specialty glass, ice
Pour ingredients into iced mixing glass
1 1/2 oz. Mount Gay Eclipse Rum
1 1/4 oz. Blue Curaçao
3/4 oz. Citrónge Orange Liqueur
1 oz. fresh lime juice
1 1/2 oz. orange juice
1 1/2 oz. sweet 'n' sour
Shake and strain
Near fill with club soda
Float 3/4 oz. St. James Extra Old Rhum
Lime wedge garnish

CYRANO
Rocks glass, chilled
Pour ingredients into iced mixing glass
1 oz. Baileys Irish Cream
1 oz. Grand Marnier
3/4 oz. Chambord
Shake and strain

DACTYL NIGHTMARE
Presentation shot glass, chilled
Layer ingredients
1/2 fill Baileys Irish Cream
1/2 fill Midori
4 drops grenadine

DAIQUIRI
House specialty glass, ice
Pour ingredients into iced mixing glass
1 1/4 oz. Light Rum
1/2 oz. Rose's Lime Juice
2 oz. sweet 'n' sour
Shake and strain
Lime wedge garnish

STOLICHNAYA®
CITROS VODKA

No one has proved the point better than Russian-born Stolichnaya that vodkas taste better if given a flavor or two. A few minutes alone with any member of the Stoli flavor family should be enough to appreciate why they have attained preeminence. It's all about flavor—innovative, satiny smooth, true-to-fruit flavor. Case in point is STOLICHNAYA CITROS VODKA.

Introduced in 2003, Stoli Citros is a lemon-lime sensation with a svelte body and a bouquet of sun-drenched citrus zest. The refreshing and mildly tart flavors of lemon and lime play out equally on the palate and linger long after the vodka has gone on its way.

The makers of Stolichnaya are clearly intent on world domination. STOLI CRANBERI is a fresh and vibrant vodka imbued with the luscious taste of cranberries. As with all of the Stoli vodkas, Cranberi is flavored with natural flavors, not artificial syrups. STOLI OHRANJ tastes like it was infused with tree-ripened oranges picked over the weekend.

As if those weren't enough to conquer the free world, the Stoli family tree also includes the hugely successful VANIL (vanilla), RAZBERI (raspberry), STRASBERI (strawberry) and PERSIK (peach).

They are wonderful in Martinis, Gimlets, Kamikazes, or many other tantalizing cocktail variations.

DAIQUIRI, BANANA
House specialty glass, chilled
Pour ingredients into blender
1 1/4 oz. Light Rum
1 oz. Cruzan Banana Rum
Peeled ripe banana
1/2 oz. Rose's Lime Juice
2 oz. sweet 'n' sour
Blend with ice
Orange and banana slice garnish

DAIQUIRI, BERRY
House specialty glass, chilled
Pour ingredients into blender
1 1/4 oz. Light Rum
1/2 cup raspberries or strawberries
1/2 oz. Rose's Lime Juice
2 oz. sweet 'n' sour
Blend with ice
Float 3/4 oz. Chambord
Pineapple wedge and cherry garnish

DAIQUIRI, CALYPSO
House specialty glass, chilled
Pour ingredients into blender
1 1/2 oz. Appleton Estate V/X Jamaica Rum
1 ripe banana
1 tsp. vanilla extract
3/4 oz. half & half cream
2 1/2 oz. sweet 'n' sour
Blend with ice
Float 3/4 oz. Rhum Barbancourt
   3-Star
Pineapple wedge and cherry garnish

DAIQUIRI, CHARLES
Cocktail glass, chilled
Pour ingredients into iced mixing glass
1 1/2 oz. Light Rum
3/4 oz. Dark Rum
3/4 oz. Cointreau
1/2 oz. Rose's Lime Juice
1 1/2 oz. sweet 'n' sour
Shake and strain
Lime wedge garnish

DAIQUIRI, COCONUT
Cocktail glass, chilled
Pour ingredients into iced mixing glass
1 1/2 oz. Light Rum
1 oz. Coconut Rum
3/4 oz. coconut cream syrup
1/2 oz. Rose's Lime Juice
1 1/2 oz. sweet 'n' sour
Shake and strain
Lime wedge garnish

DAIQUIRI, DEMERARA
Cocktail glass, chilled
Pour ingredients into iced mixing glass
1 1/4 oz. Demerara Rum
1/2 oz. Rose's Lime Juice
2 oz. sweet 'n' sour
Shake and strain
Orange slice garnish

DAIQUIRI DE PIÑA
House specialty glass, chilled
Pour ingredients into blender
1 1/2 oz. Light Rum
1 oz. Cruzan Pineapple Rum
2-3 slices cored and peeled pineapple
1/2 oz. Rose's Lime Juice
2 oz. sweet 'n' sour
Blend with ice
Orange slice, pineapple wedge and
  cherry garnish

DAIQUIRI, DERBY
Cocktail glass, chilled
Pour ingredients into blender
1 oz. Kuya Fusion Rum
1/2 oz. Rose's Lime Juice
1 oz. orange juice
1 1/2 oz. sweet 'n' sour
Blend with ice
Float 3/4 oz. Kuya Fusion Rum
Pineapple wedge and cherry garnish

DAIQUIRI, DON ROLAND
Cocktail glass, chilled
Pour ingredients into iced mixing glass
1 1/2 oz. Light Rum
1/2 oz. Green Crème de Menthe
1/2 oz. Cointreau
2 mint leaves
1/2 oz. Rose's Lime Juice
1 1/2 oz. sweet 'n' sour
Shake and strain
Mint sprig garnish

DAIQUIRI, FLIGHT OF FANCY
House specialty glass, chilled
Pour ingredients into blender
2 oz. Kuya Fusion Rum
1/2 oz. Rose's Lime Juice
1/2 cup raspberries
3 oz. sweet 'n' sour
Blend with ice

DAIQUIRI, FLORIDA
Cocktail glass, chilled
Pour ingredients into iced mixing glass
1 1/2 oz. Light Rum
1/4 oz. grenadine
1/2 oz. Rose's Lime Juice
1/2 oz. grapefruit juice
1 1/2 oz. sweet 'n' sour
Shake and strain
Lime wedge garnish

DAIQUIRI, FRENCH (1)
Cocktail glass, chilled
Pour ingredients into iced mixing glass
1 3/4 oz. St. James Extra Old Rhum
3/4 oz. Crème de Cassis
1/2 oz. Rose's Lime Juice
2 oz. sweet 'n' sour
Shake and strain
Orange twist garnish

DAIQUIRI, FRENCH (2)
Cocktail glass, chilled
Pour ingredients into iced mixing glass
1 3/4 oz. J. Bally Rhum Vieux 7 Year
1/2 oz. Rose's Lime Juice
1 oz. passion fruit juice
2 oz. sweet 'n' sour
Shake and strain
Orange twist garnish

DAIQUIRI, FRUIT (BASIC)
House specialty glass, chilled
Pour ingredients into blender
1 1/2 oz. Light Rum
1/2 cup requested fruit
1/2 oz. Rose's Lime Juice
1 1/2 oz. sweet 'n' sour
Blend with ice
Fresh fruit garnish

DAIQUIRI, HEMINGWAY
Cocktail glass, chilled
Pour ingredients into iced mixing glass
1 3/4 oz. Light Rum
1/2 oz. Maraschino Liqueur
1 oz. grapefruit juice
1 1/2 oz. fresh lime juice
Shake and strain
Lime wheel garnish

DAIQUIRI, LA FLORIDITA
Cocktail glass, chilled
Pour ingredients into iced mixing glass
1 1/2 oz. Light Rum
3/4 oz. Cointreau
3/4 oz. fresh lime juice
2 oz. sweet 'n' sour
Shake and strain
Lime wedge garnish

CHAMBORD® LIQUEUR ROYALE DE FRANCE

It is hard to imagine sipping a liqueur more luscious than CHAMBORD LIQUEUR ROYALE DE FRANCE. Long a favorite of King Louis XIV, Chambord is an elegant and refined crème de framboise. It became an overnight success when introduced in the United States and was a fixture on back bars moments after its arrival. Now twenty years later, Chambord is the featured performer in a large repertoire of cocktails and permanently enrolled in the "must have" class.

Appropriately enough, Chambord Liqueur is made in the town of Chambord, which is located in the center of France. The liqueur is crafted on a base of neutral spirits that is infused with a mixture of fresh *framboise noires* (small black raspberries), herbs and other fruits. The maceration of fruit is steeped in cognac; then the infusion is blended and bottled at 33 proof.

Everything about Chambord is sensational. The intrigue begins with its opaque appearance and extremely deep, ruby/purple hue. The liqueur has a luxuriously textured, medium-weight body and a wafting herbal and fruit bouquet. The semisweet palate is a lavish affair featuring raspberries, spice, herbs and a taste of honey. The flavors persist on the palate for a remarkably long finish.

In the hands of the inspired, Chambord has no creative limitations.

DAIQUIRI, LECHTHALER'S
House specialty glass, chilled
Pour ingredients into iced mixing glass
1 oz. Light Rum
1 oz. Gold Rum
1/2 oz. Rose's Lime Juice
2 oz. sweet 'n' sour
Shake and strain
Lime wedge and orange slice garnish

DAIQUIRI, MULATTA
House specialty glass, chilled
Pour ingredients into iced mixing glass
1 oz. Appleton Estate V/X Jamaica Rum
1 oz. Mount Gay Eclipse Rum
3/4 oz. Dark Crème de Cacao
3/4 oz. Maraschino Liqueur
1/2 oz. Rose's Lime Juice
2 oz. sweet 'n' sour
Shake and strain
Lime wedge garnish

DAIQUIRI, PAPA HEMINGWAY
Cocktail glass, chilled
Pour ingredients into iced mixing glass
1 1/2 oz. Light Rum
1/2 oz. Maraschino Liqueur
1 oz. fresh lime juice
1 1/2 oz. grapefruit juice
Shake and strain
Lime wedge garnish

DAIQUIRI, PASSION
Cocktail glass, chilled
Pour ingredients into iced mixing glass
1 1/2 oz. Light Rum
1/2 oz. Rose's Lime Juice
1 1/2 oz. passion fruit juice
1 1/2 oz. sweet 'n' sour
Shake and strain
Orange twist garnish

DAIQUIRI, PRICKLY PEAR
House specialty glass, chilled
Pour ingredients into iced mixing glass
2 oz. Bacardi Limón Rum
1/2 oz. grenadine
1 oz. sweetened lime juice
1 oz. sweet 'n' sour
2 oz. prickly pear syrup (puree)
Shake and strain
Lime wedge garnish

DAIQUIRI, PYRAT
Cocktail glass, chilled
Pour ingredients into iced mixing glass
1 3/4 oz. Pyrat XO Reserve Rum
1 oz. orange juice
1 1/4 oz. sweetened lime juice
Shake and strain
Orange twist garnish

DAIQUIRI, RASPBERRY
Cocktail glass, chilled
Pour ingredients into iced mixing glass
1 1/2 oz. Dark Rum
3/4 oz. Raspberry Liqueur
1/2 oz. Rose's Lime Juice
2 oz. sweet 'n' sour
Shake and strain
Berry garnish

DAIQUIRI, RHUM
Cocktail glass, chilled
Pour ingredients into iced mixing glass
2 oz. Rhum Barbancourt 5-Star
3/4 oz. Chambord
3/4 oz. Crème de Banana
2 oz. sweetened lime juice
Shake and strain
Lime wedge and orange slice garnish

DAIQUIRI, SUMMER SKY
Cocktail glass, chilled
Pour ingredients into iced mixing glass
1 3/4 oz. Mount Gay Eclipse Rum
1 1/2 oz. orange juice
1 1/2 oz. sweetened lime juice
Shake and strain
Orange twist garnish

DAIQUIRI, SWEET TART
House specialty glass, ice
Pour ingredients into iced mixing glass
1 1/4 oz. Doorly's XO Barbados Rum
3/4 oz. Limoncello Liqueur
1/2 oz. Rose's Lime Juice
2 oz. sweet 'n' sour
Shake and strain
Strawberry garnish

DAIQUIRI, WHALE SMOOCH
House specialty glass, ice
Pour ingredients into iced mixing glass
1 1/4 oz. Whaler's Dark Rum
3/4 oz. Whaler's Original Vanille Rum
1/2 oz. Rose's Lime Juice
2 oz. sweet 'n' sour
Shake and strain
Lime wedge garnish

DALE'S SOUR APPLE
Cocktail glass, chilled
Pour ingredients into iced mixing glass
1 1/2 oz. Vox Vodka
3/4 oz. DeKuyper Pucker Sour Apple
3/4 oz. Cointreau
1/2 oz. fresh lemon juice
1 oz. sweet 'n' sour
Shake and strain
Green apple wedge garnish

DAMRAK 75
Champagne glass, chilled
Pour ingredients into iced mixing glass
1 3/4 oz. Damrak Amsterdam Gin
1/2 oz. Cointreau
2 oz. sweet 'n' sour
Shake and strain
Fill with Champagne
Lemon twist garnish

DAMRAK BLUE LADY
Cocktail glass, chilled
Pour ingredients into iced mixing glass
1 1/2 oz. Damrak Amsterdam Gin
3/4 oz. Blue Curaçao
1 tsp. sugar
1 oz. fresh lemon juice
Shake and strain
Lime wheel and lemon twist garnish

DANGEROUS LIAISONS
Cocktail glass, chilled
Pour ingredients into iced mixing glass
1 oz. Brandy
1 oz. Cointreau
2 oz. sweet 'n' sour
Shake and strain
Lemon wheel garnish

DARK CONTINENT CAFÉ
Coffee mug, pre-heated
Build in glass
1 1/2 oz. Amarula Cream Liqueur
1 oz. Kahlúa
3/4 oz. Dark Crème de Cacao
Fill with hot coffee
Dollop whipped cream
Shaved chocolate garnish

DARK 'N' STORMY
House specialty glass, ice
Build in glass
1 3/4 oz. Gosling's Black Seal Rum
Fill with Ginger Beer
Lime wedge garnish

DARK WATERS
House specialty glass, ice
Pour ingredients into iced mixing glass
1 oz. RémyRed Red Berry Infusion
1 oz. Bacardi Limón Rum
1/2 oz. grenadine
2 oz. orange juice
2 oz. pineapple juice
Shake and strain
Float 3/4 oz. Appleton Estate
    V/X Jamaica Rum

SAUZA® HORNITOS® REPOSADO TEQUILA

Sauza struck pay dirt with the introduction of HORNITOS REPOSADO 100% AGAVE TEQUILA. It has for years been the best-selling reposado in the United States. More importantly, Sauza Hornitos is likely the best value in the entire category, earning it the distinction of being the "most tequila for the buck."

Hornitos is distilled entirely from mature blue agave at the Sauza La Perseverancia Distillery in Jalisco, Mexico. The harvested agaves are baked, shredded, fermented and double-distilled in both an alembic still and a stainless steel column still. Sauza then ages Hornitos for 4 to 6 months in large oak vats, which is just enough time to soften its character without being appreciably affected by the tannins in the wood. As a result, Hornitos has the exuberance and fresh agave character of a blanco tequila with a touch of the mellow refinement of an añejo.

A quick sniff, sip and swallow will reveal why Hornitos has become such a runaway success. The pale, golden color belies its complexity and full, rounded body. The tequila has an alluring bouquet concentrated with the aromas of pepper, caramel and citrus. Its semisweet palate features the flavors of caramel, pepper, ripe fruit and the herbaceous taste of agave.

Sauza Hornitos Reposado is a tequila that knows no creative limitations and is fit for any tequila-based assignment.

DC-3 SHOOTER
Rocks glass, chilled
Pour ingredients into iced mixing glass
1 oz. Campari Aperitivo
1 oz. Vodka
1 oz. grapefruit juice
1 oz. orange juice
Shake and strain
Orange twist garnish

DEAD EYE DICK'S RED EYE
Pilsner glass, chilled
Build in glass
3/4 fill Draft Beer
Near fill with Bloody Mary mix
Float whole egg on top (optional)

DEAD GRIZZLY
Rocks glass, ice
Build in glass
3/4 oz. Yukon Jack Liqueur
3/4 oz. Añejo Tequila
3/4 oz. Bourbon
2 dashes Tabasco Sauce

DEAD GRIZZLY SHOOTER
Presentation shot glass, chilled
Build in glass
1/2 oz. Yukon Jack Liqueur
1/2 oz. Añejo Tequila
1/2 oz. Bourbon
2 dashes Tabasco Sauce

DEATH BY CHOCOLATE
House specialty glass, chilled
Pour ingredients into blender
1 oz. Baileys Irish Cream
1 oz. Godiva Chocolate Liqueur
3/4 oz. Dark Crème de Cacao
1 oz. milk
2 scoops chocolate ice cream
Blend ingredients (with ice optional)
Whipped cream garnish
Float 3/4 oz. Kahlúa

DEATH OF A VIRGIN
Bucket glass, ice
Build in glass
1 1/4 oz. Midori
1 1/4 oz. Peach Schnapps
1/2 oz. Rose's Lime Juice
1/2 fill orange juice
1/2 fill Seven-Up
Orange slice and cherry garnish

DEATHWISH
Presentation shot glass, chilled
Build in glass
3/4 oz. Wild Turkey 101° Bourbon
3/4 oz. Bacardi Gold Rum
1/2 oz. Rumple Minze Schnapps
1/2 oz. grenadine

DEAUVILLE
Cocktail glass, chilled
Pour ingredients into iced mixing glass
1 1/4 oz. Calvados Apple Brandy
1/2 oz. Cointreau
1/2 oz. grenadine
1 1/2 oz. sweet 'n' sour
Shake and strain

DEBONAIR
Brandy snifter, ice
Build in glass
1 1/2 oz. Irish Liqueur
3/4 oz. Baileys Irish Cream

DEBUTANTE
Cocktail glass, chilled
Pour ingredients into iced mixing glass
1/2 oz. Tequila
1/2 oz. Peach Schnapps
1/2 oz. White Crème de Menthe
1 1/2 oz. sweet 'n' sour
Shake and strain
Lemon twist garnish

DEEP SEA DIVER
House specialty glass, ice
Pour ingredients into iced mixing glass
1 1/4 oz. Bacardi Gold Rum
3/4 oz. Mount Gay Eclipse Rum
3/4 oz. Grand Marnier
1/2 oz. Rose's Lime Juice
2 oz. sweet 'n' sour
Shake and strain
Float 3/4 oz. Cruzan Estate Diamond Rum
Lime, lemon and orange wedge garnish

DEEP THROAT
Presentation shot glass, chilled
Build in glass
3/4 oz. Vodka
3/4 oz. Tia Maria
1/2 oz. Baileys Irish Cream
Whipped cream garnish

DEFROSTER
House specialty glass, chilled
Pour ingredients into blender
2 oz. Canadian Whisky
1/2 oz. Limoncello Liqueur
1/2 oz. RémyRed Red Berry Infusion
1 1/2 oz. peach puree
2 oz. sweet 'n' sour
Blend with ice

DE GAULLE COCKTAIL
Champagne glass, chilled
Pour ingredients into iced mixing glass
3/4 oz. VS Cognac
3/4 oz. Chambord
1 1/2 oz. sweet 'n' sour
Shake and strain
Fill with Champagne
Lemon wheel garnish

DE GAULLE'S DESSERT
House specialty glass, chilled
Pour ingredients into blender
1 1/2 oz. B & B Liqueur
1/2 oz. simple syrup
1/2 oz. grenadine
2 scoops vanilla ice cream
Blend ingredients (with ice optional)
Sprinkle shaved chocolate

DELICIAS DE LA HABANA
House specialty glass, chilled
Pour ingredients into blender
1 1/4 oz. Matusalem Light Dry Rum
1 1/4 oz. Matusalem Golden Dry Rum
1 oz. Midori
3/4 oz. Blue Curaçao
1 oz. coconut cream syrup
1 oz. pineapple juice
2 oz. peach nectar
Blend with ice
Pineapple and peach wedge garnish

DEPTH CHARGE
Shot glass and beer mug, chilled
Build in shot glass
1 1/2 oz. Whiskey
Build in mug
3/4 fill Draft Beer
Drop shot glass of whiskey into beer

DESERT PASSION
House specialty glass, ice
Pour ingredients into iced mixing glass
1 oz. RémyRed Strawberry Kiwi Infusion
1 oz. RémyRed Red Berry Infusion
1 oz. Midori
1/2 oz. grenadine
1/2 oz. Rose's Lime Juice
1 oz. tangerine juice
3 oz. pineapple juice
Shake and strain
Pineapple wedge garnish

DEKUYPER® PUCKER® SOUR APPLE

If you're still capable of cranking out a smile, then you still have enough life in you to enjoy DEKUYPER PUCKER SOUR APPLE. Everything about this product screams of fun, from the lighthearted packaging to its spry, low-proof character. DeKuyper did their homework and created a winner.

Pucker Sour Apple is one of a line of similarly constructed sweet 'n' sour schnapps that are balanced with surgical precision to be just this side of tart. What differentiates this snazzy line of schnapps from the rest of the field is that they have just enough zing to make them something special; any more tartness and the effect would be dashed. The tartness works, especially when it is used as the principal flavoring agent in cocktails.

The liqueur has a light, delicate body and a cheerful apple green hue, two qualities ideal for drink making. Sipped neat, the liqueur will bring about a pucker, but when mixed, the tangy tartness acts as a counterbalance. The sour apple flavor seems true enough and persists for a remarkably long time.

Pucker Sour Apple burst into the spotlight when it debuted in the Appletini and has never looked back. You can now find it in uptown cocktails and downtown shooters. What this Pucker hasn't found yet is its creative limitations.

DESERT STORM
Bucket glass, ice
Pour ingredients into iced mixing glass
1 1/2 oz. Cruzan Pineapple Rum
1 oz. Disaronno Amaretto
1/2 oz. fresh lime juice
1 1/2 oz. pineapple juice
1 1/2 oz. orange juice
Shake and strain
Orange wedge garnish

DESERT SUNRISE
Bucket glass, ice
Build in glass
1 1/4 oz. Jose Cuervo Tradicional Tequila
3/4 oz. Blue Curaçao
1/2 fill orange juice
1/2 fill lemonade
Lime wedge garnish

DESIGNER JEANS
Presentation shot glass, chilled
Build in glass
1/3 fill Baileys Irish Cream
1/3 fill DeKuyper Raspberry Pucker
1/3 fill Appleton Estate V/X Jamaica Rum

DEWAR'S HIGHLAND COOLER
Bucket glass, ice
Build in glass
2 oz. Dewar's White Label Scotch Whisky
1/4 oz. simple syrup
Near fill with club soda
Long spiral lemon twist garnish

DEWAR'S TANGO
Cocktail glass, chilled
Pour ingredients into iced mixing glass
1 oz. Dewar's White Label Scotch Whisky
1 oz. sweet 'n' sour
1 oz. orange juice
Shake and strain
Orange slice and cherry garnish

DEW DROP DEAD
Mason jar, ice
Build in glass
2 1/2 oz. Georgia Moonshine Corn Whiskey
1/2 oz. Triple Sec
Fill with white grape juice

DHARAMA RUM
House specialty glass, chilled
Pour ingredients into blender
1 1/2 oz. Appleton Estate V/X Jamaica Rum
3/4 oz. Dark Crème de Cacao
3/4 oz. Crème de Banana
Peeled, ripe banana
2 scoops vanilla ice cream
Blend ingredients (with ice optional)
Pineapple wedge and banana slice garnish

DIABLO
Cocktail glass, chilled
Pour ingredients into iced mixing glass
1 1/2 oz. Brandy
1/2 oz. Dry Vermouth
1/2 oz. Triple Sec
2 dashes Angostura Bitters
Stir and strain
Lemon twist garnish

DIKI-DIKI
Cocktail glass, chilled
Pour ingredients into iced mixing glass
1 1/2 oz. Laird's Applejack Brandy
3/4 oz. Gin
2 oz. grapefruit juice
Shake and strain

DINGO
House specialty glass, ice
Pour ingredients into iced mixing glass
1 oz. Light Rum
3/4 oz. Disaronno Amaretto
1/2 oz. Southern Comfort
3/4 oz. grenadine
2 oz. sweet 'n' sour
2 oz. orange juice
Shake and strain
Float 3/4 oz. Jamaican Rum
Orange slice garnish

DINGY GINGER
Highball glass, ice
Build in glass
1 1/4 oz. Bourbon
Fill with ginger ale
Float 3/4 oz. RémyRed Red Berry Infusion
Lemon wedge garnish

DIPLOMATIC IMMUNITY
Cocktail glass, chilled
Pour ingredients into iced mixing glass
1 3/4 oz. Knappogue Castle Irish Whiskey
3/4 oz. Cruzan Banana Rum
3/4 oz. Gran Gala Orange Liqueur
1 1/2 oz. sweet 'n' sour
Shake and strain
Speared banana slice and cherry garnish

DIRE STRAITS
aka **Dirty Mother F'er**
Rocks glass, ice
Build in glass
1 1/2 oz. Brandy
1/2 oz. Kahlúa
1/2 oz. Galliano Liqueur
3/4 oz. half & half cream

DIRTY BANANA
Cocktail glass, chilled
Pour ingredients into iced mixing glass
3/4 oz. Dark Crème de Cacao
3/4 oz. Crème de Banana
2 oz. half & half cream
Shake and strain

DIRTY DOG
Bucket glass, ice
Rim glass with salt
Build in glass
1 1/4 oz. Vodka
1/4 oz. olive juice (brine)
Fill with grapefruit juice

DIRTY GIN 'N' JUICE
Bucket glass, ice
Build in glass
1 1/4 oz. Gin
1/4 oz. olive juice (brine)
Fill with grapefruit juice

DIRTY HARRY
Presentation shot glass, chilled
Build in glass
1 oz. Tia Maria
1 oz. Grand Marnier

DIRTY LEMONADE
Bucket glass, ice
Build in glass
1 1/4 oz. Gin
1/2 oz. Triple Sec
2 1/2 oz. sweet 'n' sour
2 dashes olive juice (brine)
Splash cranberry juice
Splash club soda

DIRTY MOTHER
aka **Dirty White Mother**
Rocks glass, ice
Build in glass
1 1/2 oz. Brandy
3/4 oz. Kahlúa
3/4 oz. half & half cream

DIZZY LIZZY
Bucket glass, ice
Pour ingredients into iced mixing glass
1 1/2 oz. Bourbon
1 1/2 oz. Sherry
1 oz. sweet 'n' sour
Shake and strain
Fill with club soda

Nº TEN
BY TANQUERAY®

Nº TEN BY TANQUERAY is unlike any gin that has come before it. Instead of deriving its flavor from botanicals such as dried roots, berries, rinds, barks and seeds, this innovative spirit is made using only fresh ingredients, such as ripe grapefruits, oranges, and limes. In addition, the recipe calls for handpicked juniper berries from Tuscany and herbs such as coriander and chamomile.

The fresh fruit and botanicals are distilled in a swan-necked, small batch still long known as "Nº Ten." This singular still produces what is lovingly referred to as "the heart of the gin," which is then added to a larger batch of premium botanicals and redistilled for a total of four distillations.

Nº Ten by Tanqueray is a gin enthusiast's dream come true. The light bodied gin has a generous and layered bouquet comprised of citrus, spice and evergreen aromas. It has a dry, crisp palate, one that completely fills the mouth with a luscious medley of fresh fruit, juniper and a slight hint of chamomile. The gin finishes cool, flavorful and relaxed.

Nº Ten by Tanqueray is so smooth and refreshing that you won't even notice that it's 94.6 proof. While seemingly bred for a chilled cocktail glass, in the right hands the gin has no creative limitations.

DOCTOR'S ADVICE
Cocktail glass, chilled
Pour ingredients into iced mixing glass
1 oz. Peppermint Schnapps
1 oz. Kahlúa
1 oz. White Crème de Cacao
Shake and strain

DOCTOR'S ELIXIR
Rocks glass, ice
Build in glass
1 oz. Chambord
1 oz. Peppermint Schnapps

DOCTOR'S ORDERS
Presentation shot glass, chilled
Build in glass
1/2 fill Vanilla Rum
1/2 fill Canadian Club Whisky

DODO BIRD
Highball glass, ice
Build in glass
3/4 oz. Razzmatazz Raspberry Liqueur
3/4 oz. Cruzan Banana Rum
Fill with orange juice

DOG SLED
Rocks glass, chilled
Pour ingredients into iced mixing glass
1 1/2 oz. Canadian Club Whisky
1/2 oz. fresh lemon juice
1/2 oz. grenadine
2 oz. orange juice
Shake and strain

DOLLAR BILL
Cocktail glass, chilled
Pour ingredients into iced mixing glass
1 3/4 oz. Irish Whiskey
1/2 oz. Sweet Vermouth
1/2 oz. Dubonnet Rouge
Stir and strain
Lemon twist garnish

DONE & BRADSTREET
Cocktail glass, chilled
Pour ingredients into iced mixing glass
1 1/4 oz. Absolut Vodka
3/4 oz. Absolut Citron Vodka
3/4 oz. Midori
1/2 oz. Blue Curaçao
1/4 oz. Rose's Lime Juice
Stir and strain
Lime wheel garnish

DOUBLE AGENT
Bucket glass, ice
Pour ingredients into iced mixing glass
1 1/2 oz. Vodka
1/2 oz. Rose's Lime Juice
1/2 oz. grenadine
1 oz. sweet 'n' sour
Shake and strain
Fill with Seven-Up

DOUBT RAISER
Champagne glass, chilled
Build in glass
3/4 oz. Chambord
3/4 oz. Grand Marnier
1/2 oz. Vodka
1 dash grenadine
Fill with Champagne
Lemon twist garnish

DOWNEASTER
Highball glass, ice
Build in glass
1 1/4 oz. Vodka
1/2 fill cranberry juice
1/2 fill pineapple juice

DOWN UNDER
House specialty glass, ice
Pour ingredients into iced mixing glass
1 1/2 oz. Disaronno Amaretto
1 1/2 oz. orange juice
1 1/2 oz. sweet 'n' sour
Shake and strain
Fill with Champagne

DOWN UNDER SNOWBALL
House specialty glass, chilled
Pour ingredients into blender
1 1/2 oz. Light Rum
3/4 oz. Peach Schnapps
1 oz. grenadine
4 oz. orange juice
Blend with ice
Orange slice garnish

DR. BERRY VANILLA
Bucket glass, ice
Build in glass
1 3/4 oz. Vanilla Rum
3/4 oz. Raspberry Liqueur
Near fill with club soda
Splash half & half cream

DR. PEPPER (1)
aka **Easy Rider**
Highball glass, ice
Build in glass
1 1/4 oz. Disaronno Amaretto
Fill with club soda

DR. PEPPER (2)
Shot glass and beer mug, chilled
Build in shot glass
1 1/4 oz. Disaronno Amaretto
Build in mug
3/4 fill Draft Beer
Drop shot glass of Amaretto into beer

DR. PEPPER FROM HELL
Shot glass and beer mug, chilled
Build in shot glass
1/2 fill Disaronno Amaretto
1/2 fill 151° Rum
Build in mug
3/4 fill Draft Beer
Drop shot glass into beer mug

DR. SEUSS GO-GO JUICE
House specialty glass, ice
Pour ingredients into iced mixing glass
1 1/2 oz. Jose Cuervo Especial Tequila
1/2 oz. Raspberry Liqueur
1/2 oz. Rose's Lime Juice
1 1/2 oz. white cranberry juice
1 1/2 oz. sweet 'n' sour
Shake and strain
Lime wedge garnish

DR. VANILLA DREAMSICLE
House specialty glass, chilled
Rim glass with powdered cocoa (optional)
Pour ingredients into blender
2 oz. Vanilla Rum
1 oz. orange juice
2 scoops vanilla ice cream
Blend ingredients (with ice optional)
Orange slice garnish

DRAGOON
Sherry glass, chilled
Build in glass
1/3 fill Black Sambuca
1/3 fill Kahlúa
1/3 fill Baileys Irish Cream

DREAM CATCHER
Champagne glass, chilled
Build in glass
3/4 oz. Orange Liqueur
3/4 oz. Chambord
1/2 oz. Raspberry Vodka
1/4 oz. grenadine
Fill with Champagne
Lemon twist garnish

MAGADANSKAYA® VODKA

In July 1945, with World War II drawing to an end, Harry Truman, Winston Churchill and Josef Stalin met in Potsdam, Germany. The historic conference set into motion events that would change world politics for the next 45 years. Stalin hosted a state dinner for his American and British counterparts, at which he toasted the assembled dignitaries with a rare spirit called MAGADANSKAYA VODKA.

This award winning, super-premium Russian vodka has been made for over 100 years in the once closed city of Magadan in Siberia. It is a quadruple-distilled vodka skillfully produced from grain, potatoes and the pure mineral water from the Tal'skaya Springs. To attain essential purity, it is filtered ten times through sand and Taiga Birch charcoal.

Magadanskaya—the first vodka that Truman and Churchill had ever tasted—is now available in the United States. The vodka is crystal clear with a velvet-textured, medium-weight body and a subtle, floral bouquet. Even at room temperature the vodka barely generates any heat on the palate while completely filling the mouth with delicately crisp flavors. The vodka finishes long and semisweet.

Magadanskaya is a classy, museum-quality vodka, the certain choice to make the next time you're toasting heads of state.

DREAM MAKER
House specialty glass, ice
Pour ingredients into iced mixing glass
2 1/4 oz. RémyRed Red Berry Infusion
1 oz. RémyRed Kiwi Strawberry Infusion
3/4 oz. Chambord
1 1/4 oz. pineapple juice
1 1/2 oz. coconut cream syrup
2 oz. orange juice
Shake and strain
Pineapple wedge garnish

DREAMSICLE (1)
Highball glass, ice
Build in glass
1 1/4 oz. Disaronno Amaretto
3/4 oz. half & half cream
Near fill with orange juice
Float 3/4 oz. Galliano Liqueur (optional)

DREAMSICLE (2)
House specialty glass, chilled
Pour ingredients into blender
1 1/4 oz. Disaronno Amaretto
3/4 oz. Triple Sec
2 oz. orange juice
2 scoops vanilla ice cream
Blend ingredients (with ice optional)
Vanilla wafer garnish

DREAMSICLE (3)
Bucket glass, ice
Build in glass
1 1/4 oz. Licor 43 (Cuarenta y Tres)
1/2 fill half & half cream
1/2 fill orange juice
Orange slice garnish

DREAMSICLE (4)
Bucket glass, ice
Build in glass
1 3/4 oz. Licor 43 (Cuarenta y Tres)
3/4 oz. Limoncello Liqueur
Fill with orange juice
Orange slice garnish

DRUNKEN MONKEY
Large house specialty glass, ice
Pour ingredients into iced mixing glass
3/4 oz. Bacardi Light Rum
3/4 oz. Mount Gay Eclipse Rum
3/4 oz. Malibu Caribbean Rum
3/4 oz. Midori
3/4 oz. Crème de Banana
1 1/2 oz. orange juice
1 1/2 oz. pineapple juice
Shake and strain
Float 3/4 oz. Appleton Estate
    V/X Jamaica Rum
Lime, lemon and orange wedge garnish

DRY ARROYO
Champagne glass, chilled
Pour ingredients into iced mixing glass
3/4 oz. Tia Maria
3/4 oz. Chambord
3/4 oz. orange juice
3/4 oz. sweet 'n' sour
Shake and strain
Fill with Champagne
Orange twist garnish

DRY CREEK
Rocks glass, ice
Build in glass
2 oz. Canadian Whisky
3/4 oz. Saké
Lemon twist garnish

DUBONNET COCKTAIL
Cocktail glass, chilled
Pour ingredients into iced mixing glass
1 1/2 oz. Gin
1 1/2 oz. Dubonnet Rouge
Stir and strain
Lemon twist garnish

DUBONNET FUZZY
Bucket glass, ice
Build in glass
2 oz. Dubonnet Rouge
3/4 oz. Disaronno Amaretto
1 1/4 oz. pineapple juice
Pineapple wedge garnish

DUCK FART
Presentation shot glass, chilled
Layer ingredients
1/3 fill Kahlúa
1/3 fill Baileys Irish Cream
1/3 fill Crown Royal

DUDLEY DOES RIGHT
House specialty glass, ice
Pour ingredients into iced mixing glass
1 3/4 oz. Canadian Whisky
1/2 oz. RémyRed Red Berry Infusion
1 1/2 oz. sweet 'n' sour
Shake and strain
Fill with Squirt
Lemon wheel garnish

DUKE OF EARL
Coffee mug, heated
Build in glass
1 1/4 oz. Kahlúa
3/4 oz. Dark Rum
1/2 oz. Disaronno Amaretto
1/2 fill hot coffee
1/2 fill frothed milk
Sprinkle shaved chocolate

DU MONDE
Champagne glass, chilled
Build in glass
1 3/4 oz. Limoncello Liqueur
Fill with Champagne
Lemon twist garnish

DUNHAM GOOD
Presentation shot glass, chilled
Build in glass
1 1/4 oz. Goldschläger
1/2 oz. Disaronno Amaretto

DUSTY ROSE
Presentation shot glass, chilled
Build in glass
1 oz. Chambord
1 oz. Baileys Irish Cream

DUTCH COFFEE
Coffee mug, heated
Build in glass
1 oz. Vandermint Liqueur
Near fill with hot coffee
Whipped cream garnish

DUTCH VELVET
Cocktail glass, chilled
Pour ingredients into iced mixing glass
1 oz. Vandermint Liqueur
3/4 oz. Crème de Banana
2 oz. half & half cream
Shake and strain
Sprinkle shaved chocolate

DYING NAZI FROM HELL
Presentation shot glass, chilled
Build in glass
1/3 fill Jägermeister
1/3 fill Baileys Irish Cream
1/3 fill Vodka

EARL OF GREY
Tea cup or coffee mug, heated
Build in glass
1 1/4 oz. Scotch Whisky
Fill with Earl Grey tea
Lemon wedge garnish

EAST INDIA
Cocktail glass, chilled
Pour ingredients into iced mixing glass
1 1/2 oz. Brandy
3/4 oz. Cointreau
2-3 dashes Angostura Bitters
2 oz. pineapple juice
Shake and strain
Lemon twist garnish

EVAN WILLIAMS®
SINGLE BARREL 1994
VINTAGE BOURBON

There are several intriguing things about EVAN WILLIAMS SINGLE BARREL 1994 VINTAGE BOURBON that qualify it as a world-class whiskey. First, the bourbon is drawn from a single cask, and when it's gone, that's it. The whiskey in the neighboring cask may be similar, but it won't be an exact match.

Second, the whiskey is vintage dated, a slice of life that can never be duplicated. It offers a precise snapshot of the conditions surrounding everything that went into its making. Finally, the bottle carries the Evan Williams name, and to bourbon drinkers, that means a lot.

The 1994 vintage of Evan Williams Single Barrel is a spectacular bourbon. Made in Bardstown, Kentucky, the whiskey was distilled and barreled in the autumn of 1994. After resting for nine years in charred oak casks, the whiskey is drawn straight from the barrel and diluted to 86.6 proof.

This critically acclaimed bourbon is a veritable extravaganza for the senses. The current vintage is endowed with a generous bouquet and a lavish palate with notes of caramel, vanilla and fruit. The finish is long and eminently flavorful.

This remarkable bourbon is a "must-have" for any top-shelf. Take a sip and you'll see why whiskey enthusiasts have snapped up the previous seven vintages.

EAST RIVER
Champagne glass, chilled
Pour ingredients into iced mixing glass
1 1/2 oz. Chambord
2 1/2 oz. orange juice
Shake and strain
Fill with Champagne
Orange twist garnish

EAU DE GIN
Cocktail glass, chilled
Pour ingredients into iced mixing glass
1/2 oz. Saké
1/2 oz. Rose's Lime Juice
1 1/2 oz. Citadelle Gin
Stir and strain

ECSTASY SHOOTER
Rocks glass, chilled
Pour ingredients into iced mixing glass
1 oz. Chambord
3/4 oz. Stolichnaya Strasberi Vodka
1 oz. pineapple juice
1/2 oz. cranberry juice
Shake and strain

ED SULLIVAN
House specialty glass, chilled
Pour ingredients into blender
1 1/4 oz. Light Rum
3/4 oz. Disaronno Amaretto
1/2 cup strawberries
3/4 oz. half & half cream
2 oz. sweet 'n' sour
Blend with ice
Fill with Champagne
Strawberry garnish

EIFFEL VIEW
Champagne glass, chilled
Pour ingredients into iced mixing glass
1 oz. Grey Goose Le Citron Vodka
1 oz. Grey Goose L'Orange Vodka
1/4 oz. grenadine
1 1/2 oz. sweet 'n' sour
Shake and strain
Fill with Champagne
Orange slice garnish

EL CAJON SUNRISE
Bucket glass, ice
Build in glass
1 oz. Patrón Reposado Tequila
Near fill with orange juice
Float 3/4 oz. Crème de Cassis

EL CONQUISTADOR
House specialty glass, chilled
Pour ingredients into blender
1 oz. Sauza Conmemorativo Añejo Tequila
1 oz. Sauza Hornitos Tequila
1/2 oz. Raspberry Liqueur
3/4 oz. Triple Sec
3/4 oz. Rose's Lime Juice
1/2 oz. grenadine
2 oz. sweet 'n' sour
2 oz. pineapple juice
Blend with ice
Lime wedge garnish

EL DIABLO
Bucket glass, ice
Build in glass
1 1/2 oz. Sauza Gold Tequila
3/4 oz. Crème de Cassis
1/2 oz. fresh lime juice
Fill with ginger ale
Lime wedge garnish

EL PRESIDENTÉ COCKTAIL (1)
Cocktail glass, chilled
Pour ingredients into iced mixing glass
1 1/2 oz. Light Rum
1/2 oz. Dry Vermouth
1/2 oz. Sweet Vermouth
1/2 oz. Cointreau
1/4 oz. grenadine
1/4 oz. fresh lemon juice
Stir and strain
Lime wedge garnish

EL PRESIDENTÉ COCKTAIL (2)
Cocktail glass, chilled
Pour ingredients into iced mixing glass
1 1/2 oz. Kuya Fusion Rum
1/2 oz. fresh lime juice
1 oz. orange juice
1 oz. pineapple juice
Shake and strain
Lime wedge garnish

EL PRESIDENTÉ COCKTAIL (3)
Cocktail glass, chilled
Pour ingredients into iced mixing glass
1/2 oz. Dry Vermouth
2 dashes Angostura Bitters
3/4 oz. Mount Gay Eclipse Rum
2 1/4 oz. Light Rum
Stir and strain
Lime wedge garnish

EL TORO
Bucket glass, ice
Build in glass
1 1/4 oz. Espolon Añejo Tequila
3/4 oz. Agavero Liqueur
Near fill with lemonade
Splash Seven-Up
Lime wheel garnish

ELECTRICAL STORM
Presentation shot glass, chilled
Layer ingredients
1/4 fill Baileys Irish Cream
1/4 fill Rumple Minze Schnapps
1/4 fill Goldschläger
1/4 fill Jägermeister

ELECTRIC JAM
House specialty glass, ice
Pour ingredients into iced mixing glass
1 1/4 oz. Polar Ice Vodka
3/4 oz. Hpnotiq Liqueur
2 oz. sweet 'n' sour
Shake and strain
Fill with club soda
Lemon wedge garnish

ELECTRIC LEMONADE
aka **Adios Mother**
House specialty glass, ice
Pour ingredients into iced mixing glass
3/4 oz. Absolut Vodka
3/4 oz. Bombay Gin
3/4 oz. Bacardi Limón Rum
3/4 oz. Grand Marnier
2 oz. sweet 'n' sour
Shake and strain
Fill with Seven-Up
Float 3/4 oz. Blue Curaçao

ELECTRIC WATERMELON (1)
House specialty glass, ice
Pour ingredients into iced mixing glass
1/2 oz. Midori
1/2 oz. Vodka
1/2 oz. Light Rum
1/2 oz. DeKuyper Watermelon Pucker
1/2 oz. grenadine
2 oz. orange juice
Shake and strain
Fill with Seven-Up

ELECTRIC WATERMELON (2)
Bucket glass, ice
Build in glass
3/4 oz. Southern Comfort
3/4 oz. Midori
Near fill with orange juice
Float 3/4 oz. DeKuyper Raspberry Pucker

SOUTHERN COMFORT®

SOUTHERN COMFORT is the first liqueur crafted in the United States and remains an American classic. It originated in New Orleans, where in 1874 a barman named M. W. Herron created a concoction named Cuffs and Buttons, an upscale reference to white tie and tails. He later moved to St. Louis where he renamed his luxurious potion Southern Comfort.

The liqueur is now made in Louisville, Kentucky, from the same closely guarded, proprietary recipe. The makers of Southern Comfort have let it be known that it is crafted from a base of pure grain neutral spirits and is flavored with peach liqueur, fresh peach and natural citrus extracts. After the infusion process is complete, the liqueur is filtered and bottled at 80 proof.

It is interesting to note that to this day many people think of Southern Comfort as a bourbon. This widely held misconception is easily understood. Southern Comfort has a marvelous, whiskey quality to its character. The liqueur has a flawlessly textured, medium-weight body and a delectable bouquet with floral and citrus notes. Its sensationally delicious palate features the long lasting flavors of fresh peaches, oranges and vanilla.

Southern Comfort is an extremely versatile liqueur and an absolute "must have" product.

ELECTRODE OVERLOAD
Coffee mug, heated
Build in glass
3/4 oz. Cruzan Estate Diamond Rum
1/2 oz. Godiva Chocolate Liqueur
1/2 oz. Peppermint Schnapps
Near fill with hot coffee
Whipped cream garnish
Drizzle 1/2 oz. Godiva Chocolate Liqueur

ELIXIR OF LOVE
House specialty glass, ice
Pour ingredients into iced mixing glass
2 oz. Disaronno Amaretto
2 oz. White Crème de Cacao
1 oz. Light Rum
2 oz. half & half cream
Shake and strain

EMBOLISM
Presentation shot glass, chilled
Build in glass
1/2 fill Baileys Irish Cream
1/2 fill DeKuyper Raspberry Pucker

EMERALD ICE
House specialty glass, chilled
Pour ingredients into blender
3/4 oz. Cinnamon Schnapps
3/4 oz. Green Crème de Menthe
1 1/2 oz. half & half cream
2 scoops vanilla ice cream
Blend ingredients (with ice optional)

EMERALD ISLE
Cappuccino cup, heated
Build in glass
3/4 oz. Irish Liqueur
3/4 oz. Baileys Irish Cream
3/4 oz. Irish Whiskey
1/4 oz. Kahlúa Especial
Near fill with hot espresso coffee
Top with frothed milk
Sprinkle shaved chocolate

EMPIRE STATE SLAMMER
Rocks glass, chilled
Pour ingredients into iced mixing glass
1 1/4 oz. Canadian Club Whisky
1/2 oz. Crème de Banana
1/2 oz. Sloe Gin
3 oz. orange juice
Shake and strain

ENCINADA HILL CLIMBER
Bucket glass, ice
Build in glass
1 1/4 oz. Sol Dios Añejo Tequila
1/2 oz. fresh lime juice
Fill with grapefruit juice

ENERGIZER BUNNY
Bucket glass, ice
Build in glass
1 1/2 oz. Vodka
1/2 fill orange juice
1/2 fill Red Bull Energy Drink

ENGLISH MULE
Beer or ale glass, ice
Build in glass
1 1/2 oz. Gin
3 oz. green ginger beer
2 1/2 oz. orange juice
Fill with club soda
Preserved ginger garnish (optional)

E PLURIBUS UNUM
House specialty glass, chilled
Pour ingredients into blender
3/4 oz. Frangelico
3/4 oz. Chambord
3/4 oz. Kahlúa
2 scoops chocolate ice cream
Blend ingredients (with ice optional)
Sprinkle shaved white chocolate

ERIE ISLE
Rocks glass, ice
Build in glass
1 1/2 oz. Irish Whiskey
1/2 oz. Irish Liqueur
1/2 oz. Baileys Irish Cream

ESTES FIZZ
Champagne glass, chilled
Build in glass
2-3 strawberries
1 1/2 oz. orange juice
Fill with Champagne
Strawberry garnish

E.T.
Presentation shot glass, chilled
Build in glass
1/3 fill Midori
1/3 fill Baileys Irish Cream
1/3 fill Stolichnaya Vodka

EVE'S APPLE
House specialty glass, chilled
Pour ingredients into blender
1 oz. DeKuyper Pucker Sour Apple
1/2 oz. Cinnamon Schnapps
1/2 oz. Blue Curaçao
1/2 oz. Rose's Lime Juice
1 1/2 oz. apple juice
2 scoops vanilla ice cream
Blend ingredients (with ice optional)
Apple wedge garnish

EVE'S PEACH
Cocktail glass, chilled
Pour ingredients into iced mixing glass
1 1/2 oz. Patrón Añejo Tequila
1/2 oz. DeKuyper Peach Pucker
1 oz. sweet 'n' sour
1 oz. orange juice
Shake and strain
Peach wedge garnish

EXPRESS MAIL DROP
House specialty glass, chilled
Pour ingredients into iced mixing glass
1 1/4 oz. Disaronno Amaretto
1/2 oz. Chambord
2 1/2 oz. orange juice
Shake and strain
Fill with Champagne

EYE TO EYE
Rocks glass, chilled
Pour ingredients into iced mixing glass
1 oz. Baileys Irish Cream
1 oz. Jameson Irish Whiskey
Shake and strain

F-16
aka **B-53**
Presentation shot glass, chilled
Layer ingredients
1/3 fill Kahlúa
1/3 fill Frangelico
1/3 fill Baileys Irish Cream

FACE ERASER
Bucket glass, crushed ice
Build in glass
1 oz. Vodka
1 oz. Kahlúa
Fill with Seven-Up

FAHRENHEIT 5000
Presentation shot glass, chilled
Build in glass
Cover bottom of glass with Tabasco Sauce
1 oz. Cinnamon Schnapps
1 oz. Absolut Peppar Vodka

FARMER'S DAUGHTER
Cocktail glass, chilled
Pour ingredients into iced mixing glass
2 oz. Jack Daniel's Tennessee Whiskey
1 oz. DeKuyper Pucker Sour Apple
2 oz. ginger beer
Stir and strain
Orange slice and cherry garnish

BELVEDERE® VODKA

Since its American debut in 1996, super-premium BELVEDERE VODKA from Poland has caught on in a seriously big way. It can be found on the back bar of any self-respecting Martini bar, and with good reason. Belvedere is a full-bodied, character-laden spirit that gives substance and meaning to any vodka-inspired cocktail.

Belvedere Vodka is crafted at the Polmos Zyrardów Distillery from premium rye and underground spring water. It is first distilled in an alembic still, a costly and relatively laborious step, but one that imbues the vodka with a substantial body and a robust character. It is then triple-distilled in a continuous still, which lightens it significantly. The vodka is filtered three times through a complex of carbon screens rendering it free of any trace congeners or impurities.

Belvedere is deserving of its world-class reputation. The vodka has ideal clarity and a subtle, pleasant bouquet of pine and dried herbs. Its velvety smooth body has heft and substance and glides over the palate completely filling the mouth with notes of pepper and citrus zest. The lingering, slightly sweet finish is flawless.

This uptown vodka is a perfect candidate for serving straight-up, over ice, or in any contemporary cocktail that showcases vodka.

FAT CAT FIZZ
Bucket glass, ice
Build in glass
1 oz. Dubonnet Rouge
1 oz. Chambord
Fill with Seven-Up
Lemon wedge garnish

FATMANCELLO
Cocktail glass, chilled
Pour ingredients into iced mixing glass
1 oz. Limoncello Liqueur
3/4 oz. Frangelico
3/4 oz. Patrón XO Café Coffee Liqueur
Shake and strain
Sprinkle shaved chocolate

FEDERAL EXPRESS
House specialty glass, chilled
Pour ingredients into iced mixing glass
1 1/4 oz. Disaronno Amaretto
1/2 oz. Chambord
2 1/2 oz. sweet 'n' sour
Shake and strain
Fill with Champagne
Lemon twist garnish

FEDORA
Cocktail glass, chilled
Pour ingredients into iced mixing glass
3/4 oz. Christian Brothers Brandy
3/4 oz. Jim Beam White Label Bourbon
3/4 oz. Myers's Jamaican Rum
1/2 oz. Cointreau
1 oz. sweet 'n' sour
Shake and strain

FINLANDIA LIME LIGHT
Cocktail glass, chilled
Pour ingredients into iced mixing glass
1 3/4 oz. Finlandia Vodka
3/4 oz. Midori
2 oz. grapefruit juice
Shake and strain
Lime wheel garnish

FIRE AND ICE (1)
House specialty glass, chilled
Pour ingredients into blender
3/4 oz. Cinnamon Schnapps
3/4 oz. White Crème de Cacao
1 1/2 oz. half & half cream
2 scoops vanilla ice cream
Blend ingredients (with ice optional)

FIRE AND ICE (2)
Rocks glass, chilled
Build in glass
1 oz. Rumple Minze Schnapps
1 oz. Cinnamon Schnapps

FIREBALL
aka **Jaw Breaker**
Presentation shot glass, chilled
Build in glass
Fill with Cinnamon Schnapps
2-3 dashes Tabasco Sauce

FIRECRACKER
Bucket glass, ice
Build in glass
1 1/2 oz. Spiced Rum
1/2 oz. 151° Rum
1/2 oz. grenadine
Fill with orange juice

FIRE IN THE HOLE
Presentation shot glass, chilled
Build in glass
1 1/2 oz. Ouzo
3 dashes Tabasco Sauce

FIRE-IT-UP
Rocks glass, ice
Build in glass
1 1/2 oz. Cinnamon Schnapps
3/4 oz. Kahlúa

FIRST AID KIT
Bucket glass, ice
Build in glass
1 1/4 oz. Corazón Silver Tequila
1/2 fill grapefruit juice
1/2 fill cranberry juice

FITZGERALD COCKTAIL
Cocktail glass, chilled
Pour ingredients into iced mixing glass
1 1/2 oz. Gin
1/2 oz. simple syrup
1 1/2 oz. fresh lemon juice
3 dashes Angostura Bitters
Shake and strain
Lemon twist garnish

FIVE DOLLAR MARGARET
Rocks glass, chilled
Pour ingredients into iced mixing glass
1 oz. Chambord
1 oz. Kahlúa
1 oz. Disaronno Amaretto
1 oz. half & half cream
Shake and strain

FLAMING ARMADILLO
Rocks glass, chilled
Pour ingredients into iced mixing glass
3/4 oz. Kahlúa Especial
3/4 oz. Disaronno Amaretto
3/4 oz. Grand Marnier
3/4 oz. Cruzan Estate Diamond Rum
Stir and strain

FLAMING BLUE BLASTER
Rocks glass, ice
Pour ingredients into iced mixing glass
1 oz. Bourbon
3/4 oz. Peppermint Schnapps
3/4 oz. Blue Curaçao
1/4 oz. Spiced Rum
Shake and strain

FLAMING BLUE JEANS
aka **Flaming Blue Jesus**
Rocks glass, ice
Pour ingredients into iced mixing glass
1 oz. Southern Comfort
3/4 oz. Peppermint Schnapps
3/4 oz. Raspberry Liqueur
1/4 oz. 151° Rum
Shake and strain

FLAMINGO (1)
Bucket glass, ice
Build in glass
1 1/2 oz. Spiced Rum
3/4 oz. grenadine
1/2 fill orange juice
Near fill with lemonade
Float 3/4 oz. Dark Rum
Lemon wedge garnish

FLAMINGO (2)
House specialty glass, ice
Pour ingredients into iced mixing glass
1 1/2 oz. Dark Rum
1/2 oz. grenadine
2 oz. sweetened lime juice
2 oz. pineapple juice
Shake and strain
Float 3/4 oz. Naval Rum
Lime wedge garnish

FLOATING HEART
Champagne glass, chilled
Pour ingredients into iced mixing glass
2 oz. RémyRed Grape Berry Infusion
1 oz. RémyRed Red Berry Infusion
1 oz. pineapple juice
1 oz. sweet 'n' sour
Shake and strain
1 1/2 oz. Champagne
Orange twist garnish

GLENDRONACH® SINGLE HIGHLAND MALT SCOTCH

Some whisky aficionados are looking for a bracing slap in the face from their favorite malts. Others think life is tough enough and want the whisky to pamper them like an attentive date. For those people, their short list must include the uncommonly smooth and delectable GLENDRONACH SINGLE HIGHLAND MALT SCOTCH.

Established in 1826, the Glendronach distillery is located in the countryside of Aberdeenshire. It is the definitive example of a traditional distillery, one that dries its own malt, uses wooden fermenting tuns and heats its stills with coal. Glendronach is renowned for producing two distinctly different types of malts—those that are aged in oak barrels and those that are matured in Spanish sherry casks.

The version of Glendronach that most Americans have become enamored with is the glorious, 100% sherry cask single Highland malt. This elegant, voluptuous malt is aged 15 years in first fill, during which it develops a golden/amber color, round, full-body and a wafting, fruity bouquet. It washes the palate with dry, malty, sherry-laced flavors. The finish is long, luscious and slightly creamy. For such a complex single malt, Glendronach is an exceptionally easy whisky to drink.

Aged for 25 years in sherry casks, The GLENDRONACH VINTAGE 1968 has a supple, medium body and a thoroughly delicious, peat and sherry-infused palate that was well worth the wait.

FLORIDA
Bucket glass, ice
Pour ingredients into iced mixing glass
1 1/2 oz. Light Rum
1/2 oz. Rose's Lime Juice
1/2 oz. pineapple juice
2 oz. grapefruit juice
Shake and strain
Near fill with club soda
Float 3/4 oz. Dark Rum
Mint sprig garnish (optional)

FLORIDA T-BACK
Bucket glass, ice
Pour ingredients into iced mixing glass
1 oz. Appleton Estate V/X Jamaica Rum
1 oz. Mount Gay Eclipse Rum
1 oz. Malibu Caribbean Rum
1/2 oz. grenadine
1/2 oz. Rose's Lime Juice
1 1/2 oz. pineapple juice
1 1/2 oz. orange juice
Shake and strain
Pineapple wedge and cherry garnish

FOGCUTTER
House specialty glass, ice
Pour ingredients into iced mixing glass
3/4 oz. Brandy
1/2 oz. Light Rum
1/2 oz. Gin
1 1/2 oz. orange juice
1 1/2 oz. sweet 'n' sour
Shake and strain
Float 3/4 oz. Oloroso Sherry
Lemon wedge garnish

FOGCUTTER, ROYAL NAVY
House specialty glass, ice
Pour ingredients into iced mixing glass
1 1/2 oz. Plymouth Gin
1 oz. Pusser's British Navy Rum
1/2 oz. Brandy
1/2 oz. orgeat syrup
1 oz. orange juice
1 oz. sweet 'n' sour
Shake and strain
Float 3/4 oz. Dry Sherry
Lemon wedge garnish

FOGHORN
Highball glass, ice
Build in glass
1 1/4 oz. Gin
1/2 oz. Rose's Lime Juice
Fill with ginger ale

FOOL'S GOLD
Rocks glass, chilled
Pour ingredients into iced mixing glass
1 oz. VooDoo Spiced Rum
3/4 oz. Goldschläger
3/4 oz. Cinnamon Schnapps
3/4 oz. sweet 'n' sour
Shake and strain

FOREIGN LEGION
Cappuccino cup, heated
Build in glass
1/2 oz. Brandy
1/2 oz. B & B Liqueur
1/2 oz. Frangelico
1/2 oz. Disaronno Amaretto
Near fill with hot espresso coffee
Top with frothed milk
Sprinkle shaved chocolate

FOREVER AMBER
Brandy snifter, heated
Build in glass
1 1/2 oz. Tuaca
1/2 oz. Brandy

FORTRESS OF SINGAPORE
Cocktail glass, chilled
Pour ingredients into iced mixing glass
1 3/4 oz. Beefeater London Dry Gin
1 1/2 oz. Van Gogh Citron Vodka
1/2 oz. Courvoisier VSOP Cognac
1/2 oz. Canton Ginger Liqueur
Stir and strain
Lemon twist garnish

FOUR WISE MEN
Presentation shot glass, chilled
Build in glass
1/2 oz. Jack Daniel's Tennessee Whiskey
1/2 oz. Jim Beam White Label Bourbon
1/2 oz. Jose Cuervo Especial Tequila
1/2 oz. Don Bacardi Gold Rum

FRAMBOISE KISS
Brandy snifter, heated
Build in glass
1 1/2 oz. XO Cognac
1/2 oz. Chambord

FRANGELICO FREEZE
House specialty glass, chilled
Pour ingredients into blender
3/4 oz. Frangelico
1/2 oz. Godiva Chocolate Liqueur
1/2 oz. Kahlúa
2 scoops vanilla ice cream
Blend ingredients (with ice optional)
Vanilla wafer garnish

FRAPPÉ
Cocktail or champagne saucer, chilled
Build in glass
Fill to a mound with crushed ice
2 oz. requested liqueur
Short straw

FRAPPÉ, APRICOT BRANDY
Cocktail or champagne saucer, chilled
Build in glass
Fill to a mound with crushed ice
1 oz. Brandy
1/2 oz. Apricot Brandy
1/2 oz. Crème de Noyaux
Short straw

FRAPPÉ, BANANA RUM
Cocktail or champagne saucer, chilled
Build in glass
Fill to a mound with crushed ice
1 1/4 oz. Light Rum
3/4 oz. Crème de Banana
1/2 oz. orange juice
Short straw

FRAPPÉ, CHOCOLATE MINT
Cocktail or champagne saucer, chilled
Build in glass
Fill to a mound with crushed ice
1 1/2 oz. Peppermint Schnapps
Drizzle 1 1/2 oz. Hershey's chocolate syrup
Cherry garnish
Short straw

FRAPPÉ, COFFEE MARNIER
Cocktail or champagne saucer, chilled
Build in glass
Fill to a mound with crushed ice
1 oz. Kahlúa
1 oz. Grand Marnier
Splash orange juice
Short straw

FRAPPÉ, DERBY MINT
Cocktail or champagne saucer, chilled
Build in glass
Fill to a mound with crushed ice
1/2 oz. Peppermint Schnapps
2 oz. Bourbon
Short straw

FRAPPÉ, LAGNIAPPE
Rocks glass, chilled
Build in glass
1/2 peach
Fill to a mound with crushed ice
1 1/2 oz. Bourbon
Note: The 'lagniappe' or 'bonus', is the
    bourbon-soaked peach

CRUZAN® SINGLE BARREL ESTATE RUM

The new standard bearer in this age of small indulgences is the unfettered pleasure of sipping añejo rums. Search as hard as you might, you will not find a more luxurious spirit to sip than CRUZAN SINGLE BARREL ESTATE RUM. As a single barrel rum, it is a once in a lifetime occurrence that must be seized when the opportunity arises.

Crafted in St. Croix, this limited production, handcrafted rum is made from a blend of triple-distilled rums that are aged between 5 and 12 years in American oak bourbon barrels. After blending, the rum is placed in new, American white oak casks for secondary aging, the insides of which are heavily charred. This extended aging allows the elements of the blend to "marry" and fully integrate. No batch is bottled until a panel of tasters deems the rum ready for release.

The result of the "Double Casking" can be perceived in every aspect of the rum's character. It has a lustrous, tawny red color and a trim, compact body. Cruzan Single Barrel Estate Rum is impressively similar to an aged brandy with rum notes on the palate and finish.

This is a spirit that should be doted over, sipped straight-up or on the rocks. If you're in the mood for a cocktail, however, Cruzan Single Barrel Estate Rum is more than ready to play.

FRAPPÉ, LEMON
Cocktail or champagne saucer, chilled
Build in glass
Fill to a mound with crushed ice
1 oz. Tuaca
3/4 oz. Limoncello Liqueur
1 1/2 oz. sweet 'n' sour
Short straw

FRAPPÉ, MOCHA
Cocktail or champagne saucer, chilled
Build in glass
Fill to a mound with crushed ice
1 oz. Kahlúa
1/2 oz. White Crème de Menthe
1/2 oz. White Crème de Cacao
1/2 oz. Cointreau
Short straw

FRAPPÉ, MULATTA
Cocktail or champagne saucer, chilled
Build in glass
Fill to a mound with crushed ice
1 1/4 oz. Gold Rum
3/4 oz. Dark Crème de Cacao
1/4 oz. Rose's Lime Juice
1/4 oz. fresh lime juice
Lime wedge garnish

FRAPPÉ, PARISIAN
Cocktail or champagne saucer, chilled
Build in glass
Fill to a mound with crushed ice
1 oz. Yellow Chartreuse
1 oz. VS Cognac
Short straw

FRAPPÉ, SAMBUCA MOCHA
Cocktail or champagne saucer, chilled
Build in glass
Fill to a mound with crushed ice
1 oz. Kahlúa
1 oz. Sambuca Romano
3 Roasted coffee beans
Short straw

FRAPPÉ, TRICONTINENTAL
Cocktail or champagne saucer, chilled
Build in glass
Fill to a mound with crushed ice
1 1/2 oz. Gold Rum
1/2 oz. grenadine
1/2 oz. Dark Crème de Cacao
Short straw

FREDDY FUDPUCKER
aka **Cactus Banger, Charlie Goodleg**
Bucket glass, ice
Build in glass
1 1/4 oz. Tequila
Near fill with orange juice
Float 3/4 oz. Galliano Liqueur

FREDDY KRUGER
Presentation shot glass, chilled
Layer ingredients
1/3 fill Sambuca
1/3 fill Jägermeister
1/3 fill Vodka

FRENCH 75 (1)
Champagne glass, chilled
Pour ingredients into iced mixing glass
1 oz. Gin
2 oz. sweet 'n' sour
Shake and strain
Fill with Champagne
Lemon twist garnish

FRENCH 75 (2)
aka **French 125**
Champagne glass, chilled
Pour ingredients into iced mixing glass
1 oz. VS Cognac
2 oz. sweet 'n' sour
Shake and strain
Fill with Champagne
Lemon twist garnish

FRENCH 95
Champagne glass, chilled
Pour ingredients into iced mixing glass
1 oz. Bourbon
2 oz. sweet 'n' sour
Shake and strain
Fill with Champagne
Lemon twist garnish

FRENCH BLUSH
Cocktail glass, chilled
Pour ingredients into iced mixing glass
2 oz. Grey Goose Le Citron Vodka
1/2 oz. Crème de Cassis
Stir and strain
Lemon twist garnish

FRENCH CONGO COOLER
Bucket glass, ice
Build in glass
1 1/2 oz. Citadelle Raspberry Vodka
3/4 oz. half & half cream
Near fill with orange juice
Float 3/4 oz. Crème de Banana

FRENCH CONNECTION
Brandy snifter, heated
Build in glass
1 1/2 oz. VS Cognac
1 1/2 oz. Grand Marnier

FRENCH CONSULATE
House specialty glass, chilled
Pour ingredients into iced mixing glass
3/4 oz. B & B Liqueur
3/4 oz. Brandy
1/2 oz. Cointreau
1/2 oz. orange juice
2 oz. sweet 'n' sour
Shake and strain
Fill with Champagne
Lemon twist garnish

FRENCH CRUSH
Bucket glass, ice
Build in glass
1 oz. Cointreau
3/4 oz. White Crème de Cacao
3/4 oz. half & half cream
Fill with orange juice
Orange slice garnish

FRENCH DREAM
Brandy snifter, ice
Build in glass
1 oz. Baileys Irish Cream
3/4 oz. Chambord
3/4 oz. Tia Maria

FRENCH HARVEST
Brandy snifter, heated
Build in glass
1 1/2 oz. Courvoisier Initiale Extra Cognac
1/2 oz. Grand Marnier
Lemon twist garnish

FRENCH KISS
Coffee mug, heated
Build in glass
3/4 oz. Kahlúa
3/4 oz. Disaronno Amaretto
Near fill with hot chocolate
Whipped cream garnish
Dust powdered cocoa

FRENCH MAID'S CAFÉ
Coffee mug, heated
Build in glass
1/2 oz. Kahlúa
1/2 oz. Grand Marnier
1/2 oz. Brandy
Near fill with hot coffee
Whipped cream garnish
Sprinkle shaved chocolate

FRENCH MANDARINE
Brandy snifter, heated
Build in glass
1 1/2 oz. Armagnac
3/4 oz. Grand Marnier

PEARL® VODKA

The Pearl Vodka Distillery is located close to the majestic Canadian Rockies. There, in the crisp thin air and surrounded by fields of wheat, the distillery has been able to accomplish something great, namely craft a spirit that captures the essence of its idyllic setting. The spirit is award winning PEARL VODKA and there's a little slice of pristine wilderness in every sip.

The vodka is distilled in small batches from Canadian winter wheat and soft spring water drawn from the leeward side of the Rockies. In total, Pearl is distilled five times and subjected to rigorous purification. The vodka contains no additives or flavor enhancers and is bottled at 80 proof.

Pearl Vodka is bracing and refreshing, created where brisk is a way of life. The vodka is perfectly clear and outfitted with a sleek, medium-weight body. Its rousing bouquet is redolent with soft, creamy aromas. The slightly sweet palate expands in the mouth quickly and then slowly fades away into a relaxed finish. Pearl Vodka is tailor-made for the nearest dry Martini.

In 2003, the distillery introduced PEARL LO COCO VODKA, a vibrantly flavorful spirit distilled with the addition of pure coconut oil essence. It is light-bodied and has an alluring bouquet. This new flavored Pearl Vodka is ideal for making refreshing, tropical cocktails.

FRENCH MOUNTIE
Cocktail glass, chilled
Pour ingredients into iced mixing glass
2 oz. Canadian Whisky
3/4 oz. VSOP Cognac
1 oz. fresh lemon juice
Shake and strain
Lemon wheel garnish

FRENCH SWEETHEART
Bucket glass, ice
Build in glass
1 1/2 oz. Cointreau
2 oz. orange juice
Fill with club soda
Orange slice garnish

FRENCH TICKLER
Presentation shot glass, chilled
Build in glass
1 1/4 oz. Goldschläger
3/4 oz. Grand Marnier

FRENCH TOAST ROYALE
Brandy snifter, heated
Build in glass
1 oz. Courvoisier VSOP Cognac
1 oz. Chambord

FRENCH TWIST
Brandy snifter, heated
Build in glass
1 oz. Courvoisier Napoleon Cognac
1 oz. Grand Marnier Centenaire

FRESH SQUEEZED BAT JUICE
Highball glass, ice
Build in glass
1 1/4 oz. Canadian Whisky
Fill with blood orange juice

FREUDIAN SLIP
Champagne glass, chilled
Pour ingredients into iced mixing glass
1 oz. Brandy
3/4 oz. Grand Marnier
1 1/2 oz. sweet 'n' sour
Shake and strain
Fill with Champagne
Orange twist garnish

FRIAR TUCK
Rocks glass, ice
Build in glass
1 1/2 oz. Canadian Club Whisky
3/4 oz. Frangelico

FROSTBITE
House specialty glass, chilled
Pour ingredients into blender
1 1/2 oz. Yukon Jack Liqueur
1/4 oz. Peppermint Schnapps
2 1/2 oz. sweet 'n' sour
Blend with ice

FROSTED COKE
Beer mug or house specialty glass, ice
Build in glass
1 1/2 oz. Vodka
1/2 oz. Kahlúa
1/2 oz. Dark Crème de Cacao
3/4 oz. half & half cream
Fill with cola

FROSTED IN THE SHADE
Cocktail glass, chilled
Pour ingredients into iced mixing glass
2 1/4 oz. Cîroc Snap Frost Vodka
3/4 oz. Grand Marnier
Stir and strain
Orange twist garnish

FROSTED PEACH BREEZE
House specialty glass, chilled
Pour ingredients into blender
1 oz. Peach Schnapps
3/4 oz. Vodka
2 oz. cranberry juice
2 oz. grapefruit juice
Blend with ice

FROSTED STRAWBERRY TEA
House specialty glass, chilled
Pour ingredients into blender
4 oz. English Breakfast tea
2 tbsp. sugar
1/2 cup frozen strawberries
2 oz. sweet 'n' sour
Blend with ice
Strawberry garnish

FROSTY NAVEL
House specialty glass, chilled
Pour ingredients into blender
1 oz. Peach Schnapps
1 1/2 oz. orange juice
1 1/2 oz. half & half cream
2 scoops vanilla ice cream
Blend ingredients (with ice optional)
Vanilla wafer garnish

FROZEN CAPPUCCINO
House specialty glass, chilled
Rim glass with cinnamon sugar (optional)
Pour ingredients into blender
3/4 oz. Baileys Irish Cream
3/4 oz. Kahlúa
3/4 oz. Frangelico
2 scoops vanilla ice cream
Blend ingredients (with ice optional)
Whipped cream garnish

FROZEN DEVOTION
House specialty glass, chilled
Pour ingredients into blender
1 1/4 oz. Cruzan Estate Diamond Rum
3/4 oz. Disaronno Amaretto
3 oz. strawberry puree
2 scoops vanilla ice cream
Blend ingredients (with ice optional)
Strawberry garnish

FROZEN MONK
House specialty glass, chilled
Pour ingredients into blender
3/4 oz. Frangelico
3/4 oz. Kahlúa
3/4 oz. Dark Crème de Cacao
2 scoops vanilla ice cream
Blend ingredients (with ice optional)

FROZEN ROSE
House specialty glass, chilled
Pour ingredients into blender
2 oz. Tequila Rose Cream Liqueur
1 oz. Tequila
1/2 oz. Triple Sec
1 oz. cranberry juice
1 oz. sweet 'n' sour
Blend with ice
Lime wedge and strawberry (rose) **garnish**

FRUIT BURST
House specialty glass, ice
Pour ingredients into iced mixing glass
1 3/4 oz. Limoncello Liqueur
3/4 oz. Vodka
3/4 oz. Raspberry Liqueur
1 oz. orange juice
1 oz. cranberry juice
1 oz. pineapple juice
Shake and strain
Pineapple wedge garnish

KELT® XO TOUR DU MONDE GRANDE CHAMPAGNE COGNAC

If you haven't had a vacation in years, you're not going to want to read any further. One of the highest rated brandies in the world—KELT XO TOUR DU MONDE GRANDE CHAMPAGNE COGNAC—takes a leisurely cruise around the world before being bottled.

The cognac takes this three month voyage shortly after blending. While en route, the brandy is stored in small, 72-liter Limousin oak barrels that are lashed to the ship's deck. The gentle rolling of the ship allows the brandies in its blend to become fully integrated, while the constantly changing climate and fresh ocean air positively influence the aging cognac. Upon its return to France, the brandy is aged an additional year in oak barrels.

Kelt XO Tour du Monde is an extraordinarily luxurious cognac with an average age of 42 years. The Grande Champagne brandy has a lush texture and medium-weight body. It has an expansive bouquet graced with rich fruity and floral aromas. The palate is a lavish affair featuring the delectable flavors of fruit, vanilla, spice and oak. The lingering, warm finish is a sublime pleasure. Kelt XO Tour du Monde is a singular cognac worthy of the critical acclaim it has received.

FRUIT STRIPE
House specialty glass, chilled
Object is to create a 2-layer drink
1—*Pour ingredients into blender*
 1 oz. Light Rum
 1/2 cup strawberries
 2 oz. sweet 'n' sour
Blend with ice
Pour first drink into glass 1/2 full
2—*Pour ingredients into blender*
 1 oz. Light Rum
 2 oz. coconut cream syrup
 3 oz. pineapple juice
Blend with ice
Fill glass with second drink

FRUITY TUTTI
Rocks glass, ice
Pour ingredients into iced mixing glass
1 oz. DeKuyper Peachtree Schnapps
1/2 oz. Chambord
1/2 oz. Midori
Splash cranberry juice
Shake and strain
Lime wedge garnish

FULL MONTE
Cocktail glass, chilled
Pour ingredients into mixing glass
3-4 mint springs
1/4 oz. simple syrup
Muddle contents
Add ice
1 1/4 oz. Woodford Reserve Bourbon
Stir and strain
Top with 1 oz. Champagne
Float 1/4 oz. Chambord

FULL MOON
Brandy snifter, heated
Build in glass
1 oz. Grand Marnier
1 oz. Disaronno Amaretto

FU MANCHU
Cocktail glass, chilled
Pour ingredients into iced mixing glass
1 1/2 oz. Gold Rum
1/2 oz. Triple Sec
1/2 oz. White Crème de Menthe
1/2 oz. Rose's Lime Juice
1 dash simple syrup
Stir and strain
Orange twist garnish

FUN IN THE SUN
Rocks glass, ice
Build in glass
1 3/4 oz. Irish Whiskey
3/4 oz. Kahlúa
1/2 oz. Chambord

FUNKY MONKEY
House specialty glass, ice
Pour ingredients into iced mixing glass
1 1/4 oz. Light Rum
1 oz. Coconut Rum
3/4 oz. Banana Rum
3/4 oz. apple-grape juice concentrate
2 oz. pineapple juice
Shake and strain
Pineapple wedge and cherry garnish

FUZZY DICK
Coffee mug, heated
Build in glass
3/4 oz. Grand Marnier
3/4 oz. Kahlúa
Near fill with hot coffee
Whipped cream garnish
Dust powdered cocoa

FUZZY MUSSY
Coffee mug, heated
Build in glass
1 oz. Frangelico
1/2 oz. Baileys Irish Cream
1/2 oz. Grand Marnier
Near fill with hot coffee
Whipped cream garnish
Dust powdered cocoa

FUZZY NAVEL
Highball glass, ice
Build in glass
1 1/4 oz. Peach Schnapps
Fill with orange juice

FUZZY WUZZIE
Cocktail glass, chilled
Pour ingredients into iced mixing glass
1 3/4 oz. Ultimat Vodka
1/2 oz. Peach Schnapps
1/2 oz. Rose's Lime Juice
1/2 oz. orange juice
Stir and strain
Peeled kiwi slice garnish

GALLIANO STINGER
Rocks glass, ice
Build in glass
1 1/2 oz. Galliano Liqueur
1/2 oz. White Crème de Menthe

GANGBUSTER (serves 2)
2 house specialty glasses, ice
Pour ingredients into iced mixing glass
1 1/2 oz. Light Rum
1 oz. Gold Rum
1 1/2 oz. guava nectar
1 1/2 oz. pineapple juice
1 1/2 oz. sweet 'n' sour
Shake and strain
Float 1/2 oz. Dark Rum
Float 1/2 oz. 151° Rum
Lime, lemon and orange wedge garnish

GANG GREEN
House specialty glass, ice
Pour ingredients into iced mixing glass
1 1/2 oz. Light Rum
1 oz. Midori
1/2 oz. Spiced Rum
3/4 oz. Blue Curaçao
2 oz. orange juice
2 oz. sweet 'n' sour
Shake and strain
Pineapple wedge and cherry garnish

GATOR JUICE
Bucket glass, ice
Build in glass
1 1/4 oz. Southern Comfort
1/4 oz. Rose's Lime Juice
Near fill with orange juice
Float 3/4 oz. Blue Curaçao

GAUGUIN
House specialty glass, chilled
Pour ingredients into blender
2 oz. Bacardi Limón Rum
1 oz. passion fruit syrup
1 1/2 oz. sweet 'n' sour
1 1/2 oz. sweetened lime juice
Blend with ice
Lime, lemon and orange wedge garnish

G-BOY
Rocks glass, chilled
Pour ingredients into iced mixing glass
3/4 oz. Grand Marnier
3/4 oz. Baileys Irish Cream
3/4 oz. Frangelico
Shake and strain

GENTLEMAN'S BOILERMAKER
Brandy snifter, heated
Build in glass
1 oz. Armagnac
1 oz. Tawny Port

GEORGIA PEACH (1)
Highball glass, ice
Build in glass
1 1/4 oz. Peach Schnapps
Fill with cranberry juice

FRANGELICO® LIQUEUR

When introduced in the early 1980s, FRANGELICO LIQUEUR immediately developed a loyal following. Nothing quite like it had ever appeared on American back bars. Its brilliant hazelnut flavor quickly became the featured attraction in scores of contemporary classics.

Legend has it that in the early 1600s an Italian friar named Fra. Angelico concocted a liqueur out of wild hazelnuts and brandy. This eventually became the inspiration for the Frangelico recipe. The liqueur is made in the Piedmont region of Italy and combines natural flavor extracts, including hazelnuts, cocoa, coffee and vanilla to deliver its complex and one of a kind character. The liqueur is then filtered for purity, sweetened and bottled at 48 proof.

The reasons for Frangelico's meteoric success are perfectly evident. The liqueur has an appealing amber hue and a supple, lightweight body. Its generous bouquet is perhaps the most seductive in the business, a wafting affair of vanilla, honey and nuts. The bakery fresh aromas expertly prepare the palate for the waves of chocolate, spicy herbs and toasted hazelnuts. The flavorful finish is warm and relaxed.

Frangelico is as versatile as it is delicious and its place on the roster of indispensable back bar products is firmly entrenched. If you haven't sipped on it neat, you're in for a genuine treat.

GEORGIA PEACH (2)
House specialty glass, ice
Pour ingredients into iced mixing glass
1 1/2 oz. Peach Schnapps
1/2 oz. grenadine
2 oz. sweet 'n' sour
Shake and strain
Peach wedge and cherry garnish

GEORGIA TURNOVER
Coffee mug, heated
Build in glass
1 1/2 oz. Peach Schnapps
1 1/2 oz. cranberry juice
Fill with hot apple cider

GEORGIA'S OWN
House specialty glass, chilled
Pour ingredients into blender
3 oz. Peach Nectar
1 1/2 oz. orange juice
3/4 oz. sweet 'n' sour
Blend with ice
Fill with club soda

GERMAN CHOCOLATE CAKE
Cocktail glass, chilled
Pour ingredients into iced mixing glass
1/2 oz. Baileys Irish Cream
1/2 oz. Kahlúa
1/2 oz. Frangelico
1 1/2 oz. half & half cream
Shake and strain
Whipped cream garnish

GERMAN ROOT BEER
Bucket glass, ice
Build in glass
1 3/4 oz. Jägermeister
Fill with root beer

GIBSON
Cocktail glass, chilled
Pour ingredients into iced mixing glass
8 drops Dry Vermouth
1 1/2 oz. Gin
Stir and strain
Cocktail onions garnish

GIBSON, DRY
Cocktail glass, chilled
Pour ingredients into iced mixing glass
4 drops Dry Vermouth
1 1/2 oz. Gin
Stir and strain
Cocktail onions garnish

GIBSON, EXTRA DRY
Cocktail glass, chilled
Pour ingredients into iced mixing glass
1 drop Dry Vermouth (optional)
1 1/2 oz. Gin
Stir and strain
Cocktail onions garnish

GIBSON, VODKA
Cocktail glass, chilled
Pour ingredients into iced mixing glass
8 drops Dry Vermouth
1 1/2 oz. Vodka
Stir and strain
Cocktail onions garnish
Note: Use less dry vermouth to make a
   Dry Vodka Gibson, use little or no
   dry vermouth to make an Extra Dry
   Vodka Gibson

GIMLET
Cocktail glass, chilled
Pour ingredients into iced mixing glass
1 1/2 oz. Gin
1/2 oz. Rose's Lime Juice
Stir and strain
Lime wedge garnish

GIMLET, CHER'S
Cocktail glass, chilled
Pour ingredients into iced mixing glass
1 3/4 oz. Bombay Gin
1/2 oz. Grand Marnier
1/2 oz. fresh lime juice
1/2 oz. Rose's Lime Juice
Shake and strain
Lime wedge garnish

GIMLET, COBBLER'S
Cocktail glass, chilled
Pour ingredients into iced mixing glass
1 3/4 oz. Broker's London Dry Gin
1/2 oz. Limoncello Liqueur
1/2 oz. Rose's Lime Juice
Shake and strain
Lime wheel and lemon twist garnish

GIMLET, IRISH
Cocktail glass, chilled
Pour ingredients into iced mixing glass
2 1/4 oz. Irish Whiskey
1/2 oz. Blue Curaçao
1/2 oz. Rose's Lime Juice
Stir and strain
Lime wedge garnish

GIMLET, KEY LIME
Cocktail glass, chilled
Pour ingredients into iced mixing glass
2 oz. Citrus Vodka
3/4 oz. key lime juice
3/4 oz. simple syrup
Stir and strain
Lime wedge garnish

GIMLET, MARTINIQUE (1)
Cocktail glass, chilled
Pour ingredients into iced mixing glass
1 3/4 oz. St. James Extra Old Rhum
3/4 oz. Cointreau
1/2 oz. fresh lime juice
1/2 oz. sweet 'n' sour
Shake and strain
Lime wedge garnish

GIMLET, MARTINIQUE (2)
Cocktail glass, chilled
Pour ingredients into iced mixing glass
1 oz. J. Bally Rhum Vieux 12 Year
1 oz. Dillon Dark Rhum
3/4 oz. Citrónge Orange Liqueur
1/2 oz. fresh lime juice
1/2 oz. sweet 'n' sour
Shake and strain
Lime wedge garnish

GIMLET, PYRAT
Cocktail glass, chilled
Pour ingredients into iced mixing glass
1 1/2 oz. Pyrat XO Reserve Rum
1/2 oz. Rose's Lime Juice
1/4 oz. fresh lime juice
1/4 oz. Citrónge Orange Liqueur
Stir and strain
Lime wedge garnish

GIMLET, RASPBERRY
Cocktail glass, chilled
Pour ingredients into iced mixing glass
1 1/2 oz. Vodka
3/4 oz. Chambord
1/2 oz. fresh lime juice
1/2 oz. Rose's Lime Juice
Stir and strain
Lime wedge garnish

GIMLET, SAPPHIRE
Cocktail glass, chilled
Pour ingredients into iced mixing glass
1 3/4 oz. Bombay Sapphire London Dry Gin
3/4 oz. Grand Marnier
1/2 oz. fresh lime juice
1/2 oz. sweet 'n' sour
Shake and strain
Lime wedge garnish

BEEFEATER®
LONDON DRY GIN

First produced in 1820 by pharmacist James Burrough, BEEFEATER LONDON DRY GIN is still made according to the same family-held recipe using time-honored production techniques. Burrough named the spirit after the Yeomen of the Guard at the Tower of London, who are commonly known as Beefeaters.

Beefeater deserves its reputation as the driest of the elite London dry gins. The botanicals and aromatics used to make Beefeater Gin are steeped in the neutral spirits for 24 hours before being redistilled in an alembic still. The recipe's botanicals include juniper berries, coriander, angelica root, licorice, cassia bark, dried Seville orange peels and Spanish lemon peels.

A quick sniff is all that's necessary to explain Beefeater's enduring popularity. The famous gin has a lavish, thoroughly engaging bouquet, one laced with floral, spice and juniper. Its lightweight body is crisp and exceptionally dry. The gin immediately fills the mouth with layers of delicious flavors, notably citrus, juniper, lavender and spice. The persistence of flavors is remarkably long. The gin is bottled at a lip tingling 94 proof.

Why is Beefeater Gin found on every back bar throughout the world? A captivating aroma, silky body, great taste, long, dry finish and tremendous versatility. That largely explains it, yes?

GIMLET, SOHO
Cocktail glass, chilled
Pour ingredients into iced mixing glass
1 3/4 oz. Beefeater London Dry Gin
1/2 oz. Gran Gala Orange Liqueur
1/2 oz. fresh lime juice
1/2 oz. sweet 'n' sour
Shake and strain
Lime wedge garnish

GIMLET, TUACA
Cocktail glass, chilled
Pour ingredients into iced mixing glass
1 1/2 oz. Vodka
3/4 oz. Tuaca
1/2 oz. Rose's Lime Juice
Stir and strain
Lime wedge garnish

GIMLET, VODKA
Cocktail glass, chilled
Pour ingredients into iced mixing glass
1 1/2 oz. Vodka
1/2 oz. Rose's Lime Juice
Stir and strain
Lime wedge garnish

GIMLET, WHALER
Cocktail glass, chilled
Pour ingredients into iced mixing glass
1 1/2 oz. Whaler's Original Vanille Rum
3/4 oz. Tuaca
1/2 oz. Rose's Lime Juice
Stir and strain
Lime wedge garnish

GIN ALEXANDER
aka **Plain Alexander**
Cocktail glass, chilled
Pour ingredients into iced mixing glass
3/4 oz. Gin
3/4 oz. White Crème de Cacao
2 oz. half & half cream
Shake and strain
Sprinkle nutmeg

GIN AND IT
Cocktail glass, chilled
Pour ingredients into iced mixing glass
1/2 oz. Sweet Vermouth
1 1/2 oz. Gin
Stir and strain

GINGER BEER SHANDY
Beer glass, chilled
Build in glass
9 oz. Amber Ale
Fill with Ginger Beer

GINGERBREAD MAN
Rocks glass, chilled
Build in glass
3/4 oz. Goldschläger
3/4 oz. Baileys Irish Cream
3/4 oz. DeKuyper Buttershots Schnapps

GINNY'S SWEET 'N' SOUR STONE SOUR
Tall house specialty glass, ice
Pour ingredients into iced mixing glass
1 1/2 oz. Wet by Beefeater
3/4 oz. grapefruit juice
3/4 oz. orange juice
1 1/2 oz. sweet 'n' sour
Shake and strain
Fill with Seven-Up
Lime wedge, orange slice and cherry garnish

GIN RICKEY
Highball glass, ice
Build in glass
1 1/4 oz. Gin
Fill with club soda
Lime wedge garnish

GIRL SCOUT COOKIE
Cocktail glass, chilled
Pour ingredients into iced mixing glass
3/4 oz. Peppermint Schnapps
3/4 oz. Kahlúa
1 1/2 oz. half & half cream
Shake and strain
Cookie garnish

GLACIER BREEZE
Bucket glass, ice
Build in glass
1 1/2 oz. Finlandia Vodka
3/4 oz. cranberry juice
3/4 oz. apple juice
Fill with orange juice

GLASNOST
Bucket glass, ice
Pour ingredients into iced mixing glass
1 oz. Spudka Vodka
1 oz. Chambord
2 oz. sweet 'n' sour
2 oz. orange juice
Shake and strain
Orange slice and cherry garnish

GLASS TOWER
House specialty glass, ice
Build in glass
1 oz. Bacardi Light Rum
1 oz. Stolichnaya Persik Vodka
1 oz. DeKuyper Peachtree Schnapps
1 oz. Triple Sec
1/2 oz. Sambuca
Fill with Seven-Up

GLENDA
Champagne flute, chilled
Build in glass
3/4 oz. Peach Schnapps
3/4 oz. Grand Marnier
Fill with Champagne
Lemon twist garnish

GLOOMRAISER
Cocktail glass, chilled
Pour ingredients into iced mixing glass
1 1/2 oz. Gin
1/4 oz. Dry Vermouth
2 dashes Pernod
2 dashes grenadine
Stir and strain
Cherry garnish (optional)

GOAL POST
Presentation shot glass, chilled
Layer ingredients
1/2 fill White Crème de Menthe
1/2 fill Tequila

GODCHILD
Rocks glass, ice
Build in glass
1 1/2 oz. Vodka
3/4 oz. Disaronno Amaretto
3/4 oz. half & half cream

GODFATHER
Rocks glass, ice
Build in glass
1 1/2 oz. Scotch Whisky
3/4 oz. Disaronno Amaretto

GODMOTHER
Rocks glass, ice
Build in glass
1 1/2 oz. Vodka
3/4 oz. Disaronno Amaretto

GOLD AND LAGER
Beer glass, chilled
Build in glass
1 1/4 oz. Goldschläger
Fill with Pilsner

GOLD AND RICHES
Brandy snifter, heated
Build in glass
1 1/2 oz. XO Cognac
1/2 oz. Godiva Chocolate Liqueur
1/2 oz. Grand Marnier Centenaire
Serve with underliner, add 3 gold-covered
    chocolate coins

JIM BEAM®
BLACK LABEL BOURBON

Jim Beam is the most famous name in bourbon and something of an international phenomenon. While the White Label and their stellar collection of small batch whiskeys get most of the attention, JIM BEAM BLACK LABEL BOURBON is making a name for itself with connoisseurs and novices alike as a super-premium bourbon with a sublime easily accessible character.

Made in Clermont, Kentucky, Jim Beam Black Label is distilled from a high proportion of white and yellow corn grown in Indiana and Kentucky, and lesser percentages of rye and malted barley. The bourbon is matured in oak a minimum of 8 years and bottled at 86 proof.

If someone does'nt immediately become enamored with Black Label's tremondous personailty and character then they likely won't become enamored with any other bourbon. It's bouquet is still irresistible—sweet and brimming with the aromas of corn, vanilla and toasted oak. While the whiskey remains enormously flavorful, the additional time in the barrel has tempered some of its natural exuberance. The finish is warm and long.

Jim Beam Black Label Bourbon has genuinely come of age. The whiskey is sophisticated enough to appreciate alone in the glass.

GOLDEN CADILLAC
Cocktail glass, chilled
Pour ingredients into iced mixing glass
3/4 oz. White Crème de Cacao
3/4 oz. Galliano Liqueur
2 oz. half & half cream
Shake and strain

GOLDEN DRAGON
House specialty glass, ice
Pour ingredients into iced mixing glass
1 1/2 oz. Bacardi 8 Reserva Rum
1/2 oz. Sweet Vermouth
1 oz. orgeat syrup
1 1/2 oz. coconut cream syrup
1 1/2 oz. half & half cream
Shake and strain
Dust ground cinnamon

GOLDEN DREAM
Cocktail glass, chilled
Pour ingredients into iced mixing glass
3/4 oz. Galliano Liqueur
3/4 oz. Triple Sec
3/4 oz. orange juice
1 1/2 oz. half & half cream
Shake and strain

GOLDEN DREAM WITH
DOUBLE BUMPERS
House specialty glass, chilled
Pour ingredients into iced mixing glass
3/4 oz. Galliano Liqueur
3/4 oz. Triple Sec
3/4 oz. Brandy
3/4 oz. B & B Liqueur
3/4 oz. orange juice
2 oz. half & half cream
Shake and strain

GOLDEN FIZZ
Bucket glass, ice
Pour ingredients into iced mixing glass
1 1/4 oz. Gin
1/2 oz. simple syrup
1 1/2 oz. sweet 'n' sour
1 1/2 oz. half & half cream
1 egg yolk (optional)
Shake and strain
Splash club soda

GOLDEN MAX
Brandy snifter, heated
Build in glass
1 1/2 oz. VS Cognac
3/4 oz. Cointreau

GOLDEN NAIL
Highball glass, ice
Build in glass
1 1/4 oz. Drambuie
Fill with grapefruit juice

GOLDEN PEACH
Bucket glass, ice
Pour ingredients into iced mixing glass
1 3/4 oz. Irish Whiskey
3/4 oz. DeKuyper Peachtree Schnapps
1 1/2 oz. orange juice
1 1/2 oz. sweet 'n' sour
Shake and strain
Orange slice garnish

GOLDEN RAM
House specialty glass, chilled
Pour ingredients into blender
1 oz. Southern Comfort
1/2 oz. Galliano Liqueur
1/2 oz. Disaronno Amaretto
1/2 oz. DeKuyper Peach Pucker
3 oz. orange juice
Blend with ice

GOLDEN SCREW
aka **Italian Screw**
Highball glass, ice
Build in glass
1 1/4 oz. Galliano Liqueur
Fill with orange juice

GOLD FURNACE
Presentation shot glass, chilled
Build in glass
1 1/2 oz. Goldschläger
2 dashes Tabasco Sauce

GOLD RUSH (1)
Cocktail glass, chilled
Rim glass with salt (optional)
Pour ingredients into iced mixing glass
1 1/2 oz. Jose Cuervo Especial Tequila
1/2 oz. Grand Marnier
1/2 oz. Rose's Lime Juice
Stir and strain
Lime wedge garnish

GOLD RUSH (2)
Presentation shot glass, chilled
Build in glass
3/4 oz. Goldschläger
3/4 oz. Gold Tequila

GOLD RUSH (3)
Cocktail glass, chilled
Pour ingredients into iced mixing glass
1 1/2 oz. Jose Cuervo Especial Tequila
3/4 oz. Licor 43 (Cuarenta y Tres)
1/2 oz. Rose's Lime Juice
Stir and strain
Lime wedge garnish

GOOD & PLENTY
Rocks glass, ice
Build in glass
1 1/2 oz. Kahlúa
1/2 oz. Anisette

GOOM BAY SMASH (1)
House specialty glass, chilled
Pour ingredients into blender
1 1/4 oz. Gold Rum
1 1/4 oz. Malibu Caribbean Rum
3/4 oz. Crème de Banana
2 oz. pineapple juice
2 oz. orange juice
Blend with ice
Banana slice garnish

GOOM BAY SMASH (2)
House specialty glass, chilled
Pour ingredients into blender
1 1/4 oz. Jamaican Rum
1 1/4 oz. Coconut Rum
3/4 oz. Crème de Banana
2 oz. pineapple juice
2 oz. orange juice
Blend with ice
Banana slice garnish

GOOSE DOWN
Cocktail glass, chilled
Pour ingredients into iced mixing glass
1 1/2 oz. Grey Goose Vodka
1 oz. Limoncello Liqueur
Shake and strain
Lemon twist garnish

GORILLA MILK
House specialty glass, chilled
Pour ingredients into blender
1 oz. Light Rum
3/4 oz. Kahlúa
3/4 oz. Baileys Irish Cream
3/4 oz. Crème de Banana
1 oz. half & half cream
1 scoop vanilla ice cream
Blend ingredients (with ice optional)
Pineapple wedge and banana slice garnish

GORKY PARK COOLER (1)
House specialty glass, ice
Pour ingredients into iced mixing glass
1 1/4 oz. Stolichnaya Strasberi Vodka
3/4 oz. Stolichnaya Vodka
3/4 oz. Malibu Caribbean Rum
1 oz. sweet 'n' sour
2 oz. pineapple juice
Shake and strain
Pineapple wedge garnish

CITADELLE® VODKA

If you're looking for a vodka with tremendous character, you've come to the right place. Made by cognac producer Cognac Ferrand, CITADELLE VODKA is a handcrafted tour de force.

It takes only a few moments alone with this cork-finished thoroughbred to determine that it is an Olympic caliber spirit. The small batch vodka is made from the hearts of wheat and spring water from the famed Angeac Champagne Springs in Cognac. It is distilled five times in traditional copper alembic stills and rendered pure using an exclusive process called micro-oxygenation.

There is much more to Citadelle Vodka than meets the eye. It has a light, voluptuously supple body, a generous semisweet bouquet and a palate imbued with the fresh fruit flavors of cherries and orange zest. The vodka's persistence of flavor borders on the remarkable.

Cognac Ferrand has also created two flavored vodkas that are every bit as classy as the original. CITADELLE RASPBERRY VODKA is created with the addition of an infusion of fresh fruit. It has a highly focused aroma and flavor of raspberries, a genuinely sublime pleasure to drink. CITADELLE APPLE VODKA is equally enticing. It is a spry and vibrant spirit with an engaging and slightly tart palate. Both versions are tailor-made for use in cocktails.

GORKY PARK COOLER (2)
House specialty glass, chilled
Pour ingredients into blender
1 1/2 oz. Stolichnaya Razberi Vodka
1/2 oz. Captain Morgan Spiced Rum
1/2 oz. Malibu Caribbean Rum
4 oz. pineapple juice
Blend with ice
Pineapple wedge garnish

GOTHAM LEMONADE
Bucket glass, ice
Build in glass
1 1/2 oz. Vox Raspberry Vodka
3/4 oz. Triple Sec
1 oz. white cranberry juice
Fill with lemonade
Lemon wheel garnish

GRAN BLISS
Champagne glass, chilled
Build in glass
3/4 oz. Gran Gala Orange Liqueur
1/2 oz. DeKuyper Peachtree Schnapps
Fill with Champagne
Lemon twist garnish

GRAN BOMBAY
Cocktail glass, chilled
Pour ingredients into iced mixing glass
1 oz. Bombay Sapphire London Dry Gin
3/4 oz. Gran Gala Orange Liqueur
1 oz. sweet 'n' sour
Shake and strain
Orange twist garnish

GRAN CAPPUCCINO
Cappuccino cup, heated
Build in glass
3/4 oz. Gran Gala Orange Liqueur
3/4 oz. Patrón XO Café Coffee Liqueur
1/2 oz. VS Cognac
Near fill with hot espresso coffee
Top with frothed milk
Sprinkle shaved chocolate

GRAND ALLIANCE
Sherry glass, chilled
Build in glass
1/2 fill Disaronno Amaretto
1/2 fill Champagne

GRAND BALL
Rocks glass, ice
Build in glass
2 oz. Crown Royal Canadian Whisky
3/4 oz. Grand Marnier Centenaire

GRANDFATHER
Tankard or pilsner glass, chilled
Build in glass
1/3 fill Guinness Stout
1/3 fill Bass
1/3 fill Harp

GRAND MARSHALL SOUR
Cocktail glass, chilled
Pour ingredients into iced mixing glass
1 oz. Jack Daniel's Single Barrel Whiskey
1/2 oz. Grand Marnier Centenaire
1 1/2 oz. sweet 'n' sour
Shake and strain
Orange and starfruit (carambola)
    slice garnish

GRAND ORANGE BLOSSOM
Cocktail glass, chilled
Pour ingredients into iced mixing glass
1 1/4 oz. Grey Goose L'Orange Vodka
3/4 oz. Grand Marnier
3/4 oz. orange juice
1/4 oz. sugar syrup
Shake and strain
Orange slice garnish

GRAN SONORAN SUNSET
Highball glass, ice
Build in glass
1 1/4 oz. El Tesoro Añejo Tequila
1 oz. fresh lime juice
Near fill with orange juice
Float 3/4 oz. Gran Gala Orange Liqueur
Lime wheel garnish

GRAPE NEHI
Rocks glass, ice
Pour ingredients into iced mixing glass
1 1/2 oz. Vodka
1 oz. DeKuyper Grape Pucker
1/4 oz. fresh lemon juice
1 1/2 oz. sweet 'n' sour
Shake and strain

GRAPES OF WRATH
Cocktail glass, chilled
Pour ingredients into iced mixing glass
2 oz. Cîroc Snap Frost Vodka
1 oz. white grape juice
Stir and strain
Grape bunch garnish

GRASSHOPPER
Cocktail glass, chilled
Pour ingredients into iced mixing glass
3/4 oz. White Crème de Cacao
3/4 oz. Green Crème de Menthe
2 oz. half & half cream
Shake and strain

GREAT LAKES TRAPPER
Coffee mug, heated
Build in glass
3/4 oz. Brandy
3/4 oz. White Crème de Menthe
Near fill with hot chocolate
Whipped cream garnish
Sprinkle nutmeg

GREEK COFFEE
Coffee mug, heated
Build in glass
3/4 oz. Metaxa 5 Star Brandy
3/4 oz. Ouzo
Fill with hot coffee

GREEN HORNET
Rocks glass, ice
Build in glass
1 1/2 oz. Brandy
1/2 oz. Green Crème de Menthe

GREEN LIZARD
Presentation shot glass, chilled
Layer ingredients
1/2 fill Green Chartreuse
1/2 fill 151° Rum

GREEN MINT FLOAT
Rocks glass, ice
Build in glass
1 3/4 oz. Irish Whiskey
1 oz. Green Crème de Menthe
1 oz. half & half cream
Cherry garnish

GREEN MONSTER
Bucket glass, ice
Build in glass
1 oz. KéKé Beach Cream Liqueur
3/4 oz. Midori
3/4 oz. Light Rum
Near fill with orange juice
Splash pineapple juice

GREEN REEF
Bucket glass, ice
Build in glass
3/4 oz. Light Rum
3/4 oz. Midori
1/2 oz. White Crème de Cacao
Near fill with pineapple juice
Float 3/4 oz. Cruzan Pineapple Rum
Pineapple wedge and cherry garnish

GREEN RUSSIAN
Rocks glass, ice
Build in glass
1 1/2 oz. Vodka
1/2 oz. Midori

TEQUILA ROSE®
STRAWBERRY FLAVORED
CREAM LIQUEUR & TEQUILA

The Tequila Rose story is a simple one to tell. It came, it saw and it conquered. Seriously, how else would you describe the liqueur's meteoric rise to stardom? When Tequila Rose debuted in 1997, there was nothing on the market remotely like it, and since it has hit the popular scene, the brand hasn't looked back.

TEQUILA ROSE is a blend of strawberry flavored cream liqueur and tequila. To call marrying these flavors together innovative would be an understatement. But as throngs of devotees will attest, the combination works exceptionally well.

Tequila Rose has a true-to-Crayola pink hue. While not necessarily the most rugged color they could have chosen, it may well be the only pink product behind the bar. The lavish bouquet is that of strawberries and cream, which also best describes the palate. To fully appreciate how its flavors fully integrate, Tequila Rose should be sampled chilled, either straight-up or on the rocks.

The liqueur may be at its best when playing a featured role in a cocktail or mixed libation. Tequila Rose is great when mixed over ice with a fruit flavored liqueur, or blended with strawberry ice cream and presented as a liquid dessert. It also works with coffee and chocolate. If you can't have fun with Tequila Rose, maybe you're no longer breathing.

GREEN SNEAKERS
Bucket glass, ice
Pour ingredients into iced mixing glass
1 1/2 oz. Citadelle Apple Vodka
3/4 oz. Midori
3/4 oz. DeKuyper Pucker Sour Apple
3/4 oz. Blue Curaçao
3/4 oz. orange juice
Shake and strain
Fill with lemonade
Lemon wedge garnish

GREEN SPIDER
Rocks glass, ice
Build in glass
1 1/2 oz. Vodka
1/2 oz. Green Crème de Menthe

GREYHOUND
Highball glass, ice
Build in glass
1 1/4 oz. Vodka
Fill with grapefruit juice
Note: May be requested made with Gin

GRIFFEN, THE
Champagne glass, chilled
Build in glass
1 oz. Pineau des Charentes
Fill with Champagne
Frozen grapes garnish

GROUND ZERO
Bucket glass, ice
Build in glass
1 1/4 oz. Cruzan Pineapple Rum
3/4 oz. Midori
Fill with pineapple juice
Pineapple wedge and cherry garnish

GUAVA COOLER
Bucket glass, ice
Pour ingredients into iced mixing glass
1 1/2 oz. Kuya Fusion Rum
1/2 oz. Raspberry Liqueur
1 1/2 oz. guava nectar
1/2 oz. simple syrup
1 oz. sweet 'n' sour
1 oz. pineapple juice
Shake and strain

GUAVA MARTINIQUE
House specialty glass, ice
Pour ingredients into iced mixing glass
1 1/2 oz. Rhum Barbancourt 5-Star
1/2 oz. Chambord
1/2 oz. Godiva Chocolate Liqueur
1 1/2 oz. guava nectar
1 1/2 oz. pineapple juice
1 1/2 oz. sweet 'n' sour
Shake and strain
Float 3/4 oz. St. James Extra Old Rhum
Orange slice and cherry garnish

GULF BREEZE
Bucket glass, ice
Build in glass
1 1/4 oz. Gin
1/2 fill grapefruit juice
1/2 fill cranberry juice

GULF STREAM SCREAM
House specialty glass, ice
Pour ingredients into iced mixing glass
1 oz. Light Rum
1 oz. Midori
1/2 oz. Peach Schnapps
2 oz. pineapple juice
2 oz. orange juice
Shake and strain
Float 3/4 oz. Mount Gay Eclipse Rum
Orange slice and cherry garnish

GULF TIDE
Highball glass, ice
Build in glass
1 1/4 oz. Gin
1/2 fill orange juice
1/2 fill cranberry juice

GULLET PLEASER
Presentation shot glass, chilled
Build in glass
1/3 fill DeKuyper Peach Pucker
1/3 fill Stolichnaya Citros Vodka
1/3 fill cranberry-grapefruit juice

GUMBY
Bucket glass, chilled
Pour ingredients into iced mixing glass
1 1/4 oz. Vodka
3/4 oz. Midori
3/4 oz. sweet 'n' sour
Shake and strain
Fill with Seven-Up
Cherry garnish

GYPSY
Cocktail glass, chilled
Pour ingredients into iced mixing glass
1 1/2 oz. Vodka
1/2 oz. B & B Liqueur
2-3 dashes Angostura Bitters
Stir and strain
Lemon twist garnish

HABANA LIBRE
House specialty glass, ice
Build in glass
1 1/2 oz. Light Rum
1/2 oz. fresh lime juice
1/4 oz. grenadine
Near fill with cola
Float 3/4 oz. Bacardi 151° Rum
Lime wedge and mint sprig garnish

HABANOS HAVANA
Cocktail glass, chilled
Pour ingredients into iced mixing glass
1 3/4 oz. Matusalem Golden Dry Rum
3/4 oz. Cointreau
1 1/2 oz. sweetened lime juice
Shake and strain
Lime wedge garnish

HAIRY SUNRISE
Bucket glass, ice
Build in glass
3/4 oz. Corazón Silver Tequila
3/4 oz. Grey Goose Vodka
3/4 oz. Grey Goose L'Orange Vodka
Near fill with orange juice
Float 3/4 oz. Raspberry Liqueur
Lime wheel garnish

HALEKULANI SUNSET
House specialty glass, ice
Pour ingredients into iced mixing glass
1 1/2 oz. Light Rum
3/4 oz. Blue Curaçao
1/2 oz. grenadine
3 oz. guava nectar
1 1/2 oz. sweet 'n' sour
Shake and strain
Float 3/4 oz. Dark Rum
Pineapple wedge and cherry garnish

HALF & HALF (1)
Cocktail glass, chilled
Pour ingredients into iced mixing glass
1 1/2 oz. Dry Vermouth
1 1/2 oz. Sweet Vermouth
Stir and strain
Lemon twist garnish

JOSE CUERVO®
ESPECIAL® TEQUILA

If you walk into a bar and don't see a bottle of JOSE CUERVO ESPECIAL TEQUILA on the back bar, turn around and leave. The brand has grown to be the world's best-selling tequila and around the world is referred to simply as "Cuervo Gold."

Made in the town of Tequila at the 200 year old family distillery, *La Rojeña*, premium Jose Cuervo Especial is produced from a special blend of reposado (rested) and other high quality Cuevo tequilas. It is bottled at 80 proof.

The explanation of why Jose Cuervo Especial has become an international phenomenon is not so much how it's made, but rather how it performs in the glass. The tequila has a lustrous amber hue, a medium-weight, seamlessly smooth body and an expansive herbal and floral bouquet. Its palate immediately fills the mouth with slightly sweet oaky and vanilla flavors that persist well into the long and warming finish.

There is but one Jose Cuervo Especial and without it all tequila-related commerce at the bar grinds to a halt. When it comes to drink making, the brand has unlimited creative range and is popularly featured in every type of contemporary cocktail. From the shot glass to Margarita glass, it is the standard bearer.

HALF & HALF (2)
Beer glass, chilled
Build in glass
1/2 fill Bitter Ale
1/2 fill Pilsner

HANGIN' ON A STICK
Rocks glass, chilled
Pour ingredients into iced mixing glass
1 oz. Jose Cuervo Especial Tequila
3/4 oz. Cointreau
1/2 oz. cranberry juice
1/2 oz. pineapple juice
3/4 oz. orange juice
Shake and strain

HAPPY HOUR
Bucket glass, ice
Build in glass
1 1/2 oz. Mount Gay Eclipse Rum
3/4 oz. Grand Marnier
Fill with papaya juice

HAPPY JACKS
Presentation shot glass, chilled
Build in glass
1/2 fill Jack Daniel's Tennessee Whiskey
1/2 fill Laird's Applejack Brandy

HARBOR LIGHTS
Presentation shot glass, chilled
Layer ingredients
1/3 fill Kahlúa
1/3 fill Tequila
1/3 fill 151° Rum

HARVARD
Cocktail glass, chilled
Pour ingredients into iced mixing glass
1 3/4 oz. Brandy
3/4 oz. Sweet Vermouth
2 dashes Angostura Bitters
1/4 oz. simple syrup
Stir and strain
Lemon twist garnish

HARVEST GROG
Coffee mug, heated
Build in glass
1 oz. Laird's Applejack Brandy
1 oz. Chambord
2 dashes cinnamon
3 cloves
6 oz. apple cider
Cinnamon stick garnish
Heat mix of apple cider and spices in small sauce pan for 5 minutes. Remove cloves, pour mixture into glass with Applejack and Chambord.

HARVEST NIGHT
House specialty glass, chilled
Pour ingredients into blender
1 1/2 oz. Finlandia Vodka
1 oz. Limoncello Liqueur
1/2 cup cubed cantaloupe
1/2 cup fresh peaches
Blend with ice
Fresh melon slice garnish

HARVEY WALLBANGER
Bucket glass, ice
Build in glass
1 1/4 oz. Vodka
Near fill with orange juice
Float 3/4 oz. Galliano Liqueur

HASTA LA VISTA, BABY
Highball glass, chilled
Pour ingredients into iced mixing glass
3/4 oz. Jose Cuervo Especial Tequila
3/4 oz. Absolut Peppar Vodka
1/2 oz. DeKuyper Peachtree Schnapps
1/4 oz. Triple Sec
1/4 oz. Crème de Noyaux
1/4 oz. B & B Liqueur
1/2 oz. Rose's Lime Juice
3/4 oz. pineapple juice
3/4 oz. orange juice
Shake and strain

HAVANA
Cocktail glass, chilled
Pour ingredients into iced mixing glass
1/2 oz. Dry Sherry
1 3/4 oz. Gold Rum
1 dash Angostura Bitters
1 1/2 oz. sweet 'n' sour
Shake and strain
Orange twist garnish

HAVANA CLUB
Cocktail glass, chilled
Pour ingredients into iced mixing glass
1/2 oz. Sweet Vermouth
1 3/4 oz. Gold Rum
1 dash Angostura Bitters
Stir and strain
Cherry garnish

HAVANA COCKTAIL
Cocktail glass, chilled
Pour ingredients into iced mixing glass
1 3/4 oz. Matusalem Golden Dry Rum
1/2 oz. fresh lemon juice
1 1/2 oz. pineapple juice
Shake and strain
Cherry garnish

HAWAIIAN HURRICANE
House specialty glass, ice
Pour ingredients into iced mixing glass
1/2 oz. Light Rum
1/2 oz. Gold Rum
1/2 oz. Jamaican Rum
1/2 oz. Tequila
1/2 oz. Vodka
2 oz. pineapple juice
2 oz. papaya juice
Shake and strain
Float 3/4 oz. 151° Rum
Orange slice and cherry garnish

HAWAIIAN PUNCH (1)
Bucket glass, ice
Pour ingredients into iced mixing glass
1 oz. Vodka
1/2 oz. Disaronno Amaretto
1/2 oz. Southern Comfort
1/2 oz. Sloe Gin
2 oz. pineapple juice
Shake and strain
Splash Seven-Up (optional)

HAWAIIAN PUNCH (2)
Bucket glass, ice
Build in glass
3/4 oz. Southern Comfort
3/4 oz. Disaronno Amaretto
3/4 oz. Crème de Noyaux
1 1/2 oz. pineapple juice
1 1/2 oz. orange juice

HAWAIIAN SHOOTER
Rocks glass, chilled
Pour ingredients into iced mixing glass
1 1/4 oz. Southern Comfort
3/4 oz. Crème de Noyaux
1/2 oz. pineapple juice
Shake and strain

HAWAIIAN SUNBURN
Bucket glass, ice
Build in glass
1 1/4 oz. Herradura Reposado Tequila
1/2 oz. Gran Gala Orange Liqueur
Near fill with cranberry juice
Splash pineapple juice

HEARTBREAK
Bucket glass, ice
Build in glass
1 1/4 oz. Canadian Club Whisky
Near fill with cranberry juice
Float 3/4 oz. Brandy

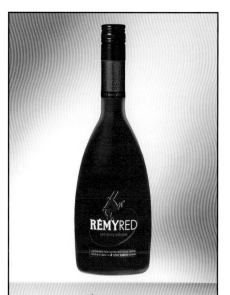

RÉMYRED®
RED BERRY INFUSION

Launched in 1999, RÉMYRED RED BERRY INFUSION is a sensational cognac-based liqueur made by one of the preeminent cognac houses, Rémy Martin. Its style is an engaging blend of tradition and contemporary living. In fact, it makes a lively cocktail in itself, just chill, pop open the bottle and let the rave reviews pour forth.

RémyRed is made in the heart of the cognac region of France from a proprietary recipe, the base of which includes the juice of freshly picked currants, apricots and peaches. Natural fruit juices are added to the mix. The firm then infuses this lively liqueur with aged, Fine Champagne Rémy Martin Cognac, a blend of Grande and Petite Champagne cognac.

The Red Berry Infusion has an exotic appearance. It is opaque with a brilliant, lustrous, red-orange color. The generous bouquet is that of freshly squeezed juice, predominantly apricot and currant, plus a hint of the underlying cognac. The aperitif has a full, luscious body, and a slightly tart palate in which no one juice flavor dominates. The cognac is the decisive element in the blend, balancing out the natural sweetness in the juice.

Thank goodness for innovation. RémyRed is a true-blue friend behind the bar. It adds a splash of personality to a wide range of cocktails, often just the thing to tip the scales of fate.

HEATHER BLUSH
Champagne glass, chilled
Build in glass
1 1/4 oz. Scotch Whisky
1 oz. Chambord
Fill with Champagne

HEAT WAVE
Bucket glass, ice
Build in glass
1 oz. Mount Gay Eclipse Rum
1/2 oz. DeKuyper Peachtree Schnapps
Near fill with pineapple juice
Float 3/4 oz. Appleton Estate
    V/X Jamaica Rum
Lime wedge garnish

HEAVENLY TODDY
Coffee mug, heated
Build in glass
2 oz. Brandy
2 tsp. honey
2 oz. fresh lemon juice
Fill with hot water
Lemon twist garnish

HEAVYWEIGHT SAILOR
Cocktail glass, chilled
Pour ingredients into iced mixing glass
1 1/4 oz. Sea Wynde Pot Still Rum
1/2 oz. Tia Maria
1/2 oz. Rose's Lime Juice
1 3/4 oz. sweet 'n' sour
Shake and strain
Lime wedge garnish

HELENE
Brandy snifter (ice optional)
Build in glass
1 1/2 oz. Poire William
    (Eau de Vie de Poire)
1/2 oz. Godiva Chocolate Liqueur

HELL ON ICE
Bucket glass, ice
Build in glass
1 oz. VooDoo Spiced Rum
1 oz. Bourbon
1/2 oz. Cinnamon Schnapps
Fill with orange juice

HEMINGWAY
aka **Death in the Afternoon**
Champagne glass, chilled
Build in glass
1 1/2 oz. Pernod
Fill with Champagne

HEMINGWAY'S FLAMBÉ COFFEE
Coffee mug, heated
Build in glass
1 oz. Frangelico
1/2 oz. Sambuca Romano
1/2 oz. Brandy
Near fill with hot coffee
Whipped cream garnish
Sprinkle nutmeg

HIGHBALL
Highball glass, ice
Build in glass
1 1/4 oz. Bourbon
Fill with ginger ale

HIGHLAND COCKTAIL
aka **Highland Fling**
Cocktail glass, chilled
Pour ingredients into iced mixing glass
1 1/2 oz. Glenmorangie Single Malt Scotch
1/2 oz. Sweet Vermouth
2-3 dashes Angostura Bitters
Stir and strain
Lemon twist garnish

HIGHLAND GOLFER
Bucket glass, ice
Build in glass
1 1/4 oz. Scotch Whisky
1/2 oz. Triple Sec
1/2 oz. Green Crème de Menthe
Fill with apple cider

HIGHLAND HIGHBALL
Highball glass, ice
Build in glass
1 1/4 oz. Scotch Whisky
Fill with ginger ale
Lemon twist garnish

HIMBEERSAFT
Highball glass, ice
Build in glass
3 oz. raspberry syrup
Fill with club soda
Mint sprig garnish

HOLE-IN-ONE
Presentation shot glass, chilled
Build in glass
1 1/4 oz. Midori
3/4 oz. Laird's Applejack Brandy
4 drops half & half cream

HOLLAND'S OPUS
Cocktail glass, chilled
Pour ingredients into iced mixing glass
2 oz. Damrak Amsterdam Gin
1/2 oz. Chambord
1 3/4 oz. sweet 'n' sour
Shake and strain
Lemon twist garnish

HOLLYWOOD
Highball glass, ice
Build in glass
3/4 oz. Raspberry Vodka
3/4 oz. Chambord
Fill with pineapple juice

HOLY HAND GRENADE
Rocks glass, chilled
Build in glass
1 1/4 oz. Chambord
3/4 oz. Absolut Kurant Vodka
1 1/2 oz. lemonade

HONEY BEE
Cocktail glass, chilled
Pour ingredients into iced mixing glass
1 oz. Myers's Jamaican Rum
1/2 oz. honey
1 1/2 oz. sweet 'n' sour
Shake and strain

HONEYBUNCH PUNCH
House specialty glass, ice
Pour ingredients into iced mixing glass
1 1/2 oz. Dark Rum
1/2 oz. Grand Marnier
1/2 oz. Rose's Lime Juice
2-3 dashes Angostura Bitters
1/4 oz. grenadine
1/2 oz. orange juice
1/2 oz. pineapple juice
Shake and strain
Orange slice and cherry garnish

HONEYDEW
Bucket glass, ice
Pour ingredients into iced mixing glass
1 1/2 oz. Midori
3 oz. lemonade
Shake and strain
Fill with Champagne

HONEYMOON
aka **Farmer's Daughter**
Cocktail glass, chilled
Pour ingredients into iced mixing glass
1 1/4 oz. Laird's Applejack Brandy
1/2 oz. B & B Liqueur
1/2 oz. Triple Sec
1 3/4 oz. sweet 'n' sour
Shake and strain

KUYA® FUSION RUM

The rum category is hot and rapidly getting hotter. Its growth to a large degree has been fueled by innovation. Bold flavors are in. Rums lacking in character are yesterday's news. Now is a great time for something like KUYA FUSION RUM.

Produced by Kahlúa, Kuya is made from a blend of rich, golden rums that are infused with natural citrus flavor extracts and an array of island spices. As it states on the label, it is best described as a fusion between the classic spiced rum and the new breed of fruit flavored rum. The result is phenomenal.

Kuya Fusion Rum has a captivating bouquet of citron, grapefruit and vanilla tinged with cloves and spice. After the first sniff you'll know good things are coming your way. It has a featherweight, seamlessly textured body that delivers a citrus and spicy vanilla palate, flavors that linger for an impressively long time. Guaranteed you've never tasted a rum like this before.

Before you start making drinks, take a moment to appreciate Kuya neat or slightly chilled. It's a 70 proof treat not to be missed. But it was bred for drink making and mixologists are going to have a field day with it behind the bar. It's a good candidate for a specialty Gimlet, Kamikaze and Cosmopolitan. The Piña Colada and classic Daiquiri are also ideal vehicles for serving Kuya.

HONEY RUM TODDY
Coffee mug, heated
Build in glass
2 oz. Gold Rum
2 tbsp. honey
1 tbsp. fresh lime juice
A thin slice of lime
Fill with boiling water
Lemon wedge and cinnamon stick garnish

HOOCHIE KÉKÉ MAMA
Bucket glass, ice
Build in glass
1 oz. KéKé Beach Cream Liqueur
1 oz. Polar Ice Vodka
3/4 oz. Kahlúa
1/2 fill with cola
1/2 fill with half & half cream

HORSE'S NECK WITH A KICK
Highball glass, ice
Build in glass
1 1/4 oz. Bourbon
Fill with ginger ale
Long lemon peel spiral garnish
 (a 'horse's neck')

HOT APPLE PIE
Coffee mug, heated
Build in glass
1 oz. Tuaca
Near fill with hot apple cider
Whipped cream garnish
Sprinkle nutmeg

HOT APPLE ROSE
Coffee mug, heated
Build in glass
1 1/4 oz. Tequila Rose Cream Liqueur
Near fill with hot apple cider
Whipped cream and cinnamon
 stick garnish

HOT BUTTERED RUM
Coffee mug, heated
Build in glass
1 1/2 oz. Appleton Estate V/X Jamaica Rum
1/2 oz. simple syrup
2 pinches nutmeg
Fill with hot water
Float pat of butter
Cinnamon stick garnish

HOT CHAMBORD DREAM
Coffee mug, heated
Build in glass
3/4 oz. Dark Crème de Cacao
3/4 oz. Chambord
Near fill with hot espresso coffee
Top with frothed milk
Sprinkle shaved chocolate

HOT HONEY POT
Cocktail glass, chilled
Pour ingredients into iced mixing glass
1 oz. Cinnamon Schnapps
1/2 oz. honey
1 1/2 oz. sweet 'n' sour
Shake and strain

HOT IRISH DREAM
Coffee mug, heated
Build in glass
1 oz. Irish Liqueur
1/2 oz. Baileys Irish Cream
1/2 oz. Frangelico
Near fill with coffee
Whipped cream garnish
Drizzle 1/2 oz. Chambord

HOT MILK PUNCH
Coffee mug, heated
Build in glass
1 1/2 oz. Bourbon
1/2 oz. simple syrup
Fill with hot milk
Sprinkle nutmeg

HOT MULLED WINE
Punch bowl or decanter
Pour ingredients into saucepan
36 oz. Dry Red Wine
1/2 cup sugar
12 oz. cranberry juice
1/4 cup mulling spices
Simmer for 30 minutes
Makes 8-10 servings

HOT RUM COW
Coffee mug, heated
Build in glass
1 3/4 oz. Gold Rum
1 tsp. powdered sugar
1 dash Angostura Bitters
2 dashes vanilla extract
2 pinches nutmeg
Fill with hot milk

HOT TIMES
Presentation shot glass
Build in glass
1/4 fill DeKuyper Pucker Sour Apple
1/4 fill Cinnamon Schnapps
1/4 fill Light Rum
1/4 fill hot apple cider

HOT TODDY
Coffee mug, heated
Build in glass
1 1/2 oz. Brandy
1 tsp. sugar
Fill with hot water
Lemon twist garnish
Note: May be requested made
    with Bourbon

HOT TROPICO MAMA
Cocktail glass, chilled
Pour ingredients into iced mixing glass
3/4 oz. RémyRed Strawberry Kiwi Infusion
3/4 oz. Crème de Banana
3/4 oz. Triple Sec
1 1/4 oz. orange juice
1 1/4 oz. half & half cream
Shake and strain
Sprinkle shaved chocolate

HOUNDSTOOTH
Rocks glass, ice
Build in glass
1 1/2 oz. Vodka
1/2 oz. White Crème de Cacao
1/2 oz. Blackberry Brandy

HOURGLASS
Cocktail glass, chilled
Pour ingredients into iced mixing glass
1 1/4 oz. Irish Whiskey
1 oz. orange juice
1 oz. cranberry juice
Shake and strain
Lime wheel garnish

HULA SKIRT
Brandy snifter, ice
Pour ingredients into iced mixing glass
1 oz. Grand Marnier
1 oz. Cruzan Estate Single Barrel Rum
3/4 oz. pineapple juice
3/4 oz. fresh lime juice
Shake and strain
Lime wedge garnish

HUMMER
House specialty glass, chilled
Pour ingredients into blender
3/4 oz. Gold Rum
3/4 oz. Kahlúa
3/4 oz. Dark Crème de Cacao
2 scoops vanilla ice cream
Blend ingredients (with ice optional)
Float 3/4 oz. Jamaican Rum
Oreo cookie garnish

CÎROC® SNAP FROST VODKA

Introduced in 2002, CÎROC SNAP FROST VODKA is the first and only vodka distilled entirely from grapes. You don't need to know how many international awards it has already earned to know that you're in the presence of something genuinely special.

Made in Gaillac, France, Cîroc is distilled from two revered varieties of grapes, namely the Mauzac Blanc and Ugni Blanc. The latter is the principal grape variety used to make cognac. The "snap-frost" Mauzac grapes are grown in high elevations and are picked late in the season, allowing them to attain a higher sugar content and fuller, fresher grape character. The grapes are cold macerated and cold fermented prior to being distilled five times in traditional copper pot stills. It is rigorously filtered and bottled at 80 proof.

If you haven't experienced Cîroc first-hand, be prepared to be wowed. The vodka is crystal clear with a luxuriously supple body. Its nose is unique among vodkas, a wafting array of spice, tangy citrus and freshly picked grapes. The vodka immediately fills the mouth with warm, spicy flavors that linger on the palate for an impressively long time.

While there are a few other world-class, pot-distilled vodkas, none seem to match Cîroc's exuberant personality. Do nothing with this vodka until you've had the pleasure of tasting it slightly chilled.

HUNTER'S COFFEE
Coffee mug, heated
Build in glass
3/4 oz. Tia Maria
3/4 oz. Cointreau
Near fill with hot coffee
Whipped cream garnish
Drizzle 1/2 oz. Tia Maria

HURRICANE (1)
House specialty glass, ice
Pour ingredients into iced mixing glass
1 1/2 oz. Light Rum
1 1/2 oz. Gold Rum
1/2 oz. Rose's Lime Juice
1/2 oz. simple syrup
1/2 oz. grenadine
2 oz. orange juice
2 oz. pineapple juice
Shake and strain
Lime, lemon and orange wedge garnish

HURRICANE (2)
House specialty glass, ice
Pour ingredients into iced mixing glass
1 1/2 oz. Light Rum
1 1/2 oz. Gold Rum
1/2 oz. simple syrup
1 1/2 oz. passion fruit juice or nectar
1 1/2 oz. fresh lime juice
1 1/2 oz. pineapple juice
Shake and strain
Float 3/4 oz. Overproof Rum
Lime, lemon and orange wedge garnish

IACOCCA
Cappuccino cup, heated
Build in glass
3/4 oz. Kahlúa
1/2 oz. Grand Marnier
1/2 oz. Baileys Irish Cream
Near fill with hot espresso coffee
Top with frothed milk
Drizzle 1 oz. Frangelico
Sprinkle shaved chocolate

ICE CHOCOLATE
Rocks glass, chilled
Build in glass
1 oz. Rumple Minze Schnapps
1 oz. Godiva Chocolate Liqueur

ICE CREAM BELLINI
House specialty glass, chilled
Pour ingredients into blender
2 scoops peach ice cream
4-5 frozen peach slices
5 oz. ginger ale
Blend ingredients (with ice optional)
Fill with Champagne
Peach wedge garnish

ICEBERG (1)
Rocks glass, ice
Build in glass
1 1/2 oz. Vodka
3/4 oz. Peppermint Schnapps

ICEBERG (2)
Rocks glass, ice
Build in glass
1 1/2 oz. Vodka
3/4 oz. Pernod

ICED TEA, AFTERBURNER
House specialty glass, ice
Pour ingredients into iced mixing glass
1/2 oz. Gin
1/2 oz. Vodka
1/2 oz. Rum
1/2 oz. Tequila
1/2 oz. Triple Sec
2 oz. sweet 'n' sour
2 oz. cola
Shake and strain
Float 3/4 oz. 151° Rum

ICED TEA, ALASKAN
House specialty glass, ice
Pour ingredients into iced mixing glass
1/2 oz. Gin
1/2 oz. Vodka
1/2 oz. Light Rum
1/2 oz. Blue Curaçao
4 oz. sweet 'n' sour
Shake and strain
Fill with Seven-Up
Lemon wedge garnish

ICED TEA, BIMINI
House specialty glass, ice
Pour ingredients into iced mixing glass
1/2 oz. Gin
1/2 oz. Vodka
1/2 oz. Light Rum
1/2 oz. Tequila
1/2 oz. Blue Curaçao
2 oz. orange juice
2 oz. pineapple juice
1 1/2 oz. sweet 'n' sour
2 oz. cola
Shake and strain
Lemon wedge garnish

ICED TEA, BLUE KANGAROO
House specialty glass, ice
Pour ingredients into iced mixing glass
1/2 oz. Gin
1/2 oz. Vodka
1/2 oz. Light Rum
1/2 oz. Tequila
1/2 oz. Blue Curaçao
2 oz. sweet 'n' sour
Shake and strain
1/2 fill Seven-Up
1/2 fill club soda
Lemon wedge garnish

ICED TEA, CALIFORNIA
House specialty glass, ice
Pour ingredients into iced mixing glass
1/2 oz. Tanqueray Gin
1/2 oz. Vox Vodka
1/2 oz. Bacardi Light Rum
1/2 oz. Sauza Hornitos Tequila
1/2 oz. Triple Sec
1 oz. cola
2 oz. sweet 'n' sour
2 oz. grapefruit juice
Shake and strain
Lemon wedge garnish

ICED TEA, DIRTY ASHTRAY
House specialty glass, ice
Pour ingredients into iced mixing glass
1/2 oz. Gin
1/2 oz. Vodka
1/2 oz. Light Rum
1/2 oz. Tequila
1/2 oz. Blue Curaçao
1/2 oz. grenadine
1 1/2 oz. pineapple juice
2 oz. sweet 'n' sour
Shake and strain
Lemon wedge garnish

ICED TEA, FLORIDA
House specialty glass, ice
Pour ingredients into iced mixing glass
1/2 oz. Gin
1/2 oz. Vodka
1/2 oz. Light Rum
1/2 oz. Tequila
1/2 oz. Triple Sec
1 oz. cola
2 oz. sweet 'n' sour
2 oz. orange juice
Shake and strain
Lemon wedge garnish

PATRÓN® XO CAFÉ
COFFEE LIQUEUR

It is estimated that more than 400 billion cups of coffee are consumed each year, easily making it the world's most popular beverage. A large percentage of those cups of Joe are consumed here in the United States. In fact, America is the largest coffee-consuming nation in the world, making super-premium PATRÓN XO CAFÉ COFFEE LIQUEUR the right product at the right time.

Imported by the same folks who make Patrón 100% Blue Agave Tequila, XO Café is made in Mexico from well aged añejo tequila and pure, natural essence of coffee. The 70 proof liqueur is crafted with the barest minimum of sweetener, which makes it more of a coffee-flavored tequila than a typical liqueur.

Patrón XO Café is a luscious, thoroughly satisfying product that has already developed a considerable following. It has a velvety smooth, medium-weight body and an engaging bouquet of cocoa, vanilla and freshly roasted coffee. Its surprisingly dry palate fills the mouth with the balanced flavors of coffee and mellow aged tequila. The liqueur is long and memorable.

Patrón XO Café is an excellent twist on the conventional. The marriage of tequila and coffee is brilliant, making it a superb ingredient in a wide array of contemporary cocktails. It is outstanding with everything from vodka and tequila to ice cream and hot chocolate.

ICED TEA, FRONT PARLOR
House specialty glass, ice
Pour ingredients into iced mixing glass
1 oz. Absolut Citron Vodka
1/2 oz. Tanqueray Gin
1/2 oz. Bacardi Light Rum
1/2 oz. Cointreau
1/2 oz. fresh lemon juice
2 oz. sweet 'n' sour
2 oz. iced tea
Splash cola
Shake and strain
Lemon wedge garnish

ICED TEA, GEORGIA
House specialty glass, ice
Pour ingredients into iced mixing glass
1/2 oz. Gin
1/2 oz. Vodka
1/2 oz. Light Rum
1/2 oz. Tequila
3/4 oz. Peach Schnapps
2 oz. sweet 'n' sour
2 oz. cola
Shake and strain
Lemon wedge garnish

ICED TEA, GREEN TEA
aka **Green Dinosaur**
House specialty glass, ice
Pour ingredients into iced mixing glass
1/2 oz. Gin
1/2 oz. Vodka
1/2 oz. Rum
1/2 oz. Tequila
1/2 oz. Triple Sec
1 1/2 oz. sweet 'n' sour
1 1/2 oz. cranberry juice
Shake and strain
Float 1 oz. Midori
Lemon wedge garnish

ICED TEA, HAVANA
House specialty glass, ice
Pour ingredients into iced mixing glass
1/2 oz. Brandy
1/2 oz. Golden Dry Rum
1/2 oz. Light Dry Rum
1/2 oz. Triple Sec
1 1/2 oz. orange juice
1 1/2 oz. sweet 'n' sour
1 1/2 oz. cola
Shake and strain
Lemon wedge garnish

ICED TEA, HAWAIIAN
House specialty glass, ice
Pour ingredients into iced mixing glass
1/2 oz. Gin
1/2 oz. Vodka
1/2 oz. Light Rum
1/2 oz. Tequila
1/2 oz. Triple Sec
1 oz. cola
2 oz. sweet 'n' sour
2 oz. pineapple juice
Shake and strain
Lemon wedge garnish

ICED TEA, ITALIAN
House specialty glass, ice
Pour ingredients into iced mixing glass
1/2 oz. Gin
1/2 oz. Vodka
1/2 oz. Light Rum
1/2 oz. Triple Sec
2 oz. sweet 'n' sour
2 oz. cola
Shake and strain
Float 3/4 oz. Disaronno Amaretto
Lemon wedge garnish

ICED TEA, JESSE'S SHOCKING
House specialty glass, ice
Pour ingredients into iced mixing glass
1/2 oz. Citrus Vodka
1/2 oz. Citrus Rum
1/2 oz. Orange Rum
1/2 oz. Chambord
1/2 oz. Cointreau
2 oz. sweet 'n' sour
2 oz. Seven-Up
Shake and strain
Lemon wedge garnish

ICED TEA, LONG BEACH
House specialty glass, ice
Pour ingredients into iced mixing glass
1/2 oz. Gin
1/2 oz. Vodka
1/2 oz. Light Rum
1/2 oz. Tequila
1/2 oz. Triple Sec
1 oz. cola
2 oz. cranberry juice
2 oz. sweet 'n' sour
Shake and strain
Lemon wedge garnish

ICED TEA, LONG ISLAND
aka **Texas Iced Tea**
House specialty glass, ice
Pour ingredients into iced mixing glass
1/2 oz. Gin
1/2 oz. Vodka
1/2 oz. Light Rum
1/2 oz. Tequila
1/2 oz. Triple Sec
2 oz. sweet 'n' sour
2 oz. cola
Shake and strain
Lemon wedge garnish

ICED TEA, MANHATTAN
House specialty glass, ice
Pour ingredients into iced mixing glass
1/2 oz. Gin
1/2 oz. Vodka
1/2 oz. Light Rum
1/2 oz. Tequila
2 oz. cola
2 oz. sweet 'n' sour
Shake and strain
Float 3/4 oz. Bourbon
Lemon wedge garnish

ICED TEA, PLANTATION
House specialty glass, ice
Pour ingredients into iced mixing glass
1/2 oz. Gin
1/2 oz. Vodka
1/2 oz. Light Rum
1/2 oz. Tequila
1/2 oz. Triple Sec
2 oz. sweet 'n' sour
2 oz. iced tea
Splash cola
Shake and strain
Lemon wedge garnish

ICED TEA, RASPBERRY
aka **Grateful Dead**, **Purple Haze**
House specialty glass, ice
Pour ingredients into iced mixing glass
1/2 oz. Gin
1/2 oz. Vodka
1/2 oz. Light Rum
1/2 oz. Tequila
1/2 oz. Triple Sec
2 oz. sweet 'n' sour
2 oz. cola
Shake and strain
Float 3/4 oz. Chambord
Lemon wedge garnish

SAUZA® CONMEMORATIVO® AÑEJO TEQUILA

Long before tequila became trendy, the brand of choice for aficionados and connoisseurs alike was SAUZA CONMEMORATIVO AÑEJO. Introduced in 1968, this super-premium embodies all of the characteristics great tequila should possess.

Sauza Conmemorativo is a *mixto* tequila, meaning that it is blended with a minimum of 51% agave. Being an extended-aged añejo, the brand is aged in wood longer than most 100% agave tequilas. Sauza matures the tequila for two years in small, white American oak barrels called *barricas de roble*.

Sauza Conmemorativo Añejo is a classically structured tequila. It has an expansive bouquet laced with the aromas of pepper, caramel and a hint of oak. In the mouth, the tequila has a full, rounded body that delivers a savory complex of semisweet flavors of vanilla, citrus and fruit with undertones of white pepper and toasty oak. It has a long, palate-warming finish.

While most purists would rightfully contend that Conmemorativo Añejo is best appreciated neat, those same purists will savor what this tequila contributes to a Margarita. It blossoms in the cocktail, adding a seemingly endless array of flavors. So don't consider using Conmemorativo Añejo in a Margarita as diluting a great tequila, think of it rather as an artistic stroke of genius.

ICED TEA, SPICED
House specialty glass, ice
Pour ingredients into iced mixing glass
1 oz. Spiced Rum
1/2 oz. Gin
1/2 oz. Vodka
1/2 oz. Tequila
3/4 oz. Triple Sec
2 oz. sweet 'n' sour
2 oz. lemon-lime soda
Shake and strain
Lemon wedge garnish

ICED TEA, STRAWBERRY
House specialty glass, ice
Pour ingredients into iced mixing glass
1/2 oz. Gin
1/2 oz. Vodka
1/2 oz. Rum
1/2 oz. Tequila
1/2 oz. Triple Sec
2 oz. sweet 'n' sour
2 oz. strawberry puree
Shake and strain
Splash cola
Lemon wedge garnish

ICED TEA, SWEDISH
House specialty glass, ice
Pour ingredients into iced mixing glass
1 oz. Absolut Kurant Vodka
1/2 oz. Gin
1/2 oz. Light Rum
1/2 oz. Tequila
3/4 oz. Triple Sec
2 oz. sweet 'n' sour
2 oz. lemon-lime soda
Shake and strain
Lemon wedge garnish

ICED TEA, TAHITI
House specialty glass, ice
Pour ingredients into iced mixing glass
1/2 oz. Gin
1/2 oz. Vodka
1/2 oz. Rum
1/2 oz. Tequila
1/2 oz. Triple Sec
1 oz. sweet 'n' sour
1 1/2 oz. orange juice
1 1/2 oz. pineapple juice
Shake and strain
Lemon wedge garnish

ICED TEA, TERMINAL
aka **Terminal Tea**
House specialty glass, ice
Pour ingredients into iced mixing glass
1/2 oz. Jose Cuervo Especial Tequila
1/2 oz. Smirnoff Vodka
1/2 oz. Tanqueray Gin
1/2 oz. Bacardi Light Rum
1/2 oz. Grand Marnier
2 oz. sweet 'n' sour
2 oz. cola
Shake and strain
Lemon wedge garnish

ICED TEA, TEXAS
House specialty glass, ice
Pour ingredients into iced mixing glass
3/4 oz. Light Rum
3/4 oz. Vodka
1/2 oz. Gin
1/2 oz. Grand Marnier
2 oz. cranberry juice
1 1/2 oz. pineapple juice
1 1/2 oz. orange juice
Shake and strain

ICED TEA, TROPICAL
House specialty glass, ice
Pour ingredients into iced mixing glass
1/2 oz. Gin
1/2 oz. Vodka
1/2 oz. Rum
1/2 oz. Tequila
1/2 oz. Triple Sec
1/2 oz. grenadine
1 oz. sweet 'n' sour
1 oz. pineapple juice
1 oz. cranberry juice
Shake and strain
Lemon wedge garnish

ICED TEA, VERANDA
House specialty glass, ice
Pour ingredients into iced mixing glass
1 oz. Citrus Vodka
1/2 oz. Gin
1/2 oz. Light Rum
1/2 oz. Triple Sec
1/2 oz. fresh lemon juice
2 oz. sweet 'n' sour
2 oz. iced tea
Splash cola
Shake and strain
Lemon wedge garnish

ICE PICK ICED TEA
Bucket glass, ice
Build in glass
1 1/4 oz. Vodka
Fill with lemon-flavored iced tea
Lemon wedge garnish

IDEAL COCKTAIL
Cocktail glass, chilled
Pour ingredients into iced mixing glass
1 1/2 oz. Gin
1/2 oz. Dry Vermouth
1 dash simple syrup
1 oz. grapefruit juice
Shake and strain

IL DUCE
House specialty glass, chilled
Rim glass with cinnamon and
    sugar (optional)
Pour ingredients into blender
1/2 oz. Baileys Irish Cream
1/2 oz. Frangelico
1/2 oz. Kahlúa
3 oz. espresso coffee
2 scoops vanilla ice cream
Blend ingredients
Whipped cream garnish
Dust powdered cocoa

IMPERIAL DUO
Champagne glass, chilled
Pour ingredients into iced mixing glass
1 1/2 oz. VS Cognac
3/4 oz. Chambord
1/4 oz. Godiva Chocolate Liqueur
2 oz. sweet 'n' sour
Shake and strain
Lemon twist garnish

IMPERIAL FUZZ
Champagne glass, chilled
Build in glass
1 1/2 oz. Peach Schnapps
2 oz. orange juice
Fill with Champagne
Orange slice and cherry garnish

INDEPENDENCE SWIZZLE
House specialty glass, crushed ice
Build in glass
1 1/2 oz. Appleton Estate V/X Jamaica Rum
3 dashes Angostura Bitters
1/4 oz. honey
1/2 oz. simple syrup
1 oz. fresh lime juice
Swizzle thoroughly with spoon
    until glass frosts
Lime wedge garnish

CHRISTIAN BROTHERS®
BRANDY

CHRISTIAN BROTHERS BRANDY is one of the oldest and best-selling American spirits. In 1882, the religious order of the Christian Brothers began distilling brandy from California grapes. Their commitment was and remains to create singularly light, flavorful brandies using locally grown grape varietals.

The Christian Brothers winery and adjacent distillery is a huge, state of the art complex located in the fertile San Joaquin Valley in California. Despite the innovations the Christian Brothers have built into their facility, little has changed in their artisan approach to making brandy.

The Christian Brothers selected the Thompson Seedless grape as the principal variety, because they possess the sought after qualities of high acidity, balanced flavor and low alcohol output. They distill their brandies in huge, copper alembic stills, as well as extremely efficient patent stills. Prior to blending, the brandies are aged in American white oak bourbon barrels a minimum of 4 to 6 years.

The enormously popular Christian Brothers Brandy has a tempting, fruity bouquet and a soft, supple texture. The full body is imbued with layers of well-balanced fruit flavors. Its finish is warm and lingering.

Superb also is the CHRISTIAN BROTHERS XO RARE RESERVE, a 6 year old blend containing a high percentage of pot-distilled brandies.

INFUSION, ALIEN SECRETION
Large covered jar
Steep in jar
Fill 1/2 full with pineapples,
    peeled and sliced
Fill 1/2 full with Midori (1/2 - 1 1/2 liters)
Fill with Malibu Caribbean Rum
    (1/2 - 1 1/2 liters)
Taste test after 3-4 days

INFUSION, ASTRAL APRICOT
Large covered jar
Steep in jar
Fill 1/2 full with apricots, pitted and halved
Add 4 cinnamon sticks
Add 2 vanilla beans
Fill with Vodka (1/2 - 2 liters)
Float 2 naval orange slices
Taste test after 4-5 days

INFUSION, BARRIER REEF
Large covered jar
Steep in jar
Fill 1/2 full with pineapples,
    peeled and sliced
Fill 1/4 full with cantaloupe,
    peeled and sliced
Fill 1/4 full with honey dew melon,
    peeled and sliced
Add 3 cups maraschino cherries
Fill with Light Rum (1/2 - 2 liters)
Taste test after 2-3 days

INFUSION, BEACH
Large covered jar
Steep in jar
Fill 1/2 full with pineapples,
    peeled and sliced
Fill 1/2 full with cranberries, fresh or frozen
Add Peach Schnapps (5 - 10 oz.)
Fill 1/2 full with Vodka (1/2 - 1 liter)
Fill with Midori (1/2 - 1 liter)
Taste test after 3-4 days

INFUSION, BEEFEATER
BLOODY CAESAR
Large covered jar
Steep in jar
Fill 1/2 full with sun-dried tomatoes
Fill 1/3 full with celery, cut into stalks
Add clam juice (5-10 oz.)
Add 3 tbsp. seasoned salt
Add 4 oz. Tabasco Sauce
Add Bloody Mary mix (8 - 16 oz.)
Fill with Beefeater London Dry Gin
    (1/2 - 1 liter)
Float lime wheels (3-4 limes)
Taste test after 3-4 days

INFUSION, BEEFEATER DELI
Large covered jar
Steep in jar
Fill 1/3 full with sun-dried tomatoes
Fill 1/3 full with large olives
Add 6 oz. sliced garlic
Add 6 oz. whole dill
Add 4 large red onions, peeled and sliced
Fill with Beefeater London Dry Gin
   (1/2 - 1 liter)
Taste test after 3-4 days

INFUSION, BRAZILIAN DAIQUIRI
Large covered jar
Steep in jar
Fill with pineapples, peeled and sliced
Add 3 vanilla beans
Add 1 cup brown sugar
Fill 1/3 full with Light Rum (1/2 - 1 liter)
Fill 1/3 full with Gold Rum (1/2 - 1 liter)
Fill with Dark Rum (1/2 - 1 liter)
Taste test after 4-5 days

INFUSION, CHERRY BOMB
Large covered jar
Steep in jar
Fill with maraschino cherries
   (1/2 - 1 gallon)
Add 3 vanilla beans
Fill with Light Rum (1 - 3 liters)
Taste test after 3-4 days

INFUSION, COSMIC COCONUT
Large covered jar
Steep in jar
Fill with pineapples, peeled and sliced
Add 8 oz. grated coconut
Fill with Vodka (1/2 - 3 liters)
Float sliced navel oranges (3-6 oranges)
Taste test after 3-4 days

INFUSION, ICE BLUE MARGARITA
Large covered jar
Steep in jar
Fill 1/3 full with lemons, sliced
Fill 1/6 full with limes, sliced
Fill 1/6 full with oranges, sliced
Fill with Tequila (1 liter)
Fill with Midori (1 liter)
Add 10 oz. Blue Curaçao
Taste test after 2-3 days
Note: Mix equal parts of infusion with
   sweet 'n' sour, shake and serve

INFUSION, LEMONEATER
Large covered jar
Steep in jar
Fill 1/3 full with lemons, sliced
Fill 1/3 full with limes, sliced
Fill 1/3 full with oranges, sliced
Add 6 oz. simple syrup
Add 16 oz. Triple Sec
Fill with Gin (2-3 liters)
Taste test after 3-4 days

INFUSION, LEMONTREE MARGARITA
Large covered jar
Steep in jar
Fill 1/4 full with lemons, sliced
Fill 1/4 full with limes, sliced
Fill 1/4 full with oranges, sliced
Add 16 oz. Triple Sec
Add 6 oz. simple syrup
Fill with Silver Tequila (1-2 liters)
Taste test after 3-4 days
Note: Mix equal parts of infusion with
   sweet 'n' sour, shake and serve

INFUSION, LIME LIGHTS
Large covered jar
Steep in jar
Fill 1/2 full with kiwis, peeled and sliced
Fill 1/2 full with limes, sliced
Fill with Vodka (1-3 liters)
Taste test after 2-3 days

INFUSION, LIME-TEQUILA
Large covered jar
Steep in jar
Fill 1/3 full with limes, sliced
Fill 1/3 full with oranges, sliced
Add 6 oz. simple syrup
Fill with Silver Tequila (1-2 liters)
Taste test after 2-3 days

INFUSION, LUMBERJACK
Large covered jar
Steep in jar
Fill with apples, cored and sliced
Add 4 vanilla beans
Add 12 cloves
Fill with Canadian Club Whisky (1-3 liters)
Taste test after 3-4 days

INFUSION, MARS MANGO
Large covered jar
Steep in jar
Fill 3/4 full with mangos, peeled and cubed
Fill 1/4 full with limes, sliced
Fill with Vodka (1-3 liters)
Taste test after 1-2 days
Note: See Mango Bloody Mary for
   serving suggestions

L'ESPRIT® DE COURVOISIER® COGNAC

The distinguished House of Courvoisier began making brandies in the mid-18th century and soon became the favorite of Napoléon Bonaparte and his court. In 1869, Chateau Courvoisier was honored as the "Purveyor by Special Appointment to the Court of Napoléon III." The brand's ascendancy into preeminence reached a pinnacle with the creation of L'ESPRIT DE COURVOISIER COGNAC.

Made in the heart of Jarnac, France, L'Esprit de Courvoisier is arguably the finest, most exclusive brandy ever created. It is handcrafted from the finest brandies distilled in the premiere *crus*, or growing regions. The brandies are double-distilled in small copper alembic stills and cellared in handmade Limousin and Tronçais oak barrels.

L'Esprit de Courvoisier is comprised of brandies from the finest vintages in the past centuries, some exceeding 200 years in age. The youngest constituent brandy is from 1930, while the oldest is from the vintage of 1802.

L'Esprit is certainly the finest, most complex brandy to grace a snifter. Hand packaged in a stunning Lalique crystal decanter, the brandy has a wafting bouquet saturated with fruity aromas. The full, satiny textured brandy glides over the palate and slowly fades into a luxuriously flavorful finish. L'Esprit de Courvoisier is an extraordinary achievement, one worthy of a museum exhibition.

INFUSION, PEPPER-TEQUILA
aka **Sonoran Spittoon Infusion**
Large covered jar
Steep in jar
Fill 1/4 full with red bell peppers, sliced
Fill 1/4 full with green bell peppers, sliced
Fill 1/4 full with yellow bell peppers, sliced
Add 4-6 jalapeño peppers
Add 1 serrano chile
Fill with Gold Tequila (1-2 liters)
Taste test after 2-3 days

INFUSION, PINEAPPLE PURPLE PASSION
Large covered jar
Steep in jar
Fill with pineapples, peeled and sliced
Add 10 oz. Blue Curaçao
Add 10 oz. grenadine
Fill with Vodka (1-3 liters)
Taste test after 3-4 days

INFUSION, PLANETARY PINEAPPLE
Large covered jar
Steep in jar
Fill 3/4 full with pineapples, peeled and sliced
Add 2 pints raspberries, washed
Fill with Vodka (1-3 liters)
Taste test after 6-7 days

INFUSION, POOL WATER
Large covered jar
Steep in jar
Fill 3/4 full with pineapples, peeled and sliced
Fill 1/4 full with oranges, sliced
Add 10 oz. Peach Schnapps
Fill with Midori (1-2 liters)
Taste test after 3-4 days

INFUSION, ROXBURY PINEAPPLE
Large covered jar
Steep in jar
Fill with pineapples, peeled and sliced
Add 1 cup sugar
Fill with Vodka (1-3 liters)
Taste test after 2-3 days

INFUSION, SICILIAN MARTINI
Large covered jar
Steep in jar
16-24 garlic cloves, peeled, crushed and wrapped in cheese cloth
Add 10 oz. Dry Vermouth
Fill with Vodka (1-3 liters)
Taste test after 24 hours
Note: See Sicilian Martini (1) for serving suggestions

INFUSION, SKY BLUE
Large covered jar
Steep in jar
Fill with lemons, washed and sliced
Add 1 cup sugar
Fill 1/2 full with Blue Curaçao (1/2 -1 liter)
Taste test after 2-3 days

INFUSION, SONORAN SPITTOON
Large covered jar
Steep in jar
Fill 1/3 full with green bell peppers, sliced
Fill 1/3 full with red bell peppers, sliced
Fill 1/3 full with yellow bell peppers, sliced
Add 8 jalapeño peppers, washed and lanced
Add 4 serrano chiles, washed
Fill with Gold Tequila (1-3 liters)
Taste test after 3-4 days
Note: Remove serrano chilis after desired
  spiciness is achieved

INFUSION, SPICE SATELLITE
Large covered jar
Steep in jar
Fill with hard apples, cored and sliced
Add 5 cinnamon sticks
Add raisins (1/2 - 1 lb.)
Fill with Vodka (1-3 liters)
Taste test after 6-7 days

INFUSION, SUMMER
SHADES MARGARITA
Large covered jar
Steep in jar
Fill 1/5 full with pineapples,
  peeled and sliced
Fill 1/5 full with cantaloupe,
  peeled and sliced
Fill 1/5 full with strawberries
Fill 1/5 full with peaches, pitted and sliced
Fill 1/2 full with Gold Tequila (1/2 - 1 liter)
Fill 1/2 full with Midori (1/2 - 1 liter)
Add 10 oz. Blue Curaçao
Taste test after 4-5 days
Note: Mix equal parts of infusion with
  sweet 'n' sour, shake and serve

INFUSION, VENUS VANILLA
Large covered jar
Steep in jar
Fill 1/2 full with peaches, pitted and sliced
Fill 1/2 full with nectarines,
  pitted and sliced
Add 2 vanilla beans
Fill with Vodka (1-3 liters)
Taste test after 4-5 days

INFUSION, VODKA CROCODILE
Large covered jar
Steep in jar
Fill 3/4 full with lemons, sliced
Add 1 liter Midori
Fill with Vodka (1-3 liters)
Taste test after 2-3 days

INOCULATION
Presentation shot glass, chilled
Layer ingredients
3/4 fill Chilled Peppermint Schnapps
1/4 fill Brandy

INSTANT CARMA
Rocks glass, chilled
Build in glass
3/4 oz. Grey Goose La Vanille Vodka
3/4 oz. Baileys Irish Cream
3/4 oz. Frangelico
3/4 oz. Kahlúa Especial

INSTANT KARMA
House specialty glass, ice
Pour ingredients into iced mixing glass
2 oz. Kuya Fusion Rum
1 oz. Stolichnaya Citros Vodka
1/4 oz. fresh lime juice
1 oz. pineapple juice
1 oz. grapefruit juice
1 oz. sweet 'n' sour
Shake and strain
Pineapple wedge garnish

INTERNATIONAL AFFAIR
Coffee mug, heated
Build in glass
1/2 oz. Grand Marnier
1/2 oz. Baileys Irish Cream
1/2 oz. Calvados Apple Brandy
Near fill with hot coffee
Whipped cream garnish
Dust powdered cocoa

INTERNATIONAL CAPPUCCINO
Cappuccino cup, heated
Build in glass
1/2 oz. Kahlúa Especial
1/2 oz. Disaronno Amaretto
1/2 oz. Vandermint Liqueur
1/2 oz. Baileys Irish Cream
Near fill with hot espresso coffee
Top with frothed milk
Sprinkle shaved chocolate

INTERNATIONAL DREAM
Presentation shot glass, chilled
Build in glass
1/4 fill Kahlúa
1/4 fill Godiva Chocolate Liqueur
1/4 fill Goldschläger
1/4 fill Cinnamon Schnapps

LIQUID ICE® VODKA

Few really extraordinary vodkas are distilled in the United States. The most notable exception is LIQUID ICE VODKA. This world-class performer is handcrafted at the Silver Creek Distillery in Rigby, Idaho. Situated by the western slopes of the Grand Teton Mountains, the award winning distillery has mastered the art and science of distillation and makes spirits as pristine as its surroundings.

Liquid Ice Vodka is quadruple-distilled entirely from a blend of five, certified organic grains—wheat, oat, barley, corn and rye. The grains are non-genetically modified and are scrutinized for uncompromised quality.

The all-important spring water used in the production of Liquid Ice Vodka is drawn from a 200-foot deep aquifer fed by the Snake River. The vodka is rigorously filtered three times through charcoal, lava rock and a sub-micron filter rendering it essentially pure. It is bottled at 80 proof.

Liquid Ice is a guaranteed crowd pleaser. The vodka has crystalline clarity and a featherweight body. The bouquet is crisp and refreshing with notes of citrus. It warms the palate with the slightly sweet flavors of grain, chocolate and lemon zest, and then gradually fades into a clean and cool finish.

To fully appreciate how superb this vodka is, sample it straight with a slight chill. After that, the sky's the limit.

INTERNATIONAL STINGER
Rocks glass, ice
Build in glass
1 1/2 oz. Metaxa 5 Star Brandy
3/4 oz. Galliano Liqueur

INTERNATIONAL VELVET CAFÉ
Cappuccino cup, heated
Build in glass
3/4 oz. Citrónge Orange Liqueur
3/4 oz. Patrón XO Café Coffee Liqueur
1/2 oz. Baileys Irish Cream
Near fill with hot espresso coffee
Top with frothed milk
Sprinkle shaved chocolate

IN THE RED
Bucket glass, ice
Build in glass
1 1/2 oz. Corazón Añejo Tequila
1/2 oz. Rose's Lime Juice
Near fill with cranberry juice
Float 1/2 oz. grenadine

INVERTED NAIL
Sherry glass, chilled
Layer ingredients
1/2 fill Drambuie
1/2 fill Glenfiddich Single Malt

I.R.A.
Presentation shot glass, chilled
Layer ingredients
1/4 fill Kahlúa
1/4 fill DeKuyper But4ershots Schnapps
1/4 fill Baileys Irish Cream
1/4 fill Irish Whiskey

IRISH ALEXANDER (1)
Cocktail glass, chilled
Pour ingredients into iced mixing glass
1 oz. Irish Mist
3/4 oz. White Crème de Cacao
2 oz. half & half cream
Shake and strain
Sprinkle nutmeg

IRISH ALEXANDER (2)
Cocktail glass, chilled
Pour ingredients into iced mixing glass
1 1/2 oz. Irish Whiskey
3/4 oz. Dark Crème de Cacao
3/4 oz. Triple Sec
1 1/2 oz. half & half cream
Shake and strain
Sprinkle nutmeg

IRISH AMERICAN
Tankard or pilsner glass, chilled
Build in glass
1/2 fill Guinness Stout
1/2 fill Budweiser

IRISH BOGGLE
Coffee mug, heated
Build in glass
1 oz. Knappogue Castle Irish Whiskey
1 oz. Celtic Crossing Irish Liqueur
1/2 oz. Kahlúa Especial
Near fill with hot coffee
Top with whipped cream
Dust powdered cocoa

IRISH BROGUE
Rocks glass, ice
Build in glass
1 1/2 oz. Jameson Irish Whiskey
3/4 oz. Irish Mist

IRISH CAR BOMB
Shot glass and tankard or
   pilsner glass, chilled
Build in shot glass
1 oz. Baileys Irish Cream
1 oz. Jameson Irish Whiskey
Build in tankard or pilsner glass
3/4 fill Guinness Stout
Drop shot glass of Baileys and Jameson
   into Guinness

IRISH CHOCOLATE KISS
Cocktail glass, chilled
Pour ingredients into iced mixing glass
2 oz. Van Gogh Chocolate Vodka
1 oz. Baileys Irish Cream
1/2 oz. Green Crème de Menthe
1/2 oz. White Crème de Cacao
Shake and strain
Orange slice garnish

IRISH-CHOCO-ORANGE
Cocktail glass, chilled
Pour ingredients into iced mixing glass
1 1/2 oz. Irish Whiskey
3/4 oz. Godiva Chocolate Liqueur
3/4 oz. Orange Liqueur
3/4 oz. Baileys Irish Cream
Shake and strain
Shaved chocolate garnish

IRISH COFFEE
Coffee mug, heated
Build in glass
1 1/4 oz. Irish Whiskey
1/2 oz. simple syrup
Near fill with hot coffee
Top with frothed milk or
   whipped cream garnish

IRISH COFFEE ROYALE (1)
Coffee mug, heated
Build in glass
1 1/4 oz. Irish Whiskey
1 oz. Kahlúa
1/2 oz. simple syrup
Near fill with hot coffee
Top with frothed milk or
   whipped cream garnish

IRISH COFFEE ROYALE (2)
Coffee mug, heated
Build in glass
1 1/4 oz. Irish Whiskey
3/4 oz. Baileys Irish Cream
1/2 oz. Irish Mist
Near fill with hot coffee
Top with frothed milk or
   whipped cream garnish

IRISH DISH
Cocktail glass, chilled
Pour ingredients into iced mixing glass
2 oz. Irish Whiskey
3/4 oz. Irish Mist
Stir and strain
Lemon twist garnish

IRISH FLOAT
Beer mug, chilled
Pour ingredients into blender
1 oz. Baileys Irish Cream
1 oz. Butterscotch Schnapps
2 scoops vanilla ice cream
Blend ingredients (with ice optional)
Fill with root beer

IRISH HEADLOCK
Rocks glass, chilled
Pour ingredients into iced mixing glass
1/2 oz. Baileys Irish Cream
1/2 oz. Irish Whiskey
1/2 oz. Disaronno Amaretto
1/2 oz. Brandy
Shake and strain

IRISH LEMONADE
Bucket glass, ice
Build in glass
1 oz. Boru Vodka
1 oz. Celtic Crossing Liqueur
Fill with lemonade
Lemon slice garnish

IRISH MARIA
Rocks glass, ice
Build in glass
1 oz. Tia Maria
1 oz. Baileys Irish Cream

LIMONCÈ®
LIQUORE DI LIMONI

Italy is well known for crafting some of the finest products on Earth. While sports cars, leather goods, cheese and wine certainly top the list, the nation is also internationally famous for making *limoncello*, a remarkably light and refreshing liqueur made from lemons. It is standard fare on back bars throughout Europe. Over the past several years, Americans have been discovering how marvelously wonderful these liqueurs can be. An outstanding example of which is LIMONCÈ LIQUORE DI LIMONI.

Made in Trieste, Italy at the renowned Stock Distillery, Limoncè gets its fabulous flavor from sun-drenched lemons grown on the Mediterranean coast. The peels of the fruit are steeped for an extended period of time in pure grain spirits, after which the infused alcohol is filtered and sweetened. The liqueur is bottled at 60 proof.

Limoncè is deserving of the critical acclaim it is receiving. The liqueur looks like freshly squeezed lemonade and has a wafting, lively bouquet with notes of citrus and flora. It has a featherweight body that rolls over the palate and immediately fills the mouth with the zesty, tangy flavor of lemons. It's a vibrant sensation brimming with life and electricity. The lingering finish is warming and bittersweet.

The liqueur is tailor-made for American mixology and can be used to invigorate a wide variety of contemporary cocktails.

IRISH RASPBERRY
House specialty glass, chilled
Pour ingredients into blender
1 1/4 oz. Irish Whiskey
3/4 oz. Chambord
3/4 oz. Baileys Irish Cream
3/4 oz. half & half cream
2 scoops vanilla ice cream
Blend ingredients
Whipped cream and berries garnish
Drizzle 3/4 oz. Kahlúa Especial

IRISH SHILLELAGH
Cocktail glass, chilled
Pour ingredients into iced mixing glass
1 1/2 oz. Irish Whiskey
1/2 oz. Sloe Gin
1/2 oz. Light Rum
1 oz. sweet 'n' sour
Shake and strain
Lemon wedge garnish

IRISH STINGER
Rocks glass, ice
Build in glass
3/4 oz. Irish Whiskey
3/4 oz. Irish Mist
1/2 oz. Peppermint Schnapps

IRISH TEA
Coffee mug, heated
Build in glass
1 oz. Irish Mist
1/2 oz. Irish Whiskey
Fill with hot tea
Lemon wedge garnish

IRISH WISH
Cocktail glass, chilled
Pour ingredients into iced mixing glass
1 3/4 oz. Irish Whiskey
1/2 oz. Sweet Vermouth
1/2 oz. Limoncello Liqueur
Stir and strain
Lemon twist garnish

ISLA DE PIÑOS
House specialty glass, ice
Pour ingredients into iced mixing glass
1 1/2 oz. Light Rum
1 1/2 oz. grapefruit juice
1/2 oz. simple syrup
1/2 oz. grenadine
Shake and strain
Grapefruit slice garnish

ISLAND DITTY
Cocktail glass, chilled
Pour ingredients into iced mixing glass
2 oz. Matusalem Gran Reserva Rum
1/2 oz. Rose's Lime Juice
1/2 oz. fresh lime juice
Shake and strain
Lime wedge garnish

ISLAND DREAM
Cocktail glass, chilled
Pour ingredients into iced mixing glass
2 oz. Cruzan Estate Single Barrel Rum
1 oz. Limoncello Liqueur
2 oz. sweetened lime juice
Shake and strain
Lime wheel garnish

ISLAND FEVER
Cocktail glass, chilled
Pour ingredients into iced mixing glass
1 1/2 oz. Cruzan Estate Single Barrel Rum
1/2 oz. fresh lime juice
1 1/2 oz. sweet 'n' sour
Shake and strain
Lime wedge garnish

ISLAND FLOWER
Cocktail glass, chilled
Pour ingredients into iced mixing glass
2 1/2 oz. Cruzan Estate Single Barrel Rum
1/2 oz. Blue Curaçao
2 dashes Rose's Lime Juice
1/2 oz. fresh lime juice
Stir and strain
Lime wheel garnish

ISLAND SUNSET
House specialty glass, ice
Pour ingredients into iced mixing glass
1 oz. Vodka
1 oz. Malibu Caribbean Rum
3/4 oz. Blue Curaçao
1 oz. pineapple juice
1 oz. orange juice
Shake and strain
Near fill with Seven-Up
Float 3/4 oz. Raspberry Liqueur
Lime wedge and orange slice garnish

ISLAND VOODOO
House specialty glass, chilled
Pour ingredients into blender
1 1/2 oz. VooDoo Spiced Rum
1 1/2 oz. RedRum
2 oz. guava juice
2 oz. mango juice
1/2 oz. fresh lime juice
1/2 oz. fresh lemon juice
Blend ingredients with ice
Pineapple wedge and cherry garnish

ISLEÑA
House specialty glass, ice
Build in glass
1 1/2 oz. Light Rum
1 1/2 oz. pineapple juice
Near fill with Perrier Sparkling Water
Float 1/2 oz. grenadine
Raspberries garnish

ISLE OF PINES
Highball glass, ice
Build in glass
1 1/2 oz. Light Rum
Fill with grapefruit juice

ISTHMUS BUFFALO MILK
House specialty glass, chilled
Pour ingredients into blender
1 1/2 oz. Cruzan Estate Dark Rum
1 1/2 oz. Cruzan Estate Light Rum
3/4 oz. Kahlúa
3/4 oz. Cruzan Banana Rum
1 peeled, ripe banana
1 1/2 oz. milk
3/4 oz. chocolate syrup
Blend with ice
Whipped cream garnish
Sprinkle nutmeg

ITALIAN COFFEE
Coffee mug, heated
Build in glass
3/4 oz. Sambuca
3/4 oz. Disaronno Amaretto
Near fill with hot coffee
Whipped cream garnish

ITALIAN PUNCH
Bucket glass, ice
Build in glass
1 oz. Disaronno Amaretto
1 oz. Bacardi Limón Rum
Fill with cranberry juice

ITALIAN STALLION
Rocks glass, ice
Build in glass
1 1/2 oz. Scotch Whisky
3/4 oz. Galliano Liqueur

ITALIAN STINGER
Rocks glass, ice
Build in glass
1 1/2 oz. Brandy
3/4 oz. Galliano Liqueur

LAIRD'S® 12 YEAR OLD RARE APPLE BRANDY

Crafted at the country's oldest distillery, LAIRD'S APPLEJACK is a venerable American brandy as old as the Republic itself. It is made from tree-ripened apples that are naturally fermented in large, 20,000-gallon oak vats. The impressively pure brandy is double-distilled and then aged a minimum of 4 years in American white oak barrels.

The distillery's crowning achievement is undoubtedly LAIRD'S 12 YEAR OLD RARE APPLE BRANDY, a sumptuous spirit worthy of international recognition and acclaim. Distilled from a blend of five varieties of American apples, the brandy is aged in American white oak barrels for a minimum of 12 years.

This classic American brandy is handcrafted in extremely limited quantity. It has an alluring, expansive bouquet laced with the aromas of fresh fruit. The luscious palate is dominated by the flavors of ripe apples and vanilla that slowly taper off into a lingering, flavorful finish.

Laird's 12 Year Old Apple Brandy is a triumphant accomplishment. It compares favorably with the finest Calvados from Normandy costing 2-3 times as much. Every bottle of 88 proof brandy is hand-filled and inscribed with a batch number, bottling date and bottle number.

This apple brandy is more spirited and exuberant than its French counterpart, Calvados, which brings to mind the phrase, *viva la différence!*

ITALIAN SUNRISE (1)
House specialty glass, ice
Build in glass
1 1/4 oz. Disaronno Amaretto
1 oz. Gold Rum
Near fill with orange juice
Float 1/2 oz. grenadine
Orange wedge garnish

ITALIAN SUNRISE (2)
Bucket glass, ice
Build in glass
1 1/4 oz. Disaronno Amaretto
Near fill with orange juice
Float 3/4 oz. Crème de Cassis

ITALIAN SURFER
Rocks glass, chilled
Pour ingredients into iced mixing glass
3/4 oz. Malibu Caribbean Rum
3/4 oz. Disaronno Amaretto
1 oz. pineapple juice
1 oz. cranberry juice
Shake and strain

ITALIAN VALIUM
Rocks glass, ice
Build in glass
1 1/2 oz. Gin
3/4 oz. Disaronno Amaretto

JACKALOPE
House specialty glass, ice
Pour ingredients into iced mixing glass
1 3/4 oz. Mount Gay Eclipse Rum
3/4 oz. Patrón XO Café Coffee Liqueur
3/4 oz. Disaronno Amaretto
3/4 oz. Dark Crème de Cacao
3 oz. pineapple juice
Shake and strain
Float 3/4 oz. Appleton Estate
    V/X Jamaica Rum
Orange slice garnish

JACKARITA
Cocktail glass, chilled
Pour ingredients into iced mixing glass
1 1/4 oz. Jack Daniel's Tennessee Whiskey
3/4 oz. Gran Gala Orange Liqueur
1 3/4 oz. sweet 'n' sour
Lime wedge garnish
Shake and strain

JACK BENNY
Rocks glass, ice
Build in glass
1 1/2 oz. Jack Daniel's Tennessee Whiskey
1/2 oz. Baileys Irish Cream
1/2 oz. Kahlúa

JACKIE SPECIAL
House specialty glass, ice
Pour ingredients into iced mixing glass
1/2 oz. Vodka
1/2 oz. Malibu Caribbean Rum
1/2 oz. Southern Comfort
1/2 oz. Disaronno Amaretto
1 1/2 oz. pineapple juice
1 1/2 oz. orange juice
Shake and strain
Float 3/4 oz. Raspberry Liqueur
Orange slice and cherry garnish

JACK ROSE COCKTAIL
Cocktail glass, chilled
Pour ingredients into iced mixing glass
1 oz. Laird's Applejack Brandy
1 1/2 oz. sweet 'n' sour
1/2 oz. grenadine
Shake and strain

JACK TAIL
Bucket glass, ice
Pour ingredients into iced mixing glass
1 1/2 oz. Jack Daniel's Tennessee Whiskey
1/2 oz. grenadine
1 1/2 oz. pineapple juice
2 oz. sweet 'n' sour
Shake and strain
Orange slice garnish

JACQUELINE
Cocktail glass, chilled
Pour ingredients into iced mixing glass
2 oz. Bacardi 8 Reserva Rum
3/4 oz. Grand Marnier Centenaire
1/2 oz. Rose's Lime Juice
1 oz. fresh lime juice
Stir and strain
Lime wedge garnish

JADE
Cocktail glass, chilled
Pour ingredients into iced mixing glass
1 1/2 oz. Light Rum
1/2 oz. Triple Sec
1/2 oz. Green Crème de Menthe
1/2 oz. Rose's Lime Juice
Stir and strain
Lime wedge garnish

JÄGERITA
Rocks glass, chilled
Pour ingredients into iced mixing glass
1/2 oz. Jägermeister
1/2 oz. Jose Cuervo Especial Tequila
1/2 oz. Cointreau
3/4 oz. fresh lime juice
Shake and strain
Lime wedge garnish

JÄGER MONSTER
Bucket glass, ice
Build in glass
1 1/4 oz. Jägermeister
1/2 oz. Disaronno Amaretto
Near fill with orange juice
Float 3/4 oz. Razzmatazz Raspberry Liqueur

JÄGER MY WORM
Presentation shot glass, chilled
Build in glass
1/2 fill Jägermeister
1/2 fill Tequila

JAMAICA JUICE
House specialty glass, chilled
Pour ingredients into blender
3/4 oz. Appleton Estate V/X Jamaica Rum
1 oz. pineapple juice
1 oz. orange juice
1 oz. cranberry juice
2 oz. coconut cream syrup
Blend with ice
Float 3/4 oz. Appleton Estate
   V/X Jamaica Rum
Pineapple wedge and cherry garnish

JAMAICA ME CRAZY (1)
Bucket glass, ice
Build in glass
1 1/2 oz. Appleton Estate V/X Jamaica Rum
3/4 oz. Tia Maria
Fill with pineapple juice
Orange slice garnish

JAMAICA ME CRAZY (2)
House specialty glass, chilled
Pour ingredients into blender
1 1/2 oz. Appleton Estate V/X Jamaica Rum
3/4 oz. Blue Curaçao
2 oz. coconut cream syrup
2 oz. pineapple juice
2 oz. orange juice
Blend with ice
Pineapple wedge and cherry garnish

JAMAICAN BARBADOS BOMBER
Rocks glass, chilled
1 3/4 oz. Appleton Estate V/X Jamaica Rum
1 3/4 oz. Mount Gay Eclipse Rum
3/4 oz. Triple Sec
1/2 oz. Rose's Lime Juice
Stir and strain
Lime wedge garnish

SCAPA® SINGLE ORKNEY MALT SCOTCH WHISKY

We are all products of our environment. It's especially true for spirits. The microclimate and local conditions of the distillery significantly influence the overall character of the finished spirit. SCAPA SINGLE ORKNEY MALT SCOTCH WHISKY is a sterling example.

The Scapa Distillery is made near Kirkwall on the island of Orkney. It is situated at roughly the same latitude as Alaska, which makes Orkney the northernmost, whisky producing locale in the world. The microclimate of this cold and wind-swept island is dominated by the North Sea and North Atlantic Ocean.

Scapa Single Malt is crafted in Lomond wash stills using traditional distilling techniques. It is made from unpeated barley malt and pure spring water impregnated with the flavor of peat and sea spray. The whisky is aged for a minimum of 12 years in American oak barrels and bottled at 80 proof.

The character of the island is deeply imbued in this extraordinary whisky. Scapa has a medium body imbued with the fresh aromas of fruit, vanilla and salty sea breeze. The palate is a complex affair that features the flavors of heather honey, flora and caramel. The finish is dry and rather tangy.

Scapa Single Orkney Malt is a classic whisky. It is loaded with charm, finesse and is exceptionally easy to drink. No one can ask more from a dram of malt.

JAMAICAN COFFEE
Coffee mug, heated
Build in glass
1 1/4 oz. Appleton Estate V/X Jamaica Rum
3/4 oz. Tia Maria
Near fill with hot coffee
Whipped cream garnish
Sprinkle shaved chocolate

JAMAICAN CRAWLER
Bucket glass, ice
Pour ingredients into iced mixing glass
1 1/2 oz. Appleton Estate V/X Jamaica Rum
1 1/2 oz. Midori
1/2 oz. grenadine
3 oz. pineapple juice
Shake and strain

JAMAICAN DUST
Presentation shot glass, chilled
Build in glass
1/3 fill Myers's Jamaican Rum
1/3 fill Tia Maria
1/3 fill pineapple juice

JAMAICAN FEVER
House specialty glass, ice
Pour ingredients into iced mixing glass
3/4 oz. Appleton Estate V/X Jamaica Rum
3/4 oz. Brandy
3/4 oz. mango syrup
1 1/2 oz. guava nectar
1 1/2 oz. pineapple juice
Shake and strain
Float 3/4 oz. Appleton Estate
   V/X Jamaica Rum
Pineapple wedge and cherry garnish

JAMAICAN HOLIDAY
Presentation shot glass, chilled
Build in glass
1/3 fill Myers's Jamaican Rum
1/3 fill Tia Maria
1/3 fill Crème de Banana

JAMAICAN ROSE
Cocktail glass, chilled
Pour ingredients into iced mixing glass
1 1/2 oz. Tequila Rose Cream Liqueur
3/4 oz. Appleton Estate V/X Jamaica Rum
3/4 oz. Godiva Chocolate Liqueur
1 1/2 oz. half & half cream
Shake and strain
Sprinkle shaved chocolate

JAMAICAN RUM COW
House specialty glass, chilled
Pour ingredients into blender
3/4 oz. Appleton Estate V/X Jamaica Rum
3/4 oz. Kahlúa Especial
1/2 oz. chocolate syrup
2 dashes Angostura Bitters
2 oz. milk
2 scoops chocolate ice cream
Blend ingredients (with ice optional)
Float 3/4 oz. Appleton Estate
   V/X Jamaica Rum
Pineapple wedge and cherry garnish

JAMAICAN SHAKE
House specialty glass, chilled
Pour ingredients into blender
1 1/4 oz. Appleton Estate V/X Jamaica Rum
3/4 oz. Tia Maria
3/4 oz. Disaronno Amaretto
1 tsp. vanilla extract
2 scoops vanilla ice cream
Blend ingredients (with ice optional)
Whipped cream garnish
Sprinkle shaved chocolate

JAMAICAN SPICE
Bucket glass, ice
Build in glass
1 oz. Appleton Estate V/X Jamaica Rum
1 oz. Captain Morgan Spiced Rum
1/2 oz. Cinnamon Schnapps
Near fill with ginger ale
Float 3/4 oz. Crème de Banana

JAMAICAN TENNIS BEADS
Bucket glass, ice
Pour ingredients into iced mixing glass
1 oz. Appleton Estate V/X Jamaica Rum
3/4 oz. Light Rum
3/4 oz. Midori
3/4 oz. Crème de Banana
3/4 oz. half & half cream
1 oz. pineapple juice
Shake and strain
Float 3/4 oz. Dark Rum

JAMAICAN TEN SPEED
Rocks glass, chilled
Pour ingredients into iced mixing glass
1 1/4 oz. Cruzan Banana Rum
3/4 oz. Midori
3/4 oz. pineapple juice
3/4 oz. cranberry juice
Shake and strain

JAMBA DAY
House specialty glass, chilled
Pour ingredients into blender
3/4 oz. Sauza Conmemorativo
   Añejo Tequila
3/4 oz. RémyRed Red Berry Infusion
1/2 oz. Crème de Banana
1/2 oz. Razzmatazz Raspberry Liqueur
1/2 cup strawberries
1 1/2 oz. sweet 'n' sour
1 1/2 oz. orange juice
Blend with ice
Strawberry garnish

JAMBA JUICE
Bucket glass, ice
Pour ingredients into iced mixing glass
3/4 oz. Captain Morgan Spiced Rum
3/4 oz. Mount Gay Eclipse Rum
1 oz. cranberry juice
1 oz. orange juice
1 oz. pineapple juice
Shake and strain
Float 3/4 oz. Appleton Estate
   V/X Jamaica Rum
Orange slice and cherry garnish

JAMESON CANNES-STYLE
Cocktail glass, chilled
Pour ingredients into iced mixing glass
1 3/4 oz. Jameson Irish Whiskey
1 oz. Crème de Banana
3/4 oz. orange juice
3/4 oz. half & half cream
Shake and strain
Speared banana slice and cherry garnish

JANE'S MILK
Presentation shot glass, chilled
Build in glass
1 oz. Banana Rum
1 oz. Baileys Irish Cream

JAPANESE COCKTAIL
Cocktail glass, chilled
Pour ingredients into iced mixing glass
1 1/2 oz. Brandy
1/2 oz. orgeat syrup
2 dashes Angostura Bitters
Stir and strain
Lemon twist garnish

MOUNT GAY® RUM ECLIPSE®

Mount Gay is quite likely the oldest brand of rum in the world. The renowned spirit is the best-selling rum on Barbados, with nearly 25% of the distillery's output being consumed on the island. The flagship of the company's portfolio, MOUNT GAY RUM ECLIPSE was created in 1910 and its name commemorates the total solar eclipse that occurred that year.

Mount Gay Eclipse is produced from estate grown sugar cane and limestone filtered spring water. It is comprised of a blend of pot still and continuous still rums aged in charred, Kentucky oak barrels for a minimum of 2 years. It is bottled at 80 proof.

Little wonder why Mount Gay Rum Eclipse has gained worldwide renown. It has a luminous, golden amber hue and a compact bouquet with notes of spice, vanilla and oak. The medium body features a complex array of flavors that settle lightly on the palate such that each individual taste can be discerned. Most prominent among its sensational flavors are tropical fruit, caramel and apricot. Eclipse sports a marvelous, semisweet, lingering finish.

The famed distillery also produces the altogether delectable MOUNT GAY EXTRA OLD and has introduced MOUNT GAY VANILLA RUM and MOUNT GAY MANGO RUM. Both rums sport brilliant flavors.

JARDINERA
House specialty glass, chilled
Pour ingredients into blender
2 oz. Tequila
1 oz. Agavero Liqueur
2 oz. coconut cream syrup
2 oz. limeade
1/2 cup pineapple cubes
Blend with ice
Coconut flakes and shaved
  chocolate garnish

JAR JUICE
Mason jar, ice
Build in glass
1 oz. Chambord
1 oz. Vodka
1/2 fill orange juice
1/2 fill pineapple juice

JAUNDICE JUICE
Highball glass, ice
Build in glass
1 1/4 oz. Bourbon
Fill with lemonade

JEALOUSY
House specialty glass, ice
Pour ingredients into iced mixing glass
1 oz. Midori
1 oz. Blue Curaçao
3/4 oz. Bourbon
3/4 oz. Light Rum
3/4 oz. Gin
3/4 oz. Rose's Lime Juice
1 oz. pineapple juice
1 oz. sweet 'n' sour
Shake and strain
Fill with ginger ale
Lemon wedge garnish

JELLY BEAN
Presentation shot glass, chilled
Layer ingredients
1/2 fill Anisette
1/2 fill Blackberry Brandy

JELLY FISH
Presentation shot glass, chilled
Layer ingredients
1/3 fill White Crème de Cacao
1/3 fill Disaronno Amaretto
1/3 fill Baileys Irish Cream
3 drops grenadine in center

JENNY WALLBANGER
Bucket glass, ice
Build in glass
1 oz. Vodka
1/2 fill orange juice
Near fill with half & half cream
Float 3/4 oz. Galliano Liqueur

JERSEY DEVIL
Cocktail glass, chilled
Pour ingredients into iced mixing glass
1 1/2 oz. Laird's Applejack Brandy
1 oz. Cointreau
1/2 oz. simple syrup
1/2 oz. cranberry juice
1/2 oz. Rose's Lime Juice
Stir and strain

JERSEY LILLY
Wine glass, chilled
Pour ingredients into iced mixing glass
5 oz. carbonated apple juice
2 dashes non-alcoholic bitters
1/4 tsp. sugar
Stir and strain
Orange slice and cherry garnish

JERSEY ROOT BEER
aka **Italian Root Beer**
Highball glass, ice
Build in glass
1 1/4 oz. Galliano Liqueur
Fill with cola

JET FUEL (1)
Bucket glass, ice
Build in glass
1/2 oz. 151° Rum
1/2 oz. Coconut Rum
1/2 oz. Naval Rum
1/2 oz. Jamaican Rum
Near fill with pineapple juice
Float 1/2 oz. grenadine
Orange slice garnish

JET FUEL (2)
Presentation shot glass, chilled
Build in glass
1/4 fill Jägermeister
1/4 fill Wild Turkey 101° Bourbon
1/4 fill Rumple Minze Schnapps
1/4 fill Bacardi 151° Rum

JEWEL
Bucket glass, ice
Pour ingredients into iced mixing glass
2 oz. Irish Whiskey
3/4 oz. DeKuyper Peachtree Schnapps
1/2 oz. Blue Curaçao
2 oz. pineapple juice
Shake and strain
Orange slice garnish

JEWEL OF RUSSIA
Champagne glass, chilled
Pour ingredients into iced mixing glass
1 3/4 oz. Stolichnaya Razberi Vodka
1/2 oz. Chambord
3/4 oz. orange juice
1 oz. sweet 'n' sour
Stir and strain
Fill with Champagne
Strawberry garnish

JEWELS AND GOLD
Cocktail glass, chilled
Pour ingredients into iced mixing glass
1 3/4 oz. Vodka
3/4 oz. Goldschläger
3/4 oz. Oro di Mazzetti Grappa Liqueur
Stir and strain
Lemon twist garnish

JOE CANOE
aka **Jonkanov**
Bucket glass, ice
Build in glass
1 oz. Light Rum
Near fill with orange juice
Float 3/4 oz. Galliano Liqueur

JOGGER
Bucket glass, ice
Build in glass
1/2 oz. Rose's Lime Juice
Fill with club soda
1 packet of artificial sweetener (optional)
Lime wedge garnish

JOHN WAYNE
Cocktail glass, chilled
Pour ingredients into iced mixing glass
2 oz. Bourbon
1/2 oz. Disaronno Amaretto
2-3 dashes Angostura Bitters
1/4 oz. orange juice
Shake and strain
Orange slice garnish

JOKE JUICE
Cocktail glass, chilled
Pour ingredients into iced mixing glass
1 1/4 oz. Southern Comfort
1/2 oz. Triple Sec
1/2 oz. Rose's Lime Juice
1/2 oz. sweet 'n' sour
Shake and strain

ULTIMAT® BLACK CHERRY FLAVORED VODKA

When Pablo Picasso was asked what three things astonished him most, his answer was, "the blues, cubism and Polish vodka." One of the finest and most innovative Polish vodkas to enter our country is ULTIMAT BLACK CHERRY FLAVORED VODKA. A few sips of this brilliantly flavored vodka and you'll understand why Picasso was astonished.

Ultimat Black Cherry Vodka is made at the Polmos distillery in Bielsko-Biala, Poland. It is crafted from a distinctive blend of 70% potato, and 15% of wheat and rye, and each contributes its own individual touch to the finished product's bouquet and taste profile. The vodka is then steeped in macerated cherries and filtered for purity. It is bottled at 80 proof.

Ultimat Black Cherry Vodka has crystal clarity and a lush, medium-weight body. The prominent aroma of cherry blossoms seems to fill the glass for a remarkably long time. The vodka rolls over the palate filling the mouth with the dry and thoroughly satisfying flavor of black cherries and spice. This vodka was bred to be cocktail friendly.

Its sibling, ULTIMAT VODKA, is a luxurious spirit made according to the same innovative blend of grains. It has a lively, semisweet bouquet. Even sampled at room temperature the vodka is completely devoid of excess heat. It has a silky body and a marvelously flavorful palate. Its best quality is a long, lingering finish.

JOLLY RANCHER (1)
Rocks glass, chilled
Pour ingredients into iced mixing glass
1/2 oz. Scotch Whisky
1/2 oz. DeKuyper Peach Pucker
1/2 oz. Midori
3/4 oz. Vodka
Shake and strain
Splash Seven-Up

JOLLY RANCHER (2)
Rocks glass, chilled
Pour ingredients into iced mixing glass
3/4 oz. Midori
1/2 oz. Disaronno Amaretto
1/2 oz. Citrus Vodka
1/2 oz. sweet 'n' sour
1/2 oz. pineapple juice
Shake and strain

JOLLY RANCHER (3)
Rocks glass, chilled
Pour ingredients into iced mixing glass
1/2 oz. DeKuyper Pucker Sour Apple
1/2 oz. Midori
3/4 oz. sweet 'n' sour
1/4 oz. pineapple juice
Shake and strain

JUBILEE COCKTAIL
Cocktail glass, chilled
Pour ingredients into iced mixing glass
1 1/2 oz. RémyRed Red Berry Infusion
1 oz. Apricot Brandy
1 oz. fresh lemon juice
Shake and strain
Lemon wheel garnish

JU JU BEE
Rocks glass, chilled
Pour ingredients into iced mixing glass
3/4 oz. Midori
3/4 oz. Vodka
1/2 oz. Malibu Caribbean Rum
Splash cranberry juice
Splash Seven-Up
Shake and strain

JULIA
House specialty glass, chilled
Pour ingredients into blender
1 oz. Light Rum
1 oz. Disaronno Amaretto
1 oz. Cruzan Rum Cream
1/2 cup strawberries
1 oz. sweet 'n' sour
2 scoops vanilla ice cream
Blend ingredients (with ice optional)
Float 3/4 oz. Dark Rum
Strawberry garnish

JULIO'S BUTTERSCOTCH
House specialty glass, chilled
Pour ingredients into blender
1/2 oz. Kahlúa
1/2 oz. Baileys Irish Cream
1/2 oz. DeKuyper Buttershots Schnapps
2 scoops vanilla ice cream
Blend ingredients (with ice optional)

JUMBY BAY PUNCH
Cocktail glass, chilled
Pour ingredients into iced mixing glass
1 1/2 oz. Amber Rum
1 oz. fresh lime juice
1 oz. simple syrup
3 dashes Angostura Bitters
Stir and strain
Sprinkle nutmeg
Orange slice and cherry garnish

JUMPER CABLES
Coffee mug or glass, heated
Build in glass
3/4 oz. Coconut Rum
1/2 oz. Baileys Irish Cream
1/2 oz. Disaronno Amaretto
Near fill with hot coffee
Top with frothed milk
Dust powdered cocoa

JUMP ME
Bucket glass, ice
Build in glass
1 1/2 oz. Bacardi Select Rum
1 oz. Mount Gay Eclipse Rum
2-3 dashes Angostura Bitters
1 oz. fresh lime juice
Near fill with pineapple juice
Float 3/4 oz. Gosling's Black Seal Rum

JUNGLE CREAM
Brandy snifter, ice
Build in glass
1 1/2 oz. Cruzan Estate Single Barrel Rum
3/4 oz. Tia Maria
3/4 oz. Cruzan Rum Cream

JUNGLE JUICE
Bucket glass, ice
Build in glass
1 oz. Gin
1 oz. Vodka
3/4 oz. Raspberry Liqueur
1/2 fill orange juice
1/2 fill grapefruit juice

JUNGLE MILK
Coffee mug, heated
Build in glass
3/4 oz. Baileys Irish Cream
3/4 oz. Crème de Banana
Near fill with hot chocolate
Whipped cream garnish
Sprinkle shaved chocolate

KAHLÚA CLUB
Highball glass, ice
Build in glass
1 1/4 oz. Kahlúa
Fill with club soda

KAHLÚA MINT
Cocktail glass, chilled
Pour ingredients into iced mixing glass
1 oz. Kahlúa
1/2 oz. White Crème de Menthe
1 1/2 oz. half & half cream
Shake and strain

KAMIKAZE
Cocktail glass, chilled
Pour ingredients into iced mixing glass
1 1/2 oz. Vodka
1/2 oz. Triple Sec
1/2 oz. Rose's Lime Juice
Stir and strain
Lime wedge garnish

KAMIKAZE, APPLE
Cocktail glass, chilled
Pour ingredients into iced mixing glass
1 oz. Vodka
1 oz. DeKuyper Pucker Sour Apple
1/2 oz. Triple Sec
1/2 oz. Rose's Lime Juice
Stir and strain
Lime wedge garnish

KAMIKAZE, BLOODY
Cocktail glass, chilled
Pour ingredients into iced mixing glass
1 1/4 oz. Vodka
1/2 oz. Southern Comfort
1/2 oz. Rose's Lime Juice
Stir and strain
Splash Cinnamon Schnapps
Lime wedge garnish

KAMIKAZE, BLUE
aka **Devine Wind**
Cocktail glass, chilled
Pour ingredients into iced mixing glass
1 1/2 oz. Vodka
3/4 oz. Blue Curaçao
1/2 oz. Rose's Lime Juice
Stir and strain
Lime wedge garnish

GRAN GALA®
LIQUEUR

The Stock Distillery has been producing world-class brandies in Italy for well over a century. While renown throughout Europe, the firm has yet to become a household name in the United States. That will certainly change as increasingly more Americans discover the simple pleasures of award winning GRAN GALA LIQUEUR.

This lively imported liqueur is skillfully made from a blend of premium triple oranges and mature, barrel-aged Italian brandy. The craftsmen at Stock imbue Gran Gala liqueur with a fetching bronze color and smoothly textured, medium-weight body. Its expansive bouquet is loaded with the aroma of fresh oranges and delicate notes of almonds and brandy. The lush, semisweet palate features zesty orange and lemon flavors and a healthy measure of sumptuous brandy. The liqueur sports a warm, flavorful finish.

The natural inclination is to serve a sophisticated product such as Gran Gala in a heated snifter or on the rocks. While certainly a popular way to enjoy it, the liqueur enjoys many uses behind the bar. The most noteworthy application for Gran Gala is as a modifier in a wide range of specialty Margaritas, where its brandy base and exuberant orange flavor make it an ideal substitute for triple sec.

KAMIKAZE, BRIT'S
Cocktail glass, chilled
Pour ingredients into iced mixing glass
1 3/4 oz. Wet by Beefeater
1/2 oz. Cointreau
1/4 oz. Rose's Lime Juice
3/4 oz. sweet 'n' sour
Shake and strain
Lime wedge garnish

KAMIKAZE, CITRON
aka **Citron Kami**
Cocktail glass, chilled
Pour ingredients into iced mixing glass
1 1/2 oz. Absolut Citron Vodka
1/2 oz. Triple Sec
1/2 oz. Rose's Lime Juice
Stir and strain
Lime wheel garnish

KAMIKAZE, COCONUT
Cocktail glass, chilled
Pour ingredients into iced mixing glass
2 oz. Pearl Lo Coco Vodka
1 oz. pineapple juice
1/2 oz. sweet 'n' sour
Stir and strain
Pineapple wedge garnish

KAMIKAZE, CRANBERRY
Cocktail glass, chilled
Pour ingredients into iced mixing glass
1 1/2 oz. Stolichnaya Cranberi Vodka
1/2 oz. Triple Sec
1/2 oz. Rose's Lime Juice
1/2 oz. white cranberry juice
Stir and strain
Lime wedge garnish

KAMIKAZE, FRENCH
Cocktail glass, chilled
Pour ingredients into iced mixing glass
1 1/2 oz. Grey Goose Vodka
1/2 oz. Grand Marnier Centenaire
3/4 oz. fresh lime juice
Stir and strain
Lime wedge garnish

KAMIKAZE, FUZZY
Cocktail glass, chilled
Pour ingredients into iced mixing glass
1 1/4 oz. Vodka
3/4 oz. Peach Schnapps
3/4 oz. Rose's Lime Juice
Stir and strain
Lime wedge garnish

KAMIKAZE, ITALIAN
Cocktail glass, chilled
Pour ingredients into iced mixing glass
1 1/4 oz. Artic Vodka & Thai Fruits Liqueur
3/4 oz. Limoncello Liqueur
3/4 oz. Gran Gala Orange Liqueur
1/2 oz. Rose's Lime Juice
Stir and strain
Lime wedge garnish

KAMIKAZE, KOKONUT
Cocktail glass, chilled
Pour ingredients into iced mixing glass
2 oz. Malibu Caribbean Rum
1 oz. pineapple juice
1/2 oz. sweet 'n' sour
Stir and strain
Lime wedge garnish

KAMIKAZE, MELON
aka **Melon Kami**
Cocktail glass, chilled
Pour ingredients into iced mixing glass
1 oz. Vodka
1 oz. Midori
1/2 oz. Rose's Lime Juice
Stir and strain
Lime wedge garnish

KAMIKAZE, PURPLE (1)
aka **Purple Kami**
Cocktail glass, chilled
Pour ingredients into iced mixing glass
1 1/2 oz. Vodka
3/4 oz. Chambord
1/2 oz. Cointreau
1/2 oz. Rose's Lime Juice
Stir and strain
Lime wedge garnish

KAMIKAZE, PURPLE (2)
aka **Purple Kami**
Cocktail glass, chilled
Pour ingredients into iced mixing glass
3/4 oz. Vox Raspberry Vodka
3/4 oz. Chambord
3/4 oz. cranberry juice
1/2 oz. Rose's Lime Juice
Stir and strain
Lime wheel garnish

KAMIKAZE, RADIOACTIVE
Cocktail glass, chilled
Pour ingredients into iced mixing glass
1/2 oz. Light Rum
1/2 oz. Coconut Rum
1/2 oz. 151° Rum
1/2 oz. Blue Curaçao
1 oz. Rose's Lime Juice
1/2 oz. grenadine
Stir and strain
Lime wedge garnish

KAMIKAZE, RASPBERRY
Cocktail glass, chilled
Pour ingredients into iced mixing glass
1 1/2 oz. Citadelle Raspberry Vodka
3/4 oz. Chambord
1/2 oz. Cointreau
1/2 oz. fresh lime juice
Stir and strain
Lime wedge garnish

KAMIKAZE, SOUTHERN COMFORT
Cocktail glass, chilled
Pour ingredients into iced mixing glass
1 1/2 oz. Southern Comfort
1/2 oz. Triple Sec
1/2 oz. Rose's Lime Juice
Stir and strain
Lime wedge garnish

KAPALUA BUTTERFLY
House specialty glass, chilled
Pour ingredients into blender
1 1/4 oz. Mount Gay Eclipse Rum
1 1/4 oz. Bacardi Gold Rum
1/2 oz. grenadine
1 1/2 oz. sweet 'n' sour
1 1/2 oz. pineapple juice
1 1/2 oz. coconut cream syrup
2 oz. orange juice
Blend with ice
Pineapple wedge and orange slice garnish

KATINKA
Cocktail glass, chilled
Pour ingredients into iced mixing glass
1 1/2 oz. Vodka
1/2 oz. Apricot Brandy
1/2 oz. Rose's Lime Juice
Stir and strain
Mint sprig garnish (optional)

KÉKÉ KICKER
Bucket glass, ice
Build in glass
1 1/4 oz. KéKé Beach Cream Liqueur
1/2 oz. Jose Cuervo Especial Tequila
1/2 oz. Kahlúa
Fill with orange juice

DON EDUARDO®
AÑEJO TEQUILA

One of the patriarchs of the tequila industry was Don Eduardo Orendain Gonzalez. He set out to found his own distillery in 1926. Today the family-owned Orendain Distillery ranks among the principal producers of super-premium 100% blue agave tequilas, the most prestigious of which is DON EDUARDO AÑEJO TEQUILA.

Don Eduardo Tequilas are produced at the state of the art Orendain Distillery in Jalisco. The agaves are cultivated on the family's estate outside of the town of Tequila. After harvesting, they are baked, crushed and slowly fermented using a proprietary strain of yeast. The fermented agave juice is double-distilled in pot stills.

The highly acclaimed Don Eduardo Añejo is aged in charred American oak bourbon barrels for a minimum of 2 years. During its extended stay in wood, the tequila gets an amber/golden color and a bouquet rich with the aromas of flora, vanilla and fruit. It has a mellow palate that features an array of spicy, peppery flavors. The finish is long and relaxed.

DON EDUARDO SILVER TEQUILA is a svelte, triple-distilled gem. It has a lightweight body and a fresh, somewhat spicy bouquet. The tequila's satiny body rolls over the palate without undue heat and then slowly dissipates into a flavorful finish. It is a delightfully accessible tequila.

KÉ LARGO
Presentation shot glass, chilled
Build in glass
1/2 fill KéKé Beach Cream Liqueur
1/2 fill Midori

KENTUCKY BLUEGRASS
Rocks glass, ice
Build in glass
1 1/2 oz. Bourbon
1/2 oz. Green Crème de Menthe
Splash Blue Curaçao

KENTUCKY COOLER
House specialty glass, ice
Pour ingredients into iced mixing glass
1 oz. Bourbon
1/2 oz. Cointreau Liqueur
3/4 oz. simple syrup
Shake and strain
Splash ginger ale
Fill with chilled, honey sweetened lemon tea
Lemon wedge and mint sprig garnish

KENTUCKY LONGSHOT
Cocktail glass, chilled
Pour ingredients into iced mixing glass
2 oz. Woodford Reserve Bourbon
1/2 oz. Canton Ginger Liqueur
1/4 oz. Peach Brandy
1-2 dashes Angostura Bitters
Shake and strain
Candied ginger garnish

KENTUCKY SHUFFLE
Cocktail glass, chilled
Pour ingredients into iced mixing glass
2 oz. Knob Creek Small Batch Bourbon
3/4 oz. Grand Marnier Centenaire
1/2 oz. fresh lime juice
Stir and strain

KENTUCKY SWAMP WATER
Bucket glass, ice
Build in glass
1 1/2 oz. Bourbon
1/2 oz. Blue Curaçao
1/2 oz. fresh lime juice
Fill with orange juice
Lime wedge garnish

KEOKI COFFEE
Coffee mug, heated
Build in glass
1/2 oz. Brandy
1/2 oz. Kahlúa
1/2 oz. Dark Crème de Cacao
Near fill with hot coffee
Whipped cream garnish
Dust powdered cocoa

KEOKI SHOOTER
Presentation shot glass, chilled
Build in glass
1/4 fill Kahlúa
1/4 fill Dark Crème de Cacao
1/4 fill Brandy
Near fill with hot coffee
Whipped cream garnish
Dust powdered cocoa

KEY ISLA MORADA
House specialty glass, chilled
Pour ingredients into blender
1 oz. Cruzan Estate Light Rum
3/4 oz. Cruzan Coconut Rum
3/4 oz. Cruzan Pineapple Rum
Peeled, ripe banana
1 tsp. vanilla extract
3/4 oz. half & half cream
2 oz. sweet 'n' sour
Blend with ice
Float 3/4 oz. Cruzan Estate Diamond Rum
Lime wedge and orange slice garnish

KEY LARGO
House specialty glass, ice
Pour ingredients into iced mixing glass
1 1/2 oz. Cruzan Estate Light Rum
3/4 oz. Cruzan Coconut Rum
3/4 oz. Disaronno Amaretto
Shake and strain
Near fill with club soda
Float 3/4 oz. Cruzan Estate Diamond Rum
Lime wedge and orange slice garnish

KEY LIME COOLER
Cocktail glass, chilled
Pour ingredients into iced mixing glass
1 oz. Licor 43 (Cuarenta y Tres)
1/2 oz. fresh lime juice
1 oz. half & half cream
Shake and strain
Lime wheel garnish

KEY LIME PIE (1)
Rocks glass, chilled
Pour ingredients into iced mixing glass
1 1/4 oz. Licor 43 (Cuarenta y Tres)
3/4 oz. fresh lime juice
1 1/4 oz. half & half cream
Shake and strain

KEY LIME PIE (2)
House specialty glass, ice
Pour ingredients into iced mixing glass
1 1/2 oz. Vanilla Rum
3/4 oz. fresh lime juice
3/4 oz. half & half cream
Shake and strain
Fill with Seven-Up

KEY WEST
House specialty glass, ice
Pour ingredients into iced mixing glass
1 1/2 oz. Light Rum
1 1/2 oz. Dark Rum
1/2 oz. Crème de Banana
1/2 oz. Raspberry Liqueur
2 oz. fresh lime juice
2 oz. sweet 'n' sour
2 oz. orange juice
Shake and strain
Near fill with Seven-Up
Float 3/4 oz. Jamaican Rum
Orange slice and cherry garnish

KIDDY COCKTAIL
Cocktail glass, chilled
Pour ingredients into iced mixing glass
1 oz. grenadine
2 oz. sweet 'n' sour
Shake and strain
Cherry garnish

KILLER KOOLAID
Cocktail glass, chilled
Pour ingredients into iced mixing glass
1 oz. Southern Comfort
1 oz. Midori
3/4 oz. Crème de Noyaux
1 oz. cranberry juice
Shake and strain

KILLER WHALE
House specialty glass, ice
Pour ingredients into iced mixing glass
1 1/4 oz. Gold Rum
1 1/4 oz. Jamaican Rum
1/2 oz. Raspberry Liqueur
1/2 fill cranberry juice
1/2 fill orange juice
Shake and strain
Near fill with Seven-Up
Float 3/4 oz. Grand Marnier
Orange slice garnish

KING ALFONSE
aka **King Alphonso**
Cordial or sherry glass, chilled
Layer ingredients
3/4 fill Dark Crème de Cacao
1/4 fill half & half cream

KING MIDAS
Bucket glass, ice
Build in glass
1 1/4 oz. Canadian Club Whisky
3/4 oz. Goldschläger
Fill with Seven-Up
Lime wedge garnish

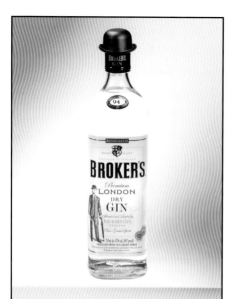

BROKER'S® LONDON DRY GIN

Creating a delicious London Dry gin is a matter of skill and artistic interpretation. Making it affordable is a stroke of genius. Fortunately for gin enthusiasts and Martini connoisseurs alike, BROKER'S LONDON DRY GIN has managed to accomplish both.

This premium gin is distilled in Birmingham, England in a single copper pot still that dates back to 1903. Crafted in a traditional style, Broker's is made from 100% pure neutral grain spirits and infused with 10 natural herbs, spices and fruit. The botanicals are crushed and steeped in the neutral spirits until their aroma and flavors have been completely integrated. The gin is then redistilled and rendered to 94 proof with purified water.

Broker's London Dry Gin is a distinctive spirit with a modest price tag. The gin has a smooth, lightweight body and a prominent citrus-laced bouquet. The pleasures continue as the gin rolls over the palate. Its entry is initially quite soft, followed quickly by a mouth-filling burst of dry, fruity flavor. The gin's elevated alcohol content tingles on the tongue, then it slowly subsides into a lingering and flavorful finish. From beginning to end, Broker's is a splendid gin experience.

No one can accuse Broker's of being stodgy or taking itself too seriously. The bowler-topped gin is ideally suited for a splash of crisp tonic or the nearest dry Martini.

KING'S CUP
Cocktail glass, chilled
Pour ingredients into iced mixing glass
1 oz. Galliano Liqueur
1/2 oz. Disaronno Amaretto
1 1/2 oz. half & half cream
Shake and strain

KIR
Wine glass, chilled
Build in glass
Near fill with White Wine
Float 3/4 oz. Crème de Cassis
Lemon twist garnish

KIR ROYALE
Champagne glass, chilled
Build in glass
Near fill with Champagne
Float 3/4 oz. Crème de Cassis
Lemon twist garnish

KISS OF THE ISLANDS
House specialty glass, ice
Pour ingredients into iced mixing glass
1 1/2 oz. Gosling's Black Seal Rum
1 1/2 oz. Mount Gay Eclipse Rum
1 oz. Crème de Banana
3/4 oz. Blue Curaçao
1 oz. coconut cream syrup
1 1/2 oz. pineapple juice
1 1/2 oz. orange juice
Shake and strain
Float 3/4 oz. Appleton Estate
    V/X Jamaica Rum
Orange slice and cherry garnish

KLONDIKE
aka **Star Cocktail**
Cocktail glass, chilled
Pour ingredients into iced mixing glass
1 1/2 oz. Laird's Applejack Brandy
1/2 oz. Dry Vermouth
3 dashes Angostura Bitters
1/4 oz. simple syrup (optional)
Stir and strain
Lemon twist garnish

KNICKERBOCKER
Bucket glass, ice
Pour ingredients into iced mixing glass
1 1/2 oz. Bacardi Limón Rum
1 oz. Mount Gay Eclipse Rum
1/2 oz. grenadine
3/4 oz. pineapple juice
1 oz. orange juice
1 oz. sweet 'n' sour
Shake and strain
Float 3/4 oz. Appleton Estate
    V/X Jamaica Rum
Orange slice and cherry garnish

KNICKERBOCKER KNEE KNOCKER
House specialty glass, chilled
Pour ingredients into blender
1 1/2 oz. Vodka
3/4 oz. Crème de Cassis
1/2 oz. fresh lime juice
1 scoop raspberry sherbet
1 scoop pineapple sherbet
Blend ingredients (with ice optional)
Berries garnish

KNICKERBOCKER KNOCKER
House specialty glass, ice
Pour ingredients into iced mixing glass
3/4 oz. Midori
3/4 oz. Peach Schnapps
3/4 oz. sweet 'n' sour
1 1/2 oz. orange juice
1 1/2 oz. cranberry juice
Shake and strain
Float 3/4 oz. Crème de Banana
Orange slice and cherry garnish

KNICKERBOCKER SPECIAL COCKTAIL
Cocktail glass, chilled
Pour ingredients into iced mixing glass
1 1/2 oz. Bacardi Limón Rum
1/2 oz. Cointreau
1/2 oz. Chambord
3/4 oz. orange juice
1 oz. sweet 'n' sour
Shake and strain
Orange slice garnish

KNICKER KNOCKER
Bucket glass, ice
Pour ingredients into iced mixing glass
3/4 oz. Southern Comfort
3/4 oz. Captain Morgan Spiced Rum
3/4 oz. Vodka
1 oz. orange juice
1 oz. sweet 'n' sour
2 oz. cranberry juice
Shake and strain
Orange slice and cherry garnish

KNOB CREEK
Rocks glass, ice
Build in glass
2 oz. Knob Creek Small Batch Bourbon
3/4 oz. branch (spring) water

KNOCKOUT
Cocktail glass, chilled
Pour ingredients into iced mixing glass
3/4 oz. Gin
3/4 oz. Pernod
3/4 oz. Dry Vermouth
1/4 oz. White Crème de Menthe
Stir and strain
Lemon twist garnish

KOALA BEAR (1)
House specialty glass, chilled
Pour ingredients into blender
1 oz. Crème de Banana
1 oz. Dark Crème de Cacao
2 scoops vanilla ice cream
Blend ingredients (with ice optional)
Whipped cream garnish
Sprinkle nutmeg

KOALA BEAR (2)
Pilsner glass, chilled 16 oz.
Build in glass
1/2 fill Foster's Lager
1/2 fill Guinness Stout

KOALA FLOAT
House specialty glass, chilled
Pour ingredients into blender
1 oz. Kahlúa
1 oz. Baileys Irish Cream
2 oz. coconut cream syrup
3 oz. pineapple juice
Blend with ice
Pineapple wedge and cherry garnish

KOOL AID (1)
Bucket glass, ice
Build in glass
3/4 oz. Vodka
3/4 oz. Midori
3/4 oz. Disaronno Amaretto
2 oz. cranberry juice

KOOL AID (2)
Bucket glass, ice
Build in glass
3/4 oz. Midori
3/4 oz. Disaronno Amaretto
3/4 oz. Southern Comfort
3/4 oz. Vodka
1/4 oz. grenadine
2 oz. cranberry juice

KOOLO
Rocks glass (ice optional)
Build in glass
1 1/4 oz. Baileys Irish Cream
1 oz. DeKuyper Butdershots Schnapps
1/2 oz. Crown Royal

COURVOISIER®
NAPOLÉON COGNAC

In a country known for making
unsurpassed brandies, the Emperor of
France preferred those crafted by
Courvoisier, so in 1869 Napoléon
Bonaparte honored the Chateau as the
exclusive purveyor to the Court of
Napoléon III. That historic
accomplishment is commemorated in an
equally prestigious achievement,
COURVOISIER NAPOLÉON COGNAC.

Made in Jarnac, France, Courvoisier
Napoléon is a Fine Champagne cognac
comprised of brandies aged for a
minimum of 15 years in oak and most
are matured in the neighborhood of 25
years. This renowned cognac possesses an
alluring, slightly spicy bouquet, a full,
velvety body and a delectable palate rich
with cocoa, fruit and spice. The brandy
has a long lasting, exceptionally flavorful
finish. It is truly a world-class brandy.

The chateau has also created the
magnificent COURVOISIER XO
IMPERIAL. This award winning cognac
is assembled from Grande and Petite
Champagne cognacs. The brandies are
aged a minimum of 20 years, with the
majority being around 35 years in age.

Courvoisier XO Imperial is a rare and
sophisticated brandy. The bouquet is
brimming with the aromas of vanilla,
cinnamon and violets. Its seamlessly
smooth body is richly textured and the
enormously flavorful palate lasts long
into the relaxed finish.

KRAKOW WITCH
Rocks glass, ice
Build in glass
1 3/4 oz. Zubrówka Bison Brand Vodka
1/2 oz. Liquore Strega
Lemon twist garnish

KURANT AFFAIR
Rocks glass, chilled
Pour ingredients into iced mixing glass
1 1/4 oz. Absolut Kurant Vodka
1 1/4 oz. orange juice
1 1/4 oz. cranberry juice
Shake and strain

KUWAITI COOLER
Bucket glass, ice
Pour ingredients into iced mixing glass
1 oz. Midori
1 oz. DeKuyper Pucker Sour Apple
2 oz. sweet 'n' sour
Shake and strain
Fill with club soda

LA BAMBA
House specialty glass, ice
Pour ingredients into iced mixing glass
1 1/4 oz. Corazón Añejo Tequila
3/4 oz. Cointreau
1 1/2 oz. pineapple juice
1 1/2 oz. orange juice
Shake and strain
Float 3/4 oz. Chambord

LA FRESCA
Bucket glass, ice
Rim glass with salt (optional)
Build in glass
2 oz. Tequila
Fill with Squirt
Lime wedge garnish

LA MOSCA
aka **Sambuca con Mosca**
Sherry glass, chilled
Build in glass
2 1/2 oz. Sambuca
Coffee beans (3) garnish

LA PALOMA
Bucket glass, ice
Build in glass
1 1/2 oz. Silver Tequila
Fill with Squirt (grapefruit soda)
Lime wedge garnish

LADIES AUXILIARY
House specialty glass, chilled
Pour ingredients into blender
1 3/4 oz. Gin
3/4 oz. Limoncello Liqueur
3/4 oz. Triple Sec
3 oz. limeade
Blend with ice
Float 3/4 oz. DeKuyper Watermelon Pucker
Lime wedge, orange slice and cherry garnish

LADY MADONNA
Brandy snifter, ice
Build in glass
1 1/2 oz. Dubonnet Rouge
1 1/2 oz. Dry Vermouth
Lemon twist

LAGER AND BLACK
Beer glass, chilled
Build in glass
1 1/2 oz. black currant juice
Fill with draft lager

LAGER AND LIME
Beer glass, chilled
Build in glass
3/4 oz. Rose's Lime Juice
Fill with draft lager

LAKE STREET LEMONADE
Bucket glass, ice
Build in glass
1 1/2 oz. Stön Vodka
1/2 oz. Disaronno Amaretto
Fill with lemonade
Lemon wedge garnish

LANDSLIDE
Presentation shot glass, chilled
Layer ingredients
1/3 fill Crème de Banana
1/3 fill Baileys Irish Cream
1/3 fill Grand Marnier

L.A.P.D.
Presentation shot glass, chilled
Rim glass with salt (optional)
Build in glass
1 oz. Tequila
1/2 oz. Blue Curaçao
1/4 oz. Raspberry Liqueur

LARCHMONT (1)
Cocktail glass, chilled
Pour ingredients into iced mixing glass
1 1/2 oz. Bacardi 8 Reserva Rum
3/4 oz. Grand Marnier
1/2 oz. Rose's Lime Juice
Stir and strain
Orange twist garnish

LARCHMONT (2)
Cocktail glass, chilled
Pour ingredients into iced mixing glass
1 1/2 oz. Pyrat XO Reserve Rum
3/4 oz. Grand Marnier
1/2 oz. Rose's Lime Juice
Stir and strain
Orange twist garnish

LARCHMONT (3)
Cocktail glass, chilled
Pour ingredients into iced mixing glass
1 1/2 oz. Cruzan Estate Single Barrel Rum
3/4 oz. Grand Marnier
1/2 oz. Rose's Lime Juice
Stir and strain
Orange twist garnish

LARRY, THE
aka **Frozen Locust**
House specialty glass, chilled
Pour ingredients into blender
3/4 oz. Van Gogh Vanilla Vodka
3/4 oz. White Crème de Cacao
3/4 oz. Green Crème de Menthe
2 scoops vanilla ice cream
Blend ingredients (with ice optional)
Whipped cream garnish
Sprinkle shaved chocolate

LASTING PASSION
House specialty glass, chilled
Pour ingredients into blender
1 1/2 oz. Mount Gay Extra Old Rum
3/4 oz. 151° Rum
3/4 oz. Rose's Lime Juice
2 oz. coconut cream syrup
2 oz. pineapple juice
2 1/2 oz. passion fruit juice
Blend with ice
Float 3/4 oz. Rhum Barbancourt
  5-Star
Pineapple wedge and orange slice garnish

LATE-NITE LEMON DROP
Cocktail glass, chilled
Rim glass with sugar (optional)
Pour ingredients into iced mixing glass
1 1/2 oz. Vox Vodka
3/4 oz. Limoncello Liqueur
3/4 oz. DeKuyper Razzmatazz
3/4 oz. fresh lemon juice
Shake and strain
Lemon twist garnish

TÜRI™ ESTONIAN VODKA

Vodka has been distilled in the tiny Baltic nation of Estonia for the past 500 years. Having finally gained its independence in 1991 after the fall of the Soviet Union, Estonia is now free to share its native spirit with the West. In a world of nearly unlimited choices in vodka, do not miss out on the singular experience that is TÜRI ESTONIAN VODKA.

Crafted at the renowned AS Onistar Distillery in Tallin, super-premium Türi is distilled from 100% hearty noble winter rye and pristine spring water. The spirit is quadruple-distilled in continuous stills and then subjected to rigorous filtration through charcoal prior to being bottled at 80 proof.

Your first sniff, sip and swallow of Türi will confirm that it rightfully belongs on the top-shelf. The vodka has brilliant clarity and a dry, featherweight body. The generous bouquet is impressively spicy with notes of pepper, flora and herbs. Its entry is remarkably soft as it gradually fills the mouth with the flavors of bittersweet chocolate and delicate citrus. The finish may be its strongest feature—long, clean and a touch sweet.

Türi is a marvelous example of how complex and thoroughly satisfying a vodka can be. It is ideally served straight-up allowing one to fully appreciate its complexity and native charm.

LATIN LOVE

House specialty glass, chilled
Rim glass with grenadine and
    shaved coconut
Pour ingredients into blender
1 oz. Coconut Rum
1 oz. Banana Rum
1 oz. raspberry juice
1 oz. coconut cream syrup
3 oz. pineapple juice
Blend with ice
Pineapple wedge and cherry garnish

LATIN LOVER (1)

House specialty glass, ice
Pour ingredients into iced mixing glass
1 1/2 oz. Dark Rum
1/2 oz. Crème de Banana
1/2 oz. grenadine
2 oz. orange juice
2 oz. pineapple juice
Shake and strain
Float 3/4 oz. Tia Maria
Lemon twist garnish

LATIN LOVER (2)

House specialty glass, chilled
Pour ingredients into blender
1 oz. Cruzan Estate Dark Rum
1 oz. Cruzan Banana Rum
3/4 oz. Chambord
1 oz. raspberry syrup
1 1/2 oz. coconut cream syrup
3 oz. pineapple juice
Blend with ice
Pineapple wedge and cherry garnish

LAUGHING COW

House specialty glass, chilled
Pour ingredients into blender
1 1/2 oz. Citrus Rum
1/2 oz. Cointreau
1/2 oz. fresh lime juice
1/2 oz. cranberry juice
2 scoops vanilla ice cream
Blend ingredients (with ice optional)
Orange twist garnish

LEAF

Cocktail or house specialty glass, chilled
Pour ingredients into iced mixing glass
1 oz. Midori
1/2 oz. Light Rum
1 1/2 oz. half & half cream
Shake and strain

LEANING TOWER
House specialty glass, ice
Pour ingredients into iced mixing glass
1 oz. Captain Morgan Spiced Rum
1 oz. Crème de Banana
1 oz. coconut cream syrup
2 oz. orange juice
2 oz. pineapple juice
Shake and strain
Float 3/4 oz. Razzmatazz Raspberry Liqueur
Orange slice and cherry garnish

LEAVE US ALONE
Coffee mug, heated
Build in glass
3/4 oz. Courvoisier VSOP Cognac
3/4 oz. Grand Marnier
1/2 oz. Godiva Chocolate Liqueur
Near fill with hot coffee
Whipped cream garnish

LE BISTRO
Cappuccino cup, heated
Build in glass
3/4 oz. B & B Liqueur
3/4 oz. Brandy
Near fill with hot espresso coffee
Top with frothed milk
Sprinkle shaved chocolate

LEFT BANK
Rocks glass, ice
Build in glass
1 1/4 oz. Baileys Irish Cream
1 1/4 oz. Chambord

LEISURE SUIT
House specialty glass, ice
Pour ingredients into iced mixing glass
1 oz. Galliano Liqueur
1 oz. Crème de Banana
2 oz. pineapple juice
2 oz. orange juice
2 oz. cranberry juice
Shake and strain

LEMONADE ROYALE
Cocktail glass, chilled
Pour ingredients into mixing glass
3-4 sliced strawberries
1/4 oz. simple syrup
1 oz. lemonade
Muddle contents
Add ice
1 1/4 oz. Vodka
Stir and strain
Top with 1 oz. Champagne
Float 1/4 oz. Chambord

LEMON DROP (1)
Cocktail glass, chilled
Rim glass with sugar (optional)
Pour ingredients into iced mixing glass
1 1/2 oz. Vodka
1/2 oz. Cointreau
1/2 oz. fresh lemon juice
Shake and strain
Lemon twist garnish

LEMON DROP (2)
Bucket glass, ice
Pour ingredients into iced mixing glass
1 1/4 oz. Vodka
2 oz. sweet 'n' sour
Shake and strain
1/2 fill club soda
1/2 fill Seven-Up

LEMON DROP (3)
Cocktail glass, chilled
Pour ingredients into iced mixing glass
1 oz. Vodka
3/4 oz. Triple Sec
1/4 oz. Rose's Lime Juice
1 oz. sweet 'n' sour
Shake and strain
Splash Seven-Up

LEMONGRAD
Highball glass, ice
Build in glass
1 1/4 oz. Stolichnaya Citros Vodka
Fill with cranberry juice

LEMON HEAVEN
Cocktail glass, chilled
Pour ingredients into iced mixing glass
1 3/4 oz. Citrus Vodka
1 oz. Limoncello Liqueur
3/4 oz. Cruzan Orange Rum
1 oz. half & half cream
Shake and strain
Lemon wheel garnish

LEMON HEIGHTS
Rocks glass, ice
Build in glass
1 1/2 oz. Citrus Vodka
1/2 oz. Limoncello Liqueur
1/2 oz. Hpnotiq Liqueur
Lemon twist garnish

LEMON LAVENDER
Cocktail glass, chilled
Pour ingredients into iced mixing glass
1 3/4 oz. Original Cristall Lemon Vodka
3/4 oz. Blue Curaçao
1/2 oz. fresh lime juice
1/2 oz. white cranberry juice
Stir and strain

B & B® LIQUEUR

B & B is about the most elegant liqueur that has ever graced a glass. It is the combination of BENEDICTINE D.O.M. LIQUEUR and noble aged cognac. Thought to be the oldest surviving proprietary liqueur, Benedictine originated in 1510 at the abbey in Fecamp, France. The legendary elixir is made with 27 herbs, spices, plants, tea and fruit. Each ingredient is distilled individually and matured in oak barrels for 3 months before blending. The liqueur is made on a base of aged cognac and rested in oak casks before being bottled at 80 proof.

B & B Liqueur was created in the 1930s. The inspiration behind the liqueur came from a barman at the famous 21 Club in Manhattan who concocted a cocktail made with Benedictine and brandy. Its soaring popularity prompted the distillery to devise its own version, and to ensure its longevity, created the liqueur on a base of old Fine Champagne cognac.

The liqueur is endowed with a flawlessly textured body and a wafting bouquet of spicy, herbal aromas and prominent notes of cognac. The palate is a sumptuous feast of zesty and spicy flavors mellowed with the refined taste of brandy. The lingering finish is sensational.

As great as B & B Liqueur is when served neat, it is equally fabulous featured in a cocktail.

LEMON NOG
Coffee mug or glass, heated
Build in glass
1 3/4 oz. Limoncello Liqueur
3/4 oz. Kahlúa
3/4 oz. Disaronno Amaretto
Near fill with hot coffee
Float 1 scoop vanilla ice cream
Drizzle chocolate syrup

LEMON PARFAIT
House specialty glass, chilled
Pour ingredients into blender
1 1/4 oz. Tequila
3/4 oz. Limoncello Liqueur
1/2 oz. fresh lemon juice
1 1/2 oz. orange juice
1 1/2 oz. sweet 'n' sour
Blend with ice

LEMON SPORTSMAN
Bucket glass, ice
Build in glass
1 3/4 oz. Spudka Vodka
Near fill with lemonade
Fill with lemon-lime soda
Lemon wedge garnish

LEMON SQUEEZE
Bucket glass, ice
Build in glass
1 oz. Limoncello Liqueur
1 oz. Citrus Rum
Fill with lemonade
Lemon wedge garnish

LEMON TART
Rocks glass, ice
Build in glass
2 oz. Vodka
3/4 oz. Limoncello Liqueur
3/4 oz. Hpnotiq Liqueur
Lemon wedge garnish

LEMON TOP
Beer glass, chilled
Build in glass
3/4 fill draft lager
1/4 fill Seven-Up

LEMON TREE TANTALIZER
House specialty glass, chilled
Pour ingredients into blender
1 1/2 oz. Citrus Vodka
2 scoops lemon sorbet
Blend ingredients (with ice optional)
Lemon wedge garnish

LE MOOSEBERRY
House specialty glass, ice
Pour ingredients into iced mixing glass
3/4 oz. Grey Goose Vodka
3/4 oz. Grey Goose L'Orange Vodka
3/4 oz. Disaronno Amaretto
2 oz. cranberry juice
2 oz. sweet 'n' sour
Shake and strain
Float 3/4 oz. Grand Marnier

LENA COCKTAIL
Cocktail glass, chilled
Pour ingredients into iced mixing glass
1/4 oz. Sweet Vermouth
1/4 oz. Dry Vermouth
1/4 oz. Campari Aperitivo
1 1/2 oz. Bourbon
Stir and strain
Lemon twist and cherry garnish

LEPRECHAUN
Highball glass, ice
Build in glass
3/4 oz. Peach Schnapps
3/4 oz. Blue Curaçao
Fill with orange juice

LETHAL INJECTION
Bucket glass, ice
Pour ingredients into iced mixing glass
1 1/4 oz. Light Rum
3/4 oz. Mount Gay Eclipse Rum
3/4 oz. Malibu Caribbean Rum
1/2 oz. Crème de Noyaux
1 1/2 oz. orange juice
1 1/2 oz. pineapple juice
Shake and strain
Float 3/4 oz. Gosling's Black Seal Rum
Pineapple wedge and cherry garnish

LET US ALONE
Cocktail glass, chilled
Pour ingredients into iced mixing glass
1 oz. Irish Liqueur
3/4 oz. Brandy
1/2 oz. Orange Liqueur
1 1/2 oz. sweet 'n' sour
Shake and strain
Orange twist garnish

LIAM'S PASSION
House specialty glass, chilled
Pour ingredients into blender
2 oz. Myers's Jamaican Rum
2 oz. coconut cream syrup
2 oz. pineapple juice
2 oz. passion fruit juice
Blend with ice

LICKETY-SPLIT
Bucket glass, ice
Build in glass
1 1/4 oz. Casa Noble Reposado Tequila
1/2 oz. Gran Gala Orange Liqueur
Fill with cranberry juice

LIFESAVER (1)
House specialty glass, ice
Pour ingredients into iced mixing glass
1 oz. Mount Gay Eclipse Rum
1 oz. Cruzan Estate Diamond Rum
2 oz. orange juice
2 oz. sweet 'n' sour
Shake and strain
Float 3/4 oz. Grand Marnier
Orange slice and cherry garnish

LIFESAVER (2)
Bucket glass, ice
Build in glass
1 1/2 oz. Malibu Caribbean Rum
1 oz. DeKuyper Butourshots Schnapps
Near fill with pineapple juice
Float 3/4 oz. Razzmatazz Raspberry Liqueur
Orange slice and cherry garnish

LIGHTHOUSE
Rocks glass, ice
Build in glass
1/2 oz. Tequila
1/2 oz. Kahlúa
1/2 oz. Peppermint Schnapps
1/2 oz. 151° Rum

LILLET CHAMPAGNE ROYALE
Champagne glass, chilled
Build in glass
2 oz. Lillet Blonde
1/2 oz. Crème de Cassis
Fill with Champagne
Lemon twist

LIMERICK
Bucket glass, ice
Pour ingredients into iced mixing glass
1 1/2 oz. Boru Vodka
3/4 oz. Celtic Crossing Irish Liqueur
3/4 oz. Midori
1/2 oz. Rose's Lime Juice
1 1/2 oz. sweet 'n' sour
Shake and strain
Lemon wedge garnish

DRAMBUIE® LIQUEUR

If you could pick your family, a good choice would be the Mackinnons of the Isle of Skye. They are the family that makes world famous DRAMBUIE LIQUEUR. Legend has it that its recipe was brought to Scotland in 1745 by Charles Edward Stuart—better known as Bonnie Prince Charles. After his armies were defeated at the Battle of Culloden Moor, Stuart took refuge on the Isle of Skye at the home of Captain Mackinnon. In gratitude the Prince gave his protector the recipe for present day Drambuie.

The Mackinnons introduced the liqueur to the world in 1906. Gaelic for "the drink that satisfies," Drambuie is now made in Edinburgh, Scotland, from a base of single Highland malt and straight grain whiskies. The blend is then infused with a measured dose of spice, herbs and heather honey and bottled at 80 proof.

Ultra-premium Drambuie has a striking amber hue and a medium-weight, satiny textured body. The liqueur has an intriguing bouquet laced with the prominent aromas of anise, dried herbs and subtle notes of peat. The palate is an elegant offering of spice, honey and a satisfying taste of whisky. The finish is especially long and flavorful.

Drambuie is a classic liqueur with unlimited creative possibilities. For a delectable change of pace sample DRAMBUIE'S SYLK CREAM LIQUEUR.

LIMÓN FITZGERALD
Cocktail glass, chilled
Pour ingredients into iced mixing glass
1 1/2 oz. Bacardi Limón Rum
1/2 oz. Limoncello Liqueur
4 dashes Angostura Bitters
1 oz. sweet 'n' sour
Stir and strain
Lemon wheel garnish

LIMÓN ORANGE BREEZE
House specialty glass, ice
Pour ingredients into iced mixing glass
1 1/2 oz. Bacardi Limón Rum
1/2 oz. Cointreau
2 oz. orange juice
2 oz. cranberry juice
Shake and strain
Orange twist garnish

LIMÓN RUNNER
House specialty glass, ice
Pour ingredients into iced mixing glass
1 1/2 oz. Bacardi Limón Rum
1/2 oz. Crème de Banana
1/2 oz. grenadine
2 oz. orange juice
2 oz. pineapple juice
Shake and strain
Lemon twist garnish

LIQUID GOLD
Brandy snifter, ice
Build in glass
1 1/2 oz. Patrón Añejo Tequila
1 oz. Patrón XO Café Coffee Liqueur
3/4 oz. Gran Gala Orange Liqueur
3/4 oz. Baileys Irish Cream
Shaved chocolate garnish

LIZARD BITCH
House specialty glass, ice
Pour ingredients into iced mixing glass
1 oz. Vodka
1 oz. Midori
1/2 oz. Southern Comfort
1 oz. sweet 'n' sour
1 oz. cranberry juice
1 oz. pineapple juice
Shake and strain
Lime wedge garnish

LOBOTOMY
Champagne glass, chilled
Pour ingredients into iced mixing glass
3/4 oz. Disaronno Amaretto
3/4 oz. Chambord
3/4 oz. pineapple juice
Shake and strain
Fill with Champagne

LOCH LOMOND (1)
Cocktail glass, chilled
Pour ingredients into iced mixing glass
2 oz. Scotch Whisky
2 dashes simple syrup
1 dash Angostura Bitters
Stir and strain
Lemon twist garnish

LOCH LOMOND (2)
House specialty glass, ice
Pour ingredients into iced mixing glass
1 1/4 oz. Scotch Whisky
1/2 oz. DeKuyper Peachtree Schnapps
1/2 oz. Blue Curaçao
1/2 oz. fresh lemon juice
2 1/2 oz. grapefruit juice
Shake and strain
Starfruit (carambola) garnish

LOCKHART ZOO
House specialty glass, ice
Pour ingredients into iced mixing glass
3/4 oz. Vodka
3/4 oz. Gin
3/4 oz. Silver Tequila
3 oz. cranberry juice
Shake and strain
Fill with draft beer

LOCO EN LA CABEZA (1)
House Specialty glass, ice
Pour ingredients into iced mixing glass
1 1/2 oz. Espolon Añejo Tequila
1/2 oz. Grand Marnier
1/2 oz. Chambord
1 1/2 oz. orange juice
1/2 oz. Rose's Lime Juice
Shake and strain
Lime wedge garnish

LOCO EN LA CABEZA (2)
House Specialty glass, ice
Pour ingredients into iced mixing glass
1 1/2 oz. Tequila
1/2 oz. Triple Sec
1 1/2 oz. orange juice
1/2 oz. Rose's Lime Juice
1/2 oz. grenadine
Shake and strain
Lime wedge garnish

LONDON GOLD
Cocktail glass, chilled
Pour ingredients into iced mixing glass
2 oz. Miller's London Dry Gin
1 oz. Goldschläger
3/4 oz. Cointreau
Shake and strain
Orange slice garnish

LONDON LEMONADE
Cocktail glass, chilled
Pour ingredients into iced mixing glass
1 3/4 oz. Broker's London Dry Gin
1 oz. lemonade
1/2 oz. Rose's Lime Juice
1/2 oz. Cointreau
Stir and strain
Lemon twist garnish

LONDON NIGHTCLUB
Highball glass, ice
Build in glass
1 1/4 oz. Wet by Beefeater
Near fill with club soda
Float 3/4 oz. grapefruit juice
Lime wedge garnish

LONDON REDHEAD
Cocktail glass, chilled
Pour ingredients into iced mixing glass
3/4 oz. Gin
3/4 oz. Dubonnet Rouge
3/4 oz. Dubonnet Blanc
2-3 dashes Angostura Bitters
1 1/2 oz. orange juice
Shake and strain

LOOKING FOR TROUBLE
House specialty glass, ice
Pour ingredients into iced mixing glass
1/2 oz. Gin
1/2 oz. Vodka
1/2 oz. Light Rum
1/2 oz. Tequila
1/2 oz. Canadian Whisky
1/2 oz. Triple Sec
1/2 oz. grenadine
1 oz. sweet 'n' sour
1 oz. pineapple juice
1 oz. cranberry juice
Shake and strain

LOOKOUT POINT
Cocktail glass, chilled
Pour ingredients into iced mixing glass
1 1/2 oz. Sea Wynde Pot Still Rum
3/4 oz. Chambord
3/4 oz. sweet 'n' sour
Shake and strain
Lime wedge garnish

MARTINI & ROSSI®
EXTRA DRY VERMOUTH

Martini & Rossi Vermouths are arguably the finest vermouths in the world. In 1863, Alessandro Martini and Luigi Rossi took over the operation of an existing vermouth producer in Turin, Italy. They soon became the leading exporter of vermouth led by their flagship brand, MARTINI & ROSSI EXTRA DRY VERMOUTH.

No self-respecting cocktail emporium would be caught without Martini & Rossi Vermouths behind the bar. The renowned Extra Dry is made from a blend of premium white wines that are infused with a secret recipe of herbs, spices and aromatics. After it is infused, the vermouth is aged for 3 to 6 months. It is then filtered and bottled at 18% alcohol by volume (abv).

This most famous brand of dry vermouth is crystal clear with no trace of color. It has a medium-weight body with a subtle yet tantalizing bouquet of spices and herbs. On the palate, the vermouth is soft and loaded with herbal and fruity nuances. The finish is long and flavorful. MARTINI & ROSSI ROSSO (SWEET) VERMOUTH is equally sensational. It is made from a blend of red wines that are infused with botanical and aromatics and is bottled at 16% abv. MARTINI & ROSSI BIANCO VERMOUTH (16% abv) is made from infused white wine and is delectably sweet and refreshing. It makes an ideal aperitif.

LOST LOVERS
House specialty glass, chilled
Pour ingredients into blender
3/4 oz. Light Rum
3/4 oz. Spiced Rum
3/4 oz. Mount Gay Eclipse Rum
3/4 oz. Crème de Banana
1 oz. coconut cream syrup
2 oz. orange juice
2 oz. pineapple juice
Blend with ice
Float 3/4 oz. Chambord
Orange slice and cherry garnish

LOUISIANA SHOOTER
Presentation shot glass, chilled
Build in glass
1 1/2 oz. Absolut Peppar Vodka
1/4 tsp. horseradish
3 dashes Tabasco Sauce
1 small raw oyster

LOUNGE LIZARD
House specialty glass, ice
Build in glass
1 oz. Gold Rum
1 oz. Spiced Rum
1/2 oz. Disaronno Amaretto
Fill with cola
Lime wedge garnish

LOUVRE ME ALONE
Cappuccino cup, heated
Build in glass
1/2 oz. Grand Marnier
1/2 oz. VS Cognac
1/2 oz. Tia Maria
Near fill with hot espresso coffee
Top with frothed milk
Sprinkle shaved chocolate

LOVE CANAL
Bucket glass, ice
Build in glass
1 3/4 oz. Jose Cuervo Clásico Tequila
3/4 oz. Disaronno Amaretto
Near fill with lemonade
Splash Squirt (grapefruit) soda
Lemon wedge garnish

LOVE POTION #9
House specialty glass, chilled
Pour ingredients into blender
1 oz. Gold Rum
1 oz. Mount Gay Eclipse Rum
2 oz. strawberry puree
1 1/2 oz. coconut cream syrup
3 oz. pineapple juice
Blend with ice
Whipped cream garnish
Drizzle 1/2 oz. chocolate syrup

LOVER'S LANE
Cocktail glass, chilled
Pour ingredients into iced mixing glass
1 3/4 oz. Dark Rum
3/4 oz. Grand Marnier
1/2 oz. fresh lime juice
1 1/2 oz. sweet 'n' sour
Shake and strain
Lime wedge garnish

LUAU
Bucket glass, ice
Build in glass
1 oz. Malibu Caribbean Rum
1 oz. Midori
Fill with pineapple juice
Orange slice and cherry garnish

LUNCH BOX
Rocks glass, chilled
Build in glass
1 oz. Disaronno Amaretto
1 oz. orange juice
3-4 oz. Draft Beer

LYNCHBURG LEMONADE
Bucket glass, ice
Pour ingredients into iced mixing glass
1 oz. Jack Daniel's Tennessee Whiskey
3/4 oz. Triple Sec
1 1/2 oz. sweet 'n' sour
Shake and strain
Fill with Seven-Up

MACINTOSH PRESS
Highball glass, ice
Build in glass
1 1/4 oz. DeKuyper Pucker Sour Apple
1/2 fill ginger ale
1/2 fill club soda

MACKENZIE GOLD
Highball glass, ice
Build in glass
1 1/2 oz. Yukon Jack Liqueur
Fill with grapefruit juice

MACKINNON ROAD
Coffee mug, heated
Build in glass
1 oz. Drambuie
1 oz. Sylk Cream Liqueur
1/2 oz. Kahlúa
Near fill with hot coffee
Whipped cream garnish
Dust powdered cocoa

MADAME BUTTERFLY
Cocktail glass, chilled
Pour ingredients into iced mixing glass
2 oz. Cîroc Snap Frost Vodka
1/4 oz. Saké
1/4 oz. VSOP Cognac
Stir and strain
Lemon twist garnish

MADAME MANDARINE
Cocktail glass, chilled
Pour ingredients into iced mixing glass
1 1/2 oz. Vodka
1/2 oz. Mandarine Napoléon
1/2 oz. Oro di Mazzetti Grappa Liqueur
Shake and strain
Orange twist garnish

MAD HATTER
Coffee mug, heated
Build in glass
3/4 oz. Dark Rum
3/4 oz. Spiced Rum
Near fill with hot chocolate
Whipped cream garnish
Sprinkle shaved chocolate

MADONNA'S BRASSIERE
Cocktail glass, chilled
Pour ingredients into iced mixing glass
3/4 oz. Vox Raspberry Vodka
3/4 oz. DeKuyper Raspberry Pucker
3/4 oz. DeKuyper Watermelon Pucker
3/4 oz. Baileys Irish Cream
Stir and strain

MADRAS
Highball glass, ice
Build in glass
1 1/4 oz. Vodka
1/2 fill orange juice
1/2 fill cranberry juice

MADTOWN MILKSHAKE
House specialty glass, chilled
Pour ingredients into blender
1 oz. Baileys Irish Cream
1 oz. Chambord
3/4 oz. Frangelico
3/4 oz. half & half cream
2 scoops vanilla ice cream
Blend ingredients (with ice optional)
Whipped cream garnish
Sprinkle shaved chocolate

CRUZAN® ESTATE DIAMOND RUM

Cruzan Rum originated on the island of St. Croix in 1760 on the Estate Diamond Plantation. The rums produced there quickly became highly sought after exports. The ruins of the original plantation serve as the site for the present day Cruzan Distillery and CRUZAN ESTATE DIAMOND RUM remains one of the most successful brands of Caribbean rum in the world.

For those looking for a savory añejo with an amazingly low price tag, this rum is just the ticket. Cruzan Estate Diamond is a blend of triple-distilled rums aged in charred American oak barrels for 5 to 10 years. The blend is then lightly filtered through activated charcoal to remove impurities and particulates.

Cruzan Estate Diamond Rum has a medium-weight body and an alluring bouquet that fills a glass with the toasty aromas of vanilla, chocolate and spice. The rum enters the mouth without a trace of heat and then bathes the palate with the delectable flavors of coffee, caramel and vanilla. The finish is dry and warming.

The Cruzan range also includes ESTATE LIGHT, which is a blend of triple-distilled rums aged in oak bourbon barrels for a minimum of 2 years. It is then filtered through charcoal to remove the color it obtained during aging. CRUZAN ESTATE DARK RUM is essentially the same, but the color is left intact.

MAGELLAN SAUCE
Cocktail glass, chilled
Pour ingredients into iced mixing glass
2 oz. Magellan Gin
3/4 oz. Cointreau
3/4 oz. fresh lime juice
Shake and strain
Lime wedge garnish

MAGIC POTION
House specialty glass, ice
Pour ingredients into iced mixing glass
1 3/4 oz. Gin
3/4 oz. RémyRed Red Berry Infusion
1/2 oz. Triple Sec
1 oz. fresh lime juice
1 oz. sweet 'n' sour
Shake and strain
Top with club soda
Lime wedge garnish

MAHOGANY GOLD
Sherry glass, chilled
Layer ingredients
1/2 fill Oro di Mazzetti Grappa Liqueur
1/2 fill Scotch Whisky

MAIDEN'S REPRIEVE
Cocktail glass, chilled
Pour ingredients into iced mixing glass
1 1/2 oz. Plymouth Gin
1/2 oz. Cointreau
1 dash orange juice
1 dash Angostura Bitters
1 oz. sweet 'n' sour
Shake and strain

MAI TAI (1)
House specialty glass, ice
Pour ingredients into iced mixing glass
1 3/4 oz. Light Rum
1/2 oz. Crème de Noyaux
1/2 oz. Triple Sec
2 oz. sweet 'n' sour
Shake and strain
Orange slice and cherry garnish

MAI TAI (2)
House specialty glass, ice
Pour ingredients into iced mixing glass
2 1/2 oz. Light Rum
1 oz. Gold Rum
1 oz. Triple Sec
3/4 oz. grenadine
3/4 oz. orgeat syrup
1 oz. fresh lime juice
1 3/4 oz. sweet 'n' sour
Shake and strain
Float 3/4 oz. Overproof Rum
Pineapple wedge and cherry garnish

MAI TAI (3)
House specialty glass, ice
Pour ingredients into iced mixing glass
1 oz. Overproof Rum
1 oz. Gold Rum
1 oz. Light Rum
3/4 oz. Orange Curaçao
1/2 oz. grenadine
1 1/2 oz. orange juice
1 3/4 oz. fresh lime juice
Shake and strain
Lime wedge, orange slice and
     mint sprig garnish

MAI TAI, MOBAY
House specialty glass, ice
Pour ingredients into iced mixing glass
1 oz. Appleton Estate V/X Jamaica Rum
1 oz. Mount Gay Eclipse Rum
1 oz. Triple Sec
1 oz. orgeat syrup
3/4 oz. grenadine
1 3/4 oz. sweet 'n' sour
1 3/4 oz. sweetened lime juice
Shake and strain
Mint sprig garnish

MALIBU BEACH
Bucket glass, ice
Build in glass
1 1/2 oz. Malibu Caribbean Rum
3/4 oz. Myers's Jamaican Rum
Fill with papaya juice

MALIBU FIZZ
Bucket glass, ice
Build in glass
1 oz. Malibu Caribbean Rum
3/4 oz. Midori
Near fill with ginger ale
Float 3/4 oz. Baileys Irish Cream

MALIBU RUNNER
Bucket glass, ice
Build in glass
1 oz. Malibu Caribbean Rum
3/4 oz. Disaronno Amaretto
Near fill with pineapple juice
Float 3/4 oz. Razzmatazz Raspberry Liqueur

MALIBU SLIDE
Bucket glass, ice
Build in glass
1 1/2 oz. Malibu Caribbean Rum
1/2 oz. Kahlúa
1/2 oz. Irish Cream
2 oz. pineapple juice
2 oz. milk

MALIBU SUNSET
Bucket glass, ice
Build in glass
1 1/2 oz. Malibu Caribbean Rum
1/2 oz. Peach Schnapps
Near fill with orange juice
Float 3/4 oz. Razzmatazz Raspberry Liqueur

MAMA CITRON
Rocks glass, ice
Build in glass
1 1/2 oz. Absolut Citron Vodka
1/2 oz. Disaronno Amaretto

MAMIE'S SISTER
Highball glass, ice
Build in glass
1 1/4 oz. Gin
Fill with ginger ale
Lemon wedge garnish

MAMIE'S SOUTHERN SISTER
Highball glass, ice
Build in glass
1 1/4 oz. Bourbon
Fill with ginger ale
Lemon wedge garnish

MAMIE TAYLOR
Highball glass, ice
Build in glass
1 1/4 oz. Scotch Whisky
Fill with ginger ale
Lemon wedge garnish

MANDARINE DREAM
House specialty glass, ice
Pour ingredients into iced mixing glass
2 oz. Orange Liqueur
3/4 oz. Chambord
1 1/2 oz. sweet 'n' sour
1 1/2 oz. orange juice
Shake and strain
Orange slice garnish

MANDARIN MIMOSA
Champagne glass, chilled
Build in glass
1 oz. Absolut Mandarin Vodka
1 1/2 oz. orange juice
Fill with Champagne
Lemon twist garnish

MANGO-A-GOGO
Cocktail glass, chilled
Pour ingredients into blender
1 3/4 oz. Vodka
1/4 oz. Rose's Lime Juice
1 scoop mango sorbet
Blend ingredients (with ice optional)
Mango cube garnish

BORU® VODKA

Brian Boru was the first High King of Ireland, having defeated the Norse invaders at the Battle of Clontarf in 1014 A.D. It is one of the most celebrated events in Irish history. Nearly a millennium later, the product that bears his name—BORU VODKA—is solidifying its own international celebrity.

Made at the Cavan and Canbery Distillery in Ballineen, Ireland, Boru Vodka is quadruple-distilled in small batches from grain and soft, pristine spring water. After distillation, the vodka is filtered through ten feet of Atlantic Irish oak charcoal. It is bottled at 80 proof.

Boru Vodka is a classy dram with a universally appealing taste. It has crystalline clarity, a delicate, featherweight body and an intriguing bouquet that features floral and vanilla notes. Its nose alone is a noteworthy achievement. The vodka rolls over the palate without bite, burn, or harshness filling the mouth with the comforting flavors of mocha and milk chocolate. The finish is long and delectable.

The Boru range also includes BORU ORANGE-FLAVORED VODKA, a spry vodka with an expansive, orange blossom bouquet and a satisfying, orange-tangerine palate. BORU CITRUS-FLAVORED VODKA is imbued with the aroma of sliced lemons and a delicate yet appealing flavor of lemons and limes, with notes of grapefruit and tangerine.

MANGO IN THE WYNDE
House specialty glass, chilled
Pour ingredients into blender
1 1/2 oz. Sea Wynde Pot Still Rum
2 scoops mango sorbet
Blend ingredients (with ice optional)
Mango cube garnish

MANGO MINGLE
House specialty glass, ice
Pour ingredients into blender
3/4 oz. Cruzan Estate Diamond Rum
1/2 oz. Cruzan Vanilla Rum
2 oz. peach puree
2 oz. mango cubes
Blend with ice
Float 3/4 oz. Cruzan Estate Diamond Rum
Mango cube and cherry garnish

MANGO MONSOON
Highball glass, ice
Build in glass
1 1/4 oz. Cruzan Mango Rum
1 oz. mango juice
Fill with pineapple juice

MANHATTAN
Cocktail glass, chilled
Pour ingredients into iced mixing glass
1/2 oz. Sweet Vermouth
1 dash Angostura Bitters (optional)
1 1/2 oz. Bourbon
Stir and strain
Cherry garnish

MANHATTAN, AFFINITY
aka **Affinity Cocktail, Perfect Rob Roy**
Cocktail glass, chilled
Pour ingredients into iced mixing glass
1/2 oz. Dry Vermouth
1/2 oz. Sweet Vermouth
2 dashes Angostura Bitters
1 1/2 oz. Scotch Whisky
Stir and strain
Lemon twist garnish

MANHATTAN, ALGONQUIN
Cocktail glass, chilled
Pour ingredients into iced mixing glass
1/4 oz. Dry Vermouth
1/4 oz. pineapple juice
3 dashes Angostura Bitters
1 1/2 oz. Bourbon
Stir and strain
Orange slice and cherry garnish

MANHATTAN, APPLE

Cocktail glass, chilled
Pour ingredients into iced mixing glass
2 oz. Maker's Mark Bourbon
1 oz. Beretzen Apple Liqueur
Stir and strain
Granny apple wedge garnish

MANHATTAN BEACH

House specialty glass, ice
Pour ingredients into iced mixing glass
1 1/4 oz. Light Rum
1 1/4 oz. Gold Rum
3/4 oz. Disaronno Amaretto
1/2 oz. grenadine
3 oz. pineapple juice
Shake and strain
Float 3/4 oz. Dark Rum
Lime, lemon and orange wedge garnish

MANHATTAN, BENEDICTINE

Cocktail glass, chilled
Pour ingredients into iced mixing glass
1/4 oz. Dry Vermouth
1 1/2 oz. Benedictine
Stir and strain
Lemon twist or cherry garnish

MANHATTAN, BIG APPLE

Cocktail glass, chilled
Pour ingredients into iced mixing glass
1/2 oz. Sweet Vermouth
1 1/2 oz. Laird's Applejack Brandy
Stir and strain
Orange twist garnish

MANHATTAN, BISCAYNE

Cocktail glass, chilled
Pour ingredients into iced mixing glass
1/2 oz. Sweet Vermouth
3 dashes B & B Liqueur
1/2 oz. Triple Sec
1 1/2 oz. Bourbon
Stir and strain
Lemon twist or cherry garnish

MANHATTAN, BLOOD AND SAND

Cocktail glass, chilled
Pour ingredients into iced mixing glass
1 3/4 oz. Brandy
1/2 oz. Chambord
1/2 oz. Sweet Vermouth
1/2 oz. orange juice
Stir and strain
Orange slice garnish

MANHATTAN, BLUE GRASS BLUES

Cocktail glass, chilled
Pour ingredients into iced mixing glass
1/2 oz. Dry Vermouth
3 dashes Angostura Bitters
1/4 oz. Blue Curaçao
1 1/2 oz. Woodford Reserve Bourbon
Stir and strain
Lemon twist or cherry garnish

MANHATTAN, BOULEVARD

Cocktail glass, chilled
Pour ingredients into iced mixing glass
1/4 oz. Dry Vermouth
1/4 oz. Grand Marnier
3 dashes orange bitters
1 1/2 oz. Old Forester Bourbon
Stir and strain
Orange slice and cherry garnish

MANHATTAN, BRANDY

aka **Delmonico**
Cocktail glass, chilled
Pour ingredients into iced mixing glass
1/2 oz. Sweet Vermouth
2-3 dashes Angostura Bitters
1 1/2 oz. Brandy
Stir and strain
Cherry garnish

MANHATTAN, CHERBOURG

Cocktail glass, chilled
Pour ingredients into iced mixing glass
1/2 oz. Dry Vermouth
1/2 oz. Sweet Vermouth
1/4 oz. fresh lemon juice
3 dashes Angostura Bitters
1 3/4 oz. Evan Williams Single Barrel
　　Vintage Bourbon
Stir and strain
Orange slice and cherry garnish

MANHATTAN, CONTINENTAL PERFECT

Cocktail glass, chilled
Pour ingredients into iced mixing glass
3/4 oz. Dry Vermouth
3/4 oz. Sweet Vermouth
3 dashes Angostura Bitters
1 1/2 oz. Bourbon
Stir and strain
Orange slice garnish

CELTIC CROSSING® LIQUEUR

Made in Bailieboro, Ireland, CELTIC CROSSING is a delicious, ideally balanced liqueur made from a recipe first devised over 150 years ago. It is skillfully crafted from a blend of barrel-aged Irish whiskies and cognac, and then sweetened with a touch of heather honey. The real question surrounding Celtic Crossing is how did it become so flavorful without sporting a hefty body and syrupy consistency?

Clearly someone knows the answer, but they're not talking. What is known about this liqueur is that it has an exceptionally light body and a velvety smooth texture. Its wafting bouquet is laced with the comforting aromas of honey, vanilla and toasted oak.

Perhaps Celtic Crossing's most laudable quality is its palate, which features the sumptuous flavors of honey, spice and a dram-sized taste of Irish whiskey. The finish is delectably long and soothing.

Like most top-notch products, Celtic Crossing is best appreciated sipped neat, or with a single cube of ice. It does, however, also enjoy numerous applications behind the bar. It blends marvelously with coffee, cappuccino and hot cocoa, as well as adding a complimentary flavor to a wide range of whiskies and many other liqueurs. Celtic Crossing is a guaranteed crowd pleaser. When you find it, grab it.

MANHATTAN, CUBAN
Cocktail glass, chilled
Pour ingredients into iced mixing glass
3/4 oz. Sweet Vermouth
2-3 dashes Angostura Bitters
1 3/4 oz. Light Rum
Stir and strain
Cherry garnish

MANHATTAN, CUBAN MEDIUM
Cocktail glass, chilled
Pour ingredients into iced mixing glass
1/2 oz. Sweet Vermouth
1/2 oz. Dry Vermouth
2-3 dashes Angostura Bitters
1 3/4 oz. Light Rum
Stir and strain
Cherry garnish

MANHATTAN, DANISH
Cocktail glass, chilled
Pour ingredients into iced mixing glass
1/4 oz. Peter Heering Cherry Heering
1/4 oz. Kirschwasser
1 1/2 oz. Bourbon
Stir and strain
Lemon twist or cherry garnish

MANHATTAN, DIJON
Cocktail glass, chilled
Pour ingredients into iced mixing glass
1/2 oz. Dry Vermouth
1/2 oz. Crème de Cassis
1 1/2 oz. Bourbon
Stir and strain
Lemon twist or cherry garnish

MANHATTAN, DRY
Cocktail glass, chilled
Pour ingredients into iced mixing glass
1/4 oz. Dry Vermouth
1 dash Angostura Bitters (optional)
1 1/2 oz. Bourbon
Stir and strain
Lemon twist garnish

MANHATTAN, DRY BRANDY
Cocktail glass, chilled
Pour ingredients into iced mixing glass
1/4 oz. Dry Vermouth
1 dash Angostura Bitters (optional)
1 1/2 oz. Brandy
Stir and strain
Lemon twist garnish

MANHATTAN, DUBONNET
Cocktail glass, chilled
Pour ingredients into iced mixing glass
1/4 oz. Dry Vermouth
3/4 oz. Dubonnet Rouge
3 dashes Angostura Bitters
1 3/4 oz. Bourbon
Stir and strain
Lemon twist or cherry garnish

MANHATTAN, GALLIANO
Cocktail glass, chilled
Pour ingredients into iced mixing glass
1/4 oz. Galliano Liqueur
1 1/2 oz. Bourbon
Stir and strain
Lemon twist or cherry garnish

MANHATTAN GLITZ
Cocktail glass, chilled
Pour ingredients into iced mixing glass
3/4 oz. Oro di Mazzetti Grappa Liqueur
2 oz. Jack Daniel's Single Barrel Whiskey
Stir and strain
Lemon twist garnish

MANHATTAN, IRISH
aka **Paddy**
Cocktail glass, chilled
Pour ingredients into iced mixing glass
1/2 oz. Sweet Vermouth
3 dashes Angostura Bitters
1 1/2 oz. Irish Whiskey
Stir and strain
Lemon twist or cherry garnish

MANHATTAN, ITALIAN
Cocktail glass, chilled
Pour ingredients into iced mixing glass
1/4 oz. maraschino cherry juice
1/2 oz. Disaronno Amaretto
1 1/2 oz. Maker's Mark Bourbon
Stir and strain
Orange slice and cherry garnish

MANHATTAN, JACK'S BEST
Cocktail glass, chilled
Pour ingredients into iced mixing glass
1/4 oz. Sweet Vermouth
3 dashes orange bitters
2 oz. Jack Daniel's Single Barrel Whiskey
Stir and strain
Orange slice and cherry garnish

MANHATTAN, LAFAYETTE
Cocktail glass, chilled
Pour ingredients into iced mixing glass
3/4 oz. Dubonnet Rouge
3 dashes Angostura Bitters
2 oz. Bourbon
Stir and strain
Lemon twist or cherry garnish

MANHATTAN, LATIN
Cocktail glass, chilled
Pour ingredients into iced mixing glass
1/4 oz. Sweet Vermouth
1/4 oz. Dry Vermouth
2 dashes Angostura Bitters (optional)
1 3/4 oz. Light Rum
Stir and strain
Lemon twist garnish

MANHATTAN, LORETTO
Cocktail glass, chilled
Pour ingredients into iced mixing glass
1/2 oz. Sweet Vermouth
3 dashes Amer Picon
1/4 oz. B & B Liqueur
1 1/2 oz. Maker's Mark Bourbon
Stir and strain
Lemon twist or cherry garnish

MANHATTAN, MAPLE LEAF
Cocktail glass, chilled
Pour ingredients into iced mixing glass
1/2 oz. Sweet Vermouth
1/4 oz. maraschino cherry juice
1 1/2 oz. Canadian Whisky
Stir and strain
Cherry garnish

MANHATTAN, MARIANNE
Cocktail glass, chilled
Pour ingredients into iced mixing glass
1/4 oz. Dry Vermouth
1/2 oz. Byrrh
3 dashes Angostura Bitters
1 1/2 oz. Bourbon
Stir and strain
Lemon twist or cherry garnish

MANHATTAN, MAZATLAN
Cocktail glass, chilled
Pour ingredients into iced mixing glass
1/2 oz. Dubonnet Rouge
1/2 oz. fresh lime juice
1/4 oz. maraschino cherry juice
2 oz. Bourbon
Stir and strain
Cherry garnish

MANHATTAN, METS
Cocktail glass, chilled
Pour ingredients into iced mixing glass
1/2 oz. Dry Vermouth
1/4 oz. Fraise Liqueur
1 1/2 oz. Canadian Whisky
Stir and strain
Lemon twist or cherry garnish

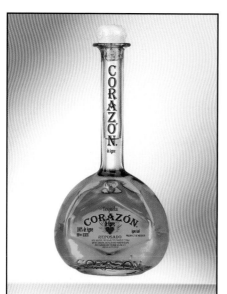

TEQUILA CORAZÓN®
DE AGAVE REPOSADO

One would expect that people in Mexico know a thing or two about tequila. Reposados are the best-selling type of tequila in its country of origin, possibly because they strike a balance between the fresh exuberance of a silver tequila and the mellow refinement of an añejo. Few demonstrate this balancing act as masterfully as TEQUILA CORAZÓN DE AGAVE REPOSADO.

Distilled in the Arandas Mountains, Corazón tequilas are handcrafted entirely at the Destiladora San Nicholas Estate. The 100% agave tequilas are made using traditional, century-old methods abandoned by most as cost prohibitive.

Tequila Corazón fully deserves the critical acclaim it is receiving. The 80 proof range of tequilas is made from mature, estate grown agaves. After harvesting, the agaves are baked in stone ovens, slowly fermented and distilled in the estate's copper pot stills.

Corazón Reposado is a supremely enjoyable spirit. It is matured in small, Canadian oak barrels for up to one year, which is a sufficient amount of time to soften its character, while leaving the inherent quality of the agave unaffected by the tannins in the wood.

The reposado has a lightweight body and a generous vanilla and floral bouquet. Its mouth-filling palate features an array of spicy, slightly peppery flavors that last long into the relaxed finish.

MANHATTAN, MOON OVER MANHATTAN
Cocktail glass, chilled
Pour ingredients into iced mixing glass
1/4 oz. cranberry juice
1/2 oz. Disaronno Amaretto
1 3/4 oz. Crown Royal
Stir and strain
Cherry garnish

MANHATTAN, NAPOLEON
Cocktail glass, chilled
Pour ingredients into iced mixing glass
1/2 oz. Sweet Vermouth
2 oz. Courvoisier VSOP Cognac
Stir and strain
Orange twist garnish

MANHATTAN, NEW ORLEANS
Cocktail glass, chilled
Pour ingredients into iced mixing glass
Swirl 1/2 oz. Frangelico, discard excess
1/2 oz. Sweet Vermouth
1 1/2 oz. Bourbon
Stir and strain
Cherry garnish

MANHATTAN, PAPARAZZI
Cocktail glass, chilled
Pour ingredients into iced mixing glass
1/2 oz. Sweet Vermouth
1/4 oz. Fernet Branca
3 dashes Pernod
1 1/2 oz. Bourbon
Stir and strain
Orange slice and cherry garnish

MANHATTAN, PARK PARADISE
Cocktail glass, chilled
Pour ingredients into iced mixing glass
1/2 oz. Sweet Vermouth
3 dashes Angostura Bitters
3 dashes Maraschino Liqueur
1 1/2 oz. Canadian Whisky
Stir and strain
Lemon twist or cherry garnish

MANHATTAN, PERFECT
aka **Medium Manhattan**
Cocktail glass, chilled
Pour ingredients into iced mixing glass
1/4 oz. Dry Vermouth
1/4 oz. Sweet Vermouth
1 dash Angostura Bitters (optional)
1 1/2 oz. Bourbon
Stir and strain
Lemon twist garnish

MANHATTAN, PERFECT BRANDY
Cocktail glass, chilled
Pour ingredients into iced mixing glass
1/4 oz. Dry Vermouth
1/4 oz. Sweet Vermouth
1 dash Angostura Bitters (optional)
1 1/2 oz. Brandy
Stir and strain
Lemon twist garnish

MANHATTAN, PERFECT SOUTHERN COMFORT
Cocktail glass, chilled
Pour ingredients into iced mixing glass
1/4 oz. Dry Vermouth
1/4 oz. Sweet Vermouth
1 1/2 oz. Southern Comfort
Stir and strain
Lemon twist garnish

MANHATTAN, POOR TIM
Cocktail glass, chilled
Pour ingredients into iced mixing glass
1/2 oz. Dry Vermouth
1/2 oz. Chambord
1 1/2 oz. Bourbon
Stir and strain
Lemon twist or cherry garnish

MANHATTAN, PREAKNESS
Cocktail glass, chilled
Pour ingredients into iced mixing glass
1/2 oz. Sweet Vermouth
3 dashes Angostura Bitters
3/4 oz. B & B Liqueur
1 1/2 oz. Bourbon
Stir and strain
Lemon twist garnish

MANHATTAN, PROHIBITION
Cocktail glass, chilled
Pour ingredients into iced mixing glass
1 oz. Sweet Vermouth
3 dashes orange bitters
1 oz. Rye Whiskey
Stir and strain
Lemon twist garnish

MANHATTAN, QUEBEC
Cocktail glass, chilled
Pour ingredients into iced mixing glass
1/2 oz. Dry Vermouth
3 dashes Amer Picon
3 dashes Maraschino Liqueur
1 1/2 oz. Canadian Whisky
Stir and strain
Lemon twist garnish

MANHATTAN, RASPBERRY
Cocktail glass, chilled
Pour ingredients into iced mixing glass
1/2 oz. Dry Vermouth
1/2 oz. Chambord
1 1/2 oz. Bourbon
Stir and strain
Lemon twist garnish

MANHATTAN, ROMAN
Cocktail glass, chilled
Pour ingredients into iced mixing glass
1/2 oz. Sweet Vermouth
1/4 oz. Sambuca Romano
1 1/2 oz. Canadian Whisky
Stir and strain
Lemon twist or cherry garnish

MANHATTAN, ROSE
Cocktail glass, chilled
Pour ingredients into iced mixing glass
1/2 oz. Dry Vermouth
1/2 oz. Crème de Cassis
1/4 oz. fresh lemon juice
1 1/2 oz. Bourbon
Stir and strain
Lemon twist or cherry garnish

MANHATTAN, ROSEBUD
Cocktail glass, chilled
Pour ingredients into iced mixing glass
1/2 oz. RémyRed Red Berry Infusion
1 1/2 oz. Bourbon
Stir and strain
Lemon twist garnish

MANHATTAN, SATIN
Cocktail glass, chilled
Pour ingredients into iced mixing glass
1/2 oz. Sweet Vermouth
1/2 oz. Grand Marnier
1 1/2 oz. Gentleman Jack
    Tennessee Whiskey
Stir and strain
Lemon twist garnish

MANHATTAN, SHAMROCK
Cocktail glass, chilled
Pour ingredients into iced mixing glass
1/2 oz. Sweet Vermouth
3 dashes Angostura Bitters
1/2 oz. Green Crème de Menthe
1 1/2 oz. Bourbon
Stir and strain
Lemon twist garnish

MAGELLAN® GIN

Premium gins are made from recipes that endow them with well-developed characters and individual personalities. They constitute a rarefied lot, with the fewest number of premium brands of all major spirits. Add to this that no two gins taste alike, and you'll see why each brand name gin is truly a singular commodity. One of the unique top-shelf performers to cross our shores is MAGELLAN GIN and we are genuinely pleased it has.

Created by spirits guru Michel Roux, Magellan Gin is made in small batches in Cognac, France from triple-distilled neutral spirits, spring water and 11 freeze-dried botanicals, a mix that includes cloves. During the fourth and final distillation, the gin is infused with deep-blue Iris petals. The result is a sensationally flavorful, 88 proof spirit with a captivating, light blue tint.

Magellan Gin is a bona fide headliner. The gin has a supple, medium-weight body and an engaging bouquet laced with the aromas of flora, citrus and spice. It has a delightfully soft entry that quickly entertains the mouth with a fanciful array of tantalizing flavors. The finish is cool and crisp.

Martini savvy haunts will want to be the first on their block to carry Magellan Gin. It was created with a cocktail glass in mind. Great looks and an incomparable taste make Magellan unbeatable.

MANHATTAN, SHEEPSHEAD BAY
Cocktail glass, chilled
Pour ingredients into iced mixing glass
1/4 oz. Sweet Vermouth
1/4 oz. B & B Liqueur
3 dashes Angostura Bitters
1 1/2 oz. Bourbon
Stir and strain
Lemon twist or cherry garnish

MANHATTAN, SMOKY
Cocktail glass, chilled
Swirl and coat inside of glass
1/3 oz. Maker's Mark Bourbon
Pour ingredients into iced mixing glass
1/2 oz. Dry Vermouth
1 1/2 oz. Ketel One Vodka
Stir and strain
Lemon twist garnish

MANHATTAN, SOUTHERN COMFORT
Cocktail glass, chilled
Pour ingredients into iced mixing glass
1/4 oz. Dry Vermouth
1 1/2 oz. Southern Comfort
Stir and strain
Cherry garnish

MANHATTAN, SPICED APPLE BRANDY
Cocktail glass, chilled
Pour ingredients into iced mixing glass
1/2 oz. Dry Vermouth
1/2 oz. Celtic Crossing Irish Liqueur
1 1/2 oz. Laird's 12 Year Apple Brandy
Stir and strain
Cherry garnish

MANHATTAN, ST. MORITZ
aka **Sidney Manhattan**
Cocktail glass, chilled
Pour ingredients into iced mixing glass
1/4 oz. Dry Vermouth
1/4 oz. Green Chartreuse
3 dashes orange bitters
1 1/2 oz. Bourbon
Stir and strain
Lemon twist garnish

MANHATTAN, TENNESSEE BLUSH
Cocktail glass, chilled
Pour ingredients into iced mixing glass
1/2 oz. RémyRed Red Berry Infusion
2 oz. Jack Daniel's Single Barrel Whiskey
Stir and strain
Lemon twist and cherry garnish

MANHATTAN, MARKET
Cocktail glass, chilled
Pour ingredients into iced mixing glass
1/2 oz. Sweet Vermouth
1/2 oz. Champagne
2-3 dashes Angostura bitters
2 oz. Maker's Mark Bourbon
Stir and strain
Orange slice and cherry garnish

MANHATTAN, TIVOLI
Cocktail glass, chilled
Pour ingredients into iced mixing glass
1/2 oz. Sweet Vermouth
1/2 oz. Aquavit
3 dashes Campari Aperitivo
1 1/2 oz. Bourbon
Stir and strain
Orange slice and cherry garnish

MANHATTAN, TWIN PEAKS
Cocktail glass, chilled
Pour ingredients into iced mixing glass
1/2 oz. Dubonnet Rouge
1/4 oz. Cointreau
1 1/2 oz. Gentleman Jack
     Tennessee Whiskey
Stir and strain
Lemon twist or cherry garnish

MANHATTAN, VINTAGE (1)
Cocktail glass, chilled
Pour ingredients into iced mixing glass
1 oz. Dubonnet Rouge
2-3 dashes Angostura Bitters
2 1/2 oz. Evan Williams Single Barrel
     Vintage Bourbon
Stir and strain
Cherry garnish

MANHATTAN, VINTAGE (2)
Cocktail glass, chilled
Pour ingredients into iced mixing glass
1/2 oz. Dubonnet Rouge
2 oz. Evan Williams Single Barrel
     Vintage Bourbon
Stir and strain
Lemon twist garnish

MANHATTAN, WALDORF
Cocktail glass, chilled
Pour ingredients into iced mixing glass
1/2 oz. Sweet Vermouth
1/4 oz. Pernod
3 dashes Angostura Bitters
1 1/2 oz. Bourbon
Stir and strain
Orange slice and cherry garnish

MANHATTAN, WESTCHESTER
Cocktail glass, chilled
Pour ingredients into iced mixing glass
1/4 oz. Dry Vermouth
1/4 oz. Rose's Lime Juice
3 dashes Angostura Bitters
1 1/2 oz. Woodford Reserve Bourbon
Stir and strain
Lemon twist or cherry garnish

MARASCHINO RUM MIST
House specialty glass, ice
Build in glass
1 1/2 oz. Gold Rum
1 1/2 oz. maraschino cherry juice
1 oz. Rose's Lime Juice
Fill with club soda
Orange slice and cherry garnish

MARGARITA, AGAVE JUICE
House specialty glass, ice
Rim glass with salt (optional)
Pour ingredients into iced mixing glass
1 1/2 oz. Don Eduardo Silver Tequila
1/2 oz. Triple Sec
1/2 oz. Rose's Lime Juice
1-2 dashes Angostura Bitters
1/2 oz. grenadine
1 oz. orange juice
1 oz. sweet 'n' sour
Shake and strain
Lime wedge garnish

MARGARITA, AGAVERO
House specialty glass, chilled
Rim glass with salt (optional)
Pour ingredients into iced mixing glass
1 1/2 oz. Añejo Tequila
3/4 oz. Agavero Liqueur
1/2 oz. orange
1/2 oz. fresh lime juice
3/4 oz. grapefruit juice
1 1/2 oz. sweet 'n' sour
Shake and strain
Lime wedge garnish

MARGARITA, ANITA
House specialty glass, ice
Rim glass with salt (optional)
Pour ingredients into iced mixing glass
1 1/4 oz. Jose Cuervo Tradicional Tequila
1/2 oz. Grand Marnier
1/2 oz. Rose's Lime Juice
1 1/2 oz. sweet 'n' sour
1 oz. cranberry juice
Shake and strain
Lime wedge garnish

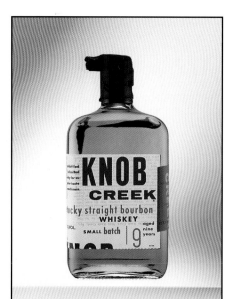

KNOB CREEK® KENTUCKY STRAIGHT BOURBON

KNOB CREEK KENTUCKY STRAIGHT BOURBON is bourbon the way it used to be. Fortunately, great taste is timeless, which is why Jim Beam included Knob Creek as a charter member of the Original Small Batch Bourbon Collection, an unparalleled set of four distinctively different styles of bourbon.

Knob Creek Bourbon is distilled in small batches and aged for a minimum of 9 years in new white oak barrels. These barrels are first seared over a low flame to bring out the natural sugars in the wood, and then "flash-fired" to create a deep char. Underneath the charcoal is a rich layer of red caramelized wood that touches every aspect of the bourbon.

A few moments alone with Knob Creek are all it takes to grasp why the 100 proof bourbon is critically acclaimed and universally popular. It has a bouquet laden with bakery fresh aromas and a semisweet palate found no where else on Earth.

The collection also includes BOOKER'S, which is aged 6 to 8 years and bottled unfiltered and uncut at about 126 proof. Booker's is a tremendous traditional bourbon. BASIL HAYDEN'S is an 8 year old bourbon made with a higher percentage of rye and barley malt for a more flavorful, peppery whiskey. BAKER'S BOURBON is an accessible 7 year old whiskey with the character of a well aged brandy.

MARGARITA AZUL
House specialty glass, ice
Rim glass with salt (optional)
Pour ingredients into iced mixing glass
1 1/4 oz. Tarantula Azul
1/2 oz. Disaronno Amaretto
1/2 oz. Blue Curaçao
1/4 oz. fresh lime juice
1 1/2 oz. sweet 'n' sour
Shake and strain
Lime wedge garnish

MARGARITA, BAHAMA MAMA
House specialty glass, ice
Rim glass with sugar (optional)
Pour ingredients into iced mixing glass
1 oz. Sauza Conmemorativo Añejo Tequila
1 oz. Malibu Caribbean Rum
1/2 oz. Triple Sec
1/2 oz. Rose's Lime Juice
1 1/2 oz. pineapple juice
1 1/2 oz. sweet 'n' sour
Shake and strain
Pineapple wedge and cherry garnish

MARGARITA, BAJA
aka **Agavero Margarita**
Cocktail glass, chilled
Rim glass with salt (optional)
Pour ingredients into iced mixing glass
1 1/4 oz. Sauza Gold Tequila
3/4 oz. Agavero Liqueur
1 1/2 oz. sweet 'n' sour
Shake and strain
Lime wedge garnish

MARGARITA, BAY BREEZE
House specialty glass, chilled
Pour ingredients into iced mixing glass
1 oz. Citrus Rum
1 oz. Orange Rum
3/4 oz. fresh lime juice
2 oz. sweet 'n' sour
Shake and strain
Float 3/4 oz. Dark Rum
Pineapple wedge and lime wheel garnish

MARGARITA, BLACK FOREST
aka **Black Cherry Margarita**
House specialty glass, ice
Rim glass with salt (optional)
Pour ingredients into iced mixing glass
1 1/4 oz. Reposado Tequila
3/4 oz. Cherry Schnapps
1/2 oz. Rose's Lime Juice
2 oz. sweet 'n' sour
2 oz. orange juice
Shake and strain
Lime wedge garnish

MARGARITA, BLACK GOLD
House specialty glass, ice
Rim glass with salt (optional)
Pour ingredients into iced mixing glass
1 oz. Añejo Tequila
1 oz. Lime-infused Silver Tequila
3/4 oz. Chambord
1/2 oz. Rose's Lime Juice
2 oz. sweet 'n' sour
Shake and strain
Lime wedge garnish

MARGARITA, BLOODY
House specialty glass, ice
Rim glass with salt and pepper (optional)
Pour ingredients into iced mixing glass
1 1/4 oz. Silver Tequila
3/4 oz. Triple Sec
1/2 oz. Rose's Lime Juice
1/4 oz. jalapeño pepper juice
1-2 dashes Tabasco Sauce
2 oz. Sangrita Mix
Shake and strain
Sprinkle ground habanero chile
    (use sparingly)
Lime wedge garnish
Note: See Sangrita Mix

MARGARITA, BLUE
aka **Midnight Margarita**
House specialty glass, ice
Rim glass with salt (optional)
Pour ingredients into iced mixing glass
1 1/4 oz. Jose Cuervo Especial Tequila
3/4 oz. Blue Curaçao
1/2 oz. Rose's Lime Juice
1 1/2 oz. sweet 'n' sour
Shake and strain
Lime wedge garnish

MARGARITA, BLUE
    MAESTRO GRAN
House specialty glass, ice
Rim glass with salt (optional)
Pour ingredients into iced mixing glass
1 1/2 oz. Mezcal del Maestro Añejo
1/2 oz. Grand Marnier
3/4 oz. Blue Curaçao
1/4 oz. Rose's Lime Juice
1 1/2 oz. sweet 'n' sour
Shake and strain
Lime wedge garnish

MARGARITA, BLUE MOON
House specialty glass, chilled
Rim glass with salt (optional)
Pour ingredients into blender
1 1/4 oz. Corazón Añejo Tequila
3/4 oz. Blue Curaçao
1/2 oz. Rose's Lime Juice
1 1/2 oz. sweet 'n' sour
1-2 scoops lemon sorbet
Blend ingredients (with ice optional)
Lime wedge garnish

MARGARITA BRITANNIA (1)
Cocktail glass, chilled
Pour ingredients into iced mixing glass
3/4 oz. Silver Tequila
3/4 oz. Gin
1/2 oz. Triple Sec
1 1/2 oz. sweet 'n' sour
Shake and strain
Lime wedge garnish

MARGARITA BRITANNIA (2)
Cocktail glass, chilled
Pour ingredients into iced mixing glass
3/4 oz. Sauza Tres Generaciones
    Plata Tequila
3/4 oz. Beefeater London Dry Gin
1/2 oz. Grand Marnier
1 1/2 oz. sweet 'n' sour
Shake and strain
Lime wedge garnish

MARGARITA, CADILLAC
House specialty glass, ice
Rim glass with salt (optional)
Pour ingredients into iced mixing glass
1 1/4 oz. 1800 Tequila
3/4 oz. Grand Marnier
1/2 oz. Rose's Lime Juice
1 1/2 oz. sweet 'n' sour
Shake and strain
Lime wedge garnish

MARGARITA, CAJUN
Cocktail glass, chilled
Rim glass with salt and pepper (optional)
Pour ingredients into iced mixing glass
1 1/4 oz. Pepper-infused Silver Tequila
1-2 dashes Tabasco Sauce
1-2 dashes jalapeño pepper juice
2 oz. sweet 'n' sour
Shake and strain
Small jalapeño peppers garnish

POLAR ICE® VODKA

For true enthusiasts, the final exam of a great vodka is how it performs once it hits the glass. It really doesn't matter how it looks on the shelf, or what its suggested retail price is. In the final analysis, it's either got what it takes to compete with the big boys, or it doesn't. Well, meet a serious contender. It is POLAR ICE VODKA and it's more than ready to play.

New to the United States, Polar Ice is made in Canada by the internationally renowned Corby Distilleries. It is made from 100% Canadian wheat that is meticulously scrutinized for quality. The vodka is quadruple-distilled in state of the art column stills, which is not necessarily unusual. What makes the production of Polar Ice unique is the use of a patented pressurized extraction process, which rids the spirit of even microscopic impurities. The vodka is then filtered three times for purity and bottled at 80 proof.

Again, it doesn't matter where or how it's made if it doesn't perform like an Olympian in the glass. Fortunately, Polar Ice is a world-class performer. The featherweight vodka has a satin-like texture and a delicate, faintly citrus bouquet. It lilts over the palate like mist leaving behind a most satisfying nothingness, exactly what its trainers were shooting for. Its finish is warm and relaxed.

Polar Ice Vodka is a savvy premium spirit priced to move.

MARGARITA, CAMINO REAL
House specialty glass, ice
Rim glass with salt (optional)
Pour ingredients into iced mixing glass
1 1/4 oz. El Tesoro Platinum Tequila
3/4 oz. Cruzan Banana Rum
1/2 oz. Rose's Lime Juice
1 oz. orange juice
1 oz. sweet 'n' sour
Shake and strain
Lime wedge garnish

MARGARITA, CANTINA WINE
House specialty glass, ice
Rim glass with salt (optional)
Build in glass
2 oz. Dry White Wine
1 oz. Triple Sec
1/4 oz. Rose's Lime Juice
2 oz. sweet 'n' sour
Fill with club soda
Lime wedge garnish

MARGARITA, CAPTAIN
House specialty glass, ice
Rim glass with salt (optional)
Pour ingredients into iced mixing glass
1 1/4 oz. Captain Morgan Spiced Rum
1/2 oz. Triple Sec
1/2 oz. Rose's Lime Juice
2 oz. sweet 'n' sour
Shake and strain
Lime wedge garnish

MARGARITA, CARIBBEAN
aka **Caribbean 'Rita**
House specialty glass, ice
Rim glass with pink lemonade mix (optional)
Pour ingredients into iced mixing glass
1 oz. Herradura Silver Tequila
1 oz. Appleton Estate V/X Jamaica Rum
1/2 oz. Triple Sec
1/2 oz. Rose's Lime Juice
1 1/2 oz. orange juice
1 1/2 oz. sweet 'n' sour
Shake and strain
Pineapple wedge and cherry garnish

MARGARITA, CATALINA
House specialty glass, ice
Rim glass with sugar (optional)
Pour ingredients into iced mixing glass
1 1/4 oz. Patrón Silver Tequila
1/2 oz. Blue Curaçao
1/2 oz. Peach Schnapps
1/4 oz. Rose's Lime Juice
2 oz. sweet 'n' sour
Shake and strain
Lime wedge garnish

MARGARITA, CATALINA ISLAND
Cocktail glass, chilled
Rim glass with salt (optional)
Pour ingredients into iced mixing glass
1 1/4 oz. Patrón Añejo Tequila
3/4 oz. Agavero Liqueur
1/2 oz. Rose's Lime Juice
1/2 oz. orange juice
1 1/2 oz. sweet 'n' sour
Shake and strain
Lime wedge garnish

MARGARITA, CHAMPAGNE
Champagne glass, chilled
Rim glass with Cointreau and
    sugar (optional)
Pour ingredients into iced mixing glass
1 oz. Patrón Añejo Tequila
1/2 oz. Cointreau
1/2 oz. Rose's Lime Juice
1/2 oz. orange juice
Shake and strain
Fill with Champagne
Lemon twist garnish

MARGARITA, CHAPALA
House specialty glass, ice
Rim glass with salt (optional)
Pour ingredients into iced mixing glass
1 1/4 oz. Corazón Reposado Tequila
1/2 oz. Cointreau
1/2 oz. orange juice
1/2 oz. Rose's Lime Juice
1/4 oz. grenadine
1-2 dashes of orange flower water
1 1/2 oz. sweet 'n' sour
Shake and strain
Lime wedge garnish

MARGARITA, CIAO ITALIAN
Cocktail glass, chilled
Rim glass with salt (optional)
Pour ingredients into iced mixing glass
1 1/4 oz. Don Eduardo Añejo Tequila
1 oz. Limoncello Liqueur
3/4 oz. Cointreau
1/2 oz. Rose's Lime Juice
1/2 oz. cranberry juice
2 oz. sweet 'n' sour
Shake and strain
Lime wedge garnish

MARGARITA, CITRONITA
House specialty glass, ice
Rim glass with salt (optional)
Pour ingredients into iced mixing glass
1 1/4 oz. Absolut Citron Vodka
1/2 oz. Cointreau
1/2 oz. Rose's Lime Juice
3/4 oz. cranberry juice
2 oz. sweet 'n' sour
Shake and strain
Lemon wedge garnish

MARGARITA CLASSICO
Cocktail glass, chilled
Rim glass with salt (optional)
Pour ingredients into iced mixing glass
1 1/4 oz. Silver Tequila
1/2 oz. Triple Sec
1/4 oz. Rose's Lime Juice (optional)
1/4 oz. orange juice (optional)
1 1/2 oz. sweet 'n' sour
Shake and strain
Lime wedge garnish

MARGARITA, CONGA
Cocktail glass, chilled
Pour ingredients into iced mixing glass
1 oz. Cruzan Banana Rum
1 oz. Cruzan Pineapple Rum
3/4 oz. Citrónge Orange Liqueur
1/2 oz. Rose's Lime Juice
1 1/2 oz. sweet 'n' sour
Shake and strain
Lime wedge garnish

MARGARITA, COYOTE (1)
House specialty glass, ice
Rim glass with salt and pepper (optional)
Pour ingredients into iced mixing glass
1 1/4 oz. Jose Cuervo Clásico Tequila
1/2 oz. Triple Sec
1/2 oz. Rose's Lime Juice
1/4 oz. jalapeño pepper juice
1 oz. cranberry juice
1 1/2 oz. sweet 'n' sour
Shake and strain
Lime wedge garnish

MARGARITA, COYOTE (2)
House specialty glass, ice
Rim glass with salt and pepper (optional)
Pour ingredients into iced mixing glass
1 1/2 oz. Sol Dios Añejo Tequila
1/2 oz. Triple Sec
1/2 oz. Rose's Lime Juice
1 1/2 oz. prickly pear juice
1 1/2 oz. sweet 'n' sour
Shake and strain
Lime wedge garnish

SYLK CREAM® LIQUEUR

Don't be surprised if the first sip of SYLK CREAM LIQUEUR leaves you with the unmistakable impression that you've just tasted something unique. That's because there is nothing remotely like it.

This highly innovative liqueur is made in Scotland by the House of Drambuie. Sylk Cream Liqueur is an artistic creation crafted from a base of fresh dairy cream imported from Holland, which contains 40% less fat than the leading cream liqueurs. To the base is added heather honey, premium Scotch malt whiskies aged between 15 and 17 years and the same secret recipe of herbs and spices used in Drambuie. The liqueur is bottled at 34 proof.

Everything about this liqueur screams of elegance. Sylk has an attractive ivory color and a light, velvety smooth body that is noticeably less thick than its contemporaries. The prominent bouquet features the aromas of herbs, spices and fine malt whisky. Its true moment of glory comes when it washes over the palate and leaves behind a delectable array of flavors that could only be created by Drambuie. The finish is long and dessert-like.

Sylk Cream Liqueur is a highly sophisticated product that is best served chilled, although it does enjoy loads of creative applications behind the bar. Don't overlook the obvious, Sylk Cream Liqueur and Drambuie are a natural pair.

MARGARITA, CRANBERRY (1)
House specialty glass, chilled
Rim glass with salt (optional)
Pour ingredients into blender
1 1/2 oz. Silver Tequila
1/2 oz. Grand Marnier
3/4 oz. Rose's Lime Juice
3/4 oz. sweet 'n' sour
2 oz. cranberry juice
2 oz. strawberry puree
Blend with ice
Lime wedge garnish

MARGARITA, CRANBERRY (2)
House specialty glass, chilled
Rim glass with sugar (optional)
Pour ingredients into blender
1 1/2 oz. Silver Tequila
1/2 oz. Triple Sec
1/4 cup jellied cranberry sauce
1 1/2 oz. sweet 'n' sour
Blend with ice
Fresh strawberry garnish

MARGARITA, DAMRAK 'RITA
House specialty glass, ice
Rim glass with salt (optional)
Pour ingredients into iced mixing glass
2 oz. Damrak Amsterdam Gin
1/2 oz. Cointreau
1/4 oz. orange juice
1 1/2 oz. fresh lime juice
Shake and strain
Lime wedge garnish

MARGARITA DE FRUTA
aka **Fruit Margarita**
House specialty glass, chilled
Rim glass with sugar (optional)
Pour ingredients into blender
1 1/4 oz. Silver Tequila
1/2 oz. Triple Sec
1/2 oz. Rose's Lime Juice
1/2 cup requested fruit
1 dash orange juice (optional)
1 1/2 oz. sweet 'n' sour
Blend with ice
Fresh fruit garnish
Note: Fruit choices include apple, apricot, banana, kiwi, melon, peach, pomegranate, raspberry, strawberry and watermelon

MARGARITA DE MEXICO
Cocktail glass, chilled
Rim glass with salt (optional)
Pour ingredients into iced mixing glass
1 oz. Silver Tequila
1 oz. Controy Licor de Naranjas
1 oz. fresh lime juice
Shake and strain
Lime wedge garnish

MARGARITA, DIABLO
aka **Red Hot Margarita**
House specialty glass, ice
Rim glass with cinnamon and
    sugar (optional)
Pour ingredients into iced mixing glass
1 1/4 oz. Reposado Tequila
3/4 oz. Cinnamon Schnapps
1/2 oz. Rose's Lime Juice
1 1/2 oz. orange juice
1 1/2 oz. sweet 'n' sour
Shake and strain
Lime wedge garnish

MARGARITA, EL CIEN
Cocktail glass, chilled
Rim glass with salt (optional)
Pour ingredients into iced mixing glass
1 1/2 oz. Herradura Seleccion
    Suprema Tequila
1 oz. El Tesoro Paradiso Añejo Tequila
3/4 oz. Cointreau
1/2 oz. fresh lime juice
1/2 oz. fresh lemon juice
1/2 oz. orange juice
1 1/2 oz. sweet 'n' sour
Shake and strain
Float 3/4 oz. Grand Marnier Centenaire
Lime wedge garnish

MARGARITA, EL CONQUISTADOR
House specialty glass, ice
Rim glass with salt (optional)
Pour ingredients into iced mixing glass
3/4 oz. Sauza Conmemorativo
    Añejo Tequila
3/4 oz. Sauza Hornitos Tequila
1/2 oz. Chambord
1/2 oz. Grand Marnier
1/2 oz. Rose's Lime Juice
1 1/2 oz. sweet 'n' sour
1 1/2 oz. pineapple juice
Shake and strain
Lime wedge garnish

MARGARITA, ELEGANTÉ
House specialty glass, ice
Rim glass with salt (optional)
Pour ingredients into iced mixing glass
3/4 oz. Sauza Conmemorativo
    Añejo Tequila
3/4 oz. Sauza Hornitos Tequila
1/2 oz. Cointreau
1/2 oz. Rose's Lime Juice
1 1/2 oz. sweet 'n' sour
Shake and strain
Lime wedge garnish

MARGARITA, FLORIDITA
aka **Floridita 'Rita**
House specialty glass, ice
Rim glass with pink lemonade
    mix (optional)
Pour ingredients into iced mixing glass
1 1/4 oz. Tequila
1/2 oz. Triple Sec
1/4 oz. Rose's Lime Juice
1/2 oz. cranberry juice
1 1/2 oz. grapefruit juice
1 1/2 oz. sweet 'n' sour
Shake and strain
Lime wedge garnish

MARGARITA FRAMBOISE
House specialty glass, ice
Rim glass with salt and sugar (optional)
Pour ingredients into iced mixing glass
1 1/2 oz. El Tesoro Paradiso Añejo Tequila
3/4 oz. Chambord
1/4 oz. Cointreau
1/4 oz. Grand Marnier Centenaire
1/4 oz. orange juice
1/2 oz. fresh lime juice
2 oz. sweet 'n' sour
Shake and strain
Float red raspberries
Lime wheel garnish

MARGARITA, FRENCH/RUSSIAN
House specialty glass, ice
Rim glass with salt (optional)
Pour ingredients into iced mixing glass
1 1/4 oz. Stolichnaya Ohranj Vodka
1/2 oz. Grand Marnier
1/4 oz. orange juice
1/2 oz. Rose's Lime Juice
1 1/2 oz. sweet 'n' sour
Shake and strain
Orange twist garnish

MARGARITA, GEORGIA
House specialty glass, ice
Rim glass with sugar (optional)
Pour ingredients into iced mixing glass
1 1/4 oz. El Tesoro Platinum Tequila
3/4 oz. DeKuyper Peachtree Schnapps
1/2 oz. Rose's Lime Juice
1 1/2 oz. sweet 'n' sour
Shake and strain
Lime wedge garnish

GRAND MARNIER® CUVEE DE CENT CINQUANTENAIRE

GRAND MARNIER CUVEE DE CENT CINQUANTENAIRE may very well be the pinnacle of elegance and sophistication. Introduced in 1977 to commemorate the 150ᵗʰ anniversary of Marnier-Lapostolle, this magnificent liqueur is the company's crowning achievement.

Cuvee de Cent Cinquantenaire is skillfully crafted at the Marnier-Lapostolle distillery in Neauphle-le-Château. After the infusion of Haitian orange peels and barrel-aged cognacs have been redistilled, they are blended with exceptionally old, Grande Champagne cognacs ranging in age up to 50 years. The liqueur is then aged in Limousin oak barrels in the Marnier-Lapostolle cognac cellars.

The Cuvee de Cent Cinquantenaire is a luxurious liqueur. It has a burnished amber hue and a delicate, silky smooth body. The bouquet is lavishly endowed with the aromas of well aged cognac and citrus. It has a sensationally full and rich palate prominently featuring the flavor of cognac with vibrant orange notes. The finish is delectably long and warming.

To fully appreciate its grandeur, allow it to fully breathe in a snifter.

In 1927, the company released GRAND MARNIER CUVEE DE CENTENAIRE. This world-class version of Grand Marnier is made on a base of cognacs ranging in age up to 25 years. It is marvelously aromatic and flavorful, a masterfully crafted liqueur in every respect.

MARGARITA, GEORGIA PEACH
House specialty glass, ice
Rim glass with sugar (optional)
Pour ingredients into iced mixing glass
1 1/4 oz. Corazón Añejo Tequila
1/2 oz. DeKuyper Peachtree Schnapps
1/2 oz. Triple Sec
1/2 oz. Rose's Lime Juice
1 1/2 oz. orange juice
1 1/2 oz. sweet 'n' sour
Shake and strain
Orange slice garnish

MARGARITA, GUAYMAS
House specialty glass, ice
Rim glass with salt (optional)
Pour ingredients into iced mixing glass
1 1/4 oz. Sauza Tres Generaciones
    Plata Tequila
3/4 oz. Cointreau
1/2 oz. Rose's Lime Juice
1 1/2 oz. sweet 'n' sour
Shake and strain
Lime wedge garnish

MARGARITA, HAWAIIAN
aka **Giggling Margarita**
House specialty glass, chilled
Rim glass with sugar (optional)
Pour ingredients into blender
1 1/4 oz. Jose Cuervo Clásico Tequila
3/4 oz. Disaronno Amaretto
3/4 oz. Blue Curaçao
3-4 slices of cored pineapple
2 oz. sweet 'n' sour
Blend with ice
Lime and pineapple wedge garnish

MARGARITA, HERBA BUENA
aka **Margarita Mojito**
House specialty glass, chilled
Rim glass with salt (optional)
Muddle 5-6 mint leaves with 1/2 oz. simple
    syrup then add ice
Pour ingredients into iced mixing glass
1 1/4 oz. Añejo Tequila
1/2 oz. Triple Sec
1/2 oz. Rose's Lime Juice
2 oz. lemon/lime soda
2 oz. sweet 'n' sour
Shake and strain
Lime wedge and mint sprig garnish

MARGARITA, HONEYDEW THIS
House specialty glass, chilled
Rim glass with sugar (optional)
Pour ingredients into blender
1 1/4 oz. Gold Tequila
1/2 oz. Rose's Lime Juice
1/2 cup diced honeydew melon
2 oz. sweet 'n' sour
Blend with ice
Honeydew slice garnish

MARGARITA, HORNI (1)
House specialty glass, ice
Rim glass with salt (optional)
Pour ingredients into iced mixing glass
1 1/2 oz. Sauza Hornitos Tequila
1/2 oz. Cointreau
1/4 oz. Rose's Lime Juice
2 oz. fresh lime juice
2 oz. sweet 'n' sour
Shake and strain
Lime wedge garnish

MARGARITA, HORNI (2)
House specialty glass, ice
Rim glass with salt (optional)
Pour ingredients into iced mixing glass
1 1/4 oz. Sauza Hornitos Tequila
3/4 oz. Triple Sec
1/2 oz. Rose's Lime Juice
1/2 oz. cranberry juice
1 3/4 oz. sweet 'n' sour
Shake and strain
Lime wedge garnish

MARGARITA, HYPNOTIC
Cocktail glass, chilled
Rim glass with salt (optional)
Pour ingredients into iced mixing glass
1 3/4 oz. Silver Tequila
1 oz. Hpnotiq Liqueur
1/2 oz. Blue Curaçao
1 oz. white cranberry juice
1/2 oz. fresh lime juice
1 1/2 oz. sweet 'n' sour
Shake and strain
Lime wedge garnish

MARGARITA, ICE CREAM
House specialty glass, chilled
Pour ingredients into blender
1 1/4 oz. Espolon Añejo Tequila
3/4 oz. Crème de Banana
1/2 oz. Triple Sec
2 oz. sweet 'n' sour
1-2 scoops vanilla ice cream
Blend ingredients (with ice optional)
Orange slice and cherry garnish

MARGARITA, ITALIAN
House specialty glass, ice
Rim glass with sugar (optional)
Pour ingredients into iced mixing glass
1 1/4 oz. Corazón Reposado Tequila
3/4 oz. Disaronno Amaretto
1/2 oz. Triple Sec
1/2 oz. orange juice
2 oz. sweet 'n' sour
Shake and strain
Lime wedge, orange slice and cherry garnish

MARGARITA, JALAPEÑO
aka **Jalapeñorita**
House specialty glass, ice
Rim glass with salt and pepper (optional)
Pour ingredients into iced mixing glass
1 1/4 oz. Xalixco Tequila
3/4 oz. Grand Marnier
1/2 tsp. Tabasco Jalapeño Sauce
2 oz. sweet 'n' sour
Shake and strain
Lime wedge garnish

MARGARITA, JAMAICAN
Cocktail glass, chilled
Pour ingredients into iced mixing glass
1 1/4 oz. Appleton Estate V/X Jamaica Rum
3/4 oz. Cointreau
1/2 oz. Rose's Lime Juice
1/2 oz. orange juice
1 1/2 oz. sweet 'n' sour
Shake and strain
Lime wedge garnish

MARGARITA, JIMMIE DAVIS
House specialty glass, chilled
Rim glass with salt (optional)
Pour ingredients into iced mixing glass
1 1/2 oz. Tequila
1/2 oz. Triple Sec
1/4 oz. orgeat syrup
1 oz. simple syrup
2 oz. fresh lime juice
Shake and strain
Lime wedge garnish

MARGARITA, KAMIKAZE
aka **Kami 'Rita**
House specialty glass, ice
Rim glass with salt (optional)
Pour ingredients into iced mixing glass
1 oz. Corazón Añejo Tequila
1 oz. Grey Goose Le Citron Vodka
1/2 oz. Cointreau
1/2 oz. Rose's Lime Juice
1 1/2 oz. sweet 'n' sour
Shake and strain
Lime wedge garnish

ESPOLON® 100% AGAVE AÑEJO TEQUILA

Introduced into the American market in 2002, ESPOLON 100% AGAVE AÑEJO TEQUILA is a classy new "don't miss" spirit. The entire range of super-premium Espolon tequilas are made from mature agaves grown in the rich, red clay soil of the 600 acre Plascencia family estate located high in the mountains surrounding Arandas, Jalisco. In fact, the entire production and bottling process takes place on the estate.

The agaves are slowly fermented over 7 to 10 days and then double-distilled in stainless steel pot stills inlaid with copper. The tequila is made without any chemicals, flavorings, colorings, or alterations of any kind.

Espolon Añejo is aged for a year in French white oak barrels, which because of the wood's wide grain pattern, allows the tequila to extract more flavorants from the wood. It has a medium-weight body and a floral and herbaceous bouquet. The añejo rolls lightly over the palate filling the mouth with the flavors of vanilla, butterscotch and black pepper. The finish is flavorful and long lasting.

Enthusiasts of blanco tequila will thoroughly enjoy the Espolon Silver. It has a lightweight body and a wafting floral bouquet. The palate is superb, an exuberant offering of peppery and spicy flavors. The Espolon Reposado is aged in oak for a minimum of 6 months. It is a savory and refined spirit.

MARGARITA, KENTUCKY
Cocktail glass, chilled
Pour ingredients into iced mixing glass
1 1/4 oz. Maker's Mark Bourbon
1/2 oz. Grand Marnier
1/4 oz. fresh lime juice
1 1/2 oz. sweet 'n' sour
Shake and strain
Lime wedge garnish

MARGARITA, KEY LIME
Cocktail glass, chilled
Rim glass with salt (optional)
Pour ingredients into iced mixing glass
1 1/4 oz. Lime-infused Silver Tequila
1/2 oz. Triple Sec
1/4 oz. Rose's Lime Juice
1 1/2 oz. sweet 'n' sour
Shake and strain
Lime wedge garnish

MARGARITA, LA BAMBA
House specialty glass, ice
Rim glass with sugar (optional)
Pour ingredients into iced mixing glass
1 1/4 oz. Patrón Añejo Tequila
1/2 oz. Cointreau
1/4 oz. grenadine
1 1/2 oz. pineapple juice
1 1/2 oz. orange juice
Shake and strain
Lemon wedge garnish

MARGARITA LA PERSEVERANCIA
Cocktail glass, chilled
Rim glass with salt (optional)
Pour ingredients into iced mixing glass
1 1/4 oz. Sauza Tres Generaciones
Añejo Tequila
3/4 oz. Cointreau
1 1/2 oz. sweet 'n' sour
Shake and strain
Lime wedge garnish

MARGARITA LA REYNA DEL PLAYA
House specialty glass, ice
Rim glass with salt (optional)
Pour ingredients into iced mixing glass
1 1/2 oz. Jose Cuervo Reserva
de la Familia Tequila
3/4 oz. Lillet Blonde
1/2 oz. Midori
1/4 oz. pineapple juice
1/4 oz. orange juice
2 oz. sweet 'n' sour
Shake and strain
Lime wedge and orange slice garnish

MARGARITA, LUNA AZUL
House specialty glass, ice
Rim glass with salt (optional)
Pour ingredients into iced mixing glass
1 1/2 oz. Tarantula Azul
3/4 oz. Blue Curaçao
1/2 oz. Cointreau
1/2 oz. Rose's Lime Juice
1 1/2 oz. sweet 'n' sour
Shake and strain
Lime wedge garnish

MARGARITA, MAD RUSSIAN
House specialty glass, ice
Rim glass with salt (optional)
Pour ingredients into iced mixing glass
1 1/4 oz. Jose Cuervo Tradicional Tequila
3/4 oz. Blue Curaçao
1/2 oz. Grand Marnier
1/2 oz. cranberry juice
2 oz. sweet 'n' sour
Shake and strain
Lime wedge garnish

MARGARITA, MALTA'S GRAPPARITA
House specialty glass, ice
Rim glass with salt (optional)
Pour ingredients into iced mixing glass
1 1/4 oz. Grappa
3/4 oz. Triple Sec
1/2 oz. Rose's Lime Juice
1/2 oz. orange juice
2 oz. sweet 'n' sour
Shake and strain
Lime wedge garnish

MARGARITA, MANGO
aka **Mangorita**
House specialty glass, chilled
Rim glass with salt (optional)
Pour ingredients into blender
1 1/4 oz. XXX Siglo Treinta Tequila
1/2 cup mango cubes
1/2 oz. Rose's Lime Juice
2 oz. sweet 'n' sour
Blend with ice
Lime wedge garnish

MARGARITA MARTINI
Cocktail glass, chilled
Rim glass with salt (optional)
Pour ingredients into iced mixing glass
1 1/4 oz. Patrón Añejo Tequila
1/4 oz. Cointreau
1/4 oz. Rose's Lime Juice
1/4 oz. sweet 'n' sour
Shake and strain
Lime wedge garnish

MARGARITA MAS FINO
House specialty glass, ice
Rim glass with salt (optional)
Pour ingredients into iced mixing glass
3/4 oz. El Tesoro Añejo Tequila
3/4 oz. El Tesoro Platinum Tequila
3/4 oz. Cointreau
1/2 oz. orange juice
1/2 oz. Rose's Lime Juice
1 1/2 oz. sweet 'n' sour
Shake and strain
Lime wedge garnish

MARGARITA, MAUI (1)
House specialty glass, chilled
Rim glass with salt (optional)
Pour ingredients into blender
1 1/4 oz. XXX Siglo Treinta Tequila
1/2 oz. Triple Sec
1/2 oz. Rose's Lime Juice
1 1/2 oz. orange juice
2 oz. sweet 'n' sour
Blend with ice
Lime wedge garnish

MARGARITA, MAUI (2)
House specialty glass, ice
Rim glass with salt (optional)
Pour ingredients into iced mixing glass
1 1/2 oz. El Tesoro Platinum Tequila
3/4 oz. Grand Marnier
1/2 oz. pineapple juice
1 1/2 oz. sweet 'n' sour
Shake and strain
Lime wedge garnish

MARGARITA, MAXIMILIAN
House specialty glass, ice
Rim glass with salt (optional)
Pour ingredients into iced mixing glass
1 1/4 oz. Jose Cuervo Reserva
   de la Familia Tequila
3/4 oz. Cointreau
1/2 oz. Rose's Lime Juice
1/4 oz. orange juice
1 1/2 oz. sweet 'n' sour
Shake and strain
Lime wedge garnish

ARDBEG® SINGLE ISLAY MALT SCOTCH WHISKY

There are few spirits on Earth that capture unbridled passion and the sense of discovery as the peaty and iodine-laced flavors in ARDBEG SINGLE ISLAY MALT SCOTCH WHISKY. If you're looking for an exotic adventure but still have to show up for work in the morning, we recommend saving the airfare and having a dram or two of this magnificent, award winning whisky.

Ardbeg is made on Islay ("eye-luh"), a wind-swept island located off the rugged west coast of Scotland. Its blustery climate is dominated by the sea of Hebrides and the unpredictable North Atlantic. Built in 1815, the famed Ardbeg distillery sits by the waters edge and is one of the oldest and smallest distilleries in Scotland. The local peat used in production is floor malted and the pure, soft water comes from two lochs several miles uphill. Ardbeg single malt is aged for 10 years in seasoned American oak casks, chill filtered and bottled at 92 proof.

Arbeg is a bold and robust whisky with the distinction of being the most heavily peated single malt. It is generously graced with the aromas of iodine, peaty smoke and sea air. On the palate, the medium-weight body delivers a huge array of briny and salty flavors. The finish is long with a muscular heft to it.

Ardbeg is a classic malt for the ages.

MARGARITA, MELTDOWN

House specialty glass, chilled
Rim glass with salt (optional)
Pour ingredients into blender
1 1/4 oz. Sauza Hornitos Tequila
1/2 oz. Grand Marnier
1/2 oz. Rose's Lime Juice
1/2 oz. cranberry juice
1 1/2 oz. pureed raspberries
2 oz. sweet 'n' sour
Blend with ice
Float 3/4 oz. Chambord
Lime wedge garnish

MARGARITA, MEZCAL

House specialty glass, ice
Rim glass with salt (optional)
Pour ingredients into iced mixing glass
1 1/4 oz. Añejo Mezcal
1/2 oz. Brandy
2-3 dashes Peychaud bitters
1/2 oz. simple syrup
2 oz. sweet 'n' sour
Shake and strain
Lime wedge garnish

MARGARITA, MIDNIGHT MADNESS

House specialty glass, chilled
Rim glass with salt (optional)
Object is to create a 2-layer drink
1—*Pour ingredients into blender*
3/4 oz. Sauza Gold Tequila
3/4 oz. Blue Curaçao
1/2 oz. Rose's Lime Juice
1 1/2 oz. sweet 'n' sour
Blend with ice
Pour first drink into glass 1/2 full
2—*Pour ingredients into blender*
3/4 oz. Sauza Gold Tequila
3/4 oz. Chambord
Blend with ice
Fill glass with second drink

MARGARITA, MIDORI

aka **Melon Margarita, Green Iguana**
Cocktail glass, chilled
Rim glass with salt (optional)
Pour ingredients into iced mixing glass
1 oz. Tequila
1 oz. Midori
1 1/2 oz. sweet 'n' sour
Shake and strain
Lime wedge garnish

MARGARITA, MIMOSA
aka **Mimosarita**
Tulip champagne glass, chilled
Pour ingredients into iced mixing glass
1 1/2 oz. Corazón Añejo Tequila
1/2 oz. Triple Sec
1/4 oz. Rose's Lime Juice
1 oz. orange juice
1 oz. sweet 'n' sour
Shake and strain
Fill with champagne
Orange twist garnish

MARGARITA, MONTEGO
Cocktail glass, chilled
Pour ingredients into iced mixing glass
1 1/2 oz. Appleton Estate V/X Jamaica Rum
3/4 oz. Citrónge Orange Liqueur
1/2 oz. Rose's Lime Juice
1/2 oz. orange juice
1 1/2 oz. sweet 'n' sour
Shake and strain
Lime and lemon wedge garnish

MARGARITA, MOONBURN
Cocktail glass, chilled
Rim glass with salt (optional)
Pour ingredients into iced mixing glass
1 3/4 oz. Tequila
3/4 oz. Cointreau
1/2 oz. fresh lime juice
1/2 oz. Rose's Lime Juice
1 oz. sweet 'n' sour
3 oz. blood orange juice
Shake and strain
Lime wedge garnish

MARGARITA, MOSCOW
House specialty glass, ice
Rim glass with salt (optional)
Pour ingredients into iced mixing glass
1 1/2 oz. Russian Vodka
1/2 oz. Triple Sec
1/2 oz. Rose's Lime Juice
2 oz. sweet 'n' sour
Shake and strain
Lime wedge garnish

MARGARITA, MOUNT FUGI
House specialty glass, ice
Rim glass with salt (optional)
Pour ingredients into iced mixing glass
2 oz. Saké
1/2 oz. Triple Sec
2 oz. sweet 'n' sour
Shake and strain
Lemon wheel garnish

MARGARITA, MY BABY GRAND
Cocktail glass, chilled
Rim glass with salt (optional)
Pour ingredients into iced mixing glass
2 oz. Jose Cuervo Tradicional Tequila
3/4 oz. Grand Marnier
1/2 oz. Rose's Lime Juice
1/2 oz. fresh lime juice
1 oz. grapefruit juice
Stir and strain
Lime wedge garnish

MARGARITA, NEON WATERMELON
House specialty glass, chilled
Rim glass with sugar (optional)
Pour ingredients into blender
1 1/4 oz. Espolon Silver Tequila
1 oz. Midori
3/4 oz. Blue Curaçao
1/2 cup frozen seedless watermelon cubes
3 oz. sweet 'n' sour
Blend with ice
Watermelon slice garnish

MARGARITA, NORMANDY
aka **Apple Margarita**
House specialty glass, chilled
Rim glass with cinnamon and sugar
Pour ingredients into blender
1 oz. Silver Tequila
1 oz. Calvados Apple Brandy
1/2 oz. Grand Marnier
1/2 oz. apple juice or cider
1/2 oz. apple sauce (optional)
1 1/2 oz. sweet 'n' sour
Blend with ice
Apple wedge garnish

MARGARITA, ORANGITA
House specialty glass, ice
Rim glass with sugar (optional)
Pour ingredients into iced mixing glass
1 1/4 oz. Don Eduardo Añejo Tequila
3/4 oz. Triple Sec
1/2 oz. Rose's Lime Juice
1 oz. sweet 'n' sour
1 3/4 oz. orange juice
Shake and strain
Lime wedge garnish

MARGARITA, ORIGINAL ™
aka **Margarita Sames' Margarita**
Cocktail glass, chilled
Rim glass with salt
Pour ingredients into iced mixing glass
1 1/2 oz. Silver Tequila
3/4 oz. Cointreau
3/4 oz. fresh lime juice
Shake and strain
Lime wedge garnish

MALIBU® CARIBBEAN RUM

When one operator chooses to carry a brand, it's a solitary decision. When darn near every beverage operator on the planet elects to carry a spirits brand, it's a sweeping mandate. Such is the case with universally accepted MALIBU CARIBBEAN RUM. Since its introduction in 1980, the phenomenally successful brand has become synonymous with coconut rum and for good reason.

Founded in 1893, this famed facility produces both light- and full-bodied rums in several different types of stills. These spirits are blended together along with natural coconut flavorings to achieve a balanced rum with taste and personality. It is bottled at 42 proof.

Malibu Rum is well deserving of its back bar preeminence. The crystal clear spirit has a lightweight body and an alluring bouquet laced with the aromas of fresh citrus and coconut. The marriage of rum and coconut is sublime. Its semisweet flavor gently washes over the palate like a wave and lingers well into the extended finish. From start to finish, this savory rum is a feast for the senses.

It's hard to fathom life behind the bar without Malibu on the top shelf. It is the featured performer in scores of popular shooters, Piña Coladas, Daiquiris and Margaritas. In fact, there isn't a category of mixology that Malibu hasn't made an impression on. Your first sip will confirm why it's the world's preferred coconut rum.

MARGARITA, OSCAR NIGHT
House specialty glass, ice
Rim glass with sugar (optional)
Pour ingredients into iced mixing glass
1 1/4 oz. Patrón Silver Tequila
3/4 oz. Agavero Liqueur
3/4 oz. Disaronno Amaretto
1 1/2 oz. orange juice
1 1/2 oz. sweet 'n' sour
Shake and strain
Lime wedge garnish

MARGARITA, PACIFIC BLUE
House specialty glass, chilled
Rim glass with salt (optional)
Pour ingredients into iced mixing glass
1 1/2 oz. Corazón Silver Tequila
1 1/2 oz. Hpnotiq Liqueur
1/2 oz. Blue Curaçao
1/2 oz. fresh lime juice
1 1/2 oz. sweet 'n' sour
Shake and strain
Lime wedge garnish

MARGARITA, PASSION
House specialty glass, chilled
Rim glass with salt (optional)
Pour ingredients into iced mixing glass
1 1/2 oz. RémyRed Red Berry Infusion
1 oz. Sauza Tres Generaciones Plata Tequila
1/2 oz. Cointreau
1 1/2 oz. sweet 'n' sour
1 1/2 oz. cranberry juice
Shake and strain
Lime wedge garnish

MARGARITA, PEAR
aka **Pearita**
House specialty glass, chilled
Rim glass with salt (optional)
Pour ingredients into blender
1 3/4 oz. XXX Siglo Treinta Tequila
1/2 oz. Triple Sec
1 whole canned Bartlett pear
1/2 oz. Rose's Lime Juice
1 1/2 oz. sweet 'n' sour
Blend with ice
Lime wheel garnish

MARGARITA PICANTE
House specialty glass, ice
Rim glass with salt and pepper (optional)
Pour ingredients into iced mixing glass
1 1/4 oz. Jose Cuervo Especial Tequila
3/4 oz. Absolut Peppar Vodka
1/2 oz. Triple Sec
1-2 dashes Tabasco Sauce
2 pinches black pepper
4-6 drops jalapeño pepper juice
2 oz. sweet 'n' sour
Shake and strain
Small jalapeño peppers garnish

MARGARITA, PICOSITA
House specialty glass, ice
Rim glass with salt and pepper (optional)
Pour ingredients into iced mixing glass
3/4 oz. Tequila
3/4 oz. Pepper-infused Silver Tequila
1/2 oz. Triple Sec
1/2 oz. Rose's Lime Juice
1/2 oz. orange juice
1 3/4 oz. sweet 'n' sour
Shake and strain
Lime wedge and small jalapeño
    pepper garnish

MARGARITA, PINEAPPLE
aka **Piñarita**
Cocktail or house specialty glass, chilled
Pour ingredients into blender
1 1/4 oz. Jose Cuervo Clásico Tequila
3/4 oz. Triple Sec
1/2 cup pineapple cubes
1 1/2 oz. pineapple juice
Blend with ice
Lime wedge garnish

MARGARITA, PINK CADILLAC
House specialty glass, ice
Rim glass with salt (optional)
Pour ingredients into iced mixing glass
1 1/4 oz. 1800 Tequila
1/2 oz. Cointreau
1/2 oz. Rose's Lime Juice
1/2 oz. cranberry juice
1 1/2 oz. sweet 'n' sour
Shake and strain
Lime wedge garnish

MARGARITA, PRESIDENTÉ
House specialty glass, ice
Rim glass with salt (optional)
Pour ingredients into iced mixing glass
1 oz. Sauza Conmemorativo Añejo Tequila
1 oz. Presidenté Brandy
3/4 oz. Cointreau
1/4 oz. orange juice
1/2 oz. Rose's Lime Juice
2 oz. sweet 'n' sour
Shake and strain
Lime wedge and orange slice garnish

MARGARITA, PRICKLY PEAR (1)
House specialty glass, chilled
Rim glass with salt (optional)
Pour ingredients into blender
1 1/4 oz. Silver Tequila
1/2 oz. Triple Sec
1/2 oz. Rose's Lime Juice
1/4 oz. grenadine
3/4 oz. prickly pear juice
1 1/2 oz. sweet 'n' sour
Blend with ice
Lime wedge garnish

MARGARITA, PRICKLY PEAR (2)
House specialty glass, chilled
Rim glass with salt (optional)
Pour ingredients into blender
1 1/4 oz. Silver Tequila
1/2 oz. Triple Sec
3/4 oz. Rose's Lime Juice
1 1/2 oz. prickly pear juice
2 oz. sweet 'n' sour
Blend with ice
Lime wheel garnish

MARGARITA, PRICKLY PINEAPPLE
Cocktail glass, chilled
Rim glass with salt (optional)
Pour ingredients into iced mixing glass
1 1/4 oz. Espolon Añejo Tequila
1/2 oz. Grand Marnier
1/2 oz. prickly pear syrup
3/4 oz. pineapple juice
1 1/2 oz. sweet 'n' sour
Shake and strain
Lime wedge garnish

STÖN® VODKA

For five decades while the Iron Curtain was drawn, scores of small distilleries throughout Eastern Europe languished with no access to markets in the west. Now in this time of enlightenment, we're seeing fabulous new vodkas emigrating from the former Warsaw Pact countries. One of the finest examples is STÖN VODKA, a marvelous and skillfully crafted spirit made in Kiiu, Estonia by the country's most acclaimed distillery, Remedia.

Stön Vodka is quadruple-distilled from locally grown wheat and pure, icy water from deep artesian wells fed by ancient glaciers. The vodka is then filtered four times through limestone to attain its essential purity and bottled at 80 proof.

Stön is a classically structured Eastern European vodka—aromatic, flavorful and slightly edgy. It is impeccably clear with substantial heft and body. The vodka fills the glass with the delectable and semisweet combination of grainy and citrus aromas. Its entry on the palate is soft and warming, and then it quickly blossoms into an expansive array of tangy and spicy flavors. The finish is outstanding—clean, lingering and semisweet.

Stön is an ideal vodka to serve to those people who insist that vodkas have no character or personality. It is perhaps best presented with a slight chill alone in a cocktail glass. Stön Vodka, welcome to America!

MARGARITA PRIMERO CLASE
House specialty glass, ice
Rim glass with salt (optional)
Pour ingredients into iced mixing glass
1 3/4 oz. El Tesoro Añejo Tequila
3/4 oz. El Tesoro Paradiso Añejo
3/4 oz. Cointreau
1/2 oz. fresh lime juice
1 1/2 oz. sweet 'n' sour
Shake and strain
Lime wedge garnish

MARGARITA PUNCH
Punch Bowl (256 oz.), quarter-full with ice
Pour ingredients into punch bowl
2 liters Gold Tequila
1.5 (750ml) bottles of chilled champagne
20 oz. Triple Sec
10 oz. Rose's Lime Juice
10 oz. orange juice
5 oz. fresh lime juice
18 oz. ginger ale
45 oz. sweet 'n' sour
Stir thoroughly
Lime, lemon and orange slice garnish

MARGARITA, PURPLE (1)
aka **Purple Gecko, Purple Haze Margarita**
House specialty glass, ice
Rim glass with salt (optional)
Pour ingredients into iced mixing glass
1 1/4 oz. Reposado Tequila
1/2 oz. Blue Curaçao
1/2 oz. Chambord
1/2 oz. Rose's Lime Juice
1 oz. cranberry juice
1 1/2 oz. sweet 'n' sour
Shake and strain
Lime wedge garnish

MARGARITA, PURPLE (2)
House specialty glass, ice
Rim glass with salt (optional)
Pour ingredients into iced mixing glass
1 1/4 oz. Corazón Reposado Tequila
3/4 oz. Chambord
3/4 oz. Blue Curaçao
1/2 oz. Rose's Lime Juice
1 oz. Welch's 100% Grape Juice
1 1/2 oz. sweet 'n' sour
Shake and strain
Lime wedge garnish

MARGARITA, RASPBERRY
House specialty glass, chilled
Rim glass with sugar (optional)
Pour ingredients into blender
1 1/2 oz. Jose Cuervo Especial Tequila
3/4 oz. Triple Sec
1 1/2 oz. raspberry puree
1 1/2 oz. orange juice
1 1/2 oz. sweet 'n' sour
Blend with ice
Lime wedge and orange slice garnish

MARGARITA, RASPBERRY TORTE
House specialty glass, chilled
Rim glass with sugar (optional)
Object is to create a 3-layer drink
1—*Pour ingredients into blender*
 1 1/2 oz. Silver Tequila
 1/2 oz. Triple Sec
 2 oz. sweet 'n' sour
Blend with ice
Pour blended drink into glass 1/2 full
2—*Add in glass*
 2 oz. raspberry puree
3—*Slowly fill glass with blended drink to create a third layer*
Lime wedge and orange slice garnish

MARGARITA, RED CACTUS
House specialty glass, chilled
Rim glass with sugar (optional)
Pour ingredients into blender
1 1/4 oz. Sauza Hornitos Tequila
1/2 oz. Triple Sec
1/2 oz. Chambord
1/2 oz. Rose's Lime Juice
1/2 cup frozen raspberries
1 1/2 oz. sweet 'n' sour
Blend with ice
Lime wedge garnish

MARGARITA, RIO GRANDE
House specialty glass, ice
Rim glass with salt (optional)
Pour ingredients into iced mixing glass
3/4 oz. Sol Dios Añejo Tequila
3/4 oz. Tia Maria
3/4 oz. Triple Sec
1 1/2 oz. orange juice
1 1/2 oz. sweet 'n' sour
Shake and strain
Lime wedge garnish

MARGARITA, RIVER SPEY
Cocktail glass, chilled
Rim glass with salt (optional)
Pour ingredients into iced mixing glass
1 1/4 oz. Glenlivet Single Malt Whisky
1/2 oz. Cointreau
1 1/2 oz. sweet 'n' sour
Shake and strain
Lime wedge garnish

MARGARITA, ROCKY POINT
Cocktail glass, chilled
Rim glass with salt (optional)
Pour ingredients into iced mixing glass
1 1/4 oz. Patrón Silver Tequila
3/4 oz. Cruzan Orange Rum
3/4 oz. Damiana Liqueur
1/2 oz. fresh lime juice
1 1/2 oz. sweet 'n' sour
Shake and strain
Lime wedge garnish

MARGARITA, ROSARITA
House specialty glass, ice
Rim glass with salt (optional)
Pour ingredients into iced mixing glass
1 1/4 oz. Sauza Tres Generaciones
 Plata Tequila
3/4 oz. Grand Marnier
1/2 oz. cranberry juice
1/2 oz. Rose's Lime Juice
1 1/2 oz. sweet 'n' sour
Shake and strain
Lime wedge garnish

MARGARITA, ROSE
House specialty glass, chilled
Rim glass with sugar (optional)
Pour ingredients into blender
2 oz. Tequila Rose Cream Liqueur
1 oz. Gran Gala Orange Liqueur
1/2 oz. Rose's Lime Juice
2 oz. sweet 'n' sour
2 oz. frozen strawberries
Blend with ice
Lime wedge garnish

MARGARITA, R-RATED
House specialty glass, ice
Rim glass with salt (optional)
Pour ingredients into iced mixing glass
3/4 oz. Herradura Silver Tequila
3/4 oz. Herradura Reposado Tequila
1/2 oz. Cointreau
1/2 oz. Rose's Lime Juice
1/2 oz. orange juice
1 1/2 oz. sweet 'n' sour
Shake and strain
Float 3/4 oz. Herradura Añejo Tequila
Lime wedge garnish

AGAVERO® TEQUILA LIQUEUR

Tequila has captured the collective imagination of Americans. For the past 20 years, it has been a headliner in the popular scene. Now the robust and exotic flavor of tequila has been captured in a liqueur, one that can only be described as sensational. The product is AGAVERO TEQUILA LIQUEUR.

For more than a century, the Gallardo family has produced Tequila Gran Centenario at Los Camichines Hacienda in Jalisco, Mexico. In 1857, the head of the family, Don Lazaro Gallardo, created Agavero to savor after dinner. The liqueur is made with a singular blend of a reserve, barrel-aged tequila, a reposado and a 2 year old añejo.

The secret ingredient in Agavero's well-guarded recipe is a unique tea brewed from the Damiana flower, which is an aromatic flower indigenous to the mountains of Jalisco. It is a revered plant in Mexico and is purported to be an aphrodisiac. It is bottled at 64 proof.

You have to taste Agavero Tequila Liqueur to fully appreciate how delicious it is. The liqueur has a supple, medium-weight body and a spicy, floral bouquet. Its palate delivers a well-balanced array of herbal-enriched, semisweet flavors. The character of the tequilas are revealed in the relaxed finish.

Agavero is a romantic hit. It has scores of applications behind the bar, most notably as a modifier in specialty Margaritas.

MARGARITA, SAKÉ
Cocktail glass, chilled
Rim glass with salt (optional)
Pour ingredients into iced mixing glass
1 1/4 oz. Saké
3/4 oz. Grand Marnier
1/2 oz. Rose's Lime Juice
2 oz. sweet 'n' sour
Shake and strain
Lime wheel garnish

MARGARITA, SANGRITA
aka **Sangria 'Rita**
House specialty glass, ice
Rim glass with sugar (optional)
Pour ingredients into iced mixing glass
1 oz. Silver Tequila
2 oz. Dry Red Wine
1/2 oz. Triple Sec
1/2 oz. Peach Schnapps
1/2 oz. Rose's Lime Juice
2 oz. sweet 'n' sour
Shake and strain
Lime, lemon and orange slice garnish

MARGARITA, SANTA RITA
House specialty glass, ice
Rim glass with salt (optional)
Pour ingredients into iced mixing glass
1 1/4 oz. Espolon Reposado Tequila
1/2 oz. Chambord
1/2 oz. Peach Schnapps
2 oz. sweet 'n' sour
Shake and strain
Lime wedge garnish

MARGARITA, SANTIAGO
House specialty glass, ice
Rim glass with pink lemonade
    mix (optional)
Pour ingredients into iced mixing glass
1 1/4 oz. Herradura Silver Tequila
3/4 oz. Midori
1/2 oz. Grand Marnier
1/2 oz. Rose's Lime Juice
1/4 oz. grenadine
1 1/2 oz. grapefruit juice
2 oz. sweet 'n' sour
Shake and strain
Orange slice garnish

MARGARITA, SAUZA PURE
House specialty glass, ice
Rim glass with salt (optional)
Pour ingredients into iced mixing glass
1 1/2 oz. Sauza Hornitos Tequila
3/4 oz. Triple Sec
1 1/2 oz. fresh lime juice
Shake and strain
Lime wedge garnish

MARGARITA, SEA BREEZE
House specialty glass, chilled
Rim glass with salt (optional)
Pour ingredients into iced mixing glass
1 3/4 oz. Tarantula Azul
3/4 oz. Gran Gala Orange Liqueur
1/2 oz. Rose's Lime Juice
1 oz. sweet 'n' sour
1 oz. cranberry juice
2 oz. grapefruit juice
Shake and strain
Lime wedge garnish

MARGARITA, SEÑORITA
House specialty glass, ice
Rim glass with salt (optional)
Pour ingredients into iced mixing glass
1 1/4 oz. Espolon Reposado Tequila
1/2 oz. Cointreau
1/4 oz. Rose's Lime Juice
1/4 oz. fresh lime juice
1 1/2 oz. sweet 'n' sour
Shake and strain
Float 3/4 oz. Espolon Reposado Tequila
Lime wedge garnish

MARGARITA, SHOOTAH
aka **Shootah 'Rita**
Presentation shot glass, chilled
Rim glass with salt (optional)
Pour ingredients into iced mixing glass
1 oz. Tequila
1/2 oz. Triple Sec
1/4 oz. sweet 'n' sour
1/4 oz. fresh lime juice
Shake and strain
Lime wedge garnish

MARGARITA, SONORAN
House specialty glass, ice
Rim glass with salt (optional)
Pour ingredients into iced mixing glass
1 1/4 oz. Jose Cuervo Especial Tequila
3/4 oz. Grand Marnier
1/2 oz. Rose's Lime Juice
3/4 oz. white cranberry juice
1 1/2 oz. sweet 'n' sour
Shake and strain
Lime wedge garnish

MARGARITA, SONORAN SPITTOON
Cocktail glass, chilled
Rim glass with salt and pepper (optional)
Pour ingredients into iced mixing glass
1 1/4 oz. Pepper-infused Silver Tequila
1/2 oz. Triple Sec
1/2 oz. Rose's Lime Juice
1 1/2 oz. sweet 'n' sour
Shake and strain
Lime wedge and small jalapeño
    pepper garnish

MARGARITA, SPANISH
aka **Gold Rush Margarita**
House specialty glass, ice
Rim glass with salt (optional)
Pour ingredients into iced mixing glass
1 1/2 oz. Herradura Reposado Tequila
3/4 oz. Licor 43 (Cuarenta y Tres)
1/2 oz. Rose's Lime Juice
1 1/2 oz. sweet 'n' sour
Shake and strain
Lime wedge garnish

MARGARITA SPLASH
House specialty glass, ice
Rim glass with salt (optional)
Pour ingredients into iced mixing glass
1 3/4 oz. Tarantula Azul
3/4 oz. Blue Curaçao
1 1/2 oz. fresh lime juice
1 1/2 oz. sweet 'n' sour
Shake and strain
Fill with Squirt (grapefruit)
Lime wedge garnish

MARGARITA, STRAWBERRY LOVER'S
House specialty glass, chilled
Rim glass with sugar (optional)
Pour ingredients into blender
1 oz. Sauza Tres Generaciones Plata Tequila
1 oz. Stolichnaya Strasberi Vodka
1/2 oz. Grand Marnier
1/3 cup fresh or frozen strawberries
2 oz. sweet 'n' sour
Blend with ice
Strawberry garnish

MARGARITA, SUNNY
House specialty glass, chilled
Rim glass with salt (optional)
Pour ingredients into blender
1 1/4 oz. XXX Siglo Treinta Tequila
3/4 oz. Triple Sec
1/2 oz. Rose's Lime Juice
2 oz. sweet 'n' sour
2 scoops orange sorbet
Blend ingredients (with ice optional)
Lime wedge garnish

KAHLÚA® LIQUEUR

The exact origins of the KAHLÚA LIQUEUR recipe are a matter of debate. Those that contend it originated in Morocco, point to the Moorish archway depicted on the label as one piece of evidence.

What is known, however, is that Kahlúa has been made in Mexico for nearly a century and that it steadfastly remains one of the best-selling liqueurs in the world.

Kahlúa is made from a base of distilled sugar cane that is steeped with vanilla and mountain-grown Mexican coffee. The liqueur has a deep brown color, a velvety smooth texture and a freshly ground coffee bouquet. Kahlúa's well-rounded body delivers the rich flavors of roasted coffee, cocoa and mint. While moderately sweet, it is never cloying or overbearing. The liqueur has a long, flavorful finish.

Kahlúa was first imported into the United States after the repeal of prohibition and quickly became a favorite with this country's mixologists. One of the liqueur's strong suits is that it mixes with a seemingly endless combination of products.

As testimony to its nearly universal mixability, Kahlúa is one of the most frequently used ingredients in this or any other drink guide. Without it, much of American mixology simply isn't possible. Obviously this is a "must have" product.

MARGARITA, SUNSET
House specialty glass, ice
Rim glass with salt (optional)
Pour ingredients into iced mixing glass
1 1/4 oz. Don Eduardo Silver Tequila
3/4 oz. Blue Curaçao
1/2 oz. Chambord
1/2 oz. Rose's Lime Juice
1 1/2 oz. sweet 'n' sour
1 1/2 oz. grapefruit
Shake and strain
Float 3/4 oz. grenadine
Orange wheel garnish

MARGARITA, TEA-ARITA
House specialty glass, ice
Rim glass with salt (optional)
Pour ingredients into iced mixing glass
1 1/4 oz. Corazón Silver Tequila
1/2 oz. Triple Sec
1/2 oz. Rose's Lime Juice
2 oz. iced tea
2 oz. sweet 'n' sour
Shake and strain
Lime and lemon wedge garnish

MARGARITA, TEAL
House specialty glass, ice
Rim glass with salt (optional)
Pour ingredients into iced mixing glass
1 1/2 oz. Don Eduardo Silver Tequila
3/4 oz. Blue Curaçao
1/2 oz. Grand Marnier
1/2 oz. cranberry juice
1 1/2 oz. sweet 'n' sour
Shake and strain
Lime wedge garnish

MARGARITA, THREE AMIGOS
House specialty glass, ice
Rim glass with salt (optional)
Pour ingredients into iced mixing glass
3/4 oz. Sauza Conmemorativo
  Añejo Tequila
3/4 oz. Sauza Hornitos Tequila
1/2 oz. Cointreau
1/2 oz. Rose's Lime Juice
1 oz. lemon/lime soda
1 1/4 oz. sweet 'n' sour
Shake and strain
Float 3/4 oz. Sauza Tres Generaciones
  Añejo Tequila
Lime wedge garnish

MARGARITA, TRES COMPADRES
House specialty glass, ice
Rim glass with salt (optional)
Pour ingredients into iced mixing glass
1 1/2 oz. El Tesoro Añejo Tequila
1/2 oz. Cointreau
1/2 oz. Chambord
1/2 oz. Rose's Lime Juice
3/4 oz. fresh lime juice
3/4 oz. orange juice
3/4 oz. grapefruit juice
Shake and strain
Lime wedge garnish

MARGARITA, TRIPLE GOLD
House specialty glass, ice
Rim glass with salt (optional)
Pour ingredients into iced mixing glass
3/4 oz. Sauza Tres Generaciones
    Añejo Tequila
3/4 oz. Sauza Conmemorativo
    Añejo Tequila
1/2 oz. Cointreau
1 1/2 oz. sweet 'n' sour
Shake and strain
Float 3/4 oz. Goldschläger
Lime wedge garnish

MARGARITA, TUACA
Cocktail glass, chilled
Rim glass with sugar (optional)
Pour ingredients into iced mixing glass
1 oz. Silver Tequila
1 oz. Tuaca
1 1/2 oz. sweet 'n' sour
Splash lemon/lime soda (optional)
Shake and strain
Lime wedge garnish

MARGARITA, TWO-TONED
House specialty glass, 3/4 fill with ice
Rim glass with salt (optional)
Pour ingredients into iced mixing glass
1 1/2 oz. Tequila
3/4 oz. Triple Sec
1/2 oz. Rose's Lime Juice
1 1/2 oz. orange juice
2 oz. sweet 'n' sour
Shake, strain and fill glass 3/4 full
Pour remaining contents into blender
Add 1 oz. Chambord or Midori
Blend with ice and pour blended drink
    on top of iced margarita
Lime wedge garnish

MARGARITA, ULTIMATE SHOT
aka **Ultimate 'Rita Shot**
Presentation shot glass, chilled
Rim glass with salt (optional)
Pour ingredients into iced mixing glass
3/4 oz. Sauza Tres Generaciones
    Añejo Tequila
3/4 oz. Cointreau
1/4 oz. sweet 'n' sour
1/4 oz. fresh lime juice
Shake and strain
Lime wedge garnish

MARGARITA, VINTNER'S
House specialty glass, ice
Rim glass with salt (optional)
Pour ingredients into iced mixing glass
3 oz. Dry White Wine
1/2 oz. Triple Sec
1/2 oz. Rose's Lime Juice
1/2 oz. orange juice
2 oz. sweet 'n' sour
Shake and strain
Lime wedge and orange slice garnish

MARGARITA, VIRGIN (1)
Cocktail glass, chilled
Rim glass with salt (optional)
Pour ingredients into iced mixing glass
2 oz. sweet 'n' sour
1/2 oz. Alcohol-Free Triple Sec
1 oz. orange juice
3/4 oz. Rose's Lime Juice
Shake and strain
Lime wedge garnish

MARGARITA, VIRGIN (2)
House specialty glass, ice
Pour ingredients into iced mixing glass
1 oz. Alcohol-Free Triple Sec
2 oz. sweet 'n' sour
1/2 oz. Rose's Lime Juice
1/2 oz. orange juice
Shake and strain
Lime wedge garnish

MARGARITA, WATERMELON
House specialty glass, chilled
Rim glass with sugar (optional)
Pour ingredients into blender
1 1/4 oz. Silver Tequila
3/4 oz. Triple Sec
3/4 oz. DeKuyper Watermelon Pucker
1/2 cup frozen seedless watermelon cubes
3 oz. sweet 'n' sour
Blend with ice
Watermelon slice garnish

BOMBAY® SAPPHIRE® GIN

BOMBAY SAPPHIRE LONDON DRY GIN took the world by storm with its release in 1988, quickly establishing itself as the category's first and only super-premium entry. Packaged in an elegant, readily identifiable blue bottle, it has become a popular favorite of the Martini-craving public.

One of the secrets behind Bombay Sapphire's phenomonal success can be found in the singular way that it is distilled. The gin is crafted using four . Carter Head stills, the only examples of this type in the world. Neutral grain spirits are double-distilled, and then during their final distillation the rising vapors pass through a copper still basket holding the gin's 10 botanicals and aromatics.

The proprietary mix includes herbs, spices, roots, fruit and juniper berries from exotic places around the world. All of the ingredients are crushed or grated prior to distillation to fully release their flavors. It is bottled at 94 proof.

Bombay Sapphire richly deserves its universal ranking as a "must have" brand. The gin is crystal clear with a plush, medium-weight body. Its bouquet is absolutely mesmerizing. It is a sensational mélange of citrus, spice and juniper. Sapphire is brimming with crisp, mouth filling flavors that linger on the palate for a consummate finish.

MARGARITA, ZINFUL
House specialty glass, ice
Rim glass with salt (optional)
Pour ingredients into iced mixing glass
1 1/4 oz. Gold Tequila
3 oz. White Zinfandel
1/2 oz. Chambord
1 oz. sweet 'n' sour
1/2 oz. Rose's Lime Juice
1 1/2 oz. orange juice
Shake and strain
Lime wedge and orange slice garnish

MARGO MOORE
Bucket glass, ice
Build in glass
1 1/2 oz. Brandy
3/4 oz. Light Rum
1/2 oz. Blue Curaçao
Fill with bitter lemon soda

MARIACHI LOCO
Bucket glass, ice
Pour ingredients into iced mixing glass
1 1/4 oz. RémyRed Red Berry Infusion
3/4 oz. Silver Tequila
1/4 oz. Rose's Lime Juice
1 1/2 oz. sweet 'n' sour
2 oz. cranberry juice
Shake and strain
Lime wedge garnish

MARIA SANGRITA
House specialty glass, ice
Rim glass with salt (optional)
Build in glass
1 1/2 oz. Tequila
1/2 oz. fresh lime juice
2 pinches each, salt and black pepper
1/2 tsp. grated red onion
Fill with Sangrita Mix
Lime wedge garnish
Note: See Sangrita Mix

MARITIME SUNRISE
Bucket glass, ice
Build in glass
2 oz. Türi Vodka
4 oz. grapefruit juice
1 oz. cranberry juice
Float 3/4 oz. Chambord

MARQUIS
Rocks glass, ice
Build in glass
3/4 oz. B & B Liqueur
3/4 oz. Kahlúa
1/4 oz. Orange Liqueur
3/4 oz. half & half cream

MARSEILLES STOCKINGS
Brandy snifter, heated
Build in glass
1 1/2 oz. VSOP Cognac
3/4 oz. Grand Marnier

MARTINI
Cocktail glass, chilled
Pour ingredients into iced mixing glass
6 drops Dry Vermouth
1 1/2 oz. Gin
Stir and strain
Olives or lemon twist garnish

MARTINI, 007
Champagne or cocktail glass, chilled
Pour ingredients into iced mixing glass
1/4 oz. Lillet Blonde
1 oz. Vodka
1 oz. Gin
Shake and strain
Lemon twist garnish

MARTINI, 008
Champagne or cocktail glass, chilled
Pour ingredients into iced mixing glass
1/4 oz. Dubonnet Blonde
1 oz. Spudka Vodka
1 oz. Broker's London Dry Gin
Shake and strain
Lemon twist garnish

MARTINI, ABSOLUT MANDARIN
Cocktail glass, chilled
Pour ingredients into iced mixing glass
1/4 oz. Cointreau
2 1/4 oz. Absolut Mandarin Vodka
Stir and strain
Orange twist garnish

MARTINI, ALEXANDER NEVSKY
Cocktail glass, chilled
Pour ingredients into iced mixing glass
1/4 oz. Chambord
1 oz. Bombay Sapphire London Dry Gin
1 oz. Stolichnaya Razberi Vodka
Stir and strain
Raspberries garnish

MARTINI, ALL AMERICAN
Cocktail glass, chilled
Pour ingredients into iced mixing glass
1/4 oz. Jack Daniel's Single Barrel Whiskey
1/4 oz. Dry Vermouth
1 1/2 oz. Gin
Stir and strain
Lemon twist garnish

MARTINI, AMADORA
Cocktail glass, chilled
Pour ingredients into iced mixing glass
1/4 oz. Tawny Port
1 1/2 oz. Gin
Stir and strain
Lemon twist garnish

MARTINI, AMBER SKIES
Cocktail glass, chilled
Rim glass with finely crushed
   almonds (optional)
Pour ingredients into iced mixing glass
1/2 oz. Disaronno Amaretto
1/4 oz. Frangelico
1 1/2 oz. Vodka
Stir and strain
Lemon twist garnish

MARTINI, APPLE PIE
Cocktail glass, chilled
Rim glass with chocolate syrup and
   graham crackers
Pour ingredients into iced mixing glass
1 1/2 oz. Kuya Fusion Rum
1 oz. DeKuyper Pucker Sour Apple
3/4 oz. Baileys Irish Cream
1/2 oz. apple juice
Shake and strain
Apple slice s garnish

MARTINI, APPLETINI (1)
Cocktail glass, chilled
Pour ingredients into iced mixing glass
2 1/2 oz. Vodka
3/4 oz. DeKuyper Pucker Sour Apple
Stir and strain
Green apple wedge garnish

MARTINI, APPLETINI (2)
Cocktail glass, chilled
Pour ingredients into iced mixing glass
2 1/2 oz. Vodka
3/4 oz. DeKuyper Pucker Sour Apple
1/2 oz. sweet 'n' sour
Shake and strain
Green apple wedge garnish

MARTINI, APPLETINI (3)
Cocktail glass, chilled
Rim glass with apple-flavored
   sugar (optional)
Pour ingredients into iced mixing glass
1 3/4 oz. Vodka
1 oz. DeKuyper Pucker Sour Apple
3/4 oz. sweet 'n' sour
Shake and strain
Green apple wedge garnish

WOODFORD RESERVE®
DISTILLER'S SELECT
BOURBON WHISKEY

To fully appreciate what a whiskey masterpiece WOODFORD RESERVE DISTILLER'S SELECT BOURBON WHISKEY is, you must understand something about the historic surroundings under which much of it is produced.

This bourbon is distilled in Louisville by Brown-Forman Distillery. The master distiller selects barrels that match the distinctive taste profile used in the Woodford Reserve. The barrels are then transferred to the 100 year old warehouses at the recently restored Woodford Reserve Distillery. This famous distillery began producing whiskey in 1812 and is situated on the banks of Glenn's Creek. The limestone filtered spring water of the creek is used to bring the mature whiskey down to its bottled strength of 90.4 proof.

Woodford Reserve is a luxurious sip of whiskey, one steeped in heritage. The small batch bourbon has a rich appearance and is generously aromatic with notes of flora, honey and spice. Its palate is a complex affair, a lavish offering of caramel, fruit, vanilla and several other buttery flavors too subtle to describe. The delectable flavors persist well into the slightly spicy and exceptionally long finish.

Woodford Reserve is a handcrafted whiskey born in Louisville and raised in the country. Factor in its relatively modest price tag and you've got a top-shelf contender of Olympic proportions.

MARTINI, BALD HEAD
Cocktail glass, chilled
Pour ingredients into iced mixing glass
1/4 oz. Dry Vermouth
1/4 oz. Sweet Vermouth
1/4 oz. Pernod
1 1/2 oz. Gin
Stir and strain
Lemon twist garnish

MARTINI, BALTIC SEA
Cocktail glass, chilled
Rim glass with seas salt (optional)
Pour ingredients into iced mixing glass
1/8 oz. Dry Vermouth
1/8 oz. olive juice (brine)
2 oz. Türi Vodka
Stir and strain
Three black olives stuffed with red caviar

MARTINI, BANANA CREME PIE
Cocktail glass, chilled
Pour ingredients into iced mixing glass
2 oz. Mount Gay Eclipse Rum
3/4 oz. Crème de Banana
1 1/2 oz. half & half cream
Shake and strain
Banana slice and cherry garnish

MARTINI, BECCO
Cocktail glass, chilled
Pour ingredients into iced mixing glass
1 1/2 oz. Orange Vodka
1/2 oz. Campari Aperitivo
1/2 oz. Sweet Vermouth
Stir and strain
Orange peel

MARTINI, BEL-AIR
Cocktail glass, chilled
Pour ingredients into iced mixing glass
1/2 oz. Sherry
2 oz. Vodka
Stir and strain
Lemon twist garnish

MARTINI, BELLINI
Cocktail glass, chilled
Pour ingredients into iced mixing glass
1 oz. Limoncé Limoncello
1/2 oz. Gran Gala Orange Liqueur
1/2 oz. Crème de Banana
1/2 oz. Peach Schnapps
1/2 oz. orange juice
Stir and strain
Orange wheel garnish

MARTINI, BENTLEY
Cocktail glass, chilled
Pour ingredients into iced mixing glass
1/2 oz. Dry Vermouth
1/2 oz. Sweet Vermouth
1/4 oz. B & B Liqueur
1 1/2 oz. Gin
Stir and strain
Lemon twist garnish

MARTINI, BITCHIN'
Cocktail glass, chilled
Pour ingredients into iced mixing glass
1/2 oz. Dry Vermouth
2 dashes White Crème de Menthe
2 dashes Pernod
1 1/2 oz. Gin
Stir and strain
Lemon twist garnish

MARTINI, BLACK (1)
Cocktail glass, chilled
Pour ingredients into iced mixing glass
1/2 oz. Chambord
2 oz. Vodka
Stir and strain
Lemon twist garnish

MARTINI, BLACK (2)
Cocktail glass, chilled
Pour ingredients into iced mixing glass
1/2 oz. Crème de Cassis
1 1/2 oz. Vodka
Stir and strain
Lemon twist garnish

MARTINI, BLACK (3)
Cocktail glass, chilled
Pour ingredients into iced mixing glass
1/2 oz. Quady Elysium Wine
1/2 oz. Quady Essensia Wine
1 3/4 oz. Vodka
Stir and strain
Orange slice garnish

MARTINI, BLACK & ORANGE
Cocktail glass, chilled
Pour ingredients into iced mixing glass
2 oz. Jim Beam Black Label Bourbon
3/4 oz. Disaronno Amaretto
Dash Angostura Bitters
1/2 oz. fresh orange juice
1/2 oz. fresh lime juice
Stir and strain
Orange wheel garnish

MARTINI, BLACK COFFEE & CREAMTINI
Cocktail glass, chilled
Pour ingredients into iced mixing glass
1 1/2 oz. Jim Beam Black Label Bourbon
3/4 oz. Tia Maria
3/4 oz. Baileys Irish Cream
Shake and strain
Sprinkle cinnamon garnish

MARTINI, BLACK DEVIL
Cocktail glass, chilled
Pour ingredients into iced mixing glass
1/4 oz. Dry Vermouth
2 oz. Cruzan Estate Light Rum
Stir and strain
Black olives garnish

MARTINI, BLACK TIE (1)
Cocktail glass, chilled
Pour ingredients into iced mixing glass
1/4 oz. Dry Vermouth
2 oz. Appleton Estate Extra Jamaica Rum
Stir and strain
Black olives garnish

MARTINI, BLACK TIE (2)
Cocktail glass, chilled
Pour ingredients into iced mixing glass
2 dashes Campari Aperitivo
1/4 oz. Scotch Whisky
1 1/2 oz. Vodka
Stir and strain
Cocktail onions and black olive garnish

MARTINI, BLEU
Cocktail glass, chilled
Pour ingredients into iced mixing glass
1/2 oz. Dry Vermouth
1 1/2 oz. Vodka
Stir and strain
Olives stuffed with bleu cheese

MARTINI, BLOOD ORANGE
Cocktail glass, chilled
Pour ingredients into iced mixing glass
1/2 oz. Campari Aperitivo
1 1/2 oz. Orange Vodka
Stir and strain
Lemon twist garnish

MARTINI, BLOOD SHOT
Cocktail glass, chilled
Pour ingredients into iced mixing glass
1/4 oz. Absolut Peppar Vodka
1/2 oz. Campari Aperitivo
1 1/2 oz. Vodka
Stir and strain
Chile pepper garnish

FINLANDIA® VODKA

Finland had been producing spirits for over 400 years when the country enacted Prohibition. Mirroring what was happening in the United States, the ban ended in 1932, at which point the state assumed control over the production of spirits. Thus began the storied existence of FINLANDIA VODKA.

The highly acclaimed vodka was originally produced at the historic Rajamäki Distillery, located just outside of Helsinki, which had been producing vodka since 1888. A century later, production moved to the state of the art facilities of the Koskenkorva Distillery.

Finlandia Vodka is distilled entirely from premium, six row barley and glacier-fed spring water. It is triple-distilled in continuous column stills, where it is rectified to 96% alcohol by volume, then diluted with the same glacial spring water to its bottle strength of 80 proof.

Finlandia is an exemplary neutral vodka possessing a silky texture, medium-weight body and a prominent bouquet of grain and dried herbs. It glides over the palate without a trace of harshness, filling the mouth with warmth before it slips away in a clean, crisp finish.

The distillery also produces two flavored vodkas, FINLANDIA CRANBERRY FUSION and FINLANDIA LIME FUSION. These refreshing, cocktail friendly spirits are crystal clear and loaded with flavor.

MARTINI, BLUE DIAMOND
Cocktail glass, chilled
Pour ingredients into iced mixing glass
1 1/2 oz. DeKuyper Island Blue Pucker
3/4 oz. DeKuyper Pucker Sour Apple
3/4 oz. Absolut Citron Vodka
Stir and strain
Splash of cola
Orange wheel garnish

MARTINI, BLUE MOON (1)
Cocktail glass, chilled
Pour ingredients into iced mixing glass
1/2 oz. Blue Curaçao
1 1/2 oz. Bombay Sapphire London Dry Gin
1 1/2 oz. Stolichnaya Vodka
Stir and strain
Lemon twist garnish

MARTINI, BLUE MOON (2)
Cocktail glass, chilled
Pour ingredients into iced mixing glass
1/2 oz. Blue Curaçao
1 1/2 oz. Beefeater London Dry Gin
Stir and strain
Lemon twist garnish

MARTINI, BLUE PACIFIC
Cocktail glass, chilled
Pour ingredients into iced mixing glass
1/4 oz. Dry Vermouth
1/4 oz. Blue Curaçao
1 1/2 oz. Magellan Gin
1 1/2 oz. Absolut Vodka
Stir and strain
Lemon twist garnish

MARTINI, BLUE SHOCK
Cocktail glass, chilled
Pour ingredients into iced mixing glass
1 1/2 oz. Crown Royal
1/2 oz. Disaronno Amaretto
1/2 oz. Blue Curaçao
3/4 oz. sweet 'n' sour
3/4 oz. cranberry juice
1/2 oz. Seven-Up
Stir and strain
Orange slice and cherry garnish

MARTINI BLUES
Cocktail glass, chilled
Pour ingredients into iced mixing glass
1/2 oz. Blue Curaçao
1 oz. Broker's London Dry Gin
1 oz. Spudka Vodka
Stir and strain
Lemon twist garnish

MARTINI, BOOTLEGGER
Cocktail glass, chilled
Pour ingredients into iced mixing glass
1/4 oz. Dry Vermouth
1/2 oz. Southern Comfort
1 1/2 oz. Gin
Stir and strain
Lemon twist garnish

MARTINI, BOSTON
Cocktail glass, chilled
Pour ingredients into iced mixing glass
3 dashes Dry Vermouth
2 oz. Gin
Stir and strain
Anchovy-wrapped or almond-stuffed
   olives garnish

MARTINI, BRAZEN
Cocktail glass, chilled
Pour ingredients into iced mixing glass
1/4 oz. Crème de Cassis
2 1/2 oz. Grey Goose Vodka
Stir and strain
Kumquat garnish

MARTINI, BRONX
Cocktail glass, chilled
Pour ingredients into iced mixing glass
1/4 oz. Dry Vermouth
1/4 oz. Sweet Vermouth
1/4 oz. orange juice
1 1/2 oz. Gin
Stir and strain
Lemon twist garnish

MARTINI, BUBBLEGUM
Cocktail glass, chilled
Pour ingredients into iced mixing glass
1/4 oz. Chambord
1/4 oz. Rose's Lime Juice
2 oz. Gin
Shake and strain
Lime wedge garnish

MARTINI, BUCKEYE
Cocktail glass, chilled
Pour ingredients into iced mixing glass
3 dashes Dry Vermouth
2 oz. Gin
Stir and strain
Black olives garnish

MARTINI, CAFÉ NUTTINI
Cocktail glass, chilled
Pour ingredients into iced mixing glass
1/2 oz. Kahlúa Especial
1/2 oz. Disaronno Amaretto
2 oz. Liquid Ice Vodka
Stir and strain
Orange twist garnish

MARTINI, CAJUN (1)
Cocktail glass, chilled
Pour ingredients into iced mixing glass
1/4 oz. Dry Vermouth
1/4 oz. Sweet Vermouth
3/4 oz. Gin
3/4 oz. jalapeño-steeped Gin
Stir and strain
Small jalapeño peppers garnish

MARTINI, CAJUN (2)
Cocktail glass, chilled
Pour ingredients into iced mixing glass
1/4 oz. Dry Vermouth
1/4 oz. Absolut Peppar Vodka
2-3 dashes Tabasco Sauce
2 oz. Gin
Stir and strain
Cooked crawfish garnish
Note: Steep crawfish in Absolut Peppar
   prior to cooking

MARTINI, CAJUN KING
Cocktail glass, chilled
Pour ingredients into iced mixing glass
2 dashes Dry Vermouth
1/2 oz. Absolut Citron Vodka
1 1/2 oz. Absolut Peppar Vodka
Stir and strain
Small jalapeño peppers garnish

MARTINI, CARIBBEAN
Cocktail glass, chilled
Pour ingredients into iced mixing glass
1/2 oz. fresh lemon juice
1 oz. Bacardi Limón Rum
2 1/2 oz. RémyRed Red Berry Infusion
Stir and strain
Lemon twist garnish

MARTINI, CARROT CAKE
Cocktail glass, chilled
Rim glass with chocolate syrup and
   graham crackers
Pour ingredients into iced mixing glass
1 1/2 oz. Baileys Irish Cream
1 oz. DeKuyper Butianshots Schnapps
3/4 oz. Cinnamon Schnapps
3/4 oz. cream
Shake and strain
Chocolate dipped strawberry garnish

MARTINI, CELTIC
Cocktail glass, chilled
Pour ingredients into iced mixing glass
1/4 oz. lemon juice
3/4 oz. Celtic Crossing Irish Liqueur
1 1/2 oz. Boru Vodka
Stir and strain
Lemon twist garnish

DEKUYPER® RAZZMATAZZ®

In Europe, raspberries have long been associated with royalty, the berries of kings, so to speak. In fact, the raspberry liqueurs made on the Continent—where they're referred to as Framboise—are regal, luxurious and quite sophisticated. Here in the U.S., however, the raspberry belongs to the people and while it is one of the most popular flavors in the country, we just want to have fun. Enter DEKUYPER RAZZMATAZZ, a raspberry liqueur born and bred for the nightlife.

DeKuyper Razzmatazz is made on a base of pure grain, neutral spirits that are liberally infused with natural raspberry flavorings. It is remarkably similar in character to Framboise. The principal difference between the two is that Razzmatazz has a slightly lighter body than most of its European counterparts, a characteristic that makes it tailor-made for drink making.

Razzmatazz has a deep, true raspberry color and a lively, fresh fruit bouquet. The liqueur is well-balanced between sweet and sour and is loaded with raspberry flavor. The finish is admirably long.

DeKuyper Razzmatazz is a contemporary gem. In the hands of a skilled mixologist it is a product with no creative boundaries. It is frequently featured in everything from Martinis, Margaritas and Daiquiris to coffee, hot cocoa and ice cream drinks. So have fun with it and give your drinks some pizzazz with Razzmatazz.

MARTINI, CHOCOLATE
Cocktail glass, chilled
Pour ingredients into iced mixing glass
1/2 oz. Godiva Chocolate Liqueur
3/4 oz. Van Gogh Vanilla Vodka
1 3/4 oz. Van Gogh Chocolate Vodka
Stir and strain
Lemon twist garnish

MARTINI, CHOCOLATE COVERED STRAWBERRY
Cocktail glass, chilled
Rim glass with chocolate syrup and powdered cocoa
Pour ingredients into iced mixing glass
2 oz. Stolichnaya Strasberi Vodka
3/4 oz. White Crème de Cacao
3/4 oz. strawberry nectar
Shake and strain
Strawberry slices garnish

MARTINI, CHOCOLATE CRANBERRY
Cocktail glass, chilled
Pour ingredients into iced mixing glass
1/2 oz. white cranberry juice
3/4 oz. Godiva Chocolate Liqueur
2 oz. Stolichnaya Cranberi Vodka
Stir and strain
Orange slice garnish

MARTINI, CHOCOLATE MINT
Cocktail glass, chilled
Pour ingredients into iced mixing glass
3/4 oz. Godiva Chocolate Liqueur
3/4 oz. White Crème de Menthe
1 3/4 oz. Van Gogh Chocolate Vodka
Stir and strain
Peppermint stick garnish

MARTINI, CHOCOLATE ORANGE DROP
Cocktail glass, chilled
Pour ingredients into iced mixing glass
3/4 oz. White Crème de Cacao
3/4 oz. Gran Gala Orange Liqueur
3/4 oz. orange juice
1 1/2 oz. Vodka
Stir and strain
Lemon wheel garnish

MARTINI, CHOCOLATE SUPREME
Cocktail glass, chilled
Pour ingredients into iced mixing glass
1 1/2 oz. Godiva Chocolate Liqueur
1 oz. Absolut Vanilia Vodka
1 oz. Grand Marnier
1 oz. Kahlúa
1/2 oz. VS Cognac
Stir and strain
Shaved white chocolate garnish

MARTINI, CHOCOLATE UTOPIA
Cocktail glass, chilled
Pour ingredients into iced mixing glass
2 oz. Van Gogh Chocolate Vodka
1 oz. Godiva Chocolate Liqueur
1/2 oz. Chambord
1/2 oz. Disaronno Amaretto
1 oz. milk
Shake and strain
Shaved chocolate garnish

MARTINI, CITRUS
Cocktail glass, chilled
Pour ingredients into iced mixing glass
3/4 oz. Blue Curaçao
3/4 oz. lemonade
2 oz. Ketel One Citroen Vodka
Stir and strain
Lemon wedge garnish

MARTINI, COLADA
Cocktail glass, chilled
Rim glass with chocolate syrup and
  graham crackers
Pour ingredients into iced mixing glass
1 1/2 oz. Pineapple Rum
1 oz. Coconut Rum
1 oz. pineapple juice
Shake and strain
Pineapple wedge garnish

MARTINI, COPPER ILLUSION
Cocktail glass, chilled
Pour ingredients into iced mixing glass
1/2 oz. Cointreau
1/2 oz. Campari Aperitivo
1 1/2 oz. Gin
Stir and strain
Lemon twist garnish

MARTINI, COSMONAUT
Cocktail glass, chilled
Pour ingredients into iced mixing glass
1 1/2 oz. lemonade
1/8 oz. Chambord
1/4 oz. Grand Marnier
2 oz. Original Cristall Vodka
Shake and strain
Starfruit (carambola) garnish

MARTINI, COZUMEL
Cocktail glass, chilled
Pour ingredients into iced mixing glass
1/4 oz. fresh lime juice
1/4 oz. Grand Marnier Centenaire
2 1/2 oz. El Tesoro Platinum Tequila
Stir and strain
Lemon twist garnish

MARTINI, CRAN-APPLETINI
Cocktail glass, chilled
Rim glass with cinnamon and
  sugar (optional)
Pour ingredients into iced mixing glass
1 oz. Jim Beam White Label Bourbon
1 oz. DeKuyper Pucker Sour Apple
1 oz. cranberry juice
Stir and strain
Green apple garnish

MARTINI, CRÈME BRÛLÉE (1)
Cocktail glass, chilled
Rim glass with brown sugar (optional)
Pour ingredients into iced mixing glass
1/4 oz. Frangelico
1/4 oz. Cointreau
1 oz. Crème Anglaise
2 oz. Grey Goose Vodka
Shake and strain
Vanilla stick swizzle

MARTINI, CRÈME BRÛLÉE (2)
Cocktail glass, chilled
Rim glass with brown sugar (optional)
Pour ingredients into iced mixing glass
1/4 oz. half & half cream
1/2 oz. Cointreau
1/2 oz. Frangelico
1 oz. Stolichnaya Vanil Vodka
Shake and strain
Orange slice garnish

MARTINI, CRÈME BRÛLÉE (3)
Cocktail glass, chilled
Paint inside of glass with ribbons of
caramel syrup
Pour ingredients into iced mixing glass
1/4 oz. half & half cream
1/4 oz. Chambord
1/2 oz. DeKuyper Butdate
2 oz. Stolichnaya Vanil Vodka
Stir and strain
Orange slice garnish

MARTINI, CREOLE
Cocktail glass, chilled
Pour ingredients into iced mixing glass
1/4 oz. Dry Vermouth
2 oz. Absolut Peppar Vodka
Stir and strain
Pepperoncini garnish

JOSE CUERVO® TRADICIONAL® REPOSADO TEQUILA

Jose Antonio de Cuervo is acknowledged as the first person to ever produce what would become known as tequila. In 1795, King Carlos IV of Spain granted his son, Jose Maria Guadalupe Cuervo, the first license to commercially produce tequila. In the 208 years since then, the Jose Cuervo brand has become internationally renowned. Few products better illustrate why the distillery has achieved preeminence than JOSE CUERVO TRADICIONAL REPOSADO TEQUILA.

Made in the town of Tequila at the Jose Cuervo distillery, *La Rojeña*, Tradicional is handcrafted entirely from mature blue agaves. The harvested agaves are steamed in clay ovens prior to being pressed and fermented. The tequila is double-distilled and aged in white oak casks for 6 months. It is made in limited production and bottled at 80 proof.

Jose Cuervo Tradicional Reposado is the best-selling 100% agave tequila in Mexico. The straw-colored tequila has a medium-weight body with a generous helping of long lasting oak and herbaceous aromas. On the palate the tequila offers the flavors of caramel and vanilla that taper to a warm and spicy finish.

Most tequila enthusiasts don't know that Jose Cuervo Tradicional is actually vintage dated. The bottle above—produced in 2003—is marked with a "208" to commemorate the 208th year of production. *Salud!*

MARTINI, CRYSTAL PEARLESSENCE
Cocktail glass, chilled
Pour ingredients into iced mixing glass
1/2 oz. VSOP Cognac
2 oz. Pearl Vodka
Stir and strain
Lemon twist garnish

MARTINI, CUPID'S BOW
Cocktail glass, chilled
Pour ingredients into iced mixing glass
1/2 oz. Dry Vermouth
1/2 oz. Lillet Blonde
1 1/2 oz. Miller's London Dry Gin
Stir and strain
Lemon twist and cherry garnish

MARTINI, DIAMOND
Cocktail glass, chilled
Rim glass with sugar (optional)
Pour ingredients into iced mixing glass
1 oz. VSOP Cognac
1 oz. Vodka
1/4 oz. fresh lemon juice
1 oz. pineapple juice
Stir and strain
Lemon wheel garnish

MARTINI, DIRTY (1)
Cocktail glass, chilled
Pour ingredients into iced mixing glass
2 dashes Dry Vermouth
1 1/2 oz. Vodka
1/4 oz. olive juice (brine)
Stir and strain
Olives garnish

MARTINI, DIRTY (2)
Cocktail glass, chilled
Pour ingredients into iced mixing glass
1/4 oz. olive juice (brine)
1/2 oz. Vodka
1 1/2 oz. Gin
Stir and strain
Olive garnish

MARTINI, DIRTY CITRUS
Cocktail glass, chilled
Pour ingredients into iced mixing glass
1/4 oz. olive juice (brine)
2 oz. Vodka
1 oz. Citrus Vodka
Shake vigorously and strain
Lemon twist garnish

MARTINI, DIRTY GIN TWIST
Cocktail glass, chilled
Pour ingredients into iced mixing glass
1/4 oz. olive juice (brine)
2 oz. Gin
1 oz. Citrus Vodka
Shake vigorously and strain
Lemon twist garnish

MARTINI, DRAGON'S BREATH
Cocktail glass, chilled
Pour ingredients into iced mixing glass
1/4 oz. Dry Vermouth
1/2 oz. Cointreau
1/2 oz. blood orange juice
2 oz. Citadelle Gin
Stir and strain
Lemon wheel garnish

MARTINI, DRY
Cocktail glass, chilled
Pour ingredients into iced mixing glass
2 drops Dry Vermouth
1 1/2 oz. Gin
Stir and strain
Olives or lemon twist garnish

MARTINI, DRY TANQUE
Cocktail glass, chilled
Pour ingredients into iced mixing glass
2 drops Dry Vermouth
1/4 oz. Grand Marnier
1 oz. Tanqueray Gin
1 oz. Absolut Vodka
Stir and strain
Olives or lemon twist garnish

MARTINI, DRY VODKA
Cocktail glass, chilled
Pour ingredients into iced mixing glass
4 drops Dry Vermouth
1 1/2 oz. Vodka
Stir and strain
Olives or lemon twist garnish

MARTINI, DUTCH (1)
Cocktail glass, chilled
Pour ingredients into iced mixing glass
1/4 oz. Dubonnet Blonde
2 oz. Damrak Amsterdam Gin
Stir and strain
Lemon twist garnish

MARTINI, DUTCH (2)
Cocktail glass, chilled
Pour ingredients into iced mixing glass
1/4 oz. Dry Vermouth
1 1/2 oz. Genever Gin
Stir and strain
Lemon twist garnish

MARTINI, ELECTRIC BLUE
Cocktail glass, chilled
Pour ingredients into iced mixing glass
1 1/2 oz. Raspberry Vodka
1 oz. Hpnotiq Liqueur
1 oz. Blue Curaçao
Stir and strain
Top with 1 1/2 oz. Champagne
Orange twist garnish

MARTINI, ELEPHANT'S EAR
Cocktail glass, chilled
Pour ingredients into iced mixing glass
1/2 oz. Dry Vermouth
1/2 oz. Dubonnet Blonde
1 1/2 oz. Plymouth Gin
Stir and strain
Lemon twist garnish

MARTINI, ELISA'S MARTINI OF LOVE
Cocktail glass, chilled
Pour ingredients into iced mixing glass
1/2 oz. Baileys Irish Cream
1/2 oz. Frangelico
1/2 oz. Godiva Chocolate Liqueur
2 1/4 oz. Stön Vodka
Stir and strain
Hershey Kiss (unwrapped) garnish

MARTINI, EL PRESIDENTÉ
Cocktail glass, chilled
Pour ingredients into iced mixing glass
1/2 oz. Dry Vermouth
1/2 oz. Sweet Vermouth
1/2 oz. Cointreau
2 dashes grenadine
1 1/2 oz. Light Rum
Stir and strain
Lemon twist garnish

MARTINI, EMERALD
Cocktail glass, chilled
Pour ingredients into iced mixing glass
1/2 oz. Midori
1 1/2 oz. Citrus Rum
Stir and strain
Lemon twist garnish

MARTINI, ESPRESSO
Cocktail glass, chilled
Pour ingredients into iced mixing glass
1/2 oz. Tia Maria
1/2 oz. Kahlúa Especial
1 oz. espresso coffee
2 oz. Vodka
Stir and strain

RÉMYRED® STRAWBERRY KIWI INFUSION

Launched in 2003, RÉMYRED STRAWBERRY KIWI INFUSION is unlike any other liqueur you've ever tried…guaranteed. It is so luscious and bursting with juicy flavors that it's hard to imagine how it all fit into the bottle. One thing is for certain though, this new French sensation is capable of standing alone in a glass wearing nothing but a chill and drawing nothing but praise.

RémyRed Strawberry Kiwi Infusion is made in the heart of the cognac region of France by the legendary cognac house of Rémy Martin. The liqueur is produced on a base of aged, Fine Champagne Rémy Martin Cognac, a blend of Grande and Petite Champagne cognacs. The cognac is then infused with the natural juice of strawberries and kiwis. The infusion is rested and bottled at 32 proof.

This version of RémyRed possesses every characteristic for sustained popularity. The liqueur has a beckoning pink color with orange highlights and looks like freshly squeezed strawberry juice. It has a lightweight body and a generous bouquet laced with the succulent aromas of ripe, juicy fruit. The palate features a diverse array of flavors, including mangos, nectarines and oranges, as well as strawberries and kiwis. It's genuinely a luscious experience.

In addition to being delicious served as an aperitif, this RémyRed is marvelous used as an ingredient in cocktails.

MARTINI, ESPRESSO FRAMBOISE
Cocktail glass, chilled
Pour ingredients into iced mixing glass
1/2 oz. Godiva Chocolate Liqueur
1/2 oz. Chambord
1/2 oz. chilled espresso coffee
1 1/2 oz. Absolut Vanilia Vodka
Stir and strain
Coffee beans (3) garnish

MARTINI, EVERGLADES
Cocktail glass, chilled
Pour ingredients into iced mixing glass
1/4 oz. Dry Vermouth
1/4 oz. Grand Marnier
2 oz. Tanqueray N⁰ Ten Gin
Stir and strain
Lemon twist garnish

MARTINI, EXTRA DRY
Cocktail glass, chilled
Pour ingredients into iced mixing glass
1 drop Dry Vermouth (optional)
1 1/2 oz. Gin
Stir and strain
Olives or lemon twist garnish

MARTINI, EXTRA DRY VODKA
Cocktail glass, chilled
Pour ingredients into iced mixing glass
1 drop Dry Vermouth (optional)
1 1/2 oz. Vodka
Stir and strain
Olives or lemon twist garnish

MARTINI, FANTINO
Cocktail glass, chilled
Pour ingredients into iced mixing glass
2 dashes Campari Aperitivo
1/2 oz. Limoncello Liqueur
2 oz. Vodka
Stir and strain
Lemon twist garnish

MARTINI, F.D.R.
Cocktail glass, chilled
Pour ingredients into iced mixing glass
1/2 oz. Dry Vermouth
1/4 oz. olive juice (brine)
2 oz. Gin
Stir and strain
Twist lemon peel, rub glass with
 peel, discard.
Olive garnish

MARTINI, FIDEL'S
Cocktail glass, chilled
Pour ingredients into iced mixing glass
1/2 oz. Cruzan Banana Rum
1 1/2 oz. Stolichnaya Vodka
Stir and strain
Banana slice garnish

MARTINI, FINLANDIA PEPPER
Cocktail glass, chilled
Pour ingredients into iced mixing glass
1/4 oz. Dry Vermouth
2 oz. Finlandia Vodka
3-4 dashes Louisiana Gold Pepper Sauce
Stir and strain
Red peppers (2) garnish

MARTINI, FINO
Cocktail glass, chilled
Pour ingredients into iced mixing glass
1/2 oz. Fino Sherry
2 oz. Gin
Stir and strain
Lemon twist garnish

MARTINI, FLAN
Cocktail glass, chilled
Rim glass with chocolate syrup and
   powdered cocoa
Pour ingredients into iced mixing glass
2 oz. Captain Morgan Spiced Rum
3/4 oz. Baileys Irish Cream
1/2 oz. White Crème de Cacao
1/2 oz. caramel syrup
Shake and strain
Strawberry slice s garnish

MARTINI, FLIRTINI (1)
Champagne glass, chilled
Muddle 4 raspberries in bottom of glass
Pour ingredients into iced mixing glass
1 oz. Vodka
1/2 oz. Cointreau
1/2 oz. Rose's Lime Juice
1/2 oz. cranberry juice
1/2 oz. pineapple juice
Shake and strain
Fill with Champagne
Mint sprig garnish

MARTINI, FLIRTINI (2)
Champagne glass, chilled
Pour ingredients into iced mixing glass
1 oz. Vox Raspberry Vodka
2 oz. pineapple juice
Shake and strain
Fill with Champagne

MARTINI, FOREIGN LEGION
Cocktail glass, chilled
Pour ingredients into iced mixing glass
1 1/2 oz. Amarula Cream Liqueur
1 oz. Appleton Estate V/X Jamaica Rum
3/4 oz. Dark Crème de Cacao
Shake and strain
Orange slice and cherry garnish

MARTINI, FOURTH DEGREE
Cocktail glass, chilled
Pour ingredients into iced mixing glass
1/2 oz. RémyRed Red Berry Infusion
1/2 oz. Dubonnet Blonde
1 3/4 oz. Beefeater London Dry Gin
Stir and strain
Lemon twist garnish

MARTINI, FRENCH (1)
Cocktail glass, chilled
Pour ingredients into iced mixing glass
1/4 oz. Dry Vermouth
3/4 oz. Grand Marnier
1 3/4 oz. Grey Goose Vodka
Stir and strain
Lemon twist garnish

MARTINI, FRENCH (2)
Cocktail glass, chilled
Pour ingredients into iced mixing glass
1/2 oz. Chambord
1 oz. pineapple juice
2 oz. Grey Goose Vodka
Stir and strain
Orange twist garnish

MARTINI, FRENCH (3)
aka **Golden Drop**
Cocktail glass, chilled
Pour ingredients into iced mixing glass
1/4 oz. Scotch Whisky
1/4 oz. Dry Vermouth (optional)
1 1/2 oz. Gin
Stir and strain
Lemon twist garnish

MARTINI, FRENCH GRAPE
Cocktail glass, chilled
Pour ingredients into iced mixing glass
1/2 oz. Grand Marnier
3/4 oz. red grape juice
1/2 oz. Blue Curaçao
2 oz. Cîroc Snap Frost Vodka
Stir and strain
Orange wheel garnish

RHUM BARBANCOURT® FIVE STAR RÉSERVE SPÉCIALE

Rhum Barbancourt was founded in 1862 by Frenchman Dupré Barbancourt. His ambition was to apply the techniques that he had learned making cognac to the rhum making process. He achieved his dream with RHUM BARBANCOURT FIVE STAR RÉSERVE SPÉCIALE.

This revered spirit is an agricole rhum fermented for three days and double-distilled, first in a single-column still and then in a copper alembic still. The final distillate is diluted with purified rain water prior to being aged a minimum of 8 years in large, Limousin oak vats. It is then bottled at 80 proof.

The Five Star Réserve Spéciale is a genuinely elegant rhum. It has a medium body and a seamlessly smooth texture. The rhum's pronounced bouquet offers up a bevy of warm, toasty aromas. It's on the palate that this exceptional spirit shines. The rhum is brimming with the flavors of chocolate, honey and toffee. The flavors persist on the palate for an extended amount of time, eventually tapering off into a brandy-like finish.

RHUM BARBANCOURT ESTATE RÉSERVE DU DOMAINE was once the private reserve of the distillery. It is aged a minimum of 15 years in large, French oak vats. The extended aging has a profound affect on the rhum, which makes it comparable to a well aged cognac. It has tremendous complexity and a character full of charm and sophistication.

MARTINI, FRIAR PAUL
Cocktail glass, chilled
Pour ingredients into iced mixing glass
4 drops Dry Vermouth
1 1/2 oz. Plymouth Gin
Stir and strain
Cocktail onions garnish

MARTINI, FULL MOON (1)
Cocktail glass, chilled
Pour ingredients into iced mixing glass
3/4 oz. Grand Marnier
3/4 oz. Disaronno Amaretto
3/4 oz. Stolichnaya Vodka
Stir and strain
Lemon twist garnish

MARTINI, FULL MOON (2)
Cocktail glass, chilled
Pour ingredients into iced mixing glass
3/4 oz. Gran Gala Orange Liqueur
3/4 oz. Disaronno Amaretto
Stir and strain
Lemon twist garnish

MARTINI, FULL NELSON
Cocktail glass, chilled
Pour ingredients into iced mixing glass
4 drops Dry Vermouth
1 1/2 oz. Dry Gin
Stir and strain
Cocktail onion and green olives garnish

MARTINI, GOLDEN GIRL
Cocktail glass, chilled
Pour ingredients into iced mixing glass
3/4 oz. Dry Sherry
2 dashes Angostura Bitters
2 dashes orange bitters
1 1/2 oz. Tanqueray Gin
Stir and strain
Lemon twist garnish

MARTINI, GOTHAM
Cocktail glass, chilled
Pour ingredients into iced mixing glass
1/4 oz. Opal Nera Black Sambuca
1/4 oz. Crème de Cassis
2 oz. Vodka
Stir and strain
Lemon twist garnish

MARTINI, GRAND OPERA
Cocktail glass, chilled
Pour ingredients into iced mixing glass
1 1/2 oz. Tanqueray Nº Ten Gin
1/2 oz. Grand Marnier
1/2 oz. fresh lime juice
1 oz. pineapple juice
Shake and strain
Kumquat garnish

MARTINI, GREEN APPLE
Cocktail glass, chilled
Rim glass with sugar
Pour ingredients into iced mixing glass
1 1/2 oz. Van Gogh Wild Appel Vodka
1 1/2 oz. DeKuyper Pucker Sour Apple
Splash sweet 'n' sour
Shake and strain
Apple wedge garnish

MARTINI, GREEN LANTERN
Cocktail glass, chilled
Pour ingredients into iced mixing glass
1/2 oz. Midori
1/4 oz. Rose's Lime Juice
1/4 oz. sweet 'n' sour
2 oz. Vodka
Stir and strain
Lemon twist garnish

MARTINI, GUMMIE BARE
Cocktail glass, chilled
Pour ingredients into iced mixing glass
1 oz. Midori
1 oz. Peach Schnapps
3/4 oz. cranberry juice
1 oz. sweet 'n' sour
Shake and strain
Gummie Bears (3) garnish

MARTINI, HARPER'S
Cocktail glass, chilled
Pour ingredients into iced mixing glass
3/4 oz. Dubonnet Rouge
1/4 oz. Chambord
2 oz. Stolichnaya Persik Vodka
Stir and strain
Orange slice garnish

MARTINI, HAVANA
Cocktail glass, chilled
Pour ingredients into iced mixing glass
1/2 oz. Vintage Tawny Port
1 1/2 oz. Bacardi 8 Reserva Rum
Stir and strain
Cherry garnish

MARTINI, HAWAIIAN
Cocktail glass, chilled
Pour ingredients into iced mixing glass
1/4 oz. Dry Vermouth
1/4 oz. Sweet Vermouth
1/4 oz. pineapple juice
1 1/2 oz. Vodka
Stir and strain
Pineapple wedge garnish

MARTINI, HENNESSY
Cocktail glass, chilled
Pour ingredients into iced mixing glass
1/4 oz. fresh lemon juice
2 oz. Hennessy VS Cognac
Stir and strain
Lemon twist garnish

MARTINI, HIGHLANDER
Cocktail glass, chilled
Pour ingredients into iced mixing glass
1/2 oz. Glenlivet Single Malt Scotch
2 oz. Gin
Stir and strain
Lemon twist garnish

MARTINI, HOT
Cocktail glass, chilled
Pour ingredients into iced mixing glass
1/4 oz. Dry Vermouth
1/4 oz. pickled jalapeño juice
1/4 oz. fresh lime juice
2 oz. Vodka
Stir and strain
Jalapeño-stuffed olive garnish

MARTINI, HOT MARTI
Cocktail glass, chilled
Pour ingredients into iced mixing glass
1/2 oz. Dry Vermouth
1/4 oz. pickled jalapeño juice
1/4 oz. fresh lime juice
2 oz. Vodka
Stir and strain
Cocktail onions garnish

MARTINI, ICEBERG
Cocktail glass, chilled
Pour ingredients into iced mixing glass
1/4 oz. White Crème de Menthe
2 oz. Gin
Stir and strain
Mint sprig garnish

MARTINI, IMPERIAL
Cocktail glass, chilled
Pour ingredients into iced mixing glass
3 dashes Dry Vermouth
3 dashes Angostura Bitters
1/4 oz. Chambord
1 1/2 oz. Gin
Stir and strain
Lemon twist garnish

GREY GOOSE®
LE CITRON VODKA

We are a country that loves the flavor of lemons. So when one of the world's elite vodkas introduces a sophisticated lemon-infused vodka, Americans are going to take notice. Such was the enthusiastic response that welcomed the release of GREY GOOSE LE CITRON.

The entire range of Grey Goose Vodkas is skillfully produced in the heart of Cognac. They are distilled in small batches beginning in copper stills from a choice blend of grains. The pure grain vodkas are produced with pristine, limestone-filtered water drawn from the famous Genté Springs. Natural citrus flavors are added to the vodka, which is then rigorously filtered and bottled at 80 proof.

Grey Goose Le Citron is refreshing and exceptionally delicious. Take a long moment to appreciate it wearing nothing but a slight chill before you go off and begin making cocktails with it. The vodka is crystal clear and possesses a soft, smooth, medium-weight body. The generous bouquet is redolent with the fresh aroma of sun-ripened lemons. It immediately fills the mouth with the warm, tingling flavor of citrus before it gradually resides into a relaxed and surgically clean finish.

This Olympic caliber spirit is one of the Grey Goose family of flavored vodkas that also includes L'ORANGE and LA VANILLE.

MARTINI, INFUSED
Cocktail glass, chilled
Pour ingredients into iced mixing glass
1/4 oz. Dry Vermouth
1/4 oz. Sweet Vermouth
3/4 oz. Gin
3/4 oz. Lemoneater Infused Gin
Stir and strain
Lemon twist garnish

MARTINI, IRISH
Cocktail glass, chilled
Rim glass with cinnamon and
   sugar (optional)
Pour ingredients into iced mixing glass
3/4 oz. Irish Liqueur
3/4 oz. Baileys Irish Cream
1 3/4 oz. Irish Whiskey
Stir and strain
Orange slice garnish

MARTINI, ITALIAN (1)
Cocktail glass, chilled
Pour ingredients into iced mixing glass
1/2 oz. Gran Gala Orange Liqueur
1 1/4 oz. Mezzaluna Limoncello Liqueur
1 1/4 oz. Mezzaluna Italian Vodka
Stir and strain
Lemon wedge garnish

MARTINI, ITALIAN (2)
Cocktail glass, chilled
Pour ingredients into iced mixing glass
1/2 oz. Marsala Wine
2 oz. Gin
Stir and strain
Lemon twist garnish

MARTINI, JACKSON
Cocktail glass, chilled
Pour ingredients into iced mixing glass
1/2 oz. Dubonnet Blonde
3 dashes Angostura Bitters
2 oz. Gin
Stir and strain
Lemon twist garnish

MARTINI, JADED
Cocktail glass, chilled
Pour ingredients into iced mixing glass
1/4 oz. Limoncello Liqueur
1/4 oz. Midori
2 oz. Magellan Gin
Stir and strain
Orange twist garnish

MARTINI, JALISCO
Cocktail glass, chilled
Pour ingredients into iced mixing glass
1/4 oz. Grand Marnier
1 1/2 oz. Chili-infused Tequila
Stir and strain
Chile peppers garnish

MARTINI, JOURNALIST
Cocktail glass, chilled
Pour ingredients into iced mixing glass
1/4 oz. Dry Vermouth
1/4 oz. Southern Comfort
1/4 oz. Triple Sec
2 dashes Angostura Bitters
2 dashes fresh lemon juice
1 1/2 oz. Gin
Stir and strain
Lemon twist garnish

MARTINI, KÉKÉ V
Cocktail glass, chilled
Pour ingredients into iced mixing glass
3/4 oz. KéKé Beach Cream Liqueur
2 oz. Vodka
Shake and strain
Lime wedge garnish

MARTINI, KENTUCKY
Cocktail glass, chilled
Pour ingredients into iced mixing glass
1/2 oz. Disaronno Amaretto
1 1/2 oz. Maker's Mark Bourbon
Stir and strain
Lemon twist garnish

MARTINI, KETEL ONE
Cocktail glass, chilled
Pour ingredients into iced mixing glass
1/4 oz. Tomolive juice (optional)
2 1/2 oz. Ketel One Vodka
Stir and strain
Tomolive (3) garnish

MARTINI, KEY LIME
Cocktail glass, chilled
Rim glass with chocolate syrup and crushed
  graham crackers
Pour ingredients into iced mixing glass
3/4 oz. KéKé Beach Cream Liqueur
3/4 oz. Stolichnaya Vanil Vodka
3/4 oz. Whaler's Originale Vanille Rum
1/2 oz. fresh lime juice
1 oz. sweet 'n' sour
Shake and strain

MARTINI, KEY LIME PIE
Cocktail glass, chilled
Rim glass with lime juice and crushed
  graham crackers
Pour ingredients into iced mixing glass
3/4 oz. Midori
1/4 oz. Rose's Lime Juice
1/4 oz. half & half cream
1 1/4 oz. Stolichnaya Citros Vodka
1 1/4 oz. Stolichnaya Vanil Vodka
Shake and strain

MARTINI, KOHV
Cocktail glass, chilled
Pour ingredients into iced mixing glass
1/2 oz. Frangelico
1 oz. cold black coffee
1 oz. skim milk
1 1/2 oz. Türi Vodka
Shake and strain
Three sliced almonds

MARTINI, LEFT BANK
Cocktail glass, chilled
Pour ingredients into iced mixing glass
1/2 oz. Cointreau
3/4 oz. sweet 'n' sour
3/4 oz. VSOP Cognac
1 oz. Hpnotiq Liqueur
1 3/4 oz. Türi Vodka
Stir and strain
Lemon wheel garnish

MARTINI, LEMON GROVE
Cocktail glass, chilled
Pour ingredients into iced mixing glass
2 dashes Grand Marnier
2 dashes fresh lemon juice
1 1/2 oz. Grey Goose Le Citron Vodka
Stir and strain
Lemon twist garnish

MARTINI, LEMONEATER
Cocktail glass, chilled
Pour ingredients into iced mixing glass
1/2 oz. Limoncello Liqueur
1 1/2 oz. Lemon-infused Beefeater
  London Dry Gin
Stir and strain
Lemon twist garnish

AMARULA® CREAM LIQUEUR

Creativity is the benchmark of American mixology. Devising drinks with innovative and singularly different tastes is a straight shot to success. If people like the drinks you create, they only have one place to get them. One way to achieve that distinctive taste is to open a bottle of AMARULA CREAM LIQUEUR and let your imagination run wild.

If you're looking for something exotic, this is it. Amarula is something of an international phenomenon that currently ranks as the second best-selling cream liqueur in the world. It is made in South Africa from the fruit of the marula tree, which is better known as the Elephant Tree. The fruit is harvested and fermented in a process similar to wine making. It is then distilled in copper pot stills and aged for a minimum of two years in small French oak barrels. The liqueur masters then blend the aged liqueur with fresh dairy cream and bottle it at 34 proof.

Your first sip is likely all it will take for you to become an instant fan of Amarula Cream Liqueur. It has a medium-weight body and a subtle, cocoa-enriched bouquet. The liqueur washes the palate with the rich flavors of chocolate, mocha, vanilla, caramel and butterscotch. The finish is clean and quite memorable.

To call Amarula delicious is an understatement. It's a beverage program in a bottle, a guaranteed crowd pleaser.

MARTINI, LITTLE DEBBY
Cocktail glass, chilled
Pour ingredients into iced mixing glass
Rim glass with chocolate syrup and
    powdered cocoa
2 oz. Absolut Vanilia Vodka
3/4 oz. Dark Crème de Cacao
3/4 oz. Baileys Irish Cream
1/2 oz. chocolate syrup
Shake and strain
Strawberry slice s garnish

MARTINI, LOBSTER
Cocktail glass, chilled
Pour ingredients into iced mixing glass
1/4 oz. Dry Vermouth
2 oz. Gin
Stir and strain
Lobster claw meat garnish

MARTINI, LONDON DRY
Cocktail glass, chilled
Pour ingredients into iced mixing glass
1 oz. Dry Vermouth
2 oz. Miller's London Dry Gin
Stir and strain
Lemon twist and olive garnish

MARTINI, LOS ALTOS
Cocktail glass, chilled
Pour ingredients into iced mixing glass
2 dashes Chardonnay
2 oz. El Tesoro Platinum Tequila
Stir and strain
Lemon twist garnish

MARTINI, LYCHEE
Cocktail glass, chilled
Pour ingredients into iced mixing glass
2 oz. Absolut Citron Vodka
1 oz. lychee juice
Stir and strain
Lychee fruit garnish

MARTINI, MANDARINE
Cocktail glass, chilled
Pour ingredients into iced mixing glass
1 3/4 oz. Ketel One Vodka
1 3/4 oz. Mandarine Napoléon Liqueur
Stir and strain
Orange slice garnish

MARTINI, MARGUERITE
Cocktail glass, chilled
Pour ingredients into iced mixing glass
1/4 oz. Dry Vermouth
3 dashes orange bitters
1 3/4 oz. Gin
Stir and strain
Orange twist garnish

MARTINI, MARITIME
Cocktail glass, chilled
Pour ingredients into iced mixing glass
1/2 oz. Cherry-infused Light Rum
1 1/2 oz. Pineapple-infused Vodka
Stir and strain
Orange slice and cherry garnish

MARTINI, MARSEILLES
Cocktail glass, chilled
Pour ingredients into iced mixing glass
1/2 oz. Dry Vermouth
3 dashes Dubonnet Blonde
1 1/2 oz. Gin
Stir and strain
Lemon twist garnish

MARTINI, MARTINIQUE
Cocktail glass, chilled
Pour ingredients into iced mixing glass
Powdered sugar rim
1/2 oz. fresh lime juice
3/4 oz. sugar cane syrup
1 1/2 oz. St. James Extra Old Rhum
Stir and strain
Lime wedge garnish

MARTINI, MAYFLOWER
Cocktail glass, chilled
Pour ingredients into iced mixing glass
2 1/4 oz. Plymouth Gin
1/2 oz. Harvey's Bristol Cream Sherry
1/2 oz. Courvoisier VSOP Cognac
Stir and strain
Orange twist garnish

MARTINI, MEDICI
Cocktail glass, chilled
Pour ingredients into iced mixing glass
1/2 oz. Grappa
2 dashes Chambord
2 oz. Vodka
Stir and strain
Lemon twist garnish

MARTINI, METROPOLIS
Cocktail glass, chilled
Pour ingredients into iced mixing glass
1/2 oz. Chambord
1 1/2 oz. Vox Vodka
Stir and strain
Splash Champagne
Lemon twist garnish

MARTINI, MIDNIGHT (1)
Cocktail glass, chilled
Pour ingredients into iced mixing glass
1/2 oz. cranberry juice
1/2 oz. Chambord
1 1/2 oz. Liquid Ice Vodka
Stir and strain
Lemon twist garnish

MARTINI, MIDNIGHT (2)
Cocktail glass, chilled
Pour ingredients into iced mixing glass
3/4 oz. Black Sambuca
2 oz. Vodka
Stir and strain
Coffee beans (3) garnish

MARTINI, MIGHTY
Cocktail glass, chilled
Pour ingredients into iced mixing glass
1/4 oz. Dry Vermouth
2 1/2 oz. Zubrówka Bison Brand Vodka
Stir and strain
Green olives (3) garnish

MARTINI, MIKHAIL'S
Cocktail glass, chilled
Pour ingredients into iced mixing glass
1/2 oz. Stolichnaya Vanil Vodka
1 1/2 oz. Stolichnaya Ohranj Vodka
Stir and strain
Orange twist garnish

MARTINI, MONASTERY
Cocktail glass, chilled
Pour ingredients into iced mixing glass
1/2 oz. B & B Liqueur
2 oz. Türi Vodka
Stir and strain
Lemon twist garnish

MARTINI, MORO
Cocktail glass, chilled
Pour ingredients into iced mixing glass
1/2 oz. Dry Vermouth
2 1/4 oz. Ultimat Vodka
3/4 oz. blood orange juice
Stir and strain
Blood orange slice garnish

MARTINI, MOSCOW CHILL
Cocktail glass, chilled
Pour ingredients into iced mixing glass
3/4 oz. Godiva Chocolate Liqueur
3/4 oz. Grand Marnier
2 oz. Stolichnaya Vodka
Stir and strain
Orange slice garnish

MARTINI, MOUNDS-TINI
Cocktail glass, chilled
Pour ingredients into iced mixing glass
Rim glass with cocoa and shaved coconut
1 3/4 oz. Malibu Rum
3/4 oz. Dark Crème de Cacao
3/4 oz. Baileys Irish Cream
Shake and strain

GOSLING'S®
BLACK SEAL RUM

GOSLING'S BLACK SEAL RUM is the national spirit of Bermuda. In the spring of 1806, English wine and spirits merchant James Gosling arrived in St George's, Bermuda, where he and his family decided to set up shop. To this day, Gosling Brothers remains the oldest surviving business in Bermuda. The company's claim to international fame is being the creator of Gosling's Black Seal Rum.

The Gosling brothers introduced the brand in 1860 after having experimented with different blends of barrel-aged Caribbean rum until they created a masterpiece, which they initially named the "Old Rum." During World War I, the company began filling champagne bottles reclaimed from the British Officer's mess. The corks were secured in place with the use of black sealing wax. It soon became known as the "Black Seal" brand.

Gosling's Black Seal Rum has a dark amber/brown color and a compact bouquet of coffee, sugar cane, caramel and toasted oak. Its palate is a medley of roasted and spicy flavors that completely fill the mouth before slipping away in a warm, lingering finish.

It is understandable why Gosling's Black Seal Rum is the best-selling spirit in Bermuda. While a pleasure to drink neat, it is a delight to mix in cocktails, and is the core of such classics as the Dark 'n Stormy and Rum Swizzle.

MARTINI, MUSCOVY
Cocktail glass, chilled
Pour ingredients into iced mixing glass
1 oz. Stolichnaya Vodka
1 oz. Stolichnaya Ohranj Vodka
1/2 oz. Triple Sec
1/2 oz. orange juice
1 pinch cinnamon
Stir and strain
Orange twist garnish

MARTINI, MY PRECIOUS
Cocktail glass, chilled
Pour ingredients into iced mixing glass
2 oz. Bacardi O Rum
1 1/2 oz. Red Bull Energy Drink
1 1/2 oz. orange juice
Shake and strain

MARTINI, MYSTIC
Cocktail glass, chilled
Pour ingredients into iced mixing glass
2 oz. Bacardi Razz Rum
1/2 oz. Chambord
1 oz. cranberry juice
1/2 oz. sweet 'n' sour
Shake and strain

MARTINI, MYSTICAL
Cocktail glass, chilled
Pour ingredients into iced mixing glass
1/4 oz. Blonde Lillet
1 1/2 oz. Encantado Mezcal
Stir and strain
Lemon twist garnish

MARTINI, NAPOLEON
Cocktail glass, chilled
Pour ingredients into iced mixing glass
1/2 oz. Dubonnet Rouge
1/2 oz. Grand Marnier
1 1/2 oz. Gin
Stir and strain
Lemon twist garnish

MARTINI, NEW BOND
Cocktail glass, chilled or rocks glass, ice
Pour ingredients into iced mixing glass
1/2 oz. Lillet Blonde
2 oz. Citadelle Vodka
Shake and strain
Lemon twist garnish

MARTINI, NEWBURY
Cocktail glass, chilled
Pour ingredients into iced mixing glass
1/2 oz. Sweet Vermouth
2 dashes Triple Sec
1 1/2 oz. Gin
Stir and strain
Lemon and orange twist garnish

MARTINI, NITELIFE
Cocktail glass, chilled
Pour ingredients into iced mixing glass
3/4 oz. Chambord
1 1/4 oz. Orange Vodka
1 oz. cranberry juice
3/4 oz. Seven-Up
Stir and strain
Lime wedge garnish

MARTINI, NUTCRACKER
Cocktail glass, chilled
Pour ingredients into iced mixing glass
2 dashes Frangelico
1 1/2 oz. Citadelle Vodka
Stir and strain
Lemon twist garnish

MARTINI, ORANGE GROVE
Cocktail glass, chilled
Pour ingredients into iced mixing glass
1/2 oz. Cointreau
2 dashes orange juice
2 dashes Angostura Bitters
1 1/2 oz. Orange Vodka
Stir and strain
Orange twist garnish

MARTINI, ORCHID
Cocktail glass, chilled
Pour ingredients into iced mixing glass
1 1/2 oz. Tanqueray Nº Ten Gin
1/2 oz. Chambord
1 1/2 oz. sweet 'n' sour
Shake and strain
Splash ginger ale

MARTINI, OSTERIA
Cocktail glass, chilled
Pour ingredients into iced mixing glass
2 1/2 oz. Absolut Mandarin Vodka
1/2 oz. Peach Schnapps
1/2 oz. Chambord
1/2 oz. sweet 'n' sour
1 oz. cranberry juice
Shake and strain
Orange twist garnish

MARTINI, PACIFIC PEARL
Cocktail glass, chilled
Pour ingredients into iced mixing glass
1 oz. Pearl Lo Coco Vodka
1 oz. Midori
1 oz. pineapple juice
Stir and strain

MARTINI, PAISLEY
Cocktail glass, chilled
Pour ingredients into iced mixing glass
1/2 oz. Scotch Whisky
1/2 oz. Dry Vermouth
2 oz. Gin
Stir and strain
Lemon twist garnish

MARTINI, PALM ISLAND
Cocktail glass, chilled
Pour ingredients into iced mixing glass
1/4 oz. White Crème de Cacao
1/2 oz. Dry Vermouth
1 1/2 oz. Gin
Stir and strain
Lemon twist garnish

MARTINI, PASSION
Cocktail glass, chilled
Pour ingredients into iced mixing glass
1 oz. sweet 'n' sour
3/4 oz. Chambord
2 oz. Absolut Mandarin Vodka
Stir and strain
Raspberry garnish

MARTINI, P. B. & J.
Cocktail glass, chilled
Pour ingredients into iced mixing glass
1 1/2 oz. Frangelico
1/2 oz. Baileys Irish Cream
1/2 oz. Stolichnaya Razberi Vodka
1/2 oz. Chambord
Stir and strain

MARTINI, PEAR
Cocktail glass, chilled
Pour ingredients into iced mixing glass
3/4 oz. Poire William (Eau de Vie de Poire)
2 oz. Vodka
Stir and strain
Pear slice garnish

MARTINI, PEARL BAILEY
Cocktail glass, chilled
Pour ingredients into iced mixing glass
Rim glass with cocoa and shaved chocolate
1 oz. Pearl Lo Coco Vodka
1 oz. Baileys Irish Cream
1 oz. Dark Crème de Cacao
Stir and strain

MARTINI, PEARL JAM
Cocktail glass, chilled
Pour ingredients into iced mixing glass
1 tsp. strawberry jelly
2 1/2 oz. Pearl Vodka
Shake and strain
Strawberry garnish

CITADELLE® GIN

CITADELLE GIN is an intriguingly complex and thoroughly engaging gin. A quick appraisal of its considerable attributes supports the contention that this savory ultra-premium gin is going to enjoy a long and prosperous stay on American top-shelves.

Handcrafted by Cognac Ferrand, one of France's renowned producers of cognacs, liqueurs and fine spirits, Citadelle is quadruple-distilled in small batches in traditional copper alembic stills. It is formulated based on a centuries old recipe that combines nineteen, high-grade botanicals and aromatics from four continents with spring water from the famous Angeac Champagne Springs in Cognac. Balancing these exotic ingredients—including French juniper, Moroccan coriander, Spanish lemon peels, Indian cardamom and cassia bark from Indochina—is a daunting challenge, one masterfully accomplished in this gin. It is bottled at 88 proof.

Citadelle is a highly aromatic spirit with a genuinely distinctive taste. Its light, fresh bouquet is laced with juniper, spice and citrus. The gin has a full, sultry body—unusual for such a delicate spirit—and a crisp, clean palate lavishly endowed with spicy, herbal flavors. Not surprising in a gin of this world-class stature, the vibrant flavor of alpine juniper berries is most predominant. The finish is relaxed and memorable.

MARTINI, PERFECT
aka **Perfect Cocktail**
Cocktail glass, chilled
Pour ingredients into iced mixing glass
1/4 oz. Sweet Vermouth
1/4 oz. Dry Vermouth
1 dash Angostura Bitters (optional)
1 3/4 oz. Gin
Stir and strain
Lemon twist garnish

MARTINI, PIÑA
Cocktail glass, chilled
Pour ingredients into iced mixing glass
3/4 oz. pineapple juice
1 oz. Pineapple Rum
1 1/2 oz. Vodka
Stir and strain
Small pineapple wedge

MARTINI, PINK RIBBON
Cocktail glass, chilled
Pour ingredients into iced mixing glass
1 1/2 oz. Stolichnaya Cranberi Vodka
1 1/2 oz. Stolichnaya Ohranj Vodka
1/4 oz. Triple Sec
1/2 oz. sweet 'n' sour
1 1/2 oz. cranberry juice
Stir and strain

MARTINI, POINSETTIA
Cocktail glass, chilled
Pour ingredients into iced mixing glass
1/4 oz. Chambord
1/4 oz. pineapple juice
2 oz. Liquid Ice Vodka
Stir and strain
Lemon twist garnish

MARTINI, PRINCETON
Cocktail glass, chilled
Pour ingredients into iced mixing glass
1/2 oz. Dry Vermouth
1/2 oz. fresh lime juice
2 oz. Gin
Stir and strain
Lemon twist garnish

MARTINI, PURPLE HAZE
Cocktail glass, chilled
Pour ingredients into iced mixing glass
1 1/2 oz. Absolut Kurant Vodka
3 oz. RémyRed Grape Berry Infusion
Stir and strain
Lemon twist garnish

MARTINI, PYRAT
Cocktail glass, chilled
Pour ingredients into iced mixing glass
1/2 oz. Godiva Chocolate Liqueur
1 3/4 oz. Pyrat XO Reserve Rum
Stir and strain
Lemon twist garnish

MARTINI, RASPBERRY (1)
Cocktail glass, chilled
Pour ingredients into iced mixing glass
1/2 oz. Chambord
1 1/2 oz. Gin
Stir and strain
Raspberry garnish

MARTINI, RASPBERRY (2)
Cocktail glass, chilled
Pour ingredients into iced mixing glass
2 oz. Vox Raspberry Vodka
3/4 oz. Chambord
1 oz. raspberry puree
Shake and strain
Fresh raspberries (3) garnish

MARTINI, RAVING RHINO
Cocktail glass, chilled
Pour ingredients into iced mixing glass
1/4 oz. jalapeño juice
3-4 dashes Tabasco Sauce
2 1/2 oz. Absolut Peppar Vodka
Stir and strain
Speared jalapeño garnish

MARTINI, RED APPLE
Cocktail glass, chilled
Pour ingredients into iced mixing glass
3/4 oz. DeKuyper Pucker Sour Apple
1 3/4 oz. DeKuyper Raspberry Pucker
1/2 oz. sweet 'n' sour
Shake and strain
Green apple wedge garnish

MARTINI, RED DEVIL
Cocktail glass, chilled
Pour ingredients into iced mixing glass
1 1/2 oz. Absolut Vanilia Vodka
3 oz. RémyRed Grape Berry Infusion
1/2 oz. fresh lime juice
1/2 oz. white cranberry juice
Stir and strain
Lemon twist garnish

MARTINI, RED RAIN
Cocktail glass, chilled
Pour ingredients into iced mixing glass
3/4 oz. RémyRed Red Berry Infusion
2 oz. Vodka
Stir and strain
Orange slice and cherry garnish

MARTINI, RIVERS
Cocktail glass, chilled
Pour ingredients into iced mixing glass
1/4 oz. Cointreau
2 oz. London Dry Gin
Stir and strain
Anchovy-stuffed olives garnish

MARTINI, RIVIERA
Cocktail glass, chilled
Pour ingredients into iced mixing glass
1/2 oz. Sweet Vermouth
2-3 dashes orange flower water
2-3 dashes Angostura Bitters
2 1/4 oz. Gin
Stir and strain
Lemon twist garnish

MARTINI, ROLLS ROYCE
Cocktail glass, chilled
Pour ingredients into iced mixing glass
1/2 oz. Dry Vermouth
1/2 oz. Sweet Vermouth
1/2 oz. B & B Liqueur
1 3/4 oz. London Dry Gin
Stir and strain
Lemon twist garnish

MARTINI, ROMANA
Cocktail glass, chilled
Pour ingredients into iced mixing glass
1/4 oz. Dry Vermouth
3 dashes Campari Aperitivo
1 1/2 oz. Gin
Stir and strain
Lemon twist garnish

MARTINI, ROSALIND RUSSELL
Cocktail glass, chilled
Pour ingredients into iced mixing glass
1/4 oz. Aquavit
2 oz. Vodka
Stir and strain
Lemon twist garnish

MARTINI, ROSEBUD
Cocktail glass, chilled
Pour ingredients into iced mixing glass
1/4 oz. Campari Aperitivo
2 oz. Vox Vodka
Stir and strain
Lemon twist garnish

MARTINI, RUSSIAN TEA ROOM
Cocktail glass, chilled
Pour ingredients into iced mixing glass
1/4 oz. Dry Vermouth
1/4 oz. Sweet Vermouth
2 oz. Magadanskaya Vodka
Stir and strain
Black olive garnish

NYAK® VERY SPECIAL COGNAC

Today, cognac is as equally popular with Baby Boomers and the after dinner set as it is with the hip-hop generation. Kudos to the good people at A. de Fussigny, one of the renowned makers of cognac. As remarkable as their cognacs are, what is equally impressive is their apparent willingness to step out from under the cloak of nobility and embrace cognac's raging popularity. Their first foray into the mainstream is NYAK VERY SPECIAL COGNAC.

Celler master Alain Royer, owner of the A. de Fussigny brand, and his family have been making fine cognac since the early 1700s. As a smaller producer, Royer has access to many of the older, privately owned lots of fine aged cognac. These brandies are blended in small batches to create what has become an unparalleled line of cognacs.

Nyak Very Special Cognac is comprised of a blend of 6 to 8 year old cognacs, with a high proportion being from the Grande Champagne region. By comparison, similarly priced cognacs are made from a blend of 3 to 4 year old brandies. It has a rich amber color, delicate vanilla and oak notes, and a light floral bouquet. It compares in quality to many VSOP cognacs on the market.

Appropriately named, Nyak Very Special Cognac is a brandy that will simultaneously appeal to many different generations and cultures and whose value is as exquisite as its taste.

MARTINI, SAHARAN
Cocktail glass, chilled
Pour ingredients into iced mixing glass
1 1/2 oz. Amarula Cream Liqueur
1 oz. Frangelico
1 oz. Finlandia Vodka
Shake and strain
Orange slice and cherry garnish

MARTINI, SAKÉ
Cocktail glass, chilled
Pour ingredients into iced mixing glass
1/2 oz. Saké
1 1/2 oz. Gin
Stir and strain
Olive garnish

MARTINI, SAKÉTINI
Cocktail glass, chilled
Pour ingredients into iced mixing glass
1/2 oz. Blue Curaçao
1 3/4 oz. London Dry Gin
1 3/4 oz. Saké
Stir and strain

MARTINI, SAMTINI
Cocktail glass, chilled
Pour ingredients into iced mixing glass
1/2 oz. Sambuca
2 oz. Grey Goose Vodka
Stir and strain
Float 3/4 oz. Kahlúa
Coffee beans (3) garnish

MARTINI, SAN FRANCISCO
Cocktail glass, chilled
Pour ingredients into iced mixing glass
1/4 oz. Tawny Port
1 3/4 oz. Gin
2 dashes Angostura Bitters
Stir and strain
Lemon twist garnish

MARTINI, SAPPHIRE SIN
Cocktail glass, chilled
Pour ingredients into iced mixing glass
1/4 oz. Dry Vermouth
3/4 oz. Citrus Vodka
2 oz. Bombay Sapphire London Dry Gin
Stir and strain
Lemon twist garnish

MARTINI, SHADE TREE
Cocktail glass, chilled
Pour ingredients into iced mixing glass
1/2 oz. lemonade
3/4 oz. Limoncello Liqueur
2 oz. Stön Vodka
Stir and strain
Lemon wedge garnish

MARTINI, SHAGGED
Cocktail glass, chilled
Pour ingredients into iced mixing glass
1/4 oz. Sweet Vermouth
1/4 oz. Grand Marnier
1 3/4 oz. Beefeater London Dry Gin
Stir and strain
Orange twist garnish

MARTINI, SICILIAN (1)
Cocktail glass, chilled
Pour ingredients into iced mixing glass
1/4 oz. Dry Vermouth
2 oz. Garlic-infused Vodka
Stir and strain
Garlic-stuffed olive garnish
Note: See Sicilian Martini Infusion

MARTINI, SICILIAN (2)
Cocktail glass, chilled
Pour ingredients into iced mixing glass
1/2 oz. Opal Nera Black Sambuca
1 1/2 oz. Vodka
Stir and strain
Lemon twist garnish

MARTINI, SMOKED (1)
Cocktail glass, chilled
Pour ingredients into iced mixing glass
1/4 oz. Laphroaig Scotch Whisky
1 1/2 oz. Tanqueray Gin
Stir and strain
Lemon twist garnish

MARTINI, SMOKED (2)
Cocktail glass, chilled
Pour ingredients into iced mixing glass
3/4 oz. Rhum Barbancourt 5-Star
1 1/2 oz. Gin
Stir and strain
Lemon twist garnish

MARTINI, SMOKY APPLETINI
Cocktail glass, chilled
Pour ingredients into iced mixing glass
2-3 dashes Angostura bitters
1 1/2 oz. Chivas Regal Scotch
1 1/2 oz. DeKuyper Pucker Sour Apple
1/4 oz. apple juice
Stir and strain

MARTINI, SNICKERTINI
Cocktail glass, chilled
Rim glass with powdered cocoa (optional)
Pour ingredients into iced mixing glass
3/4 oz. Frangelico
3/4 oz. Godiva Chocolate Liqueur
1 1/2 oz. Ketel One Vodka
Shake and strain
Orange slice garnish

MARTINI, SPANISH
Cocktail glass, chilled
Pour ingredients into iced mixing glass
1/2 oz. Dry Sack Sherry
1 1/2 oz. Gin
Stir and strain
Lemon twist garnish

MARTINI, STAR'S
Cocktail glass, chilled
Pour ingredients into iced mixing glass
1/2 oz. El Tesoro Platinum Tequila
1 3/4 oz. Magellan Gin
Stir and strain
Lemon wedge garnish

MARTINI, STAR'S JEWEL
Cocktail glass, chilled
Pour ingredients into iced mixing glass
1/4 oz. Absolut Peppar Vodka
1 1/2 oz. Gin
Stir and strain
Lemon twist garnish

MARTINI, STARLIGHT
Cocktail glass, chilled
Pour ingredients into iced mixing glass
3/4 oz. Opal Nera Black Sambuca
2 oz. Vodka
Stir and strain
Lemon twist garnish

MARTINI, STRAWBERRY (1)
Cocktail glass, chilled
Pour ingredients into iced mixing glass
3/4 oz. White Crème de Cacao
2 oz. Stolichnaya Strasberi Vodka
Stir and strain
Strawberry garnish

MARTINI, STRAWBERRY (2)
Cocktail glass, chilled
Pour ingredients into iced mixing glass
1/2 oz. Chambraise or Fraise
1 1/2 oz. Gin
Stir and strain
Strawberry garnish

MARTINI, SUSHI
Cocktail glass, chilled
Pour ingredients into iced mixing glass
1 oz. Saké
1/2 oz. Chambord
2 oz. Vodka
Stir and strain
Lemon twist garnish

STOLICHNAYA® VODKA

STOLICHNAYA VODKA is among the most widely recognized spirit brands in the world. It is also the first Russian vodka that most Americans had ever tasted when it debuted here in the mid-1970s. For that, the country is eternally grateful. In its own way, Stolichnaya Vodka may have hastened the end of the Cold War.

Made with skillful precision, this famed, Russian-built vodka is double-distilled from winter wheat and soft purified water. After distillation, the vodka is filtered four times through crushed quartz, charcoal and tightly woven cloth before being rested in stainless-steel holding tanks. It is bottled at both 80 and 100 proof.

Once in the glass, the reasons for Stolichnaya's world-class reputation are self-evident. The vodka is crystal clear with a light, herbal and pine bouquet. The fun really begins when the medium-weight body glides over the palate, immediately filling the mouth with warmth and sweet, slightly peppery flavors. The vodka has a long, lemon-citrus finish.

Beginning in 1997, Stolichnaya introduced the Martini-starved world to a line of flavored vodkas, including VANIL (vanilla), RAZBERI (raspberry), STRASBERI (strawberry), CITROS (lemon), OHRANJ (orange), CRANBERI (cranberry) and PERSIK (peach). Seemingly overnight mixologists were able to change the flavor of their favorite drinks with a mere flick of the wrist. As a family they're a creative bonanza.

MARTINI, TAJ MAJAL
Cocktail glass, chilled
Pour ingredients into iced mixing glass
1/4 oz. Dry Vermouth
1/4 oz. Gin
2 oz. Vodka
Stir and strain
Lemon twist garnish

MARTINI, TARTINI
Cocktail glass, chilled
Pour ingredients into iced mixing glass
1/2 oz. Chambord
1/2 oz. cranberry juice
1/2 oz. sweet 'n' sour
1 1/2 oz. Liquid Ice Vodka
Stir and strain
Lime wedge garnish

MARTINI, THE LIBERTINI
Cocktail glass, chilled
Pour ingredients into iced mixing glass
1 oz. Absolut Citron Vodka
1 oz. DeKuyper Peachtree Schnapps
1/2 oz. Midori
1/2 oz. Blue Curaçao
Stir and strain

MARTINI, THREE MILE ISLAND
Cocktail glass, chilled
Pour ingredients into iced mixing glass
2 oz. RedRum
1 oz. Blue Curaçao
2 1/2 oz. pineapple juice
Shake and strain

MARTINI THYME
Cocktail glass, chilled
Pour ingredients into iced mixing glass
1/2 oz. Green Chartreuse
2 oz. Gin
Stir and strain
Thyme sprig garnish

MARTINI, TIRAMISU (1)
Cocktail glass, chilled
Rim glass with powdered hot chocolate mix (optional)
Pour ingredients into iced mixing glass
1 1/2 oz. Absolut Vanilia Vodka
1/2 oz. Kahlúa
1/2 oz. Godiva White Chocolate Liqueur
1/4 oz. Disaronno Amaretto
Stir and strain
Sprinkle shaved chocolate

MARTINI, TIRAMISU (2)
Cocktail glass, chilled
Pour ingredients into iced mixing glass
Rim glass with chocolate syrup and
   powdered cocoa
2 oz. Vodka
3/4 oz. Kahlúa
3/4 oz. Disaronno Amaretto
3/4 oz. Baileys Irish Cream
Shake and strain
Strawberry slice s garnish

MARTINI, TITIAN
Cocktail glass, chilled
Pour ingredients into iced mixing glass
1 oz. Orange Vodka
1 oz. Grand Marnier
1 oz. passion fruit juice
1 oz. fresh lime juice
1 oz. pomegranate syrup
Shake and strain
Raspberry garnish

MARTINI, TOASTED NUTS
Cocktail glass, chilled
Rim glass with powdered cocoa (optional)
Pour ingredients into iced mixing glass
3/4 oz. Godiva Chocolate Liqueur
3/4 oz. Disaronno Amaretto
2 1/2 oz. Vox Vodka
Stir and strain

MARTINI, TOPAZ
Cocktail glass, chilled
Pour ingredients into iced mixing glass
1/4 oz. Dark Crème de Cacao
1/4 oz. Frangelico
2 oz. Stön Vodka
Stir and strain
Coffee beans (3) garnish

MARTINI, TROPICAL
Cocktail glass, chilled
Pour ingredients into iced mixing glass
1/2 oz. Godiva Chocolate Liqueur
1 oz. Malibu Caribbean Rum
2 1/2 RémyRed Red Berry Infusion
Stir and strain
Lemon twist garnish

MARTINI, TY-WON-ON
Cocktail glass, chilled
Pour ingredients into iced mixing glass
1/2 oz. Chambord
3/4 oz. Saké
1 3/4 oz. Vodka
Stir and strain
Lemon twist garnish

MARTINI, VANILLA NUT
Cocktail glass, chilled
Pour ingredients into iced mixing glass
Rim glass with cocoa and shaved chocolate
1 3/4 oz. Absolut Vanilia Vodka
3/4 oz. Frangelico
Stir and strain

MARTINI, VIRGIN ISLAND
Cocktail glass, chilled
Pour ingredients into iced mixing glass
2 1/4 oz. Dry Gin
3/4 oz. Cruzan Orange Rum
Stir and strain
Orange slice garnish

MARTINI, VODKA
aka **Kangaroo**
Cocktail glass, chilled
Pour ingredients into iced mixing glass
8 drops Dry Vermouth
1 1/2 oz. Vodka
Stir and strain
Olives or lemon twist garnish

MARTINI, WATERMELON
Cocktail glass, chilled
Pour ingredients into iced mixing glass
1/2 oz. DeKuyper Watermelon Pucker
1/2 oz. watermelon juice
1 1/2 oz. Vox Raspberry Vodka
Stir and strain
Small watermelon wedge garnish

MARTINI, WET BLUE
Cocktail glass, chilled
Pour ingredients into iced mixing glass
1/2 oz. Blue Curaçao
1 1/2 oz. sweet 'n' sour
2 oz. Wet by Beefeater
Stir and strain
Lemon twist garnish

MARTINI, WILLY NILLY
Cocktail glass, chilled
Pour ingredients into iced mixing glass
1/2 oz. blood orange juice
3/4 oz. RémyRed Red Berry Infusion
1 1/2 oz. Vodka
Stir and strain
Blood orange slice garnish

MARTINI, YELLOW RATTLER
Cocktail glass, chilled
Pour ingredients into iced mixing glass
1/2 oz. Dry Vermouth
2-3 dashes orange bitters
2 oz. Gin
Stir and strain
Lemon twist garnish

CRUZAN® RUM CREAM

It's hard to imagine a product that has more marketable attributes and contemporary appeal than CRUZAN RUM CREAM. In fact, its name handily explains why the liqueur has found a niche. It enjoys great name recognition and rums are blistering hot. Because cream liqueurs are most comparable to desserts in a bottle, they are a small indulgence that we afford ourselves. This is one liqueur earmarked for greatness.

Cruzan Rum Cream is produced in Ireland with dairy-fresh Irish cream, caramel and vanilla. The Cruzan light rum used in the liqueur is a blend of triple-distilled rums, aged 2 to 3 years in oak bourbon barrels and filtered through activated charcoal.

The Cruzan Rum Cream has a light coffee color and a compact, creamy bouquet of vanilla, cream and toffee. It has a medium body that immediately coats the palate with the prominent flavors of caramel, vanilla and dairy fresh cream. The rum shines through in the lingering finish. The liqueur is marketed at 34 proof.

To get the most out of the experience, sample Cruzan Rum Cream neat with a slight chill, or with the addition of ice. The liqueur is easy to drink and devoid of the cloying finish that plague some other cream liqueurs. It is also delectable when added to coffee, mixed with Tia Maria, amaretto, or a score of other complementary flavors.

MARTINI, ZANZABAR
Cocktail glass, chilled
Pour ingredients into iced mixing glass
1 1/2 oz. Amarula Cream Liqueur
1 oz. Kahlúa
3/4 oz. Brandy
1/2 oz. half & half cream
Shake and strain
Orange slice and cherry garnish

MARTINI, ZORBATINI
Cocktail glass, chilled
Pour ingredients into iced mixing glass
1/2 oz. Metaxa Ouzo
2 oz. Vodka
Stir and strain
Green olives garnish

MARTIN'S BULL
Bucket glass, ice
Build in glass
1 3/4 oz. Miller's London Dry Gin
Near fill with Red Bull
Splash white cranberry juice

MARZ BAR
Rocks glass, chilled
Pour ingredients into iced mixing glass
3/4 oz. Pearl Vodka
3/4 oz. Godiva Chocolate Liqueur
3/4 oz. Disaronno Amaretto
3/4 oz. half & half cream (optional)
Shake and strain

MASSAPPEAL
Cocktail glass, chilled
Pour ingredients into iced mixing glass
2 oz. Limoncello Liqueur
1/2 oz. Peach Schnapps
1 oz. orange juice
3/4 oz. half & half cream
Shake and strain
Sprinkle nutmeg

MAUI BREEZER
House specialty glass, chilled
Pour ingredients into blender
1 1/2 oz. Disaronno Amaretto
1/2 oz. Triple Sec
1/2 oz. Brandy
1 oz. sweet 'n' sour
2 oz. orange juice
2 oz. guava juice
Blend with ice
Fresh fruit garnish

MAUI WOWIE
Cocktail glass, chilled
Pour ingredients into iced mixing glass
3/4 oz. Light Rum
3/4 oz. Coconut Rum
3/4 oz. Midori
1 oz. pineapple juice
1 oz. orange juice
Shake and strain
Float 3/4 oz. Dark Rum
Orange slice garnish

MAXIM'S A LONDRES
Champagne glass, chilled
Pour ingredients into iced mixing glass
1 1/2 oz. Brandy
1/2 oz. Cointreau
1/2 oz. orange juice
Shake and strain
Fill with Champagne
Orange twist garnish

MCGOODY'S CREAM SODA
Bucket glass, ice
Build in glass
1 3/4 oz. Vanilla Rum
Fill with cola

MEADOWLARK LEMON
Cocktail glass, chilled
Pour ingredients into iced mixing glass
1 1/2 oz. Stolichnaya Citros Vodka
3/4 oz. Cointreau
1/2 oz. fresh lemon juice
Stir and strain
Lemon wedge garnish

MEADOW SNOW
House specialty glass, chilled
Pour ingredients into blender
2 oz. Gin
3/4 oz. Midori
1 1/2 oz. sweet 'n' sour
Blend with ice
Cantaloupe cube garnish

MEDITERRANEAN FREEZE
House specialty glass, chilled
Pour ingredients into blender
1 oz. Vodka
3/4 oz. Midori
1/2 oz. Peach Schnapps
2 oz. sweet 'n' sour
3 oz. orange juice
Blend with ice
Orange slice and cherry garnish

MEISTER-BATION
House specialty glass, chilled
Pour ingredients into blender
1 1/4 oz. Jägermeister
3/4 oz. Crème de Banana
2 oz. half & half cream
2 oz. coconut cream syrup
Blend with ice
Pineapple wedge garnish

MELLONAIRE
Cocktail glass, chilled
Pour ingredients into iced mixing glass
1 3/4 oz. Cruzan Banana Rum
1 oz. Midori
1/2 oz. Triple Sec
2 oz. sweet 'n' sour
Shake and strain

MELLOW DRAMATIC
Presentation shot glass, chilled
Build in glass
1/3 fill Chambord
1/3 fill White Crème de Cacao
1/3 fill Baileys Irish Cream

MELON BALL (1)
Highball glass, ice
Build in glass
1 1/4 oz. Midori
1/2 oz. Vodka
Fill with orange juice

MELON BALL (2)
Rocks glass, chilled
Pour ingredients into iced mixing glass
1 1/2 oz. Midori
1/2 oz. Vodka
1/2 oz. orange juice
1/2 oz. pineapple juice
Shake and strain

MELON BALL COOLER
House specialty glass, ice
Pour ingredients into iced mixing glass
1 1/2 oz. Midori
3/4 oz. Vodka
1 oz. pineapple juice
1 oz. orange juice
Shake and strain
Fill with ginger ale

MELON BREEZE
Highball glass, ice
Build in glass
1 oz. Midori
1/2 oz. Vodka
1/2 fill cranberry juice
1/2 fill pineapple juice

SOL DIOS® AÑEJO TEQUILA

Introduced in 2003, SOL DIOS AÑEJO TEQUILA is a classically structured, 100% agave tequila that is unafraid to be robust and exuberant. It is deliciously different than most of the other ultra-premium añejos on the market and admirably represents the school of thought that even a well aged tequila should retain a vivacious spirit, one that's a bit feisty and enthusiastic.

Sol Dios is made at the Fabrica de Tequilas Finos situated in the highlands of Jalisco, Mexico. The agaves used in production are allowed to age for 9 years prior to harvesting. Once at the distillery, the agaves are steamed, pressed, fermented and double-distilled in traditional copper pot stills. The tequila is filtered four times in small batches to ensure purity. Sol Dios Añejo is aged for a minimum of 3 years in small American white oak barrels. It is bottled at 80 proof.

Sol Dios Añejo is a true top-shelf performer with a distinctive character and highly individualistic personality. The tequila has an enticing golden/yellow hue, and a lush, medium-weight body. Its initial attack is warm and assertive that quickly delivers a palate loaded with floral and herbaceous flavors. The flavorful finish is warming, but not the least bit harsh.

There is nothing passive or demur about Sol Dios Añejo tequila. It is an authentic spirit from start to finish.

MELON GRIND
Bucket glass, ice
Build in glass
1 1/2 oz. Vodka
3/4 oz. Midori
1/2 oz. Light Rum
Fill with pineapple juice

MELON MOOSE
Bucket glass, ice
Build in glass
3/4 oz. Light Rum
3/4 oz. Midori
Near fill with pineapple juice
Float 1 oz. Dark Rum

MELON SCOOP
House specialty glass, chilled
Pour ingredients into blender
1 3/4 oz. Mount Gay Eclipse Rum
1 1/2 oz. Midori
3/4 oz. Kahlúa
1/2 oz. grenadine
1 oz. sweet 'n' sour
2 scoops vanilla ice cream
Blend ingredients (with ice optional)
Float 3/4 oz. Appleton Estate
   V/X Jamaica Rum
Orange slice and cherry garnish

MEL'S CHOCOLATE
BUTTERSCOTCH SHAKE
House specialty glass, chilled
Pour ingredients into blender
1 1/2 oz. Kahlúa
3/4 oz. Appleton Estate V/X Jamaica Rum
2 oz. butterscotch topping
1 oz. chocolate syrup
4 oz. whole milk
2 scoops vanilla ice cream
Blend ingredients (with ice optional)
Whipped cream garnish
Sprinkle shaved chocolate

MEL'S CHOC/PB/NANA SHAKE
House specialty glass, chilled
Pour ingredients into blender
1 1/2 oz. Kahlúa
3/4 oz. Appleton Estate V/X Jamaica Rum
1 peeled, ripe banana
1 oz. chocolate syrup
2 tbsp. creamy peanut butter
4 oz. whole milk
2 scoops vanilla ice cream
Blend ingredients (with ice optional)
Whipped cream garnish
Sprinkle shaved chocolate

MÉNAGE À TROIS
Bucket glass, ice
Build in glass
1 1/2 oz. Brandy
1 1/2 oz. Kahlúa
1 oz. cream
3 oz. club soda

MERRY WIDOW (1)
Cocktail glass, chilled
Pour ingredients into iced mixing glass
1 1/2 oz. Dubonnet Rouge
1/2 oz. Dry Vermouth
1 dash Angostura Bitters
2 dashes Pernod
2 dashes B & B Liqueur
Stir and strain
Lemon twist garnish

MERRY WIDOW (2)
Bucket glass, ice
Pour ingredients into iced mixing glass
1 1/2 oz. Gin
1 oz. orange juice
1 oz. sweet 'n' sour
Shake and strain
Fill with club soda

METRO COCKTAIL
Champagne glass, chilled
Pour ingredients into iced mixing glass
1 oz. Vox Vodka
1 oz. Vox Raspberry Vodka
1/4 oz. Cointreau
1/4 oz. fresh lime juice
1/2 oz. cranberry juice
Shake and strain
Fill with Champagne
Lemon twist garnish

MEXICAN BLACKJACK
Rocks glass, chilled
Pour ingredients into iced mixing glass
1/2 oz. Jose Cuervo Especial Tequila
1/2 oz. Black Velvet Canadian
1/2 oz. Jack Daniel's Tennessee Whiskey
1/2 oz. Triple Sec
Shake and strain

MEXICAN BULLFROG
Highball glass, ice
Build in glass
1 1/4 oz. Xalixco Tequila
Fill with lemonade
Lime wheel garnish

MEXICAN COCOA
Coffee mug, heated
Build in glass
3/4 oz. Kahlúa
3/4 oz. Brandy
Near fill with hot chocolate
Whipped cream garnish
Sprinkle nutmeg

MEXICAN COFFEE
Coffee mug, heated
Build in glass
3/4 oz. Tequila
3/4 oz. Kahlúa
Near fill with hot coffee
Whipped cream garnish (optional)

MEXICAN FLAG
Cordial or sherry glass, chilled
Layer ingredients
1/3 fill grenadine
1/3 fill Green Crème de Menthe
1/3 fill 151° Rum

MEXICAN GRASSHOPPER
Cocktail glass, chilled
Pour ingredients into iced mixing glass
1/2 oz. White Crème de Cacao
1/2 oz. Green Crème de Menthe
1/2 oz. Kahlúa
2 oz. half & half cream
Shake and strain

MEXICAN ITCH
Presentation shot glass, chilled
Rim glass with salt (optional)
Build in glass
1/3 fill El Tesoro Añejo Tequila
1/3 fill Grand Marnier
1/3 fill lime juice
Lime wedge garnish

MEXICAN MELON
House specialty glass, ice
Rim glass with sugar (optional)
Pour ingredients into iced mixing glass
1 oz. Corazón Reposado Tequila
1 oz. Midori
1/2 oz. Chambord
1/2 oz. fresh lime juice
1 oz. orange juice
2 oz. sweet 'n' sour
Shake and strain
Lime wedge garnish

LAPHROAIG® SINGLE ISLAY MALT SCOTCH WHISKY

Laphroaig is the best known of the Islay single malts. It is an intriguing whisky, whose persona cannot be separated from the island on which it was created. Its international celebrity has everything to do with flavor—powerful, untamed and unabashedly exuberant. While not for the faint of heart, LAPHROAIG SINGLE ISLAY MALT SCOTCH WHISKY offers aficionados a rare and singular taste experience.

The Laphroaig Distillery was built in the 1820s by the waters edge on the southeast shore of Islay. It is one of only a handful of distilleries that malts its own barley. They use locally grown peat and the water used in production is drawn from the Kilbride River. The whisky is aged in first fill ex-bourbon barrels in warehouses built on the edge of the Atlantic, where the ocean air is allowed to swirl around the aging casks.

The most widely known expression of Laphroaig is the acclaimed 10 year old. This grand malt is brimming with a salty array of aromas with notes of seaweed and peaty smoke. For all of its vigor, the malt is quite accessible, sporting a full body and a palate imbued with smoke, peat, salt and iodine. The finish is supple and dry.

The famed Laphroaig range also includes a 10 year cask strength, 15 year, 30 year and 40 year malt. Each is an intriguing spirit graced with the flavor of the sea.

MEXICAN MONK
Coffee mug, heated
Build in glass
1 oz. Kahlúa
1 oz. Frangelico
1/2 oz. Dark Crème de Cacao
Near fill with hot coffee
Whipped cream garnish
Dust powdered cocoa

MEXICAN NAZI KILLER
Presentation shot glass, chilled
Layer ingredients
1/3 fill Jägermeister
1/3 fill Rumple Minze Schnapps
1/3 fill Tequila

MEXICAN RUNNER
House specialty glass, chilled
Pour ingredients into blender
3/4 oz. Patrón Reposado Tequila
3/4 oz. Cruzan Estate Diamond Rum
1/2 oz. Chambord
1/2 oz. Cruzan Banana Rum
1/2 oz. grenadine
1/2 oz. fresh lime juice
1 oz. sweet 'n' sour
2 oz. limeade
Blend with ice
Lime wheel garnish

MEXICAN SIESTA
Rocks glass, chilled
Rim glass with salt (optional)
Pour ingredients into iced mixing glass
3/4 oz. El Tesoro Añejo Tequila
3/4 oz. Grand Marnier
1 1/4 oz. sweet 'n' sour
Shake and strain
Lime wedge garnish

MIAMI ICE
House specialty glass, ice
Pour ingredients into iced mixing glass
3/4 oz. Beefeater London Dry Gin
3/4 oz. Van Gogh Vodka
3/4 oz. Cruzan Estate Light Rum
3/4 oz. DeKuyper Peach Pucker
1 oz. orange juice
1 oz. sweet 'n' sour
Shake and strain
Splash Seven-Up

MIAMI VICE (1)
House specialty glass, chilled
Pour ingredients into blender
1 1/4 oz. Ypioca Cachaça
3/4 oz. Blue Curaçao
1 1/2 oz. sweet 'n' sour
Blend with ice
Lime wedge garnish

MIAMI VICE (2)
Bucket glass, ice
Build in glass
1/2 oz. chocolate syrup
2 oz. root beer
2 oz. half & half cream
Fill with cola

MICHELADA
Pilsner or pint glass, ice
Rim glass with salt (optional)
Build in glass
1/2 oz. fresh lime juice
Fill with Mexican Lager
Serve with bottle
Lime wedge garnish

MICHELADA, CALIENTE
Pilsner or pint glass, ice
Rim glass with salt (optional)
Build in glass
1/2 oz. fresh lime juice
1/4 oz. jalapeño pepper juice
1 oz. Tequila
Fill with Mexican Lager
Serve with bottle
Lime wedge garnish

MICHELADA, SAUZA
Pilsner or pint glass, ice
Rim glass with salt (optional)
Build in glass
1 1/4 oz. Sauza Hornitos Tequila
1/2 oz. Rose's Lime Juice
6-7 oz. Mexican Lager
Serve with bottle
Lime wedge garnish

MIDNIGHT EXPRESS (1)
Cocktail glass, chilled
Pour ingredients into iced mixing glass
1 3/4 oz. Dark Rum
3/4 oz. Cointreau
1/2 oz. fresh lime juice
1/2 oz. sweet 'n' sour
Shake and strain
Lime wedge garnish

MIDNIGHT EXPRESS (2)
Cocktail glass, chilled
Pour ingredients into iced mixing glass
1 3/4 oz. Dark Rum
3/4 oz. Cointreau
1/2 oz. fresh lime juice
1/2 oz. sweet 'n' sour
Shake and strain
Lime wedge garnish

MIDNIGHT EXPRESS (3)
Cocktail glass, chilled
Pour ingredients into iced mixing glass
1 3/4 oz. Rhum Barbancourt 5-Star
3/4 oz. Cointreau
1/2 oz. fresh lime juice
1/2 oz. sweet 'n' sour
Shake and strain
Lime wedge garnish

MIDNIGHT LACE
Coffee mug, heated
Build in glass
1 1/2 oz. B & B Liqueur
1/2 oz. Orange Liqueur
1 sugar cube
Near fill with hot coffee
Lemon twist garnish
Whipped cream garnish (optional)

MIDNIGHT OIL
Tankard or pilsner glass, chilled
Build in glass
2 1/2 oz. Tawny Port
Fill with Guinness Stout

MIDNIGHT ORCHID
Cocktail glass, chilled
Pour ingredients into iced mixing glass
1 oz. Ketel One Citroen Vodka
3/4 oz. Raspberry Liqueur
3/4 oz. cranberry juice
2 oz. pineapple juice
Shake and strain

MIDORABLE
Cocktail glass, chilled
Pour ingredients into iced mixing glass
1 oz. Midori
3/4 oz. Crème de Banana
1/2 oz. fresh lime juice
1 oz. sweet 'n' sour
Shake and strain

MIDORI CANUCK
Rocks glass, ice
Build in glass
1 oz. Pearl Vodka
1 oz. Midori
1/2 oz. Canadian Club Whisky

MIDORI COOLER
Bucket glass, ice
Build in glass
1 oz. Midori
1/2 oz. DeKuyper Peach Pucker
1/2 oz. DeKuyper Raspberry Pucker
Fill with pineapple juice

PYRAT® XO RESERVE RUM

Located five miles north of St. Maarten, Anguilla is a scant 35 square miles in area. The tiny island is the home of Anguilla Rums, Ltd., makers of one of the world-renowned alembic rums, PYRAT XO RESERVE — PLANTER'S GOLD.

Introduced in 1998, Pyrat XO Reserve is a blend of nine pot-distilled rums aged in French oak barrels according to the Solera aging system. The blend ranges in age from 8 to 40 years. After aging, the rum is reduced in proof using coral-filtered spring water and bottled at 80 proof.

Pyrat XO Reserve is a genuine treat from start to finish. The rum has a lustrous amber color and a medium-weight body. The expansive bouquet is laced with aromas of vanilla, allspice and molasses. The XO quickly fills the mouth with warmth and lavish flavor. The finish is long and exceptionally flavorful.

The famed Pyrat line of handcrafted rums also includes the light and savory PYRAT SUPERIOR BLANCO RUM, a blend of Solera-aged, pot-distilled rums. The color in the rum is carefully filtered out and reduced in proof with spring water.

The crown jewel of the line is the limited release PYRAT CASK 23 RUM, an assertive rum, brimming with high-ester character and taste. This luxurious and sophisticated rum has a palate and finish similar to that of an upper echelon cognac.

MIDORI DRIVER
Highball glass, ice
Build in glass
1 1/4 oz. Midori
Near fill with orange juice
Splash club soda

MIDORI STINGER
Rocks glass, ice
Build in glass
1 oz. Midori
1 oz. Brandy
1/2 oz. White Crème de Menthe

MIDWAY MANHATTAN
House specialty glass, ice
Pour ingredients into iced mixing glass
1 1/4 oz. Bacardi Gold Rum
1 1/4 oz. Mount Gay Eclipse Rum
3/4 oz. Disaronno Amaretto
3/4 oz. Tia Maria
2 oz. orange juice
2 oz. sweet 'n' sour
Shake and strain
Orange slice and cherry garnish

MIDWAY RAT (1)
Rocks glass, chilled
Pour ingredients into iced mixing glass
1/2 oz. Light Rum
1/2 oz. Disaronno Amaretto
1/2 oz. Tia Maria
1/2 oz. pineapple juice
Shake and strain

MIDWAY RAT (2)
Bucket glass, ice
Build in glass
1 oz. Light Rum
3/4 oz. Disaronno Amaretto
3/4 oz. Tia Maria
3 oz. pineapple juice
Orange slice and cherry garnish

MIGHTY BULL SHOOTER
Presentation shot glass, chilled
Layer ingredients
1/2 fill Kahlúa Especial
1/2 fill Sauza Tres Generaciones
    Plata Tequila

MIGHTY KONG
Rocks glass, chilled
Build in glass
3/4 oz. Cruzan Banana Rum
3/4 oz. Kahlúa
3/4 oz. Baileys Irish Cream

MIKHAIL COCKTAIL
House specialty glass, ice
Pour ingredients into iced mixing glass
3/4 oz. Stolichnaya Vodka
3/4 oz. Chambord
1 oz. orange juice
1 1/2 oz. sweet 'n' sour
Shake and strain
Fill with Champagne
Lemon wedge garnish

MILK OF AMNESIA
Presentation shot glass, chilled
Build in glass
1/2 fill Jägermeister
1/2 fill Baileys Irish Cream

MILLIONAIRE COCKTAIL
Cocktail glass, chilled
Pour ingredients into iced mixing glass
1 1/2 oz. Bourbon
1/2 oz. Triple Sec
1/2 oz. grenadine
1 oz. sweet 'n' sour
1 egg white (optional)
Shake and strain

MILLIONAIRE'S COFFEE
Coffee mug, heated
Build in glass
1/2 oz. Kahlúa
1/2 oz. Baileys Irish Cream
1/2 oz. Grand Marnier
Near fill with hot coffee
Whipped cream garnish
Drizzle 1/2 oz. Frangelico

MILWAUKEE RIVER
Presentation shot glass, chilled
Layer ingredients
1/3 fill Kahlúa
1/3 fill Blue Curaçao
1/3 fill Baileys Irish Cream

MIMOSA
aka **Buck's Fizz**
Champagne glass, chilled
Build in glass
1/2 fill orange juice
1/2 fill Champagne
Orange slice garnish

MINCEMEAT MOCHA
Coffee mug, heated
Build in glass
1 1/2 oz. Gold Rum
3/4 oz. Tuaca
1 oz. Hershey's chocolate syrup
Near fill with hot coffee
Whipped cream garnish
Drizzle 1/2 oz. Apple Schnapps

MIND BENDER
Rocks glass, ice
Build in glass
1 1/2 oz. Absolut Kurant Vodka
3/4 oz. Chambord
Splash club soda

MIND ERASER (1)
Rocks glass, crushed ice
Build in glass
3/4 oz. Vodka
3/4 oz. Kahlúa
3/4 oz. Rumple Minze Schnapps

MIND ERASER (2)
Highball glass, ice
Build in glass
1 1/2 oz. Vodka
1 1/2 oz. Kahlúa
Fill with club soda

MINI BEER
Presentation shot glass, chilled
Build in glass
1 oz. Licor 43 (Cuarenta y Tres)
Whipped cream garnish

MINISKIRT LIMBO
Bucket glass, ice
Build in glass
1 3/4 oz. KéKé Beach Cream Liqueur
3/4 oz. Orange Rum
1/2 fill with orange juice
1/2 fill with half & half cream

MINNEHAHA
Bucket glass, ice
Pour ingredients into iced mixing glass
1 1/2 oz. Gin
1/2 oz. Dry Vermouth
1/2 oz. Sweet Vermouth
1/2 oz. Pernod
2 oz. orange juice
Shake and strain

MINT FREEZE
House specialty glass, chilled
Pour ingredients into blender
1 3/4 oz. Irish Whiskey
3/4 oz. Green Crème de Menthe
2 scoops vanilla ice cream
Blend ingredients (with ice optional)
Whipped cream garnish
Drizzle 3/4 oz. Kahlúa

DANZKA® VODKA

Denmark is an ideal country in which to distill vodka. It has easy access to high quality cereal grain, pristine water sources and a populous that appreciates world-class vodka. One of the most respected brands of Danish spirits is the highly innovative DANZKA VODKA.

DANZKA is made in Copenhagen at the Danish Distillers complex, a firm with over 150 years experience producing impeccable spirits. The vodka is distilled from 100% wheat in the facility's state of the art continuous six-column still. After distillation it is filtered three times in huge columns of activated charcoal. The vodka is rendered to 80 proof using pure, demineralized water.

DANZKA Vodka is an excellent spirit, especially considering its modest price tag. The vodka has a medium-weight body and a prominent bouquet of ripe tangerines and grapefruits. It quickly rolls over the palate and fills the mouth with warmth, then gradually fades into a pleasant finish.

Danish Distillers recently extended the DANZKA line with the release of several enticing flavors, including CITRUS and GRAPEFRUIT—a lively vodka with a wafting, grapefruit bouquet and a zesty, slightly bitter palate. DANZKA CRANBERYRAZ™ is a singular combination of tart cranberry and sweet raspberry flavors.

Packaged in stylish, attention-grabbing aluminum bottles, the DANZKA Vodkas are highly mixable, profit-oriented spirits.

MINT JULEP
Collins or chimney glass, frosted
Build in glass
3-4 mint sprigs
3 oz. Bourbon
1/2 oz. simple syrup
Muddle contents
Add crushed ice
Mint leaf garnish

MINT JULEP, GENTLEMAN'S
Rocks glass
Build in glass
3-4 mint sprigs
3 oz. Gentleman Jack Tennessee Whiskey
1/2 oz. Limoncello Liqueur
Muddle contents
Add crushed ice
Mint leaf garnish

MINT JULEP, KENTUCKY
Bucket glass
Build in glass
1/2 oz. fresh lime juice
1/2 oz. simple syrup
3-4 mint sprigs
2 lime wedges
Muddle contents
Add ice
2 oz. Bourbon
2-3 splashes club soda
Lime wedge and mint sprig garnish

MINT JULEP, ON THE MARK
Collins or chimney glass, chilled
Build in glass
3-4 mint sprigs
3 oz. Maker's Mark Bourbon
1/2 oz. RémyRed Red Berry Infusion
Muddle contents
Add crushed ice
Mint leaf garnish

MINT JULEP, PINEAPPLE
Collins or chimney glass, frosted
Build in glass
Muddle 3 mint sprigs
3 oz. Jack Daniel's Tennessee Whiskey
1/2 oz. simple syrup
1/2 oz. Green Crème de Menthe
2 oz. pineapple juice
Stir ingredients
Fill with crushed ice
Mint leaf garnish

MISS UBE DARN
House specialty glass, ice
Pour ingredients into iced mixing glass
1 oz. Polar Ice Vodka
1 oz. Chambord
2 oz. sweet 'n' sour
2 oz. orange juice
Shake and strain

MIST
Rocks glass, crushed ice
Build in glass
1 1/2 oz. requested liquor

MOBAY RUNNER
Bucket glass, ice
Build in glass
1 oz. Appleton Estate V/X Jamaica Rum
1 oz. Mount Gay Eclipse Rum
1 oz. Malibu Caribbean Rum
Fill with papaya juice
Orange slice garnish

MOCHA JAMOCHA
Coffee mug, heated
Build in glass
3/4 oz. Appleton Estate V/X Jamaica Rum
1/2 oz. Cruzan Rum Cream
1/2 oz. Tia Maria
1/2 oz. Dark Crème de Cacao
Near fill with hot coffee
Whipped cream garnish
Dust powdered cocoa

MOCHA MY EYE
House specialty glass, chilled
Pour ingredients into blender
1 oz. Van Gogh Chocolate Vodka
1 oz. Kahlúa Especial
3/4 oz. Nestle's chocolate syrup
2 tbsp. vanilla yogurt
2 scoops vanilla ice cream
Blend ingredients (with ice optional)
Whipped cream and chocolate-covered
    pretzel garnish
Sprinkle shaved chocolate

MOJITO (1)
Bucket glass
Build in glass
3/4 oz. fresh lime juice
1/2 oz. simple syrup
3-4 mint sprigs
2 lime wedges
Muddle contents
Add ice
2 oz. Light Rum
2-3 splashes club soda
Lime wedge and mint sprig garnish

MOJITO (2)
Bucket glass
Build in glass
1 oz. fresh lime juice
2 lime wedges
2-3 dashes Angostura Bitters
4 mint leaves
1 1/2 tbsp. superfine sugar
Muddle contents
Add ice
2 oz. Light Rum
2-3 splashes club soda
Lime wedge and mint sprig garnish

MOJITO, BLACKBERRY
Bucket glass
Build in glass
3/4 oz. fresh lime juice
1/2 oz. simple syrup
3-4 mint sprigs
3 lime wedges
4-5 fresh blackberries
Muddle contents
Add ice
2 oz. Absolut Kurant Vodka
2-3 splashes club soda
Lime wedge and mint sprig garnish

MOJITO, CELLO
Bucket glass
Build in glass
1 oz. fresh lemon juice
1/2 oz. simple syrup
3-4 mint sprigs
Muddle contents
Add ice
2 oz. Limoncello Liqueur
2-3 splashes club soda
Lime wedge and mint sprig garnish

MOJITO, CITRUS
Bucket glass
Build in glass
3/4 oz. fresh lime juice
1/2 oz. simple syrup
3-4 mint sprigs
3 lime wedges
Muddle contents
Add ice
2 oz. Citrus Rum
2-3 splashes club soda
Splash lemon-lime soda
Lime wedge and mint sprig garnish

VILLA MASSA® LIMONCELLO

Limoncello has long been one of the favorite types of liqueurs in Europe. This classic lemon liqueur was often made at home according to a family recipe and passed from one generation to the next. Such was the beginning of VILLA MASSA LIMONCELLO.

Villa Massa Limoncello is a semisweet liqueur made on a base of pure grain neutral spirits infused with succulent Sorrento lemons that are renowned for being sweet, aromatic and thick skinned. The peels contain an abundance of essential oils that imbue the liqueur with its singularly luscious flavor.

Villa Massa Limoncello has a true lemon color and an impressively light body. Its generous bouquet is rich with the aroma of freshly squeezed lemons laced with floral notes. The palate of the liqueur is balanced between the natural astringency of the lemon juice and the tangy bitterness of the peel. The resulting flavor is delicious and refreshing. The limoncello has a crisp and relaxed finish.

This sensational limoncello, 60 proof, is particularly amenable to being mixed, adding a zesty pizzazz to cocktails and scores of other libations.

Villa Massa recently introduced MANDARIN LIQUEUR, an impressively light-bodied product with a delicate orange bouquet and a soft, tangerine-like palate. The protracted finish is smooth and flavorful.

MOJITO, FUSION
Bucket glass
Build in glass
3/4 oz. fresh lime juice
1/2 oz. simple syrup
3-4 mint sprigs
2 lime wedges
Muddle contents
Add ice
2 oz. Kuya Fusion Rum
2-3 splashes club soda
Lime wedge and mint sprig garnish

MOJITO, JALISCO
Bucket glass
Build in glass
3/4 oz. fresh lime juice
1/2 oz. simple syrup
3-4 mint sprigs
3 lime wedges
Muddle contents
Add ice
1 oz. Sauza Hornitos Tequila
1 oz. Midori
2-3 splashes club soda
Lime wedge and mint sprig garnish

MOJITO, MY KENTUCKY
House specialty glass, ice
Pour ingredients into mixing glass
1/2 oz. simple syrup
5-6 mint sprigs
Muddle contents
Add ice
1 1/4 oz. Bourbon
1/2 oz. Cointreau
1/2 oz. Rose's Lime Juice
1 1/2 oz. sweet 'n' sour
1 1/2 oz. iced tea
Shake and strain
Orange slice and mint sprig garnish

MOJITO, RASPBERRY
Bucket glass
Build in glass
3/4 oz. fresh lime juice
1/2 oz. simple syrup
3-4 mint sprigs
3 lime wedges
4-5 fresh raspberries
Muddle contents
Add ice
1 1/2 oz. Van Gogh Raspberry Vodka
3/4 oz. Van Gogh Chocolate Vodka
2-3 splashes club soda
Lime wedge and mint sprig garnish

MOJITO, RASPBERRY VANILLA MOJITO
Bucket glass
Build in glass
3/4 oz. fresh lime juice
1/2 oz. simple syrup
3-4 mint sprigs
2 lime wedges
Muddle contents
Add ice
1 oz. Bacardi Razz Rum
1 oz. Absolut Vanilia Vodka
2-3 splashes club soda
Lime wedge and mint sprig garnish

MOJITO, REGGAE
Bucket glass
Build in glass
1 oz. fresh lime juice
1/2 oz. Rose's Lime Juice
2 lime wedges
2-3 dashes Angostura Bitters
4 mint leaves
1 1/2 tbsp. brown sugar
Muddle contents
Add ice
2 oz. Appleton Estate V/X Jamaica Rum
2-3 splashes club soda
Lime wedge and mint sprig garnish

MOJITO, WATERMELON
Bucket glass
Build in glass
3/4 oz. fresh lime juice
1/2 oz. simple syrup
3-4 mint sprigs
3 lime wedges
Muddle contents
Add ice
2 oz. Bacardi Light Rum
1 oz. fresh watermelon juice
2-3 splashes club soda
Lime wedge and mint sprig garnish

MOJITO, WAYWARD WYNDE
Bucket glass
Build in glass
1 oz. fresh lime juice
1/2 oz. Rose's Lime Juice
2 lime wedges
2-3 dashes Angostura Bitters
4 mint leaves
1 1/2 tbsp. brown sugar
Muddle contents
Add ice
2 oz. Sea Wynde Pot Still Rum
2-3 splashes club soda
Lime wedge and mint sprig garnish

MOLOTOV'S COCKTAIL
Rocks glass, ice
Build in glass
2 1/4 oz. Magadanskaya Vodka
1/2 oz. Rumple Minze Schnapps
Cinnamon stick garnish

MONKEY BITE
Rocks glass, chilled
Build in glass
3/4 oz. Cruzan Banana Rum
3/4 oz. Malibu Caribbean Rum
3/4 oz. pineapple juice

MONKEY GLAND
Cocktail glass, chilled
Pour ingredients into iced mixing glass
1 1/2 oz. Gin
1/2 oz. Pernod
1/2 oz. grenadine
1 oz. orange juice
Shake and strain

MONKEY JUICE
Rocks glass, ice
Build in glass
1 3/4 oz. Cruzan Estate Diamond Rum
3/4 oz. Cruzan Rum Cream
3/4 oz. Crème de Banana

MONK'S COFFEE
Coffee mug, heated
Build in glass
1 1/4 oz. B & B Liqueur
3/4 oz. Orange Liqueur
Near fill with hot coffee
Whipped cream garnish
Dust powdered cocoa

MONSOON
Rocks glass, chilled
Build in glass
1/2 oz. Vodka
1/2 oz. Kahlúa
1/2 oz. Disaronno Amaretto
1/2 oz. Baileys Irish Cream
1/2 oz. Frangelico

MONSTER APPEASER
Rocks glass, chilled
Pour ingredients into iced mixing glass
1/2 oz. Vodka
1/2 oz. Midori
1/2 oz. Blue Curaçao
1/2 oz. Disaronno Amaretto
1/2 oz. Crown Royal
1 1/2 oz. orange juice
Shake and strain

SAUZA® TRES GENERACIONES® PLATA TEQUILA

Sauza is the best-selling line of tequila in Mexico, which speaks volumes about the authenticity of their tequilas. The newest member of the distillery's Estate Collection is SAUZA TRES GENERACIONES PLATA, a satiny smooth, 100% agave silver tequila.

To make Tres Generaciones Plata, the master distiller sends the tequila through the alembic still a third time and bottles within 24 hours of distillation. Since the tequila isn't aged in oak, its inherent attributes are readily apparent and exceptional.

Tres Generaciones Plata has brilliant clarity and a sleek, featherweight body. It is exceptionally aromatic, far more pronounced and alluring than most silver tequilas. The bouquet offers up the captivating aromas of citrus and spice. The tequila lilts over the palate without a trace of heat or harshness, then slowly builds in intensity revealing layers of spicy, peppery flavor. The finish is lingering and flavorful.

Sauza's premium silver deserves to be served neat in a snifter. Sipping Tres Generaciones Plata reinforces why so many are enamored with silver tequila. It is fresh and lively, yet every bit as sophisticated as a fine *eau-de-vie*.

This should not imply that the tequila isn't ready for some fun. It enjoys scores of applications behind the bar and is a fabulous choice for Margaritas served straight-up in elegant cocktail glasses.

MONTE CRISTO SHOOTER
Presentation shot glass
Build in glass
1/3 fill Grand Marnier
1/3 fill Kahlúa
Near fill with hot coffee
Whipped cream garnish

MONTEGO BAY (1)
Coffee mug, heated
Build in glass
3/4 oz. Tia Maria
3/4 oz. Appleton Estate V/X Jamaica Rum
3/4 oz. Cruzan Banana Rum
Near fill with hot coffee
Whipped cream garnish
Sprinkle shaved chocolate

MONTEGO BAY (2)
House specialty glass, ice
Pour ingredients into iced mixing glass
2 oz. sweet 'n' sour
2 oz. orange juice
1/2 oz. Rose's Lime Juice
1/2 oz. grenadine
1 egg yolk (optional)
Shake and strain
Fill with club soda
Lime wedge garnish

MONTMARTE
Champagne glass, chilled
Pour ingredients into iced mixing glass
1 1/2 oz. Brandy
1/2 oz. Benedictine
2-3 dashes Angostura Bitters
1/2 oz. sweet 'n' sour
Shake and strain
Fill with Champagne
Lemon twist garnish

MOOSE MILK
Highball glass, ice
Build in glass
1 1/4 oz. Kahlúa
Fill with milk

MOP IN A BUCKET
Bucket glass, ice
Build in glass
1 oz. Myers's Jamaican Rum
1/2 fill orange juice
1/2 fill pineapple juice

MORNING SUN
House specialty glass, chilled
Pour ingredients into blender
1 1/2 oz. Gin
2 oz. grapefruit juice
2 oz. orange juice
1/4 oz. maraschino cherry juice
2-3 dashes Angostura Bitters
Blend with ice
Whipped cream garnish
Dust powdered cocoa

MOSCOW MULE
Highball glass, ice
Build in glass
1 1/4 oz. Vodka
Fill with Ginger Beer
Lime wedge garnish

MOTHER
Rocks glass, ice
Build in glass
1 1/2 oz. Brandy
1/2 oz. Kahlúa

MOTHER LODE
Rocks glass, ice
Build in glass
1 1/2 oz. Canadian Club Whisky
1/2 oz. Peppermint Schnapps

MOTHER MASON'S DELIGHT
House specialty glass, chilled
Pour ingredients into blender
3/4 oz. Disaronno Amaretto
3/4 oz. Dark Crème de Cacao
1/2 cup strawberries
3/4 oz. half & half cream
2 oz. sweet 'n' sour
Blend with ice
Strawberry garnish

MOULIN ROUGE
Brandy snifter, heated
Build in glass
1 1/2 oz. Crème de Cassis
1/2 oz. VSOP Cognac
1/2 oz. Dry Sherry
1-2 dashes Angostura Bitters
Lemon twist garnish

MOUNTAIN RETREAT
Cocktail glass, chilled
Pour ingredients into iced mixing glass
1 oz. Gin
1/2 oz. honey
1/2 oz. fresh lemon juice
1 1/2 oz. sweet 'n' sour
Shake and strain

MOUNT GAY CAFÉ
Cocktail glass, chilled
Sugar rim (optional)
Pour ingredients into iced mixing glass
1 1/4 oz. Mount Gay Eclipse Rum
1 oz. Tia Maria
3/4 oz. Grand Marnier
1 oz. cold coffee
Shake and strain
Top with frothed milk
Dust powdered cocoa

MR. MURPHY
Rocks glass, ice
Build in glass
1 1/2 oz. Irish Mist
3/4 oz. Baileys Irish Cream

MRS. BAILEYS' BUSH
Rocks glass, ice
Build in glass
1 oz. Irish Whiskey
1 oz. Baileys Irish Cream

MRS. BAILEYS' FAVOR
Cappuccino cup, heated
Build in glass
1/2 oz. Irish Whiskey
1/2 oz. Baileys Irish Cream
1/2 oz. Frangelico
Near fill with hot espresso coffee
Top with frothed milk
Sprinkle shaved chocolate

MUD PUDDLE
Cocktail glass, chilled
Pour ingredients into iced mixing glass
1 3/4 oz. Van Gogh Chocolate Vodka
3/4 oz. Godiva Chocolate Liqueur
1/2 oz. Frangelico
1/2 oz. Baileys Irish Cream
Shake and strain
Sprinkle shaved chocolate

MUDSLIDE (1)
Bucket glass, ice
Build in glass
1 1/2 oz. Vodka
1/2 oz. Kahlúa
1/2 oz. Baileys Irish Cream
Fill with cola

MUDSLIDE (2)
Rocks glass, ice
Build in glass
3/4 oz. Vodka
3/4 oz. Kahlúa
3/4 oz. Baileys Irish Cream

MARTIN MILLER'S®
LONDON DRY GIN

MARTIN MILLER'S LONDON DRY GIN may currently reside in the 21st century, but its character is something straight out of the 19th. Miller's is crafted at a 150 year old distillery in England's oldest operational pot still. Then, prior to bottling, the gin is taken on a remarkable voyage to Iceland. It's an intriguing beginning for an equally engaging spirit.

Miller's Gin is made in Langley, England in a copper pot still first put into service in 1903. The master distiller uses only fresh botanicals and aromatics for distillation. The botanicals are steeped in neutral grain spirits overnight and distilled in small batches.

From England the spirit then travels 3,000 miles to the remote Icelandic village of Borganes, the source of the famed Selyri Spring. The glacier-fed waters are considered among the purest, softest water on earth and are used to dilute the gin to 80 proof. The award winning Westbourne Strength is bottled at 90.4 proof.

This super-premium spirit is a veritable feast for the senses. Miller's Gin has a substantial body and a wafting, fresh bouquet loaded with the aromas of fruit and flora. It fills the mouth with a rich complex of crisp flavors, the most prominent of which are spice and zesty citrus. The gin finishes long and flavorful.

Miller's Gin has vim and vitality, an ideal choice for any gin-based assignment.

MULTIPLE ORGASM
Rocks glass, chilled
Pour ingredients into iced mixing glass
1 1/2 oz. Tia Maria
3/4 oz. Disaronno Amaretto
3/4 oz. half & half cream
Shake and strain

MYSTIC RUNNER
House specialty glass, chilled
Pour ingredients into blender
3/4 oz. XXX Siglo Treinta Tequila
3/4 oz. Coconut Rum
3/4 oz. Banana Rum
1/2 oz. Rose's Lime Juice
2 oz. strawberry puree
2 oz. sweet 'n' sour
Blend with ice

NÁCIONAL
Cocktail glass, chilled
Pour ingredients into iced mixing glass
1 1/2 oz. Gold Rum
3/4 oz. Apricot Liqueur
3/4 oz. fresh lime juice
3/4 oz. pineapple juice
Shake and strain
Lime wedge garnish

NAKED PRETZEL
Bucket glass, ice
Build in glass
3/4 oz. Vodka
1 oz. Midori
1/2 oz. Crème de Cassis
Fill with pineapple juice

NATIVE SUN
Cocktail glass, chilled
Pour ingredients into iced mixing glass
1 1/2 oz. Casa Noble Reposado Tequila
1 oz. Disaronno Amaretto
1/2 oz. Rose's Lime Juice
1/2 oz. orange Juice
1/2 oz. cranberry juice
Shake and strain
Orange slice garnish

NAVAL COMMISSION
House specialty glass, ice
Pour ingredients into iced mixing glass
1 1/2 oz. Pusser's British Navy Rum
3/4 oz. Light Rum
3/4 oz. Gold Rum
1/2 oz. Rose's Lime Juice
1/2 oz. grenadine
1 1/2 oz. orange juice
1 1/2 oz. pineapple juice
Shake and strain
Float 1/2 oz. Dark Rum
Lime, lemon and orange wedge garnish

NAVY GROG
Bucket glass, ice
Pour ingredients into iced mixing glass
1 1/2 oz. Myers's Jamaican Rum
3/4 oz. Light Rum
3/4 oz. Cadenhead's Green Label
    Demerara 151° Rum
1 1/2 oz. orange juice
1 1/2 oz. pineapple juice
1/2 oz. Rose's Lime Juice
Shake and strain

NAVY GROG, MODERN
House specialty glass, chilled
Pour ingredients into blender
2 oz. Pusser's British Navy Rum
1/2 oz. fresh lime juice
1/4 oz. Falernum (sugar cane liqueur)
1 oz. orange juice
1 oz. pineapple juice
1 oz. guava nectar
Blend with ice
Orange slice garnish

NAVY GROG, NOR'EASTER
Coffee mug, heated
Build in glass
1 oz. Dark Rum
1 oz. Navy Rum
1/2 oz. Cointreau
1/2 oz. Tia Maria
1/2 oz. Disaronno Amaretto
1 tsp. brown sugar
1 pinch cinnamon
Near fill with hot coffee
Whipped cream garnish
Drizzle 3/4 oz. Baileys Irish Cream
Sprinkle shaved chocolate

NAVY GROG, ORIGINAL
Coffee mug, heated
Build in glass
2 oz. Gold Rum
1 oz. Brandy
1 oz. fresh lemon juice
1 sugar cube
1 cinnamon stick
6 cloves
1 slice lemon
Fill with hot water
Lemon wedge garnish

NEAPOLITAN
Cocktail glass, chilled
Pour ingredients into iced mixing glass
2 oz. Alizé Gold Passion
1 oz. Absolut Vanilia
1/2 oz. orange juice
Shake and strain
Orange slice garnish

NEGRONI
Cocktail glass, chilled
Pour ingredients into iced mixing glass
3/4 oz. Gin
3/4 oz. Campari Aperitivo
3/4 oz. Sweet Vermouth
Stir and strain
Lemon twist garnish

NEGRONI, UPTOWN
Cocktail glass, chilled
Pour ingredients into iced mixing glass
1/2 oz. Sweet Vermouth
1/2 oz. Campari Aperitivo
1 1/2 oz. Bombay Sapphire London Dry Gin
Stir and strain
Lemon twist garnish

NELSON'S BLOOD (1)
Rocks glass, ice
Build in glass
2 oz. Pusser's British Navy Rum
1/2 oz. fresh lime juice
2 oz. Ginger Beer
Lime wedge garnish

NELSON'S BLOOD (2)
Bucket glass, ice
Build in glass
2 oz. Pusser's British Navy Rum
1/2 fill with cranberry juice
1/2 fill pineapple juice
Lime wedge garnish

NELSON'S BLOOD (3)
Champagne glass, chilled
Build in glass
1 1/2 oz. Tawny Port
Fill with Champagne
Orange twist garnish

NEON TWISTER
House specialty glass, ice
Pour ingredients into iced mixing glass
1/2 oz. Light Rum
1/2 oz. Midori
1/2 oz. DeKuyper Peach Pucker
1 1/2 oz. sweet 'n' sour
1 1/2 oz. orange juice
1 1/2 oz. pineapple juice
Shake and strain
Orange slice and cherry garnish

NEUTRON BOMB
Presentation shot glass, chilled
Layer ingredients
1/3 fill Kahlúa
1/3 fill Baileys Irish Cream
1/3 fill DeKuyper Buttershots Schnapps

JACK DANIEL'S®
SINGLE BARREL
TENNESSEE WHISKEY

Acclaimed as one of America's *grand cru* whiskies, Jack Daniel's Tennessee Whiskey has been produced in Lynchburg, Tennessee since 1866. Jack Daniel founded the distillery when he was just 16 years old, already having owned a whiskey still for the previous 3 years. Now Jack Daniel's Tennessee Whiskey can be found behind nearly every bar in the world.

JACK DANIEL'S SINGLE BARREL TENNESSEE WHISKEY is the real thing, a spirit to be doled out in drams and savored. The handcrafted spirit is drawn straight from the cask, exactly as Jack Daniel had envisioned it. Master distiller Jimmy Bedford carefully selects barrels of whiskey that have fully matured, displaying the aroma and full flavor that has become the brand's hallmark. The whiskey is hand-bottled one barrel at a time at 94 proof.

Since no two barrels of whiskey are identical, each bottle of Jack Daniel's Single Barrel is a slice of whiskey immortality. This is the whiskey that was once reserved solely for the master distiller and Jack Daniel himself. The Single Barrel has a disarming bouquet, rich with the aromas of oak, sweet corn and roasted pepper. It has a supple, round palate and a memorable, long lasting finish.

The whiskey's elegant decanter should be the first indication that this whiskey is meant for sipping and special occasions.

NEW ENGLAND
SUMMER SPRITZER
House specialty glass, ice
Build in glass
1 3/4 oz. Citrus Rum
3 oz. White Zinfandel
3 oz. cranberry juice
Lemon wedge garnish

NEW ORLEANS BUCK
House specialty glass, ice
Pour ingredients into iced mixing glass
1 3/4 oz. Citrus Rum
1 oz. orange juice
1 oz. sweet 'n' sour
Shake and strain
Fill with ginger ale
Lemon wedge garnish

NEW ORLEANS FIZZ
House specialty glass, ice
Pour ingredients into iced mixing glass
1 oz. Gin
1 oz. sweet 'n' sour
2 oz. half & half cream
1 egg white (optional)
Shake and strain
Splash club soda
Orange slice and cherry garnish

NEW ORLEANS JAZZ TIME
Champagne glass, chilled
Pour ingredients into iced mixing glass
1 1/2 oz. Light Rum
1/2 oz. Peach Schnapps
1/2 oz. orange juice
1/2 oz. Rose's Lime Juice
Shake and strain
Fill with Champagne
Orange twist garnish

NEW YORK NUT
Cocktail glass, chilled
Pour ingredients into iced mixing glass
1 1/2 oz. Absolut Vanilia Rum
3/4 oz. Absolut Vodka
1/2 oz. Disaronno Amaretto
1/2 oz. Frangelico
1/2 oz. Tia Maria
1 oz. half & half cream
Shake and strain

NICOLAS
House specialty glass, ice
Pour ingredients into iced mixing glass
2 oz. orange juice
2 oz. sweet 'n' sour
2 oz. grapefruit juice
1/2 oz. grenadine
1 egg white (optional)
Shake and strain
Fill with club soda

NINA'S COFFEE
Coffee mug, heated
Build in glass
3/4 oz. Tuaca
3/4 oz. Disaronno Amaretto
Near fill with hot coffee
Whipped cream garnish
Drizzle grenadine and Green
    Crème de Menthe

NINJA
Presentation shot glass, chilled
Build in glass
1/3 fill Dark Crème de Cacao
1/3 fill Midori
1/3 fill Frangelico

NOBLE HOLIDAY
Rocks glass, ice
Build in glass
1 1/2 oz. Casa Noble Reposado Tequila
3/4 oz. Kahlúa Especial
3/4 oz. Baileys Irish Cream

NOBLE NYMPH
Cocktail glass, chilled
Pour ingredients into iced mixing glass
1 oz. Tanqueray Gin
1/2 oz. Grand Marnier Centenaire
1/2 oz. fresh lime juice
1/2 oz. fresh lemon juice
Shake and strain
Orange slice garnish

N'ORLEANS CHILLER
House specialty glass, ice
Pour ingredients into iced mixing glass
1 1/2 oz. Citrus Rum
1 1/2 oz. Orange Rum
1 oz. orange juice
1 oz. sweet 'n' sour
2 oz. iced herbal tea
Shake and strain
Orange slice garnish

NORTHERN LIGHTS (1)
Coffee mug, heated
Build in glass
1 oz. Yukon Jack Liqueur
3/4 oz. Grand Marnier
Fill with hot coffee

NORTHERN LIGHTS (2)
Highball glass, ice
Build in glass
1 oz. Yukon Jack Liqueur
1/2 oz. DeKuyper Peachtree Schnapps
1/2 fill cranberry juice
1/2 fill orange juice

NOSFERATU
Cocktail glass, chilled
Pour ingredients into iced mixing glass
2 oz. Grey Goose La Vanille Vodka
3/4 oz. Baileys Irish Cream
3/4 oz. Godiva Chocolate Liqueur
Shake and strain
Cherry garnish

NOSFERATU'S SHOOTER
Presentation shot glass, chilled
Layer ingredients
1/3 fill Godiva Chocolate Liqueur
1/3 fill Peppermint Schnapps
1/3 fill Vodka
Speared Cherry Garnish

NO TELL MOTEL
Presentation shot glass, chilled
Layer ingredients
1/2 fill Peppermint Schnapps
1/2 fill Jack Daniel's Tennessee Whiskey

NUCKIN FUTS
House specialty glass, chilled
Pour ingredients into blender
1 oz. Disaronno Amaretto
3/4 oz. Kahlúa
3/4 oz. DeKuyper Cherry Pucker
2 oz. chocolate milk
2 scoops vanilla ice cream
Blend ingredients (with ice optional)
Splash Dr. Pepper
Pineapple wedge garnish

NUN OUT OF HABIT
Brandy snifter, ice
Build in glass
1 1/2 oz. VSOP Cognac
3/4 oz. Baileys Irish Cream
3/4 oz. Godiva Chocolate Liqueur

NUT CREAM COFFEE
Coffee mug, heated
Build in glass
1/2 oz. Baileys Irish Cream
1/2 oz. Frangelico
1/2 oz. Irish Whiskey
Near fill with hot coffee
Whipped cream garnish
Sprinkle nutmeg

GREY GOOSE®
L'ORANGE VODKA

One of the unmistakable consumer trends over the past few years is that flavor rules supreme. It's as true in the spirit world as it is in the culinary one. One noteworthy brand that nailed the true flavor of sun-ripened oranges is the altogether elegant GREY GOOSE L'ORANGE.

All of the Grey Goose Vodkas are crafted in the heart of Cognac. The pure grain vodka is distilled in small batches beginning in copper stills from a choice blend of grains, and then blended with limestone-filtered water drawn from the famous Genté Springs. Natural orange flavors are then blended with Grey Goose Vodka. It undergoes extensive filtration and is bottled at 80 proof.

Grey Goose L'Orange is a genuine pleasure from the first sip until well-after its lingering finish. The vodka has pristine clarity and a flawlessly smooth body. Its bouquet is especially pleasing, laced with the fresh, wafting aroma of ripe oranges. The vodka glides easily over the palate and the warm and zesty flavor of oranges slowly takes charge and lingers an impressively long time.

Before playing with this thoroughbred in mixed drinks, take a moment to enjoy it slightly chilled. It's well worth it. Then stick a spout in the bottle and begin discovering exactly how versatile this orange vodka is.

NUT 'N' HOLLI
Rocks glass, chilled
Pour ingredients into iced mixing glass
1/2 oz. Irish Mist
1/2 oz. Disaronno Amaretto
1/2 oz. Baileys Irish Cream
1/2 oz. Frangelico
Shake and strain

NUT 'N' HONEY
Rocks glass, chilled
Pour ingredients into iced mixing glass
1/2 oz. Vodka
1/2 oz. Frangelico
1/2 oz. Baileys Irish Cream
1/2 oz. Kahlúa
1/2 oz. Tuaca
Shake and strain

NUTS & BERRIES
Cocktail glass, chilled
Pour ingredients into iced mixing glass
1 1/2 oz. Frangelico
1 1/2 oz. Raspberry Liqueur
Shake and strain

NUTS TO YOU
Cocktail glass, chilled
Pour ingredients into iced mixing glass
3/4 oz. White Crème de Cacao
3/4 oz. Frangelico
2 oz. half & half cream
Shake and strain

NUTTY IRISHMAN
Rocks glass, ice
Build in glass
1 1/2 oz. Baileys Irish Cream
1/2 oz. Frangelico

NUTTY MEXICAN
Rocks glass, ice
Build in glass
1 oz. Frangelico
1 oz. Kahlúa
3/4 oz. Silver Tequila
3/4 oz. Baileys Irish Cream

NUTTY PROFESSOR
Rocks glass, ice
Build in glass
1 1/2 oz. Añejo Tequila
1/2 oz. Disaronno Amaretto
1/2 oz. Kahlúa

NYMPHOMANIAC (1)
Bucket glass, chilled
Build in glass
1 1/4 oz. Bacardi Limón Rum
3/4 oz. Midori
1 oz. sweet 'n' sour
1 oz. Seven-Up

NYMPHOMANIAC (2)
Presentation shot glass, chilled
Build in glass
1 oz. Captain Morgan Spiced Rum
1/2 oz. DeKuyper Peachtree Schnapps
1/2 oz. Malibu Caribbean Rum

OATMEAL COOKIE (1)
Rocks glass, chilled
Pour ingredients into iced mixing glass
1/2 oz. Goldschläger
1/2 oz. Frangelico
1/2 oz. Baileys Irish Cream
1/2 oz. Disaronno Amaretto
3/4 oz. half & half cream (optional)
Shake and strain

OATMEAL COOKIE (2)
Rocks glass, chilled
Pour ingredients into iced mixing glass
1/2 oz. Goldschläger
1/2 oz. Jägermeister
1/2 oz. Baileys Irish Cream
1/2 oz. DeKuyper Buttershots Schnapps
3/4 oz. half & half cream (optional)
Shake and strain

O'BRAIN FREEZE
House specialty glass, chilled
Pour ingredients into blender
1 1/2 oz. Irish Liqueur
1/2 oz. Frangelico
1/2 oz. Kahlúa
2 scoops vanilla ice cream
Blend ingredients (with ice optional)

OCEAN BREEZE
Bucket glass, ice
Build in glass
1 1/2 oz. Vodka
1/2 oz. Midori
Fill with lemonade

OCHO RIOS
Champagne glass, chilled
Pour ingredients into iced mixing glass
3/4 oz. Light Rum
3/4 oz. Cruzan Banana Rum
2-3 dashes orange bitters
Shake and strain
Fill with Champagne
Lemon twist garnish

OCTOPUS INK
Cocktail glass, chilled
Pour ingredients into iced mixing glass
1 1/2 oz. Artic Vodka & Thai Fruits Liqueur
1 oz. Blue Curaçao
1 1/4 oz. cranberry juice
Stir and strain
Lime wedge garnish

OFFENBURG FLIP
House specialty glass, chilled
Pour ingredients into blender
3/4 oz. Coconut Rum
3/4 oz. Banana Rum
1/2 oz. Rose's Lime Juice
1/2 oz. fresh lemon juice
1 peeled, ripe banana
1 egg yolk (optional)
2 oz. orange juice
Blend with ice
Float 3/4 oz. Dark Rum
Banana slice and cherry garnish

OLD FASHION
Rocks or old fashion glass
Build in glass
3 dashes Angostura Bitters
1/2 oz. simple syrup
Add ice
1 1/2 oz. Bourbon
Splash club soda
Orange slice and cherry garnish
Note: Old Fashions may be made with any
requested dark liquor

OLD FASHION, APPLE
Rocks or old fashion glass, ice
Build in glass
3 dashes Angostura Bitters
1/2 oz. simple syrup
2 1/2 oz. Laird's Applejack Brandy
Splash club soda
Orange slice and cherry garnish

OLD FASHION, CARIBBEAN
Rocks or old fashion glass
Build in glass
3 dashes Angostura Bitters
1/2 oz. simple syrup
1/2 oz. fresh lime juice
1 orange slice and cherry
Muddle contents
2 oz. Dark Rum
Add ice
Splash club soda

OLD FASHION, KNOB CREEK
Rocks or old fashion glass
Build in glass
3 dashes Angostura Bitters
1/2 oz. simple syrup
1 peeled peach slice
Muddle contents
2 1/2 oz. Knob Creek Small Batch Bourbon
Add ice
Splash club soda

DEKUYPER® ORIGINAL PEACHTREE® SCHNAPPS

When DEKUYPER ORIGINAL PEACHTREE SCHNAPPS was introduced in the early 1980s, it immediately shot to the top of the charts like a bullet. Drinks such as the Fuzzy Navel, Silk Panties and Sex on the Beach became all the rage, making DeKuyper Peachtree Schnapps indispensable behind the bar. Today it remains a "must have" brand.

Peach schnapps is produced by distilling a blend of neutral grain spirits and natural peach flavoring. While the purity of the grain spirits is a factor, what significantly differentiates one brand from another is the quality of the natural peach flavoring. Peachtree Schnapps is made from a blend of several different peach varieties, some selected for their bouquet, others for their taste.

The art and science of making high quality schnapps came together in DeKuyper Peachtree. It has a satiny, light/medium body and a robust bouquet of freshly sliced peaches. The fresh fruit experience continues on the palate, where the flavor of peach is predominant. The finish is long and flavorful.

DeKuyper Peachtree Schnapps has become something of a modern classic, the brand synonymous with the peach schnapps category. The wide variety of specialty drinks that it can create is bounded only by one's imagination.

OLD FASHION, MUDDLED
Rocks or old fashion glass
Build in glass
3 dashes Angostura Bitters
1/2 oz. simple syrup
1 orange slice and cherry
Muddle contents
1 1/2 oz. Bourbon
Add ice
Splash club soda

OLD FASHION, NEW AGE
Rocks or old fashion glass
Build in glass
3 dashes Angostura Bitters
1/2 oz. Limoncello Liqueur
Lemon and orange slice, cherry
Muddle contents
2 oz. Bourbon
Add ice
Splash Champagne

OLD FASHIONED, RUM
Bucket glass
Build in glass
1/2 oz. simple syrup
2-3 dashes Angostura Bitters
1-2 splashes club soda
Orange slice and cherry
Muddle contents
Add ice
2 oz. Light Rum
1/2 oz. 151° Rum
Lime wedge garnish

OLD FASHION, SANTA ANITA
Rocks or old fashion glass
Build in glass
3 dashes Angostura Bitters
1/2 oz. simple syrup
1 orange slice
5 fresh raspberries
Muddle contents
2 1/2 oz. Bourbon
Add ice
Splash club soda

OLD FLAME
Cocktail glass, chilled
Pour ingredients into iced mixing glass
1 oz. Bombay Sapphire London Dry Gin
1/2 oz. Sweet Vermouth
1/2 oz. Campari Aperitivo
1 oz. orange juice
1 oz. simple syrup
Shake and strain
Orange zest garnish

OPERA COCKTAIL
Cocktail glass, chilled
Pour ingredients into iced mixing glass
1 1/2 oz. Gin
1/2 oz. Dubonnet Rouge
1/2 oz. Maraschino Liqueur
Stir and strain
Orange twist garnish

OPULENT COFFEE
Coffee mug, heated
Build in glass
3/4 oz. Grand Marnier Liqueur
1/2 oz. Kahlúa Especial
1/2 oz. Baileys Irish Cream
1/2 oz. Frangelico
Near fill with hot coffee
Whipped cream garnish

ORANGE BLOSSOM (1)
Cocktail glass, chilled
Rim glass with sugar (optional)
Pour ingredients into iced mixing glass
1 oz. Gin
1/2 oz. simple syrup
1 1/2 oz. orange juice
Shake and strain

ORANGE BLOSSOM (2)
aka **Left-Handed Screwdriver**
Highball glass, ice
Build in glass
1 1/4 oz. Gin
Fill with orange juice

ORANGE CHILLER
Highball glass, ice
Build in glass
1 1/4 oz. requested liquor
1/2 fill orange juice
1/2 fill cranberry juice

ORANGE CRANBERRY TODDY
Coffee mug, heated
Pour into saucepan
1 oz. Grand Marnier
1 oz. Chambord
1/2 tsp. fine granulated sugar
2 oz. cranberry juice
4 oz. orange juice
1 cinnamon stick
1 clove
Simmer and pour into heated mug
Orange slice garnish

ORANGE DELIGHT
Cocktail glass, chilled
Pour ingredients into iced mixing glass
1 3/4 oz. Vodka
3/4 oz. Grand Marnier
2-3 dashes Angostura Bitters
Stir and strain
Orange twist garnish

ORANGE DREAM
Cocktail glass, chilled
Pour ingredients into iced mixing glass
1 1/2 oz. Vodka
3/4 oz. Vanilla Rum
1/2 oz. Grand Marnier
1/2 oz. orange juice
3/4 oz. half & half cream
Shake and strain
Orange slice garnish

ORANGE FRAPPÉ
House specialty glass, chilled
Pour ingredients into blender
1 3/4 oz. Orange Liqueur
3/4 oz. Dark Crème de Cacao
3/4 oz. Vodka
1 oz. sweet 'n' sour
1 3/4 oz. orange juice
2 scoops vanilla ice cream
Blend ingredients (with ice optional)
Whipped cream garnish
Drizzle 3/4 oz. Disaronno Amaretto

ORANGE JULIUS
Presentation shot glass, chilled
Build in glass
1/4 fill Vodka
1/4 fill Disaronno Amaretto
1/4 fill orange juice
1/4 fill Draft Beer

ORANGE-U-GLAD-2-C-ME
Cocktail glass, chilled
Pour ingredients into iced mixing glass
1 1/2 oz. Bourbon
1/2 oz. RémyRed Red Berry Infusion
1 1/2 oz. sweet 'n' sour
Shake and strain
Orange twist garnish

ORCHARD HAZE
Coffee mug, heated
Build in glass
3/4 oz. DeKuyper Pucker Sour Apple
1/2 oz. Cinnamon Schnapps
1/2 oz. Light Rum
Near fill with hot apple cider
Whipped cream garnish
Sprinkle nutmeg

XALIXCO® GOLD TEQUILA

XALIXCO GOLD TEQUILA is a singular product because it is made by the largest grower of agaves in Mexico. The Fonseca family began cultivating agaves in 1891 and in 1989 they purchased a state of the art distillery from Bacardi and began making tequila from the agaves they grew.

The Fonseca's distillery—called Tequileña—is located in the town of Tequila and the agaves used to make Xalixco are grown in the highlands of the Los Altos region. The red volcanic soil is ideal for cultivating blue agaves. The distillery is equipped with traditional copper pot stills and modern double-column continuous stills, which are highly efficient at producing light, clean alcohol.

Xalixco is a blended, or *mixto* tequila. It is made from a premium blend of 70% agave, significantly higher than most *mixtos* available on the market and is bottled at 80 proof. The tequila has a pale golden color and a smooth textured, lightweight body. The bouquet is spicy and quite herbaceous. Its initial attack is impressively soft and restrained. It slowly fills the mouth with warmth and spice and earthy flavors, but never gets hot or harsh. The finish is slightly peppery and moderately long.

Xalixco Gold Tequila is a sensational value. It is made entirely in Mexico from people who control production from the ground up. The gold tequila is well suited for the shot glass and is especially great in Margaritas.

ORCHID COCKTAIL
Cocktail glass, chilled
Pour ingredients into iced mixing glass
1 1/2 oz. VSOP Cognac
1/2 oz. Chambord
3/4 oz. sweet 'n' sour
Shake and strain
Lemon wheel garnish

ORGASM (1)
Bucket glass, ice
Build in glass
1/2 oz. Kahlúa
1/2 oz. Disaronno Amaretto
1/2 oz. Baileys Irish Cream
1/2 fill half & half cream
1/2 fill club soda

ORGASM (2)
Presentation shot glass, chilled
Layer ingredients
1/2 fill Peppermint Schnapps
1/2 fill Baileys Irish Cream

ORIGINAL MONK
Cocktail glass, chilled
Pour ingredients into iced mixing glass
1 3/4 oz. Original Cristall Vodka
1/2 oz. Hardy Noces d'Or Cognac
1/2 oz. Benedictine
Stir and strain
Orange twist garnish

ORIGINAL SIN
Coffee mug, heated
Build in glass
1 1/2 oz. Van Gogh Wild Appel Vodka
Near fill with hot apple cider
Whipped cream and cinnamon
    stick garnish

ORSINI
House specialty glass, chilled
Pour ingredients into blender
1 oz. Gin
3/4 oz. Triple Sec
1 oz. half & half cream
2 oz. sweet 'n' sour
2 oz. orange juice
Blend with ice

OSMOSIS
Bucket glass, ice
Build in glass
1 1/4 oz. Tequila
1/2 fill lemonade
1/2 fill Squirt
Float 3/4 oz. Midori
Lime wedge garnish

OTTER WATER
House specialty glass, ice
Build in glass
3/4 oz. Light Rum
3/4 oz. Gold Rum
3/4 oz. Mount Gay Eclipse Rum
1/2 oz. Chambord
1 oz. orange juice
1 oz. pineapple juice
Near fill with Seven-Up
Float 3/4 oz. Dark Rum
Orange slice garnish

OUTRIGGER
Cocktail Glass, chilled
Pour ingredients into iced mixing glass
1 oz. Cruzan Citrus Rum
1/2 oz. Disaronno Amaretto
1 1/2 oz. cranberry juice
1 1/2 oz. pineapple juice
Shake and strain
Float 3/4 oz. Cruzan Estate Diamond Rum
Orange slice and cherry garnish

OYSTER SHOOTER
Rocks glass, chilled
Build in glass
2 dashes Tabasco Sauce
1/2 tsp. horseradish
3 oz. Draft Beer
1 raw oyster

PACIFIC RIM
House specialty glass, chilled
Pour ingredients into iced mixing glass
1/2 oz. Midori
1/2 oz. Peach Schnapps
1/2 oz. sweet 'n' sour
1 1/2 oz. orange juice
1 1/2 oz. cranberry juice
Shake and strain
Fill with Champagne
Lemon twist garnish

PADDY
Cocktail glass, chilled
Pour ingredients into iced mixing glass
1 dash Angostura Bitters (optional)
1/2 oz. Sweet Vermouth
1 1/2 oz. Irish Whiskey
Stir and strain
Cherry garnish

PADDY O'ROCCO
Bucket glass, ice
Build in glass
1 1/2 oz. Irish Mist
3/4 oz. half & half cream (optional)
Near fill with orange juice
Float 3/4 oz. Disaronno Amaretto

PAIN IN THE BUTT
House specialty glass, chilled
1—Make 1/2 recipe Piña Colada
Blend with ice
Pour first drink into glass 1/2 full
2—Make 1/2 recipe Strawberry Daiquiri
Blend with ice
Fill glass with second drink
Pineapple wedge and cherry garnish

PAINKILLER
House specialty glass, ice
Build in glass
2 oz. Pusser's British Navy Rum
1 oz. orange juice
1 oz. coconut cream syrup
4 oz. pineapple juice
Stir ingredients
Orange slice and cherry garnish
Sprinkle nutmeg

PALACE GUARD
Cocktail glass, chilled
Pour ingredients into iced mixing glass
2 oz. Gin
1/4 oz. Dry Vermouth
1/4 oz. B & B Liqueur
Stir and strain
Lemon twist garnish

PANAMA JACK
Bucket glass, ice
Build in glass
1 1/2 oz. Yukon Jack Liqueur
1/2 fill pineapple juice
Near fill with cranberry juice
Splash club soda

PANAMA RED
Rocks glass, chilled
Pour ingredients into iced mixing glass
1 oz. Jose Cuervo Especial Tequila
3/4 oz. Triple Sec
1/2 oz. grenadine
1 1/4 oz. sweet 'n' sour
Shake and strain

PANTHER
Rocks glass, ice
Pour ingredients into iced mixing glass
1 1/2 oz. Tequila
3/4 oz. sweet 'n' sour
Shake and strain

DEWAR'S® WHITE LABEL SCOTCH WHISKY

DEWAR'S WHITE LABEL SCOTCH WHISKY is the preeminent blended whisky in the world. The origins of this most famous brand began in Perth, Scotland. In 1846, John Dewar opened a business as a wine and spirits merchant. After years of patient experimentation, he perfected a recipe for a blended Scotch whisky that became so popular its success prompted him to be the first to market his whisky in bottles.

Long the best-selling Scotch whisky in the United States, Dewar's White Label is a skillfully crafted blend of malt and straight grain whiskies. At the core of its blend are the renowned malts of Dewar's Highland distilleries, most notably Aberfeldy, Lochnagar and Glen Ord. It is bottled at 80 proof.

Dewar's White Label has a rich amber hue and flawlessly textured body. The wafting bouquet is peppery, fruity and lightly peated. The whisky comes alive on the palate featuring a balanced offering of mildly smoky, semisweet grain flavor. It has a somewhat long and peaty finish.

The firm also produces DEWAR'S SPECIAL RESERVE, an extraordinary blend of individually aged, 12 year old single malt whiskies distilled in different regions of Scotland. After blending, the whisky is further matured in oak barrels to allow the blend to "marry." It is bottled at 86 proof.

PAPA DOBLES
House specialty glass, chilled
Pour ingredients into blender
1 3/4 oz. Light Rum
3/4 oz. maraschino cherry juice
1 1/4 oz. fresh lime juice
1 1/4 oz. grapefruit juice
Blend with ice
Float 1 oz. Mount Gay Eclipse Rum
Lime wedge and cherry garnish

PARANOIA
Bucket glass, ice
Build in glass
1 oz. Malibu Caribbean Rum
1 oz. Disaronno Amaretto
1/2 fill orange juice
Near fill with pineapple juice
Float 3/4 oz. Gosling's Black Seal Rum
Orange slice garnish

PARFAIT
House specialty glass, chilled
Pour ingredients into blender
1 1/2 oz. requested liqueur
2 scoops vanilla ice cream
Blend ingredients (with ice optional)
Whipped cream garnish

PARIS BURNING
Brandy snifter, heated
Build in glass
1 1/2 oz. VS Cognac
1 1/2 oz. Chambord

PARPLE THUNDER
Bucket glass, ice
Pour ingredients into iced mixing glass
1 oz. Dark Rum
1 oz. Light Rum
1/2 oz. Triple Sec
1 1/2 oz. grape juice
1 1/2 oz. cranberry juice
Shake and strain
Splash club soda

PARSON'S PARTICULAR
Wine glass, ice
Pour ingredients into iced mixing glass
3 oz. orange juice
1 1/2 oz. sweet 'n' sour
1 egg yolk (optional)
1/2 oz. grenadine
Shake and strain
Orange slice and cherry garnish

PASSION ALEXANDER
Cocktail glass, chilled
Pour ingredients into iced mixing glass
3/4 oz. Opal Nera Black Sambuca
3/4 oz. White Crème de Cacao
1 1/2 oz. half & half cream
Shake and strain

PASSIONATE FRUIT
Bucket glass, ice
Pour ingredients into iced mixing glass
1 oz. RémyRed Red Berry Infusion
1 oz. Orange Vodka
1/2 oz. Peach Schnapps
1 oz. lemonade
Shake and strain
Lemon wedge garnish

PASSIONATE POINT
House specialty glass, ice
Pour ingredients into iced mixing glass
1 3/4 oz. Mount Gay Eclipse Rum
3/4 oz. Grand Marnier
3/4 oz. DeKuyper Peachtree Schnapps
2 oz. orange juice
2 oz. cranberry juice
Shake and strain
Float 3/4 oz. Mount Gay Extra Old Rum

PASSIONATE SCREW
Bucket glass, ice
Pour ingredients into iced mixing glass
1 1/4 oz. Citrus Rum
1 oz. Pineapple Rum
1 oz. Chambord
1/2 oz. grenadine
2 oz. orange juice
2 oz. sweet 'n' sour
Shake and strain
Orange slice and cherry garnish

PASSIONATE SUNSET
House specialty glass, ice
Pour ingredients into iced mixing glass
1 1/2 oz. RémyRed Red Berry Infusion
1 oz. Tequila
1/2 oz. grenadine
1 oz. orange juice
1 oz. grapefruit juice
1 oz. sweet 'n' sour
Shake and strain
Float 3/4 oz. Grand Marnier
Orange slice garnish

PASSION POTION
House specialty glass, ice
Pour ingredients into iced mixing glass
3/4 oz. Gin
3/4 oz. Vodka
3/4 oz. Light Rum
1/2 oz. grenadine
2 1/2 oz. orange juice
2 1/2 oz. pineapple juice
Shake and strain
Splash Seven-Up

PASSION PUNCH
Bucket glass, ice
Pour ingredients into iced mixing glass
2 oz. RémyRed Red Berry Infusion
2 oz. orange juice
2 oz. pineapple juice
1/2 oz. grenadine
2-3 dashes Angostura Bitters
Shake and strain
Orange slice garnish

PASSION ROYALE
Champagne glass, chilled
Pour ingredients into iced mixing glass
1 1/2 oz. VSOP Cognac
2 oz. sweet 'n' sour
Shake and strain
Fill with Champagne
Lemon twist garnish

PAZZO GRAND SPANISH COFFEE
Coffee mug, heated
Build in glass
1 oz. Patrón XO Café Coffee Liqueur
1 oz. VS Cognac
3/4 oz. Citrónge Orange Liqueur
1/2 oz. 151° Rum
2 pinches cinnamon
1 1/2 oz. espresso coffee
Fill with hot coffee
Whipped cream garnish
Dust powdered cocoa

PEACH BLASTER
Highball glass, ice
Build in glass
1 1/4 oz. Peach Schnapps
Fill cranberry juice

PEACH BOMB
Presentation shot glass, chilled
Build in glass
1/4 fill Vodka
1/4 fill Peach Schnapps
1/4 fill orange juice
1/4 fill cranberry juice

WHALER'S® ORIGINAL VANILLE RUM

WHALER'S ORIGINAL VANILLE RUM isn't likely to be shelved at a highbrow haunt. This Hawaiian classic was created for joints where the bar hops and people appreciate a good time.

This enticing spirit was originated by Hawaiian Distillers of Honolulu. The rum is distilled using molasses from locally grown sugar cane. Whaler's Original Vanille (Van-ee) is a dark, highly aromatic rum infused with natural vanilla flavors. The rum has a creamy texture and a delicious palate brimming with vanilla and hints of cocoa. Little wonder why it is the featured act in many contemporary drinks.

The popular Whaler's line of rums also includes GREAT WHITE, a sleek silver rum with a clean, lively palate, and ORIGINAL DARK, an energized spirit endowed with warm, sumptuous flavors. WHALER'S SPICED RUM has a palate saturated with the flavors of vanilla, caramel and spice.

The dean of the group is WHALER'S RARE RESERVE DARK RUM, an elegant aged rum with a beckoning bouquet and a deliciously complex palate. New to the team are KILLER COCONUT, a vibrant rum loaded with the fresh flavor of coconut, PINEAPPLE PARADISE, a lavishly flavored pineapple rum and BIG ISLAND BANANA, which is made with natural banana flavorings.

Whaler's Hawaiian Rums are a bona fide good time waiting to happen.

PEACH BREEZE
Highball glass, ice
Build in glass
1 oz. Peach Schnapps
3/4 oz. Vodka
1/2 fill cranberry juice
1/2 fill grapefruit juice

PEACH COBBLER
Cocktail glass, chilled
Pour ingredients into iced mixing glass
1 oz. Reposado Tequila
3/4 oz. Peach Schnapps
3/4 oz. Spiced Rum
3/4 oz. Vanilla Rum
1 1/2 oz. sweet 'n' sour
Shake and strain
Lemon twist garnish

PEACHES AND DREAMS
House specialty glass, ice
Pour ingredients into iced mixing glass
1 3/4 oz. Knappogue Castle Irish Whiskey
3/4 oz. DeKuyper Peachtree Schnapps
3/4 oz. Whaler's Original Vanille Rum
1 1/2 oz. orange juice
1 1/2 oz. half & half cream
Shake and strain
Orange slice garnish

PEACHES 'N' BERRIES
Rocks glass, ice
Build in glass
1 1/2 oz. Tequila Rose Cream Liqueur
1 oz. DeKuyper Peachtree Schnapps
Splash half & half cream

PEACH FUZZ
Rocks glass, chilled
Pour ingredients into iced mixing glass
1 1/4 oz. Vodka
3/4 oz. Peach Schnapps
1/2 oz. orange juice
1/2 oz. cranberry juice
Shake and strain

PEACHIE KEEN
House specialty glass, chilled
Pour ingredients into blender
1 oz. Peach Schnapps
1 oz. Galliano Liqueur
3/4 oz. half & half cream
2 scoops vanilla ice cream
Blend ingredients (with ice optional)

PEACHY CONGO COOLER
Bucket glass, ice
Build in glass
1 1/4 oz. Peach Schnapps
3/4 oz. half & half cream
Near fill with orange juice
Float 3/4 oz. Crème de Banana
Peach wedge garnish

PEARL DIVER
Rocks glass, chilled
Pour ingredients into iced mixing glass
1 oz. Pearl Vodka
1/2 oz. DeKuyper Pucker Sour Apple
1/4 oz. Galliano Liqueur
1/2 oz. grapefruit juice
Shake and strain

PEARL HARBOR
Highball glass, ice
Build in glass
1 1/2 oz. Midori
3/4 oz. Vodka
Fill with pineapple juice

PECKERHEAD
Rocks glass, chilled
Pour ingredients into iced mixing glass
3/4 oz. Yukon Jack Liqueur
3/4 oz. Disaronno Amaretto
3/4 oz. pineapple juice
Shake and strain

PEPPERMINT COOLER
Highball glass, ice
Build in glass
1 1/2 oz. Peppermint Schnapps
Fill with Seven-Up

PEPPERMINT PATTIE
Cocktail glass, chilled
Pour ingredients into iced mixing glass
3/4 oz. White Crème de Cacao
3/4 oz. Peppermint Schnapps
2 oz. half & half cream
Shake and strain

PERFECT 10
Cocktail glass, chilled
Pour ingredients into iced mixing glass
2 oz. Tanqueray № Ten Gin
1/2 oz. Limoncello Liqueur
1/2 oz. fresh lime juice
Stir and strain
Lemon twist garnish

PERFECT FIT
Bucket glass, ice
Build in glass
1 1/4 oz. Silver Tequila
1/2 fill grapefruit juice
1/2 fill orange juice

PERIODISTA (1)
Cocktail glass, chilled
Pour ingredients into iced mixing glass
1 3/4 oz. Light Rum
1/2 oz. Cointreau
1/2 oz. Apricot Brandy
1/2 oz. simple syrup
1 oz. fresh lime juice
Shake and strain
Lime wedge garnish

PERIODISTA (2)
Cocktail glass chilled
Pour ingredients into iced mixing glass
1 1/4 oz. Dark Rum
3/4 oz. Cointreau
1/2 oz. Apricot Brandy
1/2 oz. simple syrup
1 oz. fresh lime juice
Shake and strain
Lime wedge garnish

PERSUADER
Highball glass, ice
Build in glass
3/4 oz. Disaronno Amaretto
3/4 oz. Brandy
Fill with orange juice

PETER PRESCRIPTION
Coffee mug, heated
Build in glass
1 1/4 oz. Appleton Estate V/X Jamaica Rum
1/2 oz. Tia Maria
1/2 oz. Grand Marnier
1/2 oz. Chambord
Near fill with hot coffee
Whipped cream garnish
Sprinkle shaved chocolate

PHILIPPI CREEK
Coffee mug, heated
Build in glass
1 oz. Sambuca
1 oz. VS Cognac
4 oz. hot espresso coffee
Splash half & half cream
Lemon twist garnish

PILGRIM
House specialty glass, chilled
Pour ingredients into blender
1 1/2 oz. Light Rum
1/2 oz. grenadine
4 oz. cranberry juice
1 scoop orange sherbet
Blend ingredients (with ice optional)

SPUDKA® VODKA

Established in 1934, Oregon's Hood River Distillers is the oldest, independent and proprietary distillery in the western United States. One of the gems of their repertoire is SPUDKA VODKA, the first premium American spirit distilled solely from potatoes.

Introduced in 1962, Spudka is quite the achievement. Producing a great tasting, high quality spirit from potatoes is a relatively costly proposition. It is far more complicated to convert potato starches into fermentable sugars than it is cereal grains. The vodka is distilled from premium grade Northwest potatoes in a complex, 139-plate continuous still that is designed to render the vodka eminently pure. It is then double-filtered through activated charcoal and diluted to 82 proof with glacier-fed spring water from Mount Hood.

Spudka Vodka carries a mighty small price tag for such a premium spirit. It has a lightweight, satiny body and a full bouquet of sun-ripened citrus. On the palate the vodka is deliciously neutral with only hints of underlying flavor. The finish is long, warm and slightly sweet.

Only a fraction of the world's vodkas are distilled from potatoes of which Spudka is an excellent example. The vodka is ideally suited for a broad range of cocktails and mixed drinks. If you're someone who places a premium on value, then Spudka Vodka should be on your short list.

PILGRIM'S PRIDE
House specialty glass, chilled
Pour ingredients into blender
1 1/2 oz. Light Rum
1 oz. Orange Rum
1/2 oz. grenadine
3 oz. cranberry juice
2 scoops orange sherbet
Blend ingredients (with ice optional)
Float 3/4 oz. Dark Rum
Orange slice garnish

PILLOWTALK
Brandy snifter, heated
Build in glass
1 1/2 oz. Scotch Whisky
1/2 oz. Irish Liqueur

PIMM'S CUP
Collins or bucket glass, ice
Build in glass
1 1/2 oz. Pimm's Cup No. 1
Fill with Seven-Up
Lemon twist and cucumber slice garnish

PIÑA COLADA
House specialty glass, chilled
Pour ingredients into blender
1 oz. Light Rum
3/4 oz. half & half cream (optional)
2 oz. coconut cream syrup
3 oz. pineapple juice
Blend with ice
Pineapple wedge and cherry garnish

PIÑA COLADA, ACAPULCO
House specialty glass, chilled
Pour ingredients into blender
1 oz. Reposado Tequila
1/2 oz. Rose's Lime Juice
2 oz. coconut cream syrup
3 oz. pineapple juice
Blend with ice
Pineapple wedge and cherry garnish

PIÑA COLADA, AMARETTO
aka **Italian Colada**
House specialty glass, chilled
Pour ingredients into blender
1 oz. Disaronno Amaretto
1 oz. Light Rum
3/4 oz. half & half cream (optional)
2 oz. coconut cream syrup
3 oz. pineapple juice
Blend with ice
Pineapple wedge and cherry garnish

PIÑA COLADA, AUSSIE
aka **Flying Kangaroo**
House specialty glass, chilled
Pour ingredients into blender
1 oz. Light Rum
1/2 oz. Galliano Liqueur
1/2 oz. Vodka
1/2 oz. orange juice
2 oz. coconut cream syrup
3 oz. pineapple juice
3/4 oz. half & half cream (optional)
Blend with ice
Pineapple wedge and cherry garnish

PIÑA COLADA, BAHAMA
House specialty glass, chilled
Pour ingredients into blender
1 1/4 oz. Midori
1 oz. Crème de Banana
1 oz. orange juice
2 oz. coconut cream syrup
2 oz. pineapple juice
3/4 oz. half & half cream (optional)
Blend with ice
Pineapple wedge and cherry garnish

PIÑA COLADA, BELLEVUE
House specialty glass, chilled
Pour ingredients into blender
1 1/2 oz. Gold Rum
3/4 oz. Orange Liqueur
1/2 oz. Rose's Lime Juice
2 oz. coconut cream syrup
3 oz. pineapple juice
Blend with ice
Float 3/4 oz. Dark Rum
Pineapple wedge and cherry garnish

PIÑA COLADA, BERMUDA
House specialty glass, chilled
Pour ingredients into blender
2 3/4 oz. Gosling's Black Seal Rum
2 oz. coconut cream syrup
3 oz. pineapple juice
Blend with ice
Pineapple wedge and cherry garnish

PIÑA COLADA, BLACK PEARL
House specialty glass, chilled
Pour ingredients into blender
1 1/4 oz. Mount Gay Eclipse Rum
1 oz. Gold Rum
3/4 oz. Tia Maria
2 oz. coconut cream syrup
3 oz. pineapple juice
Blend with ice
Float 3/4 oz. Gosling's Black Seal Rum
Pineapple wedge and cherry garnish

PIÑA COLADA, BRAZILIAN
House specialty glass, chilled
Pour ingredients into blender
1 oz. Light Rum
1 oz. Ypióca Cachaça
1/2 cup cored, peeled pineapple
2 oz. coconut cream syrup
3 oz. pineapple juice
Blend with ice
Pineapple wedge and cherry garnish

PIÑA COLADA, CACTUS
aka **Cactus Colada**
House specialty glass, chilled
Pour ingredients into blender
1 1/4 oz. Reposado Tequila
3/4 oz. Midori
1/2 oz. grenadine
1 oz. orange juice
1 oz. pineapple juice
2 oz. coconut cream syrup
Blend with ice
Pineapple wedge and cherry garnish

PIÑA COLADA, CANNE BAY
House specialty glass, chilled
Pour ingredients into blender
1 1/2 oz. Cruzan Coconut Rum
1 1/2 oz. Cruzan Pineapple Rum
1/2 oz. Rose's Lime Juice
1/2 oz. fresh lemon juice
2 oz. coconut cream syrup
3 oz. pineapple juice
Blend with ice
Pineapple wedge and cherry garnish

PIÑA COLADA, CHOCOLATE (1)
House specialty glass, chilled
Pour ingredients into blender
1 1/2 oz. Gold Rum
1 oz. chocolate syrup
2 oz. coconut cream syrup
3 oz. pineapple juice
2 scoops chocolate ice cream
Blend ingredients (with ice optional)
Float 3/4 oz. Dark Rum
Pineapple wedge and cherry garnish

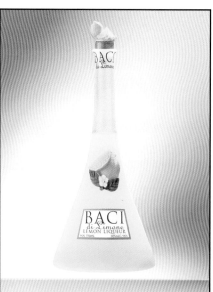

BACI DI LIMONE®
LEMON LIQUEUR

Leave it to one of the oldest cultures on Earth to devise something so luscious as *limoncello*. Imminently light and refreshing, this Italian lemon liqueur is exceptionally popular on the Continent and can be found in virtually every café, bistro and *ristorante* throughout Europe. Now one of the leading brands of *limoncello*, BACI DI LIMONE LEMON LIQUEUR, has finally arrived on our shores.

Baci di Limone is made in Agropoli, Italy, from handpicked, Cilento lemons. On the day of harvest, the tree-ripened fruit is washed and peeled. The lemon peels are then immediately immersed in spirits. The slow infusion process lasts for days. The lemon peels are then removed and the infused alcohol is filtered and sweetened. It is bottled at 60 proof.

Baci di Limone is a delectable taste sensation. It has the appearance of freshly squeezed lemonade and a soft, medium-weight body. The liqueur has a subtle bouquet laced with delicate citrus aromas. Its lemon-infused palate is a balanced affair, semisweet and naturally tangy. The finish is crisp, flavorful and of medium duration.

This succulent liqueur is extremely versatile behind the bar and can be featured in cocktails, frappés and numerous specialty drinks.

PIÑA COLADA, CHOCOLATE (2)
House specialty glass, chilled
Pour ingredients into blender
3/4 oz. Spiced Rum
3/4 oz. Gold Rum
3/4 oz. Mount Gay Eclipse Rum
3/4 oz. Kahlúa
3/4 oz. chocolate syrup
1 3/4 oz. coconut cream syrup
2 oz. pineapple juice
2 scoops vanilla ice cream
Blend ingredients (with ice optional)
Float 3/4 oz. Godiva Chocolate Liqueur
Pineapple wedge and cherry garnish

PIÑA COLADA, EMERALD ISLE
House specialty glass, chilled
Pour ingredients into blender
1 3/4 oz. Mount Gay Eclipse Rum
1 oz. Malibu Caribbean Rum
1 oz. Blue Curaçao
2 oz. coconut cream syrup
4 oz. pineapple juice
1 scoop vanilla ice cream
Blend ingredients (with ice optional)
Float 3/4 oz. Gosling's Black Seal Rum
Pineapple wedge and cherry garnish

PIÑA COLADA, FRENCH
House specialty glass, chilled
Pour ingredients into blender
1 3/4 oz. Rhum Barbancourt 5-Star
3/4 oz. VS Cognac
3/4 oz. Crème de Cassis
3/4 oz. half & half cream
1 oz. coconut cream syrup
1 1/2 oz. orange juice
2 oz. pineapple juice
Blend with ice
Pineapple wedge and cherry garnish

PIÑA COLADA, FRUIT (BASIC)
House specialty glass, chilled
Pour ingredients into blender
1 1/2 oz. Light Rum
1/2 cup requested fruit
2 oz. coconut cream syrup
3 oz. pineapple juice
Blend with ice
Fresh fruit garnish

PIÑA COLADA, FUNKY MONKEY
House specialty glass, chilled
Pour ingredients into blender
Rim glass with grenadine and
   shaved coconut
2 oz. Banana Rum
1 oz. Dark Crème de Cacao
1 ripe banana
2 oz. coconut cream syrup
3 oz. pineapple juice
Blend ingredients with ice
Pineapple wedge and cherry garnish

PIÑA COLADA, GOLDEN BACARDI
House specialty glass, chilled
Pour ingredients into blender
1 1/2 oz. Bacardi Gold Rum
3/4 oz. Bacardi Light Rum
3/4 oz. half & half cream
1 1/2 oz. orange juice
2 oz. coconut cream syrup
2 oz. pineapple juice
Blend with ice
Float 3/4 oz. Galliano Liqueur
Pineapple wedge and cherry garnish

PIÑA COLADA, HAWAIIAN LION
House specialty glass, chilled
Pour ingredients into blender
1 1/2 oz. Mount Gay Eclipse Rum
1 oz. Chambord
1/2 cup raspberries
2 oz. coconut cream syrup
3 oz. pineapple juice
Blend with ice
Float 3/4 oz. Kahlúa
Pineapple wedge and cherry garnish

PIÑA COLADA, HOLIDAY ISLE
House specialty glass, chilled
Pour ingredients into blender
1 1/4 oz. Bacardi 151° Rum
3/4 oz. Grand Marnier
2 scoops French vanilla ice cream
Blend ingredients (with ice optional)
Float 3/4 oz. Mount Gay Extra Old Rum
Pineapple wedge and cherry garnish

PIÑA COLADA, ITALIAN (1)
House specialty glass, chilled
Pour ingredients into blender
1 1/2 oz. Gold Rum
3/4 oz. Mount Gay Eclipse Rum
3/4 oz. half & half cream
2 oz. coconut cream syrup
3 oz. pineapple juice
Blend with ice
Float 3/4 oz. Disaronno Amaretto
Pineapple wedge and cherry garnish

PIÑA COLADA, ITALIAN (2)
House specialty glass, chilled
Pour ingredients into blender
1 1/2 oz. Limoncello Liqueur
3/4 oz. Gran Gala Liqueur
2 oz. coconut cream syrup
3 oz. pineapple juice
Blend ingredients (with ice optional)
Float 3/4 oz. Disaronno Amaretto
Pineapple wedge and cherry garnish

PIÑA COLADA, KAHLÚA
aka **Kahlúa Colada**
House specialty glass, chilled
Pour ingredients into blender
1 1/2 oz. Light Rum
3/4 oz. Kahlúa
3/4 oz. half & half cream
2 oz. coconut cream syrup
3 oz. pineapple juice
1 scoop vanilla ice cream
Blend ingredients (with ice optional)
Float 1 oz. Kahlúa
Pineapple wedge and cherry garnish

PIÑA COLADA, KÉKÉ COLADA
House specialty glass, chilled
Pour ingredients into blender
1 1/2 oz. KéKé Beach Cream Liqueur
1 1/2 oz. Rum
2 oz. coconut cream syrup
3 oz. pineapple juice
Blend with ice
Pineapple wedge and cherry garnish

PIÑA COLADA, KINGSTON
House specialty glass, chilled
Pour ingredients into blender
1 3/4 oz. Appleton Estate V/X Jamaica Rum
3/4 oz. Cointreau
1 1/2 oz. orange juice
1 1/2 oz. pineapple juice
2 oz. coconut cream syrup
Blend with ice
Float 3/4 oz. Tia Maria
Pineapple wedge and orange slice garnish

PIÑA COLADA, KOKOMO JOE
House specialty glass, chilled
Pour ingredients into blender
3/4 oz. Light Rum
3/4 oz. Gold Rum
3/4 oz. Mount Gay Eclipse Rum
3/4 oz. Crème de Banana
1 oz. orange juice
2 oz. coconut cream syrup
3 oz. pineapple juice
Blend with ice
Pineapple wedge and banana slice garnish

TEQUILA CORAZÓN®
DE AGAVE AÑEJO

In the spirit world, America's fascination with artisan 100% agave tequilas borders on the phenomenal. TEQUILA CORAZÓN DE AGAVE AÑEJO will serve only to fuel the trend. For those who are looking for a lush, elegant tequila to sip and enjoy, pull up a snifter and sample this handcrafted gem.

Tequila Corazón is distilled in the highlands of Arandas, which is widely considered to be among the most prestigious growing regions in Jalisco. The Corazón range of 100% agave tequilas is produced entirely on the sprawling Destiladora San Nicholas Estate using traditional, century-old methods.

The tequilas are made from mature, estate grown agaves. After harvesting, the hand-cultivated agaves are baked in stone ovens, slowly fermented and distilled in the estate's copper pot stills. The result is highly sophisticated spirits worthy of *grand cru* status.

Tequila Corazón Añejo is aged in small, Canadian oak barrels for up to 2 years. Its supple body has a velvet-like texture and an alluring floral and fruit bouquet. The tequila is brimming with spice, pepper and oaky vanilla that last well into the long, relaxed finish. The 80 proof tequila is packaged in a striking hand-blown decanter, a perfect presentation for an impressive, elegant spirit.

PIÑA COLADA, LEMONADA (1)
House specialty glass, chilled
Pour ingredients into blender
1 1/2 oz. Citrus Rum
1 1/4 oz. Limoncello Liqueur
1 oz. Amber Rum
2 oz. cranberry juice
2 oz. coconut cream syrup
2 oz. pineapple juice
Blend with ice
Pineapple wedge and cherry garnish

PIÑA COLADA, LEMONADA (2)
House specialty glass, chilled
Pour ingredients into blender
1 3/4 oz. Vanilla Rum
1 oz. Limoncello Liqueur
3/4 oz. Disaronno Amaretto
1 scoop vanilla ice cream
2 oz. coconut cream syrup
3 oz. pineapple juice
Blend ingredients (with ice optional)
Pineapple wedge and cherry garnish

PIÑA COLADA, LIQUEUR-FLAVORED
House specialty glass, chilled
Pour ingredients into blender
1 oz. Light Rum
1 oz. requested liqueur
2 oz. coconut cream syrup
3 oz. pineapple juice
3/4 oz. half & half cream (optional)
Blend with ice
Pineapple wedge and cherry garnish

PIÑA COLADA, LT. KIJE'S
House specialty glass, chilled
Pour ingredients into blender
1 1/2 oz. Absolut Kurant Vodka
1/2 oz. Cruzan Banana Rum
1/2 small ripe banana
1/2 cup strawberries
1 oz. coconut cream syrup
3 oz. pineapple juice
Blend with ice
Pineapple wedge garnish

PIÑA COLADA, MALIBU ORANGE
House specialty glass, chilled
Pour ingredients into blender
1 1/2 oz. Malibu Caribbean Rum
1 oz. Triple Sec
1 oz. orange juice
2 oz. coconut cream syrup
2 oz. pineapple juice
Blend with ice
Pineapple wedge and cherry garnish

PIÑA COLADA, MIDORI
aka **Green Eyes**
House specialty glass, chilled
Pour ingredients into blender
1 1/2 oz. Midori
1 1/2 oz. Citrus Rum
3/4 oz. half & half cream
2 oz. coconut cream syrup
3 oz. pineapple juice
Blend with ice
Pineapple wedge and cherry garnish

PIÑA COLADA, MONKALADA
Large house specialty glass, chilled
Pour ingredients into blender
1 oz. Appleton Estate V/X Jamaica Rum
1 oz. Mount Gay Eclipse Rum
1 oz. Cruzan Banana Run
2 oz. coconut cream syrup
2 oz. pineapple juice
2 scoops vanilla ice cream
Blend ingredients (with ice optional)
Float 1/2 oz. Tia Maria
Pineapple wedge and cherry garnish

PIÑA COLADA, PACIFIC BLUE
House specialty glass, chilled
Pour ingredients into blender
1 oz. Light Rum
1 3/4 oz. Hpnotiq Liqueur
2 oz. coconut cream syrup
3 oz. pineapple juice
Blend ingredients (with ice optional)
Float 3/4 oz. Blue Curaçao
Pineapple wedge and cherry garnish

PIÑA COLADA, PORT ROYAL
House specialty glass, chilled
Pour ingredients into blender
1 3/4 oz. Appleton Estate V/X Jamaica Rum
1 oz. Chambord
1 1/2 oz. strawberry juice
1 1/2 oz. orange juice
1 1/2 oz. pineapple juice
2 oz. coconut cream syrup
Blend with ice
Float 1 oz. Tia Maria
Pineapple wedge and strawberry garnish

PIÑA COLADA, PUSSER'S ISLAND
House specialty glass, chilled
Pour ingredients into blender
1 3/4 oz. Pusser's British Navy Rum
3/4 oz. Sloe Gin
2 oz. coconut cream syrup
3 1/2 oz. pineapple juice
Blend with ice
Pineapple wedge and cherry garnish

PIÑA COLADA, RÉMY COLADA
House specialty glass, chilled
Pour ingredients into blender
1 oz. Rémy Martin VS Cognac
1 oz. Mount Gay Eclipse Rum
2 oz. coconut cream syrup
4 oz. pineapple juice
Blend with ice
Pineapple wedge and cherry garnish

PIÑA COLADA, SPANISH
House specialty glass, chilled
Pour ingredients into blender
1 1/4 oz. Licor 43 (Cuarenta y Tres)
1 1/4 oz. Gold Rum
2 oz. coconut cream syrup
3 oz. pineapple juice
Blend with ice
Pineapple wedge and cherry garnish

PIÑA COLADA, STRAMARETTO
House specialty glass, chilled
Pour ingredients into blender
1 oz. Gold Rum
1 oz. Disaronno Amaretto
1/2 cup strawberries
3/4 oz. half & half cream
2 oz. coconut cream syrup
3 oz. pineapple juice
Blend with ice
Float 3/4 oz. Dark Rum
Pineapple wedge and strawberry garnish

PIÑA COLADA, STRAWBERRY BANANA
House specialty glass, chilled
Pour ingredients into blender
1 3/4 oz. Dark Rum
1 oz. Banana Rum
3/4 oz. Kahlúa
1 peeled, ripe banana
1 1/2 oz. coconut cream syrup
2 oz. pureed strawberries
2 oz. pineapple juice
Blend with ice
Pineapple wedge and cherry garnish
Whipped cream garnish (optional)

TANQUERAY®
LONDON DRY GIN

There is a mystique surrounding gin that no other light liquor evokes. To explain its nearly universal appeal, aficionados point to its light body, incomparable aroma and engaging and pervasive flavor. Few brands prove the point as well as TANQUERAY LONDON DRY GIN.

Created in 1830 by Charles Tanqueray, it has become one of the most successful spirit brands in the world, one still crafted according to the original recipe and blend of botanicals and aromatics. Tanqueray is distilled in Finsbury, England, which at one time was world-renowned for its health spa and pure, health-rejuvenating waters. The gin is still distilled in an exact replica of the copper pot still used at the gin's creation. It is bottled at 94.6 proof.

Tanqueray Gin is an intriguing, highly sophisticated spirit. It has crystalline clarity and a satiny, medium-weight body. The expansive bouquet is quite compelling, a complex of fresh, herbal aromas lightly sprinkled with a trace of sweetness. It immediately fills the mouth with a palate comprised of floral, herbal and spicy flavors that linger well into the long, relaxed finish.

From start to finish, Tanqueray Gin is a consummate performer. It is ideally suited for any cocktail requiring well-rounded flavor and a dry touch of elegance.

PIÑA COLADA, TOASTED ALMOND
House specialty glass, chilled
Pour ingredients into blender
1 1/4 oz. Gold Rum
3/4 oz. Kahlúa
3/4 oz. Disaronno Amaretto
3/4 oz. half & half cream
2 oz. coconut cream syrup
3 oz. pineapple juice
Blend with ice
Float 1/2 oz. Kahlúa
Float 1/2 oz. Disaronno Amaretto
Pineapple wedge and cherry garnish

PIÑA COLADA, TROPICAL MOON
House specialty glass, chilled
Pour ingredients into blender
1 1/2 oz. Light Rum
3/4 oz. Disaronno Amaretto
3/4 oz. Blue Curaçao
2 oz. coconut cream syrup
3 oz. pineapple juice
2 scoops chocolate ice cream
Blend ingredients (with ice optional)
Float 3/4 oz. Appleton Estate
  V/X Jamaica Rum
Pineapple wedge and cherry garnish

PIÑA COLADA, TROPICAL SPLASHES
House specialty glass, chilled
Pour ingredients into blender
1 oz. Mount Gay Eclipse Rum
2 oz. coconut cream syrup
3 oz. pineapple juice
1 scoop vanilla ice cream
Blend ingredients (with ice optional)
Float 1 oz. Appleton Estate
  V/X Jamaica Rum
Pineapple wedge and cherry garnish

PINEAPPLE FIZZ
Cocktail glass, chilled
Pour ingredients into iced mixing glass
1 3/4 oz. Dark Rum
3/4 oz. fresh lemon juice
2 oz. pineapple juice
Shake and strain
Orange slice garnish

PINEAPPLE SMOOCH
Cocktail glass, chilled
Pour ingredients into iced mixing glass
1 1/2 oz. RémyRed Red Berry Infusion
3/4 oz. Cointreau
2-3 dashes Angostura Bitters
2 oz. pineapple juice
Shake and strain
Orange twist garnish

PINK BABY
Cocktail glass, chilled
Pour ingredients into iced mixing glass
1 1/2 oz. Citrus Vodka
1/2 oz. RémyRed Red Berry Infusion
1/2 oz. fresh lemon juice
Stir and strain
Lemon twist garnish

PINK CADILLAC
Champagne glass, chilled
Pour ingredients into blender
1 oz. Chambord
1/2 oz. sweet 'n' sour
1/2 cup strawberry puree
Blend with ice
Fill with Champagne
Strawberry garnish

PINK COCONUT
Bucket glass, ice
Build in glass
1 3/4 oz. Coconut Rum
1 oz. Chambord
1 1/2 oz. pineapple juice
1 1/2 oz. orange juice
Lime wedge garnish

PINK CREOLE
Cocktail glass, chilled
Pour ingredients into iced mixing glass
1 1/4 oz. Dark Rum
3/4 oz. Chambord
1 oz. orange juice
1 oz. pineapple juice
1 oz. sweet 'n' sour
Shake and strain
Orange slice garnish

PINK FLAMINGO
House specialty glass, ice
Pour ingredients into iced mixing glass
1 1/2 oz. Raspberry Liqueur
2 oz. cranberry juice
2 oz. sweet 'n' sour
Shake and strain
Splash club soda

PINK GATOR
Bucket glass, ice
Build in glass
1 1/4 oz. Light Rum
1/2 fill orange juice
Near fill with pineapple juice
Float 3/4 oz. Raspberry Liqueur

PINK GIN
Cocktail glass, chilled
Pour ingredients into iced mixing glass
2 oz. Gin
3-4 dashes Angostura Bitters
Stir and strain
Splash water or club soda (optional)

PINK HIGHLITER
House specialty glass, ice
Pour ingredients into iced mixing glass
1 3/4 oz. Tequila
3/4 oz. Light Rum
3/4 oz. Banana Rum
2 oz. cranberry juice
2 oz. pineapple juice
Shake and strain
Orange slice and cherry garnish

PINK LADY (1)
Cocktail glass, chilled
Pour ingredients into iced mixing glass
1 oz. Gin
1/2 oz. grenadine
1 1/2 oz. half & half cream
Shake and strain

PINK LADY (2)
Cocktail glass, chilled
Pour ingredients into iced mixing glass
1 oz. Laird's Applejack Brandy
1 oz. Gin
1/2 oz. grenadine
1 1/2 oz. sweet 'n' sour
1 egg white (optional)
Shake and strain

PINK LEMONADE (1)
Rocks glass, chilled
Pour ingredients into iced mixing glass
1 1/2 oz. Vodka
1/2 oz. grapefruit juice
1/2 oz. cranberry juice
1/2 oz. sweet 'n' sour
Shake and strain

PINK LEMONADE (2)
House specialty glass, ice
Pour ingredients into iced mixing glass
1 1/4 oz. Citrus Rum
1 1/4 oz. Citrus Vodka
1/2 oz. grenadine
3 oz. lemonade
2 oz. cranberry juice
Shake and strain
Splash Seven-Up
Orange slice and cherry garnish

JIM BEAM®
WHITE LABEL BOURBON

An American institution, Jim Beam is the benchmark by which all other bourbons are measured. The Beam family has been distilling whiskey at their distillery in Clermont, Kentucky since 1795. It is among the largest and most sophisticated in the world. But for all of their technical sophistication, they have stayed true to the family tradition of quality and craftsmanship. Nothing illustrates this better than JIM BEAM WHITE LABEL BOURBON.

The best-selling bourbon in the world, Jim Beam White Label is distilled from a high proportion of white and yellow corn grown in Indiana and Kentucky, and lesser percentages of rye and malted barley. The other two crucial ingredients are sweet, limestone water from the Long Lick Creek and spontaneous-type yeast, discovered by Jim Beam himself.

The White Label Jim Beam bourbon is aged a minimum of 4 years in oak barrels. During that time it develops a soft, medium-weight body and an enticing bouquet of vanilla, baking spices, cocoa and toasted oak. On the palate, the whiskey reveals the savory flavors of caramel, vanilla, fruit and a hint of smoke. The finish is warm and relaxed.

Quality, price and versatility make Jim Beam White Label an absolute necessity behind the bar.

PINK MOMENT
Cocktail glass, chilled
Pour ingredients into iced mixing glass
1 1/2 oz. Vodka
1/2 oz. RémyRed Red Berry Infusion
1/2 oz. DeKuyper Peachtree Schnapps
1/2 oz. orange juice
1/2 oz. cranberry juice
1/2 oz. lemonade
Shake and strain
Whipped cream and peach wedge garnish

PINK PANTHER (1)
Tankard or pilsner glass, chilled
Build in glass
1/2 fill Guinness Stout
1/2 fill Raspberry-Flavored Ale

PINK PANTHER (2)
Champagne glass, chilled
Pour ingredients into iced mixing glass
1 1/4 oz. Disaronno Amaretto
1/4 oz. grenadine
1 oz. orange juice
1 1/2 oz. cranberry juice
Shake and strain
Fill with Champagne
Orange slice garnish

PINK PARADISE
House specialty glass, ice
Pour ingredients into iced mixing glass
1 oz. Appleton Estate V/X Jamaica Rum
1 oz. Mount Gay Eclipse Rum
1 oz. Disaronno Amaretto
1 1/2 oz. pineapple juice
3 oz. cranberry juice
Shake and strain
Pineapple wedge and cherry garnish

PINK PASSION
House specialty glass, ice
Build in glass
1 oz. Captain Morgan Spiced Rum
1 oz. Malibu Caribbean Rum
1/2 oz. grenadine
2 oz. orange juice
2 oz. pineapple juice
Orange slice and cherry garnish

PINK SLIPPER
House specialty glass, chilled
Pour ingredients into blender
1 1/2 oz. Light Rum
3/4 oz. Gold Rum
1 1/2 oz. coconut cream syrup
3 oz. pink lemonade concentrate
Blend with ice
Whipped cream garnish
Drizzle 3/4 oz. Chambord

PINK SQUIRREL
Cocktail glass, chilled
Pour ingredients into iced mixing glass
3/4 oz. White Crème de Cacao
3/4 oz. Crème de Noyaux
2 oz. half & half cream
Shake and strain

PINK SUNSET
Bucket glass, ice
Build in glass
1 1/4 oz. Vodka
3/4 oz. Grand Marnier
1/2 oz. fresh lemon juice
1 1/2 oz. grapefruit juice
1 1/2 oz. cranberry juice
Kiwi slice garnish

PIRANHA
House specialty glass, ice
Pour ingredients into iced mixing glass
3/4 oz. Light Rum
3/4 oz. Gold Rum
3/4 oz. Malibu Caribbean Rum
1 oz. grapefruit juice
1 oz. cranberry juice
1 oz. pineapple juice
Shake and strain
Orange slice and cherry garnish

PIRANHA CLUB INITIATION
Bucket glass, ice
Build in glass
1 1/2 oz. 151° Rum
3/4 oz. Blue Curaçao
1/2 oz. Peach Schnapps
1 1/2 oz. sweet 'n' sour
Near fill with orange juice
Float 3/4 oz. Dark Rum

PIRANHA PUNCH
Punch Bowl, ice
Build in bowl
26 oz. Dark Rum
12 oz. Gold Rum
12 oz. fresh lime juice
12 oz. strawberry syrup
32 oz. orange juice
32 oz. pineapple juice
32 oz. mango or peach nectar
Thoroughly stir ingredients
Lime, lemon and orange wedge garnish

PIRATE LOVE
House specialty glass, chilled
Pour ingredients into blender
1 1/2 oz. Pyrat XO Reserve Rum
3/4 oz. Tia Maria
3/4 oz. Disaronno Amaretto
1 tsp. vanilla extract
2 scoops vanilla ice cream
Blend ingredients (with ice optional)
Whipped cream garnish
Sprinkle shaved chocolate

PIRATE'S HICCUP
Bucket glass, ice
Build in glass
1 1/2 oz. Vanilla Rum
3/4 oz. Kahlúa
1/2 fill cola
1/2 fill half & half cream

PISCO SOUR
Sour glass, chilled
Rim glass with sugar (optional)
Pour ingredients into iced mixing glass
3 dashes Angostura Bitters
1 1/4 oz. Pisco Brandy
2 oz. sweet 'n' sour
Shake and strain
Orange slice and cherry garnish

PISTACHIO MINT ICE CREAM
House specialty glass, chilled
Pour ingredients into blender
3/4 oz. Frangelico
3/4 oz. Green Crème de Menthe
3/4 oz. Kahlúa
2 scoops vanilla ice cream
Blend ingredients (with ice optional)
Mint leaf garnish

PITLESS SHOT
Presentation shot glass, chilled
Build in glass
1/3 fill Peach Schnapps
1/3 fill Vodka
1/3 fill orange juice

PIZZETTI
Champagne glass, chilled
Build in glass
1/4 fill orange juice
1/4 fill grapefruit juice
Fill with Champagne

PEARL® LO COCO VODKA

It only stands to reason that the first coconut-flavored vodka would be created by the innovators at Pearl. It seems that they've been ahead of the curve for years. The 2004 introduction of PEARL LO COCO VODKA will only solidify their reputation.

The Pearl Vodka Distillery is located high in the Canadian Rockies. Its award winning vodka is distilled in small batches from Canadian winter wheat and soft, mountain spring water. The wheat is meticulously scrutinized for its quality and consistency. Pure coconut oil essence is added to create Lo Coco. In total, Pearl Vodka is distilled five times and subjected to repeated purification. The result is a refreshing and essentially pure 70 proof vodka.

Pearl Lo Coco Vodka is a light and vibrantly flavorful spirit, singular in character among the other top-shelf players. The perfectly clear vodka has a medium-weight, ideally textured body. As expected, the alluring aroma of fresh coconuts dominates the bouquet. The vodka rolls over the palate delivering its flavor payload with nary a trace of sweetness. The vodka finishes long, cool and flavorful.

Pearl Lo Coco Vodka is especially well cast as the star performer in a broad range of signature cocktails. Give it an audition and see if you don't agree.

PLANTER'S PUNCH (1)
House specialty glass, ice
Pour ingredients into iced mixing glass
1 1/2 oz. Dark Jamaican Rum
1/2 oz. grenadine
2 dashes Angostura Bitters
1 1/2 oz. sweet 'n' sour
1 1/2 oz. orange juice
Shake and strain
Orange slice and cherry garnish

PLANTER'S PUNCH (2)
House specialty glass, ice
Pour ingredients into iced mixing glass
1 1/2 oz. Appleton Estate V/X Jamaica Rum
1 oz. Light Rum
3/4 oz. Triple Sec
2-3 dashes Angostura Bitters
1/2 oz. grenadine
1/2 oz. Rose's Lime Juice
2 oz. orange juice
2 oz. pineapple juice
Shake and strain
Lime, lemon and orange wedge garnish

PLANTER'S PUNCH (3)
House specialty glass, ice
Pour ingredients into iced mixing glass
1 1/2 oz. Appleton Estate V/X Jamaica Rum
1 1/4 oz. Bacardi Select Rum
3/4 oz. Orange Curaçao
2-3 dashes Angostura Bitters
3/4 oz. fresh lime juice
1/2 oz. grenadine
1 1/2 oz. orange juice
1 1/2 oz. pineapple juice
Shake and strain
Float 3/4 oz. Mount Gay Eclipse Rum
Lime, lemon and orange wedge garnish

PLANTER'S RUM PUNCH
House specialty glass, ice
Pour ingredients into iced mixing glass
2 oz. Myers's Jamaican Rum
1 oz. simple syrup
3 dashes Angostura Bitters
3/4 oz. fresh lime juice
2 oz. fresh water
Shake and strain
Sprinkle nutmeg
Lemon wedge garnish

PLATA V.I.P. COCKTAIL
Bucket glass, ice
Build in glass
1 1/2 oz. Sauza Tres Generaciones
    Plata Tequila
Fill with Squirt (grapefruit) soda
Orange wedge garnish

PLYMOUTH ROCKS
Bucket glass, ice
Build in glass
1 1/2 oz. Light Rum
1/2 fill grape juice
1/2 fill club soda
Lime wedge garnish

POIREISSE
Champagne glass, chilled
Build in glass
3/4 oz. Poire William (Eau de Vie de Poire)
3/4 oz. Godiva Chocolate Liqueur
Fill with Champagne

POM POM
Wine glass, ice
Pour ingredients into iced mixing glass
1 1/2 oz. sweet 'n' sour
4 1/2 oz. lemonade
1 egg white (optional)
1/2 oz. grenadine
Shake and strain
Fill with club soda
Lemon wedge garnish

POPE ON VACATION
Rocks glass, chilled
Pour ingredients into iced mixing glass
1/2 oz. Frangelico
1/2 oz. Malibu Caribbean Rum
1/2 oz. Jamaican Rum
1/2 oz. Chambord
3/4 oz. orange juice
3/4 oz. sweet 'n' sour
Shake and strain

POPPYCOCK ROCK
Presentation shot glass, chilled
Layer ingredients
1/3 fill Kahlúa
1/3 fill Chilled Peppermint Schnapps
1/3 fill Raspberry Liqueur

PORT AND LEMON
Wine glass, chilled
Build in glass
2 oz. Tawny Port
Fill with Seven-Up

PORT IN A STORM
Wine glass or house specialty glass, ice
Pour ingredients into iced mixing glass
2 oz. Tawny Port
3/4 oz. Brandy
4 oz. Dry Red Wine
Stir and strain
Mint sprig garnish

PORT O' CALL
Bucket glass, ice
Build in glass
1 1/2 oz. Tawny Port
Near fill with cranberry juice
Splash orange juice

POT O' GOLD
Presentation shot glass, chilled
Build in glass
1/2 fill Goldschläger
1/2 fill Baileys Irish Cream

POUSSE CAFÉ (1)
Cordial or sherry glass, chilled
Layer ingredients
1/5 fill grenadine
1/5 fill Green Crème de Menthe
1/5 fill Triple Sec
1/5 fill Sloe Gin
1/5 fill Brandy

POUSSE CAFÉ (2)
Cordial or sherry glass, chilled
Layer ingredients
1/6 fill grenadine
1/6 fill Yellow Chartreuse
1/6 fill White Crème de Menthe
1/6 fill Apricot Brandy
1/6 fill Green Chartreuse
1/6 fill Brandy

POUSSE CAFÉ (3)
Cordial or sherry glass, chilled
Layer ingredients
1/7 fill grenadine
1/7 fill Kahlúa
1/7 fill White Crème de Menthe
1/7 fill Blue Curaçao
1/7 fill Galliano Liqueur
1/7 fill Green Chartreuse
1/7 fill Brandy

POUSSE CAFÉ, FOUR-WAY
Cordial or sherry glass, chilled
Layer ingredients
1/4 fill Kahlúa
1/4 fill White Crème de Menthe
1/4 fill Galliano Liqueur
1/4 fill Baileys Irish Cream

POUSSE CAFÉ, TUACA
Cordial or sherry glass, chilled
Layer ingredients
1/4 fill grenadine
1/4 fill White Crème de Menthe
1/4 fill Midori
1/4 fill Tuaca

DEKUYPER®
ISLAND BLUE PUCKER®

If someone doesn't have a good time with DEKUYPER ISLAND BLUE PUCKER behind the bar, check his or her pulse and call a medic. This new, brilliantly colored schnapps is an unpretentious, great tasting product that's chaffing at the bit to have some fun.

Island Blue Pucker is one of a line of similarly concocted sweet 'n' sour schnapps. What differentiates the Pucker line of schnapps from the rest of the field is that they are brimming with tart and zesty flavor, just enough zing to make them something special.

There is simply nothing else behind the bar to compare with this spry, Pacific blue schnapps. The taste is a refreshing blast of citrus and a hint of pineapple with the trademark sweet and sour finish. Its tangy flavor persists on the palate for an impressively long time and is completely free of any cloying sweetness.

This latest addition to the Pucker family is tailor-made for life behind bars and is capable of giving a cocktail the blues without adding unwanted sweetness. It is a popular addition in specialty drinks, everything from specialty Cosmopolitans, Margaritas and Martinis, to Piña Coladas, Daiquiris and Gimlets. Add up its attributes and you've got a back bar winner.

PRAIRIE FIRE
Presentation shot glass, chilled
Build in glass
1 1/4 oz. Gold Tequila
5 dashes Tabasco Sauce

PRAIRIE OYSTER (1)
Rocks glass
Build in glass
1 1/2 oz. Brandy (optional)
1 egg yolk (optional)
2 dashes wine vinegar
1 tsp. Worcestershire sauce
2 dashes Tabasco Sauce
1/2 tsp. salt
2 oz. tomato juice
Stir gently, do not break egg yolk

PRAIRIE OYSTER (2)
Rocks glass, chilled
Build in glass
1 1/2 oz. Chile-infused Vodka
3 dashes Tabasco Sauce
1 tsp. oyster sauce
1 raw oyster

PRESBYTERIAN
Highball glass, ice
Build in glass
1 1/4 oz. requested liquor
1/2 fill ginger ale
1/2 fill club soda

PRESIDENTÉ
Cocktail glass, chilled
Pour ingredients into iced mixing glass
1 1/2 oz. Light Rum
1/2 oz. Dry Vermouth
1/2 oz. Sweet Vermouth
1/2 oz. Cointreau
2 dashes grenadine
Stir and strain
Lemon twist garnish

PRESIDENTIAL JUICE
Rocks glass, ice
Build in glass
1 3/4 oz. Patrón Silver Tequila
3/4 oz. Patrón XO Café Coffee Liqueur
3/4 oz. Baileys Irish Cream

PRESUMPTION COCKTAIL
Cocktail glass, chilled
Pour ingredients into iced mixing glass
1 1/4 oz. Wet by Beefeater
1/2 oz. Cointreau
3/4 oz. fresh lime juice
3/4 oz. sweet 'n' sour
Shake and strain
Orange slice garnish

PRIMAL SHOOTER
Presentation shot glass, chilled
Layer ingredients
1/2 fill Patrón XO Café Coffee Liqueur
1/2 fill Light Rum

PRIMO BACIO
Champagne glass, chilled
Pour ingredients into iced mixing glass
1 oz. Absolut Citron Vodka
1/2 oz. Chambord
1 oz. sweet 'n' sour
1 oz. orange juice
Shake and strain
Fill with Champagne
Orange twist garnish

PRINCESS MARGARET
House specialty glass, chilled
Pour ingredients into blender
Rim glass with grenadine and sugar
(optional)
1 1/2 oz. sweet 'n' sour
1 1/2 oz. orange juice
3 dashes raspberry syrup
6 strawberries
1 pineapple slice
Blend with ice
Strawberry garnish

PROVINCE TOWN
House specialty glass, ice
Pour ingredients into iced mixing glass
1 oz. Vodka
1/2 oz. Citrus Vodka
2 oz. grapefruit juice
2 oz. cranberry juice
Shake and strain
Fill with club soda
Lemon wedge garnish

PUCCINI
Champagne glass, chilled
Build in glass
1/2 fill tangerine juice
1/2 fill Champagne

PUCKER-UP
Presentation shot glass, chilled
Build in glass
1/3 fill Cruzan Rum Cream
1/3 fill DeKuyper Raspberry Pucker
1/3 fill Cruzan Estate Diamond Rum

PULLMAN PORTER
House specialty glass, chilled
Pour ingredients into blender
1 1/2 oz. Vodka
1/2 oz. grenadine
1 oz. lemonade concentrate
2 scoops raspberry sorbet
Blend ingredients (with ice optional)
Berries garnish

PURPLE DEATH
Pilsner glass, chilled 16 oz.
Build in glass
3/4 fill Bass Ale
1 oz. Chambord
Top with Cider

PURPLE FLIRT
Rocks glass, chilled
Pour ingredients into iced mixing glass
1 oz. Dark Rum
1/4 oz. Blue Curaçao
1/2 oz. sweet 'n' sour
1/4 oz. grenadine
1 oz. pineapple juice
Shake and strain
Orange slice and cherry garnish

PURPLE HOOTER (1)
Cocktail glass, chilled
Pour ingredients into iced mixing glass
1 oz. Vodka
1/2 oz. Triple Sec
1/2 oz. Chambord
1/4 oz. Rose's Lime Juice
Shake and strain
Lime wedge garnish

PURPLE HOOTER (2)
Rocks glass, chilled
Pour ingredients into iced mixing glass
1 oz. Vodka
1 oz. Chambord
1 oz. sweet 'n' sour
Shake and strain
Splash Seven-Up

PURPLE MATADOR
Sherry glass, chilled
Pour ingredients into iced mixing glass
1 1/2 oz. Disaronno Amaretto
1/2 oz. Chambord
1/2 oz. pineapple juice
Shake and strain

JAMESON®
IRISH WHISKEY

Irish whiskey remains one of the most popular types of spirits in the world, and the best-selling brand of Irish whiskey—by a wide margin—is JAMESON IRISH WHISKEY. The brand's namesake, John Jameson, began crafting whiskey at the Bow Street Distillery he built in the heart of Dublin in 1780 and the whiskey has become something of a phenomenon ever since.

Jameson Irish Whiskey is a blend of grain, and malted and unmalted barley whiskies, triple-distilled in both pot and continuous stills. The blend is aged a minimum of 6 years in American oak barrels and sherry casks. The result is a magnificently light and accessible whiskey. Its lush bouquet is an alluring mix of honey and fruit. On the palate, the whiskey presents a delicious array of semisweet flavors, including toasted oak, vanilla, fruit and a hint of caramel. The finish is soft, relaxed and of medium-duration.

Jameson has extended its line with the release of several other stellar Irish whiskies, including JAMESON 1780, an elegant, 12 year old blend comprised of higher proportions of pot-still and sherry cask finished whiskies; and the appropriately named JAMESON GOLD, an ultra-premium blend of pure pot still whiskies aged in both new and seasoned oak casks.

PURPLE PASSION
Bucket glass, ice
Build in glass
1 oz. DeKuyper Peach Pucker
1/3 fill orange juice
1/3 fill cranberry juice
Near fill with pineapple juice
Float 3/4 oz. Razzmatazz Raspberry Liqueur

PURPLE PEOPLE BEEFEATER
House specialty glass, chilled
Pour ingredients into blender
1 3/4 oz. Beefeater London Dry Gin
1 oz. Chambord
1/2 oz. Rose's Lime Juice
1 1/2 oz. sweet 'n' sour
2 oz. cranberry juice
Blend with ice
Lime wedge garnish

PURPLE PIRANHA
House specialty glass, ice
Pour ingredients into iced mixing glass
3/4 oz. Light Rum
3/4 oz. Gold Rum
3/4 oz. Mount Gay Eclipse Rum
1 oz. Blue Curaçao
1 oz. cranberry juice
1 3/4 oz. sweet 'n' sour
Shake and strain
Float 3/4 oz. 151° Rum
Orange slice and cherry garnish

PUSSER'S DAILY RATION
House specialty glass, ice
Pour ingredients into iced mixing glass
2 oz. Pusser's British Navy Rum
1/2 oz. fresh lime juice
2 oz. sweet 'n' sour
Shake and strain
Fill with lemon/lime soda
Lime wedge garnish

PUSSER'S PAIN KILLER
House specialty glass, chilled
Pour ingredients into blender
2 oz. Pusser's British Navy Rum
1 oz. coconut cream syrup
1 oz. orange juice
4 oz. pineapple juice
Blend with ice
Sprinkle nutmeg

PUSSER'S STALEMATE
Coffee mug, heated
Build in glass
1 1/2 oz. Pusser's British Navy Rum
1/2 oz. Patrón XO Café Coffee Liqueur
1/2 oz. Dark Crème de Cacao
Near fill with hot chocolate
Whipped cream garnish
Sprinkle shaved chocolate

PUTTING ON THE RITZ
Cocktail glass, chilled
Pour ingredients into iced mixing glass
1 3/4 oz. Patrón Silver Tequila
1/2 oz. DeKuyper Peachtree Schnapps
3/4 oz. cranberry juice
1 1/2 oz. sweet 'n' sour
Shake and strain
Lemon twist garnish

PYRAT PETE COCKTAIL
Cocktail glass, chilled
Pour ingredients into iced mixing glass
1 3/4 oz. Pyrat XO Reserve Rum
3/4 oz. Citrónge Orange Liqueur
1/2 oz. Rose's Lime Juice
1 oz. grapefruit juice
1 oz. sweet 'n' sour
Shake and strain
Lime wedge garnish

QUAALUDE
Rocks glass, chilled
Pour ingredients into iced mixing glass
1/2 oz. Vodka
1/2 oz. Frangelico
1/2 oz. Kahlúa
1/2 oz. Dark Crème de Cacao
3/4 oz. half & half cream
Shake and strain

QUAALUDE, ALASKAN
Rocks glass, ice
Build in glass
1 1/2 oz. Vodka
1/2 oz. White Crème de Cacao
1/2 oz. Frangelico

QUAALUDE, IRANIAN
Rocks glass, chilled
Pour ingredients into iced mixing glass
1/2 oz. Vodka
1/2 oz. Kahlúa
1/2 oz. Baileys Irish Cream
1/2 oz. Disaronno Amaretto
1/2 oz. Frangelico
Shake and strain

QUAALUDE, IRISH
Presentation shot glass, chilled
Build in glass
1/2 oz. Vodka
1/2 oz. Baileys Irish Cream
1/2 oz. Frangelico
1/2 oz. Dark Crème de Cacao

QUAALUDE, RUSSIAN
Rocks glass, chilled
Build in glass
1/2 oz. Stolichnaya Vodka
1/2 oz. Frangelico
1/2 oz. Kahlúa
1/2 oz. Baileys Irish Cream

QUARTER DECK
aka **QuarterMaster**
Rocks glass, ice
Build in glass
1 oz. Appleton Estate V/X Jamaica Rum
1 oz. Mount Gay Eclipse Rum
3/4 oz. Sherry
1 dash Rose's Lime Juice
Lime wedge garnish

RABID DOG
Beer mug, chilled
Build in glass
3/4 oz. Bourbon
3/4 oz. Disaronno Amaretto
Fill with Draft Beer

RAINBOW HOLIDAY CUP
House specialty glass, ice
Build in glass
1 1/2 oz. Light Rum
1/4 oz. Cinnamon Schnapps
2 dashes bitters
2 dashes grenadine
4 oz. orange juice
Fill with club soda
Orange slice and cinnamon stick garnish

RAINBOW INTERNATIONAL COCKTAIL
Cocktail glass, chilled
Pour ingredients into iced mixing glass
1/2 oz. Dry Sack Sherry
2-3 dashes Angostura Bitters
2 1/2 oz. Gentleman Jack
 Tennessee Whiskey
Stir and strain
Orange twist garnish

RAINBOW SHOOTER (1)
Presentation shot glass, chilled
Layer ingredients
1/3 fill Crème de Noyaux
1/3 fill Midori
1/3 fill White Crème de Menthe

RÉMYRED®
GRAPE BERRY INFUSION

RémyRed is one of the most popular fruit liqueurs and their stock is about to take a giant leap skyward. In late 2003, Rémy Martin introduced RÉMYRED GRAPE BERRY INFUSION, a new, creative version of their highly successful liqueur. Like the original, RémyRed Grape Berry Infusion is generating rave reviews, both as a mixable ingredient and as a fashionable cocktail.

This lively contemporary liqueur is made in the cognac region of France from an infusion of vine-ripened grapes, blueberries and apples. Natural fruit juices are then added to the mix. The crowning touch is the addition of famed Rémy Martin Fine Champagne Cognac, a blend of aged Grande and Petite Champagne cognacs.

Everything about RémyRed Grape Berry Infusion is singular and imminently appealing. The liqueur is opaque with a vibrant purple hue. It has a voluptuously full body and an alluring bouquet that features the aromas of fresh grapes, citrus and a prominent apple finish. The liqueur lilts over the palate immediately filling the mouth with vibrant, slightly tart flavors. As is the case with the original RémyRed, the cognac base is pivotal in balancing out the natural sweetness in the juice.

This new addition to the RémyRed range is marvelous served chilled as an aperitif or used in a broad array of classy cocktails.

RAINBOW SHOOTER (2)
Rocks glass, chilled
Build in glass
3/4 oz. Malibu Caribbean Rum
3/4 oz. Midori
3/4 oz. Crème de Noyaux

RAIN MAN
House specialty glass, ice
Pour ingredients into iced mixing glass
1 1/4 oz. Dark Rum
3/4 oz. Midori
4 oz. orange juice
Shake and strain
Orange slice garnish

RAMOS FIZZ
House specialty glass, ice
Pour ingredients into iced mixing glass
1 oz. Gin
1 oz. sweet 'n' sour
3 oz. half & half cream
1 egg white (optional)
1/2 oz. simple syrup
2 dashes orange flower water
Shake and strain
Splash club soda
Orange twist garnish

RANCHO VALENCIA RUM PUNCH
Wine goblet, ice
Pour ingredients into iced mixing glass
1 oz. Light Rum
1 oz. Mount Gay Eclipse Rum
2-3 dashes Angostura Bitters
1 1/2 oz. pineapple juice
1 1/2 oz. orange juice
Shake and strain
Float 3/4 oz. Appleton Estate
    V/X Jamaica Rum
Lime, lemon and orange wedge garnish

RANDY BRANDY EGG NOG
House specialty glass, ice
Pour ingredients into iced mixing glass
1 1/2 oz. Christian Brothers Brandy
1 oz. Whaler's Original Vanille Rum
1 tsp. sugar
1 egg (optional)
4 oz. half & half cream
Shake and strain
Sprinkle nutmeg

RASPBERRY BANANA SPLIT
House specialty glass, chilled
Object is to create a 3-layer drink
1—*Pour ingredients into blender*
1 oz. Kahlúa
1 scoop vanilla ice cream
Blend ingredients (with ice optional)
Pour first drink into glass 1/3 full
2—*Pour ingredients into blender*
1 oz. Crème de Banana
1 scoop vanilla ice cream
Blend ingredients (with ice optional)
Pour second drink into glass 2/3 full
3—*Pour ingredients into blender*
1 oz. Chambord
1 scoop vanilla ice cream
Blend ingredients (with ice optional)
Fill glass with third drink
Whipped cream garnish

RASPBERRY CREAM
House specialty glass, chilled
Pour ingredients into blender
1 oz. Light Rum
3/4 oz. White Crème de Cacao
1/2 oz. Chambord
1 1/2 oz. raspberry yogurt
1 1/2 oz. half & half cream
2 scoops raspberry ice cream
Blend ingredients (with ice optional)
Whipped cream garnish
Drizzle 1/2 oz. Chambord

RASPBERRY KISS
House specialty glass, ice
Pour ingredients into iced mixing glass
6 oz. cran-raspberry drink (Ocean Spray)
1 oz. orange juice
1/2 oz. Rose's Lime Juice
Shake and strain
Fill with club soda

RASPBERRY SOUR
House specialty glass, ice
Pour ingredients into iced mixing glass
1 3/4 oz. Irish Whiskey
3/4 oz. Grand Marnier
1 oz. orange juice
2 oz. sweet 'n' sour
Shake and strain
Whipped cream garnish
Drizzle 3/4 oz. Chambord

RASPBERRY SWEET TART
Rocks glass, chilled
Pour ingredients into iced mixing glass
1 oz. Chambord
1 oz. Triple Sec
1 oz. Rose's Lime Juice
Stir and strain
Lime wedge garnish

RASPBERRY TORTE
Cordial or sherry glass, chilled
Layer ingredients
1/2 fill Chambord
1/2 fill Vox Raspberry Vodka

RASTA MAN
Presentation shot glass, chilled
Layer ingredients
1/3 fill Tia Maria
1/3 fill Godiva Chocolate Liqueur
1/3 fill Baileys Irish Cream

RASTA SPLEEF
Bucket glass, ice
Build in glass
1 1/2 oz. Myers's Jamaican Rum
2 oz. orange juice
Fill with pineapple juice

RAZORBACK HOGCALLER
Rocks glass, ice
Build in glass
1 1/2 oz. 151° Rum
1/2 oz. Green Chartreuse

RAZTINI
Rocks glass, chilled
Pour ingredients into iced mixing glass
1 1/2 oz. Chambord
1/2 oz. Vodka
1/2 oz. Orange Liqueur
1 oz. sweet 'n' sour
Shake and strain

RAZZLE DAZZLE
Highball glass, ice
Build in glass
1 1/4 oz. Razzmatazz Raspberry Liqueur
Near fill with cranberry juice
Splash club soda

RAZZLE DAZZLE ROSE
Cocktail glass, chilled
Pour ingredients into iced mixing glass
1 1/2 oz. Vodka
1/2 oz. Razzmatazz Raspberry Liqueur
1/2 oz. raspberry puree
1 1/2 oz. sweet 'n' sour
Shake and strain
Raspberry garnish

RAZZMATAZZ
Rocks glass, ice
Build in glass
1 oz. Disaronno Amaretto
1 oz. Razzmatazz Raspberry Liqueur

CRUZAN® MANGO RUM

If it's true that variety is the spice of life, then the new cocktail-friendly CRUZAN MANGO RUM will jazz things up for years to come. This brilliantly flavored spirit is the latest release from Caribbean rum giant Cruzan, who over the past several years has been releasing one tremendous rum after another.

Made in St. Croix in the U.S. Virgin Islands, this latest flavor sensation is produced from a blend of triple-distilled rums aged in oak bourbon barrels between 2 and 3 years. After aging, the rum is filtered through activated charcoal to remove impurities and any color. Natural mango flavorings are added to create the finished product.

Cruzan Mango Rum is a feast for the senses. It has a lightweight body with a ripe mango bouquet and a touch of natural fruit sweetness in the relaxed finish. Everything about this flavored gem screams of fun, which clearly is why it was created.

The other flavored rums in the range include CRUZAN COCONUT, CRUZAN BANANA, CRUZAN PINEAPPLE, CRUZAN ORANGE, CRUZAN VANILLA and the dry and tangy CRUZAN CITRUS. Because they are relatively low in alcohol (55 proof), their fruit flavors stay on the palate for a considerably long time making them ideal for drink making.

RAZZPUTENEE
Presentation shot glass, chilled
Build in glass
Rim glass with salt (optional)
1 oz. Silver Tequila
1/2 oz. Razzmatazz Raspberry Liqueur
1/4 oz. cranberry juice

RECESSION DEPRESSION
Cocktail glass, chilled
Pour ingredients into iced mixing glass
1 1/2 oz. Grey Goose Le Citron Vodka
1/2 oz. Cointreau
1/2 oz. fresh lemon juice
3 dashes Rose's Lime Juice
Stir and strain
Lime wedge garnish

RED BEER
aka **Tom Boy**
Beer glass or mug, chilled
Build in glass
Near fill with Draft Beer
2 oz. Bloody Mary mix or tomato juice

RED BEER SHOOTER
Presentation shot glass, chilled
Build in glass
3 dashes Tabasco Sauce
1/2 fill Draft Beer
1/2 fill Bloody Mary mix

RED DEATH
Presentation shot glass, chilled
Build in glass
1/2 oz. Vodka
1/2 oz. Cinnamon Schnapps
1/2 oz. Yukon Jack Liqueur
1/2 oz. 151° Rum

RED DEVIL
Rocks glass, chilled
Pour ingredients into iced mixing glass
1/2 oz. Disaronno Amaretto
1/2 oz. Southern Comfort
1/2 oz. Sloe Gin
1/2 oz. Vodka
1/2 oz. Triple Sec
Splash Rose's Lime Juice
Splash cranberry juice
Shake and strain

RED ECLIPSE
Bucket glass, ice
Build in glass
2 oz. RémyRed Red Berry Infusion
Near fill with orange juice
Float 3/4 oz. Chambord
Orange slice garnish

RED HAWAIIAN SUNSET
House specialty glass, ice
Pour ingredients into iced mixing glass
2 oz. RedRum
3/4 oz. Triple Sec
1 oz. coconut syrup
3 oz. pineapple juice
Shake and strain
Float 3/4 oz. grenadine
Pineapple wedge garnish

RED LION
Cocktail glass, chilled
Rim glass with sugar (optional)
Pour ingredients into iced mixing glass
1 oz. Gin
3/4 oz. Grand Marnier
1 oz. sweet 'n' sour
1 oz. orange juice
Shake and strain

RED RHUMBA
House specialty glass, chilled
Pour ingredients into blender
2 oz. RedRum
3/4 oz. Triple Sec
3/4 oz. grenadine
1 ripe banana
1 oz. orange juice
3 oz. pineapple juice
Blend ingredients with ice
Pineapple wedge and cherry garnish

RED RUSSIAN
Rocks glass, ice
Build in glass
1 1/2 oz. Vodka
3/4 oz. Cherry Heering

RED SKY
House specialty glass, chilled
Pour ingredients into blender
1 1/2 oz. Vodka
1 3/4 oz. RémyRed Red Berry Infusion
2 oz. cranberry juice
2 scoops vanilla ice cream
Blend ingredients (with ice optional)
Pineapple wedge garnish

RED TAIL DRAGON
House specialty glass, ice
Pour ingredients into iced mixing glass
1 oz. Midori
1/2 oz. Gin
1/2 oz. Rum
3/4 oz. grenadine
2 oz. sweet 'n' sour
Shake and strain
Lime wedge garnish

RED ZIPPER
Bucket glass, ice
Build in glass
3/4 oz. Galliano Liqueur
3/4 oz. Vodka
Fill with cranberry juice

REEF AND TIDE WATER
Cocktail glass, chilled
Pour ingredients into iced mixing glass
2 oz. Tarantula Azul
3/4 oz. Cointreau
1/2 oz. fresh lime juice
Stir and strain
Float 1/2 oz. Blue Curaçao
Lime wedge garnish

REGGAE SUNSPLASH
House specialty glass, ice
Build in glass
1 1/4 oz. Citrus Vodka
1/2 oz. Malibu Caribbean Rum
1/2 oz. Crème de Cassis
1/2 oz. grenadine
2 oz. orange juice
Fill with club soda

REGGAE WALKER
House specialty glass, chilled
Pour ingredients into blender
1 1/4 oz. Peach Schnapps
3 oz. pineapple juice
Blend with ice
Float 3/4 oz. Tia Maria
Pineapple wedge and cherry garnish

RELEASE VALVE
Highball glass, ice
Build in glass
3/4 oz. Vodka
3/4 oz. Light Rum
Near fill with pineapple juice
Float 3/4 oz. Raspberry Liqueur

RÉMYRED PUNCH
Bucket glass, ice
Build in glass
1 1/2 oz. RémyRed Red Berry Infusion
1 1/2 oz. Mount Gay Eclipse Rum
Fill with pineapple juice
Pineapple wedge garnish

RÉMYRED SUNRISE
Bucket glass, ice
Build in glass
1 1/2 oz. RémyRed Red Berry Infusion
Near fill with orange juice
Float 1 oz. RémyRed Strawberry
   Kiwi Infusion

BAK'S ZUBRÓWKA®
BISON GRASS VODKA

Long revered by enthusiasts and aficionados, Zubrówka is a traditional Polish vodka flavored with buffalo grass. For years this spectacular spirit was trapped behind the Iron Curtain and unavailable in America. Hopes for its importation rose with the end of the Cold War, only to be dashed when a trace element in the grass—coumarin—resulted in the vodka being banned in America.

Well, worry not, and welcome the long awaited arrival of BAK'S ZUBRÓWKA BISON GRASS VODKA. Produced at the Polmos Poznan Distillery, the vodka is triple-distilled in column stills from potatoes and artesian well water. It is then infused with the essential oils of the buffalo grass before being filtered through charcoal and oak chips. It is bottled at 82 proof.

Bak's Zubrówka is free of coumarin and is a dead ringer for the original infused version. The bottle even contains a long, slender blade of buffalo grass. The vodka has a pale, yellow hue, lightweight body and a generous bouquet of fresh, grassy aromas. The palate is loaded with spicy, sweet flavors that gradually fade into a warm and relaxed finish.

The buffalo grass in the Zubrówka is said to give one vitality and strength. Others say it has aphrodisiac properties. Whatever the motivation, this vodka is an experience not to be missed.

RENDEZVOUS MUUMUU
Bucket glass, ice
Pour ingredients into iced mixing glass
1 1/2 oz. Cruzan Estate Diamond Rum
3/4 oz. Cruzan Estate Light Rum
1/2 oz. grenadine
1/2 oz. Rose's Lime Juice
1 oz. pineapple juice
1 1/2 oz. sweet 'n' sour
Shake and strain
Lime wedge garnish

RENDEZVOUS PUNCH
Coffee mug, heated
Build in glass
3/4 oz. Gold Rum
3/4 oz. Chambord
Fill with hot spiced apple cider
Cinnamon stick garnish

RESERVA COCKTAIL
Cocktail glass, chilled
Rim glass with sugar
Pour ingredients into iced mixing glass
2 oz. Bacardi 8 Reserva Rum
3/4 oz. Cointreau
1/2 oz. fresh lime juice
1 oz. sweet 'n' sour
Shake and strain
Lime wedge garnish

RESTORATION
Bucket glass, ice
Pour ingredients into iced mixing glass
4 oz. Dry Red Wine
3/4 oz. Brandy
3/4 oz. Chambord
1 1/2 oz. sweet 'n' sour
Shake and strain
Lemon twist garnish

REVEREND CRAIG
Bucket glass, ice
Pour ingredients into iced mixing glass
1 1/2 oz. Bourbon
1 1/2 oz. sweet 'n' sour
Shake and strain
Fill with Draft Beer

REVERSE RUSSIAN
Sherry glass, chilled
Layer ingredients
1/2 fill Kahlúa
1/2 fill Vodka

R. F. & E.
Rocks glass, chilled
Pour ingredients into iced mixing glass
1/2 oz. Light Rum
1/2 oz. Dark Rum
1/2 oz. Coconut Rum
1/2 oz. Spiced Rum
1/2 oz. Jamaican Rum
1/4 oz. grenadine
1 oz. sweet 'n' sour
1 oz. pineapple juice
Shake and strain

RHETT BUTLER
Bucket glass, ice
Pour ingredients into iced mixing glass
1 oz. Southern Comfort
1/2 oz. Triple Sec
1 1/2 oz. sweet 'n' sour
1/2 oz. Rose's Lime Juice
Shake and strain
Fill with club soda
Lime wedge garnish

RHODODENDRON
House specialty glass, chilled
Pour ingredients into blender
1 1/2 oz. Light Rum
3/4 oz. Crème de Noyaux
1/2 oz. fresh lemon juice
1/2 oz. fresh lime juice
1/2 oz. simple syrup
2 oz. pineapple juice
Blend with ice
Float 3/4 oz. Dark Rum
Lime wedge garnish

RHUMBA ESCAPADES
House specialty glass, chilled
Pour ingredients into blender
1 1/4 oz. Light Rum
3/4 oz. Mount Gay Eclipse Rum
3/4 oz. Crème de Banana
1/2 oz. grenadine
1 1/2 oz. pineapple juice
1 peeled, ripe banana
1 scoop vanilla ice cream
Blend ingredients (with ice optional)
Whipped cream garnish

RHUM BARBANCOURT FREEZE
House specialty glass, chilled
Pour ingredients into blender
1 3/4 oz. Rhum Barbancourt 3-Star
1 oz. Blue Curaçao
1 oz. grapefruit juice
1 oz. sweet 'n' sour
2 oz. orange juice
Blend with ice
Float 3/4 oz. Rhum Barbancourt
   5-Star
Lime, lemon and orange wedge garnish

RICKEY
Highball glass, ice
Build in glass
1 1/4 oz. requested light liquor
Fill with club soda
Lime wedge garnish

RIDE THE GLIDE SLIDE
Bucket glass, ice
Build in glass
1 1/2 oz. Coconut Rum
3/4 oz. Kahlúa
3/4 oz. Baileys Irish Cream
2 oz. milk
2 oz. pineapple juice
Float 3/4 oz. Dark Rum

RIGOR MORTIS
Rocks glass, chilled
Pour ingredients into iced mixing glass
1 1/2 oz. Vodka
3/4 oz. Disaronno Amaretto
1 oz. pineapple juice
1 oz. orange juice
Shake and strain

RIN TIN GIN TONIC
Bucket glass, ice
Build in glass
1 3/4 oz. Beefeater London Dry Gin
1/2 oz. Limoncello Liqueur
Fill with tonic water
Lemon twist garnish

RIO RITA
Cocktail glass, chilled
Pour ingredients into iced mixing glass
1 1/2 oz. Ypioca Cachaça
1/2 oz. simple syrup
2 oz. sweet 'n' sour
Shake and strain
Lime wheel garnish

KÉKÉ BEACH® KEY LIME CREAM LIQUEUR

Few products have enjoyed the international success that Baileys Irish Cream has. Scores of other cream-based liqueurs have come and gone, most of which attempted to replicate Baileys now famous chocolate, whiskey and fresh dairy cream formula. Instead of mirroring something that had already been perfected, the creators of KÉKÉ BEACH KEY LIME CREAM LIQUEUR set off in an entirely different direction altogether. Fortunately for us, they did.

As clearly stated on its label, the objective was to create a cream liqueur with the bakery fresh flavors of key lime pie. You'll know with your first sip that they hit the mark spot on.

For all intents and purposes, KéKé is the popular dessert in a glass. It is made from a base of pure grain, neutral spirits with a blend of cream and natural flavorings, the exact composition of which is a proprietary secret.

The liqueur has an exotic lime green color and a creamy bouquet of graham cracker, vanilla, spice and freshly sliced citrus. It has a surprisingly lightweight body that immediately delivers on the promise of key lime pie, down to the tantalizing hint of graham cracker.

KéKé Beach Key Lime Cream Liqueur is a natural behind the bar, and in the hands of a skilled mixologist, it's a slam dunk.

RITZ AMERICANA
Champagne glass, chilled
Pour ingredients into iced mixing glass
1 1/4 oz. Bourbon
2-3 dashes Angostura Bitters
1 1/2 oz. sweet 'n' sour
Shake and strain
Fill with Champagne
Peach wedge garnish

RITZ FIZZ
House specialty glass, ice
Pour ingredients into iced mixing glass
1 oz. Disaronno Amaretto
1/2 oz. Blue Curaçao
1 1/2 oz. sweet 'n' sour
Shake and strain
Fill with Champagne
Lemon twist garnish

RITZ PICK-ME-UP
Champagne glass, chilled
Pour ingredients into iced mixing glass
1 oz. VS Cognac
1 oz. Cointreau
2 oz. orange juice
Shake and strain
Fill with Champagne

RIVER MADNESS
Bucket glass, ice
Build in glass
1 1/4 oz. Corazón Reposado Tequila
2 oz. limeade
Fill with club soda
Lime wedge garnish

RIVER SEINE CAPPUCCINO
Cappuccino cup, heated
Build in glass
1 oz. Kahlúa
3/4 oz. VS Cognac
Near fill with hot espresso coffee
Top with frothed milk
Sprinkle shaved chocolate

RIVIERA
Cocktail glass, chilled
Pour ingredients into iced mixing glass
1 oz. Dubonnet Rouge
1/2 oz. Grand Marnier
1 oz. fresh blood orange juice
Shake and strain
Orange slice garnish

RIVIERA DAYS
Rocks glass, ice
Build in glass
3/4 oz. Light Rum
3/4 oz. Cointreau
3/4 oz. Chambord
Lemon wedge garnish

RIVIERA NIGHTS
Rocks glass, ice
Build in glass
3/4 oz. Gold Rum
3/4 oz. Dark Rum
3/4 oz. Orange Liqueur
3/4 oz. Chambord
Lemon wedge garnish

ROASTED TOASTED ALMOND
Cocktail glass, chilled
Pour ingredients into iced mixing glass
1/2 oz. Disaronno Amaretto
1/2 oz. Kahlúa
1/2 oz. Vodka
2 oz. half & half cream
Shake and strain

ROB ROY
Cocktail glass, chilled
Pour ingredients into iced mixing glass
1/2 oz. Sweet Vermouth
2-3 dashes Angostura Bitters (optional)
1 1/2 oz. Scotch Whisky
Stir and strain
Cherry garnish

ROB ROY, DRY
Cocktail glass, chilled
Pour ingredients into iced mixing glass
1/4 oz. Dry Vermouth
2-3 dashes Angostura Bitters (optional)
1 1/2 oz. Scotch Whisky
Stir and strain
Lemon twist garnish

ROB ROY, HIGHLAND FLING
Cocktail glass, chilled
Pour ingredients into iced mixing glass
1/2 oz. Sweet Vermouth
2-3 dashes Angostura Bitters
2 oz. Scotch Whisky
Stir and strain
Cherry garnish

ROB ROY, OH JOY
Cocktail glass, chilled
Pour ingredients into iced mixing glass
1/2 oz. Dubonnet Rouge
1/2 oz. Tawny Port
1 1/2 oz. Single Malt Scotch Whisky
Stir and strain
Cherry garnish

ROB ROY, PERFECT
aka **Affinity Cocktail**, **Affinity Manhattan**
Cocktail glass, chilled
Pour ingredients into iced mixing glass
1/4 oz. Dry Vermouth
1/4 oz. Sweet Vermouth
2-3 dashes Angostura Bitters (optional)
1 1/2 oz. Scotch Whisky
Stir and strain
Lemon twist garnish

ROCK-A-FELLOW'S FANCY
Brandy snifter, ice
Build in glass
1 3/4 oz. Matusalem Gran Reserva Rum
1/2 oz. Grand Marnier
1/2 oz. Kahlúa Especial

ROCKET
Bucket glass, ice
Build in glass
1 1/2 oz. Yukon Jack Liqueur
Near fill with lemonade
Float 3/4 oz. 151° Rum

ROCK LOBSTER
House specialty glass, chilled
Pour ingredients into blender
1 oz. Malibu Caribbean Rum
1/2 oz. Crème de Banana
1/2 oz. Myers's Jamaican Rum
1/2 oz. grenadine
1 1/2 oz. orange juice
1 1/2 oz. pineapple juice
Blend with ice
Float 3/4 oz. Myers's Jamaican Rum
Orange slice and cherry garnish

ROCK 'N' BOCK
Pilsner glass, chilled
Build in glass
1/2 fill Rolling Rock
1/2 fill Shiner Double Bock

RODÉO DRIVER
Bucket glass, ice
Pour ingredients into iced mixing glass
1 1/2 oz. Reposado Tequila
3/4 oz. Orange Liqueur
1 oz. pineapple juice
1 oz. grapefruit juice
1 1/2 oz. sweet 'n' sour
Shake and strain
Fill with club soda
Orange slice garnish

JOSE CUERVO®
CLÁSICO® TEQUILA

In 1795, King Carlos III of Spain granted the first license to commercially produce tequila to Jose Maria Guadalupe Cuervo. The company has since grown to be the largest producer of tequila in Mexico and the best-known tequila brand throughout the world. The distillery's run of success will certainly continue with the 2003 release of the new, silver-styled JOSE CUERVO CLÁSICO TEQUILA.

Jose Cuervo Clásico is a singular blend of unaged tequilas and specially selected, high quailty Cuervo tequilas mellowed in oak barrels. Crafted under the watchful eye of Cuervo's famous Maestro Tequilero, the handpicked aged tequilas are used to soften the natural exuberance of the young silver spirits. The result is sublime.

Clásico is a classy addition to the Jose Cuervo portfolio. Don't be mislead by its apparent simplicity; this is an elegant tequila brimming with complexity and appeal. The spirit has a seamlessly smooth body and crystalline clarity. The tequila has a compact fruit and floral bouquet that slowly opens up with time. It enters the palate without a trace of harshness or excess heat, and then fills the mouth with soft, spicy flavor. This new gem from Cuervo has a delectably clean, crisp finish.

Clásico is a versatile and highly mixable spirit that adds a marvelous twist to a wealth of cocktails.

ROLLS ROYCE
Cocktail glass, chilled
Pour ingredients into iced mixing glass
1 oz. Gin
1 oz. Benedictine
1/2 oz. Dry Vermouth
1/2 oz. Sweet Vermouth
Stir and strain
Lemon twist garnish

ROOM SERVICE AT THE RITZ
Champagne glass, chilled
Pour ingredients into iced mixing glass
1 oz. Courvoisier VSOP Cognac
3/4 oz. Grand Marnier
1 1/2 oz. sweet 'n' sour
Shake and strain
Fill with Champagne
Lemon twist garnish

ROOT BEER
Bucket glass, ice
Build in glass
1 oz. Kahlúa
3/4 oz. Galliano Liqueur
3/4 oz. Vodka
Fill with cola

ROOT BEER FLOAT
Bucket glass, ice
Build in glass
1 oz. Kahlúa
3/4 oz. Galliano Liqueur
1/2 oz. Vodka (optional)
1/2 fill cola
1/2 fill half & half cream

ROOT BEER TOOTER
Highball glass, ice
Build in glass
3/4 oz. Root Beer Schnapps
3/4 oz. Vodka
3/4 oz. half & half cream
Fill with cola

ROOT CANAL
House specialty glass, ice
Pour ingredients into iced mixing glass
1/2 oz. Light Rum
1/2 oz. Gin
1/2 oz. Vodka
1/2 fill orange juice
Near fill with pineapple juice
Shake and strain
Float 1/2 oz. Jamaican Rum
Float 1/2 oz. Raspberry Liqueur

ROSE BEAM
Sherry glass, chilled
Layer ingredients
1/3 fill Tequila Rose Cream Liqueur
1/3 fill Kahlúa
1/3 fill Crème de Banana

ROSEBUD
House specialty glass, chilled
Pour ingredients into blender
2 oz. Tequila Rose Cream Liqueur
1 1/2 oz. Godiva White Chocolate Liqueur
2 scoops vanilla ice cream
Blend with ice
Strawberry garnish

ROSE PETAL
House specialty glass, chilled
Pour ingredients into blender
1 oz. Disaronno Amaretto
1/2 oz. Baileys Irish Cream
1/2 oz. grenadine
2 oz. strawberry puree
1 scoop vanilla ice cream
Blend ingredients (with ice optional)
Whipped cream garnish (optional)

ROSY PIPPIN
Wine glass, ice
Pour ingredients into iced mixing glass
4 1/2 oz. apple juice
1/2 oz. grenadine
1/2 oz. sweet 'n' sour
Shake and strain
Fill with ginger ale
Apple wedge garnish

ROUGH SEAS COCKTAIL
Cocktail glass, chilled
Pour ingredients into iced mixing glass
2 1/2 oz. Bacardi Limón Rum
1/2 oz. DeKuyper Pucker Sour Apple
1 1/2 oz. grapefruit juice
Shake and strain

ROXANNE
Cocktail glass, chilled
Pour ingredients into iced mixing glass
1 1/4 oz. Liquid Ice Vodka
3/4 oz. Peach Schnapps
1/2 oz. Disaronno Amaretto
1/2 oz. orange juice
1/2 oz. cranberry juice
Shake and strain

ROYAL BAY BREEZE
Cocktail glass, chilled
Pour ingredients into iced mixing glass
1 1/2 oz. Ultimat Black Cherry Vodka
3/4 oz. Chambord
1 1/2 oz. pineapple juice
1 1/2 oz. cranberry Juice
Shake and strain

ROYAL CANADIAN
Presentation shot glass, chilled
Build in glass
1/3 fill Kahlúa
1/3 fill Disaronno Amaretto
1/3 fill Crown Royal

ROYAL FIZZ
House specialty glass, ice
Pour ingredients into iced mixing glass
1 oz. Gin
2 oz. half & half cream
1 egg (optional)
1 oz. sweet 'n' sour
1/2 oz. simple syrup
Shake and strain
Splash club soda

ROYAL FLUSH
Rocks glass, chilled
Pour ingredients into iced mixing glass
1/2 oz. Crown Royal
1/2 oz. DeKuyper Peachtree Schnapps
1/2 oz. Chambord
1/2 oz. pineapple juice
1/2 oz. sweet 'n' sour
Shake and strain

ROYAL GODIVA
Highball glass, ice
Build in glass
3/4 oz. Godiva Chocolate Liqueur
3/4 oz. Chambord
Fill with club soda

ROYAL STREET COFFEE
Coffee mug, heated
Build in glass
3/4 oz. Disaronno Amaretto
3/4 oz. Kahlúa
1/2 tsp. nutmeg
Near fill with hot coffee
Whipped cream garnish (optional)

ROY ROGERS
Collins or bucket glass, ice
Build in glass
Near fill with cola
Float 1 oz. grenadine
Cherry garnish

WET BY BEEFEATER™

The people at Burroughs are raising the bar within the gin category with the release of WET BY BEEFEATER™. What at first seems like an unusual name for a super-premium gin makes immediate sense with the first sip. WET by Beefeater™ is innovation at its finest, one guaranteed to tickle the fancy of gin enthusiasts and Martini aficionados alike.

WET by Beefeater™ is an exuberant break from convention. It is a 100% pure grain, london-distilled spirit produced in specially designed stills. The spirits are then redistilled with a select cast of botanicals. The magic of WET by Beefeater™ involves what takes place next. A delicate essence of pear is introduced into the gin. The fruit adds lushness to the gin that has been heretofore unimagined. It is bottled at an accessible 70 proof.

Be good to yourself and sample WET by Beefeater™ wearing nothing but a chill. The bouquet is clean, fresh and loaded with soft, fruity aromas. As the featherweight gin glides over the palate, it gradually fills the mouth with an array of delicate flavors, a balanced offering of citrus and ripe pear. Because of its lower proof the flavors persist well into the extended finish.

WET by Beefeater™ is surprisingly light and brimming with flavor, but not the flavor we've grown accustomed to all these years. No, this is an altogether new set of sensations.

RUBY RED
Bucket glass, ice
Build in glass
1 1/2 oz. Citrus Vodka
Fill with ruby red grapefruit juice

RUDDY MIMOSA
Champagne glass, chilled
Build in glass
3 oz. Champagne
1 1/2 oz. orange juice
1 1/2 oz. cranberry juice
1/2 oz. Peach Schnapps

RUE DE LA PAIX
Champagne glass, chilled
Pour ingredients into iced mixing glass
1 oz. Chambord
1 oz. VSOP Cognac
Stir and strain
Fill with Champagne
Lemon twist garnish

RUM ALEXANDER
aka **Panama**
House specialty glass, chilled
Pour ingredients into blender
1 1/4 oz. Light Rum
1 oz. White Crème de Cacao
1 oz. half & half cream
2 scoops vanilla ice cream
Blend ingredients (with ice optional)
Whipped cream garnish
Sprinkle nutmeg

RUM AND BLACK
Rocks glass, chilled
1 3/4 oz. Dillon Dark Rhum
3/4 oz. black currant juice or syrup

RUMBA
Bucket glass, ice
Pour ingredients into iced mixing glass
1 1/2 oz. Myers's Jamaican Rum
3/4 oz. Light Rum
3/4 oz. Gin
1/2 oz. grenadine
1/2 oz. Rose's Lime Juice
1 1/2 oz. sweet 'n' sour
Shake and strain

RUMBALL
Brandy snifter, heated
1 3/4 oz. Dark Rum
3/4 oz. Godiva Chocolate Liqueur

RUM FIX
Bucket glass, ice
Build in glass
2 1/2 oz. Light Rum
2 1/2 oz. sweet 'n' sour
Fill with water
Lemon wedge garnish

RUM MILK PUNCH
Bucket glass, ice
Pour ingredients into iced mixing glass
1 tsp. powdered sugar
2 oz. Light Rum
4 oz. milk
Shake and strain
Sprinkle nutmeg

RUM MINT JULEP
House specialty glass
Build in glass
3-4 mint sprigs
1/2 oz. simple syrup
2 oz. water
Muddle contents
2 1/2 oz. Light Rum
Add crushed ice
Mint sprig garnish

RUMPLEMEISTER
aka **Screaming Nazi**
Presentation shot glass, chilled
Build in glass
1 oz. Rumple Minze Schnapps
1 oz. Jägermeister

RUM PUNCH
Bucket glass, ice
Pour ingredients into iced mixing glass
1 1/2 oz. Overproof Rum (strong)
1/2 oz. fresh lemon juice (sour)
2-3 dashes Angostura Bitters (bitters)
1 oz. grenadine (sweet)
2 oz. fresh fruit juice (weak)
Shake and strain
Sprinkle nutmeg
Pineapple wedge and cherry garnish

RUM RUNNER (1)
House specialty glass, ice
Pour ingredients into iced mixing glass
3/4 oz. Bacardi Light Rum
3/4 oz. Bacardi Gold Rum
3/4 oz. Crème de Banana
3/4 oz. Blackberry Brandy
2 oz. orange juice
2 oz. sweet 'n' sour
Shake and strain
Float 3/4 oz. Appleton Estate
   V/X Jamaica Rum
Orange slice garnish

RUM RUNNER (2)
House specialty glass, ice
Pour ingredients into iced mixing glass
1 1/4 oz. Dark Rum
1 1/4 oz. Mount Gay Eclipse Rum
3/4 oz. Blackberry Brandy
3/4 oz. Crème de Banana
1 1/2 oz. orange juice
1 1/2 oz. sweet 'n' sour
Shake and strain
Orange slice garnish

RUMSCAPES
House specialty glass, ice
Build in glass
1 1/4 oz. Gold Rum
1 1/4 oz. Mount Gay Eclipse Rum
3/4 oz. Chambord
3/4 oz. Crème de Banana
Fill with ginger ale
Lime wedge garnish

RUM SCREW
Highball glass, ice
Build in glass
1 1/4 oz. Light Rum
Fill with orange juice

RUM SWIZZLE
House specialty glass, crushed ice
Build in glass
2 1/2 oz. Dark Rum
3/4 oz. fresh lime juice
1/2 oz. simple syrup
2-3 dashes Angostura Bitters
2 oz. club soda
Orange slice and cherry garnish

RUM TODDY
Coffee mug, heated
Build in glass
2 oz. Gold Rum
1/2 oz. simple syrup
Fill with hot water
Lemon wedge garnish

RUN, SKIP AND GO NAKED
House specialty glass, ice
Pour ingredients into iced mixing glass
1/2 oz. Brandy
1/2 oz. Light Rum
1/2 oz. Gin
1/2 oz. Triple Sec
1 1/2 oz. sweet 'n' sour
Shake and strain
Fill with Draft Beer

COURVOISIER®
VSOP COGNAC

Courvoisier makes its cognacs from the finest brandies distilled in the premiere *crus*, or growing regions. The brandies are double-distilled in small copper alembic stills and cellared in handmade Limousin and Tronçais oak barrels. At any one point, the chateau has over 45,000 casks of brandy aging and adds about 3000 new barrels each year.

The chateau's line of cognacs is a work of art in itself. Famed COURVOISIER VSOP is a Fine Champagne cognac, a blend of brandies from the prized Grande Champagne and Petite Champagne districts of Cognac. The brandies used in its blend are matured a minimum of 6 years, with most aged in excess of 10 years.

Courvoisier VSOP is a classically structured cognac. It has a soft, round body and an assertive bouquet loaded with fruity and floral notes. The brandy has a seamlessly smooth entry and a layered palate of chocolate, citrus and nuts. The finish is fruity, spicy and of medium duration.

COURVOISIER VS is indeed something special. It is crafted from a blend of brandies from the premiere *crus*. The blend contains brandies aged for 4 years, as well as those aged a minimum of 7 years. The marriage of young and old brandies creates a cognac with a lush, floral bouquet and a delectable fruity palate with some oak undertones.

RUSSIAN' ABOUT
Cocktail glass, chilled
Pour ingredients into iced mixing glass
1 1/2 oz. Stolichnaya Vodka
1/2 oz. Baileys Irish Cream
1/2 oz. Tia Maria
1/2 oz. Frangelico
Shake and strain

RUSSIAN BEAR
Cocktail glass, chilled
Pour ingredients into iced mixing glass
1 1/2 oz. Kahlúa
3/4 oz. Vodka
1 1/2 oz. half & half cream
Shake and strain

RUSSIAN NIGHTS
Champagne glass, chilled
Pour ingredients into iced mixing glass
1 1/2 oz. Stolichnaya Citros Vodka
1 1/2 oz. orange juice
1 1/2 oz. cranberry juice
Shake and strain
Fill with Champagne
Lemon wheel garnish

RUSSIAN POLAR BEAR
House specialty glass, ice
Pour ingredients into iced mixing glass
1 1/4 oz. Stolichnaya Vodka
3/4 oz. Baileys Irish Cream
3/4 oz. Kahlúa
1/2 oz. Peppermint Schnapps
2 oz. milk
Shake and strain
Fill with cola
Orange slice and cherry garnish

RUSSIAN SUNRISE
Bucket glass, ice
Build in glass
1 oz. Magadanskaya Vodka
1/2 fill with orange juice
1/2 fill with grapefruit juice
Float 3/4 oz. Hpnotiq Liqueur

RUSTY NAIL
aka **Scotch Plaid**
Rocks glass, ice
Build in glass
1 1/2 oz. Scotch Whisky
3/4 oz. Drambuie

RUSTY NICKEL
Presentation shot glass, chilled
Build in glass
Fill with Light Rum
3 dashes Tabasco Sauce

SACRIFICE FLY
Coffee mug, heated
Build in glass
1/2 oz. Brandy
1/2 oz. DeKuyper Butldershots Schnapps
1/2 oz. Godiva Chocolate Liqueur
Near fill with hot chocolate
Whipped cream garnish
Sprinkle shaved chocolate

SAGINAW SNOOZE
Coffee mug, heated
Build in glass
3 oz. cranberry juice
3 oz. apple juice
1 tsp. honey
Heat and serve
Lemon wheel and cinnamon stick garnish

SAIL OF THE CENTURY
Cocktail glass, chilled
Pour ingredients into iced mixing glass
1 3/4 oz. Sea Wynde Pot Still Rum
3/4 oz. Grand Marnier Centenaire
1/2 oz. fresh lime juice
Shake and strain
Lime wedge garnish

SAINT MORITZ
Cordial or sherry glass, chilled
Layer ingredients
3/4 fill Chambord
1/4 fill half & half cream

SAKÉ PASSION
Cocktail glass, chilled
Pour ingredients into iced mixing glass
1 1/2 oz. Canadian Club Whisky
1/2 oz. RémyRed Red Berry Infusion
1/2 oz. Saké
1 1/2 oz. sweet 'n' sour
Shake and strain

SAKÉ PASSION CLUB
House specialty glass, ice
Pour ingredients into iced mixing glass
1 1/2 oz. Canadian Club Whisky
1/2 oz. RémyRed Red Berry Infusion
1/2 oz. Saké
1 1/2 oz. sweet 'n' sour
Shake and strain
Fill with club soda

SAKÉ-RAMA
Brandy snifter, ice
Build in glass
1 3/4 oz. Gold Tequila
1 3/4 oz. Saké

SALTY BULL
Highball glass, ice
Rim glass with salt
Build in glass
1 1/4 oz. Tequila
Fill with grapefruit juice

SALTY DOG
Highball glass, ice
Rim glass with salt
Build in glass
1 1/4 oz. Vodka
Fill with grapefruit juice
Note: May be requested made with gin

SALTY DOGITRON
Highball glass, ice
Rim glass with salt
Build in glass
1 1/2 oz. Absolut Citron Vodka
1/2 oz. grenadine
Fill with grapefruit juice

SAMMY JÄGER
Presentation shot glass, chilled
Build in glass
1/2 fill Sambuca
1/2 fill Jägermeister

SAN ANDREAS FAULT
Coffee mug, heated
Build in glass
1 oz. Dark Rum
3/4 oz. Banana Rum
3/4 oz. Godiva Chocolate Liqueur
Near fill with hot coffee
Whipped cream garnish
Dust powdered cocoa

SAND BAR SMASH
House specialty glass, chilled
Pour ingredients into iced mixing glass
1 1/2 oz. Banana Rum
3/4 oz. Dark Rum
3/4 oz. lime juice
1 1/2 oz. orange juice
1 1/2 oz. pineapple juice
Shake and strain
Float 3/4 oz. Dark Rum
Pineapple wedge and cherry garnish

SAND BLASTER
House specialty glass, ice
Build in glass
1 1/2 oz. Jägermeister
3/4 oz. Light Rum
Fill with cola
Lime wedge garnish

GREY GOOSE®
LA VANILLE VODKA

Consumers are going to be initially
attracted to thoroughbred GREY
GOOSE LA VANILLE because of its
highly recognizable name. After all, Grey
Goose has been one of the great vodka
success stories of this or any other time.
But the first sip will confirm that this is
a spirit worthy of merit because of its
own individuality, not pedigree.

All of the Grey Goose Vodkas are
crafted in the heart of Cognac. The
pure grain vodka is distilled in small
batches beginning in copper stills from a
choice blend of grains, and then blended
with limestone-filtered water drawn
from the famous Genté Springs. Natural
vanilla flavor is added to Grey Goose
Vodka. It then undergoes extensive
filtration to achieve purity and is
bottled at 80 proof.

Grey Goose La Vanille is a class act,
completely in step with contemporary
tastes. The vodka has a crystalline
appearance and a lightweight,
voluptuously rounded body. A few
minutes in the glass are sufficient for the
vodka to release its alluring, vanilla-
laced bouquet. La Vanille is graced with
enough vanilla flavor to be compelling
without being overpowering.

This Grey Goose masterpiece is a true
top-shelf performer. The vanilla-laced
palete is ideally suited to be the star
attraction in a wide range of cocktails.

SANDY BEACH BAY
Champagne glass, chilled
Rim glass with sugar
Pour ingredients into iced mixing glass
1 oz. Vanilla Rum
2 oz. Chambord
Shake and strain
Fill with Champagne
Pineapple wedge garnish

SANDY SMILE
House specialty glass, ice
Pour ingredients into iced mixing glass
1 1/2 oz. Light Rum
1 oz. Mount Gay Eclipse Rum
3/4 oz. Blue Curaçao
1 1/4 oz. apple juice
3 oz. pineapple juice
Shake and strain
Float 3/4 oz. Dark Rum
Pineapple wedge and cherry garnish

SAN FRANCISCO
House specialty glass, ice
Pour ingredients into iced mixing glass
1 1/2 oz. orange juice
1 1/2 oz. pineapple juice
1 1/2 oz. sweet 'n' sour
1 1/2 oz. grapefruit juice
1/2 oz. grenadine
1 egg white (optional)
Shake and strain
Fill with club soda
Fresh fruit garnish

SANGRIA
Wine glass or goblet, ice
Build in glass
4 oz. Dry Red Wine
3/4 oz. Peach Schnapps
3/4 oz. grenadine
3/4 oz. Rose's Lime Juice
1 1/2 oz. orange juice
1 1/2 oz. sweet 'n' sour
Lime, lemon, and orange wheel garnish

SANGRIA, MARGARITA (serves 6-8)
Pitcher (64 oz.), quarter-full with ice
Build in pitcher
20 oz. Dry Red Wine
12 oz. Gold Tequila
5 oz. Peach Schnapps
2 oz. Rose's Lime Juice
1 oz. grenadine
4 oz. orange juice
4 oz. sweet 'n' sour
Stir thoroughly
Float lime, lemon and orange wheels
Serve over ice

SANGRIA, NEW WORLD PUNCH (serves 2)
Wine goblet or house specialty glass, ice
Pour ingredients into iced mixing glass
5 oz. Dry Red Wine
3/4 oz. Peach Schnapps
3 oz. Champagne, Brut
3/4 oz. cranberry juice
3/4 oz. grenadine
3/4 oz. Rose's Lime Juice
1 oz. orange juice
1 1/2 oz. sweet 'n' sour
Shake and strain
Float 3/4 oz. Crème de Cassis
Lime, lemon and orange wheel garnish

SANGRIA PUNCH, BERRY NEW (serves 6-8)
Pitcher (64 oz.), quarter-full with ice
Build in pitcher
750ml Dry Red Wine
2 1/2 oz. Peach Schnapps
16 oz. cran-raspberry juice
3 oz. raspberry puree, sweetened
3 oz. strawberry puree, sweetened
1 1/2 oz. grapefruit juice
1 1/2 oz. orange juice
2 oz. sweet 'n' sour
Stir thoroughly
Refrigerate for 2-3 hours
Serve over ice

SANGRITA MIX
aka **Sangrita Camino Real**
Pitcher (64 oz.), 1/4 fill with ice
Build in pitcher
1 cup tomato juice
1 cup orange juice
4 oz. grenadine
4 oz. fresh lime juice
5 oz. Worcestershire sauce
1/2 tsp. black pepper
1 tsp. salt
12 dashes Tabasco Sauce
1 tsp. red onion, grated
1 pinch allspice

SANTA CLAUS IS COMING
Presentation shot glass, chilled
Layer ingredients
1/2 oz. Rumple Minze Schnapps
1/2 oz. Cinnamon Schnapps
1/2 oz. Midori
Whipped cream garnish
Sprinkle nutmeg

SANTIAGO (1)
House specialty glass, ice
Pour ingredients into iced mixing glass
1 1/4 oz. Dark Rum
1 1/4 oz. Mount Gay Eclipse Rum
3/4 oz. Cointreau
1/2 oz. Rose's Lime Juice
2 oz. sweet 'n' sour
2 dashes Angostura Bitters
Shake and strain
Fill with Champagne
Lime wedge garnish

SANTIAGO (2)
House specialty glass, ice
Pour ingredients into iced mixing glass
1 1/2 oz. Light Rum
3/4 oz. Dark Rum
3/4 oz. Triple Sec
2-3 dashes Angostura Bitters
1/2 oz. Rose's Lime Juice
1 1/2 oz. sweet 'n' sour
Shake and strain
Orange slice garnish

SAOCO
Highball glass, ice
Build in glass
1 3/4 oz. Light Rum
Fill with coconut milk

SASSAFRAS SUNSET
House specialty glass, ice
Pour ingredients into iced mixing glass
1 oz. Light Rum
1 oz. Gold Rum
3/4 oz. Triple Sec
1 oz. orange juice
1 1/2 oz. cranberry juice
1 1/2 oz. sweet 'n' sour
Shake and strain
Fill with club soda
Float 3/4 oz. Raspberry Liqueur
Orange slice and cherry garnish

SATIN PILLOW
Rocks glass, chilled
Build in glass
1/2 oz. Tia Maria
1/2 oz. Frangelico
1/2 oz. Triple Sec
1/2 oz. Raspberry Liqueur

LICOR 43®
(CUARENTA Y TRES)

LICOR 43 is a fascinating product with an equally fascinating heritage. Better known as CUARENTA Y TRES in its homeland of Spain, it is conjectured that its origin dates back to ancient times and the seafaring Phoenicians. The earliest version of the present day liqueur, however, can be traced back to the 16th century, with the mastering of distillation and the discovery of vanilla in Mexico by the Spanish Conquistadors.

Today the Diego Zamora Company makes Licor 43 in Cartegena, Spain. This delectable liqueur is made from a base of neutral grain spirits with an infusion of berries, citrus fruit and fragrant herbs. The "43" in the liqueur's name refers to the number of ingredients used in its proprietary recipe. It is bottled at 62 proof.

Licor 43 is wildly popular in Spain and can be found in over 60 countries around the world. The liqueur has a lustrous golden hue with brilliant amber highlights and a richly textured, medium-weight body. It is endowed with a generous bouquet of butterscotch, citrus and vanilla. Licor 43 presents a sweet, lively palate of citrus, herbs and vanilla that persist well into the warm and flavorful finish.

Savory Licor 43 is a versatile player behind the bar. The liqueur adds a wonderful vanilla and light citrus essence to mixed drinks.

SAUZA THREESOME
Cocktail glass, chilled
Pour ingredients into iced mixing glass
1 1/2 oz. Sauza Tres Generaciones
   Añejo Tequila
1 oz. Triple Sec
3/4 oz. orange juice
3/4 oz. fresh lime juice
3/4 oz. sweet 'n' sour
Shake and strain
Lime wedge garnish

SAVANNAH
Cocktail glass, chilled
Pour ingredients into iced mixing glass
1 1/2 oz. Gin
1 oz. orange juice
1 egg white (optional)
1 dash White Crème de Cacao
Shake and strain

SAVOY CHAMPAGNE COCKTAIL
Champagne glass, chilled
Build in glass
Sugar cube soaked with 1/4 oz.
   Angostura Bitters
1/2 oz. Grand Marnier
1/2 oz. VS Cognac
Fill with Champagne
Lemon twist garnish

SAX WITH BILL
Cocktail glass, chilled
Pour ingredients into iced mixing glass
1 1/2 oz. Gin
1/2 oz. simple syrup
1 oz. orange juice
3 dashes Angostura Bitters
Shake and strain
Lemon twist garnish

SAY HEY MARSEILLES
Coffee mug, heated
Build in glass
1 oz. Kahlúa
1 oz. Chambord
1/2 oz. Frangelico
3/4 oz. half & half cream
Near fill with hot coffee
Whipped cream garnish
Sprinkle shaved chocolate

SAZERAC
Rocks glass or brandy snifter
Build in glass
Swirl 1/2 oz. Pernod in glass, discard excess
2 dashes Angostura Bitters
2 dashes Peychaud bitters
Add ice
2 oz. Rye Whiskey
Lemon twist garnish

SCARLETT O'HARA
Highball glass, ice
Build in glass
1 1/2 oz. Southern Comfort
1/2 oz. Rose's Lime Juice
Fill with cranberry juice

SCORPION
House Specialty glass, ice
Pour ingredients into iced mixing glass
1 1/4 oz. Light Rum
1 1/4 oz. Gold Rum
1 oz. White Wine
3/4 oz. Gin
3/4 oz. Brandy
3/4 oz. Crème de Noyaux
1/2 oz. Rose's Lime Juice
1 1/2 oz. orange juice
1 1/2 oz. sweet 'n' sour
Shake and strain
Pineapple wedge and cherry garnish

SCOTCH BOUNTY
House specialty glass, ice
Pour ingredients into iced mixing glass
1 1/2 oz. Scotch Whisky
1 oz. Malibu Caribbean Rum
1/2 oz. White Crème de Cacao
1/2 oz. grenadine
1 oz. sweet 'n' sour
2 oz. orange juice
Shake and strain
Orange slice and cherry garnish

SCOTCH COFFEE
Coffee mug, heated
Build in glass
3/4 oz. Scotch Whisky
3/4 oz. Drambuie
Fill with hot coffee

SCOTTISH DREAMS
Brandy snifter, heated
Build in glass
1 1/2 oz. Scotch Whisky
1/2 oz. Drambuie
Lemon twist garnish

SCOTTISH TAN
Rocks glass, ice
Build in glass
1 1/2 oz. Single Highland Malt Scotch Whisky
3/4 oz. Kahlúa Especial
3/4 oz. Baileys Irish Cream

SCREAMING FUZZY NAVEL
Highball glass, ice
Build in glass
1 oz. Peach Schnapps
1/2 oz. Vodka
Fill with orange juice

SCREAMING GOOD TIMES
House specialty glass, chilled
Pour ingredients into blender
1 1/2 oz. Gold Rum
3/4 oz. Citrus Rum
3/4 oz. Midori
2 scoops vanilla ice cream
Blend ingredients (with ice optional)
Whipped cream garnish

SCREAMING HAWAIIAN
House specialty glass, ice
Pour ingredients into iced mixing glass
1/2 oz. Vodka
1/2 oz. Midori
1/2 oz. Malibu Caribbean Rum
Splash pineapple juice
Splash Seven-Up
Splash grenadine
Shake and strain
Orange slice and cherry garnish

SCREAMING ORGASM
House specialty glass, ice
Build in glass
1/2 oz. Vodka
1/2 oz. Kahlúa
1/2 oz. Disaronno Amaretto
1/2 oz. Baileys Irish Cream
1/2 fill half & half cream
1/2 fill club soda

SCREAMING WEEBIES
House specialty glass, ice
Pour ingredients into iced mixing glass
1 oz. Cruzan Estate Light Rum
1/2 oz. Cruzan Coconut Rum
1/2 oz. Midori
1/2 oz. grenadine
2 oz. pineapple juice
2 oz. Seven-Up
Shake and strain
Orange slice and cherry garnish

SCREWDRIVER
Highball glass, ice
Build in glass
1 1/4 oz. Vodka
Fill with orange juice

SCURVEY ABATOR
Cocktail glass, chilled
Pour ingredients into iced mixing glass
1 1/2 oz. Plymouth Gin
1/2 oz. Grand Marnier
1/2 oz. orange juice
1/2 oz. fresh lime juice
1/2 oz. sweet 'n' sour
Shake and strain
Orange slice garnish

SAUZA® EXTRA GOLD TEQUILA

Sauza has been distilling SAUZA EXTRA GOLD TEQUILA for more than a century. As a premium *joven abocado* tequila, it is rested in stainless steel vats for four months prior to bottling. Caramel coloring and flavorings are added to give it an amber/golden hue with a touch of sweetness and wood/oak flavor.

There is something wonderfully appealing about gold tequila, which is why it's the most popular type of tequila in America. Extra Gold possesses every quality that one looks for in a traditional tequila, namely an assertive character, a lush, golden hue and a rich, agave and oak flavor.

By their very nature, gold tequilas have a robust, exuberant spirit and Sauza Extra is no exception. While not overly complex, it is well structured with good agave flavor. Sauza Gold has a round, smooth body and a light earthy bouquet with floral and agave undertones. On the palate the tequila has a peppery, spicy flavor that finishes warm and restrained. It is by any measure an excellent tequila at an excellent price.

Sauza Extra Gold is an unpretentious spirit, popularly served in a shooter or mixed drink. It is also an excellent candidate for use in Margaritas, or any other tequila-based cocktail for that matter.

SEABREEZE
Highball glass, ice
Build in glass
1 1/4 oz. Vodka
1/2 fill grapefruit juice
1/2 fill cranberry juice

SEA DEW
Brandy snifter, ice
Build in glass
1 3/4 oz. Sea Wynde Pot Still Rum
3/4 oz. Grand Marnier
3/4 oz. Baileys Irish Cream

SEA SIDE LIBERTY
House specialty glass, chilled
Pour ingredients into blender
1 oz. Mount Gay Eclipse Rum
1 oz. Malibu Caribbean Rum
3/4 oz. Patrón XO Café Coffee Liqueur
3/4 oz. half & half cream
1 oz. coconut cream syrup
3 oz. pineapple juice
Blend with ice
Pineapple wedge and cherry garnish

SEATTLE'S 6.3
Cocktail glass, chilled
Pour ingredients into iced mixing glass
2 oz. Tanqueray Gin
1/4 oz. fresh lemon juice
1/4 oz. cranberry juice
1/2 oz. fresh lime juice
1/2 oz. simple syrup
Stir and strain
Orange slice garnish

SEA WATER
House specialty glass, ice
Pour ingredients into iced mixing glass
1 1/4 oz. Tarantula Azul
3/4 oz. Blue Curaçao
1 1/2 oz. orange juice
2 1/2 oz. sweet 'n' sour
Shake and strain
Lime wedge garnish

SEELBACH COCKTAIL
Champagne glass, chilled
Pour ingredients into iced mixing glass
1 oz. Old Forester Bourbon
1/4 oz. Triple Sec
1-2 dashes Peychaud Bitters
1-2 dashes Angostura Bitters
Shake and strain
Fill with Champagne
Orange twist garnish

SEPARATOR (1)
Cordial or sherry glass, chilled
Layer ingredients
1/3 fill Kahlúa
1/3 fill half & half cream
1/3 fill Brandy

SEPARATOR (2)
Rocks glass, ice
Build in glass
1 oz. Brandy
1 oz. Kahlúa
3/4 oz. half & half cream

SEVEN & SEVEN
Highball glass, ice
Build in glass
1 1/4 oz. Seagram's 7 Whisky
Fill with Seven-Up

SEVEN OF HEARTS
Bucket glass, ice
Build in glass
2 oz. RémyRed Red Berry Infusion
Fill with Seven-Up

SEVENTH AVENUE
Cocktail or house specialty glass, chilled
Pour ingredients into iced mixing glass
3/4 oz. Disaronno Amaretto
3/4 oz. Godiva Chocolate Liqueur
3/4 oz. Drambuie
3/4 oz. Sylk Cream Liqueur
Shake and strain

SEVENTH HEAVEN
Highball glass, ice
Build in glass
1 oz. Seagram's 7 Whisky
1/2 oz. Disaronno Amaretto
Fill with orange juice

SEVEN TWENTY-SEVEN (727)
Rocks glass, ice
Build in glass
3/4 oz. Vodka
3/4 oz. Kahlúa
3/4 oz. Baileys Irish Cream
3/4 oz. Grand Marnier

SEX AT THE BEACH
Rocks glass, chilled
Pour ingredients into iced mixing glass
1/2 oz. Vodka
1/2 oz. DeKuyper Peachtree Schnapps
1/2 oz. DeKuyper Pucker Sour Apple
1/2 oz. Grand Marnier
1/2 oz. Southern Comfort
1/2 oz. cranberry juice
1/2 oz. orange juice
3/4 oz. half & half cream
Shake and strain

SEX IN THE COAL REGION
Bucket glass, ice
Build in glass
1 oz. Vodka
1/2 oz. Raspberry Liqueur
1/2 oz. Blackberry Brandy
Splash Seven-Up
Splash club soda
Near fill with Draft Beer
Float 3/4 oz. Malibu Caribbean Rum

SEX IN THE TROPICS
House specialty glass, ice
Pour ingredients into iced mixing glass
1 1/2 oz. RémyRed Red Berry Infusion
1 1/2 oz. Malibu Caribbean Rum
2 oz. pineapple juice
2 oz. sweet 'n' sour
Shake and strain
Pineapple wedge garnish

SEX IN THE WOODS
House specialty glass, chilled
Pour ingredients into blender
1 1/2 oz. Vodka
3/4 oz. Disaronno Amaretto
1/2 oz. Tia Maria
2 1/2 oz. pineapple juice
Blend with ice

SEX ON A BLACK SANDY BEACH
Rocks glass, ice
Build in glass
3/4 oz. Pearl Lo Coco Vodka
3/4 oz. Chambord
1/2 oz. Licor 43 (Cuarenta y Tres)
Fill with pineapple juice

SEX ON THE BEACH (1)
Highball glass, ice
Build in glass
1/2 oz. Vodka
1/2 oz. Chambord
1/2 oz. Tia Maria
Fill with pineapple juice

SEX ON THE BEACH (2)
Highball glass, ice
Build in glass
3/4 oz. Midori
3/4 oz. Chambord
Fill with pineapple juice

SEX ON THE BEACH (3)
Rocks glass, chilled
Pour ingredients into iced mixing glass
1 oz. Southern Comfort
3/4 oz. Chambord
1 oz. pineapple juice
1 oz. orange juice
Shake and strain

TORMORE® SINGLE SPEYSIDE MALT SCOTCH WHISKY

The largest of the Scotch producing regions, the Highlands is located in the northern part of Scotland and is the home of the majority of the country's distilleries. The revered heartland of the region is the Speyside, which is located between the cities of Inverness and Aberdeen. It is the watershed of several river systems, most notably the rivers Livet and Spey. It is in the center of this noble region that TORMORE SINGLE SPEYSIDE MALT SCOTCH WHISKY is made.

Affectionately known as the "Pearl of the Speyside," the Tormore Distillery is situated on the banks of the Auchvochkie Burn, one of the streams that feed into the River Spey. It is a state of the art facility that has the capacity to produce light, yet complex and sultry whiskies.

The distillery is perhaps best known for the 12 year old Tormore Single Speyside Malt. The whisky has a deep, rich golden color, and a memorable bouquet of nutty, malty and citrus aromas. The malt is quite accessible and brimming with the flavors of almonds, spice and sliced oranges. The finish is round and satisfying.

Tormore Single Speyside Malt, 80 proof, is easy to drink, an ideal choice for whisky novices and enthusiasts alike. It's a Scotch that requires no learning to thoroughly enjoy. Pour a dram or two and see if you don't agree.

SEX ON THE BEACH (4)
Rocks glass, chilled
Pour ingredients into iced mixing glass
3/4 oz. Vodka
3/4 oz. Chambord
1/2 oz. Peach Schnapps
3/4 oz. sweet 'n' sour
3/4 oz. orange juice
Shake and strain

SEX ON THE BEACH (5)
Rocks glass, chilled
Pour ingredients into iced mixing glass
1 1/2 oz. Midori
3/4 oz. Chambord
1/2 oz. Peach Schnapps
1 oz. sweet 'n' sour
Shake and strain

SEX ON THE BEACH ON A CLOUDY DAY
Rocks glass, ice
Build in glass
1 oz. Malibu Caribbean Rum
1/2 oz. Disaronno Amaretto
1/2 oz. Baileys Irish Cream
1 oz. pineapple juice

SEXUAL CHOCOLATE
Rocks glass, chilled
Build in glass
3/4 oz. Jägermeister
3/4 oz. Baileys Irish Cream
3/4 oz. Kahlúa
3/4 oz. Dark Crème de Cacao

SEX WITH AN ALLIGATOR (1)
Cocktail glass, chilled
Pour ingredients into iced mixing glass
1 1/2 oz. Midori
1/2 oz. Chambord
1/2 oz. Jägermeister
1 1/2 oz. sweet 'n' sour
Shake and strain

SEX WITH AN ALLIGATOR (2)
Cocktail glass, chilled
Pour ingredients into iced mixing glass
1 1/2 oz. DeKuyper Pucker Sour Apple
1/2 oz. Razzmatazz Raspberry Liqueur
1/2 oz. Vodka
1/2 oz. Jägermeister
1/2 oz. Rose's Lime Juice
1 1/2 oz. sweet 'n' sour
Shake and strain

SEX WITH AN ALLIGATOR (3)
Cocktail glass, chilled
Pour ingredients into iced mixing glass
3/4 oz. Midori
3/4 oz. Malibu Caribbean Rum
3/4 oz. Jägermeister
1 1/2 oz. pineapple juice
Shake and strain
Float 1/2 oz. Chambord

SHANDY GAFF
Large beer glass or mug, chilled
Build in glass
1/2 fill Draft Deer
1/2 fill ginger ale

SHARK ATTACK
Bucket glass, ice
Build in glass
1 1/4 oz. Light Rum
Near fill with lemonade
Float 3/4 oz. Blue Curaçao
Orange slice garnish

SHARK BITE
Bucket glass, ice
Build in glass
1 oz. Appleton Estate V/X Jamaica Rum
Near fill with orange juice
Float 3/4 oz. grenadine
Orange slice garnish
Note: Immerse orange slice
to resemble shark's fin

SHARK'S TOOTH
House specialty glass, chilled
Pour ingredients into blender
1 1/2 oz. Light Rum
1 oz. Blue Curaçao
3/4 oz. White Crème de Cacao
2 scoops vanilla ice cream
Blend ingredients (with ice optional)
Whipped cream garnish
Drizzle 1/2 oz. grenadine

SHERRY'S BLOSSOM
Cocktail glass, chilled
Pour ingredients into iced mixing glass
1 1/2 oz. Vodka
1/2 oz. Mount Gay Eclipse Rum
1/2 oz. Grand Marnier
1/4 oz. Rose's Lime Juice
Stir and strain
Orange twist garnish

SHILLELAGH
Bucket glass, ice
Build in glass
2 oz. Light Rum
1 oz. Green Crème de Menthe
1 oz. fresh lime juice
1/2 oz. Rose's Lime Juice
Green cherry garnish

SHIP WRECK
Bucket glass, ice
Build in glass
1 oz. Malibu Caribbean Rum
1 oz. Silver Tequila
Fill with pineapple juice

SHIRLEY TEMPLE
Collins or bucket glass, ice
Build in glass
Near fill with Seven-Up
Float 1 oz. grenadine
Cherry garnish

SHORE BOAT
Coffee mug, heated
Build in glass
1 oz. Pusser's British Navy Rum
3/4 oz. Appleton Estate V/X Jamaica Rum
3/4 oz. Cruzan Rum Cream
3/4 oz. Patrón XO Café Coffee Liqueur
Near fill with hot coffee
Whipped cream garnish

SHORE BREEZE
Bucket glass, ice
Build in glass
1 1/2 oz. Light Rum
2-3 dashes Angostura Bitters
2 oz. cranberry juice
2 oz. pineapple juice
Float 3/4 oz. Mount Gay Eclipse Rum

SHOT IN THE DARK
Presentation shot glass
Build in glass
1/3 fill Yukon Jack Liqueur
1/3 fill Grand Marnier
1/3 fill hot coffee

SHOT THRU THE HEART
Rocks glass, chilled
Build in glass
3/4 oz. Dark Rum
3/4 oz. Kahlúa
3/4 oz. Baileys Irish Cream
3/4 oz. Orange Liqueur

PATRÓN® CITRÓNGE® EXTRA FINE ORANGE LIQUEUR

Aficionados of exceptional spirits already know and appreciate the authentic character of PATRÓN CITRÓNGE EXTRA FINE ORANGE LIQUEUR. Its vitality and vibrant personality make it a contemporary classic and give it permanent resident status on even the most crowded top-shelves.

Produced in Mexico by the fine people who make Patrón Tequila, Citrónge Extra Fine is made on a base of premium, high proof neutral grain spirits. Its flavor is derived from organically grown oranges from Jamaica and bittersweet oranges from Haiti. Peels from these oranges are steeped in the alcohol for an extended period and then fermented. Pure cane sugar is added to give the liqueur a touch of sweetness. No artificial flavors or chemical enhancers are added.

Citrónge Extra Fine Orange Liqueur is in fact extra fine. It has pristine clarity and a satiny, featherweight body. The liqueur has a compact bouquet that features the straightforward aroma of orange zest. At 80 proof, it tingles on the palate and fill the mouth with spice and broad splashes of fresh orange flavor. The medium to long finish is warm and flavorful.

Patrón Citrónge Extra Fine Orange Liqueur is capable of great things behind the bar. It is superb in both a supporting role or as a featured performer.

SIBERIAN
Rocks glass, ice
Build in glass
1 1/2 oz. Magadanskaya Vodka
1/2 oz. Brandy
1/2 oz. Kahlúa

SICILIAN KISS
Rocks glass, ice
Build in glass
1 oz. Disaronno Amaretto
1 oz. Southern Comfort

SICILIAN SUNRISE
Bucket glass, ice
Build in glass
1 oz. Espolon Silver Tequila
Near fill with Orange Pelligrino
Float 1 oz. cranberry juice
Orange slice garnish

SIDECAR (1)
Cocktail glass, chilled
Rim glass with sugar (optional)
Pour ingredients into iced mixing glass
1 oz. VS Cognac
1/2 oz. Cointreau
1 1/2 oz. sweet 'n' sour
Shake and strain

SIDECAR (2)
Cocktail glass, chilled
Rim glass with sugar (optional)
Pour ingredients into iced mixing glass
1 oz. Brandy
1/2 oz. Triple Sec
1 1/2 oz. sweet 'n' sour
Shake and strain

SIDECAR, AUTUMN
Cocktail glass, chilled
Rim glass with sugar (optional)
Pour ingredients into iced mixing glass
1 1/2 oz. VS Cognac
1/2 oz. Tuaca
1/2 oz. Frangelico
1 3/4 oz. sweet 'n' sour
Shake and strain
Orange slice garnish

SIDECAR, CUBAN
Cocktail glass, chilled
Pour ingredients into iced mixing glass
1 1/2 oz. Matusalem Light Dry Rum
1 oz. Triple Sec
1 oz. fresh lime juice
Shake and strain
Lime wedge garnish

SIDECAR, GRAND
Brandy snifter, ice
Rim glass with sugar (optional)
Pour ingredients into iced mixing glass
1 1/4 oz. Brandy
3/4 oz. Grand Marnier
1 1/2 oz. sweet 'n' sour
Shake and strain

SIDECAR, HAVANA (1)
Cocktail glass, chilled
Rim glass with sugar (optional)
Pour ingredients into iced mixing glass
1 1/2 oz. Gold Rum
3/4 oz. Cointreau
1 1/2 oz. sweet 'n' sour
Shake and strain
Lime wedge garnish

SIDECAR, HAVANA (2)
Cocktail glass, chilled
Rim glass with sugar (optional)
Pour ingredients into iced mixing glass
1 1/2 oz. Bacardi 8 Reserva Rum
3/4 oz. Cointreau
3/4 oz. sweet 'n' sour
Shake and strain
Lemon wedge garnish

SIDECAR, IMPERIAL
Cocktail glass, chilled or brandy snifter, ice
Pour ingredients into iced mixing glass
1 1/4 oz. Calvados Apple Brandy
3/4 oz. Gran Gala Orange Liqueur
1 1/2 oz. sweet 'n' sour
Shake and strain
Orange twist

SIDECAR IN BOMBAY
Cocktail glass, chilled
Rim glass with sugar (optional)
Pour ingredients into iced mixing glass
1 3/4 oz. Bombay Sapphire London Dry Gin
3/4 oz. Grand Marnier Centenaire
3/4 oz. fresh lemon juice
Shake and strain

SIDECAR, IRISH
Cocktail glass, chilled
Rim glass with sugar (optional)
Pour ingredients into iced mixing glass
1 1/2 oz. Irish Whiskey
3/4 oz. Cointreau
2 oz. sweet 'n' sour
Shake and strain

SIDECAR ROYALE
Cocktail glass, chilled
Rim glass with sugar (optional)
Pour ingredients into iced mixing glass
1 oz. VS Cognac
1/2 oz. Cointreau
1/2 oz. Benedictine
1 1/2 oz. sweet 'n' sour
Shake and strain

SIDECAR, TUACA
Cocktail glass, chilled
Rim glass with sugar (optional)
Pour ingredients into iced mixing glass
1 1/4 oz. Tuaca
1/2 oz. Triple Sec
2 1/2 oz. fresh orange juice
2 1/2 oz. fresh lemon juice
Shake and strain
Orange slice garnish

SIDE SHOT
Rocks glass, chilled
Pour ingredients into iced mixing glass
1 1/4 oz. Absolut Kurant Vodka
1 1/2 oz. cranberry juice
Shake and strain

SILKEN VEIL
Brandy snifter, ice
Build in glass
1 1/2 oz. Vodka
1 1/2 oz. Dubonnet Rouge
Lemon twist garnish

SILK PANTIES (1)
aka **Pink Silk Panties, Woo-Woo**
Highball glass, ice
Build in glass
1 oz. Peach Schnapps
1/2 oz. Vodka
Fill with cranberry juice

SILK PANTIES (2)
Rocks glass, ice
Build in glass
1 1/2 oz. Vodka
1/2 oz. Peach Schnapps

SILK ROSE
Cocktail glass, chilled
Pour ingredients into iced mixing glass
1 oz. Tequila Rose Cream Liqueur
1/2 oz. DeKuyper Buttershots Schnapps
1/2 oz. Banana Rum
1/2 oz. whole milk
1/4 oz. half & half cream
Shake and strain

ARTIC® VODKA & THAI FRUITS LIQUEUR

For the past 100 years, the Illva Saronno Distillery of Saronno, Italy has been perfecting the art and science of capturing the essential flavors of fruit and infusing them with distilled spirits. Perhaps best known for making Disaronno Amaretto, the Italian giant is also becoming known for a line of flavorful, contemporary spirits, an ensemble led by ARTIC VODKA & THAI FRUITS LIQUEUR.

This highly innovative liqueur is made from a base of pure grain neutral spirits and then blended with a liqueur made from a mixture of spices and fresh fruit, including the exotic and uncommonly delicious Thai Lemon.

Artic Vodka & Thai Fruits Liqueur looks and tastes like a skillfully prepared cocktail. It has an intriguing, light blue color and a supple, medium-weight body. The bouquet is complex with wafting citrus aromas. The liqueur washes over the palate filling the mouth with the flavors of lime, orange and spices, an overall taste reminiscent of a Kamikaze. It has a fairly long, flavorful finish.

The Artic expedition also includes ARTIC VODKA & MELON LIQUEUR, ARTIC VODKA & PEACH LIQUEUR and ARTIC VODKA & STRAWBERRY LIQUEUR. In addition to their light, pleasing flavors, these "New Age" spirits are relatively low in alcohol (50 proof), making them fashionably hip and well suited for use in cocktails.

SILK TIE
House specialty glass, ice
Pour ingredients into iced mixing glass
2 oz. Jameson Irish Whiskey
1 oz. Scotch Whisky
1/2 oz. Rose's Lime Juice
1 oz. orange juice
2 3/4 oz. sweet 'n' sour
Shake and strain
Lime wheel garnish

SILVER BULLET
Rocks glass, ice
Build in glass
1 1/2 oz. Tequila
1/2 oz. White Crème de Menthe

SILVER CLOUD
House specialty glass, chilled
Pour ingredients into iced mixing glass
3/4 oz. Kahlúa
1/2 oz. Disaronno Amaretto
1/2 oz. Dark Crème de Cacao
1/2 oz. Vodka
1 1/2 oz. half & half cream
Shake and strain

SILVER FIZZ
House specialty glass, chilled
Pour ingredients into iced mixing glass
1 oz. Gin
2 oz. half & half cream
1 egg white (optional)
1 oz. sweet 'n' sour
1/2 oz. simple syrup
Shake and strain
Splash club soda

SILVER SHADOW
Coffee mug, heated
Build in glass
1 1/4 oz. Disaronno Amaretto
Fill with English Breakfast tea
Lemon wedge garnish

SILVER SPIDER
Rocks glass, chilled
Pour ingredients into iced mixing glass
1/2 oz. Vodka
1/2 oz. Light Rum
1/2 oz. Triple Sec
1/2 oz. White Crème de Menthe
Stir and strain

SIMPLY CRIMSON
Cocktail glass, chilled
Pour ingredients into iced mixing glass
1 1/2 oz. Cointreau
4 dashes Angostura Bitters
1 1/2 oz. cranberry juice
Stir and strain
Splash club soda
Orange slice and cherry garnish

SIN & FRENCH GIN
Cocktail glass, chilled
Pour ingredients into iced mixing glass
2 oz. Citadelle Gin
1/2 oz. Gran Gala Orange Liqueur
1/4 oz. grenadine
3/4 oz. orange juice
3/4 oz. sweet 'n' sour
Shake and strain
Lemon wheel garnish

SIN IN HAWAII
Cocktail glass, chilled
Pour ingredients into iced mixing glass
1 1/2 oz. Van Gogh Wild Appel Vodka
1 oz. pineapple juice
1 oz. cranapple juice
Shake and strain
Apple wedge garnish

SINGAPORE SLING (1)
House specialty glass, ice
Pour ingredients into iced mixing glass
1 oz. Gin
1/2 oz. grenadine
1 1/2 oz. sweet 'n' sour
Shake and strain
Near fill with club soda
Float 3/4 oz. Cherry Brandy
Orange slice and cherry garnish

SINGAPORE SLING (2)
House specialty glass, ice
Pour ingredients into iced mixing glass
1 oz. Gin
1/2 oz. Cointreau
1/2 oz. Benedictine
1/2 oz. Cherry Brandy
2 dashes Angostura Bitters
1/2 oz. fresh lime juice
2 oz. pineapple juice
Shake and strain
Orange slice and cherry garnish

SKANKY HEAD
Rocks glass, chilled
Pour ingredients into iced mixing glass
3/4 oz. Jägermeister
3/4 oz. Rumple Minze
3/4 oz. Jose Cuervo Especial Tequila
Shake and strain

SKINNY DIPPING
House specialty glass, ice
Build in glass
3/4 oz. Vodka
3/4 oz. Peach Schnapps
3/4 oz. Disaronno Amaretto
1/2 fill cranberry juice
1/2 fill orange juice

SKIP AND GO NAKED
Bucket glass, ice
Pour ingredients into iced mixing glass
1 1/2 oz. Gin
1/2 oz. grenadine
1 1/2 oz. sweet 'n' sour
Shake and strain
Fill with Draft Beer

SKY HIGH
House specialty glass, chilled
Pour ingredients into blender
1 oz. Vodka
3/4 oz. Baileys Irish Cream
3/4 oz. Frangelico
3/4 oz. Gran Gala Liqueur
2 oz. milk
Blend with ice
Whipped cream garnish
Drizzle 3/4 oz. Kahlúa

SKYSCRAPER
Highball glass, ice
Build in glass
1 1/4 oz. Bourbon
1/2 oz. Rose's Lime Juice
2 dashes Angostura Bitters
Fill with cranberry juice
Cucumber garnish (optional)

SLAM DUNK
Bucket glass, ice
Build in glass
1 1/2 oz. Southern Comfort
1/2 fill cranberry juice
1/2 fill orange juice

SLEIGH RIDE
Coffee mug, heated
Build in glass
1 1/4 oz. Canadian Whisky
3/4 oz. Vanilla Rum
1/2 oz. Cinnamon Schnapps
1/2 fill warm cranberry juice
1/2 fill warm apple cider
Cinnamon stick garnish

LUNA® TOP SHELF TRIPLE SEC

Why hasn't someone thought of this before? Considering that the Margarita is the country's most frequently requested specialty drink, it only seems natural that there would be a premium, high-grade triple sec. Welcome LUNA TOP SHELF TRIPLE SEC, the right product at exactly the right time.

This savory orange liqueur is made in Mexico at the Ibara Distillery. Founded in 1891 by French nationals, the distillery is owned and operated by the fourth generation of the Ibara family. The liqueur is made from a base of pure grain neutral spirits that are infused with oranges from Veracruz, Mexico and the Caribbean island of Curaçao. The oranges are carefully peeled so as to remove the bitter pith and sun-dried for several days. The alcohol is infused with the essential oils of the oranges and then twice filtered for purity. It is bottled at 81 proof.

Perhaps the best way to appreciate the enhanced taste and quality of Luna Top Shelf is to sip it next to the triple sec you're currently using. Be prepared to immediately switch brands afterwards. Luna has a medium-weight, velvety smooth body and a captivating citrus bouquet. The palate is brilliantly flavored with the vibrant flavor of fresh oranges. The finish is relaxed with absolutely no trace of excess heat or harshness.

While Luna Triple Sec belongs on the top-shelf, the liqueur was created to mix it up.

SLIPPED DISK
House specialty glass, chilled
Pour ingredients into blender
1 1/4 oz. Bacardi Gold Rum
1 oz. Captain Morgan Spiced Rum
3/4 oz. Disaronno Amaretto
3/4 oz. Grand Marnier
1/2 oz. cranberry juice
1/2 oz. orange juice
1/2 oz. grenadine
1/2 oz. sweet 'n' sour
1 oz. coconut cream syrup
1 oz. pineapple juice
Blend with ice

SLIPPERY BANANA
Presentation shot glass, chilled
Layer ingredients
1/3 fill Kahlúa
1/3 fill Crème de Banana
1/3 fill Baileys Irish Cream

SLIPPERY DICK
Rocks glass, chilled
Build in glass
1 oz. Peppermint Schnapps
1 oz. DeKuyper Butianshots Schnapps

SLIPPERY GREEK
Presentation shot glass, chilled
Layer ingredients
1/3 fill Ouzo
2/3 fill Baileys Irish Cream

SLIPPERY NIPPLE
Presentation shot glass, chilled
Layer ingredients
1/2 fill Sambuca
1/2 fill Baileys Irish Cream

SLOE COMFORTABLE SCREW
Highball glass, ice
Build in glass
3/4 oz. Sloe Gin
Near fill with orange juice
Float 3/4 oz. Southern Comfort

SLOE COMFORTABLE SCREW UP AGAINST THE WALL
Bucket glass, ice
Build in glass
1/2 oz. Sloe Gin
1/2 oz. Southern Comfort
Near fill with orange juice
Float 3/4 oz. Galliano Liqueur

SLOE GIN FIZZ
Bucket glass, ice
Pour ingredients into iced mixing glass
1 1/2 oz. Sloe Gin
2 oz. sweet 'n' sour
Shake and strain
Fill with club soda

SLOE POKE
Highball glass, ice
Build in glass
1 1/4 oz. Sloe Gin
Fill with cola

SLOE SCREW
aka **Cobra**
Highball glass, ice
Build in glass
1 1/4 oz. Sloe Gin
Fill with orange juice

SLOPPY JOE'S COCKTAIL
Cocktail glass, chilled
Pour ingredients into iced mixing glass
1 1/2 oz. Light Rum
1/2 oz. Dry Vermouth
1/4 oz. Triple Sec
1/4 oz. grenadine
1/2 oz. fresh lime juice
Shake and strain
Lime wedge garnish

SLOW TROPICAL CRUISE
Bucket glass, ice
Build in glass
1 1/4 oz. Orange Rum
3/4 oz. Sloe Gin
1 1/2 oz. pineapple juice
1 1/2 oz. orange juice
Orange slice garnish

SMILES FOR MILES
Rocks glass, ice
Build in glass
3/4 oz. Canadian Club Whisky
3/4 oz. Disaronno Amaretto
3/4 oz. Peppermint Schnapps

SMITH & KERNS
Brandy snifter, ice
Build in glass
1 1/2 oz. Kahlúa
1/2 fill half & half cream
1/2 fill club soda

SMITH & WESSON
Brandy snifter, ice
Build in glass
1 1/2 oz. Kahlúa
1/2 fill half & half cream
1/2 fill cola

SMOOTH DRIVER
Highball glass, ice
Build in glass
1 oz. Vodka
Near fill with orange juice
Float 3/4 oz. Cointreau

SMOOTH GENTLEMAN
Bucket glass, ice
Build in glass
1 1/4 oz. Gentleman Jack
    Tennessee Whiskey
1/2 oz. Disaronno Amaretto
Fill with cranberry juice
Orange slice and cherry garnish

SMOOTH SCREW
House specialty glass, chilled
Pour ingredients into blender
3/4 oz. Appleton Estate V/X Jamaica Rum
3/4 oz. Mount Gay Eclipse Rum
3/4 oz. Tia Maria
1 1/2 oz. pineapple juice
1 1/2 oz. orange juice
Blend with ice
Float 3/4 oz. Dark Rum

SMURF PISS
Rocks glass, chilled
Pour ingredients into iced mixing glass
1/2 oz. Light Rum
1/2 oz. Blueberry Schnapps
1/2 oz. Blue Curaçao
1 oz. sweet 'n' sour
1 oz. Seven-Up
Shake and strain

SNAKE BITE (1)
Rocks glass, ice
Build in glass
1 1/2 oz. Yukon Jack Liqueur
1/2 oz. Rose's Lime Juice
Lime wedge garnish

SNAKE BITE (2)
Beer glass, chilled
Build in glass
1/2 fill Draft Ale
1/2 fill hard apple cider

SNAKE BITE (3)
Presentation shot glass, chilled
Layer ingredients
1/2 fill White Crème de Cacao
1/2 fill Southern Comfort

TARANTULA® AZUL

In this fast paced world, a little help now and again is a welcome relief. For example, there are those days when there's just not enough time to carefully prepare a fabulous tasting Blue Margarita. In the past, the only options would have been to go without or hastily throw something together. Those dark days are over, thanks to the introduction of TARANTULA AZUL, a captivating and altogether enjoyable tequila product laced with the fresh and lively flavor of citrus and a splash of Pacific blue.

This one-of-a-kind spirit is made in America from a blend of premium blanco tequila and natural citrus liqueur. Somewhere along the line it obtains its signature blue color and the package is complete.

Tarantula Azul is an innovative treat. The product has a round, medium-weight body and a fresh, lively citrus bouquet. Its entry onto the palate is soft and smooth that fills the mouth with spice and fruit flavors. The tequila doesn't overstay its welcome, finishing clean and crisp.

Poured over ice, one could easily mistake Tarantula Azul for a skillfully crafted cocktail. The taste and appearance are so well conceived that it appeals to the senses as a complete thought. Indeed, add a spot of lime and lemon juice and you have a Blue Margarita that will rival your best efforts.

SNEAK & PEAK COCKTAIL
Cocktail glass, chilled
Pour ingredients into iced mixing glass
1 1/4 oz. Bacardi Limón Rum
1 oz. Stolichnaya Razberi Vodka
1/2 oz. Chambord
1 oz. Seven-Up
1 oz. sweet 'n' sour
Shake and strain
Lemon twist and raspberry garnish

SNEAKY PEACH
House specialty glass, chilled
Pour ingredients into blender
1 1/2 oz. Peach Schnapps
3/4 oz. grenadine
1 oz. sweet 'n' sour
2 oz. orange juice
2 oz. coconut cream syrup
Blend with ice

SNO-CAP
House specialty glass, chilled
Pour ingredients into blender
1 oz. Polar Ice Vodka
1 oz. Baileys Irish Cream
1/2 oz. Kahlúa
2 oz. espresso coffee
2 oz. coffee
2 scoops chocolate ice cream
Blend ingredients (with ice optional)
Whipped cream garnish
Drizzle 1/2 oz. Kahlúa

SNOWBALL
Cocktail glass, chilled
Pour ingredients into iced mixing glass
1 oz. Gin
1/2 oz. Anisette
1 1/2 oz. half & half cream
Shake and strain

SNOWSHOE (1)
Rocks glass, ice
Build in glass
1 1/2 oz. Bourbon
1/2 oz. Peppermint Schnapps

SNOWSHOE (2)
Rocks glass, ice
Build in glass
1 1/2 oz. Bourbon
3/4 oz. Rumple Minze Schnapps

SOCIALITE
Rocks glass, ice
Build in glass
1 1/2 oz. Original Cristall Vodka
3/4 oz. Godiva Chocolate Liqueur
3/4 oz. half & half cream
Reception stick candy garnish

SOCIALITE PRIZE FIGHT
House specialty glass, chilled
Pour ingredients into blender
2 oz. Doorly's XO Barbados Rum
2 oz. coconut cream syrup
1 oz. mango fruit juice
2 oz. pineapple juice
Blend with ice
Pineapple wedge garnish

SOMBRERO
aka **Kahlúa & Cream, Muddy River**
Brandy snifter, ice
Build in glass
1 1/2 oz. Kahlúa
3/4 oz. half & half cream

SOMOSA BAY
House specialty glass, ice
Pour ingredients into iced mixing glass
1 oz. Vodka
1/2 oz. Grand Marnier
1/2 oz. Chambord
1 oz. orange juice
1/4 oz. fresh lime juice
2 oz. sweet 'n' sour
Shake and strain
Lime wedge and orange slice garnish

SON OF A PEACH
House specialty glass, ice
Pour ingredients into iced mixing glass
1 1/2 oz. Vodka
1 oz. Peach Schnapps
1 oz. sweet 'n' sour
2 oz. pineapple juice
3 oz. orange juice
Shake and strain
Orange slice and cherry garnish

SONOMA CHILLER
Wine glass, ice
Build in glass
1 3/4 oz. Vodka
1/2 oz. fresh lemon juice
Fill with Chardonnay Wine

SONOMA NOUVEAU
Wine glass, ice
Build in glass
5 oz. alcohol-free Dry White Wine
Near fill with club soda
Float 3/4 oz. cranberry juice
Lemon twist garnish

SONORAN SUNRISE
Bucket glass, ice
Build in glass
3/4 oz. Sauza Hornitos Tequila
3/4 oz. Sauza Conmemorativo
  Añejo Tequila
1/2 oz. Gran Gala Orange Liqueur
Near fill with orange juice
Float 1/2 oz. grenadine
Lime wheel garnish

SONORAN SUNSET
Highball glass, ice
Build in glass
1 1/4 oz. El Tesoro Añejo Tequila
1/2 oz. Grand Marnier Centenaire
1/2 oz. cranberry juice
1 1/2 oz. fresh lime juice
Lime wheel garnish

SOUR
Cocktail glass, chilled
Pour ingredients into iced mixing glass
1 oz. requested liquor/liqueur
2 oz. sweet 'n' sour
Shake and strain
Orange slice and cherry garnish

SOUR MELON PATCH
Cocktail glass, chilled
Pour ingredients into iced mixing glass
1 3/4 oz. Irish Whiskey
3/4 oz. Midori
3/4 oz. fresh lime juice
1 1/2 oz. orange juice
1 1/2 oz. pineapple juice
Shake and strain
Lemon wheel garnish

SOUR MINT
Brandy snifter, ice
Pour ingredients into iced mixing glass
1 oz. Light Rum
1/2 oz. Peppermint Schnapps
2 oz. sweet 'n' sour
Shake and strain

SOUR, SPARKLING
  SWEET APPLE
House specialty glass, ice
Pour ingredients into iced mixing glass
1 1/4 oz. Canadian Club Whisky
3/4 oz. DeKuyper Pucker Sour Apple
2 oz. sweet 'n' sour
Shake and strain
Splash Seven-Up
Lemon wedge garnish

KETEL ONE®
CITROEN VODKA

KETEL ONE CITROEN is an ultra-premium vodka born with a 21st century personality from 300+ year old stock. Introduced in 2000, it is a spirit with impeccable pedigree that is every bit in step with contemporary tastes. It is a balancing act that likely only famed Ketel One could so masterfully pull off.

This handcrafted vodka is crafted at the Nolet family distillery in Schiedam, Holland. It is distilled in small batches entirely from wheat and all natural citrus flavors using the alembic copper pot still method. The final distillation occurs in a centuries old, alembic copper pot still, referred to as "Ketel #1." The Ketel One name is derived from the original "Distiller Ketel #1." After distillation, the vodka is rested in tile-lined tanks.

Like its world-class sibling, Ketel One Vodka, the Citroen is elegant and essentially flawless. The vodka has a pale yellow hue and a wafting bouquet of tree-ripened limes and lemons. The zesty palate is endowed with a refreshing, true-to-fruit citrus flavor that persists well into the relaxed and lingering finish. From stem to stern, this is an unsurpassed treat for the senses.

While it is a vodka without creative limitations behind the bar, do not miss out on the opportunity of first sampling Ketel One Citroen neat or slightly chilled. It will be well worth it.

SOUTH BEACH TWIST
Cocktail glass, ice
Pour ingredients into iced mixing glass
1 1/4 oz. Limoncello Liqueur
3/4 oz. Citrus Vodka
1/2 oz. Hpnotiq Liqueur
1/2 oz. Gran Gala Orange Liqueur
Shake and strain
Orange slice garnish

SOUTHERN BELLE
Rocks glass, chilled
Build in glass
2-3 mint sprigs
1/2 oz. simple syrup
1/2 oz. sweet 'n' sour
Muddle contents
Add ice
Fill with ginger ale
Mint sprig garnish

SOUTHERN SLIDE
House specialty glass, chilled
Pour ingredients into blender
1 1/2 oz. Southern Slide
1 1/2 oz. Kahlúa
3/4 oz. chocolate syrup
2 scoops vanilla ice cream
Blend ingredients
Pineapple wedge and cherry garnish

SOUTHERN SUICIDE
Rocks glass, chilled
Pour ingredients into iced mixing glass
3/4 oz. Jack Daniel's Tennessee Whiskey
3/4 oz. Southern Comfort
1/2 oz. orange juice
1/4 oz. Seven-Up
1/4 oz. grenadine
Shake and strain

SOUTH OF FRANCE
House specialty glass, chilled
Pour ingredients into blender
1 1/2 oz. Light Rum
1 oz. B & B Liqueur
1 1/2 oz. coconut cream syrup
2 1/2 oz. pineapple juice
Blend with ice
Pineapple wedge and cherry garnish

SOUTH-OF-THE-BORDER MANGO MASH
House specialty glass, chilled
Pour ingredients into blender
1 3/4 oz. Reposado Tequila
3/4 oz. Gran Gala Orange Liqueur
1 oz. pineapple juice
2 oz. coconut cream syrup
3 oz. mango puree
Blend with ice
Orange slice garnish

SOVEREIGNTY
Cappuccino cup, heated
Build in glass
1 oz. Chambord
1/2 oz. Tia Maria
1/2 oz. White Crème de Cacao
Near fill with hot espresso coffee
Top with frothed milk
Sprinkle shaved chocolate

SOYER-AU-CHAMPAGNE
House specialty glass, chilled
Pour ingredients into iced mixing glass
1/2 oz. Brandy
1/2 oz. Blue Curaçao
1/2 oz. grenadine
1 tbsp. vanilla ice cream
Shake and strain
Fill with Champagne
Strawberry garnish

SPANISH FLY
Bucket glass, ice
Pour ingredients into iced mixing glass
1 1/4 oz. Vodka
2 oz. sweet 'n' sour
2 oz. pineapple juice
Shake and strain
Float 3/4 oz. Blue Curaçao

SPATS COLUMBO
House specialty glass, ice
Build in glass
1 1/2 oz. Light Rum
1 oz. Midori
2 oz. orange juice
2 oz. pineapple juice
Float 3/4 oz. Sloe Gin
Pineapple wedge and cherry garnish

SPEARMINT ICED TEA
Bucket glass, ice
Build in glass
1 1/4 oz. Spearmint Schnapps
Fill with iced herbal tea
Lemon wedge garnish

SPERM BANK
Presentation shot glass, chilled
Layer ingredients
1/3 fill Baileys Irish Cream
1/3 fill White Crème de Cacao
1/3 fill Disaronno Amaretto
1 drop grenadine in center with straw

SPIDER CIDER
Bucket glass, ice
Build in glass
1 oz. DeKuyper Pucker Sour Apple
1 oz. Vodka
1/2 fill cranberry juice
1/2 fill orange juice

SPIKED SMOOTHIE
House specialty glass, chilled
Pour ingredients into blender
1 oz. Bourbon
1 oz. DeKuyper Peachtree Schnapps
3 oz. orange juice
1 cup diced peaches
1/2 ripe banana
2 scoops vanilla ice cream
Blend ingredients
Orange slice and cherry garnish

SPILT MILK (1)
House specialty glass, ice
Pour ingredients into iced mixing glass
1 oz. Baileys Irish Cream
1/2 oz. Canadian Club Whisky
1/2 oz. Light Rum
1/2 oz. Crème de Noyaux
1 1/2 oz. half & half cream
Shake and strain

SPILT MILK (2)
Rocks glass, chilled
Build in glass
1 1/2 oz. Baileys Irish Cream
1/2 oz. Crown Royal
1/2 oz. Disaronno Amaretto
Splash half & half cream

SPIRIT OF ERIE COFFEE
Coffee mug or glass, heated
Build in glass
1 1/4 oz. Knappogue Castle Irish Whiskey
3/4 oz. Coconut Rum
Near fill with hot coffee
Whipped cream garnish
Drizzle 1/2 oz. Celtic Crossing Irish Liqueur

OLD FORESTER®
KENTUCKY STRAIGHT
BOURBON WHISKEY

George Garvin Brown worked in the pharmaceutical industry in the 1860s. Looking to create a bourbon that was pure enough to prescribe as both an anesthetic and medicinal whiskey, he and his brother in 1870 formed the J.T.S. Brown and Brother Distillery in Louisville. The company blended whiskeys based on quality and taste and were the first in America to market their whiskey in sealed bottles to ensure purity, a brand they called OLD FORESTER KENTUCKY STRAIGHT BOURBON WHISKEY.

Today, the flagship of the distillery is the critically acclaimed, 86 proof Old Forester. It is a traditionally structured whiskey with a higher proportion of rye in its mash bill. The bourbon has a semisweet bouquet with the unmistakable notes of vanilla and maple syrup. Its palate is laced with the flavors of spice, caramel and fruit. The finish is long and decidedly spicy. From start to finish, Old Forester is an excellent illustration of why so many people are returning to America's whiskey.

The company has also created the limited release, vintage dated OLD FORESTER BIRTHDAY BOURBON. The first two issues in the line were distilled in 1989 (95 proof) and 1990 (93 proof). Each is subtly different from the other, but both are magnificent whiskeys, imbued with mesmerizing aromas and loaded with bakery-fresh flavors.

SPLENDID GIN
Cocktail glass, chilled
Pour ingredients into iced mixing glass
1 1/2 oz. Tanqueray N⁰ Ten Gin
3/4 oz. Dubonnet Rouge
3/4 oz. Limoncello Liqueur
Shake and strain
Lemon twist garnish

SPRING BREAK
Bucket glass, ice
Build in glass
1 3/4 oz. Malibu Caribbean Rum
1/2 fill cranberry juice
1/2 fill Seven-Up

SPRITZER
Wine glass or goblet, ice
Build in glass
1/2 fill White Wine
1/2 fill club soda
Lime or lemon wedge garnish
Note: May be requested made with
    Red or Rosé Wine

SPUTNIK
Champagne glass, chilled
Rim glass with grenadine and
    sugar (optional)
Pour ingredients into iced mixing glass
1 oz. Stolichnaya Ohranj Vodka
1 oz. orange juice
1/4 oz. grenadine
Stir and strain
Fill with Champagne
Lemon twist garnish

SPY'S DEMISE
House specialty glass, ice
Pour ingredients into iced mixing glass
3/4 oz. Vodka
3/4 oz. Gin
3/4 oz. Sloe Gin
1/2 oz. Light Rum
1/2 oz. grenadine
1 oz. sweet 'n' sour
Shake and strain
Fill with Seven-Up

ST. PATRICK'S DAY
Cocktail glass, chilled
Pour ingredients into iced mixing glass
1 1/2 oz. Jameson Irish Whiskey
3/4 oz. Blue Curaçao
1/2 oz. DeKuyper Peachtree Schnapps
1 oz. orange juice
Shake and strain
Orange slice garnish

ST. PETERSBURG SUNDAE
House specialty glass, chilled
Pour ingredients into blender
1 1/4 oz. Stolichnaya Vanil Vodka
3/4 oz. Disaronno Amaretto
1 oz. milk
2 scoops chocolate ice cream
Blend ingredients (with ice optional)
Whipped cream garnish
Drizzle 1/2 oz. Kahlúa
Sprinkle chopped roasted almonds

ST. TROPEZ
Bucket glass, ice
Build in glass
2 oz. Dubonnet Rouge
1 1/2 oz. orange juice
1 1/2 oz. cranberry juice
Orange slice garnish

STARBOARD TACK
House specialty glass, ice
Build in glass
1 1/2 oz. Mount Gay Eclipse Rum
1 oz. Mount Gay Special Reserve Rum
1/2 fill cranberry juice
Near fill with orange juice
Float 3/4 oz. Mount Gay Extra Old Rum
Orange slice and cherry garnish

STARBURST
House specialty glass, chilled
Pour ingredients into blender
1 1/2 oz. Dark Rum
1 1/2 oz. Citrus Rum
1 oz. Rose's lime juice
2 oz. pureed strawberries
3 oz. orange juice
Blend with ice
Strawberry garnish

STAR GAZER
Rocks glass, ice
Build in glass
1 1/2 oz. Corazón Reposado Tequila
3/4 oz. Kahlúa Especial
3/4 oz. Grand Marnier

STARLIGHT
Cocktail glass, chilled
Pour ingredients into iced mixing glass
2 oz. Vodka
1/2 oz. Opal Nera Black Sambuca
Stir and strain
Lemon twist garnish

STARS AT NIGHT
Presentation shot glass, chilled
Layer ingredients
1/2 fill Goldschläger
1/2 fill Jägermeister

STARS & STRIPES
Sherry glass, chilled
Layer ingredients
1/3 fill Blue Curaçao
1/3 fill grenadine
1/3 fill half & half cream

STATON ISLAND BERRY
House specialty glass, chilled
Pour ingredients into blender
1/2 oz. Gin
1/2 oz. Vodka
1/2 oz. Rum
1/2 oz. Tequila
1/2 oz. Triple Sec
2 oz. sweet 'n' sour
2 oz. strawberries, frozen
Blend with ice
Splash cola
Lemon wedge garnish

STEALTH BOMBER (1)
House specialty glass, ice
Pour ingredients into iced mixing glass
1 1/4 oz. Light Rum
1 1/4 oz. Gold Rum
3/4 oz. Blue Curaçao
1 1/2 oz. grapefruit juice
1 1/2 oz. cranberry juice
Shake and strain
Float 1 oz. Dark Rum

STEALTH BOMBER (2)
Bucket glass, ice
Pour ingredients into iced mixing glass
1 1/4 oz. Myers's Jamaican Rum
1/2 oz. Triple Sec
1 1/2 oz. grapefruit juice
1 1/2 oz. cranberry juice
Shake and strain
Splash club soda (optional)

STEEPLECHASE
House specialty glass, ice
Pour ingredients into iced mixing glass
1 1/2 oz. Bourbon
1/2 oz. Triple Sec
1/4 oz. Blackberry Brandy
2 dashes Angostura Bitters
2 oz. orange juice
Shake and strain
Mint sprigs (2) garnish

CASA NOBLE®
REPOSADO TEQUILA

Artisan in nature, Casa Noble 100% Agave Tequilas are highly sophisticated spirits worthy of *grand cru* status. For people who are looking for tequilas that will gently seduce their senses, here's the ticket.

The agaves used for Casa Noble Tequilas are slow baked in stone ovens and then spontaneously fermented. The natural yeast lends an intriguing flavor to the finished spirit. All of the Casa Noble tequilas are triple-distilled in alembic stills.

CASA NOBLE REPOSADO strikes a balance between the spirited character of a silver tequila and the mellow refinement of an añejo. It is aged 364 days, just long enough to soften its character, while leaving the inherent quality of the agave unaffected by the tannins in the wood.

The distillery also produces CASA NOBLE CRYSTAL, a superb, blanco tequila with a sleek body and engaging bouquet. The palate features a balanced offering of floral and spice, and the finish is long and relaxed.

CASA NOBLE AÑEJO LIMITED RESERVE is a regal añejo tequila extended aged in French White Oak casks rather than ex-bourbon barrels. Made in limited quantities, the Casa Noble Añejo has a silky texture, a spicy palate and a slightly sweet, smoky finish.

These delectable spirits deserve their day in a snifter and the opportunity to show what they're really made of. Frankly, they've earned the right.

STEEPLE JACK
Bucket glass, ice
Pour ingredients into iced mixing glass
1 1/2 oz. Laird's Applejack Brandy
1/2 oz. Rose's Lime Juice
2 1/2 oz. apple juice
Shake and strain
Fill with club soda
Lime wedge garnish

STIFF DICK
Rocks glass, chilled
Build in glass
1 oz. Baileys Irish Cream
1 oz. DeKuyper Buttershots Schnapps

STILETTO
House specialty glass, ice
Pour ingredients into iced mixing glass
1 oz. Disaronno Amaretto
3/4 oz. Crème de Banana
1/2 fill orange juice
1/2 fill pineapple juice
Shake and strain

STINGER
Rocks glass, ice
Build in glass
1 1/2 oz. Brandy
3/4 oz. White Crème de Menthe

STOCK MARKET ZOO
Bucket glass, ice
Pour ingredients into iced mixing glass
1/2 oz. Silver Tequila
1/2 oz. Gin
1/2 oz. Spiced Rum
1/2 oz. Bourbon
1/2 oz. grenadine
1 oz. orange juice
2 oz. pineapple juice
Shake and strain

STOLI AROUND THE WORLD
House specialty glass, ice
Pour ingredients into iced mixing glass
1/2 oz. Stolichnaya Ohranj Vodka
1/2 oz. Stolichnaya Vanil Vodka
1/2 oz. Stolichnaya Razberi Vodka
1/2 oz. Stolichnaya Citros Vodka
2 oz. sweet 'n' sour
2 oz. cola
Shake and strain
Lemon wedge garnish

STOLICHNAYA LEMONADE
House specialty glass, ice
Build in glass
1 1/4 oz. Stolichnaya Citros Vodka
1/2 oz. Grand Marnier
1/2 fill sweet 'n' sour
1/2 fill lemon-lime soda
Lemon wheel garnish

STONE SOUR
Cocktail glass, chilled
Pour ingredients into iced mixing glass
1 oz. requested liquor/liqueur
1 oz. sweet 'n' sour
1 oz. orange juice
Shake and strain
Orange slice and cherry garnish

STORM-A-LONG BAY
House specialty glass, chilled
Pour ingredients into blender
1 1/2 oz. Dark Rum
3/4 oz. Chambord
1 oz. cranberry juice
2 oz. pineapple juice
2 scoops vanilla ice cream
Blend ingredients (with ice optional)
Whipped cream garnish

STRAIGHT SHOOTER
Presentation shot glass, chilled
Build in glass
1/3 fill Midori
1/3 fill Vodka
1/3 fill orange juice

STRAWBERRIES 'N' CREAM
aka **Wimbleton**
House specialty glass, chilled
Pour ingredients into blender
1 1/2 oz. Strawberry Schnapps
1/2 oz. simple syrup
1/2 cup strawberries
1 oz. sweet 'n' sour
2 oz. half & half cream
Blend with ice
Strawberry garnish

STRAWBERRY ALEXANDRA
House specialty glass, chilled
Pour ingredients into blender
1 oz. Brandy
1 oz. White Crème de Cacao
3 oz. strawberry puree
2 scoops vanilla ice cream
Blend ingredients (with ice optional)
Whipped cream garnish
Sprinkle shaved chocolate

STRAWBERRY BANANA SPLIT
House specialty glass, chilled
Pour ingredients into blender
1 1/4 oz. Mount Gay Old Rum
3/4 oz. Crème de Banana
1/2 cup strawberries
1 oz. half & half cream
1/2 tsp. vanilla
2 scoops vanilla ice cream
Blend ingredients (with ice optional)
Whipped cream and banana slice garnish

STRAWBERRY NUT
House specialty glass, chilled
Pour ingredients into blender
1 1/4 oz. Frangelico
3/4 oz. half & half cream
1/2 cup strawberries
2 scoops macadamia ice cream
Blend ingredients (with ice optional)
Whipped cream garnish
Dust powdered cocoa

STRAWBERRY QUICKIE
Rocks glass, chilled
Pour ingredients into iced mixing glass
1 1/4 oz. Tequila Rose Cream Liqueur
1 oz. DeKuyper Buttershots Schnapps
3/4 oz. Baileys Irish Cream
Shake and strain

STRAWBERRY ROSE
House specialty glass, ice
Pour ingredients into iced mixing glass
1 1/2 oz. Tequila Rose Cream Liqueur
1 oz. White Crème de Cacao
2 oz. half & half cream
Shake and strain
Strawberry garnish

STRAWBERRY SHAKE
House specialty glass, chilled
Pour ingredients into blender
1 1/2 oz. Disaronno Amaretto
1/2 cup strawberries
1 1/2 oz. half & half cream
2 scoops vanilla ice cream
Blend ingredients (with ice optional)
Strawberry garnish

DEKUYPER® BUTTERSHOTS® SCHNAPPS

No one can call DEKUYPER BUTTERSHOTS SCHNAPPS a stuffy or uptight liqueur. Quite to the contrary, it is a butterscotch-flavored schnapps born and bred for fun. While many flavored schnapps have fallen out of fashion, DeKuyper Buttershots continues to thrive, primarily because butterscotch is a timeless favorite and this schnapps is devoid of the cloying sweetness that plagues many of its contemporaries.

DeKuyper Buttershots is produced by combining pure grain neutral spirits with butterscotch flavoring. The clear, 30 proof liqueur possesses several characteristics that make it ideal for drink making. It is exceptionally aromatic for a schnapps and the wafting aroma of butterscotch and vanilla is downright enticing. It has a light to medium-weight body that is jam packed with the semisweet flavor of butterscotch and a hint of caramel.

Versatility must be DeKuyper Buttershots' middle name. While the schnapps initially earned its reputation for greatness as the primary ingredient in numerous shooters, bartenders discovered it also worked perfectly in hot cocoa, coffee and cappuccinos. It is an ideal flavor to pair with a wide assortment of other liqueurs, such as Baileys, Kahlúa and Godiva. To top it off, Buttershots is tailor-made for milkshakes and ice cream drinks.

STRAWBERRY SMASH
House specialty glass, chilled
Pour ingredients into blender
1 oz. Gold Rum
1 oz. Chambord
1/2 oz. 151° Rum
1/2 cup strawberries
1 ripe banana
1 oz. orange juice
2 oz. sweet 'n' sour
Blend with ice
Strawberry garnish

STRAW HOUSE HUMMER
House specialty glass, chilled
Pour ingredients into blender
1 1/4 oz. Light Rum
3/4 oz. Crème de Banana
3/4 oz. Disaronno Amaretto
1 peeled, ripe banana
1 oz. orange juice
1 oz. sweet 'n' sour
Blend with ice
Whipped cream and banana slice garnish
Drizzle 3/4 oz. Dark Rum

STRUMMER HUMMER
House specialty glass, chilled
Pour ingredients into blender
3/4 oz. Light Rum
3/4 oz. Cruzan Banana Rum
3/4 oz. Disaronno Amaretto
1 ripe banana
Blend with ice
Banana slice garnish

STUBB'S AYERS ROCK
House specialty glass, ice
Pour ingredients into iced mixing glass
1 1/2 oz. Stubb's Queensland Rum
2 oz. sweet 'n' sour
3 oz. cranberry juice
Shake and strain

SUFFERING BASTARD
House specialty glass, ice
Pour ingredients into iced mixing glass
1 1/2 oz. Amber Rum
3/4 oz. Light Rum
3/4 oz. Crème de Noyaux
3/4 oz. Cointreau
1/2 oz. simple syrup
1 1/2 oz. fresh lime juice
Shake and strain
Cucumber peel garnish

SUGAR BABY
Rocks glass, chilled
Pour ingredients into iced mixing glass
3/4 oz. Kahlúa
3/4 oz. DeKuyper Buttershots Schnapps
3/4 oz. Vanilla Rum
3/4 oz. Baileys Irish Cream
Shake and strain

SUGAR DADDY
Rocks glass, ice
Build in glass
1 1/2 oz. VSOP Cognac
1 1/2 oz. Kahlúa
Orange twist garnish

SUISSESSE
House specialty glass, ice
Pour ingredients into iced mixing glass
1 oz. Pernod
2 oz. sweet 'n' sour
Shake and strain
Fill with club soda

SUMMER BREEZE
Highball glass, ice
Build in glass
1 1/4 oz. Rum
1/2 fill grapefruit juice
1/2 fill cranberry juice

SUMMER DAZE
Tall house specialty glass, ice
Build in glass
1 1/2 oz. Raspberry Vodka
1 oz. Hpnotiq Liqueur
3/4 oz. orange juice
Fill with lemonade
Float 3/4 oz. Blue Curaçao
Lemon wedge garnish

SUMMER HUMMER
Cocktail glass, chilled
Pour ingredients into iced mixing glass
1 3/4 oz. Gin
1/2 oz. Chambord
1 3/4 oz. sweet 'n' sour
Shake and strain
Lime wedge garnish

SUMMER IN THE PARK
Champagne glass, chilled
Pour ingredients into iced mixing glass
2 oz. RémyRed Red Berry Infusion
1 oz. cranberry juice
1 oz. sweet 'n' sour
Shake and strain
Fill with Champagne
Orange twist garnish

SUMMER LEMONADE
Bucket glass, ice
Build in glass
1 1/2 oz. Citrus Vodka
1/2 oz. Blue Curaçao
1/2 fill lemonade
1/2 fill Seven-Up

SUMMER MEMORIES
Cocktail glass, chilled
Pour ingredients into iced mixing glass
2 oz. Vodka
3/4 oz. fresh watermelon juice
Stir and strain
Watermelon cube garnish

SUMMER SLAMMER
House specialty glass, ice
Pour ingredients into iced mixing glass
1/2 oz. Galliano Liqueur
1/2 oz. Crème de Banana
1/2 oz. Myers's Jamaican Rum
1/2 oz. sweet 'n' sour
1/2 oz. grenadine
1 1/2 oz. orange juice
1 1/2 oz. pineapple juice
Shake and strain
Cherry garnish

SUMMER TONIC
House specialty glass, chilled
Rim glass with lemon flavored
    salt (optional)
Pour ingredients into blender
2 oz. Gin
1 oz. Limoncello Liqueur
1 oz. tonic water
3 oz. sweet 'n' sour
Blend with ice
Float 3/4 oz. Crème de Cassis
Lemon wheel garnish

SUMMERCELLO
Bucket glass, ice
Build in glass
1 1/2 oz. Limoncello Liqueur
3/4 oz. Stolichnaya Citros Vodka
3/4 oz. Stolichnaya Persik Vodka
1 3/4 oz. orange juice
1 3/4 oz. pineapple juice
Orange slice garnish

SUNBURNT SEÑORITA
Cocktail glass, chilled
Pour ingredients into iced mixing glass
1 1/4 oz. El Tesoro Añejo Tequila
1 oz. fresh lime juice
3/4 oz. watermelon juice
Shake and strain
Lime wedge garnish

HARDY® NOCES D'OR COGNAC

The esteemed cognac house of A. Hardy was founded in 1863, and within a decade became one of the preeminent brandy distillers in Europe. Their sales were helped in no small measure by Czar Nicholas II, who regularly served Hardy Cognac de l'Alliance at all royal functions, formal or not.

Despite its rapid rise in popularity, A. Hardy began bottling their extraordinary brandies for the first time shortly after World War II. While the limelight shines brightly on all of the Hardy cognacs, it is the legendary HARDY NOCES D'OR COGNAC that deservedly draws much of the attention.

Introduced in 1946 to commemorate the 50th wedding anniversary of Armand Hardy, handcrafted Noces d'Or is a *Tres Ancienne Grande Champagne* cognac, meaning it is a blend of very old brandies, all of which were double-distilled entirely from grapes grown in the Grande Champagne district of Cognac. The vintage, barrel-matured brandies used in its blend average in age an extraordinary 50 years.

Hardy Noces d'Or Cognac is a magnificent brandy. It has a lustrous, deep copper color and a firm, lightweight body. The expansive bouquet features an array of savory aromas, including ripe fruit, spice, honey and toasted oak. The brandy has a remarkably lush, sophisticated palate and a warm, lingering finish.

SUNDAY BRUNCH PUNCH COCKTAIL
Cocktail glass, chilled
Pour ingredients into iced mixing glass
2 oz. Tanqueray N° Ten Gin
1/2 oz. Grand Marnier Centenaire
1 oz. orange juice
3 dashes Angostura Bitters
Shake and strain
Orange twist garnish

SUNFLOWER
Cocktail glass, chilled
Pour ingredients into iced mixing glass
2 oz. Van Gogh Vodka
1/2 oz. Grand Marnier
3/4 oz. orange juice
Stir and strain
Orange slice garnish

SUNGLOW
Cocktail glass, chilled
Pour ingredients into iced mixing glass
2 oz. Vodka
1/2 oz. XO Cognac
3-4 drops orange flower water
Stir and strain
Orange twist garnish

SUNKNEE DELITE
Bucket glass, ice
Pour ingredients into iced mixing glass
1 1/2 oz. Canadian Club Whisky
3/4 oz. Limoncello Liqueur
2 oz. sweet 'n' sour
Shake and strain
Fill with Squirt
Lemon wheel garnish

SUNRISE
Bucket glass, ice
Build in glass
1 1/2 oz. Light Rum
1/2 oz. Triple Sec
3/4 oz. orange juice
Near fill with grapefruit juice
Float 1/2 oz. grenadine

SUN SEEKER
House specialty glass, ice
Build in glass
1 1/4 oz. Bacardi Light Rum
1 oz. Mount Gay Eclipse Rum
1 oz. Crème de Banana
2 oz. pineapple juice
2 oz. orange juice
Splash Seven-Up
Orange slice and cherry garnish

SUNSTROKE
Cocktail glass, chilled
Pour ingredients into iced mixing glass
1 oz. Vodka
1/2 oz. Grand Marnier
2 oz. grapefruit juice
Shake and strain

SUNTAN TEASER
Rocks glass, chilled
Pour ingredients into iced mixing glass
1 1/2 oz. Malibu Caribbean Rum
1/2 oz. Cruzan Banana Rum
1/4 oz. Triple Sec
1/4 oz. Captain Morgan Spiced Rum
1/2 oz. pineapple juice
1 dash grenadine
Shake and strain

SURF SIDER (1)
Cocktail glass, chilled
Pour ingredients into iced mixing glass
1 1/4 oz. Dark Rum
3/4 oz. Blue Curaçao
3/4 oz. Grand Marnier
1/2 oz. Rose's Lime Juice
1 1/4 oz. pineapple juice
Shake and strain
Lime wedge garnish

SURF SIDER (2)
Bucket glass, ice
Build in glass
1 1/4 oz. Malibu Caribbean Rum
1/2 oz. Rose's Lime Juice
Near fill with cranberry juice
Splash club soda

SURFERS ON ACID
Rocks glass, chilled
Pour ingredients into iced mixing glass
3/4 oz. Malibu Caribbean Rum
3/4 oz. Jägermeister
1 1/2 oz. pineapple juice
Shake and strain

SUSIE TAYLOR
Highball glass, ice
Build in glass
1 1/4 oz. Light Rum
Fill with ginger ale
Lemon wedge garnish

SWAMP WATER
Mason jar, ice
Build in glass
1 1/2 oz. Green Chartreuse
Fill with grapefruit juice

SWAMP WATER STINGER
House specialty glass, ice
Pour ingredients into iced mixing glass
1 1/2 oz. Vodka
3/4 oz. Southern Comfort
1/2 oz. DeKuyper Peachtree Schnapps
1/2 oz. Blue Curaçao
1/2 oz. pineapple juice
1/2 oz. cranberry juice
1 oz. orange juice
Shake and strain

SWEATY BETTY
House specialty glass, chilled
Pour ingredients into blender
1 oz. Yukon Jack Liqueur
1 oz. Peppermint Schnapps
2 1/2 oz. sweet 'n' sour
Blend with ice
Lemon wedge garnish

SWEET (IRISH) DREAMS
Brandy snifter, ice
Pour ingredients into iced mixing glass
1 oz. Irish Whiskey
1 oz. Baileys Irish Cream
1 oz. Irish Liqueur
Shake and strain

SWEET RED KISS
Cocktail glass, chilled
Rim glass with sugar (optional)
Pour ingredients into iced mixing glass
1 1/2 oz. Dubonnet Rouge
3/4 oz. Chambord
3/4 oz. Absolut Kurant Vodka
1/2 oz. orange juice
1/2 oz. of pineapple juice
1/2 oz. cranberry juice
Shake and strain
Orange slice garnish

SWEET TART (1)
House specialty glass, chilled
Pour ingredients into blender
2 oz. Vodka
1/4 oz. Rose's Lime Juice
2 oz. cranberry juice
2 oz. pineapple juice
Blend with ice
Lime wheel garnish

SWEET TART (2)
Bucket glass, ice
Pour ingredients into iced mixing glass
1 1/4 oz. Vodka
3/4 oz. Chambord
1/4 oz. simple syrup (optional)
3 oz. sweet 'n' sour
Shake and strain
Fill with Seven-Up

DAMRAK® AMSTERDAM GIN

Founded in 1575, the Lucas Bols Company of Amsterdam is one of the oldest spirits companies in Europe. From the onset, the distillery has made a juniper-infused grain spirit called *jenever*. Bols became the spirits purveyor to the Dutch East India Company, which also secured the company a steady source of spices and herbs from Indonesia, Ceylon, Malaya and the Spice Islands. These exotic flavorings would eventually give birth to DAMRAK AMSTERDAM GIN.

Introduced in 2001, this ultra-premium spirit is crafted from a proprietary recipe dating back to the 1600s. It combines 17 fruits, berries, herbs and spices, each individually distilled to lock in its distinctive flavor and fragrance. The spirit base of the gin is made from grain and malt, which after it has been infused with botanicals, undergoes a total of five distillations. The gin is bottled at 83.6 proof.

Damrak Amsterdam Gin is absolutely superb in every respect. It has pristine clarity and a lightweight, silky smooth body. The generous bouquet is a captivating array of floral, citrus and herbal aromas. Initially, the flavor of succulent juniper berries is most prevalent on the palate, followed by a surge of the tart, zesty flavors of the botanical mix. The gin has a crisp and flavorful finish.

Damrak Amsterdam Gin makes a marvelous Martini, but is also ideally suited for any gin-based assignment.

SWEET TART (3)
Rocks glass, chilled
Pour ingredients into iced mixing glass
3/4 oz. Chambord
3/4 oz. Disaronno Amaretto
1 1/2 oz. sweet 'n' sour
Shake and strain

SWIMMING NAKED AT SUNSET
Bucket glass, ice
Build in glass
1 1/2 oz. Dark Rum
1/2 oz. Orange Liqueur
1/2 oz. orange juice
1/4 oz. grenadine
Fill with grapefruit juice
Orange wedge garnish

SYLK CAFÉ
Brandy snifter, ice
Build in glass
1 1/2 oz. Kahlúa
1 1/2 oz. Sylk Cream Liqueur

SYLK STOCKINGS
Brandy snifter, ice
Build in glass
1 3/4 oz. Drambuie
3/4 oz. Sylk Cream Liqueur

SYLK TOP HAT
Brandy snifter, ice
Build in glass
1 3/4 oz. Dewar's 12 Year Special Reserve
3/4 oz. Drambuie
3/4 oz. Sylk Cream Liqueur

TAHITIAN APPLE
Highball glass, ice
Build in glass
1 1/4 oz. Light Rum
Fill with apple juice

TAKE THE 'A' TRAIN
House specialty glass, ice
Pour ingredients into iced mixing glass
1 1/4 oz. Citrus Vodka
3/4 oz. orange juice
2 oz. grapefruit juice
2 oz. cranberry juice
Shake and strain
Fill with club soda
Lemon wedge garnish

TAKE THE PRIZE
Cocktail glass, chilled
Pour ingredients into iced mixing glass
1 1/2 oz. Espolon Silver Tequila
3/4 oz. Chambord
3/4 oz. Cruzan Mango Rum
1/2 oz. fresh lemon juice
1 oz. grapefruit
1 1/2 oz. sweet 'n' sour
Shake and strain
Lime wedge garnish

TAMARA LVOVA
House specialty glass, chilled
Pour ingredients into blender
1 oz. Stolichnaya Razberi Vodka
1 oz. Appleton Estate V/X Jamaica Rum
1 oz. Dark Crème de Cocao
1/4 oz. chocolate syrup
2 scoops vanilla ice cream
Blend ingredients (with ice optional)
Whipped cream and strawberry garnish
Drizzle 3/4 oz. Godiva Chocolate Liqueur

TAM-O'-SHANTER
Rocks glass, ice
Build in glass
1 1/2 oz. Kahlúa
1/2 oz. Irish Whiskey
3/4 oz. half & half cream

TANGERINE DROP
Cocktail glass, chilled
Pour ingredients into iced mixing glass
2 1/2 oz. Orange Vodka
1/4 oz. grenadine
3/4 oz. grapefruit juice
3/4 oz. cranberry juice
Stir and strain
Orange slice garnish

TARNISHED BULLET
Rocks glass, ice
Build in glass
1 1/2 oz. Tequila
1/2 oz. Green Crème de Menthe

TAVERN SUCKER, THE
Bucket glass, ice
Pour ingredients into iced mixing glass
3/4 oz. Frangelico
3/4 oz. DeKuyper Buttershots Schnapps
3/4 oz. Kahlúa
3/4 oz. Baileys Irish Cream
2 oz. chocolate milk
Shake and strain

T-BIRD
Rocks glass, chilled
Pour ingredients into iced mixing glass
1/2 oz. Vodka
1/2 oz. Grand Marnier
1/2 oz. Disaronno Amaretto
1 1/2 oz. pineapple juice
Shake and strain

TEATIME
Glass mug, heated
Build in glass
1 oz. Irish Liqueur
1 oz. Irish Whiskey
Near fill with hot tea
Serve with lemon wedge

TENDER MERCIES
Coffee mug, heated
Build in glass
1/2 oz. Tuaca
1/2 oz. Tia Maria
1/2 oz. Baileys Irish Cream
Near fill with hot coffee
Whipped cream garnish

TENNESSEE GENTLEMAN
Bucket glass, ice
Pour ingredients into iced mixing glass
1 1/4 oz. Gentleman Jack
    Tennessee Whiskey
1 1/4 oz. sweet 'n' sour
Shake and strain
Fill with ginger ale
Orange slice garnish

TENNESSEE MUD
Coffee mug, heated
Build in glass
3/4 oz. Jack Daniel's Tennessee Whiskey
3/4 oz. Disaronno Amaretto
Near fill with hot coffee
Whipped cream garnish

TENNESSEE TEA
Highball glass, ice
Build in glass
1 oz. Jack Daniel's Tennessee Whiskey
1/2 oz. Dark Crème de Cacao
Fill with cranberry juice
Lemon twist garnish

TEQUADOR
Bucket glass, ice
Build in glass
1 1/2 oz. Reposado Tequila
1/2 oz. Rose's Lime Juice
1/2 oz. Raspberry Liqueur
Fill with pineapple juice
Lime wedge garnish

REDRUM®

Best described as luscious, REDRUM is a little slice of paradise in every sip. There is absolutely nothing staid or conventional about this flavored rum and it has nothing to fear from the competition, because there is nothing on the face of the planet remotely like it.

Introduced in 1997, RedRum is made in the US Virgin Islands from a blend of light-bodied, continuous-distilled rums made from locally grown sugar cane. It is then infused with a proprietary blend of natural fruit flavors that include mango, pineapple, coconut and cherry. It is bottled at 70 proof.

RedRum is bred for drink making and having fun. It has a pale red hue and a sleek, featherweight body. The bouquet is an enticing offering of fruit where no one aroma predominates. The fun begins as it washes over the palate and fills the mouth with a satiny array of warm, nectar-like flavors. They linger on the palate for an impressively long time, and then gradually subside. The entire experience is splendid.

In 2002 the makers of RedRum released VOODOO SPICED RUM, a delectable blend of one year old añejo Virgin Island rums, cinnamon, clove and premium Madagascar vanilla. It has a delicate bouquet of vanilla with cinnamon notes and the palate is a moderately spicy dream. The rum enjoys scores of creative applications behind the bar. Little wonder why VooDoo Spiced Rum is critically acclaimed.

TEQUILA A LA BERTITA
Bucket glass, ice
Pour ingredients into iced mixing glass
2 oz. Tequila
3/4 oz. fresh lime juice
1/2 oz. Rose's Lime Juice
2 oz. lemonade
Shake and strain
Fill with Squirt
Lime wedge garnish

TEQUILA DRIVER
Highball glass, ice
Build in glass
1 1/4 oz. Tequila
Fill with orange juice

TEQUILA HIGHLANDER
Rocks glass, ice
Build in glass
1 1/2 oz. Gold Tequila
3/4 oz. Drambuie

TEQUILA MARIA
House specialty glass, chilled
Pour ingredients into blender
3/4 oz. Reposado Tequila
3/4 oz. Gold Rum
1/2 oz. Crème de Banana
1/2 oz. Blackberry Brandy
3/4 oz. grenadine
1/2 cup strawberries
1 1/2 oz. sweet 'n' sour
1 1/2 oz. fresh lime juice
Blend with ice

TEQUILA MOCKINGBIRD (1)
Cocktail glass, chilled
Pour ingredients into iced mixing glass
1 1/2 oz. Tequila
1/2 oz. Green Crème de Menthe
1 1/2 oz. fresh lime juice
Shake and strain
Lime wedge garnish

TEQUILA MOCKINGBIRD (2)
House specialty glass, ice
Pour ingredients into iced mixing glass
1 1/4 oz. Añejo Tequila
3/4 oz. Blue Curaçao
2 oz. orange juice
2 oz. sweet 'n' sour
Shake and strain
Lime wedge garnish

TEQUILA QUENCHER
Highball glass, ice
Build in glass
1 1/4 oz. Tequila
1/2 fill orange juice
1/2 fill Squirt (grapefruit) soda
Lime wedge garnish

TEQUILA ROSÉ
Bucket glass, ice
Build in glass
1 1/2 oz. Tequila
1/2 oz. Rose's Lime Juice
Near fill with grapefruit juice
Float 1/2 oz. grenadine

TEQUILA SLAMMER/POPPER
Presentation shot glass, chilled
Build in glass
1/2 fill Gold Tequila
1/2 fill ginger ale
Place napkin and palm over glass, slam glass
    down on bar top, drink while foaming

TEQUILA SLIDER
Rocks glass, chilled
Build in glass
1 1/2 oz. Tequila
2 dashes soy sauce
2 dashes Tabasco Sauce
1/2 tsp. horseradish
1/2 oz. fresh lime juice
1 medium raw oyster
1/2 tsp. caviar (optional)

TEQUILA SUNRISE
Bucket glass, ice
Build in glass
1 oz. Tequila
Near fill with orange juice
Float 1/2 oz. grenadine

TEQUILA SUNSET
Bucket glass, ice
Build in glass
1 oz. Tequila
Near fill with orange juice
Float 3/4 oz. Blackberry Brandy

TEQUILIER REAL
Rocks glass, ice
Build in glass
1 1/2 oz. Casa Noble Extra Aged Tequila
3/4 oz. Grand Marnier Centenaire

TEST-TUBE BABY (1)
Presentation shot glass, chilled
Build in glass
1/2 fill Disaronno Amaretto
1/2 fill Tequila
2 drops Baileys Irish Cream

TEST-TUBE BABY (2)
Presentation shot glass, chilled
Build in glass
3/4 oz. Disaronno Amaretto
1/2 oz. Southern Comfort
3 drops Baileys Irish Cream in center
    with straw

TEXAS TEA
Bucket glass, ice
Build in glass
3/4 oz. Absolut Vodka
3/4 oz. Absolut Kurant Vodka
3/4 oz. Chambord
Fill with pineapple juice

THREE AMIGOS
Rocks glass, chilled
Pour ingredients into iced mixing glass
1 oz. Jose Cuervo Especial Tequila
1 oz. Rumple Minze Schnapps
1 oz. Goldschläger
Stir and strain

THUG PASSION
Champagne glass, chilled
Pour ingredients into iced mixing glass
2 oz. RémyRed Red Berry Infusion
2 oz. sweet 'n' sour
Shake and strain
Fill with Champagne
Orange twist garnish

THUMPER
Rocks glass, ice
Build in glass
1 1/2 oz. Brandy
3/4 oz. Tuaca
Lemon twist garnish

TICKLE ME
Rocks glass, ice
Build in glass
1 3/4 oz. Boru Vodka
1/2 oz. Crème de Cacao
1/2 oz. Limoncello Liqueur
Lemon twist garnish

TIDAL WAVE (1)
Bucket glass, ice
Build in glass
1 1/2 oz. Laird's Applejack Brandy
Near fill with orange juice
Splash cranberry juice
Orange slice garnish

TIDAL WAVE (2)
Bucket glass, ice
Pour ingredients into iced mixing glass
3/4 oz. Gold Rum
3/4 oz. Spiced Rum
3/4 oz. Crème de Banana
2 oz. orange juice
Shake and strain
Float 3/4 oz. Galliano Liqueur

HERRADURA®
REPOSADO TEQUILA

TEQUILA HERRADURA is one of the preeminent brands of tequila. Every stage of its production takes place on the Herradura Estate in Amatitán, and it is among only a few distilleries that have always only produced 100% agave tequila. First imported in the 1950s, Herradura was the first brand of 100% agave tequilas available in the United States.

Herradura crafts its tequila using many of the same techniques perfected more than a century ago. Mature, estate grown blue agaves are baked in clay ovens, and then slowly fermented with wild, naturally occurring yeasts. Herradura tequilas are double-distilled in large, stainless steel, alembic stills and aged in both American and French oak barrels.

Herradura markets four versions of their natural, estate-bottled tequila. HERRADURA BLANCO is aromatic with a delectable palate featuring spicy, peppery and citrus flavors. HERRADURA REPOSADO is aged in oak barrels for 11 months. It has a generous, floral and dried fruit bouquet and a lavish, vanilla and oak laced palate. Both are exceptional.

The 2 year old HERRADURA AÑEJO is luxurious and loaded with the aromas and flavors of pepper, ripe apples and toasted oak. In a league of its own is ultra-premium HERRADURA SELECCIÓN SUPREMA, a 4 year old añejo brimming with sophistication and a character most similar to a well aged alembic brandy.

TIDAL WAVE (3)
Rocks glass, chilled
Pour ingredients into iced mixing glass
1/2 oz. Vodka
1/2 oz. Gold Rum
1/2 oz. Captain Morgan Spiced Rum
1/2 oz. cranberry juice
1/2 oz. sweet 'n' sour
Shake and strain

TIDY BOWL
Rocks glass, chilled
Pour ingredients into iced mixing glass
1 1/2 oz. Vodka
1/2 oz. Blue Curaçao
1/2 oz. sweet 'n' sour
Shake and strain
Raisins (2) garnish

TIE ME TO THE BED POST
Rocks glass, chilled
Pour ingredients into iced mixing glass
1/2 oz. Midori
1/2 oz. Citrus Vodka
1/2 oz. Malibu Caribbean Rum
1 oz. sweet 'n' sour
Shake and strain

TIGHTER CIDER
Coffee mug, heated
Build in glass
1 oz. Appleton Estate V/X Jamaica Rum
3/4 oz. Calvados Apple Brandy
3/4 oz. Apple Schnapps
1 tsp. apple butter
2 pinches cinnamon
Fill with hot apple cider
Apple wedge garnish

TIGHT SWEATER
Coffee mug, heated
Build in glass
1/2 oz. Frangelico
1/2 oz. Kahlúa
1/2 oz. Disaronno Amaretto
1/2 oz. Baileys Irish Cream
Near fill with hot coffee
Whipped cream garnish
Dust powdered cocoa

TIJUANA BULLDOG
Bucket glass, ice
Build in glass
1 1/4 oz. Reposado Tequila
3/4 oz. Kahlúa
2 1/2 oz. milk
Fill with cola

TIJUANA SCREW
aka **Tijuana Split**
Highball glass, ice
Build in glass
1 1/4 oz. Tequila
1/2 fill grapefruit juice
1/2 fill orange juice

TIJUANA SUNRISE
Bucket glass, ice
Build in glass
1 oz. Tequila
Fill with orange juice
6 dashes Angostura Bitters

TIKI PASSION PUNCH
House specialty glass, ice
Pour ingredients into iced mixing glass
3/4 oz. Appleton Estate V/X Jamaica Rum
3/4 oz. Mount Gay Eclipse Rum
3/4 oz. Bacardi Light Rum
1 oz. passion fruit puree
1/2 oz. grenadine
2 1/2 oz. orange juice
2 1/2 oz. pineapple juice
Shake and strain
Orange slice and cherry garnish

TIKKI DREAM
Cocktail glass, chilled
Rim glass with sugar (optional)
Pour ingredients into iced mixing glass
1 oz. Disaronno Amaretto
3/4 oz. Midori
1 1/4 oz. cranberry juice
Stir and strain
Orange slice and cherry garnish

TINTED GLASS
Cocktail glass, chilled
Pour ingredients into iced mixing glass
1/2 oz. Dry Vermouth
2 1/2 oz. Gin
4-6 drops Chambord
Stir and strain
Lemon twist garnish

TIP-TOP PUNCH
House specialty glass, ice
Pour ingredients into iced mixing glass
1 1/2 oz. Brandy
1/2 oz. Benedictine
1/2 oz. simple syrup
1 1/2 oz. sweet 'n' sour
Shake and strain
Fill with Champagne

TIRAMISU (1)
House specialty glass, chilled
Pour ingredients into blender
1 oz. Godiva Chocolate Liqueur
1 oz. Disaronno Amaretto
1 oz. Kahlúa
2 scoops vanilla ice cream
Blend ingredients (with ice optional)
Whipped cream garnish
Sprinkle shaved chocolate

TIRAMISU (2)
House specialty glass, chilled
Pour ingredients into blender
1 1/4 oz. Appleton Estate V/X Jamaica Rum
3/4 oz. White Crème de Cacao
3/4 oz. Baileys Irish Cream
1/4 oz. chocolate syrup
2 scoops vanilla ice cream
Blend ingredients (with ice optional)
Whipped cream garnish
Drizzle 3/4 oz. Tia Maria

TIZIANO
Champagne glass, chilled
Build in glass
1/2 fill white grape juice
1/2 fill Champagne
Lemon twist garnish

T.K.O.
Rocks glass, ice
Build in glass
3/4 oz. Tequila
3/4 oz. Kahlúa
3/4 oz. Ouzo

T. 'N' T.
Highball glass, ice
Build in glass
1 1/4 oz. Tanqueray Gin
Fill with tonic water
Lime wedge garnish

TOASTED ALMOND
Cocktail glass, chilled
Pour ingredients into iced mixing glass
3/4 oz. Disaronno Amaretto
3/4 oz. Kahlúa
2 oz. half & half cream
Shake and strain

TOASTED ALMOND CAFÉ
Coffee mug, heated
Build in glass
3/4 oz. Disaronno Amaretto
3/4 oz. Kahlúa
Near fill with hot coffee
Whipped cream garnish
Sprinkle nutmeg

XXX SIGLO TREINTA®
TEQUILA

The short list of brands that give you a lot of tequila for the buck certainly contains the name, XXX SIGLO TREINTA. It is gaining an international reputation for exemplary quality at an affordable price, which loosely translates to a great value. Ultra-premium, 100% agave tequilas are expensive, priced on a par with cognac, while pouring brands are inexpensive and few possess any marketable attributes other than being cheap. XXX Siglo Treinta has struck the perfect bargain. It is a high quality, superior tasting tequila with a modest price tag.

XXX Siglo Treinta is made at La Cofradia Distillery near the town of Tequila. Established in 1992, the distillery has quickly gained a reputation for quality and is the producer of award winning Casa Noble 100% Agave Tequila. XXX Siglo Treinta is a *mixto* or blended tequila, meaning that it contains at least 51% blue agave. It is double-distilled from mature blue agaves that are steamed, baked and slowly fermented. High-grade distilled sugar is added and the tequila is matured for two months in small, American white oak barrels. It is bottled at 80 proof.

XXX Siglo Treinta is an unexpectedly luxurious tequila. It has a lustrous, golden/yellow hue and wafting herbaceous bouquet. The best part is its bold, slightly smoky palate. The tequila is genuinely a pleasure to drink and makes a splendid Margarita.

TOBOGGAN TRUFFLE
Coffee mug, heated
Build in glass
1 oz. Peppermint Schnapps
1 oz. Godiva Chocolate Liqueur
Near fill with hot coffee
Whipped cream garnish
Sprinkle shaved chocolate

TOKYO SCREAM
House specialty glass, ice
Pour ingredients into iced mixing glass
1 oz. Light Rum
3/4 oz. Midori
1/2 oz. Peach Schnapps
2 oz. pineapple juice
2 oz. orange juice
Shake and strain
Orange slice and cherry garnish

TOM MIX HIGH
Highball glass, ice
Build in glass
1 1/4 oz. Seagram's 7 Whisky
1 dash Angostura Bitters
1 dash grenadine
Fill with club soda

TOOTSIE ROLL
Highball glass, ice
Build in glass
1 1/4 oz. Vodka
3/4 oz. Dark Crème de Cacao
Fill with orange juice

TOP HAT
Brandy snifter, heated
Build in glass
1 1/2 oz. Sea Wynde Pot Still Rum
3/4 oz. Grand Marnier Centenaire

TOREADOR
Cocktail glass, chilled
Pour ingredients into iced mixing glass
3/4 oz. Tequila
3/4 oz. White Crème de Menthe
2 oz. half & half cream
Shake and strain

TORONTO
Cocktail glass, chilled
Pour ingredients into iced mixing glass
2 dashes simple syrup
1 dash Angostura Bitters
3/4 oz. Fernet Branca
1 1/2 oz. Canadian Whisky
Stir and strain
Orange twist garnish

TORPEDO SLAM
Shot glass and beer mug, chilled
Build in shot glass
1 1/2 oz. Bourbon
Build in mug
2/3 fill Draft Beer
Splash Seven-Up
Drop shot glass of bourbon into beer

TORQUE WRENCH
Presentation shot glass, chilled
Build in glass
1/3 fill Midori
1/3 fill Champagne
1/3 fill orange juice

TOUR DE CARIBBEAN
House specialty glass, ice
Pour ingredients into iced mixing glass
3/4 oz. Bacardi Select Rum
3/4 oz. Mount Gay Eclipse Rum
3/4 oz. Crème de Banana
2 oz. cranberry juice
2 oz. orange juice
Shake and strain
Float 1/2 oz. Tia Maria
Float 1/2 oz. Appleton Estate
   V/X Jamaica Rum
Orange slice and cherry garnish

TOUR DE FRANCE
Champagne glass, chilled
Pour ingredients into iced mixing glass
3/4 oz. VS Cognac
3/4 oz. Chambord
1 1/2 oz. sweet 'n' sour
Shake and strain
Fill with Champagne
Lemon wheel garnish

TOUR DE PANAMA
House specialty glass, ice
Pour ingredients into iced mixing glass
3/4 oz. Jamaican Rum
1/2 oz. Dark Rum
1/2 oz. Crème de Banana
2 oz. orange juice
2 oz. pineapple juice
Shake and strain
Float 3/4 oz. Tia Maria
Orange slice and cherry garnish

TOVARICH
Cocktail glass, chilled
Pour ingredients into iced mixing glass
1 1/2 oz. Stolichnaya Vodka
1/2 oz. Stolichnaya Ohranj Vodka
1/2 oz. fresh lime juice
Stir and strain
Lime wedge garnish

TRADE DEFICIT
Coffee mug, heated
Build in glass
3/4 oz. Baileys Irish Cream
3/4 oz. Kahlúa
3/4 oz. Peppermint Schnapps
Near fill with hot coffee
Whipped cream garnish
Drizzle 3/4 oz. Godiva Chocolate Liqueur

TRADE WINDS
House specialty glass, chilled
Pour ingredients into iced mixing glass
3/4 oz. Cruzan Estate Light Rum
3/4 oz. Brandy
3/4 oz. Chambord
1 oz. orange juice
2 oz. sweet 'n' sour
Shake and strain
Lemon twist garnish

TRAFFIC LIGHT (1)
Presentation shot glass, chilled
Layer ingredients
1/3 fill Green Crème de Menthe
1/3 fill Crème de Banana
1/3 fill Sloe Gin

TRAFFIC LIGHT (2)
Cordial or sherry glass, chilled
Layer ingredients
1/3 fill Crème de Noyaux
1/3 fill Galliano Liqueur
1/3 fill Midori

TRAMONTO SUL GARDA
Champagne glass, chilled
Pour ingredients into iced mixing glass
1 oz. Gin
1/2 oz. Cointreau
1/2 oz. pink grapefruit juice
Shake and strain
Fill with Champagne
Lemon twist garnish

TRINITY
Cocktail glass, chilled
Pour ingredients into iced mixing glass
1/2 oz. Dry Vermouth
1 1/2 oz. Bourbon
2-3 dashes Angostura Bitters
1 dash White Crème de Menthe
Stir and strain
Lemon twist garnish

TRIP TO THE BEACH
House specialty glass, ice
Pour ingredients into iced mixing glass
1 oz. Gold Rum
1 oz. Citrus Rum
1/2 oz. Peach Schnapps
3 oz. orange juice
Shake and strain
Orange slice and cherry garnish

TROPHY ROOM
Coffee mug, heated
Build in glass
1/2 oz. Disaronno Amaretto
1/2 oz. Vandermint Liqueur
1/2 oz. Myers's Jamaican Rum
Near fill with hot coffee
Whipped cream garnish
Drizzle 1/2 oz. of Tia Maria

TROPICAL DEPRESSION
Coffee mug, heated
Build in glass
1 1/4 oz. Dillon Dark Rhum
1/2 oz. Disaronno Amaretto
1/2 oz. Godiva Chocolate Liqueur
Near fill with hot coffee
Whipped cream garnish
Drizzle 3/4 oz. Tia Maria

TROPICAL GOLD
Highball glass, ice
Build in glass
1 oz. Light Rum
1/2 oz. Crème de Banana
Fill with orange juice

TROPICAL HOOTER
Bucket glass, ice
Build in glass
1 1/2 oz. Malibu Caribbean Rum
1/2 oz. Midori
1/2 fill cranberry juice
1/2 fill pineapple juice

TROPICAL HURRICANE
Bucket glass, ice
Build in glass
1 oz. Citrus Rum
3/4 oz. Midori
1 1/2 oz. cranberry juice
1 1/2 oz. pineapple juice
Orange slice and cherry garnish

TROPICAL HUT
House specialty glass, ice
Pour ingredients into iced mixing glass
1 oz. Midori
1 oz. Light Rum
1/2 oz. orgeat syrup
1 1/2 oz. sweet 'n' sour
Shake and strain
Pineapple wedge and cherry garnish

TROPICAL ITCH
House specialty glass, ice
Pour ingredients into iced mixing glass
1 oz. Bacardi Gold Rum
1 oz. Mount Gay Eclipse Rum
1/2 oz. grenadine
1 oz. orange juice
1 oz. grapefruit juice
1 oz. pineapple juice
Shake and strain
Float 1/2 oz. Cruzan Banana Rum
Float 1/2 oz. Cruzan Pineapple Rum
Orange slice and cherry garnish

TROPICAL JACK
Bucket glass, ice
Build in glass
3/4 oz. Jack Daniel's Tennessee Whiskey
3/4 oz. Crème de Banana
1 dash orange juice
1 dash grenadine
Fill with pineapple juice

TROPICAL MOON
House specialty glass, chilled
Pour ingredients into blender
1 1/2 oz. Myers's Jamaican Rum
3/4 oz. Disaronno Amaretto
2 oz. coconut cream syrup
3 oz. pineapple juice
2 scoops vanilla ice cream
Blend with ice
Pineapple wedge and cherry garnish

TROPICAL SENSATION
House specialty glass, ice
Pour ingredients into iced mixing glass
1 1/2 oz. Gin
1/2 oz. Orange Liqueur
1 oz. Rose's Lime juice
1 oz. orange juice
2 oz. grapefruit juice
Shake and strain
Float 3/4 oz. Citrus Vodka
Lemon wedge garnish

TROPICAL SPECIAL
House specialty glass, ice
Pour ingredients into iced mixing glass
1 1/2 oz. Gin
1/2 oz. Triple Sec
1 oz. orange juice
1 oz. Rose's Lime Juice
2 oz. grapefruit juice
Shake and strain
Orange slice and cherry garnish

TROPICAL TANGO
House specialty glass, ice
Pour ingredients into iced mixing glass
2 oz. Orange Rum
1 oz. Citrus Rum
2 oz. cranberry juice
2 oz. orange juice
Shake and strain
Orange slice and cherry garnish

TRYST & SHOUT
Champagne glass, chilled
Pour ingredients into iced mixing glass
1 1/2 oz. Disaronno Amaretto
2 oz. sweet 'n' sour
Shake and strain
Fill with Champagne
Lemon twist garnish

TURBO MILK CHOCOLATE
Cocktail glass, chilled
Pour ingredients into iced mixing glass
2 oz. Van Gogh Chocolate Vodka
3/4 oz. Godiva Chocolate Liqueur
Stir and strain
Float 3/4 oz. Baileys Irish Cream

TURKEY SHOOTER
Presentation shot glass, chilled
Layer ingredients
1/2 fill Peppermint Schnapps
1/2 fill Bourbon

TUSCANY CHAMPAGNE
Champagne tulip glass, chilled
Build in glass
1 oz. Gran Gala Orange Liqueur
Swirl and coat inside of glass
Fill with Champagne
Orange twist garnish

TWILIGHT MOAN ZONE
Cocktail glass, chilled
Pour ingredients into iced mixing glass
1 1/4 oz. KéKé Beach Cream Liqueur
1 1/4 oz. Midori
3/4 oz. Chambord
Shake and strain
Lime wheel garnish

TWIST DE L'ORANGE
Cocktail glass, chilled
Pour ingredients into blender
1 3/4 oz. Ketel One Citroen Vodka
3/4 oz. Grand Marnier Centenaire
1 scoop orange sorbet
Blend ingredients (with ice optional)
Orange spiral twist garnish

TWISTED LEMONADE
Bucket glass, ice
Build in glass
1 1/4 oz. Citrus Rum
3/4 oz. Raspberry Liqueur
Fill with lemonade
Lemon wedge garnish

TWISTED SISTER
aka **Nun in a Blender**
House specialty glass, chilled
Pour ingredients into blender
1 oz. KéKé Beach Cream Liqueur
1 oz. DeKuyper Raspberry Pucker
3/4 oz. Midori
1 1/2 oz. sweet 'n' sour
2 scoops vanilla ice cream
Blend ingredients (with ice optional)
Whipped cream and vanilla wafer garnish

TWISTER
House specialty glass, ice
Pour ingredients into iced mixing glass
1 1/2 oz. Light Rum
3/4 oz. DeKuyper Peach Pucker
3/4 oz. DeKuyper Watermelon Pucker
3/4 oz. Malibu Caribbean Rum
3 oz. orange juice
2 oz. pineapple juice
1 oz. cranberry juice
Shake and strain

UGLY DUCKLING
Brandy snifter, ice
Build in glass
1 3/4 oz. Disaronno Amaretto
1/2 fill half & half cream
1/2 fill club soda

ULTERIOR MOTIVE
Cocktail glass, chilled
Pour ingredients into iced mixing glass
2 oz. Tanqueray Gin
3/4 oz. Limoncello Liqueur
Shake and strain
Lemon twist garnish

ULTIMATE GRAPE COCKTAIL
Champagne glass, chilled
Build in glass
1 oz. Cîroc Snap Frost Vodka
1 oz. white grape juice
Fill with champagne
Lemon twist garnish

UPSIDE DOWN SCOTTISH CROWN
Cocktail glass, chilled
Layer ingredients
1 oz. Drambuie
1 1/2 oz. Scotch Whisky
Lemon twist garnish

UP THE CREEK WITH A KICK
Highball glass, ice
Build in glass
1 1/4 oz. Canadian Whisky
3/4 oz. Cinnamon Schnapps
Fill with ginger ale

UPTOWN
Cocktail glass, chilled
Pour ingredients into iced mixing glass
1 1/2 oz. Myers's Jamaican Rum
1/2 oz. Triple Sec
1/2 oz. Rose's Lime Juice
2-3 dashes Angostura Bitters
1/4 oz. grenadine
1/2 oz. orange juice
1/2 oz. pineapple juice
Shake and strain

UPTOWN GIRL
Rocks glass, ice
Build in glass
3/4 oz. Grand Marnier
2 oz. Evan Williams Single Barrel
   Vintage Bourbon
Orange twist garnish

VAMPIRE
Rocks glass, chilled
Pour ingredients into iced mixing glass
1 1/4 oz. Vodka
3/4 oz. Chambord
1 1/2 oz. cranberry juice
Shake and strain

VAMPIRO (1)
Bucket glass, ice
Build in glass
Rim glass with salt (optional)
1 1/2 oz. Reposado Tequila
3 oz. Sangrita Mix
3 oz. grapefruit juice
3/4 oz. fresh lime juice
Grapefruit and orange slice garnish
Note: See Sangrita Mix

VAMPIRO (2)
House specialty glass, ice
Rim glass with salt (optional)
Build in glass
1 1/2 oz. Tequila
3/4 oz. orange juice
1/2 oz. fresh lime juice
3/4 oz. Squirt (grapefruit soda)
Fill with Bloody Mary Mix
Lime wedge garnish

VANDERBILT COCKTAIL
Cocktail glass, chilled
Pour ingredients into iced mixing glass
1 1/2 oz. Brandy
3/4 oz. Cherry Brandy
2 dashes simple syrup
2 dashes Angostura Bitters
Shake and strain

VANILLA ANGEL
Coffee mug, heated
Build in glass
1 1/4 oz. Vanilla Rum
1 oz. Frangelico
1 oz. Disaronno Amaretto
Near fill with hot coffee
Whipped cream garnish
Dust with powder cocoa

VANILLA MAGILLA
Rocks glass, chilled
Pour ingredients into iced mixing glass
1 1/4 oz. Spiced Rum
1 oz. Peppermint Schnapps
1/2 oz. Vanilla Rum

VANILLA PEANUT BUTTER CUP
House specialty glass, chilled
Rim glass with powdered cocoa (optional)
Pour ingredients into blender
2 oz. Vanilla Rum
1 tbsp. peanut butter
1 oz. half & half cream
2 scoops chocolate ice cream
Blend ingredients (with ice optional)
Graham cracker garnish

VANILLA SPICE ICE
Rocks glass, ice
Build in glass
2 oz. Liquid Ice Vodka
1/2 oz. Vanilla Rum
Cinnamon stick garnish

VANILLA WAFER
Rocks glass, ice
Build in glass
1 3/4 oz. Vanilla Rum
3/4 oz. DeKuyper Butatershots Schnapps
3/4 oz. half & half cream

VANIL SENSATION
House specialty glass, chilled
Pour ingredients into blender
1 oz. Stolichnaya Vanil Vodka
3/4 oz. Bombay Gin
3/4 oz. Triple Sec
1 3/4 oz. cranberry juice
2 oz. orange juice
Blend with ice

VELVET HAMMER
Cocktail glass, chilled
Pour ingredients into iced mixing glass
3/4 oz. Triple Sec
3/4 oz. White Crème de Cacao
2 oz. half & half cream
Shake and strain

VELVET SWING
Champagne glass, chilled
Build in glass
1 1/4 oz. Tawny Port
3/4 oz. Armagnac
Fill with Champagne
Lemon wheel garnish

VENETIAN SUNSET
Cocktail glass, chilled
Pour ingredients into iced mixing glass
1 1/2 oz. Grappa
1/2 oz. Campari Aperitivo
1/4 oz. simple syrup
2 oz. orange juice
Shake and strain
Orange slice and mint leaf garnish

VERMOUTH CASSIS
Cocktail glass, chilled
Pour ingredients into iced mixing glass
1 oz. Crème de Cassis
1 oz. Dry Vermouth
Stir and strain
Lemon twist garnish

VIAGRA
Bucket glass, ice
Build in glass
2 oz. Jägermeister
Fill with Red Bull Energy Drink
Lime wedge garnish

VICE ON ICE
House specialty glass, chilled
Pour ingredients into iced mixing glass
1 1/2 oz. Cruzan Pineapple Rum
3/4 oz. Dark Rum
3/4 oz. lime juice
1 oz. cranberry juice
3 oz. pink lemonade
Shake and strain
Pineapple wedge and cherry garnish

VINCENT'S BAUBLES
Cocktail glass, chilled
Pour ingredients into iced mixing glass
1 oz. Van Gogh Vodka
1 oz. Van Gogh Oranje Vodka
3/4 oz. Oro di Mazzetti Grappa Liqueur
1/2 oz. Drambuie
Stir and strain
Lemon twist garnish

V.I.P. COFFEE
Coffee mug, heated
Build in glass
1 oz. Cruzan Estate Single Barrel Rum
1/2 oz. Kahlúa
1/2 oz. Chambord
Near fill with hot coffee
Whipped cream garnish

VODKA GRAND
Cocktail glass, chilled
Pour ingredients into iced mixing glass
1 1/2 oz. Vodka
1/2 oz. Grand Marnier
1/2 oz. Rose's Lime Juice
1/4 oz. fresh lime juice
Stir and strain
Orange slice garnish

VOODOO JUICE (1)
House specialty glass, ice
Pour ingredients into iced mixing glass
2 oz. VooDoo Spiced Rum
1 oz. pineapple juice
1 oz. cranberry syrup
1 oz. orange juice
Shake and strain
Pineapple wedge garnish

VOODOO JUICE (2)
Large house specialty glass, ice
Pour ingredients into iced mixing glass
1 oz. Cruzan Orange Rum
1 oz. Cruzan Banana Rum
1 oz. Cruzan Coconut Rum
1 oz. Cruzan Pineapple Rum
1 1/2 oz. cranberry juice
1 1/2 oz. orange juice
1 1/2 oz. pineapple juice
Shake and strain
Float 3/4 oz. Cruzan Estate Diamond Rum
Orange slice and cherry garnish

VOODOO MOONDANCE
House specialty glass, ice
Pour ingredients into iced mixing glass
1 1/2 oz. Cruzan Estate Diamond Rum
1 oz. Cruzan Estate Light Rum
3/4 oz. grenadine
1 1/2 oz. pineapple juice
1 1/2 oz. orange juice
1 1/2 oz. grapefruit juice
Shake and strain
Splash club soda
Orange slice and cherry garnish

VOODOO SHOOTER
Presentation shot glass, chilled
Layer ingredients
1/3 fill Tia Maria
1/3 fill Cruzan Rum Cream
1/3 fill Bacardi Select Rum

VOODOO SNAP
Bucket glass, ice
Build in glass
1 1/2 oz. VooDoo Spiced Rum
Fill with ginger ale

VOODOO VOLCANO
Bucket glass, ice
Build in glass
1 oz. VooDoo Spiced Rum
1 oz. Kahlúa
3/4 oz. milk

VULCAN
Bucket glass, ice
Build in glass
1/2 oz. Gin
1/2 oz. Vodka
1/2 oz. Southern Comfort
1/2 oz. Malibu Caribbean Rum
1/2 fill grapefruit juice
1/2 fill Seven-Up

VULCAN MIND PROBE
Presentation shot glass, chilled
Build in glass
1/2 fill Sambuca
1/2 fill 151° Rum

WAIKÉKÉ FRATERNITY
House specialty glass, ice
Pour ingredients into iced mixing glass
1 1/2 oz. KéKé Beach Cream Liqueur
3/4 oz. Vanilla Rum
3/4 oz. Limoncello Liqueur
1 oz. sweet 'n' sour
1 oz. limeade
Shake and strain

WAIST COAT POCKET
House specialty glass, chilled
Pour ingredients into blender
1/2 oz. Kahlúa
1/2 oz. Disaronno Amaretto
1/2 oz. Godiva Chocolate Liqueur
3/4 oz. half & half cream
2 scoops vanilla ice cream
Blend ingredients (with ice optional)

WALL STREET WIZARD
Cocktail glass, chilled
Pour ingredients into iced mixing glass
1/2 oz. Gin
1/2 oz. Vodka
1/2 oz. Light Rum
1/2 oz. Blue Curaçao
1/2 oz. Midori
Stir and strain

WANDERER
Bucket glass, ice
Pour ingredients into iced mixing glass
1 oz. Ultimat Vodka
1/2 oz. Chambord
1/2 oz. DeKuyper Cherry Pucker
1/2 oz. Blue Curaçao
1 1/2 oz. pineapple juice
1 1/2 oz. cranberry juice
Shake and strain

WANNA PROBE YA
Bucket glass, ice
Build in glass
1 oz. Captain Morgan Spiced Rum
3/4 oz. Malibu Caribbean Rum
1/2 fill cranberry juice
1/2 fill pineapple juice

WARD EIGHT
Cocktail glass, chilled
Pour ingredients into iced mixing glass
1 1/2 oz. Bourbon
1/2 oz. grenadine
1 1/2 oz. sweet 'n' sour
Shake and strain

WASHINGTON APPLE
Rocks glass, chilled
Pour ingredients into iced mixing glass
1 oz. DeKuyper Pucker Sour Apple
1 oz. Crown Royal
1 oz. sweet 'n' sour
Shake and strain

WATERGATE
Presentation shot glass, chilled
Layer ingredients
1/4 fill Kahlúa
1/4 fill Baileys Irish Cream
1/4 fill Peppermint Schnapps
1/4 fill Grand Marnier

WATERMELON (1)
Rocks glass, ice
Build in glass
3/4 oz. Southern Comfort
3/4 oz. orange juice
3/4 oz. Disaronno Amaretto

WATERMELON (2)
Presentation shot glass, chilled
Build in glass
1/3 fill Vodka
1/3 fill Midori
1/3 fill Baileys Irish Cream
5 drops grenadine

WATERMELON (3)
Presentation shot glass, chilled
Build in glass
1/3 fill Vodka
1/3 fill Sloe Gin
1/3 fill orange juice

WATERMELON (4)
Bucket glass, ice
Build in glass
1 oz. Southern Comfort
1/2 oz. Midori
2 oz. orange juice
1 dash grenadine

WATERMELON (5)
Rocks glass, chilled
Pour ingredients into iced mixing glass
1 oz. Southern Comfort
3/4 oz. Vodka
1/4 oz. grenadine
2 oz. pineapple juice
Shake and strain

WATKIN'S GLEN
Bucket glass, ice
Pour ingredients into iced mixing glass
1 oz. Vodka
1/2 oz. Crème de Banana
1/2 oz. Chambord
1/2 oz. pineapple juice
1/2 oz. cranberry juice
1/2 oz. orange juice
Shake and strain
Lime wedge garnish

WEEKEND AT THE BEACH (1)
Presentation shot glass, chilled
Build in glass
3/4 oz. DeKuyper Pucker Sour Apple
3/4 oz. DeKuyper Peachtree Schnapps
Splash orange juice
Splash cranberry juice

WEEKEND AT THE BEACH (2)
Rocks glass, chilled
Pour ingredients into iced mixing glass
1 oz. Light Rum
1 oz. Peach Schnapps
1 oz. orange juice
1 oz. pineapple juice
Shake and strain

WEEK ON THE BEACH
Rocks glass, chilled
Pour ingredients into iced mixing glass
3/4 oz. DeKuyper Pucker Sour Apple
3/4 oz. DeKuyper Peachtree Schnapps
1/2 oz. orange juice
1/2 oz. pineapple juice
1/2 oz. cranberry juice
Shake and strain

WENTWORTH COCKTAIL
Cocktail glass, chilled
Pour ingredients into iced mixing glass
1 1/2 oz. Dubonnet Rouge
1 oz. Old Forester Bourbon
1 oz. cranberry juice
Shake and strain
Orange slice and dried cranberry garnish

WET DREAM
Rocks glass, chilled
Pour ingredients into iced mixing glass
3/4 oz. Chambord
3/4 oz. Crème de Banana
1/2 oz. orange juice
3/4 oz. half & half cream
Shake and strain

WET PASSION
Cocktail glass, chilled
Pour ingredients into iced mixing glass
2 oz. Wet by Beefeater
3/4 oz. Disaronno Amaretto
3/4 oz. passion fruit purée
1 oz. fresh orange juice
Shake and strain
Orange slice garnish

WHALER'S SEASON
House specialty glass, ice
Pour ingredients into iced mixing glass
1 oz. Mount Gay Eclipse Rum
3/4 oz. Captain Morgan Spiced Rum
3/4 oz. Whaler's Original Vanille Rum
1 1/2 oz. orange juice
1 1/2 oz. sweet 'n' sour
Shake and strain
Orange slice garnish

WHALE'S TAIL
House specialty glass, chilled
Pour ingredients into blender
1 oz. Van Gogh Oranje Vodka
1 oz. Whaler's Original Vanille Rum
3/4 oz. Blue Curaçao
1 1/2 oz. sweet 'n' sour
3 oz. pineapple juice
Blend with ice
Pineapple wedge garnish

WHAT CRISIS?
Rocks glass, chilled
Pour ingredients into iced mixing glass
1/2 oz. DeKuyper Peach Pucker
1/2 oz. Midori
1/2 oz. orange juice
1/2 oz. cranberry juice
Shake and strain

WHAT'S THE RUSH
House specialty glass, ice
Pour ingredients into iced mixing glass
2 oz. Jameson Irish Whiskey
2 oz. lemonade
2 oz. apple juice
Shake and strain
Splash Seven-Up
Orange slice garnish

WHAT'S YOUR HONEY DEW?
Champagne glass, chilled
Pour ingredients into iced mixing glass
1 1/4 oz. Midori
3 1/2 oz. lemonade
Shake and strain
Fill with Champagne
Lemon wedge garnish

WHEN HELL FREEZES OVER
House specialty glass, chilled
Pour ingredients into blender
3/4 oz. Cinnamon Schnapps
3/4 oz. Crème de Banana
2 oz. orange juice
2 oz. cranberry juice
Blend with ice

WHERE ARE MY UNDIES?
Bucket glass, ice
Build in glass
1 1/2 oz. KéKé Beach Cream Liqueur
3/4 oz. Vanilla Rum
Fill with orange juice

WHIP
Cocktail glass, chilled
Pour ingredients into iced mixing glass
3/4 oz. Pernod
3/4 oz. Brandy
3/4 oz. Triple Sec
3/4 oz. Dry Vermouth
Stir and strain

WHISKY-ALL-IN
Coffee mug, heated
Build in glass
1 1/2 oz. Scotch Whisky
1 tsp. sugar
1/4 oz. fresh lemon juice
Fill with hot water
Lemon wedge garnish

WHISKY GINGERBREAD
Rocks glass, chilled
Build in glass
3/4 oz. Cinnamon Schnapps
3/4 oz. Baileys Irish Cream
3/4 oz. DeKuyper Butcatershots Schnapps
3/4 oz. Canadian Club Whisky

WHISPER (1)
Brandy snifter, ice
Build in glass
1 oz. Disaronno Amaretto
1 oz. Kahlúa
1/2 fill half & half cream
1/2 fill club soda

WHISPER (2)
House specialty glass, chilled
Pour ingredients into blender
3/4 oz. Kahlúa
3/4 oz. Dark Crème de Cacao
3/4 oz. Brandy
1 oz. half & half cream
2 scoops vanilla ice cream
Blend ingredients (with ice optional)
Whipped cream garnish
Sprinkle shaved chocolate

WHITE BULL
Rocks glass, ice
Build in glass
1 1/2 oz. Tequila
3/4 oz. Kahlúa
3/4 oz. half & half cream

WHITE CADILLAC
Highball glass, ice
Build in glass
1 1/4 oz. Scotch Whisky
Fill with half & half cream

WHITE CLOUD
Cocktail glass, chilled
Rim glass with powdered cocoa (optional)
Pour ingredients into iced mixing glass
1 3/4 oz. Jameson Irish Whiskey
3/4 oz. Godiva Chocolate Liqueur
3/4 oz. White Crème de Menthe
1 1/4 half & half cream
Shake and strain

WHITE HAWAIIAN
Rocks glass, ice
Pour ingredients into iced mixing glass
Build in glass
2 oz. Pearl Lo Coco Vodka
1 oz. Kahlúa
1 oz. Baileys Irish Cream

WHITE HEART
Cocktail or house specialty glass, chilled
Pour ingredients into iced mixing glass
3/4 oz. Sambuca
3/4 oz. White Crème de Cacao
2 oz. half & half cream
Shake and strain

WHITE MINNESOTA
Highball glass, ice
Build in glass
1 1/4 oz. White Crème de Menthe
Fill with club soda

WHITE OUT
Cocktail glass, chilled
Pour ingredients into iced mixing glass
1 oz. Cointreau
1 oz. VSOP Cognac
3/4 oz. Peppermint Schnapps
Stir and strain

WHITE RUSSIAN
Rocks glass, ice
Build in glass
1 1/2 oz. Vodka
3/4 oz. Kahlúa
3/4 oz. half & half cream

WHITE RUSSIAN, PREMIUM
Rocks glass or brandy snifter, ice
Build in glass
1 1/2 oz. Stolichnaya Vodka
3/4 oz. Tia Maria
3/4 oz. Baileys Irish Cream

WHITE RUSSIAN, RASPBERRY
Bucket glass, ice
Build in glass
1 1/2 oz. Raspberry Vodka
1 1/2 oz. Kahlúa
3/4 oz. milk

WHITE RUSSIAN, SKINNY
Bucket glass, ice
Build in glass
1 1/2 oz. Vodka
1 1/2 oz. Kahlúa
3/4 oz. skim milk

WHITE RUSSIAN, TRUFFLE
Bucket glass, ice
Build in glass
1 1/2 oz. Raspberry Vodka
1 1/2 oz. Kahlúa
3/4 oz. White Crème de Cacao
3/4 oz. milk

WHITE RUSSIAN, VANILLA
Bucket glass, ice
Build in glass
1 1/2 oz. Absolut Vanilia Vodka
1 1/2 oz. Kahlúa
3/4 oz. milk

WHITE SANDS COOLER
House specialty glass, ice
Pour ingredients into iced mixing glass
3/4 oz. Casa Noble Reposado Tequila
3/4 oz. Cruzan Estate Light Rum
3/4 oz. Cruzan Banana Rum
2 oz. cranberry juice
2 oz. pineapple juice
Shake and strain
Orange slice and cherry garnish

WHITE'S CLUB
Champagne glass, chilled
Rim glass with port and sugar (optional)
Build in glass
2 oz. Tawny Port
Fill with Champagne
Lemon twist garnish

WHITE SPIDER
aka **Cossack**
Rocks glass, ice
Build in glass
1 1/2 oz. Vodka
1/2 oz. White Crème de Menthe

WHITE SWAN
Brandy snifter, ice
Build in glass
1 1/2 oz. Disaronno Amaretto
3/4 oz. half & half cream

WHITE WAY
Rocks glass, ice
Build in glass
1 1/2 oz. Gin
1/2 oz. White Crème de Menthe

WHOOTER HOOTER
Bucket glass, ice
Build in glass
1 1/2 oz. Vodka
1/2 fill cranberry juice
1/2 fill lemonade
Orange slice and cherry garnish

WIDOW WOOD'S NIGHTCAP
Coffee mug, heated
Build in glass
2 oz. Scotch Whisky
1 oz. Dark Crème de Cacao
Near fill with hot milk
Whipped cream garnish
Dust powdered cocoa

WIKI WAKI WOO
House specialty glass, ice
Pour ingredients into iced mixing glass
1 oz. Disaronno Amaretto
1/2 oz. Vodka
1/2 oz. RémyRed Strawberry Kiwi Infusion
1/2 oz. 151° Rum
1/2 oz. Silver Tequila
1 oz. pineapple juice
1 oz. orange juice
1 oz. cranberry juice
Shake and strain
Orange slice and cherry garnish
Orchid garnish (optional)

WILD ORCHID
Bucket glass, ice
Pour ingredients into iced mixing glass
1 1/4 oz. Ypioca Cachaça
3/4 oz. Crème de Noyaux
1 1/2 oz. fresh lime juice
1/2 oz. grenadine
Shake and strain
Orange slice and cherry garnish

WILE E. COYOTE
Bucket glass, ice
Build in glass
1 1/4 oz. Tuaca
3/4 oz. Jägermeister
Fill with pineapple juice
Lemon wedge garnish

WINDEX
Rocks glass, chilled
Pour ingredients into iced mixing glass
1 1/2 oz. Vodka
3/4 oz. Light Rum
1/2 oz. Blue Curaçao
1/2 oz. Rose's Lime Juice
Shake and strain

WINE COBBLER
Wine glass or goblet, ice
Build in glass
4 oz. White Wine
1 oz. Triple Sec
1/2 fill orange juice
Near fill with sweet 'n' sour
Splash club soda
Lemon twist garnish

WINE COOLER
aka **Red Wine Cooler**, **Rosé Cooler**
Wine glass or goblet, ice
Build in glass
1/2 fill Requested Wine
1/2 fill Seven-Up
Lemon twist garnish

WINNIE'S HOT HONEY POT
Coffee mug, heated
Build in glass
1 oz. Drambuie
1/2 oz. honey
1/2 oz. lemon juice
Near fill with English Breakfast tea
Serve with lemon

WINSOME WAY
Rocks glass, ice
Build in glass
3/4 oz. Gran Gala Orange Liqueur
3/4 oz. Baileys Irish Cream
3/4 oz. Frangelico

WYNBREEZER
House specialty glass, ice
Pour ingredients into iced mixing glass
2 oz. Rhum Barbancourt 3-Star
3/4 oz. Orange Liqueur
3/4 oz. Rose's Lime Juice
2 oz. orange juice
Shake and strain
Near fill with Seven-Up
Float 3/4 oz. Rhum Barbancourt
    5-Star
Orange slice garnish

XANADU
Champagne glass, chilled
Pour ingredients into iced mixing glass
1/2 oz. VSOP Cognac
1/2 oz. Cointreau
1/2 oz. sweet 'n' sour
Shake and strain
Fill with Champagne
Lemon wheel garnish

XAVIERA
Cocktail or house specialty glass, chilled
Pour ingredients into iced mixing glass
1/2 oz. Kahlúa
1/2 oz. Crème de Noyaux
1/2 oz. Triple Sec
1 1/2 oz. half & half cream
Shake and strain

XO STINGER COCKTAIL
Cocktail glass, chilled
Pour ingredients into iced mixing glass
1 oz. Patrón XO Café Coffee Liqueur
1 oz. Patrón Silver Tequila
1 oz. Citrónge Orange Liqueur
Stir and strain

YABBA-DABBA-DOO
Rocks glass, chilled
Pour ingredients into iced mixing glass
1 oz. Frangelico
1 oz. Kahlúa
1/2 oz. Green Crème de Menthe
Shake and strain

YALE COCKTAIL
Cocktail glass, chilled
Pour ingredients into iced mixing glass
1 1/2 oz. Gin
1/2 oz. Dry Vermouth
2 dashes Angostura Bitters
2 dashes simple syrup
Stir and strain
Lemon twist garnish

YANKEE PANKY
Rocks glass, ice
Build in glass
3/4 oz. Southern Comfort
3/4 oz. Disaronno Amaretto
3/4 oz. Malibu Caribbean Rum
3/4 oz. pineapple juice

YELLOW BIRD (1)
Bucket glass, ice
Build in glass
3/4 oz. Light Rum
3/4 oz. Galliano Liqueur
1/2 fill pineapple juice
1/2 fill orange juice

YELLOW BIRD (2)
House specialty glass, chilled
Pour ingredients into blender
1 oz. Light Rum
3/4 oz. Galliano Liqueur
1/2 oz. Crème de Banana
1/4 oz. simple syrup
2 oz. orange juice
2 oz. pineapple juice
Blend with ice
Pineapple wedge and cherry garnish

YELLOW DEVIL
Bucket glass, ice
Build in glass
1 oz. Mount Gay Eclipse Rum
1 oz. Galliano Liqueur
Fill with orange juice
Orange slice garnish

YELLOW JACKET
Rocks glass, chilled
Pour ingredients into iced mixing glass
3/4 oz. Jägermeister
3/4 oz. Bärenjäger Honey Liqueur
3/4 oz. Kahlúa
Shake and strain

YELLOW SNOW
House specialty glass, chilled
Pour ingredients into blender
1 1/4 oz. Bourbon
3 oz. sweet 'n' sour
Blend ingredients (with ice optional)
Lemon wheel pierced with pretzel
stick garnish

YO HOOTER HOOTER
Rocks glass, chilled
Build in glass
1 1/4 oz. Bourbon
2 dashes grenadine
1 oz. Seven-Up

YUKON STINGER
Rocks glass, ice
Build in glass
1 3/4 oz. Vodka
3/4 oz. Yukon Jack Liqueur

ZANZABAR HOLIDAY
Rocks glass, ice
Build in glass
1 oz. Brandy
1 oz. Kahlúa
1 1/2 oz. Amarula Cream Liqueur

ZANZIBAR DUNES
House specialty glass, chilled
Pour ingredients into blender
1 1/2 oz. Vodka
1 oz. Midori
1 oz. Peach Schnapps
1/2 oz. concord grape juice
1 1/2 oz. cranberry juice
2 oz. orange juice
Blend with ice

ZA-ZA
Bucket glass, ice
Pour ingredients into iced mixing glass
1 1/2 oz. Gin
1 1/2 oz. Dubonnet Rouge
1/2 oz. Triple Sec
2 oz. orange juice
Shake and strain

ZIPPER HEAD
Rocks glass, ice
Build in glass
1 1/2 oz. Vodka
3/4 oz. Chambord
Splash club soda

ZOMBIE (1)
House specialty glass, ice
Pour ingredients into iced mixing glass
2 oz. Appleton Estate V/X Jamaica Rum
3/4 oz. Crème de Noyaux
3/4 oz. Triple Sec
1 1/2 oz. sweet 'n' sour
1 1/2 oz. orange juice
Shake and strain
Float 3/4 oz. Bacardi 151° Rum
Orange slice and cherry garnish

ZOMBIE (2)
House specialty glass, ice
Pour ingredients into iced mixing glass
1 1/2 oz. Jamaican Rum
1 oz. Light Rum
3/4 oz. Triple Sec
3/4 oz. grenadine
1 1/2 oz. pineapple juice
1 1/2 oz. orange juice
1 1/2 oz. grapefruit juice
Shake and strain
Splash club soda
Float 3/4 oz. Dark Rum
Orange slice and cherry garnish

ZOMBIE, PINK
House specialty glass, ice
Pour ingredients into iced mixing glass
1 1/2 oz. Dark Rum
3/4 oz. Citrus Rum
1 oz. Crème de Banana
1/2 oz. grenadine
1 oz. fresh lime juice
2 oz. passion fruit syrup
2 oz. pineapple juice
2 oz. pink grapefruit juice
Shake and strain
Float 3/4 oz. 151° Rum
Pineapple wedge and cherry garnish

Z STREET SLAMMER
Rocks glass, chilled
Pour ingredients into iced mixing glass
1 1/4 oz. Appleton Estate V/X Jamaica Rum
3/4 oz. Crème de Banana
1 3/4 oz. pineapple juice
1/2 oz. grenadine
Shake and strain

ZUMA BUMA
Bucket glass, ice
Build in glass
1 1/2 oz. Citadelle Apple Vodka
1/2 oz. Chambord
Near fill with orange juice
Splash white cranberry juice
Splash lemon-lime soda

Glassware

The secret to glassware's success lies in its elegance, transparency and presentation. Its transparency makes it an ideal vehicle for presenting drinks of all types. In addition, glass is an excellent insulator that helps keep cold drinks cold and warm drinks warm. The best way to make a cocktail look as good as it tastes is to present it in a fabulous looking glass. The glass is one of the most important elements in defining the drink's style.

A glassware type recommendation is made with each recipe. The decision as to what size of glass you will use should be based on the size of the drink. For example, if you intend to make a champagne-based cocktail you will need a champagne or wine glass with the capacity to accommodate that size portion. If you already have a glass that you want to serve the cocktail in, but it's not the right size, you can always adjust the recipe ingredients proportionately to fit your glass.

To determine the type of glass for your cocktail, consider what the capacity of the glass will be when filled with ice. For example, a 9-ounce glass will hold approximately 3 to 4 ounces of liquid when completely filled with cubed ice.

On pages 305 and 306 are a list of beverage, cocktail, wine and beer service glassware to consider for the glassware types recommended in each recipe. The references to Libbey glassware contained in the information are intended as excellent representations of the quality, style, size and shape of glasses that are available today.

For more detailed information on glassware selection, the different types, and handling, see *Successful Beverage Management: Proven Strategies for the On-Premise Operator*, by Robert Plotkin, copyright 2000.

Drink Preparation

Each recipe contains "pouring instructions," which includes the type of glass to use and the steps to take to make the drink. The following are explanations of the italicized instructions recommended in each recipe. Any other special instructions not listed here are also italicized in the recipe.

Instructions

1. *Build in glass*
Pour the ingredients directly into the service glass.

2. *Layer ingredients*
Carefully pour each ingredient into the service glass, using the back of a spoon or the side of the glass to slow the pour of the liquid, creating a layered effect.

3. *Pour ingredients into blender*
Blend with ice
Pour a scoop of ice and each of the ingredients into the blender. Use personal judgement when adding ice. These drinks are meant to have a smooth consistency. If the scooped in ice isn't enough to freeze the drink, add another 1/4 to 1/3 scoop.

4. *Pour ingredients into blender*
Blend ingredients (with ice optional)
Pour each of the ingredients into the blender. Use personal judgement when adding ice. These drinks are meant to have a smooth consistency. The ice cream or other frozen ingredients may be enough to freeze the drink; if not, add 1/2 scoop of ice.

5. *Pour ingredients into iced mixing glass*
Shake and strain
Pour a scoop of ice and each of the ingredients into a mixing glass or cocktail shaker. The ingredients are meant to be thoroughly mixed and develop a frothy head of foam. These types of drinks are often prepared both on the rocks (over ice), and straight-up (without ice). The same process is used in preparation of either.

6. *Pour ingredients into iced mixing glass*
Stir and strain
Pour a scoop of ice and each of the ingredients into a mixing glass or cocktail shaker. The ingredients are meant to be thoroughly chilled, and gently mixed. These types of drinks are also sometimes prepared using the "Build in glass" method.

7. **Rim glass with salt**
Moisten the outside edge of the glass rim with lime juice or syrup. Dip in kosher or specialty salt to create a rim.
Rim glass with sugar
Moisten the outside edge of the glass rim with sweetened lime juice or sugar syrup. Dip in sugar to create a rim.

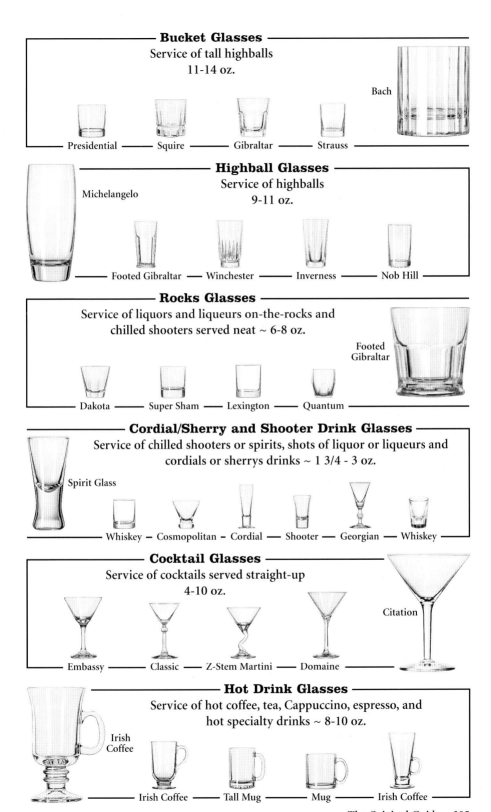

Bucket Glasses
Service of tall highballs
11-14 oz.

Bach

Presidential — Squire — Gibraltar — Strauss

Highball Glasses
Service of highballs
9-11 oz.

Michelangelo

Footed Gibraltar — Winchester — Inverness — Nob Hill

Rocks Glasses
Service of liquors and liqueurs on-the-rocks and
chilled shooters served neat ~ 6-8 oz.

Footed
Gibraltar

Dakota — Super Sham — Lexington — Quantum

Cordial/Sherry and Shooter Drink Glasses
Service of chilled shooters or spirits, shots of liquor or liqueurs and
cordials or sherrys drinks ~ 1 3/4 - 3 oz.

Spirit Glass

Whiskey — Cosmopolitan — Cordial — Shooter — Georgian — Whiskey

Cocktail Glasses
Service of cocktails served straight-up
4-10 oz.

Citation

Embassy — Classic — Z-Stem Martini — Domaine

Hot Drink Glasses
Service of hot coffee, tea, Cappuccino, espresso, and
hot specialty drinks ~ 8-10 oz.

Irish
Coffee

Irish Coffee — Tall Mug — Mug — Irish Coffee

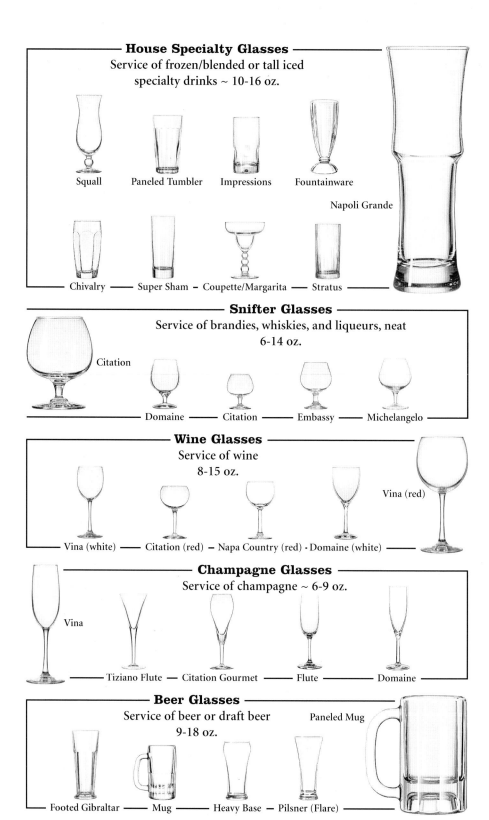

House Specialty Glasses
Service of frozen/blended or tall iced
specialty drinks ~ 10-16 oz.

Squall   Paneled Tumbler   Impressions   Fountainware

Napoli Grande

Chivalry —— Super Sham – Coupette/Margarita —— Stratus

Snifter Glasses
Service of brandies, whiskies, and liqueurs, neat
6-14 oz.

Citation

Domaine —— Citation —— Embassy —— Michelangelo

Wine Glasses
Service of wine
8-15 oz.

Vina (red)

Vina (white) —— Citation (red) – Napa Country (red) · Domaine (white)

Champagne Glasses
Service of champagne ~ 6-9 oz.

Vina

Tiziano Flute — Citation Gourmet —— Flute —— Domaine

Beer Glasses
Service of beer or draft beer
9-18 oz.

Paneled Mug

Footed Gibraltar —— Mug —— Heavy Base — Pilsner (Flare)

Find a Drink ~ Special Index

Slippery Banana
Slippery Greek
Slippery Nipple
Sno-Cap
Sperm Bank
Spilt Milk (1)
Spilt Milk (2)
Stiff Dick
Strawberry Quickie
Sugar Baby
Sweet (Irish) Dreams
Tavern Sucker, The
Tender Mercies
Test-Tube Baby (1)
Test-Tube Baby (2)
Tight Sweater
Tiramisu (2)
Trade Deficit
Turbo Milk Chocolate
Watergate
Watermelon (2)
Whisky Gingerbread
White Hawaiian
White Russian, Premium
Winsome Way

BAK'S ZUBRÓWKA
 VODKA
See Vodka, Zubrówka
BEEFEATER GIN
See Gin, Beefeater
BEER DRINKS
110 Degrees In The Shade
Baltimore Zoo
Beer Buster
Belgian Waffle
Bismark
Black And Brown
Black And Tan
Black Ape
Black Death
Black Velvet
Black Velveteen
Boilermaker
Brown Derby
Brown Velvet
Bumble Bee
Car Bomb
Dead Eye Dick's Red Eye
Depth Charge
Dr. Pepper (2)
Dr. Pepper From Hell
Ginger Beer Shandy
Gold And Lager
Grandfather
Half & Half (2)
Irish American
Irish Car Bomb
Koala Bear (2)
Lager And Black
Lager And Lime
Lemon Top
Lockhart Zoo
Michelada
Michelada, Caliente
Michelada, Sauza
Midnight Oil
Pink Panther (1)
Purple Death
Rabid Dog
Red Beer
Red Beer Shooter
Reverend Craig
Rock 'N' Bock
Sex In The Coal Region

Shandy Gaff
Skip And Go Naked
Snake Bite (2)
Torpedo Slam
BELVEDERE VODKA
See Vodka
BLENDED DRINKS
Amangani Indian
 Paintbrush
Amaretto Cruise
Appleton Planter's Punch
Ariana's Dream
Bacardi Tropical Dream
Balashi Breeze
Banana Fruit Punch
Banana Popsicle
Bananas Barbados
Berries Jubilee
Big Chill
Blackbeard's Treasure
Blizzard (1)
Blushing Berry Cooler
Borinquen
Bush Tickler
Bushwacker
Butterscotch Slide
Canyon Quake (1)
Caribbean Berry
Caribbean Cruise (1)
Caribbean Dream (2)
Caribbean Gridlock
Caribe Surfsider
Cartland Cure
Catherine Was Great
Cheap Shades
Chi-Chi
Chiquita Punch
Chocolate Milk Cooler
Cinderella
Citron Neon
Coco Loco
Coco Mocha
Cocomotion
Crimson Rose
Culture Shock
Daiquiri, Banana
Daiquiri, Berry
Daiquiri, Calypso
Daiquiri De Piña
Daiquiri, Derby
Daiquiri, Flight Of Fancy
Daiquiri, Fruit (Basic)
Defroster
Delicias De La Habana
Down Under Snowball
Ed Sullivan
El Conquistador
Frostbite
Frosted Peach Breeze
Frosted Strawberry Tea
Frozen Rose
Fruit Stripe
Gauguin
Georgia's Own
Golden Ram
Goom Bay Smash (1)
Goom Bay Smash (2)
Gorky Park Cooler (2)
Harvest Night
Island Voodoo
Isthmus Buffalo Milk
Jamaica Juice
Jamaica Me Crazy (2)
Jamba Day

Jardinera
Kapalua Butterfly
Key Isla Morada
Koala Float
Ladies Auxiliary
Lasting Passion
Latin Love
Latin Lover (2)
Lemon Parfait
Liam's Passion
Lost Lovers
Love Potion #9
Mango Mingle
Margarita, Cranberry (1)
Margarita, Cranberry (2)
Margarita De Fruta
Margarita, Hawaiian
Margarita, Honeydew This
Margarita, Mango
Margarita, Maui (1)
Margarita, Meltdown
Margarita, Midnight
 Madness
Margarita, Neon
 Watermelon
Margarita, Normandy
Margarita, Pear
Margarita, Pineapple
Margarita, Prickly Pear (1)
Margarita, Prickly Pear (2)
Margarita, Raspberry
Margarita, Raspberry Torte
Margarita, Red Cactus
Margarita, Rose
Margarita, Strawberry
 Lover's
Margarita, Two-Toned
Margarita, Watermelon
Maui Breezer
Meadow Snow
Mediterranean Freeze
Meister-Bation
Mexican Runner
Miami Vice (1)
Morning Sun
Mother Mason's Delight
Mystic Runner
Navy Grog, Modern
Offenburg Flip
Orsini
Pain In The Butt
Papa Dobles
Piña Colada
Piña Colada, Acapulco
Piña Colada, Amaretto
Piña Colada, Aussie
Piña Colada, Bahama
Piña Colada, Bellevue
Piña Colada, Bermuda
Piña Colada, Black Pearl
Piña Colada, Brazilian
Piña Colada, Cactus
Piña Colada, Canne Bay
Piña Colada, French
Piña Colada, Fruit (Basic)
Piña Colada, Funky
 Monkey
Piña Colada, Golden
 Bacardi
Piña Colada, Hawaiian
 Lion
Piña Colada, Italian (1)
Piña Colada, Italian (2)
Piña Colada, Kéké Colada

Piña Colada, Kingston
Piña Colada, Kokomo Joe
Piña Colada, Lemonada
 (1)
Piña Colada, Liqueur-
 Flavored
Piña Colada, Lt. Kije's
Piña Colada, Malibu
 Orange
Piña Colada, Midori
Piña Colada, Pacific Blue
Piña Colada, Port Royal
Piña Colada, Pusser's
 Island
Piña Colada, Rémy Colada
Piña Colada, Spanish
Piña Colada, Stramaretto
Piña Colada, Strawberry
 Banana
Piña Colada, Toasted
 Almond
Pink Cadillac
Pink Slipper
Princess Margaret
Purple People Beefeater
Pusser's Pain Killer
Red Rhumba
Reggae Walker
Rhododendron
Rhum Barbancourt Freeze
Rock Lobster
Sea Side Liberty
Sex In The Woods
Sky High
Slipped Disk
Smooth Screw
Sneaky Peach
Socialite Prize Fight
South Of France
South-Of-The-Border
 Mango Mash
Starburst
Staton Island Berry
Strawberries 'N' Cream
Strawberry Smash
Straw House Hummer
Strummer Hummer
Summer Tonic
Sweaty Betty
Sweet Tart (1)
Tequila Maria
Vanil Sensation
Whale's Tail
When Hell Freezes Over
Yellow Bird (2)
Yellow Snow
Zanzibar Dunes
BLOODY MARY DRINKS
See "Bloody Mary" In
 Alphabetized Recipes
BLUE CURAÇAO
Adios Mother
Aqua Zest
Balashi Breeze
Beach Bum Blue
Big Blue Shooter
Black & Blue Bayou
Black 'N' Blue
Black Orchid
Blast-Off Punch
Blue Bayou (2)
Blue Devil
Blue Duck
Blue Flute

Blue Hawaii
Blue Hawaiian
Blue Lagoon (1)
Blue Lagoon (2)
Blue Lemonade
Blue Marlin
Blue Moon Café
Blue Tail Fly
Blue Wave (1)
Blue Wave (2)
Blue Whale
Calypso Highway
Cold Gold
Cool Mint Listerine
Cosmopolitan, Midnight
  Blue
Cosmopolitan, Purple (1)
Cosmopolitan, Purple (2)
Cuervo Nation Cocktail
Curaçao Cooler
Damrak Blue Lady
Delicias De La Habana
Desert Sunrise
Done & Bradstreet
Electric Lemonade
Eve's Apple
Flaming Blue Blaster
Gang Green
Gator Juice
Gimlet, Irish
Green Sneakers
Halekulani Sunset
Iced Tea, Alaskan
Iced Tea, Bimini
Iced Tea, Blue Kangaroo
Iced Tea, Dirty Ashtray
Infusion, Ice Blue
  Margarita
Infusion, Pineapple Purple
  Passion
Infusion, Sky Blue
Infusion, Summer Shades
  Margarita
Island Flower
Island Sunset
Jamaica Me Crazy (2)
Jealousy
Jewel
Kamikaze, Blue
Kamikaze, Radioactive
Kentucky Bluegrass
Kentucky Swamp Water
Kiss Of The Islands
L.A.P.D.
Lemon Lavender
Leprechaun
Loch Lomond (2)
Manhattan, Blue Grass
  Blues
Margarita Azul
Margarita, Blue
Margarita, Blue Maestro
  Gran
Margarita, Blue Moon
Margarita, Catalina
Margarita, Hawaiian
Margarita, Hypnotic
Margarita, Luna Azul
Margarita, Mad Russian
Margarita, Midnight
  Madness
Margarita, Neon
  Watermelon
Margarita, Pacific Blue

Margarita, Purple (1)
Margarita, Purple (2)
Margarita Splash
Margarita, Sunset
Margarita, Teal
Margo Moore
Martini, Blue Moon (1)
Martini, Blue Moon (2)
Martini, Blue Pacific
Martini, Blue Shock
Martini Blues
Martini, Citrus
Martini, Electric Blue
Martini, French Grape
Martini, Libertini
Martini, Sakétini
Martini, Three Mile Island
Martini, Wet Blue
Miami Vice (1)
Milwaukee River
Monster Appeaser
Octopus Ink
Piña Colada, Emerald Isle
Piña Colada, Pacific Blue
Piña Colada, Tropical
  Moon
Piranha Club Initiation
Pousse Café (3)
Purple Flirt
Purple Piranha
Reef And Tide Water
Rhum Barbancourt Freeze
Ritz Fizz
Sandy Smile
Sea Water
Shark Attack
Shark's Tooth
Smurf Piss
Soyer-Au-Champagne
Spanish Fly
St. Patrick's Day
Stars & Stripes
Stealth Bomber (1)
Summer Daze
Summer Lemonade
Surf Sider (1)
Swamp Water Stinger
Tequila Mockingbird (2)
Tidy Bowl
Wall Street Wizard
Wanderer
Whale's Tail
Windex
BOMBAY SAPPHIRE GIN
  See Gin, Bombay
BORU VODKA
  See Vodka, Boru
BOURBON WHISKEY
  Evan William's Bourbon
  Manhattan, Cherbourg
  Manhattan, Vintage (1)
  Manhattan, Vintage (2)
  Uptown Girl
  Jim Beam Bourbons
  Apple Spice
  Black Beauty (2)
  Black Citrus Sin
  Black Knight
  Black Smooth & Sour
  Bomb
  Fedora
  Four Wise Men
  Martini, Black &
  Orange

Martini, Black Coffee &
  Creamtini
Martini, Cran-
  Appletini
Knob Creek Bourbon
  Kentucky Shuffle
  Knob Creek
  Old Fashion, Knob
  Creek
Maker's Mark Bourbon
  Manhattan, Apple
  Manhattan, Italian
  Manhattan, Loretto
  Manhattan, Market
  Manhattan, Smoky
  Margarita, Kentucky
  Martini, Kentucky
  Mint Julep, On The
  Mark
Old Forester Bourbon
  Manhattan, Boulevard
  Seelbach Cocktail
  Wentworth Cocktail
**Woodford Reserve
  Bourbon**
  Bourbon Ball
  Full Monte
  Kentucky Longshot
  Manhattan, Blue Grass
  Blues
  Manhattan, Westchester
**BOURBON WHISKEY
DRINKS**
  Better Than N.E.1
  Black-Eyed Susan
  Blizzard (1)
  Brooklyn
  Brown Cow
  Brown Cow Milkshake
  Buffalo Sweat
  Bull And Bear
  Burnt Sienna
  Canyon Slider
  City Tavern Cooler
  Collins, Jamie
  Collins, John
  Collins, Red Turkey
  Dead Grizzly
  Dead Grizzly Shooter
  Deathwish
  Dingy Ginger
  Dizzy Lizzy
  Flaming Blue Blaster
  Frappé, Derby Mint
  Frappé, Lagniappe
  French 95
  Hell On Ice
  Highball
  Horse's Neck With A
  Kick
  Hot Milk Punch
  Hot Toddy
  Iced Tea, Manhattan
  Jaundice Juice
  Jealousy
  Jet Fuel (2)
  John Wayne
  Kentucky Bluegrass
  Kentucky Cooler
  Kentucky Swamp Water
  Lena Cocktail
  Mamie's Southern
  Sister
  Manhattan

Manhattan, Algonquin
Manhattan, Biscayne
Manhattan,
  Continental Perfect
Manhattan, Danish
Manhattan, Dijon
Manhattan, Dry
Manhattan, Dubonnet
Manhattan, Galliano
Manhattan, Lafayette
Manhattan, Marianne
Manhattan, Mazatlan
Manhattan, New
  Orleans
Manhattan, Paparazzi
Manhattan, Perfect
Manhattan, Poor Tim
Manhattan, Preakness
Manhattan, Raspberry
Manhattan, Rose
Manhattan, Rosebud
Manhattan, Shamrock
Manhattan, Sheepshead
  Bay
Manhattan, St. Moritz
Manhattan, Tivoli
Manhattan, Waldorf
Millionaire Cocktail
Mint Julep
Mint Julep, Kentucky
Mojito, My Kentucky
Old Fashion
Old Fashion, Santa
  Anita
Old Fashion, Muddled
Old Fashion, New Age
Orange-U-Glad-2-C-
  Me
Rabid Dog
Reverend Craig
Ritz Americana
Skyscraper
Snowshoe (1)
Snowshoe (2)
Spiked Smoothie
Steeplechase
Stock Market Zoo
Torpedo Slam
Trinity
Turkey Shooter
Ward Eight
Yellow Snow
Yo Hooter Hooter
BRANDY
  Calvados Apple Brandy
  Apple Grand Marnier
  Champagne Normande
  Corpse Reviver (1)
  Deauville
  International Affair
  Margarita, Normandy
  Sidecar, Imperial
  Tighter Cider
  **Christian Brothers
  Brandy**
  Carte Blanche
  Chocolate Milk Cooler
  Fedora
  Randy Brandy Egg Nog

Laird's 12 Year Rare Apple Brandy
Apple Cart
Apple Works
Aprés Ski
Café Brûlot
Manhattan, Spiced Apple Brandy
Laird's Applejack Brandy
Ambrosia (2)
Applejack Cream
Apple Sting
Apple Toddy
Aprés Ski
Chef Dieter's Apple Pie Cocktail
Collins, Jack
Diki-Diki
Happy Jacks
Harvest Grog
Hole-In-One
Honeymoon
Jack Rose Cocktail
Jersey Devil
Klondike
Manhattan, Big Apple
Old Fashion, Apple
Pink Lady (2)
Steeple Jack
Tidal Wave (1)
BRANDY DRINKS
38th Parallel
Aching Bach
Alexander The Great
Alpine Glow
Apple Brandy Cooler
Aunt Bea's Cure-All Hot Milk Punch
B & B
Barcelona Coffee
Basin Street Balm
Benson Bomber
Betsy Ross
Between The Sheets
Black Hooter
Blizzard (2)
Blood And Sand (1)
Blood And Sand (2)
Blue Train Special
Bosom Caresser
Brandy Alexander
Brandy Egg Nog (1)
Brandy Egg Nog (2)
Brandy Gump
Café Charles
Café Correcto
Café Royale
Canyon Quake (1)
Canyon Quake (2)
Cappa 21
Cappo De Tutti Cappi
Caribe Surfsider
Champs Elysees Cocktail (1)
Cherry Amore
Cherry Bean
Cherry Blossom
Chicago
Chocolate Squirrel
Classic Vette
Cookie Mint Rookie
Corpse Reviver (2)
Creamy Dreamy Isotope

Dangerous Liaisons
Diablo
Dire Straits
Dirty Mother
East India
Fogcutter
Fogcutter, Royal Navy
Foreign Legion
Forever Amber
Frappé, Apricot Brandy
French Consulate
French Maid's Café
Freudian Slip
Golden Dream With Double Bumpers
Great Lakes Trapper
Greek Coffee
Green Hornet
Harvard
Heartbreak
Heavenly Toddy
Hemingway's Flambé Coffee
Hot Toddy
Houndstooth
Iced Tea, Havana
Inoculation
International Stinger
Irish Headlock
Italian Stinger
Jamaican Fever
Japanese Cocktail
Jelly Bean
Jubilee Cocktail
Katinka
Kentucky Longshot
Keoki Coffee
Keoki Shooter
Le Bistro
Let Us Alone
Manhattan, Blood And Sand
Manhattan, Brandy
Manhattan, Dry Brandy
Manhattan, Perfect Brandy
Margarita, Mezcal
Margarita, Presidenté
Margo Moore
Martini, Zanzabar
Maui Breezer
Maxim's A Londres
Ménage À Trois
Mexican Cocoa
Midori Stinger
Montmarte
Mother
Navy Grog, Original
Periodista (1)
Periodista (2)
Persuader
Pisco Sour
Port In A Storm
Pousse Café (1)
Pousse Café (2)
Pousse Café (3)
Prairie Oyster (1)
Restoration
Rum Runner (1)
Rum Runner (2)
Run, Skip And Go Naked
Sacrifice Fly
Scorpion

C

Separator (1)
Separator (2)
Sex In The Coal Region
Siberian
Sidecar (2)
Sidecar, Grand
Singapore Sling (1)
Singapore Sling (2)
Soyer-Au-Champagne
Steeplechase
Stinger
Strawberry Alexandra
Tequila Maria
Tequila Sunset
Thumper
Tip-Top Punch
Trade Winds
Vanderbilt Cocktail
Whip
Whisper (2)
Zanzabar Holiday
BROKER'S GIN
See Gin, Broker's

CALVADOS APPLE BRANDY
See Brandy, Calvados
CAMPARI APERITIVO
Americano
Americano Highball
Campari & Soda
Dc-3 Shooter
Lena Cocktail
Manhattan, Tivoli
Martini, Becco
Martini, Black Tie (2)
Martini, Blood Orange
Martini, Blood Shot
Martini, Copper Illusion
Martini, Fantino
Martini, Romana
Martini, Rosebud
Negroni
Negroni, Uptown
Old Flame
Venetian Sunset
CANADIAN CLUB WHISKY
See Canadian Whisky
CANADIAN WHISKY
Canadian Club Whisky
Club Sherry
Doctor's Orders
Dog Sled
Empire State Slammer
Friar Tuck
Heartbreak
Infusion, Lumberjack
King Midas
Midori Canuck
Mother Lode
Saké Passion
Saké Passion Club
Smiles For Miles
Sour, Sparkling Sweet Apple
Spilt Milk (1)
Sunknee Delite
Whisky Gingerbread

Crown Royal Whisky
Duck Fart
Grand Ball
Koolo
Manhattan, Moon Over Manhattan
Martini, Blue Shock
Monster Appeaser
Royal Canadian
Royal Flush
Spilt Milk (2)
Washington Apple
CANADIAN WHISKY DRINKS
Bettor's Dream
Canadian
Canadian Bliss
Canadian Foot Warmer
Canadian Stone Fence
Canadian Tart
Celeste's Cocktail
Defroster
Dry Creek
Dudley Does Right
French Mountie
Fresh Squeezed Bat Juice
Looking For Trouble
Manhattan, Maple Leaf
Manhattan, Mets
Manhattan, Park Paradise
Manhattan, Quebec
Manhattan, Roman
Mexican Blackjack
Sleigh Ride
Toronto
Up The Creek With A Kick
CAPPUCCINO DRINKS
Apple Grand Marnier
Baileys Express
Blast From The Past
Café Correcto
Café Framboise
Cappa 21
Cappo De Tutti Cappi
Emerald Isle
Foreign Legion
Gran Cappuccino
Hot Chambord Dream
Iacocca
International Cappuccino
International Velvet Café
Le Bistro
Louvre Me Alone
Mrs. Bailey's Favor
Pazzo Grand Spanish Coffee
Philippi Creek
River Seine Cappuccino
Sovereignty
CAPTAIN MORGAN RUM
See Rum, Captain Morgan
CASA NOBLE TEQUILAS
See Tequila, Casa Noble

CELTIC CROSSING LIQUEUR
Castle Coffee
Celtic Kiss
Irish Boggle
Irish Lemonade
Limerick
Manhattan, Spiced Apple Brandy
Martini, Celtic
Spirit Of Erie Coffee

CHAMBORD LIQUEUR
38th Parallel
1701 Fog
Abbey Road
Absolut Mandarinade
Aviation Cocktail
Banilla Boat
Bank Shot
Beachcomber (1)
Bellinisimo
Berries Jubilee
Betty Grable
Big Bamboo (1)
Bikini Line
Black And White
Blackbeard's Treasure
Black Hooter
Black Stockings
Blast From The Past
Bleacher's Twist
Brut 'N' Bogs
Burgundy Cocktail
Burnt Sienna
Café Contenté
Californian
Caribbean Sour
Caribbean Sunset
Caribe Sunset
Cartel Shooter
C.C. Rider
Chambord Dream
Chambord Repose
Champagne Framboise
Cherrillo
Cocaine Shooter (1)
Cocaine Shooter (2)
Colorado Avalanche
Comfortable Crush
Cosmopolitan, Euro
Cosmopolitan, Purple (2)
Cosmopolitan, Raspberry (1)
Crab House Shooter
Cranberry Squeeze
Cyrano
Daiquiri, Berry
Daiquiri, Rhum
De Gaulle Cocktail
Doctor's Elixir
Doubt Raiser
Dream Catcher
Dream Maker
Dry Arroyo
Dusty Rose
East River
Ecstasy Shooter
E Pluribus Unum
Express Mail Drop
Fat Cat Fizz
Federal Express
Five Dollar Margaret
Framboise Kiss
French Dream

French Toast Royale
Fruity Tutti
Full Monte
Fun In The Sun
Gimlet, Raspberry
Glasnost
Guava Martinique
Harvest Grog
Heather Blush
Holland's Opus
Hollywood
Holy Hand Grenade
Hot Chambord Dream
Hot Irish Dream
Iced Tea, Jesse's Shocking
Iced Tea, Raspberry
Imperial Duo
Irish Raspberry
Jar Juice
Jewel Of Russia
Kamikaze, Purple (1)
Kamikaze, Purple (2)
Kamikaze, Raspberry
Knickerbocker Special Cocktail
La Bamba
Latin Lover (2)
Left Bank
Lemonade Royale
Lobotomy
Loco En La Cabeza (1)
Lookout Point
Lost Lovers
Madtown Milkshake
Mandarine Dream
Manhattan, Blood And Sand
Manhattan, Poor Tim
Manhattan, Raspberry
Margarita, Black Gold
Margarita, El Conquistador
Margarita Framboise
Margarita, Meltdown
Margarita, Midnight Madness
Margarita, Purple (1)
Margarita, Purple (2)
Margarita, Red Cactus
Margarita, Santa Rita
Margarita, Sunset
Margarita, Tres Compadres
Margarita, Two-Toned
Margarita, Zinful
Maritime Sunrise
Martini, Alexander Nevsky
Martini, Black (1)
Martini, Bubblegum
Martini, Chocolate Utopia
Martini, Cosmonaut
Martini, Crème Brûlée (3)
Martini, Espresso Framboise
Martini, French (2)
Martini, Harper's
Martini, Imperial
Martini, Medici
Martini, Metropolis
Martini, Midnight (2)
Martini, Mystic
Martini, Nitelife
Martini, Orchid
Martini, Osteria

Martini, Passion
Martini, P. B. & J.
Martini, Poinsettia
Martini, Raspberry
Martini, Raspberry (2)
Martini, Sushi
Martini, Tartini
Martini, Ty-Won-On
Mellow Dramatic
Mexican Melon
Mexican Runner
Mikhail Cocktail
Mind Bender
Miss Ube Darn
Orange Cranberry Toddy
Orchid Cocktail
Otter Water
Paris Burning
Passionate Screw
Peter Prescription
Piña Colada, Hawaiian Lion
Piña Colada, Port Royal
Pink Cadillac
Pink Coconut
Pink Creole
Pink Slipper
Pope On Vacation
Primo Bacio
Purple Death
Purple Hooter (1)
Purple Hooter (2)
Purple Matador
Purple People Beefeater
Raspberry Banana Split
Raspberry Cream
Raspberry Sour
Raspberry Sweet Tart
Raspberry Torte
Raztini
Red Eclipse
Rendezvous Punch
Restoration
Riviera Days
Riviera Nights
Royal Bay Breeze
Royal Flush
Royal Godiva
Rue De La Paix
Rumscapes
Saint Moritz
Sandy Beach Bay
Say Hey Marseilles
Sex On A Black Sandy Beach
Sex On The Beach (1)
Sex On The Beach (2)
Sex On The Beach (3)
Sex On The Beach (4)
Sex On The Beach (5)
Sex With An Alligator (1)
Sex With An Alligator (3)
Sneak & Peak Cocktail
Somosa Bay
Sovereignty
Storm-A-Long Bay
Strawberry Smash
Summer Hummer
Sweet Red Kiss
Sweet Tart (2)
Sweet Tart (3)
Take The Prize
Texas Tea
Tinted Glass

Tour De France
Trade Winds
Twilight Moan Zone
V.I.P. Coffee
Vampire
Wanderer
Watkin's Glen
Wet Dream
Zipper Head
Zuma Buma

CHAMPAGNE DRINKS
Ambrosia (1)
Ambrosia (2)
April In Paris
Banalini
Beautiful In Blue
Bellini
Bellinisimo
Betelgeuse
Beverly Hills Cooler
Bismark
Black Velvet
Blood Orange Champagne Cocktail
Blue Flute
Blue Mimosa
Blue Moon Café
Blue Train Special
Blushing Angel
Brut 'N' Bogs
Bubble Zaza
Buzz Bomb
Cajun Mimosa
Caribbean Champagne
Caribbean Contessa
C.C. Rider
Celestial Fizz
Cesar Ritz
Champagne Cocktail
Champagne Cornucopia
Champagne Framboise
Champagne Imperial
Champagne Jubilee
Champagne Marseille
Champagne Normande
Champs Elysees Cocktail (2)
Cherry Amore
Chicago
Club Macanudo
Code Red
Cognac Ritz
Concorde
Damrak 75
De Gaulle Cocktail
Doubt Raiser
Down Under
Dream Catcher
Dry Arroyo
Du Monde
East River
Eiffel View
Estes Fizz
Express Mail Drop
Federal Express
Floating Heart
French 75 (1)
French 75 (2)
French 95
French Consulate
Freudian Slip
Full Monte
Glenda
Gran Bliss

Madonna's Brassiere
Magellan Sauce
Maiden's Reprieve
Manhattan
Manhattan Glitz
Massappeal
Meadowlark Lemon
Merry Widow (1)
Midnight Express (1)
Midnight Express (2)
Midnight Express (3)
Midnight Orchid
Midorable
Millionaire Cocktail
Monkey Gland
Mountain Retreat
Mud Puddle
Nácional
Neapolitan
Negroni
Negroni, Uptown
New York Nut
Noble Nymph
Nosferatu
Nuts & Berries
Octopus Ink
Old Flame
Opera Cocktail
Orange Blossom (1)
Orange Delight
Orange Dream
Orange-U-Glad-2-C-Me
Orchid Cocktail
Original Monk
Paddy
Palace Guard
Peach Cobbler
Perfect 10
Periodista (1)
Periodista (2)
Pineapple Fizz
Pineapple Smooch
Pink Baby
Pink Creole
Pink Gin
Pink Lady (2)
Pink Moment
Pisco Sour
Presidenté
Presumption Cocktail
Purple Hooter (1)
Pyrat Pete Cocktail
Rainbow International
   Cocktail
Razzle Dazzle Rose
Recession Depression
Red Lion
Reef And Tide Water
Reserva Cocktail
Rio Rita
Riviera
Rolls Royce
Rough Seas Cocktail
Roxanne
Royal Bay Breeze
Russian' About
Sail Of The Century
Saké Passion
Sauza Threesome
Savannah
Sax With Bill
Scurvey Abator
Seattle's 6.3
Seventh Avenue

Sex With An Alligator (1)
Sex With An Alligator (2)
Sex With An Alligator (3)
Sherry's Blossom
Sidecar, Autumn
Sidecar, Cuban
Sidecar, Grand
Sidecar, Havana (1)
Sidecar, Havana (2)
Sidecar, Imperial
Silk Rose
Simply Crimson
Sin & French Gin
Sin In Hawaii
Sloppy Joe's Cocktail
Sneak & Peak Cocktail
Sour
Sour Melon Patch
Sour Mint
South Beach Twist
Splendid Gin
St. Patrick's Day
Starlight
Stone Sour
Suissesse
Summer Hummer
Summer Memories
Sunburnt Señorita
Sunday Brunch Punch
   Cocktail
Sunflower
Sunglow
Sunstroke
Surf Sider (1)
Sweet Red Kiss
Take The Prize
Tangerine Drop
Tequila Mockingbird (1)
Tikki Dream
Tinted Glass
Toronto
Tovarich
Trade Winds
Trinity
Turbo Milk Chocolate
Twilight Moan Zone
Ulterior Motive
Uptown
Vanderbilt Cocktail
Venetian Sunset
Vermouth Cassis
Vincent's Baubles
Vodka Grand
Wall Street Wizard
Ward Eight
Wentworth Cocktail
Wet Passion
Whip
White Out
XO Stinger Cocktail
Yale Cocktail

COCOA DRINKS
Cabin Fever Cure
Canadian Foot Warmer
Carte Blanche
Chicago Times
French Kiss
Great Lakes Trapper
Jungle Milk
Mad Hatter
Mexican Cocoa
Pusser's Stalemate
Sacrifice Fly

COFFEE DRINKS
38th Parallel
Abbey Road
Ambush
Aspen Coffee
Baileys Mint Kiss
Barcelona Coffee
Bay Area Garter
Black Jack
Black Maria
Black Ruby
Bukhara Coffee
Café A La Cabana
Café Amore
Café Brûlot
Café Charles
Café Chocolate (1)
Café Chocolate (2)
Café Contené
Café Diablo
Café Dublin
Café Foster
Café Kingston
Café Reggae
Café Royale
Café St. Armands
Calypso Coffee
Capo Di Sopranos
Captain's Coffee (1)
Captain's Coffee (2)
Caribbean Dream (1)
Caribe Sunset
Castle Coffee
Chambord Repose
Chicago Times
Chill-Out Café
Chip Shot
Ciao Bello
Coco Mocha
Cork Street Coffee (1)
Cork Street Coffee (2)
Dark Continent Café
Duke Of Earl
Dutch Coffee
Electrode Overload
French Maid's Café
Fuzzy Dick
Fuzzy Mussy
Greek Coffee
Hemingway's Flambé
   Coffee
Hot Irish Dream
Hunter's Coffee
International Affair
Irish Boggle
Irish Coffee
Irish Coffee Royale (1)
Irish Coffee Royale (2)
Italian Coffee
Jamaican Coffee
Jumper Cables
Keoki Coffee
Keoki Shooter
Leave Us Alone
Lemon Nog
Mackinnon Road
Martini, Kohv
Mexican Coffee
Mexican Monk
Midnight Lace
Millionaire's Coffee
Mincemeat Mocha
Mocha Jamocha
Monk's Coffee

Monte Cristo Shooter
Montego Bay (1)
Mount Gay Café
Navy Grog, Nor'easter
Nina's Coffee
Northern Lights (1)
Nut Cream Coffee
Opulent Coffee
Peter Prescription
Royal Street Coffee
San Andreas Fault
Say Hey Marseilles
Scotch Coffee
Shore Boat
Shot In The Dark
Spirit Of Erie Coffee
Tender Mercies
Tennessee Mud
Tight Sweater
Toasted Almond Café
Toboggan Truffle
Trade Deficit
Trophy Room
Tropical Depression
Vanilla Angel
V.I.P. Coffee
COGNAC
Courvoisier Cognacs
Bonaparte
Champagne Imperial
Cognac Ritz
Fortress Of Singapore
French Harvest
French Toast Royale
French Twist
Leave Us Alone
Manhattan, Napoleon
Martini, Mayflower
Room Service At The
   Ritz
COGNAC DRINKS
Amber Cloud
Andalusia
Apple Grand Marnier
Beverly Hills Cooler
Blue Mimosa
Burgundy Cocktail
Buzz Bomb
Café Amore
Café Diablo
Café Royale
C. & C.
Celestial Fizz
Champs Elysees
   Cocktail (2)
Club Macanudo
Collins, Fifi
Collins, Pierre
Corpse Reviver (1)
De Gaulle Cocktail
Framboise Kiss
Frappé, Parisian
French 75 (2)
French Connection
French Mountie
Gold And Riches
Golden Max
Gran Cappuccino
Imperial Duo
Louvre Me Alone
Madame Butterfly
Marseilles Stockings
Martini, Chocolate
   Supreme

Orchard Haze
Pearl Diver
Rough Seas Cocktail
Sex At The Beach
Sex With An Alligator (2)
Sour, Sparkling Sweet
  Apple
Spider Cider
Washington Apple
Weekend At The Beach (1)
Week On The Beach
DEKUYPER RAZZMATAZZ
Badda-Bing
Black Tequila Rose
Dodo Bird
Jäger Monster
Jamba Day
Late-Nite Lemon Drop
Leaning Tower
Lifesaver (2)
Malibu Runner
Malibu Sunset
Purple Passion
Razzle Dazzle
Razzle Dazzle Rose
Razzmatazz
Razzputenee
Sex With An Alligator (2)
DEKUYPER SCHNAPPS
See Schnapps, Dekuyper
DEWAR'S SCOTCH
See Scotch Whisky
DISARONNO AMARETTO
'57 Chevy
'57 T-Bird With Arizona
  Plates
'57 T-Bird With Florida
  Plates
'57 T-Bird With Hawaiian
  Plates
Abbey Road
A Day At The Beach
After Tan (1)
After Tan (2)
Alabama Slammer (2)
Alabama Slammer (4)
Alabama Slammer (5)
Almond Joy
Amaretto Cruise
Ambush
American Dream
Appleton Blast
August Moon
Bacardi Tropical Dream
Banana Frost
Beach Blonde
Benson Bomber
Berry Cooler
Betty Grable
Big Fat Monkey Kiss
Black Smooth Sour
Black Widow
Blue Flute
Blueberry Tea
Bocci Ball
Bocci Shooter
Brown Squirrel
Bubble Gum
Café Amore
Canyon Quake (2)
Caribbean Berry
Caribbean Dream (2)
Caribbean Romance
Catherine Was Great

Cello Amore
Cello Fellow
Champagne Jubilee
Champagne Marseille
Chicago Times
Chill-Out Café
Chip Shot
Chocolate Squirrel
Come-On-I-Wanna-Lei-Ya
Cosmopolitan, Disaronno
Cowboy Killer
Crab House Shooter
Creamsicle (2)
Desert Storm
Dingo
Down Under
Dr. Pepper (1)
Dr. Pepper (2)
Dr. Pepper From Hell
Dreamsicle (1)
Dreamsicle (2)
Dubonnet Fuzzy
Duke Of Earl
Dunham Good
Ed Sullivan
Elixir Of Love
Express Mail Drop
Federal Express
Five Dollar Margaret
Flaming Armadillo
Foreign Legion
French Kiss
Frozen Devotion
Full Moon
Godchild
Godfather
Godmother
Golden Ram
Grand Alliance
Hawaiian Punch (1)
Hawaiian Punch (2)
Iced Tea, Italian
International Cappuccino
Irish Headlock
Italian Coffee
Italian Punch
Italian Sunrise (1)
Italian Sunrise (2)
Italian Surfer
Italian Valium
Jackalope
Jackie Special
Jäger Monster
Jamaican Shake
Jelly Fish
John Wayne
Jolly Rancher (2)
Julia
Jumper Cables
Key Largo
King's Cup
Kool Aid (1)
Kool Aid (2)
Lake Street Lemonade
Lemon Nog
Le Mooseberry
Lobotomy
Lounge Lizard
Love Canal
Lunch Box
Malibu Runner
Mama Citron
Manhattan Beach
Manhattan, Italian

Manhattan, Moon Over
  Manhattan
Margarita Azul
Margarita, Hawaiian
Margarita, Italian
Margarita, Oscar Night
Martini, Amber Skies
Martini, Black & Orange
Martini, Blue Shock
Martini, Café Nuttini
Martini, Chocolate Utopia
Martini, Full Moon (1)
Martini, Full Moon (2)
Martini, Kentucky
Martini, Tiramisu (1)
Martini, Tiramisu (2)
Martini, Toasted Nuts
Marz Bar
Maui Breezer
Midway Manhattan
Midway Rat (1)
Midway Rat (2)
Monsoon
Monster Appeaser
Mother Mason's Delight
Multiple Orgasm
Native Sun
Navy Grog, Nor'easter
New York Nut
Nina's Coffee
Nuckin Futs
Nut 'N' Holli
Nutty Professor
Oatmeal Cookie (1)
Orange Frappé
Orange Julius
Orgasm (1)
Outrigger
Paddy O'rocco
Paranoia
Peckerhead
Persuader
Piña Colada, Amaretto
Piña Colada, Italian (1)
Piña Colada, Italian (2)
Piña Colada, Lemonada (2)
Piña Colada, Stramaretto
Piña Colada, Toasted
  Almond
Piña Colada, Tropical
  Moon
Pink Panther (2)
Pink Paradise
Pirate Love
Purple Matador
Quaalude, Iranian
Rabid Dog
Razzmatazz
Red Devil
Rigor Mortis
Ritz Fizz
Roasted Toasted Almond
Rose Petal
Roxanne
Royal Canadian
Royal Street Coffee
Screaming Orgasm
Seventh Avenue
Seventh Heaven
Sex In The Woods
Sex On The Beach On A
  Cloudy Day
Sicilian Kiss
Silver Cloud

Silver Shadow
Skinny Dipping
Slipped Disk
Smiles For Miles
Smooth Gentleman
Sperm Bank
Spilt Milk (2)
St. Petersburg Sundae
Stiletto
Strawberry Shake
Straw House Hummer
Strummer Hummer
Sweet Tart (3)
T-Bird
Tennessee Mud
Test-Tube Baby (1)
Test-Tube Baby (2)
Tight Sweater
Tikki Dream
Tiramisu (1)
Toasted Almond
Toasted Almond Café
Trophy Room
Tropical Depression
Tropical Moon
Tryst & Shout
Ugly Duckling
Vanilla Angel
Waist Coat Pocket
Watermelon (1)
Wet Passion
Whisper (1)
White Swan
Wiki Waki Woo
Yankee Panky
DON EDUARDO TEQUILAS
See Tequilas, Don Eduardo
DRAMBUIE LIQUEUR
Aberdeen Angus
Black Jeweled Russian
Bobby Burns
Golden Nail
Inverted Nail
Mackinnon Road
Rusty Nail
Scotch Coffee
Scottish Dreams
Seventh Avenue
Sylk Stockings
Sylk Top Hat
Tequila Highlander
Upside Down Scottish
  Crown
Vincent's Baubles
Winnie's Hot Honey Pot
DUBONNET
Appetizer
Blushing Angel
Castle In The Clouds
Club Macanudo
Cosmopolitan, Dubonnet
Cosmopolitan, Red Light
Dollar Bill
Dubonnet Cocktail
Dubonnet Fuzzy
Fat Cat Fizz
Lady Madonna
London Redhead
Manhattan, Dubonnet
Manhattan, Lafayette
Manhattan, Mazatlan
Manhattan, Twin Peaks
Manhattan, Vintage (1)
Manhattan, Vintage (2)

Martini, 008
Martini, Dutch (1)
Martini, Elephant's Ear
Martini, Fourth Degree
Martini, Harper's
Martini, Jackson
Martini, Marseilles
Martini, Napoleon
Merry Widow (1)
Opera Cocktail
Riviera
Rob Roy, Oh Joy
Silken Veil
Splendid Gin
St. Tropez
Sweet Red Kiss
Wentworth Cocktail
Za-Za

E

EL TESORO TEQUILAS
See Tequilas, El Tesoro
ESPOLON TEQUILAS
See Tequilas, Espolon
ESPRESSO DRINKS
See Cappuccino Drinks
EVAN WILLIAMS
BOURBON
See Bourbon Whiskey

F

FINLANDIA VODKA
See Vodka, Finlandia
FRANGELICO LIQUEUR
American Dream
Angel Kiss
Aspen Coffee
Banana Nuts
Bananas Over You
Bay Area Garter
Black Beauty (1)
Chicago Times
Chocolate Almond Kiss
Chocolate Squirrel
Coffee Nutcake
Cork Street Coffee (1)
Cork Street Coffee (2)
E Pluribus Unum
F-16
Fatmancello
Foreign Legion
Frangelico Freeze
Friar Tuck
Frozen Cappuccino
Frozen Monk
Fuzzy Mussy
G-Boy
German Chocolate Cake
Hemingway's Flambé
  Coffee
Hot Irish Dream
Iacocca
Il Duce
Instant Carma
Madtown Milkshake
Manhattan, New Orleans
Martini, Amber Skies
Martini, Crème Brûlée (1)

Martini, Crème Brûlée (2)
Martini, Elisa's Martini Of
  Love
Martini, Kohv
Martini, Nutcracker
Martini, P. B. & J.
Martini, Saharan
Martini, Snickertini
Martini, Topaz
Martini, Vanilla Nut
Mexican Monk
Millionaire's Coffee
Monsoon
Mrs. Baileys' Favor
Mud Puddle
New York Nut
Ninja
Nut Cream Coffee
Nut 'N' Holli
Nut 'N' Honey
Nuts & Berries
Nuts To You
Nutty Irishman
Nutty Mexican
Oatmeal Cookie (1)
O'brain Freeze
Opulent Coffee
Pistachio Mint Ice Cream
Pope On Vacation
Quaalude
Quaalude, Alaskan
Quaalude, Iranian
Quaalude, Irish
Quaalude, Russian
Russian' About
Satin Pillow
Say Hey Marseilles
Sidecar, Autumn
Sky High
Strawberry Nut
Tavern Sucker, The
Tight Sweater
Vanilla Angel
Winsome Way
Yabba-Dabba-Doo
FRAPPÉS
See "Frappé" In
  Alphabetized Recipes
FROZEN DRINKS
See Blended Drinks

G

GALLIANO LIQUEUR
Amber Cloud
Café Charles
California Root Beer
Creamy Dreamy Isotope
Dire Straits
Dreamsicle (1)
Freddy Fudpucker
Galliano Stinger
Golden Cadillac
Golden Dream
Golden Dream With
  Double Bumpers
Golden Ram
Golden Screw
Harvey Wallbanger
International Stinger
Italian Stallion
Italian Stinger

Jenny Wallbanger
Jersey Root Beer
Joe Canoe
King's Cup
Leisure Suit
Manhattan, Galliano
Peachie Keen
Pearl Diver
Piña Colada, Aussie
Piña Colada, Golden
  Bacardi
Pousse Café (3)
Pousse Café, Four-Way
Red Zipper
Root Beer
Root Beer Float
Sloe Comfortable Screw
  Up Against The Wall
Summer Slammer
Tidal Wave (2)
Traffic Light (2)
Yellow Bird (1)
Yellow Bird (2)
Yellow Devil
GENTLEMAN JACK
WHISKEY
See Tennessee Whiskey
GIBSONS
See "Gibson" In
  Alphabetized Recipes
GIMLETS
See "Gimlet" In
  Alphabetized Recipes
GIN
Beefeater Gin
Cosmopolitan, London
Fortress Of Singapore
Gimlet, Soho
Infusion, Beefeater
  Bloody Caesar
Infusion, Beefeater Deli
Margarita Britannia (2)
Martini, Blue Moon (2)
Martini, Fourth Degree
Martini, Lemoneater
Martini, Shagged
Miami Ice
Purple People Beefeater
Rin Tin Gin Tonic
Bombay Gin
Bombay Grand
Electric Lemonade
Gimlet, Cher's
Vanil Sensation
Bombay Sapphire Gin
Bombay Spider
Gimlet, Sapphire
Gran Bombay
Martini, Alexander
  Nevsky
Martini, Blue Moon (1)
Martini, Sapphire Sin
Negroni, Uptown
Old Flame
Sidecar In Bombay
Broker's Gin
Gimlet, Cobbler's
London Lemonade
Martini, 008
Martini Blues

Citadelle Gin
Collins, Beverly Hills
Eau De Gin
Martini, Dragon's
  Breath
Sin & French Gin
Damrak Gin
Collins, Rodeo Drive
Damrak 75
Damrak Blue Lady
Holland's Opus
Margarita, Damrak
  'Rita
Martini, Dutch (1)
Magellan Gin
Blue Devil
Magellan Sauce
Martini, Blue Pacific
Martini, Jaded
Martini, Star's
Miller's Gin
Aviation Cocktail
London Gold
Martini, Cupid's Bow
Martini, London Dry
Martin's Bull
Nº Ten By Tanqueray
Apple Tinker
Martini, Everglades
Martini, Grand Opera
Martini, Orchid
Perfect 10
Splendid Gin
Sunday Brunch Punch
  Cocktail
Plymouth Gin
After Hours Cocktail
Fogcutter, Royal Navy
Maiden's Reprieve
Martini, Elephant's Ear
Martini, Friar Paul
Martini, Mayflower
Scurvey Abator
Tanqueray Gin
Iced Tea, California
Iced Tea, Front Parlor
Iced Tea, Terminal
Martini, Dry Tanque
Martini, Golden Girl
Martini, Smoked (1)
Noble Nymph
Seattle's 6.3
T. 'N' T.
Ulterior Motive
Wet By Beefeater
Blitz Knight
Ginny's Sweet 'N' Sour
Stone Sour
Kamikaze, Brit's
London Nightclub
Martini, Wet Blue
Presumption Cocktail
Wet Passion
GIN DRINKS
Alaska
All American Whistler
Appendectomy
Appendicitis
Appetizer
Barbary Coast
Bee's Knees
Bloody Mary, Gin
Blue Duck
Blue Lady

Byrrh Cocktail
Cinnamon Sling
Clam Digger
Clover Club
Collins, Tom
Cream Of Gin
Diki-Diki
Dirty Gin 'N' Juice
Dirty Lemonade
Dubonnet Cocktail
English Mule
Fitzgerald Cocktail
Fogcutter
Foghorn
French 75 (1)
Gibson
Gibson, Dry
Gibson, Extra Dry
Gimlet
Gimlet, Cobbler's
Gin Alexander
Gin And It
Gin Rickey
Gloomraiser
Golden Fizz
Greyhound
Gulf Breeze
Gulf Tide
Iced Tea, Afterburner
Iced Tea, Alaskan
Iced Tea, Bimini
Iced Tea, Blue
 Kangaroo
Iced Tea, Dirty Ashtray
Iced Tea, Florida
Iced Tea, Georgia
Iced Tea, Green Tea
Iced Tea, Hawaiian
Iced Tea, Italian
Iced Tea, Long Beach
Iced Tea, Long Island
Iced Tea, Manhattan
Iced Tea, Plantation
Iced Tea, Raspberry
Iced Tea, Spiced
Iced Tea, Strawberry
Iced Tea, Swedish
Iced Tea, Tahiti
Iced Tea, Texas
Iced Tea, Tropical
Iced Tea, Veranda
Ideal Cocktail
Infusion, Lemoneater
Italian Valium
Jealousy
Jungle Juice
Knockout
Ladies Auxiliary
Lockhart Zoo
London Lemonade
London Redhead
Looking For Trouble
Magic Potion
Mamie's Sister
Margarita Britannia (1)
Martini
Martini, 007
Martini, 008
Martini, All American
Martini, Amadora
Martini, Bald Head
Martini, Bentley
Martini, Bitchin'
Martini Blues

Martini, Bootlegger
Martini, Boston
Martini, Bronx
Martini, Bubblegum
Martini, Buckeye
Martini, Cajun (1)
Martini, Cajun (2)
Martini, Copper
 Illusion
Martini, Dirty (2)
Martini, Dirty Gin
 Twist
Martini, Dry
Martini, Dutch (2)
Martini, Extra Dry
Martini, F.D.R.
Martini, Fino
Martini, French (3)
Martini, Full Nelson
Martini, Highlander
Martini, Iceberg
Martini, Imperial
Martini, Infused
Martini, Italian (2)
Martini, Jackson
Martini, Journalist
Martini, Lobster
Martini, Marguerite
Martini, Marseilles
Martini, Napoleon
Martini, Newbury
Martini, Paisley
Martini, Palm Island
Martini, Perfect
Martini, Princeton
Martini, Raspberry
Martini, Rivers
Martini, Riviera
Martini, Rolls Royce
Martini, Romana
Martini, Saké
Martini, Sakétini
Martini, San Francisco
Martini, Smoked (2)
Martini, Spanish
Martini, Star's Jewel
Martini, Strawberry (2)
Martini, Taj Majal
Martini Thyme
Martini, Virgin Island
Martini, Yellow Rattler
Meadow Snow
Merry Widow (2)
Minnehaha
Monkey Gland
Morning Sun
Mountain Retreat
Negroni
New Orleans Fizz
Opera Cocktail
Orange Blossom (1)
Orange Blossom (2)
Orsini
Palace Guard
Passion Potion
Pink Gin
Pink Lady (1)
Pink Lady (2)
Ramos Fizz
Red Lion
Red Tail Dragon
Rolls Royce
Root Canal
Royal Fizz

Rumba
Run, Skip And Go
 Naked
Salty Dog
Savannah
Sax With Bill
Scorpion
Silver Fizz
Singapore Sling (1)
Singapore Sling (2)
Skip And Go Naked
Snowball
Staton Island Berry
Stock Market Zoo
Summer Hummer
Summer Tonic
Tinted Glass
Tramonto Sul Garda
Tropical Sensation
Tropical Special
Vulcan
Wall Street Wizard
White Way
Yale Cocktail
Za-Za
GLENDRONACH SCOTCH
 See Scotch Whisky
GLENMORANGIE SCOTCH
 See Scotch Whisky
GODIVA LIQUEUR
 All Star Cast
 American Dream
 Andes Summit
 Bay Area Garter
 Black Stockings
 Butterfinger
 Café A La Cabana
 Café Amore
 Café Foster
 Carte Blanche
 Chocolate Banana (2)
 Chocolate Covered Banana
 (1)
 Chocolate Cream Soda
 Choco Laté Orange
 Chocolate White Russian
 C-Note A-Float
 Death By Chocolate
 Electrode Overload
 Frangelico Freeze
 Gold And Riches
 Guava Martinique
 Helene
 Ice Chocolate
 Imperial Duo
 International Dream
 Irish-Choco-Orange
 Jamaican Rose
 Leave Us Alone
 Martini, Chocolate
 Martini, Chocolate
  Cranberry
 Martini, Chocolate Mint
 Martini, Chocolate
  Supreme
 Martini, Chocolate Utopia
 Martini, Elisa's Martini Of
  Love
 Martini, Espresso
  Framboise
 Martini, Moscow Chill
 Martini, Pyrat
 Martini, Snickertini
 Martini, Tiramisu (1)

Martini, Toasted Nuts
Martini, Tropical
Marz Bar
Mud Puddle
Nosferatu
Nosferatu's Shooter
Nun Out Of Habit
Piña Colada, Chocolate (2)
Poireisse
Rasta Man
Rosebud
Royal Godiva
Rumball
Sacrifice Fly
San Andreas Fault
Seventh Avenue
Socialite
Tamara Lvova
Tiramisu (1)
Toboggan Truffle
Trade Deficit
Tropical Depression
Turbo Milk Chocolate
Waist Coat Pocket
White Cloud
GOLDSCHLÄGER
LIQUEUR
 24-Karat Nightmare
 Beverly Hillbilly
 Dunham Good
 Electrical Storm
 Fool's Gold
 French Tickler
 Gingerbread Man
 Gold And Lager
 Gold Furnace
 Gold Rush (2)
 International Dream
 Jewels And Gold
 King Midas
 London Gold
 Margarita, Triple Gold
 Oatmeal Cookie (1)
 Oatmeal Cookie (2)
 Pot O' Gold
 Stars At Night
 Three Amigos
GOSLING'S BLACK SEAL
RUM
 See Rum, Gosling's
GRAND MARNIER
 '57 T-Bird With Florida
  Plates
 '57 T-Bird With Hawaiian
  Plates
 Absolutely Grand
 Absolut Trouble
 A.M.F.
 Appendectomy
 Apple Grand Marnier
 B-52
 Ball Joint
 Bearing Strait
 Bettor's Dream
 Bible Belt (2)
 Big Bamboo (1)
 Blast From The Past
 Blow Job (1)
 Blow Job (2)
 Blueberry Tea
 Body Warmer
 Bombay Grand
 Bull And Bear
 Busted Rubber

Cactus Moon
Café Chocolate (1)
Café Diablo
Café Gates
Caribbean Contessa
Cartel Buster
Castle Coffee
Celestial Fizz
Champagne Marseille
Choco Laté Orange
Concorde
Corazón De León
Cosmopolitan, Margarita
Cosmo
Cosmopolitan, Sonoran
Cyrano
Deep Sea Diver
Dirty Harry
Doubt Raiser
Electric Lemonade
Flaming Armadillo
Frappé, Coffee Marnier
French Connection
French Harvest
French Maid's Café
French Mandarine
French Tickler
Freudian Slip
Frosted In The Shade
Full Moon
Fuzzy Dick
Fuzzy Mussy
G-Boy
Gimlet, Cher's
Gimlet, Sapphire
Glenda
Gold Rush (1)
Grand Orange Blossom
Happy Hour
Honeybunch Punch
Hula Skirt
Iacocca
Iced Tea, Terminal
Iced Tea, Texas
International Affair
Killer Whale
Landslide
Larchmont (1)
Larchmont (2)
Larchmont (3)
Leave Us Alone
Le Mooseberry
Lifesaver (1)
Loco En La Cabeza (1)
Louvre Me Alone
Lover's Lane
Manhattan, Boulevard
Manhattan, Satin
Margarita, Anita
Margarita, Blue Maestro
Gran
Margarita Britannia (2)
Margarita, Cadillac
Margarita, Cranberry (1)
Margarita, El
Conquistador
Margarita, French/Russian
Margarita, Jalapeño
Margarita, Kentucky
Margarita, Mad Russian
Margarita, Maui (2)
Margarita, Meltdown
Margarita, My Baby Grand
Margarita, Normandy

Margarita, Prickly
Pineapple
Margarita, Rosarita
Margarita, Saké
Margarita, Santiago
Margarita, Sonoran
Margarita, Strawberry
Lover's
Margarita, Teal
Marseilles Stockings
Martini, Chocolate
Supreme
Martini, Cosmonaut
Martini, Dry Tanque
Martini, Everglades
Martini, French (1)
Martini, French Grape
Martini, Full Moon (1)
Martini, Grand Opera
Martini, Jalisco
Martini, Lemon Grove
Martini, Moscow Chill
Martini, Napoleon
Martini, Shagged
Martini, Titian
Mexican Itch
Mexican Siesta
Millionaire's Coffee
Monte Cristo Shooter
Mount Gay Café
Northern Lights (1)
Opulent Coffee
Orange Cranberry Toddy
Orange Delight
Orange Dream
Passionate Point
Passionate Sunset
Peter Prescription
Piña Colada, Holiday Isle
Pink Sunset
Raspberry Sour
Red Lion
Riviera
Rock-A-Fellow's Fancy
Room Service At The Ritz
Savoy Champagne Cocktail
Scurvey Abator
Sea Dew
Seven Twenty-Seven (727)
Sex At The Beach
Sherry's Blossom
Shot In The Dark
Sidecar, Grand
Slipped Disk
Somosa Bay
Star Gazer
Stolichnaya Lemonade
Sunflower
Sunstroke
Surf Sider (1)
T-Bird
Uptown Girl
Vodka Grand
Watergate
GRAND MARNIER CENTENAIRE
Alice In Wonderland
All Star Cast
Ancient Mariner (1)
Ancient Mariner (2)
April In Paris
Bonaparte
Champagne Imperial
French Twist

Gold And Riches
Grand Ball
Grand Marshall Sour
Jacqueline
Kamikaze, French
Kentucky Shuffle
Margarita, El Cien
Margarita Framboise
Martini, Cozumel
Noble Nymph
Sail Of The Century
Sidecar In Bombay
Sonoran Sunset
Sunday Brunch Punch
Cocktail
Tequilier Real
Top Hat
Twist De L'orange
GRAN GALA LIQUEUR
Badda-Bing
Creamsicle (2)
Diplomatic Immunity
Gimlet, Soho
Gran Bliss
Gran Bombay
Gran Cappuccino
Gran Sonoran Sunset
Hawaiian Sunburn
Jackarita
Kamikaze, Italian
Lickety-Split
Liquid Gold
Margarita, Rose
Margarita, Sea Breeze
Martini, Bellini
Martini, Chocolate Orange
Drop
Martini, Full Moon (2)
Martini, Italian (1)
Piña Colada, Italian (2)
Sidecar, Imperial
Sin & French Gin
Sky High
Sonoran Sunrise
South Beach Twist
South-Of-The-Border
Mango Mash
Tuscany Champagne
Winsome Way
GRAPPA
Margarita, Malta's
Grapparita
Martini, Medici
Venetian Sunset
GREY GOOSE VODKAS
See Vodkas, Grey Goose

H

HARDY NOCES D'OR COGNAC
See Cognac
HERRADURA TEQUILAS
See Tequila, Herradura
HIGHBAL DRINKS
'57 Chevy
'57 T-Bird With Arizona
Plates
'57 T-Bird With Florida
Plates
'57 T-Bird With Hawaiian
Plates

Absolut Mandarinade
Acapulco Gold
Acapulco Sunburn
Alabama Slammer (3)
Alabama Slammer (4)
Alien Secretion
All American Whistler
American Graffiti
Americano Highball
Añejo Sunrise
Apple Cooler
Apple Spice
Appleton Blast
Appleton Breeze
Aqua Zest
Baileys Fizz
Banana Bay
Barn Raiser
Bat Bite
Batida
Baybreeze
Benson Bomber
Bermuda Triangle (1)
Bermuda Triangle (2)
Berry Cooler
Better Than N.E.1
Between The Sheets
Black & Blue Bayou
Black Cat
Black Cherry Sonic
Black-Eyed Susan
Black Sun
Black Widow
Blonde Teaser (1)
Blonde Teaser (2)
Blood And Sand (1)
Blue Duck
Blue Lagoon (1)
Blue Lemonade
Blue Whale
Bocci Ball
Bog Fog
Bomb Pop
Bombay Spider
Buck
Buckhead Root Beer
Bullfrog (1)
Bullfrog (2)
Cactus Juice
Cactus Moon
Californian
California Root Beer
California Screw
Campari & Soda
Candy Apple
Cape Codder
Capers Cocktail
Cello Fellow
Censored On The Beach
Cheap Sunglasses
Chihuahua
Chiller
Chocolate Cream Soda
Choco Laté Orange
Cinnamon Sling
Cinnful Apple
City Tavern Cooler
Clam Digger
Clam Fogger
Cold Gold
Colorado Bulldog
Colorado River Cooler
Comfortable Crush
Comfortable Screw

Comfort Kit
Cove Cooler
Crabapple
Cranberry Squeeze
Creamy Dreamy Isotope
Cuba Libre
Cuervo Nation Cocktail
Dark 'N' Stormy
Death Of A Virgin
Desert Storm
Desert Sunrise
Dewar's Highland Cooler
Dew Drop Dead
Dingy Ginger
Dirty Dog
Dirty Gin 'N' Juice
Dirty Lemonade
Dizzy Lizzy
Dodo Bird
Double Agent
Downeaster
Dr. Berry Vanilla
Dr. Pepper (1)
Dreamsicle (1)
Dreamsicle (3)
Dreamsicle (4)
Dubonnet Fuzzy
Dudley Does Right
El Cajon Sunrise
El Diablo
El Toro
Electric Jam
Electric Watermelon (2)
Encinada Hill Climber
Energizer Bunny
English Mule
Face Eraser
Fat Cat Fizz
Firecracker
First Aid Kit
Flamingo (1)
Florida
Foghorn
Freddy Fudpucker
French Congo Cooler
French Crush
French Sweetheart
Fresh Squeezed Bat Juice
Frosted Coke
Fuzzy Navel
Gator Juice
Georgia Peach (1)
German Root Beer
Gin Rickey
Glacier Breeze
Glass Tower
Golden Nail
Golden Screw
Gotham Lemonade
Gran Sonoran Sunset
Greyhound
Ground Zero
Gulf Breeze
Gulf Tide
Habana Libre
Hairy Sunrise
Happy Hour
Harvey Wallbanger
Hawaiian Sunburn
Heartbreak
Heat Wave
Hell On Ice
Highball
Highland Golfer

Highland Highball
Hollywood
Hoochie Kéké Mama
Horse's Neck With A Kick
In The Red
Irish Lemonade
Isle Of Pines
Italian Punch
Italian Sunrise (1)
Italian Sunrise (2)
Jäger Monster
Jamaica Me Crazy (1)
Jamaican Spice
Jar Juice
Jaundice Juice
Jenny Wallbanger
Jersey Root Beer
Joe Canoe
Jump Me
Jungle Juice
Kahlúa Club
Kéké Kicker
Kentucky Swamp Water
King Midas
Kool Aid (1)
Kool Aid (2)
La Fresca
La Paloma
Lake Street Lemonade
Lemongrad
Lemon Sportsman
Lemon Squeeze
Leprechaun
Lickety-Split
London Nightclub
Lounge Lizard
Love Canal
Luau
Lynchburg Lemonade
Macintosh Press
Mackenzie Gold
Madras
Malibu Beach
Malibu Fizz
Malibu Slide
Malibu Sunset
Mamie's Sister
Mamie's Southern Sister
Mamie Taylor
Mango Monsoon
Maraschino Rum Mist
Margo Moore
Maria Sangrita
Maritime Sunrise
Martin's Bull
Mcgoody's Cream Soda
Melon Ball (1)
Melon Breeze
Melon Grind
Melon Moose
Ménage À Trois
Merry Widow (2)
Mexican Bullfrog
Miami Vice (2)
Midori Cooler
Midori Driver
Midway Rat (2)
Mind Eraser (2)
Miniskirt Limbo
Minnehaha
Mobay Runner
Moose Milk
Mop In A Bucket
Moscow Mule

Mudslide (1)
Naked Pretzel
Nelson's Blood (2)
Northern Lights (2)
Nymphomaniac (1)
Ocean Breeze
Orange Blossom (2)
Orange Chiller
Orgasm (1)
Osmosis
Paddy O'rocco
Panama Jack
Peach Blaster
Peach Breeze
Peachy Congo Cooler
Pearl Harbor
Peppermint Cooler
Perfect Fit
Persuader
Pimm's Cup
Pink Coconut
Pink Sunset
Pirate's Hiccup
Plata V.I.P. Cocktail
Plymouth Rocks
Presbyterian
Rasta Spleef
Razzle Dazzle
Red Eclipse
Red Zipper
Release Valve
Rémyred Sunrise
Rickey
Rin Tin Gin Tonic
River Madness
Rocket
Root Beer
Root Beer Float
Root Beer Tooter
Royal Godiva
Ruby Red
Rum Fix
Rumscapes
Rum Screw
Rum Swizzle
Russian Polar Bear
Russian Sunrise
Salty Bull
Salty Dog
Salty Dogitron
Sand Blaster
Saoco
Scarlett O'hara
Screaming Fuzzy Navel
Screaming Orgasm
Screwdriver
Seabreeze
Seven & Seven
Seventh Heaven
Seven Of Hearts
Sex On The Beach (1)
Sex On The Beach (2)
Sex On The Beach (3)
Shark Attack
Shark Bite
Shillelagh
Ship Wreck
Sicilian Sunrise
Silk Panties (1)
Skyscraper
Slam Dunk
Sloe Comfortable Screw
Sloe Comfortable Screw
   Up Against The Wall

Sloe Poke
Sloe Screw
Smith & Kerns
Smith & Wesson
Smooth Driver
Smooth Gentleman
Sonoran Sunset
Spider Cider
Spring Break
St. Tropez
Steeple Jack
Summer Breeze
Summercello
Summer Lemonade
Sunknee Delite
Sunrise
Surf Sider (2)
Susie Taylor
Swamp Water
Tahitian Apple
Tavern Sucker, The
Tennessee Gentleman
Tennessee Tea
Tequador
Tequila Driver
Tequila Quencher
Tequila Rosé
Tequila Sunrise
Tequila Sunset
Texas Tea
Tidal Wave (1)
Tidal Wave (2)
Tijuana Bulldog
Tijuana Screw
Tijuana Sunrise
T. 'N' T.
Tom Mix High
Tootsie Roll
Tropical Gold
Tropical Hooter
Tropical Jack
Twisted Lemonade
Ugly Duckling
Up The Creek With A Kick
Vampiro (1)
Vampiro (2)
Viagra
Voodoo Snap
Voodoo Volcano
Vulcan
Wanderer
Wanna Probe Ya
Watermelon (4)
What's The Rush
Where Are My Undies?
Whisper (1)
White Cadillac
White Minnesota
Whooter Hooter
Wild Orchid
Wile E. Coyote
Yellow Bird (1)
Yellow Devil
Za-Za
Zuma Buma

320

KAHLÚA
Abbey Road
Aching Bach
Afterburner
After Eight
After Five
Aggravation
American Dream
Apple A Go-Gogh
Area 151
Aspen Coffee
B-52
Bahama Mama (2)
Baileys Mint Kiss
Banana Sandwich
Beam Me Up, Scottie
Benson Bomber
Black And White
Black Hawaiian
Black Mass
Black Russian
Black Watch
Blizzard (2)
Blushing Berry Cooler
Brave Bull
Bush Tickler
Bushwacker
Butterscotch Slide
Café Chocolate (2)
Café Contenté
Café Dublin
Café Framboise
California Root Beer
Canadian Foot Warmer
Canyon Quake (1)
Capo Di Sopranos
Captain's Coffee (2)
Caribbean Sunset
Cello Amore
Cherry Bomb
Chill-Out Café
Chip Shot
Chiquita Punch
Ciao Bello
C-Note A-Float
Colorado Avalanche
Colorado Bulldog
Cookie Mint Rookie
Creamy Bull
Dark Continent Café
Death By Chocolate
Dire Straits
Dirty Mother
Doctor's Advice
Dragoon
Duck Fart
Duke Of Earl
E Pluribus Unum
F-16
Face Eraser
Fire-It-Up
Five Dollar Margaret
Frangelico Freeze
Frappé, Coffee Marnier
Frappé, Mocha
Frappé, Sambuca Mocha
French Kiss
French Maid's Café
Frosted Coke
Frozen Cappuccino
Frozen Monk

Fun In The Sun
Fuzzy Dick
German Chocolate Cake
Girl Scout Cookie
Good & Plenty
Gorilla Milk
Harbor Lights
Hoochie Kéké Mama
Hummer
Iacocca
Il Duce
International Dream
I.R.A.
Irish Coffee Royale (1)
Isthmus Buffalo Milk
Jack Benny
Julio's Butterscotch
Kahlúa Club
Kahlúa Mint
Keoki Coffee
Keoki Shooter
Koala Float
Lemon Nog
Lighthouse
Mackinnon Road
Malibu Slide
Marquis
Martini, Chocolate
   Supreme
Martini, Samtini
Martini, Tiramisu (1)
Martini, Tiramisu (2)
Martini, Zanzabar
Melon Scoop
Mel's Chocolate
   Butterscotch Shake
Mel's Choc/Pb/Nana Shake
Ménage À Trois
Mexican Cocoa
Mexican Coffee
Mexican Grasshopper
Mexican Monk
Mighty Kong
Millionaire's Coffee
Milwaukee River
Mind Eraser (1)
Mind Eraser (2)
Mint Freeze
Monsoon
Monte Cristo Shooter
Moose Milk
Mother
Mudslide (1)
Mudslide (2)
Neutron Bomb
Nuckin Futs
Nut 'N' Honey
Nutty Mexican
Nutty Professor
O'brain Freeze
Orgasm (1)
Piña Colada, Chocolate (2)
Piña Colada, Hawaiian
   Lion
Piña Colada, Kahlúa
Piña Colada, Strawberry
   Banana
Piña Colada, Toasted
   Almond
Pirate's Hiccup
Pistachio Mint Ice Cream
Poppycock Rock
Pousse Café (3)
Pousse Café, Four-Way

Quaalude
Quaalude, Iranian
Quaalude, Russian
Raspberry Banana Split
Reverse Russian
Ride The Glide Slide
River Seine Cappuccino
Roasted Toasted Almond
Root Beer
Root Beer Float
Rose Beam
Royal Canadian
Royal Street Coffee
Russian Bear
Russian Polar Bear
Say Hey Marseilles
Screaming Orgasm
Separator (1)
Separator (2)
Seven Twenty-Seven (727)
Sexual Chocolate
Shot Thru The Heart
Siberian
Silver Cloud
Sky High
Slippery Banana
Smith & Kerns
Smith & Wesson
Sno-Cap
Sombrero
Southern Slide
St. Petersburg Sundae
Sugar Baby
Sugar Daddy
Sylk Café
Tam-O'-Shanter
Tavern Sucker, The
Tight Sweater
Tijuana Bulldog
Tiramisu (1)
T.K.O.
Toasted Almond
Toasted Almond Café
Trade Deficit
V.I.P. Coffee
Voodoo Volcano
Waist Coat Pocket
Watergate
Whisper (1)
Whisper (2)
White Bull
White Hawaiian
White Russian
White Russian, Raspberry
White Russian, Skinny
White Russian, Truffle
White Russian, Vanilla
Xaviera
Yabba-Dabba-Doo
Yellow Jacket
Zanzabar Holiday
KAHLÚA ESPECIAL
Baileys Butterball
Bay Area Garter
Black Beauty (1)
Black Jeweled Russian
Bleacher's Twist
Butterscotch Hop
Café Chocolate (1)
Castle Coffee
Charisma Cocktail
Chocolate Milk Cooler
Coffee Nutcake
Emerald Isle

Flaming Armadillo
Instant Carma
International Cappuccino
Irish Boggle
Irish Raspberry
Jamaican Rum Cow
Martini, Café Nuttini
Martini, Espresso
Mighty Bull Shooter
Mocha My Eye
Noble Holiday
Opulent Coffee
Rock-A-Fellow's Fancy
Scottish Tan
Star Gazer
KAMIKAZES
See "Kamikaze" In
   Alphabetized Recipes
**KÉKÉ BEACH CREAM
LIQUEUR**
Big Bamboo (2)
Cheesy Cheerleader
Green Monster
Hoochie Kéké Mama
Kéké Kicker
Ké Largo
Martini, Kéké V
Martini, Key Lime
Miniskirt Limbo
Piña Colada, Kéké Colada
Twilight Moan Zone
Twisted Sister
Waikéké Fraternity
Where Are My Undies?
KELT XO COGNAC
See Cognac
KETEL ONE VODKAS
See Vodkas, Ketel One
KNAPPOGUE CASTLE
See Irish Whiskey
KNOB CREEK BOURBON
See Bourbon Whiskey
KUYA FUSION RUM
See Rum, Kuya

LAIRD'S APPLE BRANDIES
See Brandies, Laird's
**LAPHROAIG SCOTCH
WHISKY**
See Scotch Whisky
**LAYERED CORDIAL
DRINKS**
See Shooter And Cordial
   Drinks, Layered
**LAYERED SHOOTER
DRINKS**
See Shooter And Cordial
   Drinks, Layered
**LICOR 43
(CUARENTA Y TRES)**
Barcelona Coffee
Café A La Cabana
Café St. Armands
Caipirinha (2)
Dreamsicle (3)
Dreamsicle (4)
Gold Rush (3)
Key Lime Cooler
Key Lime Pie (1)
Margarita De Mexico

Margarita, Spanish
Mini Beer
Piña Colada, Spanish
Sex On A Black Sandy
  Beach
LIMONCELLO
A Cello Mia
Cactus Moon
Canadian Bliss
Capers Cocktail
Capo Di Sopranos
Castle In The Clouds
Cello Amore
Cello Blanco
Cello Fellow
Cheesy Cheerleader
Cherrillo
Ciao Bello
Classic Vette
Collins, Jamie
Cosmopolitan, Cello
Daiquiri, Sweet Tart
Defroster
Dreamsicle (4)
Du Monde
Fatmancello
Frappé, Lemon
Fruit Burst
Gimlet, Cobbler's
Goose Down
Harvest Night
Irish Wish
Island Dream
Kamikaze, Italian
Ladies Auxiliary
Late-Nite Lemon Drop
Lemon Heaven
Lemon Heights
Lemon Nog
Lemon Parfait
Lemon Squeeze
Lemon Tart
Limón Fitzgerald
Margarita, Ciao Italian
Martini, Bellini
Martini, Fantino
Martini, Italian (1)
Martini, Jaded
Martini, Lemoneater
Martini, Shade Tree
Massappeal
Mint Julep, Gentleman's
Mojito, Cello
Old Fashion, New Age
Perfect 10
Piña Colada, Italian (2)
Piña Colada, Lemonada
  (1)
Piña Colada, Lemonada
  (2)
Rin Tin Gin Tonic
South Beach Twist
Splendid Gin
Summercello
Summer Tonic
Sunknee Delite
Tickle Me
Ulterior Motive
Waikéké Fraternity
LIMONCÈ LIQUORE DI
  LIMONI
See Limoncello
LIQUID ICE VODKA
See Vodka, Liquid Ice

LONG ISLAND ICED TEAS
See "Iced Tea" In
  Alphabetized Recipes
LUNA TOP SHELF TRIPLE
  SEC
See Triple Sec

M

MAGADANSKAYA VODKA
See Vodka, Magadanskaya
MAGELLAN GIN
See Gin, Magellan
MAKER'S MARK
  BOURBON
See Bourbon Whiskey
MALIBU RUM
See Rum, Malibu
MANHATTANS
See "Manhattan" In
  Alphabetized Recipes
MARGARITAS
See "Margarita" In
  Alphabetized Recipes
MARTINIS
See "Martini" In
  Alphabetized Recipes
MARTINI & ROSSI
  VERMOUTHS
See Vermouth (Dry) Or
  Vermouth (Sweet)
MATUSALEM RUMS
See Rum, Matusalem
MEZCAL
Margarita, Blue Maestro
  Gran
Margarita, Mezcal
Martini, Mystical
MIDORI LIQUEUR
'57 T-Bird With Arizona
  Plates
Acapulco Breeze
Alien Secretion
Artificial Intelligence
Balashi Breeze
Blue Bayou (1)
Bomb Pop
Bullfrog (2)
Burnt Sienna
Cheap Shades
Circus Peanut
Citron Neon
Clear And Present Danger
Cold Fusion
Colorado River Cooler
Cosmopolitan, Melon
Dactyl Nightmare
Death Of A Virgin
Delicias De La Habana
Desert Passion
Done & Bradstreet
Drunken Monkey
Electric Watermelon (1)
Electric Watermelon (2)
E.T.
Finlandia Lime Light
Fruity Tutti
Gang Green
Green Monster
Green Reef
Green Russian
Green Sneakers

Ground Zero
Gulf Stream Scream
Gumby
Hole-In-One
Honeydew
Iced Tea, Green Tea
Infusion, Alien Secretion
Infusion, Beach
Infusion, Ice Blue
  Margarita
Infusion, Pool Water
Infusion, Summer Shades
  Margarita
Infusion, Vodka Crocodile
Jamaican Crawler
Jamaican Tennis Beads
Jamaican Ten Speed
Jealousy
Jolly Rancher (1)
Jolly Rancher (2)
Jolly Rancher (3)
Ju Ju Bee
Kamikaze, Melon
Ké Largo
Killer Koolaid
Knickerbocker Knocker
Kool Aid (1)
Kool Aid (2)
Kuwaiti Cooler
Leaf
Limerick
Lizard Bitch
Luau
Malibu Fizz
Margarita La Reyna Del
  Playa
Margarita, Midori
Margarita, Neon
  Watermelon
Margarita, Santiago
Margarita, Two-Toned
Martini, Emerald
Martini, Green Lantern
Martini, Gummie Bare
Martini, Jaded
Martini, Key Lime Pie
Martini, Pacific Pearl
Martini, Libertini
Maui Wowie
Meadow Snow
Mediterranean Freeze
Mellonaire
Melon Ball (1)
Melon Ball (2)
Melon Ball Cooler
Melon Breeze
Melon Grind
Melon Moose
Melon Scoop
Mexican Melon
Midorable
Midori Canuck
Midori Cooler
Midori Driver
Midori Stinger
Mojito, Jalisco
Monster Appeaser
Naked Pretzel
Neon Twister
Ninja
Nymphomaniac (1)
Ocean Breeze
Osmosis
Pacific Rim

Pearl Harbor
Piña Colada, Bahama
Piña Colada, Cactus
Piña Colada, Midori
Pousse Café, Tuaca
Rainbow Shooter (1)
Rainbow Shooter (2)
Rain Man
Red Tail Dragon
Santa Claus Is Coming
Screaming Good Times
Screaming Hawaiian
Screaming Weebies
Sex On The Beach (2)
Sex On The Beach (5)
Sex With An Alligator (1)
Sex With An Alligator (3)
Sour Melon Patch
Spats Columbo
Straight Shooter
Tie Me To The Bed Post
Tikki Dream
Tokyo Scream
Torque Wrench
Traffic Light (2)
Tropical Hooter
Tropical Hurricane
Tropical Hut
Twilight Moan Zone
Twisted Sister
Wall Street Wizard
Watermelon (2)
Watermelon (4)
What Crisis?
What's Your Honey Dew?
Zanzibar Dunes
MILLER'S GIN
See Gin, Miller's
MINT JULEP DRINKS
See "Mint Julep" In
  Alphabetized Recipes
MOJITOS
See "Mojito" In
  Alphabetized Recipes
MOUNT GAY RUMS
See Rum, Mount Gay
MYERS'S RUMS
See Rum, Myers's

N

NEAT DRINKS
Amber Cloud
A.M.F.
Ancient Mariner (1)
Ancient Mariner (2)
Andalusia
Apple Sting
Baby Grand Cocktail
B & B
Beauty And The Beast
Bonaparte
C. & C.
Forever Amber
Framboise Kiss
French Connection
French Harvest
French Mandarine
French Toast Royale
French Twist
Full Moon
Gentleman's Boilermaker

Marquis
Midori Canuck
Midori Stinger
Mind Bender
Mind Eraser (1)
Mist
Molotov's Cocktail
Monkey Juice
Mother
Mother Lode
Mr. Murphy
Mrs. Baileys' Bush
Mudslide (2)
Nelson's Blood (1)
Noble Holiday
Nun Out Of Habit
Nutty Irishman
Nutty Mexican
Nutty Professor
Panther
Peaches 'N' Berries
Presidential Juice
Quaalude, Alaskan
Quarter Deck
Razorback Hogcaller
Razzmatazz
Red Russian
Riviera Days
Riviera Nights
Rock-A-Fellow's Fancy
Old Fashioned, Rum
Rusty Nail
Saké-Rama
Sazerac
Scottish Tan
Sea Dew
Separator (2)
Seven Twenty-Seven (727)
Sex On A Black Sandy
  Beach
Sex On The Beach On A
  Cloudy Day
Siberian
Sicilian Kiss
Silken Veil
Silk Panties (2)
Silver Bullet
Smiles For Miles
Snake Bite (1)
Snowshoe (1)
Snowshoe (2)
Socialite
Sombrero
Spilt Milk (2)
Star Gazer
Stinger
Sugar Daddy
Sweet (Irish) Dreams
Sylk Café
Sylk Stockings
Sylk Top Hat
Tam-O'-Shanter
Tarnished Bullet
Tequila Highlander
Tequilier Real
Thumper
Tickle Me
T.K.O.
Uptown Girl
Vanilla Spice Ice
Vanilla Wafer
Watermelon (1)
White Bull
White Hawaiian

White Russian
White Russian, Premium
White Russian, Raspberry
White Russian, Skinny
White Russian, Truffle
White Russian, Vanilla
White Spider
White Swan
White Way
Winsome Way
Yankee Panky
Yukon Stinger
Zanzabar Holiday
Zipper Head
RUM
Appleton Estate Rums
  Appleton Blast
  Appleton Breeze
  Appleton Planter's
    Punch
  Artificial Intelligence
  Bahama Mama (1)
  Black Jamaican
  Blue Marlin
  Café Kingston
  Caribbean Cruise (1)
  Caribbean Gridlock
  Chocolate Covered
    Banana (1)
  Cocomotion
  Daiquiri, Calypso
  Daiquiri, Mulatta
  Dark Waters
  Designer Jeans
  Dharama Rum
  Drunken Monkey
  Florida T-Back
  Heat Wave
  Hot Buttered Rum
  Independence Swizzle
  Jackalope
  Jamaica Juice
  Jamaica Me Crazy (1)
  Jamaica Me Crazy (2)
  Jamaican Barbados
    Bomber
  Jamaican Coffee
  Jamaican Crawler
  Jamaican Fever
  Jamaican Rose
  Jamaican Rum Cow
  Jamaican Shake
  Jamaican Spice
  Jamaican Tennis Beads
  Jamba Juice
  Kiss Of The Islands
  Knickerbocker
  Mai Tai, Mobay
  Margarita, Caribbean
  Margarita, Jamaican
  Margarita, Montego
  Martini, Black Tie (1)
  Martini, Foreign Legion
  Melon Scoop
  Mel's Chocolate
    Butterscotch Shake
  Mel's Choc/Pb/Nana
    Shake
  Mobay Runner
  Mocha Jamocha
  Mojito, Reggae
  Montego Bay (1)
  Peter Prescription
  Piña Colada, Kingston

Piña Colada,
  Monkalada
Piña Colada, Port Royal
Piña Colada, Tropical
  Moon
Piña Colada, Tropical
  Splashes
Pink Paradise
Planter's Punch (2)
Planter's Punch (3)
Quarter Deck
Rancho Valencia Rum
  Punch
Rum Runner (1)
Shark Bite
Shore Boat
Smooth Screw
Tamara Lvova
Tighter Cider
Tiki Passion Punch
Tiramisu (2)
Tour De Caribbean
Zombie (1)
Z Street Slammer
Bacardi 8 Reserva Rum
  Ancient Mariner (1)
  Andalusia
  Golden Dragon
  Jacqueline
  Larchmont (1)
  Martini, Havana
  Reserva Cocktail
  Sidecar, Havana (2)
Bacardi Gold Rum
  Amaretto Cruise
  Bacardi Tropical Dream
  Badda-Bing
  Banana Fruit Punch
  Cocomotion
  Deathwish
  Deep Sea Diver
  Four Wise Men
  Kapalua Butterfly
  Midway Manhattan
  Piña Colada, Golden
    Bacardi
  Rum Runner (1)
  Slipped Disk
  Tropical Itch
Bacardi Light Rum
  Apple Works
  Bacardi Cocktail
  Caribbean Dream (2)
  Caribbean Gridlock
  Drunken Monkey
  Glass Tower
  Iced Tea, California
  Iced Tea, Front Parlor
  Iced Tea, Terminal
  Mojito, Watermelon
  Piña Colada, Golden
    Bacardi
  Rum Runner (1)
  Sun Seeker
  Tiki Passion Punch
Bacardi Limón Rum
  Bellisimo
  Bossa Nova
  Catherine Was Great
  Cosmopolitan,
    Disaronno
  Cosmopolitan, Limón
  Daiquiri, Prickly Pear
  Dark Waters

Electric Lemonade
Gauguin
Italian Punch
Knickerbocker
Knickerbocker Special
  Cocktail
Limón Fitzgerald
Limón Orange Breeze
Limón Runner
Martini, Caribbean
Nymphomaniac (1)
Rough Seas Cocktail
Sneak & Peak Cocktail
Captain Morgan Rum
  Big Blue Shooter
  Captain's Coffee (2)
  Captain's Cooler
  Cool Captain
  Gorky Park Cooler (2)
  Jamaican Spice
  Jamba Juice
  Knicker Knocker
  Leaning Tower
  Margarita, Captain
  Martini, Flan
  Nymphomaniac (2)
  Pink Passion
  Slipped Disk
  Suntan Teaser
  Tidal Wave (3)
  Wanna Probe Ya
  Whaler's Season
Cruzan Banana Rum
  Banalini
  Banana Bay
  Banana Cow
  Banana Nuts
  Banana Popsicle
  Chocolate Banana (2)
  Cruzan Rum Punch
  Culture Shock
  Daiquiri, Banana
  Diplomatic Immunity
  Dodo Bird
  Isthmus Buffalo Milk
  Jamaican Ten Speed
  Latin Lover (2)
  Margarita, Camino Real
  Margarita, Conga
  Martini, Fidel's
  Mellonaire
  Mexican Runner
  Mighty Kong
  Monkey Bite
  Montego Bay (1)
  Ocho Rios
  Piña Colada, Lt. Kije's
  Piña Colada,
    Monkalada
  Strummer Hummer
  Suntan Teaser
  Tropical Itch
  Voodoo Juice (2)
  White Sands Cooler
Cruzan Coconut Rum
  After Tan (1)
  Blue Lagoon (1)
  Come-On-I-Wanna-
    Lei-Ya
  Cruzan Rum Punch
  Culture Shock

Key Isla Morada
Key Largo
Piña Colada, Canne
Bay
Screaming Weebies
Voodoo Juice (2)
Cruzan Diamond Rum
Banana Cow
Borinquen
Culture Shock
Deep Sea Diver
Electrode Overload
Flaming Armadillo
Frozen Devotion
Key Isla Morada
Key Largo
Lifesaver (1)
Mango Mingle
Mexican Runner
Monkey Juice
Outrigger
Pucker-Up
Rendezvous Muumuu
Voodoo Juice (2)
Voodoo Moondance
Cruzan Light Rum
Bloody Mary, Bloody
Wright
Blue Hawaii
Cosmopolitan,
Caribbean Cosmo
Isthmus Buffalo Milk
Key Isla Morada
Key Largo
Martini, Black Devil
Miami Ice
Rendezvous Muumuu
Screaming Weebies
Trade Winds
Voodoo Moondance
White Sands Cooler
Cruzan Mango Rum
Cruzan Rum Punch
Mango Monsoon
Take The Prize
**Cruzan Orange & Citrus
Rum**
After Tan (1)
Banana Cow
Cold Gold
Come-On-I-Wanna-
Lei-Ya
Cosmopolitan,
Caribbean Cosmo
Cruzan Rum Punch
Lemon Heaven
Margarita, Rocky Point
Martini, Virgin Island
Outrigger
Voodoo Juice (2)
Cruzan Pineapple Rum
Blue Lagoon (1)
Cruzan Rum Punch
Daiquiri De Piña
Desert Storm
Green Reef
Ground Zero
Key Isla Morada
Margarita, Conga
Piña Colada, Canne
Bay
Tropical Itch
Vice On Ice
Voodoo Juice (2)

Cruzan Rum Cream
Blizzard (2)
Café Kingston
Cork Street Coffee (1)
Julia
Jungle Cream
Mocha Jamocha
Monkey Juice
Pucker-Up
Shore Boat
Voodoo Shooter
Cruzan Single Barrel Rum
Hula Skirt
Island Dream
Island Fever
Island Flower
Jungle Cream
Larchmont (3)
V.I.P. Coffee
Cruzan Vanilla Rum
Candy Apple
Come-On-I-Wanna-
Lei-Ya
Mango Mingle
Gosling's Black Seal Rum
Bahama Mama (1)
Bermuda Triangle (1)
Bermuda Triangle (2)
Caribbean Gridlock
Dark 'N' Stormy
Jump Me
Kiss Of The Islands
Lethal Injection
Paranoia
Piña Colada, Bermuda
Piña Colada, Black
Pearl
Piña Colada, Emerald
Isle
Kuya Fusion Rum
Black Maria
Café Reggae
Caribbean Sour
Daiquiri, Derby
Daiquiri, Flight Of
Fancy
El Presidenté Cocktail
(2)
Guava Cooler
Instant Karma
Martini, Apple Pie
Mojito, Fusion
Malibu Rum
A Day At The Beach
After Tan (2)
Alien Secretion
Artificial Intelligence
Baileys Malibu Rum
Yum
Big Blue Shooter
Blue Lagoon (2)
Coconut Coffee Pot
Coconut Cream Pie
Drunken Monkey
Florida T-Back
Goom Bay Smash (1)
Gorky Park Cooler (1)
Gorky Park Cooler (2)
Infusion, Alien
Secretion
Island Sunset
Italian Surfer
Jackie Special
Ju Ju Bee

Kamikaze, Kokonut
Lethal Injection
Lifesaver (2)
Luau
Malibu Beach
Malibu Fizz
Malibu Runner
Malibu Slide
Malibu Sunset
Margarita, Bahama
Mama
Martini, Mounds-Tini
Martini, Tropical
Mobay Runner
Monkey Bite
Nymphomaniac (2)
Paranoia
Piña Colada, Emerald
Isle
Piña Colada, Malibu
Orange
Pink Passion
Piranha
Pope On Vacation
Rainbow Shooter (2)
Reggae Sunsplash
Rock Lobster
Scotch Bounty
Screaming Hawaiian
Sea Side Liberty
Sex In The Coal Region
Sex In The Tropics
Sex On The Beach On
A Cloudy Day
Sex With An Alligator
(3)
Ship Wreck
Spring Break
Suntan Teaser
Surfers On Acid
Surf Sider (2)
Tie Me To The Bed Post
Tropical Hooter
Twister
Vulcan
Wanna Probe Ya
Yankee Panky
Matusalem Rums
Borinquen
Cuban Cocktail
Cuban Peach
Cuban Special
Delicias De La Habana
Habanos Havana
Havana Cocktail
Island Ditty
Rock-A-Fellow's Fancy
Sidecar, Cuban
Mount Gay Rums
Amaretto Cruise
Apple Works
Artificial Intelligence
Banana Fruit Punch
Banana Monkey
Bananas Barbados
Beachcomber (2)
Bermuda Triangle (3)
Blackbeard's Treasure
Black Sun
Blue Hawaiian
Blue Marlin
Caribbean Cruise (1)
Caribbean Dream (1)
Caribbean Gridlock

Caribbean Romance
Cocomotion
Curaçao Cooler
Daiquiri, Mulatta
Daiquiri, Summer Sky
Deep Sea Diver
Drunken Monkey
El Presidenté Cocktail
(3)
Florida T-Back
Gulf Stream Scream
Happy Hour
Heat Wave
Jackalope
Jamaican Barbados
Bomber
Jamba Juice
Jump Me
Kapalua Butterfly
Kiss Of The Islands
Knickerbocker
Lasting Passion
Lethal Injection
Lifesaver (1)
Lost Lovers
Love Potion #9
Mai Tai, Mobay
Martini, Banana Creme
Pie
Melon Scoop
Midway Manhattan
Mobay Runner
Mount Gay Café
Otter Water
Papa Dobles
Passionate Point
Piña Colada, Black
Pearl
Piña Colada, Chocolate
(2)
Piña Colada, Emerald
Isle
Piña Colada, Hawaiian
Lion
Piña Colada, Holiday
Isle
Piña Colada, Italian (1)
Piña Colada, Kokomo
Joe
Piña Colada,
Monkalada
Piña Colada, Rémy
Colada
Piña Colada, Tropical
Splashes
Pink Paradise
Planter's Punch (3)
Purple Piranha
Quarter Deck
Rancho Valencia Rum
Punch
Rémyred Punch
Rhumba Escapades
Rum Runner (2)
Rumscapes
Sandy Smile
Santiago (1)
Sea Side Liberty
Sherry's Blossom
Shore Breeze
Smooth Screw
Starboard Tack
Strawberry Banana
Split

Sun Seeker
Tiki Passion Punch
Tour De Caribbean
Tropical Itch
Whaler's Season
Yellow Devil
Myers's Rum
Bucking Bronco
Caribbean Dream (1)
Fedora
Honey Bee
Jamaican Dust
Jamaican Holiday
Liam's Passion
Malibu Beach
Mop In A Bucket
Navy Grog
Planter's Rum Punch
Rasta Spleef
Rock Lobster
Rumba
Stealth Bomber (2)
Summer Slammer
Trophy Room
Tropical Moon
Uptown
Pusser's Rum
Cannonball
Captain's Coffee (1)
Cove Cooler
Fogcutter, Royal Navy
Naval Commission
Navy Grog, Modern
Nelson's Blood (1)
Nelson's Blood (2)
Painkiller
Piña Colada, Pusser's Island
Pusser's Daily Ration
Pusser's Pain Killer
Pusser's Stalemate
Shore Boat
Pyrat Rums
Ancient Mariner (2)
Big Blue Shooter
Café A La Cabana
Daiquiri, Pyrat
Gimlet, Pyrat
Larchmont (2)
Martini, Pyrat
Pirate Love
Pyrat Pete Cocktail
RedRum
Ariana's Dream
Bling Bling
Island Voodoo
Martini, Three Mile Island
Red Hawaiian Sunset
Red Rhumba
Rhum Barbancourt
Borinquen
Café Foster
Caribbean Dream (2)
Chocolate Covered Banana (1)
Daiquiri, Calypso
Daiquiri, Rhum
Guava Martinique
Lasting Passion

Martini, Smoked (2)
Midnight Express (3)
Piña Colada, French
Rhum Barbancourt Freeze
Wynbreezer
Rhum Martinque
Daiquiri, French (1)
Daiquiri, French (2)
Gimlet, Martinique (1)
Gimlet, Martinique (2)
Martini, Martinique
Rum and Black
Tropical Depression
Sea Wynde Rum
Brass Monkey
Heavyweight Sailor
Lookout Point
Mango In The Wynde
Mojito, Wayward Wynde
Sail Of The Century
Sea Dew
Top Hat
Voodoo Spiced Rum
Ariana's Dream
Bermuda Triangle (1)
Cabin Fever Cure
Fool's Gold
Hell On Ice
Island Voodoo
Voodoo Juice (1)
Voodoo Snap
Voodoo Volcano
Whaler's Hawaiian Rums
Banana Stigma
Betelgeuse
Butterscotch Hop
Daiquiri, Whale Smooch
Gimlet, Whaler
Martini, Key Lime
Peaches And Dreams
Randy Brandy Egg Nog
Whale's Tail
Whaler's Season
RUM DRINKS
American Graffiti
Baileys Mint Kiss
Baltimore Zoo
Beautiful Thing
Berlin Wall
Black Jack
Charisma Cocktail
Colombian Necktie
Fire And Ice (2)
Ice Chocolate
Iced Tea, Afterburner
Iced Tea, Green Tea
Iced Tea, Strawberry
Iced Tea, Tahiti
Iced Tea, Tropical
Mind Eraser (1)
Molotov's Cocktail
Piña Colada, Kéké Colada
Red Tail Dragon
Rumplemeister
Santa Claus Is Coming
Skanky Head
Snowshoe (2)
Staton Island Berry
Summer Breeze
Three Amigos

Amber Rum Drinks
Bush Tickler
Jumby Bay Punch
Piña Colada, Lemonada (1)
Suffering Bastard
Banana Rum Drinks
Big Bamboo (2)
Calypso Highway
Caribbean Sour
Chocolate Covered Banana (2)
Funky Monkey
Jane's Milk
Latin Love
Mystic Runner
Offenburg Flip
Piña Colada, Funky Monkey
Piña Colada, Strawberry Banana
Pink Highliter
San Andreas Fault
Sand Bar Smash
Silk Rose
Citrus Rum Drinks
Cheesy Cheerleader
Iced Tea, Jesse's Shocking
Laughing Cow
Lemon Squeeze
Margarita, Bay Breeze
Martini, Emerald
Mojito, Citrus
New England Summer Spritzer
New Orleans Buck
N'orleans Chiller
Passionate Screw
Piña Colada, Lemonada (1)
Piña Colada, Midori
Pink Lemonade (2)
Screaming Good Times
Starburst
Trip To The Beach
Tropical Hurricane
Tropical Tango
Twisted Lemonade
Zombie, Pink
Coconut Rum Drinks
Bahama Mama (2)
Big Chill
Coconut Breeze
Cosmopolitan, Chi Chi
Daiquiri, Coconut
Funky Monkey
Goom Bay Smash (2)
Jet Fuel (1)
Jumper Cables
Kamikaze, Radioactive
Latin Love
Martini, Colada
Maui Wowie
Mystic Runner
Offenburg Flip
Pink Coconut
R. F. & E.
Ride The Glide Slide
Spirit Of Erie Coffee

Dark Rum Drinks
.44 Magnum
Alpine Glow
Apple Brandy Cooler
Banana Milkshake
Barn Raiser
Bat Bite
Beach Blonde
Betty Grable
Big Bamboo (2)
Big Chill
Black Mass
Black Orchid
Blast-Off Punch
Bush Tickler
Bushwacker
Café Contenté
Calypso Highway
Cappa 21
Cappo De Tutti Cappi
Caribbean Berry
Caribbean Cruise (2)
Caribe Surfsider
City Tavern Cooler
Cocomacoque
Cool Carlos
Daiquiri, Charles
Daiquiri, Raspberry
Duke Of Earl
Flamingo (1)
Flamingo (2)
Florida
Gangbuster (Serves Two)
Halekulani Sunset
Honeybunch Punch
Infusion, Brazilian Daiquiri
Key West
Latin Lover (1)
Lover's Lane
Mad Hatter
Manhattan Beach
Margarita, Bay Breeze
Maui Wowie
Melon Moose
Midnight Express (1)
Midnight Express (2)
Naval Commission
Navy Grog, Nor'easter
Offenburg Flip
Old Fashion, Caribbean
Parple Thunder
Periodista (2)
Pilgrim's Pride
Piña Colada, Bellevue
Piña Colada, Chocolate (1)
Piña Colada, Stramaretto
Piña Colada, Strawberry Banana
Pineapple Fizz
Pink Creole
Piranha Club Initiation
Piranha Punch
Planter's Punch (1)
Purple Flirt
Rain Man
R. F. & E.
Rhododendron
Ride The Glide Slide
Riviera Nights
Rum Swizzle

Rumball
San Andreas Fault
Sand Bar Smash
Santiago (2)
Shot Thru The Heart
Starburst
Stealth Bomber (1)
Storm-A-Long Bay
Straw House Hummer
Surf Sider (1)
Swimming Naked At
Sunset
Tour De Panama
Zombie (2)
Zombie, Pink

Gold Rum Drinks
Acapulco Gold
Alpine Glow
Banana Milkshake
Big Bamboo (1)
Blast-Off Punch
Boina Roja
Cocomacoque
Commodore
Cork Street Coffee (2)
Daiquiri, Lechthaler's
Frappé, Mulatta
Frappé, Tricontinental
Fu Manchu
Gangbuster (Serves
Two)
Havana
Havana Club
Hawaiian Hurricane
Honey Rum Toddy
Hot Rum Cow
Hummer
Hurricane (1)
Hurricane (2)
Iced Tea, Havana
Infusion, Brazilian
Daiquiri
Italian Sunrise (1)
Killer Whale
Lounge Lizard
Mai Tai (2)
Mai Tai (3)
Manhattan Beach
Maraschino Rum Mist
Mincemeat Mocha
Nácional
Naval Commission
Navy Grog, Original
Piña Colada, Bellevue
Piña Colada, Chocolate
(1)
Piña Colada, Spanish
Piña Colada,
Stramaretto
Piña Colada, Toasted
Almond
Pink Slipper
Piranha Punch
Rendezvous Punch
Riviera Nights
Rum Toddy
Sassafras Sunset
Scorpion
Screaming Good Times
Sidecar, Havana (1)
Stealth Bomber (1)
Strawberry Smash

Tequila Maria
Tidal Wave (2)
Trip To The Beach
Jamaican Rum Drinks
.44 Magnum
Big Chill
Black Orchid
Caribbean Berry
Caribbean Cruise (2)
Cool Carlos
Dingo
Goom Bay Smash (2)
Hawaiian Hurricane
Hummer
Jet Fuel (1)
Key West
Killer Whale
Planter's Punch (1)
R. F. & E.
Root Canal
Tour De Panama
Zombie (2)

Light Rum Drinks
.44 Magnum
'57 Chevy
Acapulco
Amangani Indian
Paintbrush
American Graffiti
Apple Brandy Cooler
Bahama Mama (2)
Balashi Breeze
Barn Raiser
Beach Blonde
Beachcomber (1)
Between The Sheets
Blast-Off Punch
Blue Bayou (2)
Bog Fog
Boina Roja
Burgundy Bishop
Bushwacker
Caipirinha (2)
Caipirissma
Calypso Coffee
Caribbean Champagne
Caribbean Contessa
Caribbean Cruise (3)
Caribe Surfsider
Coconut Breeze
Collins, Pedro
Creole
Cuba Libre
Daiquiri
Daiquiri, Berry
Daiquiri, Charles
Daiquiri, Coconut
Daiquiri, Don Roland
Daiquiri, Florida
Daiquiri, Fruit (Basic)
Daiquiri, Hemingway
Daiquiri, La Floridita
Daiquiri, Lechthaler's
Daiquiri, Papa
Hemingway
Daiquiri, Passion
Dingo
Down Under Snowball
Ed Sullivan
El Presidenté Cocktail
(1)
Electric Watermelon
(1)
Elixir Of Love

Florida
Fogcutter
Frappé, Banana Rum
Fruit Stripe
Funky Monkey
Gangbuster (Serves
Two)
Gang Green
Gorilla Milk
Green Monster
Halekulani Sunset
Hawaiian Hurricane
Hot Times
Hurricane (1)
Hurricane (2)
Iced Tea, Alaskan
Iced Tea, Bimini
Iced Tea, Blue
Kangaroo
Iced Tea, Dirty Ashtray
Iced Tea, Florida
Iced Tea, Georgia
Iced Tea, Havana
Iced Tea, Hawaiian
Iced Tea, Italian
Iced Tea, Long Beach
Iced Tea, Long Island
Iced Tea, Manhattan
Iced Tea, Plantation
Iced Tea, Raspberry
Iced Tea, Swedish
Iced Tea, Texas
Iced Tea, Veranda
Infusion, Barrier Reef
Infusion, Brazilian
Daiquiri
Infusion, Cherry Bomb
Irish Shillelagh
Isla De Piños
Isleña
Isle Of Pines
Jade
Jealousy
Joe Canoe
Kamikaze, Radioactive
Key West
Leaf
Looking For Trouble
Mai Tai (1)
Mai Tai (2)
Mai Tai (3)
Manhattan Beach
Manhattan, Cuban
Manhattan, Cuban
Medium
Manhattan, Latin
Margo Moore
Martini, El Presidenté
Martini, Maritime
Maui Wowie
Melon Grind
Melon Moose
Midway Rat (1)
Midway Rat (2)
Mojito (1)
Mojito (2)
Naval Commission
Neon Twister
New Orleans Jazz Time
Old Fashion, Rum
Orchard Haze
Parple Thunder
Passion Potion
Periodista (1)

Pilgrim
Pilgrim's Pride
Piña Colada
Piña Colada, Amaretto
Piña Colada, Aussie
Piña Colada, Brazilian
Piña Colada, Fruit
(Basic)
Piña Colada, Kahlúa
Piña Colada, Liqueur-
Flavored
Piña Colada, Pacific
Blue
Pink Gator
Pink Highliter
Pink Slipper
Plymouth Rocks
Presidenté
Primal Shooter
Rainbow Holiday Cup
Raspberry Cream
Release Valve
R. F. & E.
Rhododendron
Riviera Days
Root Canal
Rum Alexander
Rum Fix
Rum Milk Punch
Rum Mint Julep
Rum Screw
Run, Skip And Go
Naked
Rusty Nickel
Sand Blaster
Santiago (2)
Saoco
Sassafras Sunset
Scorpion
Shark Attack
Shark's Tooth
Shillelagh
Silver Spider
Sloppy Joe's Cocktail
Smurf Piss
Sour Mint
South Of France
Spats Columbo
Spilt Milk (1)
Spy's Demise
Stealth Bomber (1)
Straw House Hummer
Suffering Bastard
Sunrise
Susie Taylor
Tahitian Apple
Tokyo Scream
Tropical Gold
Tropical Hut
Wall Street Wizard
Weekend At The Beach
(2)
Windex
Yellow Bird (1)
Yellow Bird (2)
Zombie (2)
Pineapple Rum Drinks
Cosmopolitan, Chi Chi
Martini, Colada
Martini, Piña
Passionate Screw

328

Marz Bar
Mellow Dramatic
Melon Ball (2)
Mexican Blackjack
Mexican Itch
Mexican Siesta
Midway Rat (1)
Mighty Kong
Milk Of Amnesia
Mini Beer
Monkey Bite
Monsoon
Monster Appeaser
Multiple Orgasm
Ninja
Nut 'N' Holli
Nut 'N' Honey
Nymphomaniac (2)
Oatmeal Cookie (1)
Oatmeal Cookie (2)
Orange Julius
Oyster Shooter
Panama Red
Peach Bomb
Peach Fuzz
Pearl Diver
Peckerhead
Pink Lemonade (1)
Pitless Shot
Pope On Vacation
Pot O' Gold
Prairie Fire
Prairie Oyster (1)
Prairie Oyster (2)
Pucker-Up
Purple Flirt
Purple Hooter (2)
Purple Matador
Quaalude
Quaalude, Iranian
Quaalude, Irish
Quaalude, Russian
Rainbow Shooter (2)
Raspberry Sweet Tart
Raztini
Razzputenee
Red Death
Red Devil
R. F. & E.
Rigor Mortis
Royal Canadian
Royal Flush
Rum And Black
Rumplemeister
Rusty Nickel
Sammy Jäger
Satin Pillow
Sex At The Beach
Sex On The Beach (4)
Sex On The Beach (5)
Sexual Chocolate
Shot In The Dark
Shot Thru The Heart
Side Shot
Silver Spider
Skanky Head
Slippery Dick
Smurf Piss
Southern Belle
Southern Suicide
Stiff Dick
Straight Shooter
Strawberry Quickie
Sugar Baby

Suntan Teaser
Surfers On Acid
Sweet Tart (3)
T-Bird
Tequila Slammer/Popper
Tequila Slider
Test-Tube Baby (1)
Test-Tube Baby (2)
Three Amigos
Tidal Wave (3)
Tidy Bowl
Tie Me To The Bed Post
Torque Wrench
Vampire
Vanilla Magilla
Vulcan Mind Probe
Washington Apple
Watermelon (2)
Watermelon (3)
Watermelon (5)
Weekend At The Beach (1)
Weekend At The Beach (2)
Week On The Beach
Wet Dream
What Crisis?
Whisky Gingerbread
Windex
Yabba-Dabba-Doo
Yellow Jacket
Yo Hooter Hooter
Z Street Slammer

SHOOTER AND CORDIAL DRINKS, LAYERED
After Eight
After Five
Alabama Slammer (1)
Angel's Kiss
B-52
Bam Be
Banana Sandwich
Beam Me Up, Scottie
Beverly Hillbilly
Bit-O-Honey
Black And White
Black Mass
Bleacher's Twist
Bullfighter
Busted Rubber
Butterfinger
Canyon Slider
Cartel Buster
Cherry Bean
Cherry Bomb
Chip Shot
Dactyl Nightmare
Duck Fart
Electrical Storm
F-16
Freddy Kruger
Goal Post
Green Lizard
Harbor Lights
Inoculation
Inverted Nail
I.R.A.
Jelly Bean
Jelly Fish
King Alfonse
Landslide
Mahogany Gold
Mexican Flag
Mexican Nazi Killer
Mighty Bull Shooter
Milwaukee River

Neutron Bomb
Nosferatu's Shooter
No Tell Motel
Orgasm (2)
Poppycock Rock
Pousse Café (1)
Pousse Café (2)
Pousse Café (3)
Pousse Café, Four-Way
Pousse Café, Tuaca
Primal Shooter
Rainbow Shooter (1)
Raspberry Torte
Rasta Man
Reverse Russian
Rose Beam
Saint Moritz
Santa Claus Is Coming
Separator (1)
Slippery Banana
Slippery Greek
Slippery Nipple
Snake Bite (3)
Sperm Bank
Stars & Stripes
Stars At Night
Traffic Light (1)
Traffic Light (2)
Turkey Shooter
Upside Down Scottish
Crown
Voodoo Shooter
Watergate
SIDECARS
See "Sidecar" In
Alphabetized Recipes
SLOE GIN
Alabama Slammer (1)
Alabama Slammer (4)
Alabama Slammer (5)
American Graffiti
Baltimore Zoo
Empire State Slammer
Hawaiian Punch (1)
Irish Shillelagh
Piña Colada, Pusser's
Island
Pousse Café (1)
Red Devil
Sloe Comfortable Screw
Sloe Comfortable Screw
Up Against The Wall
Sloe Gin Fizz
Sloe Poke
Sloe Screw
Slow Tropical Cruise
Spats Columbo
Spy's Demise
Traffic Light (1)
Watermelon (3)
SOL DIOS TEQUILA
See Tequila, Sol Dios
SORBET DRINKS
See Also Sherbet Drinks
And Ice Cream Drinks
Champagne Cornucopia
Creamsicle (2)
Lemon Tree Tantalizer
Mango-A-Gogo
Mango In The Wynde
Margarita, Blue Moon
Margarita, Sunny
Pullman Porter
Twist De L'orange

SOUTHERN COMFORT LIQUEUR
'57 Chevy
Alabama Slammer (1)
Alabama Slammer (2)
Alabama Slammer (3)
Alabama Slammer (4)
Alabama Slammer (5)
American Graffiti
Bible Belt (1)
Bubble Gum
Bullfrog (2)
Cello Blanco
Cocaine Shooter (1)
Comfortable Crush
Comfortable Screw
Comfort Kit
Cosmopolitan, Comfort
Cowboy Killer
Crab House Shooter
Dingo
Electric Watermelon (2)
Flaming Blue Jeans
Gator Juice
Golden Ram
Hawaiian Punch (1)
Hawaiian Punch (2)
Hawaiian Shooter
Jackie Special
Joke Juice
Kamikaze, Bloody
Kamikaze, Southern
Comfort
Killer Koolaid
Knicker Knocker
Kool Aid (2)
Lizard Bitch
Manhattan, Perfect
Southern Comfort
Manhattan, Southern
Comfort
Martini, Bootlegger
Martini, Journalist
Red Devil
Rhett Butler
Scarlett O'hara
Sex At The Beach
Sex On The Beach (3)
Sicilian Kiss
Slam Dunk
Sloe Comfortable Screw
Sloe Comfortable Screw
Up Against The Wall
Snake Bite (3)
Southern Suicide
Swamp Water Stinger
Test-Tube Baby (2)
Vulcan
Watermelon (1)
Watermelon (4)
Watermelon (5)
Yankee Panky
SPARKLING WINE DRINKS
See Champagne Drinks
SPUDKA VODKA
See Vodka, Spudka
STOLICHNAYA VODKAS
See Vodkas, Stolichnaya

STÖN VODKA
See Vodka, Stön
SYLK CREAM LIQUEUR
Black Jeweled Russian
Mackinnon Road
Seventh Avenue
Sylk Café
Sylk Stockings
Sylk Top Hat

T

TALL ICED DRINKS
.44 Magnum
Acapulco
Acapulco Breeze
A Day At The Beach
Adios Mother
Alpine Glow
Apple Brandy Cooler
Artificial Intelligence
Badda-Bing
Bahama Mama (1)
Bahama Mama (2)
Banana Monkey
Bay Bridge Commuter (1)
Bay Bridge Commuter (2)
Beach Blonde
Beach Bum Blue
Beachcomber (1)
Beachcomber (2)
Bellisimo
Big Bamboo (1)
Big Bamboo (2)
Black Orchid
Black Smooth & Sour
Blast-Off Punch
Blue Bayou (1)
Blue Hawaiian
Blue Lagoon (2)
Blue Wave (1)
Blue Wave (2)
Boina Roja
Bomb
Bossa Nova
Burnt Sienna
California Lemonade
Calypso Highway
Cannonball
Captain's Cooler
Caribbean Cruise (2)
Caribbean Romance
Celeste's Cocktail
Cheesy Cheerleader
Clear And Present Danger
Cocomacoque
Coconut Breeze
Cold Fusion
Cool Carlos
Cowboy Killer
Cruzan Rum Punch
Curaçao Cooler
Dale's Sour Apple
Dark Waters
Deep Sea Diver
Desert Passion
Dingo
Dream Maker
Dr. Seuss Go-Go Juice
Drunken Monkey
Electric Lemonade
Electric Watermelon (1)

Eve's Peach
Flamingo (2)
Florida T-Back
Fogcutter
Fogcutter, Royal Navy
Fruit Burst
Funky Monkey
Gang Green
Gangbuster (Serves Two)
Georgia Peach (2)
Ginny's Sweet 'N' Sour
   Stone Sour
Glasnost
Golden Fizz
Golden Peach
Gorky Park Cooler (1)
Green Monster
Green Reef
Green Sneakers
Guava Cooler
Guava Martinique
Gulf Stream Scream
Gumby
Halekulani Sunset
Hawaiian Hurricane
Hawaiian Punch (1)
Hawaiian Punch (2)
Honeybunch Punch
Hurricane (1)
Hurricane (2)
Independence Swizzle
Instant Karma
Isla De Piños
Island Sunset
Isleña
Jackalope
Jackie Special
Jack Tail
Jamaican Crawler
Jamaican Fever
Jamaican Tennis Beads
Jamba Juice
Jealousy
Jet Fuel (1)
Jewel
Key Largo
Key West
Killer Whale
Kiss Of The Islands
Knicker Knocker
Knickerbocker
Knickerbocker Knocker
Kuwaiti Cooler
La Bamba
Latin Lover (1)
Leaning Tower
Leisure Suit
Lemon Drop (2)
Le Mooseberry
Lethal Injection
Lifesaver (1)
Lifesaver (2)
Limerick
Limón Orange Breeze
Limón Runner
Lizard Bitch
Loco En La Cabeza (1)
Loco En La Cabeza (2)
Looking For Trouble
Magic Potion
Mai Tai (1)
Mai Tai (2)
Mai Tai (3)
Mai Tai, Mobay

Malibu Runner
Mandarine Dream
Manhattan Beach
Mariachi Loco
Maui Wowie
Melon Ball Cooler
Mexican Melon
Miami Ice
Midway Manhattan
Miss Ube Darn
Montego Bay (2)
Native Sun
Naval Commission
Navy Grog
Neon Twister
New Orleans Buck
New Orleans Fizz
Nicolas
N'orleans Chiller
Otter Water
Outrigger
Pacific Rim
Painkiller
Paranoia
Parple Thunder
Passion Potion
Passion Punch
Passionate Fruit
Passionate Point
Passionate Screw
Passionate Sunset
Peaches And Dreams
Pink Flamingo
Pink Gator
Pink Highliter
Pink Lemonade (2)
Pink Paradise
Pink Passion
Piranha
Piranha Club Initiation
Piranha Punch
Planter's Punch (1)
Planter's Punch (2)
Planter's Punch (3)
Planter's Rum Punch
Province Town
Purple Passion
Purple Piranha
Pusser's Daily Ration
Putting On The Ritz
Rainbow Holiday Cup
Rain Man
Ramos Fizz
Rancho Valencia Rum
   Punch
Raspberry Sour
Red Hawaiian Sunset
Red Tail Dragon
Reggae Sunsplash
Rémyred Punch
Rendezvous Muumuu
Rhett Butler
Ride The Glide Slide
Rodéo Driver
Root Canal
Royal Fizz
Rumba
Rum Punch
Rum Runner (1)
Rum Runner (2)
Run, Skip And Go Naked
Saké Passion Club
Sand Bar Smash
Sandy Smile

San Francisco
Santiago (2)
Sassafras Sunset
Scorpion
Scotch Bounty
Screaming Hawaiian
Screaming Weebies
Sea Water
Sex In The Tropics
Shore Breeze
Silk Tie
Singapore Sling (1)
Singapore Sling (2)
Skinny Dipping
Sloe Gin Fizz
Slow Tropical Cruise
Somosa Bay
Son Of A Peach
Sonoran Sunrise
Sour, Sparkling Sweet
   Apple
Spanish Fly
Spats Columbo
Spy's Demise
Starboard Tack
Stealth Bomber (1)
Stealth Bomber (2)
Steeplechase
Stiletto
Stock Market Zoo
Stoli Around The World
Stolichnaya Lemonade
Stubb's Ayers Rock
Suffering Bastard
Summer Daze
Summer Slammer
Sun Seeker
Swamp Water Stinger
Sweet Tart (2)
Swimming Naked At
   Sunset
Take The 'A' Train
Tequila A La Bertita
Tequila Mockingbird (2)
Tiki Passion Punch
Tokyo Scream
Tour De Caribbean
Tour De Panama
Trip To The Beach
Tropical Hurricane
Tropical Hut
Tropical Itch
Tropical Sensation
Tropical Special
Tropical Tango
Twister
Vice On Ice
Voodoo Juice (1)
Voodoo Juice (2)
Voodoo Moondance
Waikéké Fraternity
Watkin's Glen
Whaler's Season
White Sands Cooler
Wiki Waki Woo
Wynbreezer
Zombie (1)
Zombie (2)
Zombie, Pink
TANQUERAY GIN
See Gin, Tanqueray

Iced Tea, Bimini
Iced Tea, Blue
 Kangaroo
Iced Tea, Dirty Ashtray
Iced Tea, Florida
Iced Tea, Georgia
Iced Tea, Green Tea
Iced Tea, Hawaiian
Iced Tea, Long Beach
Iced Tea, Long Island
Iced Tea, Manhattan
Iced Tea, Plantation
Iced Tea, Raspberry
Iced Tea, Spiced
Iced Tea, Strawberry
Iced Tea, Swedish
Iced Tea, Tahiti
Iced Tea, Tropical
Infusion, Ice Blue
 Margarita
Jäger My Worm
Jardinera
La Fresca
L.A.P.D.
Lemon Parfait
Lighthouse
Loco En La Cabeza (2)
Looking For Trouble
Margarita, Floridita
Margarita, Jimmie
 Davis
Margarita, Midori
Margarita, Moonburn
Margarita, Picosita
Margarita, Shootah
Margarita, Two-Toned
Maria Sangrita
Mexican Coffee
Mexican Nazi Killer
Michelada, Caliente
Osmosis
Panther
Passionate Sunset
Pink Highliter
Salty Bull
Silver Bullet
Staton Island Berry
Tarnished Bullet
Tequila A La Bertita
Tequila Driver
Tequila Mockingbird
 (1)
Tequila Quencher
Tequila Rosé
Tequila Slider
Tequila Sunrise
Tequila Sunset
Test-Tube Baby (1)
Tijuana Screw
Tijuana Sunrise
T.K.O.
Toreador
Vampiro (2)
White Bull
Tequila Añejo Drinks
Añejo Sunrise
Area 151
Bandera
Brave Agave
Buddha Shooter
Chimayo Cocktail
Dead Grizzly
Dead Grizzly Shooter
Margarita, Agavero

Margarita, Black Gold
Margarita, Herba
 Buena
Nutty Professor
Tequila Mockingbird
 (2)
Tequila Gold Drinks
Gold Rush (2)
Infusion, Pepper-
 Tequila
Infusion, Sonoran
 Spittoon
Infusion, Summer
 Shades Margarita
Margarita, Honeydew
 This
Margarita Punch
Margarita, Zinful
Prairie Fire
Saké-Rama
Sangria, Margarita
Tequila Highlander
Tequila
 Slammer/Popper
Tequila Resposado Drinks
Bloody Mary, Michilata
Margarita, Black Forest
Margarita, Diablo
Margarita, Purple (1)
Peach Cobbler
Piña Colada, Acapulco
Piña Colada, Cactus
Rodéo Driver
South-Of-The-Border
 Mango Mash
Tequador
Tequila Maria
Tijuana Bulldog
Vampiro (1)
Tequila Silver Drinks
Acapulco
Infusion, Lemontree
 Margarita
Infusion, Lime-Tequila
La Paloma
Lockhart Zoo
Margarita, Black Gold
Margarita, Bloody
Margarita Britannia (1)
Margarita, Cajun
Margarita Classico
Margarita, Cranberry
 (1)
Margarita, Cranberry
 (2)
Margarita De Fruta
Margarita De Mexico
Margarita, Hypnotic
Margarita, Key Lime
Margarita, Normandy
Margarita, Original ™
Margarita, Picosita
Margarita, Prickly Pear
 (1)
Margarita, Prickly Pear
 (2)
Margarita, Raspberry
 Torte
Margarita, Sangrita
Margarita, Sonoran
 Spittoon
Margarita, Tuaca
Margarita, Watermelon
Mariachi Loco

Nutty Mexican
Perfect Fit
Razzputenee
Ship Wreck
Stock Market Zoo
Wiki Waki Woo
TEQUILA ROSE LIQUEUR
Black Tequila Rose
Crimson Rose
Frozen Rose
Hot Apple Rose
Jamaican Rose
Margarita, Rose
Peaches 'N' Berries
Rose Beam
Rosebud
Silk Rose
Strawberry Quickie
Strawberry Rose
TIA MARIA LIQUEUR
Alice In Wonderland
A.M.F.
Bam Be
Bikini Line
Black Jamaican
Black Maria
Blast From The Past
Blow Job (1)
Brahma Bull
Café Amore
Café Gates
Café Kingston
Café Reggae
Calypso Coffee
Cappa 21
Cappo De Tutti Cappi
Caribbean Sunset
Caribe Sunset
Cartel Buster
Chambord Repose
Cocomonut
Coconut Coffee Pot
Deep Throat
Dirty Harry
Dry Arroyo
French Dream
Heavyweight Sailor
Hunter's Coffee
Irish Maria
Jamaican Coffee
Jamaican Dust
Jamaican Holiday
Jamaican Shake
Jamaica Me Crazy (1)
Jungle Cream
Latin Lover (1)
Louvre Me Alone
Margarita, Rio Grande
Martini, Black Coffee &
 Creamtini
Martini, Espresso
Midway Manhattan
Midway Rat (1)
Midway Rat (2)
Mocha Jamocha
Montego Bay (1)
Mount Gay Café
Multiple Orgasm
Navy Grog, Nor'easter
New York Nut
Peter Prescription
Piña Colada, Black Pearl
Piña Colada, Kingston
Piña Colada, Monkalada

Piña Colada, Port Royal
Pirate Love
Rasta Man
Reggae Walker
Russian' About
Satin Pillow
Sex In The Woods
Sex On The Beach (1)
Smooth Screw
Sovereignty
Tender Mercies
Tiramisu (2)
Tour De Caribbean
Tour De Panama
Trophy Room
Tropical Depression
Voodoo Shooter
White Russian, Premium
TORMORE SCOTCH
See Scotch Whiskey
TRIPLE SEC
3d-Elixir
.44 Magnum
'57 T-Bird With Arizona
 Plates
Appendicitis
August Moon
Balalaika
Baltimore Zoo
Beachcomber (1)
Beachcomber (2)
Between The Sheets
Bible Belt (1)
Black Smooth & Sour
Bosom Caresser
Canadian
Canadian Stone Fence
Captain's Cooler
Cherry Blossom
Chicago
Citrus Samurai
Cold Fusion
Creamsicle (1)
Crimson Rose
Cuban Special
Dew Drop Dead
Diablo
Dirty Lemonade
Dreamsicle (2)
El Conquistador
Frozen Rose
Fu Manchu
Glass Tower
Golden Dream
Golden Dream With
 Double Bumpers
Gotham Lemonade
Hasta La Vista, Baby
Highland Golfer
Honeymoon
Hot Tropico Mama
Iced Tea, Afterburner
Iced Tea, California
Iced Tea, Florida
Iced Tea, Green Tea
Iced Tea, Havana
Iced Tea, Hawaiian
Iced Tea, Italian
Iced Tea, Long Beach
Iced Tea, Long Island
Iced Tea, Plantation
Iced Tea, Raspberry
Iced Tea, Spiced
Iced Tea, Strawberry

Iced Tea, Swedish
Iced Tea, Tahiti
Iced Tea, Tropical
Iced Tea, Veranda
Infusion, Lemoneater
Infusion, Lemontree
   Margarita
Irish Alexander (2)
Jade
Jamaican Barbados
   Bomber
Joke Juice
Kamikaze
Kamikaze, Apple
Kamikaze, Citron
Kamikaze, Cranberry
Kamikaze, Southern
   Comfort
Ladies Auxiliary
Lemon Drop (3)
Loco En La Cabeza (2)
Looking For Trouble
Lynchburg Lemonade
Magic Potion
Mai Tai (1)
Mai Tai (2)
Mai Tai, Mobay
Manhattan, Biscayne
Margarita, Agave Juice
Margarita, Bahama Mama
Margarita, Bloody
Margarita Britannia (1)
Margarita, Cantina Wine
Margarita, Captain
Margarita, Caribbean
Margarita Classico
Margarita, Coyote (1)
Margarita, Coyote (2)
Margarita, Cranberry (2)
Margarita De Fruta
Margarita, Floridita
Margarita, Georgia Peach
Margarita, Herba Buena
Margarita, Horni (2)
Margarita, Ice Cream
Margarita, Italian
Margarita, Jimmie Davis
Margarita, Key Lime
Margarita, Malta's
   Grapparita
Margarita, Maui (1)
Margarita, Mimosa
Margarita, Moscow
Margarita, Mount Fugi
Margarita, Orangita
Margarita, Pear
Margarita Picante
Margarita, Picosita
Margarita, Pineapple
Margarita, Prickly Pear (1)
Margarita, Prickly Pear (2)
Margarita Punch
Margarita, Raspberry
Margarita, Raspberry Torte
Margarita, Red Cactus
Margarita, Rio Grande
Margarita, Sangrita
Margarita, Sauza Pure
Margarita, Shootah
Margarita, Sonoran
   Spittoon
Margarita, Sunny
Margarita, Tea-Arita
Margarita, Two-Toned

Margarita, Vintner's
Margarita, Virgin (1)
Margarita, Virgin (2)
Margarita, Watermelon
Martini, Journalist
Martini, Muscovy
Martini, Newbury
Martini, Pink Ribbon
Maui Breezer
Mellonaire
Mexican Blackjack
Millionaire Cocktail
Orsini
Panama Red
Parple Thunder
Piña Colada, Malibu
   Orange
Planter's Punch (2)
Pousse Café (1)
Purple Hooter (1)
Raspberry Sweet Tart
Red Devil
Red Hawaiian Sunset
Red Rhumba
Rhett Butler
Run, Skip And Go Naked
Santiago (2)
Sassafras Sunset
Satin Pillow
Sauza Threesome
Seelbach Cocktail
Sidecar (2)
Sidecar, Cuban
Sidecar, Tuaca
Silver Spider
Sloppy Joe's Cocktail
Staton Island Berry
Stealth Bomber (2)
Steeplechase
Sunrise
Suntan Teaser
Tropical Special
Uptown
Vanil Sensation
Velvet Hammer
Whip
Wine Cobbler
Xaviera
Za-Za
Zombie (1)
Zombie (2)

TUACA LIQUEUR
Black Ruby
Bourbon Ball
Chicago Times
Forever Amber
Frappé, Lemon
Gimlet, Tuaca
Gimlet, Whaler
Hot Apple Pie
Margarita, Tuaca
Mincemeat Mocha
Nina's Coffee
Nut 'N' Honey
Pousse Café, Tuaca
Sidecar, Autumn
Sidecar, Tuaca
Tender Mercies
Thumper
Wile E. Coyote
TÜRI VODKA
See Vodka, Türi

ULTIMAT VODKAS
See Vodka, Ultimat

VAN GOGH VODKAS
See Vodka, Van Gogh
VERMOUTH (DRY)
Black Diamond
Brainstorm Cocktail
Brazil
Brooklyn
Byrrh Cocktail
Coronation
Diablo
El Presidenté Cocktail (1)
El Presidenté Cocktail (3)
Gibson
Gibson, Dry
Gibson, Extra Dry
Gibson, Vodka
Gloomraiser
Half & Half (1)
Ideal Cocktail
Infusion, Sicilian Martini
Klondike
Knockout
Lady Madonna
Lena Cocktail
Manhattan, Affinity
Manhattan, Algonquin
Manhattan, Benedictine
Manhattan, Blue Grass
   Blues
Manhattan, Boulevard
Manhattan, Cherbourg
Manhattan, Continental
   Perfect
Manhattan, Cuban
   Medium
Manhattan, Dijon
Manhattan, Dry
Manhattan, Dry Brandy
Manhattan, Dubonnet
Manhattan, Latin
Manhattan, Marianne
Manhattan, Mets
Manhattan, Perfect
Manhattan, Perfect Brandy
Manhattan, Perfect
   Southern Comfort
Manhattan, Poor Tim
Manhattan, Quebec
Manhattan, Raspberry
Manhattan, Rose
Manhattan, Smoky
Manhattan, Southern
   Comfort
Manhattan, Spiced Apple
   Brandy
Manhattan, St. Moritz
Manhattan, Westchester
Martini
Martini, All American
Martini, Bald Head
Martini, Baltic Sea
Martini, Bentley
Martini, Bitchin'
Martini, Black Devil

Martini, Black Tie (1)
Martini, Bleu
Martini, Blue Pacific
Martini, Bootlegger
Martini, Boston
Martini, Bronx
Martini, Buckeye
Martini, Cajun (1)
Martini, Cajun (2)
Martini, Cajun King
Martini, Creole
Martini, Cupid's Bow
Martini, Dirty (1)
Martini, Dragon's Breath
Martini, Dry
Martini, Dry Tanque
Martini, Dry Vodka
Martini, Dutch (2)
Martini, Elephant's Ear
Martini, El Presidenté
Martini, Everglades
Martini, Extra Dry
Martini, Extra Dry Vodka
Martini, F.D.R.
Martini, Finlandia Pepper
Martini, French (1)
Martini, French (3)
Martini, Friar Paul
Martini, Full Nelson
Martini, Hawaiian
Martini, Hot
Martini, Hot Marti
Martini, Imperial
Martini, Infused
Martini, Journalist
Martini, Lobster
Martini, London Dry
Martini, Marguerite
Martini, Marseilles
Martini, Mighty
Martini, Moro
Martini, Paisley
Martini, Palm Island
Martini, Perfect
Martini, Princeton
Martini, Rolls Royce
Martini, Romana
Martini, Russian Tea
   Room
Martini, Sapphire Sin
Martini, Sicilian (1)
Martini, Taj Majal
Martini, Vodka
Martini, Yellow Rattler
Merry Widow (1)
Minnehaha
Palace Guard
Presidenté
Rob Roy, Dry
Rob Roy, Perfect
Rolls Royce
Sloppy Joe's Cocktail
Tinted Glass
Trinity
Vermouth Cassis
Whip
Yale Cocktail
VERMOUTH (SWEET)
Adonis
Americano
Americano Highball
Blood And Sand (2)
Blood And Sand (3)
Bobby Burns

Corpse Reviver (1)
Dollar Bill
El Presidenté Cocktail (1)
Gin And It
Golden Dragon
Half & Half (1)
Harvard
Havana Club
Highland Cocktail
Irish Wish
Lena Cocktail
Manhattan
Manhattan, Affinity
Manhattan, Big Apple
Manhattan, Biscayne
Manhattan, Blood And
   Sand
Manhattan, Brandy
Manhattan, Cherbourg
Manhattan, Continental
   Perfect
Manhattan, Cuban
Manhattan, Cuban
   Medium
Manhattan, Irish
Manhattan, Jack's Best
Manhattan, Latin
Manhattan, Loretto
Manhattan, Maple Leaf
Manhattan, Market
Manhattan, Napoleon
Manhattan, New Orleans
Manhattan, Paparazzi
Manhattan, Park Paradise
Manhattan, Perfect
Manhattan, Perfect Brandy
Manhattan, Perfect
   Southern Comfort
Manhattan, Preakness
Manhattan, Prohibition
Manhattan, Roman
Manhattan, Satin
Manhattan, Shamrock
Manhattan, Sheepshead
   Bay
Manhattan, Tivoli
Manhattan, Waldorf
Martini, Bald Head
Martini, Becco
Martini, Bentley
Martini, Bronx
Martini, Cajun (1)
Martini, El Presidenté
Martini, Hawaiian
Martini, Infused
Martini, Newbury
Martini, Perfect
Martini, Riviera
Martini, Rolls Royce
Martini, Russian Tea
   Room
Martini, Shagged
Minnehaha
Negroni
Negroni, Uptown
Old Flame
Paddy
Presidenté
Rob Roy
Rob Roy, Highland Fling
Rob Roy, Perfect
Rolls Royce

**VILLA MASSA
LIMONCELLO**
See Limoncello
VODKA
Absolut Vodka
Absolutely Grand
Badda-Bing
Done & Bradstreet
Electric Lemonade
Martini, Blue Pacific
Martini, Dry Tanque
New York Nut
Texas Tea
Absolut Citron Vodka
Abo-Tron
Absolut Trouble
Citron Neon
Cosmopolitan
Cosmopolitan, Red
   Light
Cosmopolitan, White
Done & Bradstreet
Iced Tea, Front Parlor
Kamikaze, Citron
Mama Citron
Margarita, Citronita
Martini, Blue Diamond
Martini, Cajun King
Martini, Libertini
Martini, Lychee
Primo Bacio
Salty Dogitron
Absolut Kurant Vodka
Bank Shot
Holy Hand Grenade
Iced Tea, Swedish
Kurant Affair
Martini, Purple Haze
Mind Bender
Mojito, Blackberry
Piña Colada, Lt. Kije's
Side Shot
Sweet Red Kiss
Texas Tea
Absolut Mandarin Vodka
Absolut Mandarinade
Crypto Nugget
Mandarin Mimosa
Martini, Absolut
   Mandarin
Martini, Osteria
Martini, Passion
Absolut Peppar Vodka
Bay Bridge Commuter
   (1)
Bloody Mary, Bloody
   Nose (2)
Fahrenheit 5000
Hasta La Vista, Baby
Louisiana Shooter
Margarita Picante
Martini, Blood Shot
Martini, Cajun (2)
Martini, Cajun King
Martini, Creole
Martini, Raving Rhino
Martini, Star's Jewel
Absolut Vanilia Vodka
Martini, Chocolate
   Supreme
Martini, Espresso
   Framboise
Martini, Little Debby
Martini, Red Devil

Martini, Tiramisu (1)
Martini, Vanilla Nut
Mojito, Raspberry
   Vanilla Mojito
Neapolitan
New York Nut
White Russian, Vanilla
Bak's Zubrówka Vodka
Bloody Mary, Bloody
   Bison
Bloody Mary, Bloody
   Moose
Krakow Witch
Martini, Mighty
Boru Vodka
Irish Lemonade
Limerick
Martini, Celtic
Tickle Me
Ciroc Vodka
Frosted In The Shade
Grapes Of Wrath
Madame Butterfly
Martini, French Grape
Ultimate Grape
   Cocktail
Citadelle Vodkas
Apple Cooler
Café Framboise
Capers Cocktail
Cosmopolitan, Euro
French Congo Cooler
Green Sneakers
Kamikaze, Raspberry
Martini, New Bond
Martini, Nutcracker
Zuma Buma
Danzka Vodkas
Adios Mother
Finlandia Vodka
Finlandia Lime Light
Glacier Breeze
Harvest Night
Martini, Finlandia
   Pepper
Martini, Saharan
Grey Goose Vodka
Black Widow
Bloody Mary, Bloody
   French Goose
Brass Monkey
Club Macanudo
Goose Down
Hairy Sunrise
Kamikaze, French
Le Mooseberry
Martini, Brazen
Martini, Crème Brûlée
   (1)
Martini, French (1)
Martini, French (2)
Martini, Samtini
**Grey Goose La Vanille
Vodka**
Charisma Cocktail
Instant Carma
Nosferatu
**Grey Goose Le Citron
Vodka**
Eiffel View
French Blush
Margarita, Kamikaze
Martini, Lemon Grove
Recession Depression

**Grey Goose L'orange
Vodka**
Cosmopolitan, Orchard
   Peach
Eiffel View
Grand Orange Blossom
Hairy Sunrise
Le Mooseberry
Ketel One Vodka
Ball Joint
Blonde Teaser (1)
Manhattan, Smoky
Martini, Ketel One
Martini, Mandarine
Martini, Snickertini
Ketel One Citroen Vodka
Citroen Lemon Drop
Clear And Present
   Danger
Martini, Citrus
Midnight Orchid
Twist De L'orange
Liquid Ice Vodka
Martini, Café Nuttini
Martini, Midnight (2)
Martini, Poinsettia
Martini, Tartini
Roxanne
Vanilla Spice Ice
Magadanskaya Vodka
Martini, Russian Tea
   Room
Molotov's Cocktail
Russian Sunrise
Siberian
Original Cristall Vodka
Bearing Strait
Cactus Moon
Lemon Lavender
Martini, Cosmonaut
Original Monk
Socialite
Pearl Vodka
Martini, Crystal
   Pearlessence
Martini, Pearl Jam
Marz Bar
Midori Canuck
Pearl Diver
Pearl Lo Coco Vodka
Black Hawaiian
Coconut Coffee Pot
Kamikaze, Coconut
Martini, Pacific Pearl
Martini, Pearl Bailey
Sex On A Black Sandy
   Beach
White Hawaiian
Polar Ice Vodka
Black 'N' Blue
Electric Jam
Hoochie Kéké Mama
Miss Ube Darn
Sno-Cap
Spudka Vodka
Banana Stigma
Glasnost
Lemon Sportsman
Martini, 008
Martini Blues

Stolichnaya Vodka
Black Jeweled Russian
E.T.
Gorky Park Cooler (1)
Martini, Blue Moon (1)
Martini, Fidel's
Martini, Full Moon (1)
Martini, Moscow Chill
Martini, Muscovy
Mikhail Cocktail
Quaalude, Russian
Russian' About
Russian Polar Bear
Tovarich
White Russian,
Premium
Stolichnaya Citros Vodka
Bloody Mary, Bloody
Russian Bastard
Concorde
Gullet Pleaser
Instant Karma
Lemongrad
Martini, Key Lime Pie
Meadowlark Lemon
Russian Nights
Stoli Around The
World
Stolichnaya Lemonade
Summercello
Stolichnaya Cranberi
Vodka
Cranberry Squeeze
Kamikaze, Cranberry
Martini, Chocolate
Cranberry
Martini, Pink Ribbon
Stolichnaya Ohranj Vodka
Margarita,
French/Russian
Martini, Mikhail's
Martini, Muscovy
Martini, Pink Ribbon
Sputnik
Stoli Around The
World
Tovarich
Stolichnaya Persik Vodka
Glass Tower
Martini, Harper's
Summercello
Stolichnaya Razberi
Vodka
Balalaika
Gorky Park Cooler (2)
Jewel Of Russia
Martini, Alexander
Nevsky
Martini, P. B. & J.
Sneak & Peak Cocktail
Stoli Around The
World
Tamara Lvova
Stolichnaya Strasberi
Vodka
Ecstasy Shooter
Gorky Park Cooler (1)
Margarita, Strawberry
Lover's
Martini, Chocolate
Covered Strawberry
Martini, Strawberry (1)

Stolichnaya Vanil Vodka
Betelgeuse
Bukhara Coffee
Martini, Crème Brûlée
(2)
Martini, Crème Brûlée
(3)
Martini, Key Lime
Martini, Key Lime Pie
Martini, Mikhail's
St. Petersburg Sundae
Stoli Around The
World
Vanil Sensation
Stön Vodka
Lake Street Lemonade
Martini, Elisa's Martini
Of Love
Martini, Shade Tree
Martini, Topaz
Türi Vodka
1701 Fog
Angel Kiss
Maritime Sunrise
Martini, Baltic Sea
Martini, Kohv
Martini, Left Bank
Martini, Monastery
Ultimat Vodkas
Black Cherry Sonic
Fuzzy Wuzzie
Martini, Moro
Royal Bay Breeze
Wanderer
Van Gogh Vodka
Black Beauty (1)
Choco Laté Orange
Miami Ice
Sunflower
Vincent's Baubles
Van Gogh Chocolate
Vodka
Black Beauty (1)
Charisma Cocktail
Chocolate White
Russian
Irish Chocolate Kiss
Martini, Chocolate
Martini, Chocolate
Mint
Martini, Chocolate
Utopia
Mocha My Eye
Mojito, Raspberry
Mud Puddle
Turbo Milk Chocolate
Van Gogh Citron, Oranje
And Raspberry Vodka
Choco Laté Orange
Cosmopolitan, Lemon
Twisted
Fortress Of Singapore
Mojito, Raspberry
Van Gogh Vanilla Vodka
Larry, The
Martini, Chocolate
Mocha My Eye

Van Gogh Wild Appel
Vodka
Apple A Go-Gogh
Cosmopolitan, Lemon
Twisted
Martini, Green Apple
Original Sin
Sin In Hawaii
Vox Vodka
Dale's Sour Apple
Iced Tea, California
Late-Nite Lemon Drop
Martini, Metropolis
Martini, Rosebud
Martini, Toasted Nuts
Metro Cocktail
Vox Raspberry Vodka
Badda-Bing
Baileys Comet
Bikini Line
Black Stockings
Bubble Zaza
Cosmopolitan,
Raspberry (2)
Gotham Lemonade
Kamikaze, Purple (2)
Madonna's Brassiere
Martini, Flirtini (2)
Martini, Raspberry (2)
Martini, Watermelon
Metro Cocktail
Raspberry Torte
VODKA DRINKS
.44 Magnum
'57 Chevy
'57 T-Bird With
Arizona Plates
'57 T-Bird With Florida
Plates
'57 T-Bird With
Hawaiian Plates
Alabama Slammer (3)
Baltimore Zoo
Barn Raiser
Baybreeze
Beer Buster
Black Russian
Bloody Mary
Bloody Mary,
Bloodhound
Bloody Mary, Bloody
Bull
Bloody Mary, Bloody
Caesar
Bloody Mary, Bloody
Cajun
Bloody Mary, Bloody
Italian
Bloody Mary, Bloody
Nose (1)
Bloody Mary, Bloody
Tex-Mex
Bloody Mary, Dirty
Bloody Mary, Dirty
Bloody Cajun
Bloody Mary, Mango
Blue Bayou (1)
Blue Duck
Bomb Pop
Brawny Broth
Bullfrog (1)
Caipiroshka
California Screw
Cape Codder

Catherine Was Great
Cayman Cocktail
Cello Fellow
Censored On The
Beach
Champagne
Cornucopia
Champagne Marseille
Cheap Sunglasses
Chi-Chi
Chocolate Almond Kiss
Clam Fogger
Cocaine Shooter (1)
Cocaine Shooter (2)
Cold Fusion
Collins, Vodka
Colorado Bulldog
Cool Mint Listerine
Cosmopolitan, Melon
Cosmopolitan,
Raspberry (1)
Crabapple
Dc-3 Shooter
Deep Throat
Dirty Dog
Double Agent
Doubt Raiser
Downeaster
Dying Nazi From Hell
Electric Watermelon
(1)
Energizer Bunny
Face Eraser
Freddy Kruger
Frosted Coke
Frosted Peach Breeze
Fruit Burst
Gibson, Vodka
Gimlet, Raspberry
Gimlet, Tuaca
Gimlet, Vodka
Godchild
Godmother
Grape Nehi
Green Russian
Green Spider
Greyhound
Gumby
Gypsy
Harvey Wallbanger
Hawaiian Hurricane
Hawaiian Punch (1)
Houndstooth
Iceberg (1)
Iceberg (2)
Iced Tea, Afterburner
Iced Tea, Alaskan
Iced Tea, Bimini
Iced Tea, Blue
Kangaroo
Iced Tea, Dirty Ashtray
Iced Tea, Florida
Iced Tea, Georgia
Iced Tea, Green Tea
Iced Tea, Hawaiian
Iced Tea, Italian
Iced Tea, Long Beach
Iced Tea, Long Island
Iced Tea, Manhattan
Iced Tea, Plantation
Iced Tea, Raspberry
Iced Tea, Spiced
Iced Tea, Strawberry
Iced Tea, Tahiti

Iced Tea, Texas
Iced Tea, Tropical
Ice Pick Iced Tea
Island Sunset
Jackie Special
Jar Juice
Jenny Wallbanger
Jewels And Gold
Jolly Rancher (1)
Ju Ju Bee
Jungle Juice
Kamikaze
Kamikaze, Apple
Kamikaze, Bloody
Kamikaze, Blue
Kamikaze, Fuzzy
Kamikaze, Melon
Kamikaze, Purple (1)
Katinka
Knickerbocker Knee
  Knocker
Knicker Knocker
Kool Aid (1)
Kool Aid (2)
Lemonade Royale
Lemon Drop (1)
Lemon Drop (2)
Lemon Drop (3)
Lemon Tart
Lizard Bitch
Lockhart Zoo
Looking For Trouble
Madame Mandarine
Madras
Mango-A-Gogo
Martini, 007
Martini, Amber Skies
Martini, Appletini (1)
Martini, Appletini (2)
Martini, Appletini (3)
Martini, Bel-Air
Martini, Black (1)
Martini, Black (2)
Martini, Black (3)
Martini, Black Tie (2)
Martini, Bleu
Martini, Diamond
Martini, Dirty (1)
Martini, Dirty (2)
Martini, Dirty Citrus
Martini, Dry Vodka
Martini, Espresso
Martini, Extra Dry
  Vodka
Martini, Fantino
Martini, Flirtini (1)
Martini, Gotham
Martini, Green Lantern
Martini, Hawaiian
Martini, Hot
Martini, Hot Marti
Martini, Kéké V
Martini, Medici
Martini, Midnight (3)
Martini, Pear
Martini, Piña
Martini, Red Rain
Martini, Rosalind
  Russell
Martini, Sicilian (1)
Martini, Sicilian (2)
Martini, Starlight
Martini, Sushi
Martini, Taj Majal

Martini, Tiramisu (2)
Martini, Ty-Won-On
Martini, Vodka
Martini, Willy Nilly
Martini, Zorbatini
Mediterranean Freeze
Melon Ball (1)
Melon Ball (2)
Melon Ball Cooler
Melon Breeze
Melon Grind
Mind Eraser (1)
Mind Eraser (2)
Monsoon
Monster Appeaser
Moscow Mule
Mudslide (1)
Mudslide (2)
Naked Pretzel
Nosferatu's Shooter
Nut 'N' Honey
Ocean Breeze
Orange Delight
Orange Dream
Orange Frappé
Orange Julius
Passion Potion
Peach Bomb
Peach Breeze
Peach Fuzz
Pearl Harbor
Piña Colada, Aussie
Pink Lemonade (1)
Pink Moment
Pink Sunset
Pitless Shot
Province Town
Pullman Porter
Purple Hooter (1)
Purple Hooter (2)
Quaalude
Quaalude, Alaskan
Quaalude, Iranian
Quaalude, Irish
Raztini
Razzle Dazzle Rose
Red Death
Red Devil
Red Russian
Red Sky
Red Zipper
Release Valve
Reverse Russian
Rigor Mortis
Roasted Toasted
  Almond
Root Beer
Root Beer Float
Root Beer Tooter
Root Canal
Russian Bear
Salty Dog
Screaming Fuzzy Navel
Screaming Hawaiian
Screaming Orgasm
Screwdriver
Seabreeze
Seven Twenty-Seven
  (727)
Sex At The Beach
Sex In The Coal Region
Sex In The Woods
Sex On The Beach (1)
Sex On The Beach (4)

Sex With An Alligator
  (2)
Sherry's Blossom
Silken Veil
Silk Panties (1)
Silk Panties (2)
Silver Cloud
Silver Spider
Skinny Dipping
Sky High
Smooth Driver
Somosa Bay
Son Of A Peach
Sonoma Chiller
Spanish Fly
Spider Cider
Spy's Demise
Starlight
Staton Island Berry
Straight Shooter
Summer Memories
Sunglow
Sunstroke
Swamp Water Stinger
Sweet Tart (1)
Sweet Tart (2)
T-Bird
Tidal Wave (3)
Tidy Bowl
Tootsie Roll
Vampire
Vodka Grand
Vulcan
Wall Street Wizard
Watermelon (2)
Watermelon (3)
Watermelon (5)
Watkin's Glen
White Russian
White Russian, Skinny
White Spider
Whooter Hooter
Wiki Waki Woo
Windex
Yukon Stinger
Zanzibar Dunes
Zipper Head
Citrus Vodka Drinks
Blue Lemonade
Cement Mixer
Citrus Samurai
Collins, Jeff
Cosmopolitan,
  Dubonnet
Cosmopolitan, Hpnotiq
Cosmopolitan,
  Midnight Blue
Cosmopolitan, Purple
  (2)
Cosmopolitan, Summer
  Daze
Gimlet, Key Lime
Iced Tea, Jesse's
  Shocking
Iced Tea, Veranda
Jolly Rancher (2)
Lemon Heaven
Lemon Heights
Lemon Tree Tantalizer
Martini, Dirty Citrus
Martini, Dirty Gin
  Twist
Martini, Sapphire Sin
Pink Baby

Pink Lemonade (2)
Province Town
Reggae Sunsplash
Ruby Red
South Beach Twist
Summer Lemonade
Take The 'A' Train
Tie Me To The Bed Post
Tropical Sensation
Orange Vodka Drinks
Cartel Shooter
Martini, Becco
Martini, Blood Orange
Martini, Nitelife
Martini, Orange Grove
Martini, Titian
Passionate Fruit
Tangerine Drop
Raspberry Vodka Drinks
Brown Derby
Cosmopolitan, Summer
  Daze
Dream Catcher
Hollywood
Martini, Electric Blue
Summer Daze
White Russian,
  Raspberry
White Russian, Truffle
VOODOO SPICED RUM
  See Rum, Voodoo
VOX VODKAS
  See Vodka, Vox

W

WET BY BEEFEATER
  See Gin, Wet
WHALER'S RUMS
  See Rums, Whaler's
WHISKEY, BOURBON
  See Bourbon Whiskey
WHISKEY, IRISH
  See Irish Whiskey
WHISKEY, RYE
  See Rye Whiskey
WHISKEY, TENNESSEE
  See Tennessee Whiskey
WHISKY, CANADIAN
  See Canadian Whisky
WHISKY, SCOTCH
  See Scotch Whisky
WINE DRINKS
Betelgeuse
Blue Wave (2)
Burgundy Bishop
Burgundy Cocktail
Cocomacoque
Colorado River Cooler
Coronation
Hot Mulled Wine
Kir
Margarita, Cantina Wine
Margarita, Sangrita
Margarita, Vintner's
Margarita, Zinful
Martini, Black (3)
Martini, Italian (2)
Martini, Los Altos
Port In A Storm
Restoration
Sangria

Sangria, Margarita
Sangria, New World Punch
   (Serves Two)
Sangria Punch, Berry New
Scorpion
Sonoma Chiller
Sonoma Nouveau
Spritzer
Wine Cobbler
Wine Cooler
WOODFORD RESERVE
BOURBON
   See Bourbon Whiskey

X

XALIXCO GOLD TEQUILA
   See Tequila, Xalixco Gold
XXX SIGLO TREINTA
TEQUILA
   See Tequila, XXX Siglo
   Treinta

Y

YUKON JACK LIQUEUR
Burnt Sienna
Dead Grizzly
Dead Grizzly Shooter
Frostbite
Mackenzie Gold
Northern Lights (1)
Northern Lights (2)
Panama Jack
Peckerhead
Red Death
Rocket
Shot In The Dark
Snake Bite (1)
Sweaty Betty
Yukon Stinger